MW00451264

Interpreting Ethiopia

Ayana Eneyew

Interpreting Ethiopia

Observations of Five Decades

Donald N. Levine

TSEHAI
Publishers & Distributors

TSEHAI
Publishers & Distributors

Interpreting Ethiopia: Observations of Five Decades
Copyright © 2014 by Donald N. Levine. All rights reserved.

Apart from any fair dealing for the purpose of private study, research, criticism or review, as permitted under the Copyright Act, no part of this publication may be reproduced in any form, stored in a retrieval system or transmitted in any form by any means—electronic, mechanical, photocopy, recording or otherwise—without the prior permission of the publisher. Enquiries should be sent to the undermentioned address.

Tsehai books may be purchased for educational, business, or sales promotional use.
For more information, please contact our special sales department.

Tsehai Publishers
Loyola Marymount University
1 LMU Drive, UH 3012, Los Angeles, CA 90045

www.tsehaipublishers.com
info@tsehaipublishers.com

Hardcover ISBN: 978-1-59907-0957
Paperback ISBN: 978-1-59907-0964

First Edition: Fall 2014

Publisher: Elias Wondimu
Typesetting: Melanie Pagayunan and Sara Martinez
Cover Design: Sara Martinez
Cover Design Assistant: Jennifer Masuda

Library of Congress Catalog Card Number
A catalog record for this book is available from the Library of Congress.

British Library Cataloguing in Publication Data
A catalogue record for this book is available from the British Library.

10 9 8 7 6 5 4 3 2 1

Printed in the United States of America

Los Angeles | Addis Ababa | New York | Oxford

Contents

Contents

Foreword

Donald Levine's Journey through Ethiopian Civilization

by Andrew DeCort

A keen student of Ethiopian civilization for more than fifty years, Donald Levine offers in this book his observations on the ethos and worldview, education and literature, and history, politics, and cross-national connections of the cultural area that he calls Greater Ethiopia. Levine's oeuvre is the outcome of a serious scholarly odyssey through Ethiopian civilization over space and time. As a sociologist, Levine has travelled through nearly all regions of Greater Ethiopia—from Massawa to Konso, from Jigjiga to Jinka—but the heart of his journey has taken shape temporally: over extended periods of travel and in looking at increasing spans of time that together reach from prehistory to the present.

Levine's Ethiopian journey can be divided into three periods. Phase I ranged from the years of his ethnographic work in Ethiopia (1958–60) to library work in Europe and the U.S. before and after those years, which expanded his purview through documents from the 16th century onward. Phase II, centered on library and seminar work at the University of Chicago in the years 1971–74, reaches back to the first two millennia BCE, and moves forward through the reign of Emperor Haile Selassie. Phase III extends from Levine's return to Ethiopia in 1992–2012. Historically, it covers the regimes of the Derg and of the EPRDF, and relates features of those regimes back to the Aksumite kingdoms of the first few centuries CE. In this phase, Levine also attends to Ethiopia's Diaspora population, her interaction with other nations, and her comparison with Japanese civilization.

The *Wax and Gold* Phase: Tradition and Modernization

As a student at the University of Chicago in the early 1950s, Levine participated in Robert Redfield's graduate seminar on the comparison of cultures. This seminar marked a historic effort to promote the comparative study of civilizations in a non-Western-centric perspective.[1] Inspired by Redfield's vision, Levine began to search for a 'third-world' culture to which he could devote himself in his post-doctoral years. That search led him to Ethiopia, on which as a first step he studied ethnographic reports for a chapter on adolescence in his 1957 dissertation. The grant that funded his post-doctoral research in Ethiopia was tied to a project concerning adolescence in Ethiopia. However, when Levine arrived there he discovered that the assumptions on which that project rested were faulty. Remembering Redfield's more general counsel to "go and have a good look around," he went on to examine a number of different things. In due course he came to relate these to chapters of Redfield's book on ways to understand human communities, *The Little Community.* The book that brought together most of what Levine learned during this period, *Wax and Gold: Tradition and Innovation in Ethiopian Culture* (1965) was organized in seven chapters, each of which corresponded to one of the approaches of *The Little Community*. Levine's first paper on Ethiopia, "On the Conceptions of Time and Space in the Amhara World View" (Chapter 2), for the First International Conference of Ethiopian Studies in Rome in 1959, dealt with an aspect of one of those topics, "an outlook on life."

While engaged in work that led to *Wax and Gold*, Levine was looking for a symbol that would get to the heart of Ethiopian society, similar to the way Ruth Benedict's title *The Chrysanthemum and the Sword* (1946) worked for Japan. While at an event at the University College of Addis Ababa (later became Haile Selassie I University, then Addis Ababa University), Levine sat next to student Tegegn Yeteshawarq, who said, "I hope you come to understand some of the deeper features of our culture. So many foreigners have the idea that this is a savage place. We have very rich traditions." Tegegn went on to tell Levine about the genre of Ge'ez and Amharic poetry called *säm-enna-wärq* or "wax-and-gold," which plays on the ambiguity of double-meanings in compact Amharic verse "to attain a maximum of thought with a minimum of words" (see Chapter 12). Immediately captivated, he went on to study books in Amharic on wax-and-gold poetry and collect samples of such verse, and traveled to a monastery in Gojjam where *säm-enna-wärq* was taught. Soon enough, Levine knew he had discovered a valuable interpretive key for Ethiopia.

The core interpretive theme of *Wax and Gold,* as the subtitle suggests, was the conflict between traditional customs and Ethiopia's drive toward modernity.

This theme emerged both from listening to what Ethiopians of diverse sectors were talking about, which he readily theorized from prominent dichotomies in sociological theory such as Emile Durkheim's contrast between 'mechanical' and 'organic' societies and Max Weber's contrast between traditional and rational bases of legitimacy, and from such agenda-setting books as Daniel Lerner's *The Passing of Traditional Society* (1958). Levine opened his treatment of the theme in *Wax and Gold* by identifying five options for handling this conflict: Traditionalism; Modernism; Skepticism; Conciliation; and Pragmatism. He opted for the Pragmatist position, defined as a commitment "to the optimum realization of all values possible in a given historic situation." In this perspective, Levine concluded that "the wax-and-gold mentality should be regarded not only as an obstacle to Ethiopia's modernization but also, by virtue of its contribution to the continuing effectiveness of her social organization and the continuing richness of her expressive culture, as a beneficial agent."[2] This sense of evolving integration rather than zero sum conflict or revolutionary change[3] would pervade Levine's lifelong work interpreting Ethiopia.

In the academic world, *Wax and Gold* was hailed as originary in several respects as the first study of Ethiopia by a professional sociologist which, in the words of reviewers Nicholas Hopkins and Wendy Belcher, "blazed a new trail in the study of modernity and in the sympathetic understanding of a complex traditional society" and that Levine "was ahead of his time" in analyzing an African culture through the lens of "one of that culture's own philosophies." Commenting on the contribution of *Wax and Gold*, Allan Hoben put it on par with de Tocqueville's *Democracy in America*. In his own words, "Ethiopians too will profit from this outsider's analysis of the major outlines of their dominant culture, as Americans, at least in retrospect, profited by the observations of Alexis de Tocqueville."[4]

Five decades later, social scientists working on Ethiopia still drew on *Wax and Gold* as a stimulus for new research as represented by a day-long colloquium at the 2012 meetings of the African Studies association on the contemporary relevance *Wax and Gold*, organized by anthropologist Daniel Mains. In addition, in those years, it had been taken up by Ethiopians in a number of non-academic genres, as the title of two esteemed paintings, a best-selling CD by popular vocalist Gigi, and the title of a journal on East African philosophies. Addis Ababa University President Andreas Eshete, in presenting an honorary doctorate to Levine in 2004, called *Wax & Gold* "a pioneering work" that has become "an Ethiopian classic" after which "the very concept of Wax and Gold has taken on a life of its own: it figures at once in our understanding of Ethiopia's pre-modern culture and in our coming to grips with Ethiopia's reception of modernity."

On the other hand, reactions by a number of Ethiopians at the time were not nearly so positive. Those knowledgeable about traditional Ge'ez qené found Levine's understanding of its Orthodox forms superficial if not misleading, a critique Levine fully accepted with apologies that he simply did not have the time to devote to that demanding, esoteric genre. Perhaps more common and certainly more antagonistic were those who felt his appreciation of the traditional culture in the Redfieldian mode simply expressed a conservative bias. The most vehemently articulate of these critiques appeared in a nearly 20,000-word essay by Gedamu Abraha, who called Levine "a prophet of reactionary dogmatism" pursuing bourgeois science, "a prophet who has taken it upon himself to vanquish the demons of social change." Along with a number of appreciative glosses on the book, Gedamu urged Ethiopian modernists who do not share Levine's philosophy to let him "indulge his poetic muse on the enchanting medieval scenes of Ethiopia" while they "continue to strive for a new dawn," which he evokes in the words of poet Paul Eluard, "Brothers, this dawn is yours."[5]

Reactions of this sort saddened Levine, because he felt that sort of sentiment would lead precisely to the sort of despotic regime likely to follow unless more moderate, progressive changes were introduced under the government of Haile Selassie. What Levine in fact advocated in chapter five of *Wax and Gold* was two major kinds of change: for the emperor and his relevant appointees to open up a sphere of discourse in which universalistic standards could have full sway, and where people could feel free to express criticism; and for modern-educated Ethiopians to "break out of their posture of negativism and defeatism" and to push forward courageously in the light of their country's developmental needs. A possible outcome of failure to make such changes, he predicted, could be that "the modernizing infrastructure of the society would grow increasingly restless, culminating in a revolution which would install a modernizing oligarchy" (216). The obvious bearer of that infrastructure, he suggested in a subsequent paper, would be the military (Chapter 25)—a suggestion that some Ethiopian readers ridiculed.

One other form of objection to some of what Levine was doing in *Wax and Gold* concerned his forthright acknowledgement of "the fact of Amhara dominance." That objection had consequences for the next phase of Levine's journey. [Despite the criticisms, Allan Hoben, in what sounds like a fitting tribute, wrote, "Yet scholars and the general public alike should be grateful that a man of Mr. Levine's obvious brilliance rushed in where an angel would fear to tread."[6]

The *Greater Ethiopia* Phase: Ethnic Identities and Multiethnic Society

Levine's focus on the Amhara in *Wax and Gold* stemmed from a wish to study what was patently the politically and culturally dominant ethnic group in Ethiopia as a key to the major aspects of Ethiopia's tradition that might be in tension with modernization.[7] This also converged with his wish to learn Amharic, the official national language. Although this focus on Amhara culture reflected purely heuristic considerations, it led some Ethiopian readers to express concern about bias. Non-Amhara readers often read the book as too favorable toward the Amhara; Amhara readers often took it to be too critical of the Amhara. Both types of respondents worried that it might contribute to growing tensions among ethnic groups in Ethiopia—a potential effect that was the antithesis of Levine's aim in writing the book. In consequence, during a funded year off in 1971–2, Levine abandoned a planned project on social theory and decided to compensate for his earlier exclusive attention to the Amhara in what became his next full-length work, *Greater Ethiopia: The Evolution of a Multiethnic Society* (1974).[8]

Seeking to head off what he feared might be an explosive upsurge of inter-ethnic conflict following the regime of Haile Selassie, in *Greater Ethiopia* Levine sought to reveal lines of evolutionary development that contributed to the formation of Ethiopia as a cohesive, multiethnic society. The original peopling of Ethiopia with many dozens of distinct ethnic groups took place in the first two millennia BCE. *Greater Ethiopia* took shape as a response to the question: what enabled this subcontinent of diverse ethnies to become a viable multiethnic society that could withstand the attacks of external invaders and the forces of colonialism during the Scramble for Africa—a feat achieved by no other traditional African society?

The book delineated five such factors. (1) A broad basis of common cultural characteristics shared by virtually all the peoples of Greater Ethiopia. (2) Numerous patterns of inter-ethnic association over the centuries, through interacting at markets, participating in common religious rituals, going on pilgrimages, intermarriage, and fighting against common enemies. (3) The expansion of an imperial center. (4) The creation of a national epic (see Chapters 4 and 5). (5) The expansion in all directions of the Oromo peoples, who came to provide a kind of cultural glue among the various ethnies among whom they settled.

Published the same year that the emperor was overthrown by a revolution amidst a radicalizing student movement strongly influenced by Marx and Stalin, *Greater Ethiopia*'s scholarly argument took on political urgency with its implicit claim that "Greater Ethiopia" figured not only as an accurate representation of Ethiopia's past but also as an ideal with which to pursue her uncertain future. Thinking ahead to the years after the Solomonic Dynasty, which had grounded political legitimacy and self-understanding in (Highland) Ethiopia for the previous seven hundred years, Levine hoped that the idea of "Greater Ethiopia" itself might serve as a source of integrative self-understanding and political legitimacy to shape the moral imagination of post-Solomonic Ethiopia. Similar to how he interpreted the wax-and-gold culture as a "beneficial agent" of "continuing richness" for Ethiopia's modernization process, so he wrote in *Greater Ethiopia*,

> Imagine what might be done by propagating a vision of the future that integrates, rather than repudiates, the positive achievements of the past ... Animated by this understanding [of multiethnic Ethiopia], Ethiopians may now be able to transform the solidarity and courage that went into fighting the Battle of Adwa into the solidarity and courage it takes to sustain a non-violent political process that works toward a larger community based on unity, justice, and democracy.[9]

Even more than *Wax and Gold*, *Greater Ethiopia* was widely regarded as transformative in the field of Ethiopian studies. It was quickly accepted as offering a perspective beyond the narrow academic domains of Semitic philology, cultural anthropology, and modernization studies. It stimulated a number of research initiatives, including a conference on Ethiopian origins in England and a superb essay by Alula Pankhurst, "Reflections on Pilgrimages in Ethiopia."[10] Because its appendix offered the first systematic compilation of all the ethnic groups of Ethiopia in one place, the Derg even duplicated that appendix as part of its educational program for cadres. A second edition was demanded in 2000 and an Amharic translation, *Tiliqua Ityopya,* was published the following year.

And also, just like *Wax and Gold*, it became the object of criticisms from politically charged readers. In particular, even though the book represented a bold attempt to show that, while, the Amhara-Tigreans had produced a multiethnic Ethiopian *state*, the Oromo effectively contributed as much to the emergence of the modern Ethiopian *polity*, many Oromo took umbrage at how their history was represented.

In the violent years that followed *Greater Ethiopia* under the Derg regime, Levine considered himself unwelcome in the country due to his testimony before the U.S. Senate about the abuses of the regime in 1976 (Chapter 26). The turn against Western social scientists under the Derg discouraged him from trying to send doctoral students there for research. The only Ethiopianist project he undertook in those years was to take leadership in organizing the Fifth International Conference of Ethiopian Studies at The University of Chicago in 1978. Otherwise, in those years, his interests turned back to social theory.[11]

The Post-Derg Phase: Internal and External Challenges

In 1991, a different kind of turning point made its mark on Ethiopian society. The Derg regime was overthrown, Mengistu Haile Mariam fled to Zimbabwe, and the Ethiopian People's Democratic Revolutionary Front (EPRDF) took control of the country under the leadership of Meles Zenawi. This regime change and its ensuing challenges ushered in a third stage in Donald Levine's journey through Ethiopian civilization. After an absence of 32 years, broken only by a short visit in 1976 to attend a conference on Feudalism in Ethiopia, Levine returned to Ethiopia in 1992 under the auspices of the International African Institute as an official observer of the first national multi-party election.

During that visit, in an interview with President Meles facilitated by Kifle Wodajo, Levine was deeply impressed by Meles's intelligence and articulateness, and by his expressed care for the country and the rights of all its peoples. He shared Meles's ostensible grief at the departure of Ethiopia's Jews to Israel (see Chapter 17) when Meles put his hand over his heart and said, "It's like they tore out a piece of our history." And over the next two decades, he maintained a personal friendship with the man whom many of his Ethiopian friends reviled, in spite of sharp disagreements with many of Meles's actions.

Those disagreements appeared the moment Levine set foot in Ethiopia. When Levine told a taxi-driver he was there to observe Ethiopia's democratic election, the driver replied, "*Wushet demokratie*!" ("Democracy as a lie.") Rather than a free and fair election, Levine and all the other international observers were dismayed by the extent to which the government controlled, harassed, and disenfranchised the various opposition parties.

The following year more disagreements appeared. In 1993 a conference on ethnicity was to be held at Addis Ababa University, but it was abruptly canceled. The official reason for the cancellation was that there was not enough interest in the conference; in reality, more people signed up for this important conference than the planners even anticipated. It turned out that Meles simply did not want the conference and its open discussion to take place, and he shut it down by fiat. One may assume that many of the visiting scholars would object to the EPRDF manner of dealing with the ethnic question: separating different ethnic population into divisive, autonomous zones (*kilil*) rather than promoting interethnic harmony through enlightened policies.

Levine himself was in the forefront of those who opposed the *kilil* system—based on Meles's policy of "ethnic federalism" and the EPRDF's view of a united Ethiopia as a "fiction" (see Chapter 18)—since it was diametrically opposed to the argument of *Greater Ethiopia*. Rather than emphasizing the historic, multiethnic character of Ethiopia, Meles's leadership divided Ethiopia along ethnic lines, to the point of including a provision for national secession in the federal constitution (see Chapter 30).

Levine refused to heed the notice of cancellation and arranged to visit Addis Ababa University instead. On arrival, he learned that forty members of the University faculty had been summarily fired, an action that prompted him to compose a sharp critique of Meles's action (Chapter 13 in this volume, "Is Ethiopia Cutting Off Its Head Again?"). Perhaps apprehension that visiting academics would be dismayed by that destructive action was a factor in Meles's decision to cancel the conference on Ethnicity.

Three years later, Levine was invited by Meles to join a group of other American academics for a conversation at the Ethiopian Embassy in Washington, DC. Before going into this meeting, Levine encouraged his colleagues to be prepared with pointed questions about the state of free association, freedom of press, and political parties in Ethiopia. Meles's responses to these questions were disappointing and disturbing. When asked about the importance of a level playing field and the challenges that other political parties faced in getting resources, Meles defiantly replied, "If they're serious, they should do what we did: we went out into the bush, fought, and shot our way into power." For Levine, witnessing Ethiopia's Head of State declare that political participation could only be obtained by "shooting one's way into power" was a breaking point, and he turned his professional focus back to social theory and education.[12]

Nonetheless, if Levine confessed to having been "seduced by the charm of traditional Amhara life" thirty years before,[13] his life was now inextricably wedded to the future of the Greater Ethiopia he had come to love. Despite his recurrent pronouncements that he was "finished" with Ethiopia, he could not resist the idea of participating in the 13th International Conference of Ethiopian Studies in Kyoto in 1997. While teaching for a semester in Japan, Levine attended the conference and presented new work that integrated his original interests in comparisons of civilizations, fortified by a later interest in Japanese culture and the Japanese martial art of aikido (see Chapters 33 and 34).[14]

Soon after, Getachew Haile wrote Levine and asked him to renew his direct engagement with Ethiopian society. Getachew's request inspired Levine to begin writing articles for current Ethiopian publications, several of which are included in this volume (see Chapters 8, 16, 17, 28, and 29). He returned to Ethiopia in 2004 to receive an honorary doctorate from Addis Ababa University. Then, in the wake of the post-election violence in 2005 that left nearly 200 people dead and thousands imprisoned, Levine returned to Addis to serve as a mediator (*shimagele*) in the political conflict. Levine confided to Prime Minister Meles that although he was a critic of the EPRDF regime he wanted to help a friend, Ethiopia, in time of need, and hoped to secure a working relationship with the PM. Meles agreed, and promptly enabled him to visit the prisoners in jail repeatedly. Visiting Ethiopia during the critical year of 2006 inspired Levine to write a number of short pieces—*Assir Getz*, "Ten Pages"—one of which, "Two Tales of One City," appears as Chapter 22. (The experience figured in two longer pieces, included as Chapters 30 and 31.)

Although the polarization between supporters of the EPRDF regime and the primary opposition party, the Coalition for Union and Democracy, hinged on the two ideological perspectives and the two narratives ("tales") held by those political combatants, Levine was surprised by the lack of attention to what he believed would be a more serious long term opposition, between the Northerners and the Oromo activists. Apart from his global and comparative interests, his main effort from then on would be to promote bridging efforts among Oromos and with the Northern ethnic groups (see Chapter 19).

This brief map of Donald Levine's journey through Ethiopian civilization would not be complete without noting his commitment all throughout these decades to teaching courses at the University of Chicago on Ethiopian culture and civilization. His first such course was offered in the mid-1960s, and it was my distinct honor to serve as his assistant for the most recent offering of this course in 2012. Retracing a journey that had begun some 60 years before, this seminar was part of the seedbed for developing Levine's most recent academic publication on Ethiopia–a sweeping interpretation of Ethiopia's societal evolution across time and space. This article now serves as the capstone of Levine's vocation of interpreting Ethiopia (Chapter 37).

The Ethical Concern of Levine's Work

In everything that has been written above, the distinctly ethical dimensions of Donald Levine's engagement with Ethiopia should be unmistakable. From his first attempt to serve as a minister of reconciliation between "the patterns of order" in the Ethiopian past and present with *Wax & Gold*[15]; to his work as a peacemaker bringing together the peoples of Ethiopia with their interconnected "institutional orders, interactional patterns, and cultural codes" in his *Greater Ethiopia*[16]; to his role as a mediator following the violent conflicts of 2005 and faithful presence throughout significant conversations thereafter, ethics and the pursuit of peace, justice, and freedom must be a fundamental feature of any thoughtful interpretation of Donald Levine's Ethiopianist oeuvre.

In addition to building bridges, Levine's ethical concern has been especially evident in his courageous defense of press and academic freedom in Ethiopia throughout his career. From his critical 1961 article on Haile Sellassie's authoritarianism, which cost him his post at the soon to be founded Haile

Selassie I University (see Chapters 10 and 23), and his 1976 testimony at the U.S. Congress on the human rights abuses of the Derg (see Chapter 25); to his critical analysis of the violent 1993 crisis at Addis Ababa University and the "hope for freedom" (see Chapter 13 and 27); to his 2004 acceptance speech for his honorary doctorate at Addis Ababa University, in which he warned against the dangers of suppressing academic freedom and defended the University's Pauline motto *Kwillo amekkiru we-ze-senay atsni'u* ("Investigate everything, and retain what is best"—1 Thessalonians 5:21) (see Chapter 14)—Levine has been an exemplar of speaking truth to power at personal cost for the sake of protecting a public sphere in which the ingrained either/or *metazez wes meshefet* ("obey or rebel") can be overcome for a third way of "public discussion" and "loyal opposition" (see Chapters 5 and 27).

Indeed, the fundamental question of the sources and implications of ethical order and moral anarchy in Ethiopia is a pressing inheritance of Levine's lifework, which he hands on to the present and future generations of Ethiopians and Ethiopianists.[17] With his unsurpassed interpretation of the *Kibre Negest* as the source of legitimacy and self-understanding in pre-1974 Solomonic Ethiopia (see Chapters 4–7), the question remains open regarding what can provide the sources for a unifying vision of goodness and justice in an increasingly pluralistic, fragilized, constitutionally secularized Ethiopia.[18] Is the history and ideal of a "Greater Ethiopia" enough to provide this legitimacy and self-transcendence—this respect for universal human rights and the recognition of the sacredness of the person?[19] What are the possibilities for dialogue within Ethiopia's rich religious traditions (see Chapters 2 and 8) and her more recent secular constituencies as part of the "world-wide dialogue about the limitations and potentialities of human experience" described 49 years ago in *Wax & Gold*?[20] What will energize and guide the future of forgiveness, trust, freedom, excellence, and the common good—or their opposites—in Ethiopia?

Within the panorama of Donald Levine's five decades of journeying through Ethiopia's millennial civilization, these are just a few of the many questions that can no longer be "politely overlooked or furtively concealed."[21] Indeed, these pressing questions might be received as precious gifts providing renewed opportunities "for all Ethiopians to stretch out their hands—to embrace one another and to reclaim their historic heritage."[22]

***

Editorial note. In the highly diverse chapters that follow, we have not attempted to standardize the various spellings of Ethiopian toponyms or personal names. Nor have we revised rare occurrences of gendered language, allowing the texts to resonate with their original context of writing. One important exception has been made throughout: all uses of the term "Galla," now a dated and derogatory word, have been respectfully converted to "Oromo."

Notes

1 See "The Redfield-Singer Civilization Project" in Levine, *Powers of the Mind: The Reinvention of Liberal Learning in America* (Chicago, IL: University of Chicago Press, 2006), 157–62.

2 *Wax & Gold*, op. cit., 17. See the penultimate paragraph of Chapter 4: "it would be unjust to say that consequences of her traditional system of legitimacy have only negative implications for Ethiopia's capacity to rise to her contemporary challenges."

3 Ibid., 16: "The experience of history has demonstrated the futility of attempting the revolutionary implementation of a clear and distinct ideal in human society. No matter how bold and sweeping the program, traditional patterns persist tenaciously." Note the warning from 1961 in Chapter 1: "If they [traditionalists and modernists] lose the capacity to understand each other as Ethiopians and as human beings, if all their energy is consumed in conflict against each other, Ethiopia's development can never be more than halting and disjointing, and terribly wasteful." See Chapter 30 on "the seduction of revolutionary ideologies."

4 Allan Hoben, *American Anthropologist*, Volume 69, Issue 3–4 (1967), 397.

5 "Wax & Gold," *Ethiopia Observer*, volume 11 number 3 (1968), 232, 243.

6 *American Anthropologist*, Volume 69, Issue 3–4 (1967), 39.

7 Although viewing the Amhara as an ethnic group at the time made sense–and was picked up, to Levine's dismay by the EPRDF policy of making Amhara a zonal entity–Levine would later show that historically Amhara referred only to a small area in southwestern Wallo (see Chapter 18).

8 An analogous reaction that motivated a second book came to Levine's attention in a subsequent conversation with his colleague William Julius Wilson. Wilson confessed that his second major book, *The Truly Disadvantaged*, was written to balance his argument in *The Declining Significance of Race*—that the issue of race had been replaced by the issue of class and that the plight of lower-class people had been ignored, gaps that many African-American critics found to be hurtful.

9 Xxi.

10 *New Trends in Ethiopian Studies,* edited by Marcus and Hudson (Lawrenceville, NJ: The Red Sea Press, Inc, 1994), 933-953.

11 See Donald N. Levine, *The Flight from Ambiguity: Essays in Social and Cultural Theory* (Chicago, IL: University of Chicago Press, 1985).

12 See Donald N. Levine, *Visions of the Sociological Tradition* (Chicago, IL: University of Chicago Press, 1995) and *Powers of the Mind: The Reinvention of*

Liberal Learning in America (Chicago, IL: University of Chicago Press, 2006). Another participant in that meeting, Theodore Vestal, subsequently published an extended critique, *Ethiopia: A Post-Cold War African State* (Praeger, 1999).

13 *Wax & Gold*, op. cit., ix.

14 This work, too, hearkened back to the influence of Robert Redfield, whose papers on how to think about civilizations affected Levine deeply. In addition, Levine was subsequently influenced by another student of civilizations, Benjamin Nelson, and joined an organization Nelson helped found, the International Society for the Comparative Study of Civilizations. An early version of "Ethiopia and Japan in Comparative Civilizational Perspective" was presented an at ISCSC conference at the University of Utah.

15 See especially ibid, x–xi. Note Levine's description of sociology in Chapter 1: "[Sociology] has to do with the foundation of social order and the processes of social change. This means, in the framework I have found most useful to adopt, that a sociologist concerns himself with the values shared by the members of a given society in the diverse circumstances of their lives, the institutions which embody these values the modes of conflict and solidarity within and among these institutions, and the ways in which these institutions persist, develop, or become transformed."

16 See especially *Greater Ethiopia*, op. cit., xxi.

17 See the end of Chapter 1, where Levine attempts to constructively re-interpret and retrieve the traditional values of "total submissiveness to elders and superiors, individualism, equivocation, and physical aggressiveness" in terms of their "moral equivalents" suitable to "the goals of the new era."

18 Note Chapter 1: "the question of conflict in the sphere of moral values…it seems to me [is] at the heart of Ethiopia's dilemmas today and yet one of the least explored aspects of changing Ethiopia." See *Greater Ethiopia*, xvi–xvii: "Perhaps even more important [to the rise of ethnonationalism] was the threat to the national center posed by internal cultural difficulties. I refer to the problems posed by the decline in authority of the Solomonid ideology as a basis for legitimating the national center… When the shortcomings of Marxism became apparent, what was left? Ethiopia faced a cultural dilemma that proved no less formidable than the crises posed by a shattered economy and an enfeebled political structure. She stood in need of ideas and symbols that could fill the vacuum left by the overthrow both of the Solomonid royal ideology and the revolutionary ideology of Marxism." In *Visions of the Sociological Tradition*, op. cit., 1, Levine refers to this dilemma as "a shortage of ideas and ideals suitable for lending us purpose and moral direction under radically changed social and technological conditions" or "the depletion of our symbolic resources." In this way, perhaps Ethiopia can continue to serve as "a mirror against which the dilemmas of Western societies might also be viewed" (*Wax & God*, op. cit., xi).

19 This is essentially Levine's argument in the final paragraph of Chapter 30.

20 Ibid, xi–xii. See also, 15: "In its most creative outcome, the conflict may involve so genuine a dialogue between traditional and modern patterns that novel values emerge and authentic variants of modern culture are developed." In *Visions of the Sociological Tradition*, op. cit., 3, Levine similarly writes of "the dialogical narrative" as "the possibility of a constructive foundation for coping with those problems, both by linking currently disconnected parties into common universes of discourse and by providing grounds for a communal ethic based on the prerequisites of dialogue." See his *Dialogical Social Theory* (Piscataway, NJ: Transaction Publishers, forthcoming).

21 Ibid, xi.

22 *Greater Ethiopia*, op. cit., xxi. This is clearly an allusion to the famous text Psalm 68:31: "Ethiopia shall stretch out her hands to God." Now in Levine's midrash, Ethiopians are no longer "stretching out their hands" to God but to *one another*. While this may not have been Levine's original intention in revising this crucial text for Ethiopia's historic self-understanding, the case could be made from the teachings of Jesus that the only way to reach God, rather than a self-made idol, is to reach out in forgiveness and service to one's neighbors (see Matthew 6:14–15). In this case, Levine's ethical revision of Psalm 68:31 is brilliantly in line with early Christian theology. See Dietrich Bonhoeffer, *Letters and Papers from Prison*, Dietrich Bonhoeffer Works, Volume 8, edited by J.W. de Gruchy (Minneapolis, MI: Fortress Press, 2010), 510: "Our relationship to God is a new life in 'being there for others.'"

Preface

by Donald Levine

In an ad hoc lecture at Addis Ababa University in 2006, I felt an impulse to reflect on the date of my talk and realized that it was exactly a half century from when I began my scholarly work on Ethiopia. That was when, anticipating a shift into the field of Ethiopian studies, I devoted a chapter of my dissertation to Ethiopia. My dissertation work took me to publications of the International African Institute, which contained chapters based on ethnographies of the Oromo [designated in those years as "Galla"] and the Somali peoples.

The reflection took me by surprise. Five decades! Had it really been that long? Jostled by the thought, I spontaneously announced: Well, this being the anniversary of my entrance into Ethiopian Studies, I'd like to acknowledge that fact by putting together a collection of my papers from the span of five decades. Eight years and many ups and downs later, the collection has at last appeared.

In organizing this volume, I made a special effort to include unpublished pieces. I divided the selections into five thematic parts and, to convey the sense of progression of my work over the period, ordered the sections chronologically. A number of these papers were composed since 2006. During that short period, some of my ideas about Ethiopia changed a good deal. Even so, except for Chapters 8 and 9, I left the earlier pieces as originally written. Yet it might be worthwhile here to mention the main changes I am aware of.

I now have a heightened sense of the continuity of Ethiopian civilization over two millennia, with respect to certain geopolitical and cultural patterns manifested in Aksumite civilization. The core political pattern embodies what I have come to call a pharaonic complex, in which the well-being of the body politic is associated with projecting special powers to the head of state. This complex is supported by a cultural pattern of deriving special legitimacy from outside the country—in Christian epochs, from both Jerusalemic motifs and the

Alexandrian Patriarchate; and in post-monarchical regimes, from ideologies coming out of East European sources. This poses particular challenges to those Ethiopians who wish to move toward a system in which the population function as citizens with full civil rights rather than only as subjects.

I have also been struck by two other characteristics of the bimillennial continuity of Ethiopia's civilization. What I have long referred to as the multiethnic character of the Ethiopian polity really originates in the multiethnic empire of ancient Aksum. What is more, when one thinks of it, it is striking that contemporary popular music uses the ancient pentatonic system and is even performed by a group with the name Yared.

In addition, since 2006 I have come upon new ways of contributing to Ethiopia's development. Beyond working to build bridges between traditionalists and modernists, and among different ethnic groups—the focus of my efforts in previous decades—I found myself working to build bridges between those committed to ethnic federalism and those oriented toward *etiopiyawinet*, Ethiopian nationhood. This was most evident in my efforts to mediate between the Federal Government and the political leaders of the CUD Party who had been imprisoned (see Chapter 22). Subsequently, I found myself galvanized to promote understanding between the Oromo peoples and the Northern Ethiopians (see Chapter 19, and my talk to the Society of Ethiopians Established in the Diasapora [SEED] in May 2014 at *donlevine.com*). Most recently, I have been concerned to restore amicable relations among Muslims and Christians, which had begun to deteriorate following the importation of minor streams of radical Islamism (see Chapter 8).

Another area of concern was directed at Ethiopia's youth. It began with efforts to assist young people orphaned due to the deaths of their parents from AIDS—in particular, the Awassa Children's Center, supported by a Chicago NGO. I went on to work on conjoining the AIDS education circus that originated at that center with a new aikido dojo, thereby forming an NGO, the Awassa Youth Campus, which has gone on to develop a number of extracurricular programs for young people. Extending ideas articulated in Chapter 34, I sought through the aikido education in that dojo to help Ethiopians find ways in which their traditions of warriorhood could be conjoined with efforts to promote nonviolence.

To acknowledge fully the help I received in my Ethihopianist efforts over the years would take a small book. For now, let me name only those who played a key role in that work from the mid-1950s on. Lemma Frehiwot introduced me to Ethiopia, first from abroad—when we were fellow graduate students at the University of Chicago—and then at home, from my very first days in the land. His love for his land and people was contagious, his sincere religiosity moving, his practical advice invaluable. It was Lemma who advised me to spend time in the provincial area of Menz when I expressed frustration over having such a hard time learning Amharic among Anglophone Ethiopian friends in the city. Thanks to Lemma, I befriended the brothers General Mengistu and Germame Neway. General Mengistu, then Commander of the Imperial Bodyguard, was a congenial host and expected me to appear at his luncheon table regularly. My friendship with the Neway brothers became fateful at the end of my three-year sojourn in Ethiopia in December 1960 (see footnote to Chapter 23).

During the time I spent in the capital, the University College of Addis Ababa was a major place for me to hang out. I learned so much from conversations with the college students, two in particular. It was Tegegn Yeteshawarq, who first told me about the type of Ethiopian poetry called *sam-enna warq,* wax-and-gold. (Tegegn was one of the many fine Ethiopians who was executed summarily in November 1974, on what is known as Black Saturday.)

Another helpful student was Tadesse Tamrat, whose assistance spanned more than four decades. As my first quasi-official Amharic teacher, Tadesse spent thankless hours helping me to read Amharic by studying articles in the newspaper *Addis Zemen.* He went on to do doctoral work at SOAS, producing a distinguished work that has become a bedrock for Ethiopianists ever since, *Church and State in Ethiopia: 1270–1527.* Many years after that, as director of Addis Ababa University Press, Tadesse supervised the publication of the Amharic translation of my *Greater Ethiopia.*

Tadesse's monograph was soon followed by another work of distinguished historical scholarship, *Yohannes IV of Ethiopia*, by Dr. Dejazmatch Zewde Selassie, great-great-grandson of that emperor. I learned so much about Ethiopian history through conversations with Zewde over the years. Beyond that, he stood out in my mind as one of the rare Ethiopians whom, in *Wax and Gold,* I described as a moral hero. This was true under all three regimes. We shall never forget his stunning speech at the United Nations, denouncing the Derg massacres, and resigning from his position as Minister of Foreign Affairs. With companion volumes by Mordecai Abir, Sven Rubenson, and Harold Marcus, we were blessed in short compass by monographs covering the rulers of Ethiopia through the 19th century.

What can I say about the people of Menz? The six months I spent living among them figure as among the most memorable in my life. It was from them that I learned so much about the integuments of traditional Amhara life, in moments that remain fresh in my mind more than half a century later. I cherish memories of their hardiness, hospitality, humor, and vivid exemplification of a culture based on strenuous work, observant religiosity, and simple living.

During the early 1970s, when it became crucial for me to expand my ethnic horizon beyond the Amhara, I had the good fortune to befriend an Ethiopian anthropologist, Asmarom Legesse. Thanks to his path-breaking publications on Oromo social structure and a seminar which we taught jointly at the University of Chicago, I learned an enormous amount about that amazing people. I also benefited from my dissertation student John Hinnant, who supplemented Asmarom's knowledge of the Boran Oromo with research on the Guji Oromo.

The Derg years were famously a time when Western social scientists had virtually no access to first-hand reportage in Ethiopia. The great exception to this was Paul Henze, whose regular reporting on the Derg years was an invaluable source. Paul also did originary work on ancient Ethiopian architecture, about which he kindly reported in courses I taught on Ethiopia at Chicago.

I owe a great personal debt to Million Neknik, a distinguished Ethiopian educator and ambassador, and the first Ethiopian to translate Shakespeare into Amharic. Million spent a good part of his last few years translating *Greater Ethiopia* into his pearly Amharic, a task in which he had the assistance of linguist Hailu Fulass.

Other Ethiopian friends edified me by virtue of their creativity in developing contemporary art out of traditional forms. Ale Felege Selam, whom I had known when he studied at the Art Institute of Chicago, went on to teach generations of Ethiopian artists at the academy he established. Habte Selassie Tafesse took a renowned series of photographs of Ethiopians and their art in the service of the Tourism Commission he established. Vocalist Zeleke Gessesse, active with one of Ethiopia's first rock bands, promoted Ethiopian music through his noted Wild Hare nightclub in Chicago, and then returned to create the Wild Hare Addis. Tesfaye Lemma assembled a group of musicians playing traditional instruments previously used in solos to form a path-breaking Orchestra Ethiopia, and later, Mulatu Astatke and Elias Nagash showed the power of Ethiopian melodies in creating contemporary jazz. Painters Wosene Kosrof and Fikru Gebremariam brought traditional motifs into the mainstream of international modern art. Haile Gerima, whom we knew as a struggling theater student in Chicago, went on to a distinguished career in filmmaking; his film *Adwa* should be required viewing for every Ethiopian.

I have benefited from astute critical comments on some drafts of my essays by the distinguished philologist Getachew Haile. I was fortunate to reconnect with Tekalign Gedamu, a friend from 1959, some fifty years later, from whom I have learned much from his first-hand knowledge of the past three regimes beyond what he has included in his stunning work *Republicans on the Throne*. In recent years, I have befriended Ezekiel Gebissa, an extraordinary young Oromo scholar who has helped me through his masterful leadership of the *Journal of Oromo Studies*, his originary research, and his fastidious scholarship on matters Ethiopian. I am also grateful to Tesfaye Tekelu, co-founder of the Awassa Youth Campus, who shares my vision of turning Ethiopia's tradition of warriorhood into nonviolence through aikido.

This book would of course not have been published without the support of Elias Wondimu. Elias's creative stewardship of the priceless heritage of primary and secondary sources for Ethiopian history commands heartfelt thanks from Ethiopians and friends of Ethiopia now and in future generations. And finally, for the demanding task of editing this complex manuscript properly, I owe a huge amount to Andrew DeCort, one of my doctoral students, to whom I am also deeply indebted for his Foreword—and to an exceptionally able research assistant, Lucas Wehrwein.

—Donald N. Levine, August 9, 2014

I

Understanding Ethiopia Today

*Some Observations of a Sociologist (1961)**

If one wishes to gain truer understanding of any human individual or society, it is necessary to cultivate two special capacities: the capacity for detachment and the capacity for sympathy. Without detachment, understanding is biased and distorted, because of the prejudices one has unwittingly acquired and the personal interests one inevitably pursues. Without sympathy, understanding remains cold and remote, and thereby suffers from superficiality, exaggeration, and dogma.

There are three main ways in which the qualities of detachment and sympathy can be maximized in order to obtain a deeper understanding of one's own society. One is to spend a long time in another country. If one sojourns in a foreign country, not as a tourist or a playboy, but with a serious interest in learning, one's perspective broadens. This broadening of perspective appears, for example, as one of the most significant changes experienced by students abroad in such studies as *The Western-Educated Man in India*, by John Useem, and in my own research among foreign-educated Ethiopians. Thus, one of my informants, an Ethiopian who studied for several years in Canada, described the main change in his outlook as follows:

---

* An address delivered to the Second Annual Convention of the Ethiopian Students Association of North America at Africa House, Washington, D.C., on September 7, 1961.

> I learned how to discuss with people holding quite divergent views, something I could not do before. The chief experience I had abroad was the impact of different cultures, which broadened one; I learned to see others as just as good as you or better, and everything as interesting. I came to appreciate the importance of environmental differences and their effects.

The first-hand experience of a different culture enables one to look with more detachment at one's own. Thanks to this detachment, young Ethiopians who have studied abroad are often able on return to understand their society more adequately than many of their elders. They are able, moreover, to criticize certain unhappy features of their society, which their elders take for granted, and also to appreciate, with surer reason, the more valuable aspects of their society.

There is of course the danger that if one remains for too long a time outside one's society one may lose the feeling for their country. His detachment may become so pronounced, by virtue of his new attachment to his host country, that his ability to sustain sympathetic contact with his countrymen and their traditions disintegrates. Thus one finds at times the ultra-Westernized Ethiopian, whose understanding of his society is impaired by the poverty of his sympathy. This is not a necessary consequence of prolonged study abroad, however. If the experience abroad is used not only to gain detachment but also as an occasion for the exercise of sympathy with different human beings and institutions, this same sympathetic faculty can be turned to good account on return by a new effort, an adventure in the sympathetic understanding of the now somewhat estranged elements of one's native society.

A second way in which the qualities of detachment and broader human sympathy may be developed is through a properly constructed program of general education and through advanced studies in the humanistic disciplines and social science. The thorough study of the history of one's country and civilization serves, like travel, to detach one from the prejudices and passions of the moment and to open up new dimensions of sympathetic resources. The same is true, to an even greater extent, of the study of alien civilizations. It has been with this aim in mind, and not only for the (admittedly considerable) intrinsic interest of the subjects, that the College of The University of Chicago has in recent years provided for its undergraduate students courses in Islamic Civilization, Indian Civilization, and Chinese Civilization. In the various social sciences, moreover, the study of theory, comparative materials, and empirical methodology likewise gives the student new capacities for looking at his society with increased understanding.

For more than three decades now, it has been the policy of the Imperial Ethiopian Government to support both these types of experience which, among other functions, serve to equip Ethiopians with the capacity to understand themselves and their institutions more thoroughly. As is well known to all of you here, His Imperial Majesty Haile Selassie I has sent hundreds of Ethiopians abroad for study and practical experience, both before the Italian Occupation and, in greatly increased numbers, since the Liberation. These foreign-educated Ethiopians have brought back to their country not only the skills and information necessary to contribute to the modernization of Ethiopia but also a greater capacity to think about the nature of their country and to offer constructive criticism, the most valuable asset of a country which is seeking to change itself. The distressing fact that so few of the returnees have made use of this asset, by discussing their country's problems more openly and responsibly and attempting to introduce new models of thought and action, must be attributed as much to their widespread timidity, pettiness of ambition, and sheer laziness, as to the relative rigidity of their political system.

On the other hand, it has long been His Majesty's vision, a vision he has sustained, to establish in Ethiopia a national university, which would provide on "Ethiopia's soil an institution of higher learning that might eventually become comparable to the other great universities in the world." It is now a source of immense satisfaction to Ethiopia's friends in many countries, as well as to all of you here, to note that His Majesty's patient efforts in this regard are at last bearing fruit. As you have recently been informed, The Emperor and those professional educators who are entrusted with the establishment of this University are determined to create an institution of the highest quality; to select none but the most competent and dedicated personnel for its staff; to make it a vital force in raising the educational level of the Ethiopian people; and to ensure for it the fundamental conditions of intellectual life—freedom of speech and publication. For this determination, the people of Ethiopia now and for generations to come will certainly feel the most profound gratitude.

There is yet a third way in which understanding of one's society can be deepened, and that is by inviting or enabling people from other countries whose vocation is the search for truth to study one's society and present a view from the outside. Ethiopia has been fortunate in having claimed the attention of a considerable number of gifted scholars during the past few centuries, from the time of Job Ludolphus, the "founder" of Ethiopian studies in the late 17th century, to the distinguished Ethiopianists of the present century, among whom might be named Enno Littman of Germany, Marcel Cohen of France, Carlo Conti-Rossini and Enrico Gerulli of Italy, Stefan Strelcyn of Poland, H.J. Polotsky of Israel, J. Spencer Trimingham and Edward Ullendorf of England, and Wolf Leslau of the United States. The debt which all of us who are concerned about Ethiopia owe to these scholars is very great indeed.

However, the work of these renowned scholars has for the most part been restricted to the fields of humanistic study—chiefly, history and linguistics. Only in the past six or seven years have students versed in the ideas and methods of modern social science begun to do significant empirical research among the peoples of Ethiopia. The professional training of such students has given them, in addition to their natural detachment as an outsider, many special intellectual resources with which to approach their subject in a detached manner, and at the same time this training has equipped them to enlarge the scope of their sympathy so that they may be more sensitive to the experience of those living in an alien culture. Most, though not all, of this work has been conducted by young American anthropologists working under research grants from the Ford Foundation. That generous institution has also supported my own research in Ethiopia as a sociologist.

The particular perspective which a sociologist would bring to the field of Ethiopian Studies might vary considerably within my profession; but, stated in general terms, it has to do with the foundation of social order and the processes of social change. This means, in the framework I have found most useful to adopt, that a sociologist concerns himself with the values shared by the members of a given society in the diverse circumstances of their lives, the institutions which embody these values, the modes of conflict and solidarity within and among these institutions, and the ways in which these institutions persist, develop, or become transformed.

The subject-matter of the sociologist thus consists of some of the most sensitive and complicated of phenomena, yet it is often of the greatest general significance and urgency. Moreover, while the sociologist does his work with the detachment of a scientist, the results of his work may well be used to assist the rulers and public of a society to solve their outstanding social problems. Before going on now to make a few modest observations which I, as an American sociologist, would like to contribute here to the discussion of modern Ethiopia, let me give an illustration of a case in which a foreign sociologist studied a difficult social problem in this country and thereby contributed toward its practical solution.

In 1938 Dr. Gunnar Myrdal, the noted Swedish sociologist, was brought to the United States by the Carnegie Corporation in order to direct "a comprehensive study of the Negro in the United States, to be undertaken in a wholly objective and dispassionate way as a social phenomenon." For four years he and his staff studied this problem, making use of the most effective procedures and resources which sociology then had at its disposal. The main results of their research were published under the title *An American Dilemma*, a book which was quick to become a "classic" of modern sociology. *An American*

Dilemma was an important contribution to the understanding of modern American society. It had, moreover, many practical consequences. Perhaps the most notable of these is the direct influence it had on the members of the Supreme Court of the United States. Whereas the Supreme Court was always divided and vacillating on questions relating to the status of Negroes prior to the appearance of Myrdal's book, once they had read *An American Dilemma*, the Supreme Court judges voted consistently against any infringement of the rights of Negroes ever after. The historic Supreme Court decision of 1954, which ruled school segregation unconstitutional, was to some small but significant extent an effect of the impact of the work of a Swedish sociologist.

In Myrdal's analysis of the situation of the Negro in the United States, his central formulation is that the United States is racked by a major conflict of values—a conflict between the value of white supremacy, as institutionalized in the color caste system in this country, and the value of social equality, as institutionalized in the Constitution of the United States and in the hearts of Americans as the "American Creed." This conflict of values, this "American dilemma," would, Myrdal maintained, eventually have to become resolved in favor of the value of social equality. (And indeed, American society has moved a good deal in that direction since Myrdal wrote two decades ago, though needless to say the process is far from complete.)

Other conflicts of values which a sociologist might observe, however, cannot be so simply resolved. Sometimes there must be an adjustment on both sides of the conflict, a resolution by compromise. At other times, the conflicts can be handled by relegating those who embody the divergent values to different parts of the social system, thereby making use of what may be referred to as "the moral division of labor." At still other times, no manner of reconciliation is possible at all, the conflicts in question stemming from the very nature of society and human nature, a reflection of the essentially tragic character of human existence. In any case, it is one of the most important jobs of a sociologist to determine just what the value conflicts in a society are and to suggest what, if anything, should be done about them.

Ethiopia, like all other countries today, is in the throes of a dilemma, or series of dilemmas, that stem from certain conflicts of values. Many, though not all, of these conflicts can be subsumed under the broad conflict of Ethiopian versus Western, or traditional versus modern, values. Let me state at once that this is already a gross oversimplification. The traditional value systems in Ethiopia are of many kinds, representing the great variety of traditions to be found among the various peoples in the Empire. But I am concerned now with the gross conflicts within the national culture, and so I will restrict myself to considering the dominant cultural tradition in Ethiopia, that of the Amhara and Tigrean peoples. In other words, when I here refer to "traditional" or "Ethiopian" values, I shall, for present purposes, be referring to the values of *Habesha* culture. Similarly, although many Western national cultures have made an impact on modern Ethiopia—particularly French, Italian, British, and North American—I am not now concerned with the differences among these, but with their more general and common components. Nor do I raise the very important, if still largely unexplored, question of the respects in which "modernization" may be achieved without fundamental "Westernization."

In nearly every aspect of Ethiopian culture, then, one can observe a conflict between traditional *Habesha* and modern, Western values. In the cognitive sphere, it is a conflict between beliefs based on traditional superstitions and beliefs based on the methods and findings of science. With regard to religion, it is a conflict between a Christianity preoccupied with archaic rituals and customs and a Christianity attentive to moral precepts and practice; and I imagine an analogous conflict obtains among the Muslims in Ethiopia. In the domain of consumption and taste, it is a conflict about such various matters as the food one eats, the clothes one wears on national holidays, the music one plays at parties, and whether or not one should make use of tobacco. In the area of political values, there is, among others, the conflict between the traditional view that public office is a private possession, to be awarded on the basis of hereditary claims and political loyalty, and to be used for the purpose of personal aggrandizement; and the modern ideal of public office as a public trust, to be awarded on the basis of administrative and technical capacities, and to be used primarily as a means of discharging a specified set of obligations on behalf of the public. With respect to moral values, the conflicts are only now beginning to emerge, but in many ways they are bound to be the most distressing and momentous of all.

Before going into the details of some of these value conflicts in modern Ethiopia, it may be useful to consider two general points concerning the nature of ideological conflicts in contemporary Ethiopia. One is that, as a country aspiring toward rapid economic and social development, Ethiopia sorely needs the constructive use of the energies of all her people. It is important therefore to maintain many bridges between the tradition-minded and the modernists in her population. If they lose the capacity to understand each other as Ethiopians and as human beings, if all their energy is consumed in conflict against each other, Ethiopia's development can never be more than halting and disjointing, and terribly wasteful.

On the other hand, it is important to understand and discuss those conflicts which do exist, and whenever possible to use them to resolve antagonisms and to create new and more generally shared values. As a leading contemporary sociologist, Professor Lewis Coser tells us in his book on *The Functions of Social*

Conflict, a social structure in which there is little or no toleration of conflict suffers thereby. If there are no outlets for the expression of conflict, Coser has noted, "the rigidity [of the social structure]. . . permits hostilities to accumulate and to be channeled along one major line of cleavage once they break out in conflict." That is the situation of revolutionary chaos, a situation which a country like Ethiopia can ill afford to indulge in. Fortunately, there is every indication that the airing of social conflicts in Ethiopia will become more and more feasible in the years to come. Already, in the past few years, oratorical contests and debates among the secondary school and college students have begun to explore, for a limited public, many of the conflicts of values which are vexing Ethiopia today. It could be one of the major contributions of the new Haile Selassie I University to provide a forum in which such conflicts can be aired more thoroughly and for a wider public than ever before, if educated Ethiopians like those of you here are determined to make it so.

Now I, as an outsider and a professional sociologist, would like to contribute a few words to this discussion of ideological conflict in Ethiopia. In particular, I want to discuss the question of conflict in the sphere of moral values, since that is, it seems to me, at the heart of Ethiopia's dilemmas today and yet one of the least explored aspects of changing Ethiopia. The view which prevails among most educated Ethiopians is that the best hope for Ethiopia is to take from the West whatever is needed to promote national development and otherwise to retain the traditional culture. Stated in these general terms, one cannot quarrel with this formulation. At times, however, this statement appears to mean that what Ethiopia must do is to adopt from the West the knowledge of modern science and the achievements of modern technology, and otherwise to retain her traditional morality intact. This aspiration, I venture to say, is not wholly realistic: it is neither possible nor desirable. It is impossible, because, the very introduction of modern science and technology inevitably produces far-reaching changes in the sphere of moral values. It is not desirable, for the kinds of institutions and activity required to promote the development of Ethiopia require radically new kinds of moral orientation in certain respects.

There are four main aspects of traditional Ethiopian morality which appear to be inadequate guides to the kind of behavior needed in Ethiopia today. Roughly speaking, these may be identified as (1) submissiveness to elders and superiors, (2) individualism, (3) equivocation, and (4) physical aggressiveness.

Unconditional respect for one's elders and superiors is an unfailing feature of a strongly patriarchal society. Command and obedience are the primary modes of communication in such a system. The importance of transmitting faithfully the culture of the fathers means that such education as occurs will be focused on the transfer of tradition, by a pedagogy which is based on imitation and repetition. The opinions of youth are accounted of no significance; young people are to be seen little and heard less. The classical interpretation of such a society would suggest that the same relation is projected onto the political hierarchy, where political father figures are entitled to absolute obedience and subordinates are entrusted with no responsibility.

It is clear that this sort of pattern cannot remain intact in any society attempting to change itself. The primary resource for accomplishing social change is the education of young people, and these must be granted some positions of responsibility in society if their education is not to be in vain and if society is to advance. Since educated young people are likely to obtain politically subordinate positions in the political and social structure, moreover, the traditional pattern of expecting them only to follow the orders of their superiors likewise conflicts with the aspiration for progress.

In short: the traditional value of subservience to elders and superiors conflicts with the modern value of respect for youth and qualified subordinates.

Another important aspect of the traditional Habesha morality may be referred to as individualism. In this respect the Amhara peasant is very much like the American farmer, especially in the New England states, who feels that "good fences make good neighbors" and stresses the virtues of self-reliance, independence, and self-assertion. Traditional individualism is reflected in many aspects of traditional Ethiopia: the organization of the church, the organization of the armies, the lack of a viable community organization, the prominence of litigation, the sensitivity to insults, and the insistence on originality in the composition of *qine*. This is a complicated subject, and I am dealing with it at greater length in my coming book. But I think that none of you will disagree with me when I suggest that in traditional Ethiopia, the interest in oneself and one's immediate kin was always much more important than the interest in any broader societal structures.

Now Ethiopia has entered a period—in the life of her cities—where the chief restraint on unbridled individualism, the family, has become weakened; and where, on the other hand, the pursuit of narrow self-interest no longer suffices as a principle of social organization. If Ethiopia is to develop, activity on behalf of the larger community will have to become a central part of the lives of many of her citizens. Thus we have arrived at a second conflict of moral values: the traditional value of individualism versus the value of modern nationalism.

The third area of traditional morality I would like to discuss concerns the basic mode of relating to one another. According to the traditional culture, communication must be indirect. For example, one never comes out directly and asks for a position; one practices *dej tenat* for a while and eventually perhaps someone notices. One did not ask for a gift directly, but instead gave a *mamalacha* to one's superior and hoped to receive the desired object in return. Furthermore, language itself is expected to be used somewhat deviously. The central principle of Ge'ez prosody, among the masters of *qine*, is equivocation. It is the genius of the Amharic language that it lends itself so readily to such equivocation, and among the major traditional culture heroes—men like Aleqa Gabre Hanna, and Afe Negus Ishete Geda—are those who became noted for their facility with puns and double entendre.

All this is delightful; but as a basic mode of interpersonal relations it does not augur well for national development. Honest consensus among people is indispensable for meaningful concerted activity, especially of the creative sort that is required in Ethiopia today. The fact that the question of honesty is very much on the minds of Ethiopia's youth is indicated by the results of a questionnaire I administered to 700 secondary and college students in Ethiopia, where by far the greatest number of them indicated "honesty" as the best character trait of all, and a few of them even mentioned honesty as that thing they would most like their children to have that they did not have! Thus we encounter a third moral dilemma in Ethiopia today: the traditional value of subtle equivocation versus the modern value of clear and honest communication.

Finally, and here I speak primarily to the males, physical aggressiveness is very much stressed in traditional Ethiopia. It was important, in that rough and ready society, for a man to defend himself boldly against infringements on his hereditary land and his personal honor. Proper use of the *dula* was one unfailing lesson for every Ethiopian boy. Not only the soldiers by vocation but every healthy man outside of the clergy was expected to march to battle when the *negarit* sounded. Warfare was almost as common a component of the traditional round of life as was plowing.

In modern Ethiopia, however, apart from the minimal security functions of the police and the army, there is no longer any sense in which military activity is a normal part of Ethiopian life. The days of intertribal warfare are reaching an end; the military threat of European imperialism is clearly a thing of the past; nor does there appear any realistic likelihood that any of Ethiopia's African neighbors will attempt to invade her. Physical aggression, moreover, has lost a good deal of favor as a means of settling disputes. In school life, as in the civil administration, there is no need for a man to prove himself as a heroic fighter. In Ethiopia, as in all countries of the modern world, public consciousness has become increasingly informed by humanitarian concerns and impulses, despite such monstrous exceptions as Hitlerism and the atomic arms race. The opposition of this modern humanitarianism to the old virtue of physical aggressiveness thus constitutes a fourth area of moral conflict in Ethiopia today.

The foregoing considerations add up to a serious critique of some of the important elements of traditional Ethiopian morality, from the point of view of the aspirations and sentiments of progressive Ethiopians today. There are many moral values, of course, which there is no call to change, which it would be wise to leave intact or even to strengthen—such values as hospitality, respect for another's property, and politeness in everyday relations. But with these four traditional patterns at least—total submissiveness to elders and superiors, individualism, equivocation, and physical aggressiveness—the modern Ethiopian can no longer remain satisfied.

How is this aspect of Ethiopia's dilemma to be resolved? Does it mean that the modern-minded must wage an unrelenting battle against the defenders of these traditional values until they are superseded? It is to this question that I would like to turn now in concluding my remarks today.

In the course of studying Ethiopia's dilemmas during the past few years, I have been particularly drawn toward the question of how Ethiopia's own traditional motives, norms, and symbols can be used effectively in the cause of modernization. It does seem that instead of seeking to discard and replace those aspects of the traditional culture which are inadequate to serve modern purposes, it might be much more productive to redefine them in more suitable terms. Such an effort would contribute much more to the attainment of national solidarity and would be more in keeping with the true spirit of Ethiopian nationalism.

In the case of the outmoded moral values which we have just considered for example, it might well be worth some effort to try to find their "moral equivalents," to use the famous phrase of William James, in related values which may serve the goals of the new era. Let us now explore this possibility briefly.

The attitude of respect toward elders in Ethiopia, as in so many cultures which are slow to change, is connected in part with their attribute of wisdom. Those who live long in a traditional society by that fact know more about what is required to live successfully in their culture than those who have lived for a shorter time. In a rapidly changing society, however, it is the youth who know more about what is going on. The function of the elder, or *shemagle*, must then pass—in those institutions most closely connected to change—to young people who have been educated in modern ways. It is not unthinkable that young Ethiopians now come to play the role of *shemagle* in certain areas of national life. In olden times, a very young *dejazmatch* or *fitawrari* would be considered one of *ye-agar shemaglotch*. To qualify for this deference, however, the educated youth must also demonstrate the other characteristics of the *shemagle* besides wisdom. They must at all costs avoid flippancy and vanity, but show in their manner and bearing the great patience, dignity, and calm judgment which are the beloved characteristics of the Ethiopian *shemagle*. Then they too will have a chance to earn the deference of the other Ethiopians who have to deal with them.

The disposition toward individualism can likewise be redefined—perhaps even more successfully—in ways that are more appropriate to the needs of modern Ethiopia. For what Ethiopia needs more than ever today are true "individuals": personalities who can stand on their own feet and pursue a goal without being discouraged by obstacles or dismayed by the ignorant comments of public opinion. The way in which this can best be achieved is through cultivating the notion of career, whereby individual advancement is constantly pursued, but measured in terms of professional standards and actual accomplishments on behalf of the country. Individual ambition, pursued through appropriate channels, may then become a blessing rather than a curse for Ethiopia.

It may not be so easy to find a place for equivocation in the modern setting, for I believe that honest communication and the related ability to trust one another are among the most important capacities which Ethiopians have to develop today. Nevertheless, the traditional genius for ambiguous expression may also be used to good effect in the effort to achieve social change with a minimum of disruptive tension. It is possible, that is, to justify a certain innovation to someone who is content with the status quo by appealing to a more general value which both of you can accept. For example, those tradition-minded people who still oppose modern education because of its association with the heathen *ferinj* may be told that only by thorough study of *ferinj* science can Ethiopia become strong enough to repel any invader of the country's land in the future. Such double talk is often helpful in achieving desired changes with a minimum of tension. (There is good precedent in Ethiopia's own history for this sort of approach. Those of you familiar with the inscriptions of Emperor Ezana of the Fourth Century will recall how his manifestation of so radical a change as conversion to Christianity was expressed in very cautious and ambiguous language.)

There is, finally, a great place for a redefined norm of physical courage, or *gwebeznet*. For, if physical courage plays a much smaller role in Ethiopian life today, moral courage is required more desperately than ever. This is the courage to resist the temptations of corruption and nepotism when one is oneself in office. It is the courage to pursue a sound project for a long time, despite recurrent rebuffs. It is the courage to stand up to one's superior when necessary—to be tactful, but honest, with him, and tell him in a firm and rational manner when his policies are being detrimental to the country.

Beyond this, there is a real place for active aggression today. For Ethiopia still has many enemies, though they do not come armed with spears or flying airplanes. The enemies of the present day are hunger, poverty, and disease;

they are ignorance, inhumanity, and injustice. There is still need today for the Ethiopian warrior, but his *shilela* war chant needs to be rewritten:

Wadya mado hono basheta binorew;

Wadih mado hono denqurna wey alew;

Tateq y'agere lij yih neger yegna new!

"If an enemy like disease comes from afar

If an enemy like ignorance strikes from within

Take arms, my countryman, let's just deal with it!"

This sort of spirit might well provide a medium for expressing that fervent devotion to country which His Imperial Majesty has so often urged the citizens of Ethiopia to cultivate, and which I have been privileged to witness in my encounter with you here.

Part I

ETHOS AND WORLDVIEW

2

On the Conceptions of Time and Space in the Amhara World View (1959)*

The concept of world view has become increasingly prominent in recent years as one of those very general categories, like social structure or basic personality, by means of which anthropologists attempt to come to terms with the character of a society as a whole. In more generous definitions of the concept, world view refers to the sum total of a people's orientations toward the objects they confront in life. These orientations include cognitive orientations, or ideas about what is; affective orientations, or feelings about what is; and evaluative orientations, or judgments about good and bad. The kinds of objects confronted may be distinguished as physical objects, including natural objects and human artifacts; social objects, including the self, other individuals, and collectivities; and cultural objects, including symbol systems, works of art, and representations of the supernatural. In short, world view refers to the "whole meaningful universe" of a people as perceived and experienced from the inside, from their own point of view.[1]

Although the effort to depict the world view of a given people arises from the desire to characterize them as a whole, it is, strictly speaking, an impossible task.

---

* Originally presented at the First International Conference of Ethiopian Studies (Rome, April 2–4, 1959) and published in *Atti del Convegno Internazionale di Studi Etiopici* (Roma: Accademia Nazionale dei Lincei, 1960), 223–28.

Every social role that involves a distinctive way of life involves to some extent a different outlook on the world. Every society, therefore, contains a number of different world views, for it is hard to imagine even the most homogeneous society where the outlook of children is exactly the same as that of adults or where men and women do not differ in some aspects of their orientations.

Leaving aside differences based on age and sex, one may identify, within the traditional society of the Amhara people, four somewhat different world views, corresponding to the four main roles and styles of life within that society. One may speak, first of all, of the world view of the emperors. Their outlook has been conditioned by a position of theoretically absolute power and by the assumption that they are divine monarchs, descended from a holy line appointed to execute God's will.[2] Of the style of life of the emperors, many books have been written. Of their inner thoughts and feelings, we shall probably never know very much.

The upper class in Amhara society, the *mäkwannint*, may be said to have a style of life and a world view of their own. Ideas of good breeding, feelings of reserve and aplomb and an ethos of nobility and military courage are some of the elements of their outlook on life, which will be the subject of a later study.

That small proportion of the clergy who have mastered what may be called the "Great Tradition"[3] in Abyssinian culture constitute a way unto themselves. They possess a world view which is esoteric, not in the sense that it is secret and forbidden, but in the sense that many years of study are needed to acquire it. The elaboration of this world view, based on the hundred or so books in the literature of the church and on a mass of oral lore, would be a task demanding a book of its own, a task I hope some Ethiopian scholar may undertake in the future.

The Amhara peasant has received relatively little treatment in books on Ethiopia, yet of the four main branches of Amhara society, his is perhaps most accessible to empirical study, and one can never aspire to an understanding of the sense and sway of Abyssinian culture and history without making his acquaintance more intimately. In work now in progress I am exploring the world of the Amhara peasant, seeking to determine his ideas and feelings about the cosmos; supernatural beings; nature; the self; human nature; society; time and space; art; and the good life.

In the course of this research it has become apparent that the restriction of focus to the peasant class is a fruitful one, for in certain areas his views are indeed different from those of other parts of the society. For example, the cosmological ideas of the Amhara peasant are quite different from those of the learned men of the church, just as his notions about proper behavior are in many ways different from those of the nobility.

In some areas, on the other hand, all parts of traditional Amhara society are in accord.[4] The feeling that elders deserve special respect and the preference for oral literature over other forms of art are "universals" in Amhara culture. Here I shall discuss one general category—time and space—whose content seems much the same throughout Amhara society.

The topic of time and space in the Amhara world view will be considered here briefly under three headings: the secular dimension, the sacred dimension, and the basic configuration.

The Secular Dimension

Time as a medium for the pursuit of secular interests is of little explicit concern for the Amhara. Historical time does not claim his attention, for history is neither a problem nor a delight to the Amhara: the essential goals of his life are realized outside of history. Consequently, he has traditionally had little interest in his own history, and almost never knows any historical dates. He usually does not know the exact year, yet alone date, of his own birth.

Local time is equally ignored. Hours and dates do not bother him. When a man says he is going on a trip "tomorrow," everyone assumes that he means he may be going on a trip a few days later. Many appointments are made but few are kept. There is, moreover, little sense of time in the abstract. When you ask an Amhara how long a trip takes, he will not reply "x hours," but rather in the form, "if you leave here at t1, you will arrive there at ta"; and usually his estimate of the arrival time varies with whether or not he wants you to make the trip.

Parallel with this lack of rationalization of secular time we find the lack of interest in measuring and systematically ordering secular space. Land is never measured, and in traditional Amhara country the people raise a big protest if there is any suggestion that their land is to be measured. Land titles are defined loosely, by tradition and approximation, with the result—in a country where land is the most important value—that the Amharas are forever litigating about property rights. This lack of rationalizing space is conspicuous even in the capital city, where to this day there are no street numbers, so that places can only be identified roughly as near a certain police station or past a certain hospital.

The Sacred Dimension

At the beginning of each new year, a little ceremony is held in the churches. A learned *däbtära* stands before the people and calculates the dates for the important holidays and fasts during the coming year. Sometimes this is preceded by telling the story of Demetrios, the man who after long struggles succeeded in discovering the formula according to which the Orthodox calendar can be computed, so that, for example, the little fast before Lent will begin on Monday and end on Thursday. This ceremony symbolizes the extreme importance of rationalizing time for religious purposes in Amhara life.

The years and the days of the month are named after, and usually best remembered by, the various holy figures in the Ethiopian Church. Each cycle of four years is named after the Four Gospels, with that 'of Johannis (John) standing for leap year. The customary greeting at the New Year is of the form: May He bring you safely from the year of Mark to the year of Luke! Nearly every day of the month is dedicated to some saint or angel, the major days being:

Ledäta (birth of Mary)	1st of each month
Abbo (Gäbrä Mänfäs Qiddus)	5th of each month
Selasse (Trinity)	7th of each month
Mikael	12th of each month
Kidanä Meh'rät (covenant of Mercy, for Mary)	16th of each month
Gäbrael	19th of each month
Maryam	21st of each month
Giorgis	23rd of each month
Täklä Haymanot	24th of each month
Mädhäne Aläm (Savior of the world)	27th of each month
Balä Wäld	29th of each month

Certain of these days, according to local custom, are honored each month as holidays, on which no work is to be done. The schedule of these days is well implanted in the mind of each Amhara. The names of these holy figures thus *come to take the place of calendar dates.* Instead of saying, "He fell sick on the fifth" or "He is due to come on the twelfth," the Amhara normally says, "He fell sick on Abbo" or "He is due to come on Mikael."

Similarly, the Amharas are very conscious of the organization of space with regard to the distribution of the holy arks, or *tabot,* which are named after the holy figures and housed in churches of the same names. Though people are rarely clear about the precise boundaries of various place names over the country, everyone knows just where the several churches are located over a wide area. It is customary for people to locate a given place with reference to the nearest *tabot* or church. Thus they will say, "He lives near Abbo" or "We must travel past Mikael." Thus *locations in space are identified by precisely the same set of coordinates as are events in time:* the names of the saints and angels. Moreover, just as in every year some month is the occasion for an annual celebration on behalf of each holy person, so in the countryside certain churches are considered to be the holiest shrines of the various holy figures.

The Basic Configuration

The Amhara's conception of time is, I suggest, a cyclical one. This hypothesis explains both his lack of attention to historical events and the character of his prophesies. The general Amhara attitude is that the seasons come and go, people come and go, but there is not much new under the sun. The essential feature of Abyssinian history, apart from the Gragn saga and some developments of the past century, is its repetitiveness, its lack of development. As one country *däbtära* put it: "The people around here do not know much about historical figures, because our history was always the same old thing—one lord fighting another to get more power."

On the other hand, we sometimes hear of prophecies about the future, prophecies which point to the restoration of some state of things that obtained in the past. It is believed that Dejatch Kassa chose the throne name of Tewodros II because of the contemporary prophecy that a king of that name would arise to destroy Islam and bring the people peace and prosperity, repeating the happy reign that was attributed to Tewodros I of the Fifteenth Century. Likewise, some Amharas today speak of a ruler to come who will take the name of Tewodros again. He will rule with the *Bang* (a type of stick that symbolizes peace and justice) and usher in another happy time. On the darker side is a prophecy that a Muslim from Tsä'da Sa'ri in Dankali land will conquer and rule Ethiopia for a brief time. Later, he will be defeated, and a Christian will again rule over Ethiopia. This prophecy suggests that the Gragn story of the Sixteenth Century will be repeated in the future.

There is also the prophecy, related by a Gojjami peasant, that when the Eighth Millenium arrives (2508 A.D., European calendar) God will effect the destruction of the world by turning it upside down. All who live at that time will perish, while those who died first in the world's history will return to life, to a time of renewal, when a little grain will go a long way and the milk of one cow will feed a multitude. The whole thing will start all over again.

A cyclical pattern is certainly found in the Amhara's experience of months and years. The years do not run on continuously, but follow the sequence Matthew, Mark, Luke, John—again and again and again. Each month, moreover, revolves about the same set of saints' days—in contrast to the Catholic calendar, which has a different saint for each day of the year. In addition to the annual holidays of Mäsqäl (Discovery of the True Cross), Timqät (Epiphany), and Fasiqa (Easter), the Amhara gives special celebration to each of the "monthly" holy figures at least once a year, though the precise month may vary with locality. There is thus a big celebration in honor of Mikael in Hidar, one honoring Maryam in Tir, and Balä Wäld, Festival of the Son, is honored especially on His birthday, Christmas, in the month of Tah'sas. The result is a triple system of monthly cycles, annual cycles, and four-year cycles—issuing in a series of epicycles, in which the monthly rounds play themselves out within the larger circles of annual rounds.

The dominant configuration in the Amhara's experience of space seems to be that of concentric circles. Whether or not we try to relate this to the cycles and epicycles in his conception of time, the fact remains that the pattern of a highly significant center surrounded by circles of decreasing significance recurs in every dimension of traditional Amhara life.

It is to be found, first of all, in his architecture. The traditional peasant home is round, with a conical roof supported by a pole which rises in the center of the circle. This is his domestic "inner sanctum." Surrounding the compound in which the home stands is a round fence which separates the basic kin group from the whole outside world, a boundary distinction of great social and psychological importance.

This form is developed more fully in the churches. The holiest item in the church, the *tabot,* is kept (in an oblong frame, the *mänbär)* right in the middle of the church. This ark stands in an inner sanctum, the *mäqdäs,* which only ordained priests and deacons may enter. Within this innermost circle the mass is performed. Separated from this by a round wall is a second circle, the *qiddist,* where those who wish to partake of the Communion stand. Only young children and those few adults who have been married by Communion in the church enjoy this privilege. Beyond this, past another wall, is the third circle, *q'ne mah'let,* where the ordinary person may stand and where priests and *däbtäras* assemble on special days to sing hymns and perform dances. The round church building itself stands in a compound ringed by an outer wall. This represents still another gradation of ritual purity proceeding away from the center. Those who have eaten before the mass, or who have had sexual relations the night before, are not even permitted to enter the circle, and must stand outside, beyond the outer wall, during the services.

This spatial pattern is likewise found in the arrangement of people out of doors. The most notable instance is the traditional organization of the military camp of a king or ras. In the center of the camp was the big, round tent of the chief, together with tents for the *tabot,* noble visitors, and supplies. Around this were stationed the high officers: the *däjasmatch* in front, the *qägnasmatch* on the right, and the *g'rasmatch* on the left. This "inner sanctum" was circled by the tents of the cavalry. Beyond this ring, finally, was an outer circle composed of the huts of the common soldiery.[5]

Spontaneous arrangements following this sort of pattern appear during festivals. The person or persons who sing or dance are placed in the center, and the spectators form a circle around them. During religious celebrations outside, a small group of priests assemble in one place to sing and dance. Around them is an inner circle of spectators, mostly older priests and *däbtäras*. Standing at some distance is another circle, where the lay people watch from afar. It is the pattern of concentric circles once again.

These words serve merely to introduce the topic of the Amhara world view, and of Amhara conceptions of time and space in particular. They suggest a notable parallelism between the forms of time and the forms of space in the Amhara world. That sacred, rather than secular, interests are dominant in organizing time and space here is not surprising in a traditional society whose chief focus of organization has long been the church. The cyclical sense of time is perhaps related to the intimate dependence of Amhara life on the seasons, and the, relative absence of historical novelty in a world where man's will is not reckoned an efficient cause in universe.

Notes

1 For discussion of the concept of world view, Cf. R. Redfield, *The Little Community* (Chicago: University of Chicago Press, 1955), Chapter VI. For analysis of modes of orientation and types of objects, cf. also Parsons and Shils, eds., *Toward a General Theory of Action* (Cambridge: Harvard University Press, 1951), Part II.

2 Thus Tewodros, who did so much to restore the role of the emperor, is said to have declared at his coronation in 1855: "Know that I am the new Constantine of the Holy Empire of Abyssinia, of Ancient Ethiopia, the elected of God for your salvation," Quoted in B. Velat, *Un Grand Dignitaire de l'Eglise Ethiopienne,* "Les Cahiers Coptes," 1953, No. IV, p. 18.

3 For discussion of the concepts of Great Tradition and Little Tradition, cf. R. Redfield, *Peasant Society and Culture* (Chicago: University of Chicago Press, *1956),* Chapter Ill.

4 Again, it would be hard to imagine a society, however heterogeneous, where all the members did not hold *some* ideas and feelings in common. The very use of a common language already signifies some common component of world view.

5 Cf. M. Griaule. *Uti Camp Militaire Abyssin,* Journal de la Societe des Africanistes, Tome IV, 1934, pp. 117–22. For suggesting the correspondence of church and camp forms, I am indebted to S.D. Messing, *The Highland-Plateau Amhara of Ethiopia* (Unpublished Ph. D. Dissertation. University of Pennsylvania, 1957), p. 267.

3

On the History and Culture of Manz (1964)*

Manz, an Amhara area of about 850 square miles located in the northeast horn of Shoa Province,[1] is of particular interest in the field of Ethiopian studies from both the ethnographic and the historical points of view.[2] It is of ethnographic interest because the culture of Manz differs in certain respects from the standard culture of the Amhara people.[3] Some aspects of this variance are directly related to its climate which, owing to Manz's altitude and its position at the edge of an escarpment that leads eventually to a desert of the Rift valley, is one of the coldest, if not the coldest, inhabited area in all Ethiopia. Thus, in contrast with the cotton dress worn by most Amhara, the standard Manz dress is the *bānnā*, a blanket made from the natural wool of the sheep which are found in large numbers there. Further, since Manz is not warm enough for the cultivation of *tēff*, the cereal grain favoured by Amhara for use in their staple pancake *enjarā*, the Manzē typically eats *enjarā* made from barley; while consumption of *tēff*, since it is so scarce, has become there a mark of high status. Again, because of the sharp winds and because the terrain is so stony, the walls of houses in Manz are built of stone, rather than wattle as in other Amhara areas.

The culture of Manz is further distinguished by its selective emphasis on certain values which are universal in Amhara culture. Chief among these are the values of *rest*, on the one hand, and *gwabaz-nat*, on the other. *Rest*, land inherited from a relative, usually father or mother, is an object of the highest respect and devotion in Manz. The feeling against selling it to someone outside one's family is exceedingly strong among the Manzēs. Those who migrate from Manz retain

* Originally published in the *Journal of Semitic Studies* (1964) 9 (1): 204–11.

a deep sentimental attachment to any *rest* they may happen to own there, and the claim of someone who has been away from his family's land even for more than a generation is greatly respected in Manz. This sentiment is expressed in a favourite Manzē proverb:

> *Ya-Manz rest ba-shi amatu / la-bālabētu;*
>
> Manz *rest* (belongs) to its owner until the thousandth year

Gwabaz-nat, the virtue of physical courage, is also accentuated in Manzē culture. In their own eyes as in the eyes of others the men of Manz are reputed for hardiness and combativeness. *Mot ged yallam*, "Never mind death!", is the motto one governor from Manz volunteered as the key to the ethos of his people. The Manzē wants his son to be *gwabaz*, brave, and uses this term, like that of *watādar*, soldier, as a favourite compliment. The names which are characteristically given to children in Manz express this determination:

Ahidē	Thrasher
Asdangat	Frighten
Atāmantā	Don't hesitate
Balātchaw	Give It To Them
Balāy-metā	Hit On The Top
Gosheme	Shover
Latybalu	Let Them Bow
Mān Yazhal	Who Orders You?
Nādaw	Wipe Him Out
Tālārgē	Powerful
Tāsaw	Smash Him
Tchabudē	Squeezer
Tchaftchefē	Hacker
Weqātchaw	Thrash Them

The people of Manz are further distinguished from other Amhara—in their own minds, at least—by virtue of the tenacity and scrupulousness with which they adhere to the dietary laws of Ethiopian Christianity. Although with respect to the literary and monarchal aspects of Ethiopian Christianity their culture is impoverished if one compares Manz with Gojjām, Bagēmder, Lāstā, or Tigrē, the Manzēs are extremely self-conscious of their identity as Christians and ritually devout. They may be reckoned among the more fundamentalist of Amhara Christians, for which reason most of them resist sending their children to government schools because of the feeling that these schools are tainted by their connexion with the culture of the "heathen" foreigner.

While the separate identity of the Manzē is for the most part based on a celebration of these and related differences of custom and ethos, the pride of the more informed Manzē rests on the historical significance of his land. This significance derives primarily from two related phenomena which date from the seventeenth century. First, since Manz was practically the only part of Shoa not occupied by the Oromo, it was able to provide a base from which the Amhara offensive to reconquer the south was launched. It is for this reason that Shoans often refer to Manz as *ya-amārā mentch*, the source of the Amhara. Secondly, Manz was the birthplace of a line of rulers which culminated in the present family of Ethiopia.

To some extent, moreover, Manz is noted for its connexion with important events and sovereigns of earlier centuries. According to Ethiopian traditions Manz was the heir of the sole survivor of Aksumite royalty, Anbasā Wedem, who is believed to have fled south to Manz when was sacked in the 10th century.[4] Manz was the object of some attention under Emperor Zar'a Yā'qob (1434–68), who established a monastery at Ferkutā in eastern Manz and during whose reign was written a biography of the "apostle of Manz," Yohānnes the Oriental, who converted wild beasts and overcame the dragon.[5] His successor, Ba'eda Māryām (1468–78), made his camp for a while at Maryam in Manz. His sojourn there is remembered to this day, recorded in the amusing formula with which he exacted tribute from the various districts near his camp:

> From Agāntchā, fifty *koretcha* (saddles);
>
> from Hulu Dehā, fifty *deha* (servants);
>
> from Aftanak, fifty *naf* (rags);
>
> from Godambo, fifty *gambo* (jars of drink).

It was from Manz that Ba'eda Māryām brought priests to officiate at coronation in Djagno.[6] According to Shoan tradition, finally, Manz also served as a refuge during the invasions of Ahmad Gragn for the fourth son of Lebna Dengel (1507–40), Yā'qob, who is said to have fled there with the royal raiments, and who is regarded as a direct ancestor of the line of rulers which later emerged from Manz.[7]

According to *Futuh el-Habacha*, Manz was ravaged by the forces of Gragn in 1531.[8] Scarred timbers identified as pillars of churches burned during that invasion may be seen there today. Local legends concerning the history of Manz relate for the most part to the miraculous feats which were performed there, on the one hand, and to the resettlement of Gragn on the other. These legends speak of the "founding" of Manz by three men—Māmā, Lālo, and Gērā—who were sent by one of the emperors to settle and govern that territory. As the story goes, the emperor gave each of them as much land as he could cross in a single day. They set out from the Adabāy River, today a western boundary of Manz, and the result of a long day's journey was the present tripartite division of Manz into Māmā Meder, Lālo Meder, and Gērā Meder. This is why Gērā Meder is the largest of the three districts; for Gērā's horse was the strongest!

Some versions of the legend state that Māmā, Lālo and Gērā were sent by Emperor Galāwdēwos (1541–59), while others say that were sent from Gonder [founded in 1632]. In any case it does appear that they were historical personages, and from genealogical evidence and other allusions it seems reasonable to place them in the latter part of the seventeenth century.[9]

Other aspects of the history and culture of Manz will be treated in a forthcoming publication. I should like to complete this brief communication by following the Amhara folk example of treating history—*tārik*—chiefly in terms of outstanding places and related personages, and mention three *tārikāwi bota* (historical places) to which the local inhabitants attribute special significance: Agāntchā, Ferkutā, and Afqārā (all of them located in Gērā Meder).

Agāntchā is famous as the birthplace of Nagāssē Kristos Warada Q̱āl, commonly known as Nagassi. Born to a wealthy proprietor in that district, Nagāssi's valour and skill at arms won him many followers, and he emerged from a long series of battles with his neighbours, including, it seems, the mighty Gērā, as the dominant chieftain in Manz. He proceeded to expand his dominion, establishing settlements and churches in adjacent lands which he recaptured from the Oromo, thereby initiating the process of steady Amhara expansion which was to eventuate in the reassertion of Amhara hegemony over Shoa. Nagāssi proclaimed himself ruling prince of Shoa, and his authority was to some extent confirmed by Emperor Iyāsu I (1682–1706) during Nagāssi's tour to Gonder.[10] (The field on which he camped during his sojourn there still bears the name "Nagāssi Meda.") Nagāssi did not live to enjoy his long-sought investiture on Shoan soil, for he died in Gonder of smallpox. But the authority of his position was acknowledged by the people of Manz, and his chieftancy passed in unbroken succession from father to son for the next eight generations, culminating in the figure of Emperor Menelik II (1889–1913).[11] The church which Nagāssi founded at Agāntchā, Kidāna Maherat, is today one of the larger churches in Manz.

Kidana Maherat is also the name of the one important monastery in Manz. It is located in the district of Ferkutā, near the eastern escarpment. The monastery compound includes two large church buildings, the older built in the fifteenth century by Zar'a Yā'qob, the other built in this century by Emperor Lejj Iyāsu (1913–17). Ferkutā Kidāna Maherat is of note chiefly because of its association with one of the minor figures of Ethiopian hagiography, Etchē Yohānnes, who is said to be buried there and whose biography (*gadal*) is probably the only distinctive volume in the monastery library. Etchē Yohannes was a devout and wealthy monk who taught at Ferkutā during the reign of Iyasu I. The frost which occasionally ruins the crops around Ferkutā is attributed to his curse upon the locale for circulating rumours which denied his virginity.[12] The monastery was in addition peripherally involved in the political history of Manz, in that it served as a refuge for one of the rulers in Nagāssi's line, Asfa Wassan, when as a youth he fled upon learning that the woman from whom he had sired a son (the future Wassan Sagad) had been one of his father's concubines.[13]

A third place of great renown in Manz is the mountain of Afqārā. It is located about two hours' journey to the west of Alo Bāhr, a small crater lake famous throughout Manz as the chief abode of the evil spirits and connected with legends about the visit of the Virgin Mary to Manz.[14] A huge natural fortress ringed by gorges, Afqārā is sparsely populated on clearings at two levels. The lower level (considered *wayna dēgā* altitude) has a famous church dedicated to Gabre'ēl, the upper level (considered *dēgā* altitude) has a Sellāssē church which is said to date back to the time of Saint Takla Haymanot. (Some amber-coloured stones near the Sellāssē church are depicted as places where Takla Haymanot himself trod, the footsteps having turned to "gold".) The local inhabitants are enthusiastic about the mountain's military advantages. Only two paths permit access to the upper level, and only one of these can be traversed by mules. At many places access to the upper level can be prevented by dropping rocks against the invader; one of these places is called *shi fajj*, "destroyer of a thousand," for one man is supposed to have destroyed a thousand troops by this method there.

It was thus natural that Gērā, whose territory included Afqārā, should set it up as a garrison for detaining political prisoners, a purpose it served for generations of Shoan rulers until the time of the Italian invasion (1936). Menilek also built a palace and an armoury there. Its fortunate situation permitted this stronghold to survive serious assaults. According to local inhabitants, Emperor Tēwodros (1855–68) tried for three years to capture Afqara, bombarding it with cannon, but to no avail; and it took Italian troops and air-force eleven days to seize the upper level (which they left the same day it was attained).

The lower level of Afqārā was the abode of numerous descendants of Gera, including the prominent lord, his grandson Goli, the grandfather of Zanama Warq, who was the mother of King Sahle Selassie. It is also said to have been the birthplace of Ras Makonnen, father of Emperor Haile Selassie. In these and the previously mentioned connexions with the Imperial family, the people of Manz take great pride. If their land is one of bannas and barley, of fighting and fasting, it is also, they are pleased to point out, *ya-negus agar*—"king's country." Indeed, their attachment to the line of Nagāssi is periodically voiced when, on certain festive occasions, the young braves of Manz dance with their staves and intone the stirring chant:

Ya-Manz abbabā / ya-Manz abbabā / Yābbabāl genā—

The flower of Manz / the flower of Manz / it will bloom yet again.

Notes

1 GEOGRAPHICAL NOTE. Manz lies on a broad plateau at about 10,000 ft above sea level. This plateau is cross-cut by a number of rivers which flow westerly to become part of the great Blue Nile basin. The valleys of the rivers are flanked by fairly abrupt cliffs, which makes travel from one part of Manz to another slow going. These rivers form boundaries between the geographical divisions within Manz, which is divided into three major parts: Mama Meder in the south, Lalo Meder in the centre, and Gera Meder in the north. The entire area of Manz is itself bounded by steep mountains. The boundaries of Manz proper include the Mofar river in the south, the Adabay and Wantchet rivers in the west, the Qetchene' river in the north, and in the east a long chain of mountains which pour forth that waters that drain across Manz and divide it from the lowlands of Efrata, Geddem and Qawat. Accurate maps of Manz and its boundaries do not yet exist.

2 Manz has heretofore not been an object of any sustained concern in the literature on Ethiopia. Previous exploration of the area was limited to two-day trips across Manz by Krapf, a British missionary, in 1842, and Soldllet, a French explorer (and friend of Rimbaud), in 1882. Their itineraries are described in Isenberg and Krapf, *Journals* (London, 1843), and Paul Soleillet, *Voyages in Ethiopia* (Rouen, 1886).

The present communication is based on field research conducted in Ethiopia during 1958–60. The author lived for six months in Manz, as part of a larger programme of study concerning the relation between Amhara traditions and Ethiopia's modernization. The author was based in Mama Meder, but had the opportunity to travel throughout Manz.

3 Of more exotic ethnographic interest is the "monastery" called Yallema located at the north-west boundary of Manz in the district of Qaya Gabre'ēl. The inhabitants of Yallema are potters who follow a cult that appears to combine Christian, Judaic and pagan elements. The men and women who live there are said to claim that they do not perform sexual intercourse, and hide their children when any visitor approaches. They are isolated from the neighbouring Manzēs by their own rigid secrecy and by the fear of the latter, who do not consider them Christians and believe them to possess the evil eye. The only regular occasion they have for interacting with the Manzes is at the market.

4 Tekla Tsadik Mekurya, *Ya-Etyopya Tarik Ka-Atse Lebna Dengel Eske Atse Tewodros* (Addis Ababa, 1957), p. 20.

5 Enrico Cerulli, *Storia della letteratura etiopica* (Milan, 1956), pp. 101–3.

6 Jean Doresse, *L'Empire du Prêtre Jean* (Paris, 1957), p. 165.

7 This story and its implication for the special significance of Manz are celebrated in the apologetic homily, *Dersana Raguel.* Cf. A. Caquot,"L'Homélie en l'honneur de

l'archange Raguel," *Annales d'Éthiopie* (Paris, 1957), 91–122.

8 Sihad ad-Din, Ahmad, *Futuh el-Habesha*, trans. d'Abbadie and Paulitschke (Paris, 1898), p. 342.

9 All informants agreed that Mama, Lalo and Gera were contemporaries; according to some accounts, they were brothers. Both Lalo and Gera appear to be contemporaries of Nagassi; for Mama's daughter Tagunstyan was married to Nagassi's son Substyanos, and Gera's grandson was a contemporary, and antagonist, of Nagassi's grandson Abiye; and there are stories of military encounters between Nagassi and Geri. Nagassi's life can with some accuracy be placed in the latter seventeenth century, since he died during the reign of Iyasu I (1682–1706), and since by independent dating of the reigns of his successors his death can be placed about 1703.

10 Antonio Cecchi, *Da Zeila alle Frontiere del Caffa*, 1 (Rome, 1886), 238; Tekla Tsadik Makurya, *op. cit.* pp. 248–9.

11 The line of rulers following Nagassi is as follows:

Name	**Highest rank attained**	**Dates of rule (dates prior to Sāhla Sallāssē are not certain)**
Substyānos ("Substē")	Maredāzmātch	1705–10
Abiye	Maredāzmātch	1720–45
Amhā Yēsus	Maredāzmātch	1745–75
Asfā Wassan	Maredāzmātch	1775–1808
Wassan Sagad	Rās	1808–13
Sahle Selassie	Negus (King)	1813–47
Hāyla Malakot	Negus (King)	1847–55
Menelik II	Negusa nagast (Emperor)	1865–1913

12 Here are two versions of the legend of Etchē Yohannes.

A. Etchē Yohānnes was a pious and wealthy monk. The people around Ferkutā were envious of his celibacy and of his property. So they spread a rumour that he was no virgin after all, that in fact he had made one of the local women pregnant. This woman accused him in court, saying: "May God split me in two if it is not the truth!" Whereupon God split her in two, and turned her into stone. Etche Yohannes then cursed the local people, saying: "Let frost and wind destroy your crops!"; and he disappeared. For many years the people searched for him in vain. One day a group of them heard a shepherd boy saying to another: "Bring back the animals from the Etchē Yohānnes grave." The people ran to the place which the shepherds showed them and began digging. At last they unearthed a skeleton, which spoke to them: "Do not mistreat my body." The few drops of blood which were on the skeleton fell to the ground and became big cedar trees.

B. After the woman was turned into stone (and the stone can be seen not far from the monastery), Etchē Yohannes left Ferkutā and went to Gonder, where he died. Prior to that, Ferkutā had been a very fertile land. All of the *qolā* (lowland) crops grew there, even though it was *dēgā* (highland). The great expanse of wild grass that grows near Ferkutā had been then *tēff*. But after Etchē Yohānnes cursed the area and died at Gonder, nothing at all grew—not even animals or people. When a government investigator came the people complained, and insisted that his body must be brought from Gonder to Ferkutā. This was done, and thereafter the people and animals grew once more, but the only crop which grew was barley; and that is today the only crop that can be cultivated at Ferkutā.

13 Tekla Tsadik Makurya, p. 254.

14 A common version of the legend about Mary and Alo Bahr is as follows:

Mary was travelling in a district of Manz called Alo when Jesus was a young boy. She sat down by the edge of a cliff to rest and eat some food, but accidentally her *tchebbeto* (bread made from scraps of *enjarā*) fell; so she went to search for bread. She walked and walked without finding anything to eat. Finally night came, and she went up to the house of a woman and asked for lodging and bread there. The woman showed Mary a huge pile of grain and told her to grind it during the night, and she would give her bread the next day. Mary was tired and fell asleep, but during the night an angel came and ground the grain for Mary without making a sound. The woman of the house refused to give Mary bread the next day, for she claimed that the miracle had been worked as much in her behalf as in Mary's.

Mary then went around Alo to secure justice. She appealed to two groups of judges, the shepherds and the elders. The shepherds judged in her favour, and she rewarded them by giving them *dābo* (wheat bread). (Some versions of this legend connect this story with the festival of Buhē, on which shepherds are given bread.) But the elders judged against Mary, and to punish them she sent thunder and lightning so powerful that they formed a huge hole in the earth. This hole filled with water to become Alo Bahr. (In another version, she cursed the locale and it melted away to become the lake.) A similar version of this legend was recorded 120 years ago by Krapf. Cf. Isenberg and Krapf, *op. cit.* p. 309.

4

Legitimacy in Ethiopia (1964)*

I.

In December of 1960 a small group of military officers and Western-educated civilians seized power in Addis Ababa in an attempt to overthrow the established government of Ethiopia. Through radio broadcasts and leaflets they tried to rally the population to their cause. Spokesmen for the rebel government denounced the *ancien regime* in revolutionary terms. Charging that Ethiopians had been living in a state of poverty and oppression for three thousand years, they called for bold new efforts in economic development and the extension of political rights to the mass of the people. As you well know, the project was ill-fated. The high command of the Ethiopian Army objected to the leadership of the rebel group, and the *coup d'etat* was reversed—after fairly severe fighting—within three days after it had taken place.

Although this coup had been carried out with the primary purpose of replacing the rule of the present emperor, His Imperial Majesty Haile Selassie I, it is notable that it was attempted while the Emperor was safely out of the country. What is more, in all the broadcasts launched against the *ancien regime* by the rebel spokesmen, Haile Selassie was not once mentioned by name. In fact, some of the rebel troops were mobilized to fight against loyalist Army forces on the pretext that the latter were staging on insurrection against the Emperor and had to be suppressed.

---

* Prepared for delivery at the 1964 Annual Meeting of the American Political Science Association, Chicago, Illinois, Pick-Congress Hotel, September 9–12, 1964. Previously unpublished.

As a result of all this deference to him on the part of the very rebels who sought to displace him, the Emperor was able to state publicly upon his return that the rebellion had not even been directed against him in the first place. He was further able, after a few months of adjustments following his restoration, to re-establish his authority fully and to secure the domestic order and stability which Ethiopia has enjoyed ever since.

Whatever else may be said of this sequence of events, it is a remarkable testimony to the tenacity of legitimate authority in the empire of Ethiopia. At the same time that the leaders of so many other nations in Africa and Asia are engaged in a critical struggle to secure the blessings of legitimacy for their fledgling governments, the head of the Ethiopian state has been able, with little more than a flick of the wrist, to return directly to the helm after the rebellion of his most trusted supporters—the Imperial Bodyguard and the Chief of Security—and to proceed at once to undertake such ventures as the establishment of a national university, the launching of a second five-year plan, and the performance of a conspicuous and creative role in the realm of international diplomacy. Among the conditions that made this tour de force possible the peculiar character and political acumen of Haile Selassie as well as many other particular historical circumstances would have to be included. But there can be no doubt that deeply rooted traditions of respect for imperial authority in Ethiopia were an important part of the picture. This is the same cultural force that is in evidence when we bring to mind another feature that distinguishes Ethiopia among contemporary states: her claim to possess the oldest continuous national dynasty in the world, one that stretches back three thousand years to the time of King Solomon of Israel. If this claim rests on beliefs that are not historically demonstrable, it does refer to two important empirical realities. One is the fact that the present imperial line does descend, with no more than two or three brief hiatuses, from a dynasty that ascended to the throne as long as seven centuries ago. The other is the fact that tradition-minded Ethiopians at least cherish the belief that their national dynasty is as antique and sacred as the Solomonic legend suggests.

In the remarks which follow, my aim will be to analyze the foundation for this success of legitimate national authority in Ethiopia over so long a period. In so doing, I aim in addition to raise some theoretical questions concerning the foundations of legitimacy in traditional societies in general. In conclusion, I will comment on some of the apparent consequences of this pattern for Ethiopian politics today.

II.

Let me begin with a brief sketch of the normative order which has characterized the Ethiopian polity during the last seven countries. For nearly all of this period supreme authority was vested in an emperor whose legitimacy was based on membership in a line of descent of the Solomonic Dynasty and anointment by the archbishop of the Ethiopian Church, the *abuna*. The emperor's authority was virtually unlimited; but his autonomy was circumscribed in at least two ways by traditional norms. In the first place he was expected to remain faithful to the beliefs and practices of the Ethiopian Orthodox Church, the institution which embodied the paramount values of Ethiopian culture. Deviation from this norm had the effect of undermining his legitimacy. This was shown, for example, in the case of Za Dengel and Susneyos—two emperors of the early seventeenth century who were deposed because of their conversion to Catholicism. Secondly, the emperor was expected to perform a number of functions on behalf of the Ethiopian nation. He was at once supreme military commander, supreme judge, and supreme administrator, as well as symbolic guarantor of the peace and prosperity of the realm. Failure to carry out these functions weakened his reputation, if not his legitimacy. Thus, Emperor Iyasu II (1730-55) was ridiculed by the townspeople of Gonder for devoting too much time to the adornment of his palace and too little to the arts of warfare. On the other hand, in the actual performance of these various functions the emperor had a completely free hand. He had advisers and petitioners, to be sure—monks and court officials and war lords and relatives—but he was normally not bound by any of their counsel. In judging a case he might hear twelve opinions all in favor of a certain decision, and might then proceed to judge against it without any difficulty. He was free to make decisions of any sort at any level of the society, and was supposed to be obeyed by everyone in the realm. Those who countered him often paid dearly; we have a record of a chief justice under Emperor Lebna Dengel (1508–41) being flogged to the bones because he passed a judgment that displeased His Majesty. "The Kings of Abyssinia . . . are supreme in all causes, ecclesiastical and civil," wrote James Bruce, one of the earlier students of Ethiopian society.

The monarch's authority was naturally most readily obeyed in his immediate vicinity. Although he attempted to re-assert his authority from time to time throughout the empire by tours around the country and by summoning provincial officials to his capital—which much of the time was mobile, a city of tents—it was necessary to delegate a good deal of authority to other men in order to rule so spacious and geographically disjointed a land as Ethiopia. In return for their services as tax collectors, provincial judges, and military commanders, these men were rewarded with honorific titles, grants of land, and rights to tribute, judicial fees, and corvee labor. The Ethiopian system thus approximates Weber's ideal type of a patrimonial order, and its history reveals the pattern he suggests is inherent in patrimonialism, namely, a struggle between the king and the usurpers of prerogatives who attempt to establish themselves as a hereditary status group. The Ethiopian nobility did in fact cut loose from the dominion of the emperor for about a century, a troubled time in Ethiopian history known as the Age of the Princes (1755–1855). But at all times, whether subservient to the national monarch or not, they behaved like emperors in their own provinces, built up local support and promoted local dynasties, and attempted to reproduce the organization and etiquette of the imperial court in their own household and military camps.

One other group of men enjoyed a fairly diffuse pattern of authority—the clergy. Their legitimation came from ordination by the archbishop, the *abuna*, and remained for life so long as they adhered to the norms governing ritual purity. Since the clergy and the nobility had separate sources of legitimation and spheres of authority, from time to time each was effective in bringing pressure to bear on the other. The clergy, especially the monks, used their power of excommunication and their moral authority to dissuade secular powers from certain objectionable actions and to arouse the populace against them if they were intransigent. The nobility in turn used their political authority to have members of the clergy imprisoned, flogged, or executed—events which were recorded on numerous occasions in Ethiopian history. But most of the time religious and secular powers worked in harmony, encouraging and assisting one another.

These three orders—emperors, nobility, and clergy—developed and sustained a minimal national culture among provinces marked by considerable isolation, separatism, and pluralism. Despite the serious inroads made by militant Muslim invaders, dedicated Catholic missionaries, and the imperialist ambitions of Turkey, Egypt, England, France, and Italy, they succeeded in maintaining the cultural integrity and political independence of Ethiopia until well into the twentieth century. Their success bespeaks a high degree of validity in the traditional Ethiopian normative order.

The validity (*Geltung*) of a normative order is frequently taken for granted when we think of traditional societies. We tend to assume that the behavior of members of such societies is characterized by considerable readiness to uphold and obey the authority of their traditional rulers. The case of Ethiopia—where such behavior is evident to an unusual degree and forms one of the most conspicuous features of the society—suggests that something may be gained by explicitly analyzing this as a variable phenomenon.

If the validity of a moral order—the extent to which it is followed and its durability—is to be regarded as a dependent variable, then, following Weber, we may divide the independent variables affecting it into two broad categories. One of these concerns the motivation to uphold the normative order. The other concerns the principles on which the legitimacy of the order is based. Let us now analyze the constituent elements of these two variables in the Ethiopian case and thereby raise some questions about variation in the effectiveness of the normative orders of traditional societies generally.

III.

The customary behavior of Ethiopians shows a pronounced disposition to conform to the demands of all traditional authority figures. No matter how exploitative or otherwise morally objectionable the actions of such authorities may appear, so long as their status is defined as legitimate their persons are approached with much deference and their commands are customarily met with prompt compliance.

This sort of disposition may be produced by a number of different motives. Weber has identified four such motives, which we may paraphrase as, first, an emotional need to surrender to authority; second, beliefs which rationalize the value of submitting to authority; third, religious sanctions; and, fourth, personal interests which are best served by complying with authority.

None of the motives is insignificant in the Ethiopian case or, more precisely, structure, which, through following a bilateral descent system, is strongly patriarchal in character. In the Amhara family the father is the object of utmost respect. His broad jurisdiction handily includes the area of physical punishment, which he may apply to wife and servants as well as children, and which, whenever inflicted, is usually considered to be deserved and productive of salutary effects. Obedience is the prime objective in the socialization of Amhara children. They are taught to respond quickly to any parental command and to be respectful and reserved in their comportment. This ethic is illustrated in the Amhara practice of expecting children to stand silently, facing the wall, if they are at home while their elders eat their meals. Adolescence, although a period for learning the skills and norms related to adult self-sufficiency, is also a time when paternal authority is heightened and demands for obedience are greatly multiplied. In addition to filial respect and obedience, Amhara are brought up to have a sense of filial gratitude. They are taught that whatever meager benefits they have in this world they owe to the paternal bounty.

These sentiments are typically projected onto persons of superior status in many spheres outside the family. Personal patrons, ecclesiastical dignitaries, political officials, and the king himself—all are perceived in the imagery of fatherhood, all are the object of comparable feelings of deference and submissiveness and, often, of filial attachment and gratitude. Nearly every aspect of Amhara social life, moreover, is anchored in some sort of authority figures. The absence of such a relationship evokes feelings of incompleteness and malaise. Nearly all social situations among the Amhara are structured in more or less authoritarian terms, from the play groups of shepherds to the disputations of adults, which latter invariably culminate in a request for someone to serve as a "judge" and arbitrate the discussion.

It is evident how a psychological orientation of this sort favors the upholding of legitimate authority. Among the Amhara this is backstopped by both rational beliefs and religious sanctions which support the submission to authority. The central philosophical belief in question concerns the value of authority as an indispensable basis for civil peace. The Amhara outlook is fundamentally Hobbesian. Amhara ideas about human nature present man as a creature inherently unreliable and aggressive, one who is prone to molest others unless checked by such inner controls as a heavy, year-round regimen of fasting and by outer controls imposed by established authorities. The Amharic expression *ya-negus agar*—"a country with a king"—refers to a land which enjoys domestic tranquility. The Amhara further tend to believe that, if anything is to be accomplished that involves the coordinated activity of a number of men, it can only be accomplished through some sort of authoritarian arrangement.

With respect to religious beliefs, the Amhara tend to interpret the Bible in the way that stresses the importance of obedience to all earthly authorities. Thus, in responding to a survey question, "Should one always obey the order of a superior?", a number of the Amhara students who replied affirmatively gave as their reason, "because the Bible says so." In particular, Amhara culture sustains the belief that the authority of the emperor is divinely sanctioned, a belief retained in the 1955 Constitution of Ethiopia, which states that "the person of the Emperor is sacred, His dignity is inviolable and His power indisputable." The sacred authority of the Ethiopian emperor is also celebrated in the national epic of Ethiopia, a fourteenth-century work called the *Kibre Negest* or *Glory of the Kings*. This book serves a vital justification function in Ethiopia; as recently as 1872 Emperor Yohannes declared that physical possession of the manuscript was important in order for him to secure the obedience of his people. In the *Kibre Negest*, one reads: "It is not a good thing for any of those who are under the dominion of a king to revile him, for retribution belongeth to God." The book at the same time upholds the authority of the ordained clergy: "Moreover, it says, the people must not revile the bishops and priests, for they are the children of God and the men of His house."

Belief in the sacred authority of the emperor, on the one hand, and of the ordained clergy, on the other, has meant that the Amhara were induced to submit to the authority out of fear of divine recriminations if they should flaunt it. Rebelliousness might jeopardize their chances of going to heaven. Amhara culture further provides a more immediate sort of sanction in the form of excommunication. The threat of excommunication has been used not only to buttress the authority of ecclesiastical dignitaries, but also kings and noblemen have been able to use it by persuading or compelling churchmen to employ the threat on their behalf in connection with purely secular matters.

Such are the various "disinterested" or "inner" reasons, as Weber terms them, for the upholding of legitimate authority in the empire of Ethiopia. But the Amharas' inclination to follow authority is not free from ambivalence. Their orientation is marked by strong antinomian tendencies as well as by abject conformism. They are quite disposed to pursue personal interests at the expense of normative considerations. The record does not lack accounts of the rebellion of subjects, not to mention to subtle reviling of authorities. What contributes decisively to the underpinning of legitimate authority in Ethiopia, in my opinion, is the fact that, by and large, the Ethiopian social system affords far more opportunity for the pursuit of private advantage through the channel of authorities rather than outside of or against it.

Traditional Amhara social structure is practically devoid of mechanisms through which individuals can associate in the pursuit of collective interests. There are no fixed corporate structures, either in the kinship system or on a territorial or civic basis, which might serve to canalize the pursuit of common interests. There are no traditional patterns for spontaneous cooperation other than very limited, reciprocal forms for the attainment of quite specific goals such as the construction of a roof or the repair of a church. The Amhara are sociologically unequipped for banding together to confront some authority with common demands. On the contrary, the Amhara normally pursue their interests on a highly individualistic basis. And to attain their goals, individuals in Amhara society must inevitably have recourse to some figure of authority.

The three main objectives sought in traditional Amhara life are: rights to the use of land for cultivation (*rist*); rights to the tribute and corvee labor due from inhabitants of a given piece of land (*gult*); and honorific titles (*shumat*). In the pursuit of one or more of these objectives all Amhara are in a continual state of competition. Decisive gains along those lines depend on the favor of some figure of authority. Secular honorific titles can only be attained through the dispensation of the emperor or, traditionally, one of the greater noblemen; ecclesiastical titles only through the emperor or the appropriate ecclesiastical authorities—there are no hereditary titles in Ethiopia. Rights to tribute and corvee labor have normally come in the form of contingent grants awarded by the emperor. The situation with respect to land-use far exceeds the amount of land actually available for cultivation. The way in which Amhara enlarge their land claims is by submitting appeals to court. The importance of being on favorable terms with authority figures here is twofold. Being on good terms with the judges at various levels is not irrelevant to securing a sympathetic judgment in such cases. In addition, the attainment of high position, through appointment by a higher authority, is of great value to one who seeks to enlarge his land-use claims because the local people will be eager to testify on his behalf and support his claims in the expectation that they in turn will derive some benefit from his higher status.

There is a well-known alienative pattern in Amhara culture, known as *mashafat*, in which an individual may seek to advance himself by rebelling against his lord and prevailing authorities and build up a force of retainers of his own. But this is the exceptional and rarely successful alternative. The customary procedure for an individual with economic or political ambitions is to ally himself as closely as possible with some existing authority and, through clever competition against all other comers, to ingratiate himself and move upward on the coattails of his patron. This sociological pattern constitutes a powerful prop for the prevailing normative order.

In the foregoing analysis I have sought to relate the effectiveness of Ethiopia's normative order to a number of motives to conform to legitimate authority. We have seen that with respect to each of the four motives mentioned by Weber—emotional disposition, rational beliefs, religious sanctions, and ulterior personal interests—the Amhara case provides substantial support for legitimacy. Carrying Weber's assumptions further, we should expect that in other traditional societies or historical periods a decrease in the support provided by these motives should be related to the attenuation of legitimacy. What the range of alternative constellations might be is a question that poses an interesting agenda for the comparative study of traditional political systems.

IV.

I turn now to the other major variable defined by Weber, namely, the grounds on which the legitimacy of an order may be based. In this part of the discussion I shall depart somewhat from Weber's schema; for while Weber was concerned with cultural grounds of legitimacy when comparing traditional authority to other forms of authority, he did not pursue the question of cultural grounds when he came to analyze the variety of forms which traditional authority itself may take. On this subject he proceeded by delineating variations in social structure—patriarchalism, feudalism, and the like—rather than by treating variations in the cultural bases for justifying traditional authority. Regarding the latter question he rests content with the formula that traditional authority is legitimated by "established beliefs in the sanctity of immemorial traditions." The question I would now like to raise, while examining the principles of legitimacy in Ethiopia, is whether or not there might be something in the nature of the "immemorial traditions" themselves that affects the extent and durability of their authority over the members of traditional societies.

The traditions which legitimate the authority of the emperor of Ethiopia revolve about three themes, each of which imparts an aura of charisma to his status. One of these themes relates to charisma by *heredity*; one celebrates the charisma of his *historic role*; and one has to do with the charisma of the *ritual* by which he is crowned. All three of these motifs are elaborated in the *Kibre Negest* as well as in other hallowed Ethiopian writings. The themes of hereditary charisma relate, of course, to the belief in the Solomonic genealogy. The most important legend recorded in the *Kibre Negest* concerns the visit of the Queen of Sheba of King Solomon in Jerusalem, his clever seduction of her, and the destiny of their offspring—a boy who becomes Menelik I, legendary first emperor of Ethiopia. All but one of the emperors of Ethiopia since the late thirteenth century have legitimated their status by claiming to be descendants of Menelik I, a claim recently reiterated in Article 2 of the 1955 Constitution which states: "the Imperial dignity shall remain perpetually attached to the Haile Selassie I, descendant of King Sahle Selassie, whose line descends without interruption from the dynasty of Menelik I, son of the Queen of Ethiopia, the Queen of Sheba, and King Solomon of Jerusalem."

In addition to the charisma of descent from King Solomon, the *Kibre Negest* stresses the charisma of the imperial role as repository of a sacred legacy. For the Ethiopian emperor is portrayed therein as successor to both the kings of Israel and the kings of Rome—hence the sole legitimate bearer of the Judaic-Christian mission. The transfer of religious mission from the Jews is represented in the *Kibre Negest* by a prophetic dream attributed to Solomon, in which God's favor passes from Israel to Ethiopia. The transfer is somewhat literally depicted, moreover, by the story of young Menelik's theft from Jerusalem of the most sacred symbol of the Judaic mission—the Ark of the Covenant. This legendary event is symbolized in every Ethiopian Orthodox Church today by its central devotional object, the *tabot*, an oblong box which serves as a replica of the holy ark.

The transfer of religious mission from Rome to Ethiopia is a theme which is not stressed in Ethiopian tradition until the seventeenth century. But it is clearly foreshadowed in the *Kibre Negest* by two claims. The first is that, while the emperor of Rome is "the son of Solomon . . . the Emperor of Ethiopia is the *firstborn and eldest* son of Solomon." This claim to genealogical supremacy is then fortified by a claim to spiritual supremacy; for the *Kibre Negest* states that whereas Ethiopia remained true in the Monophysite Orthodox Faith, the people of the country of Rome were seduced by Satan "and they corrupted the Faith of Christ." Thus Ethiopian tradition propounds a theory, not of a third Rome, but of the Ethiopian emperor as successor to Constantine—and Constantine was in fact the throne name that was adopted by Ethiopian emperors of the fifteenth century.

The third principle which legitimates the authority of the imperial status concerns the rite of coronation. The anointment of the emperor is a ritual of particularly sacred meaning to Ethiopians. As the *Kibre Negest* says in another passage enjoining deference to royalty: "Now it is not a seemly thing to revile the king, for he is the anointed of God." Article 4 of the Ethiopian Constitution attributes the sanctity of the Emperor to two factors: his imperial blood and "the anointing which he has received." The significance of anointment is twofold. On the one hand, it refers back to the biblical ancestry of the Ethiopian monarchy. Thus another apologetic work, *The Book of the Riches of Kings*, attributes the following words to the Ethiopian monk who is credited with restoring the monarchy to the Solomonic line in the thirteenth century:

> And moreover, this day I brought the kingdom of God to Yakuno Amlak, the son of David, and to his seed forever. And the bringing of the kingdom to him shall not be the kingdom only, but it shall be accompanied by a horn of oil, according to the ordinances of the kings who were his fathers, and by the fame of having been anointed with unguents . . . .

The other reason for the charismatic significance of the act of anointment is that it can only be performed by the *abuna*, the spiritual head of the Ethiopian church. The *abuna* has traditionally been an Egyptian monk sent to Ethiopia from the Coptic Patriarchate at Alexandria. His laying on of hands thus represents a direct transmission of charisma from the ultimate source of religious justification in the traditional system.

The principles of anointment by the *abuna*, Solomonic genealogy, and sacred mission have been used to legitimate national political authority in Ethiopia for no less than seven centuries. In what ways might the nature of these principles be said to contribute to the efficaciousness of the legitimacy of Ethiopia's monarchy? The ideas I shall now present attempt to interpret this culture pattern in terms that are suitable for comparative analysis. They are highly exploratory.

The first point emerges directly from what has already been said regarding the charismatic element in the imperial office. It concerns the content of the qualities used as criteria for determining the legitimacy of authoritative status. One dimension of this content has to do with the presence or absence of charisma among the qualities. In the Ethiopian case we have seen that all of the qualities of which the emperor's legitimacy is grounded are marked by charisma, emanating ultimately from either the ancient kings of Israel or the hallowed office of the Alexandria Patriarch. This suggests a hypothesis: That the grounds of traditional authority are more valid when they include some admixture of charisma. In saying this we are simply elaborating the point made by Weber, when he wrote that "communal groups approximating the purely traditional type (of authority) . . . have never been stable indefinitely and. . . have seldom been without a head who had a personally charismatic status by heredity or office."

My second point concerns the source of the principles which provide the ultimate grounds of legitimacy for a traditional system. One aspect of this question has to do with whether they originate within the system or whether they stem from a source outside the system. In the Ethiopian case it is noteworthy that the *legitimacy of the emperor is ultimately exogenous.* The genealogical basis of the emperor's legitimacy is derived from a source outside the system—from the kings of Israel. His sacred role as bearer of a national mission stems from outside the system—from the legacy of Judaic and Christian missions. The ritual justification of his high authority again depends on a source outside the system—on anointment by an outsider, an Egyptian, sent from a distant sanctuary. Despite their parochialism, Ethiopians have traditionally reserved their highest esteem for symbols of authority which lie outside their homeland. If there is any general significance in this, it probably relates to the fact that remote authorities are in a way untouchable. They are not subject to contamination and degradation by the tensions and conflicts which prevail within any social system. This suggests a second hypothesis: that traditional authority may be most valid when it is grounded on at least some symbols which originate outside the system.

The third variable that seems significant in the Ethiopian pattern concerns the distribution of the qualities which establish legitimacy. Are they peculiar to the one, or are they shared by the many? Both alternatives are realized in the case of the Ethiopian emperor. The condition of being anointed confers a unique status upon the imperial person. His authority is upheld thereafter because he and he alone has received the anointing from the *abuna.* His authority would be greatly diminished if it were possible for the *abuna* to anoint someone else during his lifetime—a dangerous possibility which Ethiopian emperors have traditionally forestalled by having only one *abuna* in the country at a given time and by keeping him in the vicinity of the imperial court.

On the other hand, qualities that refer to the Israelite background and Christian mission of the Ethiopian emperor are in a way shared by the Amhara people as a whole. By virtue of some of the same beliefs which ascribe charisma to the imperial person they are able to view themselves as a chosen people and to affix some of that charisma to themselves. Thus, they consider themselves as a people to be descendants of the ancient chosen people of Israel. Nobility related to the imperial line have in fact traditionally been referred to as "chiefs of Israel," and Amhara with any status pretensions whatsoever delight in tracing their genealogies back into the remote past where they connect at some point with the imperial line and thence back to Solomon. Furthermore, they identify themselves as unique bearers of the Christian faith. It was, after all, the Ethiopian people as a whole, and not only the emperor, whom the *Kibre Negest* celebrates as having remained true to the Orthodox Christian faith. To this day many Amhara regard themselves as the only authentic Christians in the world. In short, the emperor's legitimacy is maintained in part because he symbolizes qualities which his people are proud of in themselves. What this suggests concerning the distribution of legitimating qualities is that the optimum distribution may involve some sort of balance between legitimating qualities which are unique to the authority figure and qualities which are shared with his people. Just what sort of variation exists along this line and how significant it may be—these are questions that await elucidation from further cooperative studies.

V.

I hope that these remarks have served to throw some light on the foundations of legitimacy in the traditional Ethiopian political system. We have seen that those foundations have been very securely laid, which helps to explain the fact that—despite severe geographical obstacles, very primitive technology, a dissentious people, and critical periods of disorganization brought about by external force—a national political order of the traditional type has survived intact up to the age of automation.

I should like, in concluding, to comment briefly on some of the consequences of this order for politics in Ethiopia today. One consequence was alluded to at the beginning of this paper: the framework of stability enjoyed by the present regime. Haile Selassie became Regent of Ethiopia in 1917, and has thus played the major role in directing Ethiopia's national politics for almost half a century. His domestic enemies—and they have been numerous—have with few exceptions refrained from any form of public criticism, let alone from any outright show of disrespect or disobedience. Many acts of rebellion have been contemplated, but few have been carried out and none have succeeded. Respect for the office of the Ethiopian emperor runs deep in the land and will doubtless preserve that office in spite of whatever political change the future may bring—so long as the Amhara remain dominant in Ethiopia.

It is interesting to note in this connection that much of the popular opposition to Haile Selassie in the thirties was related to changes which discredited his legitimacy. He was accused of not having sufficiently strong genealogical claims to the throne. He was accused of failing to abide by traditional norms which set the limits for imperial behavior, by leading his country away from hallowed practices down the road to modernization and by failing to remain in battle against the Italian invaders to the finish. Such charges did harm his reputation but were never sufficiently serious to undermine his authority.

The traditionalist critique to Haile Selassie had largely evaporated by the 1950s. In its place stepped a critique of the imperial office itself. This critique claimed, in effect, that the legitimacy of the traditional order was proving *too* successful. Its consequences, in a country opening up to modern technology, were held to be excessive centralization of the powers of government and stifling of energies needed for national development. Some Ethiopians began to refer to the regime as *Ya-Kantu weddase zaman*—the era of futile flattery. Libertarians called for representative institutions and public liberties; modernists called for separation of economic and administrative leadership from a role suited primarily for symbolic-expressive functions in the context of contemporary government. Such circumscription of imperial power is theoretically unwarranted under the traditional system, for it legitimated a diffuse, all-embracing authority, any delegation of whose power is tantamount to a loss of dignity.

This is the impasse which Ethiopia suffers today. It racks the souls of all modern-educated Ethiopians who have their country's welfare at heart. Yet it would be unjust to say that consequences of her traditional system of legitimacy have only negative implications for Ethiopia's capacity to rise to her contemporary challenges. There are at least two respects in which this traditional pattern plays a constructive role in behalf of Ethiopia's modernization. One is that by providing an established nation-wide system of authority it has facilitated swift action on a few elementary projects once the decision to undertake them was made on high. A word from the throne has been sufficient to make sure, for example, that a highway is built across a province in short order, that a medical research team is given every facility in a distant town, or that a school which has been in the planning stages for many years is suddenly constructed.

The other is that, by providing a framework for national stability for so long a period, it has been possible to develop cadres of individuals who may be ready to carry on the tasks of modern government in a more effective manner when the time for more rapid change is opportune. Following the bedlam which accompanied the unsuccessful coup attempt of December 1960, even some of the most radical Ethiopian students were beginning to consider the advantage of a few years more of tyranny over a few months of anarchy.

Bibliography

Budge, E. A. Wallis. *The Life of Takla Hymanot, the Miracles of Takla Hymanot, and the Book of the Riches of Kings*. London: W. Griggs, 1906.

______. *The Queen of Sheba and Her Only Son Menylek: A complete Translation of the Kebra Nagast*. London: Medici Society, 1922.

Ethiopia. Revised Constitution. Addis Ababa, 1955.

Hoben, Allan. 'The Role of Ambilineal Descent Groups in Gojjam Amhara Social Organization.' Unpub. Ph. D. dissertation, University of California, 1963.

Levine, Donald N. "Ethiopia . . ." *In Political Culture and Political Development*, ed. Lucien Pye and Sidney Verva. Published by Princeton University Press, 1965.

_______. *Wax and Gold: Tradition and Innovation in Ethiopian Culture*. Published by University of Chicago Press, 1965.

Perham, Margery. *The Government of Ethiopia*. London: Faber and Faver, 1948.

Weber, Max, *The Theory of Economic and Social Organization.* (Trans., A. M. Henderson and T. Parsons). New York: Oxford University Press, 1947.

5

Ethiopia

*Identity, Authority, and Realism (1965)**

I.

The political systems of nearly all the nations of Asia and Africa are "new" in one of three respects. In the extreme case, illustrated by Malaysia and Nigeria, they comprise entirely new political entities, the more or less arbitrary invention of state makers who have drawn a line around a piece of territory and given it a name. In other instances, such as Burma and Morocco, they represent a restoration to autonomous status of former nations whose rulers were displaced or subordinated by European powers. A third type of novelty is represented by countries like China and Egypt, which both have a national history and were self-governing by the end of World War II but have since experienced a revolutionary change of governmental form.

All these societies are now working to cope with the consequences of a fairly sharp break with the recent past. Insofar as they are committed to economic and social modernization they are aided by the freshness of their political institutions and the climate of dynamism in which their governments came into being. At the same time their viability as national societies is made problematic by the fact that the concept of themselves that they now seek to sustain is at such variance with their prior experience and culture.

---

* Originally published in *Political Culture and Political Development*, eds. Lucien Pye and Sidney Verba (Princeton, NJ: Princeton University Press, 1965), 245–81.

Precisely the converse constellation of circumstances is faced by a smaller group of nations whose distinguishing feature is a conspicuous degree of continuity with the past. These are the proud old nations, traditional monarchies with rich national cultures and long histories, whose indigenous leadership was never effectively dislocated by outside forces or structural change. In this group we find Afghanistan and Thailand, Iran and Ethiopia. For these countries the attainment of a national identity in the modern world has been relatively unproblematic, while the effort to modernize has been arduous and halting, palpably artificial in the context of customary national life.

When Ethiopia is examined in this comparative perspective, it is apparent that the tendency to represent Ethiopia as one of so many African nations is highly misleading despite the fact that her political and cultural ties with the rest of the continent have of late become increasingly prominent. It is true that to most of Africa's aspiring nationalists and Christian separatists Ethiopia has stood for decades as a symbol of African autonomy. It is noteworthy that the Imperial Ethiopian government, spurred by the international developments of the past decade, has turned from a policy of virtually complete alignment with the Western powers and aloofness from pan-Africanism toward a policy of greater neutralism and outspoken solidarity with the other nations of Africa, a change marked by the establishment of the UN Economic Commission for Africa in Addis Ababa in 1958 and the convocation there in 1963 of the Conference of Heads of Independent African States. It is likewise notable that the emphasis on Ethiopia's extra-African ties which has characterized most Ethiopianist scholarship in the past, an emphasis on the numerous culture complexes absorbed from Mediterranean and especially Semitic cultures during the past three millennia, is slowly giving way to an appreciation of Ethiopian culture traits which are of African origin and character. Yet for all this upsurge of interest in perceiving Ethiopia as an African nation, from the point of view of comparative politics it is clear that now, more than ever, Ethiopia is "in Africa but not of Africa."

II.

To say this is to draw attention to a number of particular aspects of Ethiopia's situation that contribute to the distinctiveness of her political system.

1. The Ethiopian polity of today is continuous with political institutions that have a recorded history of some two thousand years. Ethiopia has not shared the *élan* and the agonies that accompanied the birth of the new states of Africa. She has experienced in much milder form and more leisurely pace the problems and stimulation that come with building a contemporary state: establishing the

legitimacy of national political authority, securing recognition from other states, devising the machinery of national government, and so on.

2. Unlike the other African states which were independent in 1945—unlike Liberia and South Africa, whose elites represent alien elements, and unlike Egypt, whose native elites identify with supra-national Islam or pan-Arab nationalism—Ethiopia has traditionally been governed by indigenous elites connected with her antique institutions and bearers of a national culture. They have been custodians of a written tradition which, though partly foreign in origin, was thoroughly Ethiopianized in character and became a primary repository of Ethiopian national sentiment. However much divided by differences of region, dialect, custom, theology, and interest, they shared faint memories of ancient national glories and the symbols and practices of a national religion.

3. The Imperial Ethiopian Government has evidently never dogmatically opposed the principle of imperialism. Though the Ethiopian version of this state's name is, literally, Government of the King of Kings—and hence connotes a personal regime rather than territorial empire—it is a conspicuous fact that the Ethiopian state has emerged through the ascendance of one of the peoples in the country, the Amhara, over all others.

The Amhara came to the fore in Ethiopia by the thirteenth century. Since the beginning of what is known as the restored Solomonid Dynasty (1270) virtually all the emperors of Ethiopia have been Amhara. In the centuries following their ascendance they maintained a prosperous and expanding kingdom. After severe setbacks in the sixteenth and seventeenth centuries they began a comeback which eventuated in the victories of Menelik II (1889–1913), under whom the area subject to Amhara rule was tripled. Throughout most of the past seven centuries Amhara emperors, nobles, soldiers, and colonists have maintained their political supremacy in Ethiopia and have made their tongue, Amharic, the national language.

4. The Amhara hegemony is upheld by a number of beliefs and sentiments which in their anti-egalitarian character are likewise not typical of contemporary African ideologies. According to an Amharic saying, "The Amhara is to rule, not to be ruled." This presumptive right is legitimated, in Amhara minds at least, by fairly intense feelings of ethnic and cultural superiority. Thus the Amhara have carried on "cultural imperialism" to a limited degree as well: Amharization via the school system, the spreading of Amhara customs and religion through settlers, traders, and occasional missionaries. The most recent example of this process has been the substitution of Amharic names for indigenous place names in many parts of the empire.

5. Ethiopia was never effectively colonized. During the brief period of foreign rule (1936–1941) many if not most Ethiopians who were politically aware did not define the situation as that of being in a colony, but rather as that of suffering temporarily under an enemy invader. Furthermore, numbers of Ethiopian patriots, mostly Amhara, carried on an underground resistance during the whole period, while many others spent the years in exile. The fact that Ethiopia has been a non-colonial country distinguishes her from most other African nations in a number of respects:

> a. Ethiopians do not have the psychic scars that come from having grown up as an alien in one's own country. Rather, they enjoy a high degree of self-esteem and pride in their long tradition of independence.[1]
>
> b. Ethiopian public life has not experienced the rise of modern agitational politics, nor the related phenomenon of political movements or parties. There has thus been no serious threat to the rule of the traditional elites.
>
> c. The Ethiopian public has not been exposed to oratory promising dynamic and economic changes for the benefit of the people. There has thus developed no mass base of support for populist leaders who might seek to promote more rapid forms of change.

One may summarize the distinctive aspects of Ethiopia's situation just enumerated by observing that, unlike all other African states, the Ethiopian state represents a historic nation which has largely preserved its own institutions, elites, and culture from displacement by Western forms and authorities, chiefly through the agency of one of a large number of ethnic groups which has partially imposed its rule and its language upon the others. It is clear that any attempt to understand the nature of the Ethiopian political system must begin with the fact of Amhara dominance.

Considered numerically, the Amhara are a minority group in Ethiopia today. They are concentrated in four of the fourteen provinces of the Empire—Shoa, Wallo, Gojjam, and Bagemder—each of which contains sizeable non-Amhara populations. All together the Amhara comprise perhaps one-fifth of the total national population of some 20 to 25 million people.

Their disproportionate influence on the course of Ethiopian politics appears first of all in the fact that not only the Crown but also the great majority of important positions in the government and the armed forces are in Amhara hands (for the most part Amhara of Shoa Province, homeland of the present imperial dynasty). The Amhara are also over-represented in the one area of Ethiopian life where competition is not affected by ethnic considerations, the school system. Due to their fortunate economic position and perhaps to the location of primary schools, Amhara students make up approximately 55 percent of all Ethiopians registered in secondary schools and colleges.[2]

Without denying the significance of this factor of differential access to influential positions, it may be suggested that a more revealing measure of Amhara influence on Ethiopian political life is the extent to which the ideas, symbols, and values which govern Ethiopian politics are drawn from Amhara culture. The national politics of Ethiopia have on the whole been shaped in accordance with what may be called Amhara political culture. It is the task of the pages which follow to develop the meaning of this concept and to ask what it implies for the understanding of Ethiopia's political development.

Political culture, simply stated, consists of the complex of meanings given by a people to the objects in their political system. Yet this simplicity of definition is a hollow victory, since social scientists are far from agreement on how to define a political system and have yet to produce a viable schema for the systematic analysis of cultural meanings. Whether, in analyzing political culture, one chooses to focus on the cultural aspects of a political system or the politically relevant aspects of a culture, one is treading on unstable conceptual ground.

In keeping with the rudimentary state of our facility to deal with this concept, I shall forego the temptation to set forth a coherent and systematic account of Amhara culture and dwell instead on three themes that are of compelling relevance to any consideration of political culture: orientation to authority, to human nature, and to the polity.[3] The first two themes represent very general, basic orientations that connect with other aspects of Amhara culture as well as the narrowly political. Their content is much the same at all levels of Amhara society and presumably has changed very little over the centuries. The third theme, that of nationhood, has been somewhat more prominent in the outlook of the Amhara elites than of the masses and has undergone a historical development which we shall attempt to reconstruct.

III.

The complex of beliefs, symbols, and values regarding authority constitutes a key component of Amhara political culture. Throughout Amhara culture appears the motif that authority as such is good: indispensable for the well-being of society and worthy of unremitting deference, obeisance and praise. Every aspect of Amhara social life is anchored in some sort of relationship to authority figures, and the absence of such a relationship evokes feelings of incompleteness and malaise. The chief exceptions to this are those activities which are defined as outside the pale of society—as in the solipsistic worlds of the anchorite and the outlaw.

The psychological roots of these attitudes toward authority lie of course in the Amhara family. Although Amhara kinship rests on the principle of bilateral descent, and women enjoy substantial rights with regard to inheritance and divorce, the character of the family is unmistakably patriarchal. The father is endowed with considerable powers and is entitled to the utmost respect and obedience. His jurisdiction handily includes the area of physical punishment, which he may apply to wife and servants as well as children, and which, whenever inflicted, is usually considered to be deserved and productive of salutary effects.

Obedience is the prime objective in the socialization of Amhara children. They are taught to be inconspicuous and respectful and to respond readily to any parental commands. An illustration of this ethic is the Amhara practice during mealtime, whereby children are expected to stand quietly, facing the wall, while their elders are eating, and are only fed afterwards, with what is considered second-rate food. Adolescence, although a period for learning the skills and norms related to adult self-sufficiency, is also a time when paternal authority is heightened and demands for obedience are greatly multiplied.

This experience in the family is continuous and consistent with the rest of Amhara culture. Children and adolescents acquire a disposition to respect and obey authority which is generalized to all other spheres of their life. Even in children's play groups there is a pronounced tendency to define someone—usually the eldest—as an authority figure and to submit willingly to his ideas and impulses. Amhara students in the secular government schools, even when separated from their families by boarding arrangements, retain this traditional orientation to a large extent. In a survey of attitudes of secondary-school seniors which I conducted in 1959–1960, 67 per cent of those who identified themselves as Amhara maintained that *one should always obey the order of the superior.* The main reasons given for this response were that, "it is one's duty," "things would not go right otherwise," "the Bible says so," and, "obedience is a virtue."

Ethiopia is not a "political society" in Shils' sense inasmuch as involvement with the goals of the total society is not widely dispersed throughout the populace. But the nature of life among the Amhara is highly "political" in that the wielding of authority is a basic and pervasive feature of their social relationships and in a manner that is broadly similar for all institutional contexts. Theirs is an authoritarian and a politicking society.

Perhaps a better way of approaching this phenomenon is to say that there is but a very tenuous distinction between the occupation of high status on the one hand and the possession of authority on the other whether the latter be conceived as the legitimated capacity to influence the actions of others or as a legitimate agency for allocating values. Men who possess a good measure of one or more of the qualities for which high status is ascribed in Amhara society—family age, wealth, ecclesiastical rank, and political rank—are esteemed throughout the society, and the judgments and decisions are binding in their local contexts. Family patriarch, parish chieftain, wealthy landlord, ecclesiastical dignitary, political dignitary, military officer—all are perceived in the imagery of fatherhood; all are the objects of comparable attitudes regarding the obeisance which is due them and the benefits which may be expected from them.

Amhara culture provides numerous forms for indicating deference to superiors. Some of these are linguistic, the numerous respect forms used in reference and address to superiors. There are in addition many non-verbal gestures of respect towards superiors. For example, an inferior rises to speak when addressed by any authority figure. If eating in his home, he must rise when water is brought for washing his hands. If riding a mule, he dismounts and bows until the superior has passed. When entering his home, he twists his toga in a respectful manner and bows low to the ground, his arms crossed over his chest.

The praise of authorities is an activity which makes use of some of the most elaborate symbolic forms in Amhara culture. These include formal hymns of praise, at times composed in the classical Ethiopic language Ge'ez, in which extravagant religious imagery may be used to glorify secular authorities, as well as extemporized laudatory verses in the vernacular Amharic rendered by minstrels. Similarly, ready compliance with the wishes of any authority figure is expected of the Amhara, at least in appearance. If the subordinate disagrees with the decision of some authority, he does not express that disagreement openly—certainly never in public. If he has some public criticism to make of any authority, he may voice it only through the obscure, double-edged witticisms or verse which are the genius of Amhara culture. Related to this is a very important aspect of authority relations: acceptance of the pronouncement of a judge. Although the Amhara is quick to assert his claims and grievances in litigation, once a judge, at whatever level, has pronounced his verdict, the decision is instantly acquiesced in. If the loser is dissatisfied, which is often the case, he will go outside and appeal to a higher-level judge at a later time.

In their turn, most authority figures are looked upon as sources of certain benefits for the people. One of these is the provision of food. The function of "feeder" is closely associated with the role of father, and "big men" generally are expected to feed numerous relatives and retainers regularly and to institute annual feasts for the benefit of the poor and indigent in their area as well as for wider circles of kin and friends. Prosperous clergy sometimes do the same. The confessor, or "soul father," moreover, performs this function in reverse as it were, checking the observance of fasting requirements by his confessants and imposing additional fasts as punishment for transgressions.

Another service commonly performed by authority figures is the dispensation of justice. Local chieftain, priest, elder, landlord, as well as judges and administrative officials are continually being requested to reconcile antagonists or pass judgment on litigants. It would be considered highly improper for them to refuse such requests. Still another is the ceremonial function. The presence of "big men" in places of honor is an indispensable aesthetic ingredient on such occasions as the celebration of annual religious festivals and, more recently, of secular national holidays.

There is, finally, a sort of magical function connected with the higher political authorities. Their presence is regarded as a source of well-being in the country, a precondition for order and prosperity. This attitude is reflected in an Amharic proverb which attributes fertility of the land to the nobility, and in the story of the deposition of one local Amhara ruler in the eighteenth century because of a severe drought which occurred during the first year of his rule.

All of these themes are realized in the most complete form and on a grand scale in connection with the highest authority figure of all, the emperor. The incumbent of this role has been the recipient of the most extreme forms of obeisance. It has been customary, for example, for Ethiopian subjects to prostrate themselves and refrain from lifting their eyes in his presence. Earlier records document a comparable show of deference when royal messages were received from afar; the recipient had to hear the message outside his home, standing, and naked above the waist. Similarly, eulogies of the emperor were expressed in numerous literary forms. In royal chronicles and hymns of praise which span seven centuries the emperors are celebrated for superlative beauty and superhuman powers. In splendor of countenance they are likened to the sun; in awesomeness of power, to the lion; in religious character and divine force, to the kings of Israel and, at times, to God Himself.

Expectations of service from the emperor were on a comparably grand scale. Hundreds and at times thousands of men were periodically nourished at his feasts. Numerous cases of litigation—appeals from lower judicial levels, as well as disputes originating at the highest level—were judged by him in periodic court sessions. His appearance in any part of the country at any time was itself a momentous ceremonial occasion. And his magical function was, according to some students, the most important of all—a transcendent source of social euphoria. For this reason, again, the death of an emperor has usually been a time of acute social malaise, often bordering on anarchy, and the news of his death has often been concealed as long as possible from the public.

While it is meaningful thus to regard the orientation toward the emperor as a continuation and projection of the orientations toward authority figures at all levels in Amhara society—he is the greatest father figure of all—there are however certain discontinuous and unique elements in Amhara political culture concerning the imperial role and person. For the role of emperor is bound up with beliefs and values that are *sui generis* and that are directly connected with other more fundamental aspects of Amhara culture. These relate primarily to the conception of the emperor as a sacred personality, as "Elect of God."

This conception, probably deriving ultimately from pre-Christian notions of divine monarchy and subsequently anchored in beliefs concerning Solomonic ancestry and the transfer of divine mission from the Kings of Israel to the Kings of Ethiopia, is closely connected with the self-image of the Amhara people. By virtue of the beliefs on which the charisma of his office is grounded they are able to view themselves as a chosen people and to affix some of that charisma to themselves. On the one hand they identify themselves as descendants of the ancient chosen people of Israel. Nobles related to the imperial line have in fact traditionally been referred to as "chiefs of Israel" On the other hand they identify themselves as the unique bearers of the Christian faith, and to this day many if not most Amhara regard themselves as the only authentic Christians in the world. These beliefs provide the ideological basis for the superiority which the Amhara feel vis-à-vis the other peoples of Ethiopia (except the Tigreans, with whom they share this cultural legacy) and for their claims to be the just rulers of the land.

Because of the important symbolic function of the royal office, certain extraordinary qualifications have been required for entry into that office. One is that the emperor actually be descended from persons identified as members of the Solomonic line. Another is that his body be free from any physical defect, in order as it were to serve as an adequate symbol for the integrity of the body politic. Finally, legitimate accession to the throne has depended on two rites, anointment by oil and bestowal of the crown. Authority to conduct these rites was vested in the archbishop who, until the election of an Ethiopian to that station in 1950, had always been an Egyptian monk sent by the Coptic Patriarch at Alexandria. The act of coronation transformed the status of the new emperor, who assumed a new name and accoutred himself with such insignia as a red silk parasol and special drums, trumpets, and flutes.

The unique status of the emperor relates to other aspects of Amhara culture which are particularly important for understanding the nature and scope of the Ethiopian monarchy today. One of these is the peculiar responsibility placed on the emperor for the welfare of the Orthodox Church. Most emperors have in fact been active in one way or another in supporting the religious institutions of the country. For some the Christianizing role has been a key component of their identity—those, for example, who selected the throne name of Constantine. They have frequently granted lands to the church, constructed church buildings and monasteries, and bestowed gifts of silk robes and other precious items. Several emperors have been particularly involved in some specialized aspect of religious affairs, whether the composition of religious writings and the revision of liturgies, like Zar'a Ya'qob (1434–1468); working to resolve theological controversies, as did Yohannes the Pious (1667–1682); stimulating, like Iyasu the Great (1682–1706), religious cultural activities and education; or waging campaigns to convert the heathens, as did Yohannes IV (1872–1889).

The authority to invest the highest ranks was another distinct attribute of the emperor's position. Ethiopia did not possess a hereditary aristocracy such as those developed in most European countries. To be sure, there developed a quasi-hereditary nobility, based on the tendency for lands, office, and titles to be given to members of the same families. In practice the emperors frequently let such possessions pass from father to son, either because they were in too distant a region or because there was no good cause for taking them away, and on occasion drew up written charters assigning grants of land to a man and his future descendants. But titles never passed directly from father to son without the approval of the emperor, and however much a man might qualify for political appointment or honorific title by virtue of his father's standing, he could attain the highest distinctions only through the agency of royal favor.

Thus two kinds of variables were always involved in the assignment of status to an authority figure: the intrinsic factors of family background, wealth, and local military strength, and the extrinsic factor of investiture by the sovereign. The relative importance of these two sources of high status depended on the actual political strength of the emperor at a given time and the degree of proximity to his court.

Still another distinctive feature of the emperor's pre-eminent position was his authority to introduce culture change. While the Amhara are basically resistant to innovations of any sort, they have expected the emperor to do what is necessary to ensure the welfare of the realm and have tolerated his deviation from precedent when that has not conflicted with their ultimate values, such as allegiance to the Ethiopian Orthodox faith. At times such changes have been introduced by direct proclamation, as in the institution of new religious holidays by Zar'a Ya'qob or the introduction of smallpox vaccination by Menelik. At times they have been introduced through suggestion or by providing models for the populace to follow, as in the effort of a number of monarchs of the past century to combat the Amhara's repugnance for manual labor by themselves engaging in arduous physical work on occasion. More recently they have included the establishment of new institution such as the State Bank and the secular school, introduced by Menelik.

IV.

Another aspect of Amhara culture highly relevant to an understanding of Ethiopia's political development is its approach to human nature. This phenomenon may be examined first of all by inspecting the variety of semantic usages connected with the generic word for "man," *saw*. Perhaps the most common connotation of this term is the concept of "others." An object which is described as *ya-saw*—literally, "of man"—means an object belonging to *someone else*. So used, the word *saw* tends to have unpleasant overtones. It means someone outside the circle of kin; it means neighbors or outsiders and thus conveys a negative or at best sternly neutral sentiment. The adage that "the affairs of man [i.e. other people] are grief" illustrates this. An extraordinary instance of this negative use of the generic word for man appears in the expression *ya-saw ayn*; literally, "the eye of man," or "the eye of others." *Ya-saw ayn*, however, is an idiom which signifies the "evil eye," one of the most feared and despised objects in Amhara culture.

By adding the suffix "*ya*," *saw* takes on the meaning of a particular man. The word *sawya* is used in narrative in a neutral, descriptive sense: *and sawya nabara*, "once there was a man." But it is also used in a vocative sense, like the American *man*! or the German *Mensch*! Unlike these latter, however, it conveys no positive sentiment based on the friendly assumption of solidarity between two members of the same species. On the contrary, the term *Sawya!* tends to be spoken in a somewhat domineering tone and might best be rendered by the American expression, "Hey you!"

In other contexts *saw* takes on a more affirmative meaning. It may signify a free man as distinguished from a slave. It may also signify a human being, a fully formed member of the species. But here the Amhara attitude toward human nature is expressed in a common and very characteristic saying, *Saw yallam*—"there is no human being;" in other words, an individual who fully embodies the concept of humanity does not exist. In this sense of the term human nature in the abstract is admirable, but in actuality never so.

Extending our examination beyond such narrow semantic analyses, we find that these negative associations of the word *saw* are supported by two sets of negative ideas concerning man: the attribution of inferiority to various human types due to their possession of certain ascribed qualities, and the assumption that man is dominated by certain fundamental negative propensities.

The Amhara's conception of humanity is radically unegalitarian. A person's chief characteristics, in the Amhara view, are whether he is male or female, elder or youth, Amhara or non-Amhara, Christian or non-Christian, free or slave and well born or poor. Each of these dichotomies falls into a superior-inferior pattern. Women are considered inferior because of their alleged infidelity and the triviality of their conversation. With respect to age categories, children are considered inferior because they are governed by ignorance and passion; adolescents because, like wind, they are flighty and never settled; young men because, like fire, they are hot in picking quarrels and chasing after women. Non-Amhara people are disdained, partly on a racial basis—the "ashen-faced" European and the black man with Negroid features, both the traditional objects of racial ridicule—and partly on a cultural basis, with occupational hunters and pastoral nomads at the bottom of the status hierarchy. The distinction between Orthodox Christian and all other religions is all-or-none; Catholic, Protestant, Muslim, and pagan are to the traditional Amhara, virtually interchangeable as inferior, infidel types. Finally, slaves, ex-slaves, and poor folk generally are considered inferior by definition. Because of this strong unegalitarian ethos the Amhara have but a very dim feeling that the simple fact of being a human being is sufficient to entitle an individual to respect.[4]

Part of the reason for this is that the particular features which dominate the Amhara's image of generic human nature are man's inherent aggressiveness and his untrustworthiness. Amhara culture does not support the belief that unformed human nature is good raw material. It holds, rather, that without strict punishment for nearly a dozen years of his life a person will not grow up properly. He will be rude, untrained, tending to trample on others.

Once a person reaches adulthood, moreover, his hostility must constantly be kept in check. This belief is illustrated by the Amharic concept of *Tagābengnā*. The literal meaning of *tagābengnā* is "one who has been sated," who has had his fill of food and drink. In common usage, however, the word signifies a person who is disposed to insult and pick fights with people. A servant who becomes "uppity" or a soldier who opposes his superior's command may be called *tagābengnā*, implying that the arrogant behavior in question comes from having been too well off. A number of Amharic couplets begin with the lines, "When a peasant gets sated, he beats with his stick." In the Amhara view the specific effect of drinking alcohol is to release not Eros but the aggressive instincts. The following proverb about the Ethiopian barley-beer, *tallā*, states this forthrightly:

One [glass] whets the appetite;
Two quenches it;
Three heats one up;
Four makes one quarrel;
Five brings fighting;
Six causes killing.

The Amhara view of human nature thus conceives of aggression as a response to abundant gratification, not frustration. A corollary to this is the belief that deprivation is the proper prophylaxis against aggression. The Amhara refer to fasting as the most important part of their religion, and indeed, with respect to the number and harshness of the fasts it prescribes, Amhara custom is probably the strictest in the world. This custom is explained on the grounds that by weakening one's body thus, one is less likely to commit some wrong against others, like assaulting or insulting them.

Related to this view of man's powerful latent hostility is the notion that man is untrustworthy. *Sawan mämman ba-kantu naw*, "It is futile to trust in man"—so runs an Amharic epigram sometimes woven ornamentally into wool rugs. In part this is an expression of the otherworldly orientation of Ethiopian Christianity; the world is transient, all things pass away except God, and so it is futile to place one's trust in anyone other than God. But this epigram also expresses a very deep-rooted secular disposition, a disposition to be suspicious of everyone outside the narrow circle of kin and often within that circle as well. This disposition is institutionalized in the custom known as *wāss*, according to which virtually any sort of secular transaction—hiring a servant, lending money, litigating in court, and so on—requires as the initial step the securing of a guarantor who agrees to make good for any damages caused by the man he is backing.

The Amhara's essentially pessimistic estimate of man's potentialities does not, however, imply a dogmatic or emotional rejection of man, such as has been experienced in some other developments within the Christian tradition. The Amhara's approach to human nature may be characterized, rather, as a sort of realistic humanism. Man is accepted, with all his frailties, for what he is assumed to be. The institutions and norms of the Amhara are shaped not to overwhelm man with guilt for his shortcomings, not to pressure him into personal or social reform, not to deprive his worldly existence of all enjoyment and significance, but rather to accommodate human realities and transcendent values to one another in such a way that neither is seriously compromised. The negative propensities of man are simply acknowledged and taken into account. Where feasible, they are controlled; where not, their free sway is accepted.

The latter alternative is followed in instances where certain Christian ideals are upheld at the same time as the normal human inclination to flout them is recognized and accepted. With respect to the use of violence, for example, the Christian pacifist ideal is embodied in the requirement that those who officiate in the celebration of the Mass—priests and deacons—must never have shed human blood; and an Amhara who has been ordained as a priest must not even shed the blood of an animal. This does not mean that the clergy have constituted a social force working to oppose violence as such. Priests have gladly accompanied military expeditions and assisted the efforts of combatants by their divinations and their prayers. But by virtue of the norm that they themselves abstain from violence, the clergy have kept alive in this traditionally martial society a faint echo of the Christian ideal of non-violence.

The Amhara arrangements with respect to the Christian ideal of monogamy are equally discriminating. The Ethiopian Church recognizes as legal only those marriages which have been sanctified by a ceremony in which the husband and wife partake of the Eucharist. The parties to such a marriage, known as a *qurbān* type of marriage, are thereafter forbidden to commit adultery, to divorce, or to remarry upon the death of one of the partners. Such rules are clearly oppressive to the majority of Amhara, who prefer to contract a civil marriage and live their lives technically excommunicated by their church, which they may do and still remain fully respected members of the society. Marriage according to this Church law is, however, a prerequisite for ordination to the priesthood, and the most important single prerequisite at that. In other words, the Christian ideal of monogamy is embodied in the careers of those whose vocation is ritual purity, while the rest of the society is relatively free to follow the inclinations of the old Adam.

Still another sociological arrangement which embodies the Amhara's forbearance toward human frailty concerns the role known as *dabtarā*. The *dabtarā* is the literatus of Amhara society, and his functions as chorister, scribe, and religious poet are essential to the working of the Church. In this role the Amhara have instituted a religious vocation which requires the attainment of special knowledge but does not expect pious behavior. The *dabtarā* can be a man who has marched on the warpath or who hunts wild game. His marital life is as free of restrictions as the ordinary layman's. The role of *dabtarā* thus provides an outlet for religiously oriented Amhara who do not choose to be tied down by the strict conditions of the priesthood and for priests who, finding these conditions to be too much to live with, have divorced or remarried.

Other aspects of Amhara society and culture are organized so as to set limits to the acting out of man's presumed asocial and disruptive tendencies. One of these we have already mentioned: the subjection of all Christian Amhara to a stringent regime of fasting. The Amhara acknowledge the appropriateness and efficacy of this custom in a matter-of-fact way. They say, when questioned, that man is susceptible to the temptations of the devil, and that by weakening their bodies through fasting they will be better prepared to withstand these temptations and to refrain from committing some wrong against their fellows.

Another source of control is the subordination of all individuals to the authority of various superiors. Here two understandings are at work. One is the feeling that centrifugal and mutually destructive impulses will play themselves out unless checked by some figure of authority. As a number of secondary school and college students noted when justifying their response that "one should always obey the order of a superior," "things would not go right otherwise," and "this is necessary for people to cooperate." The other is the expectation that some judge-figure will always be available; that it is all right to unleash complaint and accusations against one's neighbor because sooner or later the antagonism will be brought into control and channeled through the agency of customary judicial procedures. The Amhara view of human nature thus complements the previously discussed orientation to authority in buttressing a disposition to respect and obey figures of authority.

The realistic acceptance of and adjustment to what are perceived as man's inherent shortcomings is an expression, furthermore, of a more general orientation to the universe that may be described as a kind of fatalism. The concept of fate—*edell*—is invoked by Amhara to account for the various accomplishments and peripeties of their lives. *Eddel* is the working of divine will as it affects human purposes, and it is believed to be more important than human effort in attaining any end. Amhara culture thus provides little justification for efforts to introduce change. On the contrary, received habit is tenaciously kept because of its association with the authority "of our fathers." Nature is regarded as a set of conditions to be accepted as found and carefully adjusted to, not to be conquered or transformed. Time is conceived as cyclical, not linear, and ordered in terms of months, years, and sequences of years of which the characteristic feature is not historical uniqueness but indefinite repetition. This cyclical feeling is mirrored in the Amhara's organization of space, which is marked by the repeated use of concentric circles![5]

The chief political implication of all this is that society no more than human nature is to be made the object of systematic efforts to apply transcendent principles or to transform the *status quo*. The task of political authority is to accept such conflicts and strains as exist and to work, by skillful manipulation, adjudication, and occasional coercion, to maintain a minimum of order and retributive justice. Another implication of some importance is that, because human beings are considered so untrustworthy, the degree to which Amhara are disposed to unite in pursuit of a common cause is a priori quite limited.

V.

Neither at the local nor the national level does Amhara culture place a high value on the notion of civil community.[6] Indeed, the concept of "community" can scarcely be rendered in idiomatic Amharic. Social cohesion has been attained not by the attachment of solidaristic sentiment to communal symbols or the organization of activities in behalf of communal ends but through the sharing of common religious, territorial, and linguistic identifications on the one hand and subordination to individual authority figures on the other. When individual and presumed communal interests come into conflict, Amhara culture tends to place greater weight on the defense of individual interests. Similarly, it values the pursuit of local, para-dynastic interests more than the subordination of parochial goals to the interests of the nation. Most of the stories which Amhara like to tell of their national history thus take the form of anecdotes related to internecine warfare and political conflict and the substance of their history has been to a large extent as described by an Amhara literatus: "Always the same old thing—one lord fighting another to gain more power." Nevertheless some sense of national community, however rare, has never been wholly absent from the Amhara consciousness. It rests on a number of national memories, symbols, and aspirations that are an inalienable part of Amhara experience.

Ethiopian nationality has for millenia been designated by the term Habasha by Orientals. The term apparently derives from the name of one of the South Arabian tribes which migrated across the Red Sea in the first millennium B.C., the Habashat. Although Ethiopians frequently use the term *hābashā* among themselves—if for no other reason than that it is simpler to pronounce than the cumbersome *etiopiyāwi*—they resent the use of the term (and its European counterpart, Abyssinian) by outsiders because of alleged pejorative overtones.

It is difficult to determine at what time the name Ethiopia gained currency as a symbol of national identity. In Aksumite antiquity it referred not to their own country but to Nilotic kingdoms to the west. The earliest recorded use of the appellation "King of Kings of Ethiopia" was by Yekuno Amlak in the late thirteenth century, and all emperors since him have followed suit. Yet whatever name it went by, some sense of nationality must have preceded this usage, and contemporary national sentiment refers back to two cultural sources which clearly antedate the rise of the Amhara as rulers of the country: the tradition of the monarchy and that of the Church.

Native king lists connect the present dynasty with a genealogy that stretches back literally to King Solomon. Associated with the antique monarchy in the national memory are the former seats of royal power which were embodied in enduring architectural constructions: the stelae of Aksum, the churches of Lalibela, and the castles of Gonder. The sense of Ethiopian nationhood is thus in part the effect of identification with a legendary and historical national dynasty shared by all Amhara.

It is also the effect of common membership in a national religion. Introduced by King Ezana in the fourth century, Christianity has expressed and stimulated the development of a national sentiment among those who have adopted it. It is in connection with her religion that Ethiopia has undergone some of the most unifying experiences in her history.

1. Although the political center of Ethiopia shifted southward from Aksum toward the end of the first millennium A.D., the cathedral of St. Mary of Zion at Aksum remained the first sanctuary of the land until the latter part of the nineteenth century. Thus some sense of an underlying unity of north and south, of Tigre and Amhara, was kept alive by the Amhara's respect for the sanctuary in the north and the custom of holding the rite of coronation of the Amhara emperors at Aksum.

2. Through a spontaneous process of geographical division of labor Ethiopia developed over the centuries a nationwide system of higher religious education. Ethiopian youth who sought a greater mastery of the religious traditions than that afforded in their local parishes left home and tramped across mountains to one or another of the more specialized centers of instruction. For study of the liturgical chants the best schools were in Bagamder and Tigre provinces; for the art of religious poetry they went to one of the monasteries in Gojjam; for religious dance and the study of the holy books the best masters were to be found, in recent centuries, at Gonder. Thus virtually all parts of the country were linked in the minds of Amhara as parts of a unified, national system for the transmission of religious culture.

3. The greatest collective trauma remembered by Ethiopians was the effect of a *jihad* led by an imam from the eastern kingdom of Adal, Ahmad Gragn. In a series of campaigns that began in 1527 and continued for fifteen years, Ahmad Gragn, fortified by firearms from the Ottoman Turks and hordes of Somali fighters, laid most of the Amhara country waste, looted and burned churches, and forced most of the inhabitants to embrace Islam. His eventual defeat was followed by the return of most of the forced converts to the Christian fold and a slow and painful reconstruction of the church. This first serious invasion of Ethiopia by an outside power thus connected the themes of national defense and Christian identity in an intimate way and stamped upon Ethiopian consciousness the self-image which was later to be made famous in the remark of Menelik, who characterized Ethiopia as "an island of Christians in a sea of pagans."

4. In the course of seeking to recover from the destruction wrought by Gragn's *jihad* a number of emperors turned to European Christian powers for religious association as well as political support and technical aid. Some of the emperors became converts to Catholicism and, encouraged by Jesuit missionaries, attempted to promote the Roman faith among their subjects. This policy in turn provoked a strong nationalist reaction, particularly during the reign of Susneyos (1607–1632). Susneyos was forced to abdicate, the Jesuits were expelled from the country, and the new emperor secured the agreement of the

pashas on the coast to execute all priests who tried to enter the country. Thus, as one historian has put it, "it was the Muslims who now became the [Ethiopians'] allies . . . against what seemed to them the greater menace—the attempt of Europeans to undermine their national religion, the very embodiment of their national spirit."[7] Through this second trauma, then, just as through the assaults of the Muslim invader, adherence to the traditional religion provided a rallying point for the crystallization of a greater sense of national unity and identity.

It was only in the nineteenth century, in response to the acute civil disorder brought on by a century of feudal separatism and the growing external threat—first from Muhammed Ali's Egypt, then from Mahdism in the Sudan and the expansion of European imperialism—that a more secular concept of nationalism began to germinate in Ethiopia. The agent of this germination was Emperor Tewodros II (Theodore, 1855–1868), whose tortuous career was devoted to the goal of unifying the country and upholding its dignity as a nation. In the words and deeds of Tewodros, the two secular aspirations which form the hard core of modern Ethiopian nationalism—territorial integrity and self-rule—received a classic formulation.

Territory has overriding emotional significance to the Ethiopian because virtually all the ideas and values of his secular national culture are derived from peasant experience. The Amhara peasant's deep attachment to his land and his readiness to defend it by fighting are projected at the national level into a determination to protect the territorial boundaries of the nation at all costs. This attitude is reflected in one of the mottoes of the Imperial Bodyguard, "Bitter as aloes for a handful of earth." In the case of Tewodros it was expressed in the story of his dealings with two British explorers who had been accused of making maps of the country. When they were about to depart, Tewodros gave them many jewels as a farewell present but sent a servant along to wash their boots before they embarked. His explanation: "Far more precious than jewels is a single grain of our country's soil."

Yet if Tewodros is remembered for anything in Ethiopia, it is for his proud determination not to be subjected to foreign rule, capped by his dramatic suicide—a highly unusual act in traditional Ethiopia—when faced with the prospect of capture by the chiefs of the British expedition in 1868. In his famous remark to M. Lejean, the French Consul, Tewodros expressed the pride of sentiment that lay behind that final act: "I know the tactics of European Governments when they desire to acquire an Eastern State. First they send out missionaries, then consuls to support the missionaries, then battalions to support the consuls. I am not a rajah of Hindustan to be made a mockery of in that way: I prefer to have to deal with the battalions right away."[8] The resurgence of interest in Tewodros by Ethiopians during the past decade, the plays written and performed about him, and his increased popularity as a national hero are based on his perfect incarnation of the Amhara wish: Give me freedom from foreign rule or give me death. Because of their long history as rulers of the country, moreover, and their deeply ingrained belief that "the Amhara are to rule, not to be ruled," the Amhara are, of all Ethiopians, most sensitive to the encroachment of foreign powers.

The elemental goals of secular nationalism were further pursued by the Tigre emperor Yohannes IV (1871–1889), who also sought to revive the association of Ethiopian nationality with Orthodox Christianity. By his time, however, the numerous Muslims in the country made such a concept no longer feasible. Yohannes' brutal policy of forcing conversions to Christianity was foredoomed to failure. The religious component of Ethiopian nationality was thereafter reduced in importance, particularly after the national boundaries were expanded to their present extent under Menelik, an expansion which added millions of Muslims and pagans to the population of the country.

In the course of Menelik's reign, on the other hand, the concept of national self-determination reached a new level of importance. Indeed, it may be said that the modern concept of Ethiopian nationhood was born of Menelik's defeat of the Italian troops at Adwa in 1896. That event represented a tremendous national undertaking, in which Tigre and Oromo as well as Amhara generals played important parts. It also gave the Ethiopian nation a considerable increase in prestige, moving European powers to acknowledge Ethiopia as a force to be reckoned with seriously and so to increase or establish diplomatic representations at Addis Ababa. The year following Adwa witnessed the adoption of an official version of the tricolor Ethiopian national flag[9] and opened a decade of negotiations with European powers in which nine border treaties were signed.[10] On the basis of this quickened intercourse with European states Menelik began to introduce a number of modern Western institutions into his country, including, as one of his last major acts, the establishment of governmental ministries.

Because of the crucial importance of the victory at Adwa in establishing Ethiopia's identity as a nation in the modern world, it is not surprising that the annual commemoration of that victory constitutes one of the five national secular holidays celebrated in contemporary Ethiopia. The other four commemorate events that have occurred during the reign of the present Emperor, Haile Selassie I.

VI.

There have been no radical changes in the Amhara orientation to nationhood under His Imperial Majesty Haile Selassie I. The values which informed this orientation under Menelik have remained much the same: the

Solomonic monarchy as the locus of sovereignty, territorial integrity, national self-determination, and a tempered emphasis on Orthodox Christianity as an embodiment of the national spirit. What has happened during Haile Selassie's long and eventful regime is that these themes have been enriched by new experiences and the accretion of new meanings. The net result has been a slow but continuous evolution of a sense of Ethiopian nationhood consistent with the traditional Amhara beliefs and values.

The idea of the Solomonic monarchy as the locus of Ethiopian sovereignty has been raised to a new level of importance. It has been given legal expression in the two constitutions which Haile Selassie presented to the people of Ethiopia, in 1931 and again in 1955. Both constitutions affirm the genealogical basis of imperial legitimacy, proclaiming that "the Imperial dignity shall remain perpetually attached to the line of Haile Selassie I . . . whose line descends without interruption from the dynasty of Menelik I, son of the Queen of Ethiopia, the Queen of Sheba, and King Solomon of Jerusalem." They further assert that "By virtue of His Imperial Blood, as well as by the anointing which He has received, the person of the Emperor is sacred, His dignity is inviolable and His power indisputable. He is consequently entitled to all the honours due Him in accordance with tradition and the present Constitution . . . The Sovereignty of the Empire is vested in the Emperor."

The person of the Sovereign has been publicized to a degree hitherto unimagined. Haile Selassie has been the subject of an unremitting cult of personality. The paraphenalia of royalty have been refined and multiplied through the incorporation of modern facilities. The image of an august, benevolent sovereign has been projected throughout the empire by means of modern media. Celebration of the anniversary of his birth and the annual commemoration of his coronation have been institutionalized as national holidays. The country has thus been permeated with the image of a legitimate national authority and has thereby moved somewhat closer to the sense of itself as a single political entity.

The main international event of this reign, the war with Italy and subsequent five-year Occupation, likewise produced and diffused a more substantial sense of nationhood. The consequences of this event were not unmixed, to be sure. Some tribal groups welcomed the Italians as liberating them from Amhara suzerainty, and many ambitious parties joined the Italian cause as collaborators. Yet for most of the Amhara, and many Tigre and Oromo, the invasion of their territory and the usurpation of their government by an alien power was not to be borne. Numbers of them spent the Occupation years as exiles in Kenya, Somalia, Sudan, Israel, or Europe; and many others conducted an effective campaign of resistance on the home front. Like Adwa, moreover, the repercussions of the

Italian invasion were such as to heighten the importance of Ethiopia in world opinion. Ethiopian prestige was at an all-time high in the international sphere in the decade following the liberation, and some awareness of this condition likewise boosted the sense of national identity at home.

A new set of national symbols and memories was one of the legacies of the Italian era. The annual holiday in honor of the "Ethiopian Martyrs of 12 Yekatit" commemorates the massacre of educated Ethiopians and clergy carried out in February 1937 in retaliation for an attempt on the life of the Italian viceroy, Marshal Graziani. Liberation from the Italian rule is the theme of another holiday, falling on May 5. This anniversary upholds the identification of the monarch with the state, for actually it is defined not as an anniversary of national liberation but rather as "His Imperial Majesty's Triumphant Return to Addis Ababa." Still another symbolic event was the martyrdom of Abuna Petros, the Ethiopian bishop who chose death rather than collaboration with the Italian regime. An imposing statue of this venerable monk was erected in the capital to commemorate, as the Ethiopian Herald put it, "the martyrdom of an Ethiopian patriot," a subject also commemorated in the form of a verse drama by a distinguished Amhara writer.

The case of Abuna Petros leads us once more to the question of the relationship between religion and Ethiopian nationality. The traditional Orthodox faith has remained a national religion under Haile Selassie in some very important respects. The 1955 Constitution states that only adherents to this faith may be counted as members of the imperial family and prescribes that the Emperor, in the oath taken upon coronation, swear to "profess and defend the Holy Orthodox Faith based on the doctrines of St. Mark of Alexandria, professed in Ethiopia, since the Holy Emperors Abreha and Atsbiha." Article 126 explicitly sets forth that "The Ethiopian Orthodox Church . . . is the Established Church of the Empire and is, as such, supported by the State."

In practice, however, a pluralistic approach has been in evidence. Haile Selassie has not attempted to force conversion to the Orthodox faith, but has adopted a policy of toleration. His conciliatory attitude toward the large Muslim minority and efforts to integrate them into a national community are indicated by his construction of mosques, bestowal of honors and benefits upon selected Muslim notables, and support of a newspaper published in Arabic as well as Amharic—a paper whose name refers to the Ethiopian national flag. He has adopted the practice of inviting leaders of the Muslim community to the palace at the close of the fast of Ramadan.

While the main Ethiopian Christian holidays are still observed as national holidays, some of them have become occasions for the expression of a more secular national spirit. On the festivals of Masqal (Finding of the True Cross) in September and Timqät (Epiphany) in January members of various tribal and religious groups congregate to perform their respective traditional dances and songs. These holidays have to some extent become media for the stimulation of feelings of national solidarity rather than divisive sentiments.

VII.

Where, as in the case of Ethiopia, a traditional culture has not been subjected to radical transformation through the agency of alien powers or internal revolutionaries, it may be expected that the most general beliefs and values concerning the political system will remain efficacious, guiding and limiting the variety of immediate adjustments in governmental structure and popular political action. Thus in Ethiopia the political culture of the Amhara, dominant in the land for many centuries, remains today the chief determinant of Ethiopia's political orientation as she is pushed by history in the direction of modernization.[11] How do the features of Amhara political culture we have discussed affect the course of political development in Ethiopia?

To answer this question we must first specify what will be meant here by "political modernization," underdeveloped though our understanding of that complicated notion may be. Three ideas are commonly regarded as central to this concept. One is that the authority of government be firmly established in the structure of a sovereign nation-state—not in a clan, a tribe, a church, a duchy, or a trust. The modern polity is first of all headed by a national government which both possesses a preponderance, if not a monopoly, of the means of physical coercion and is recognized as legitimate by a substantial majority of those living under its rule.

The second idea essential to the notion of political modernization is that of rationalization. Rationalization, an integral part of any conception of generic modernity, refers to the sustained and systematic effort to subject man's environment to rational control; more specifically here, to maximize the efficiency of operation of the various parts of the political system. With respect to the organs of government this is usually understood to entail the establishment of a bureaucratic form of public administration and a division of labor involving the separation of judicial, executive, and legislative functions. With respect to the governed it is usually understood to entail the establishment of procedures whereby their interests can be known and their support can be mobilized.

A third and related constituent of political modernization may be designated as the institutionalized capacity to generate and absorb change. A modern or modernizing polity is thus one which is disposed to experiment, to innovate, and to react to social change not as a threatening, extrinsic phenomenon but as a normal, expected feature of political life.

So conceptualized, the course of political modernization in Ethiopia may be seen to have been affected in diverse ways by the continuity of Amhara political culture. Speaking very generally, one may say that this culture has furthered the establishment of legitimate national government, has obstructed the process of rationalization, and has affected both positively and negatively the receptivity to social change.

Several features of Amhara political culture have favored the establishment of a national government accepted as legitimate by a substantial majority of the Ethiopian people. The principal one is of course the traditional belief in the transcendent dignity and authority of the King of Kings of Ethiopia. This belief has been preserved over the centuries, even when (during the "Age of the Princes," ca. 1769–1855) the emperor was a mere puppet, a shadowy figure, having no perceptible impact on Ethiopian political life. It has been sustained by the high value accorded to the Solomonic genealogy and to the sanctity of anointment. It has been used by the emperors of the past century to justify their efforts to establish autocratic authority over the entire country. Acceptance of this authority has been furthered by the Amhara's emphasis on obedience to authority figures generally. The relevance of this orientation to authority is shown by the fact that although the present emperor has numerous opponents, no one has dared to criticize him publicly. As one high official once told me, "Whether we like him or not, we must not criticize him." The tenacity of this mentality was dramatically illustrated by the behavior of the rebels of December 1960; they did not presume to stage a coup d'etat while the emperor was in the country, and in all of their revolutionary pronouncements during their brief stay in power the emperor was not once mentioned directly.

It is difficult to determine what proportion of the total population of Ethiopia accepts the suzerainty of the Amhara monarchy. It must be assumed that many Muslim and pagan tribesmen remain alienated from it. But the politically relevant elements of the population certainly accept it, even where they are critically disposed toward the present incumbent; and this has made it possible for Haile Selassie to eliminate once and for all the semi-autonomous strength of the powerful provincial nobles and to centralize power and prestige in his person to a degree never before realized in Ethiopia.

While the authority of national government in Ethiopia thus rests primarily upon a solid base of allegiance and subordination to the office of the emperor, it also gains support from the aspirations of the people of Ethiopia to maintain their national territory and freedom from alien domination. No political issue has aroused Ethiopians of all classes more in the past decade than the dispute over the Somali border. Except for the Somali elements in the population, most Ethiopians who have any awareness of the issue are passionate nationalists when it comes to the prospect of having to relinquish a single acre of the vast Ogaden desert. Furthermore, as a result of the Italian Occupation and more recently the spread of ideas about the white man's imperialism elsewhere in Africa, the Amhara passion to avoid being dominated in any way by aliens provides a further channel for the expression of nationalist sentiment.

The authority of the national government is thus further upheld by its acceptance as a spokesman for and defender of national political interests, interests which are deeply valued in Amhara political culture. It is true that the national government is scarcely perceived as an embodiment of the will of a united Ethiopian people; for feelings of solidarity among the peoples of Ethiopia are still very weak. Regional, ethnic, and religious differences remain the paramount foci of orientation for the vast majority of the population. Such differences are accentuated by the traditional notions of Amhara superiority and sense of exclusiveness. Even so, it can be said that Amhara culture provides some bases for the development of a greater sense of Ethiopian nationality.

One of these is, paradoxically, the continued association between church and state—paradoxically, because the religious composition of the Ethiopian populace is so very mixed. A rough estimate, based on Trimingham's figures,[12] would be: Christians, 49 per cent; Muslims, 27 per cent; pagans, 23 per cent; Jews, 1 per cent. Other estimates make the Christian and Muslim proportions very nearly equal. Despite this mixture the close connection between church and state may be seen as furthering the sense of Ethiopian nationality and the authority of the central government in two ways. On the one hand it provides a basis for uniting the political leaders of the country, nearly all of whom are Christians, though stemming from diverse ethnic, tribal, and linguistic backgrounds; and it gives them a greater self-esteem through the feeling that they are first-class citizens and associated with the peculiar historical mission and traditions of Ethiopia. On the other hand it contributes to a growing sense of nationality at the popular level through the secularization and universalization of some of the Christian holidays.

Another feature of Amhara culture which has not been discussed in this context is the use of Amharic as a national language. Although less than half of the population know Amharic, it is slowly becoming a lingua franca in the empire by virtue of its required use as the language of instruction in the elementary grades as well as for purposes of administration and judicial records. Some groups may resent or be disadvantaged by the suppression of their native languages in such matters, but Amharic is clearly the medium of communication in Ethiopia's future and as such a strong nationalizing factor. Even among those who are not native Amharic speakers those who are aware of the situation elsewhere in Africa tend to take pride in the fact that their national language is indigenous, not, as is true of most other African countries, an alien tongue.

It may also be noted, finally, that Amhara culture has traditionally subverted its ethnic snobbishness to some extent by favoring intermarriage for purposes of political harmony. The example set by many Amhara notables, including the present Emperor, in marrying into families of non-Amhara stock has mollified the bans against ethnic intermarriage, which were never extremely rigid anyway. When asked if they would marry someone from another tribe, 67 per cent of the Amhara secondary students and 74 per cent of Amhara college students replied affirmatively. In responding to a more general question on the relative strength of their tribal and national identifications 60 per cent of all secondary and 75 per cent of all college students indicated that their identification as Ethiopians took priority.

VIII.

With respect to rationalization, the second characteristic of political modernization as we have proposed to understand it here, Amhara culture is as much of an obstacle as it is an asset in regard to the goal just considered. For if the main criterion of rationalization in the political realm is the development of relatively specialized structures appropriate to the performance of the several functions of a political system, nothing could be further removed from this standard than the aspects of Amhara culture which define the character of Ethiopian politics. The political system as it has developed under Haile Selassie, an extrapolation from but fully consistent with traditional Amhara beliefs and practices, is designed for anything but differentiation of function. With respect to the performance of all seven functions of the political system identified by Almond—rule-making, rule application, rule adjudication, interest articulation, interest aggregation, political communication, and political recruitment[13]—it may be said that Emperor Haile Selassie has been a key agency.

In the first three of the governmental functions, this functional diffuseness is self-evident from a reading of the Ethiopian Constitution. While the 1955 Constitution represents some movement in the direction of differentiation, in that it delegates greater prerogatives to the Parliament and provides for the popular election of the Lower House, it continues to invest the monarch with supreme legislative, executive, military, and judicial powers. The Emperor is given the right to appoint the members of the Senate, to initiate legislative proposals, and to veto any legislation passed by the Parliament. He has the right to determine the "organization, powers, and duties of all Ministries, executive departments and the administrations of the Government, and appoints, promotes, transfers, suspends, and dismisses the officials of the same." He likewise appoints the heads of all municipal governments. As Commander-in-chief of the Armed Forces, he reserves the right to determine their size, organization, and duties. He appoints the members of the judiciary, and "has the right and the duty to maintain justice through the courts, and the right to grant pardons and amnesties and to commute penalties."

All this only renders explicit and in detail what have been the normal traditional functions of the Amhara emperors. Historically this diffuseness of function likewise characterized the roles of provincial governors and lesser authorities, all of whom combined rulemaking, administrative, military, judicial, and ceremonial functions as well. The situation has been changed at the local level under Haile Selassie, who has deprived provincial notables of their traditional military functions and has attempted, through the distinct organization of the Ministries of Interior, Finance, and Justice, to differentiate administrative and judicial structures. But the fusion of roles at the pinnacle of governmental authority has been a conspicuous and tenacious feature of the present regime.

This pattern, while supported by certain factors peculiar to the contemporary political situation and the actors involved, has proved especially resistant to change because it is grounded in two features of Amhara political culture discussed above: the high estimation of authority and the low estimation of human nature. The Amhara habitually look to the person of highest status in whatever hierarchy they belong to for all authoritative decisions, whether of a rule-making, administrative, or judicial nature. To delegate authority elsewhere is to deprive the functionary involved of the power and dignity that have been ascribed to him by virtue of his high status. The Emperor has been unwilling to delegate any of his basic powers and has been supported in this by a good segment of the Amhara people because of the feeling that his dignity would thereby be somewhat diminished. On the other hand he has also been reluctant to do so because of an inability to trust those to whom he might confer powers which he has wielded himself. While this intense suspiciousness and caution might reflect idiosyncratic factors, there can be no doubt that it is in some part a cultural phenomenon expressive of the typical Amhara orientation to human nature.

These factors likewise are part of the reason for the absence of structures that might serve the articulation and aggregation of interests. It is true, and important, that Amhara culture respects the rights of any individual to air his grievances or pursue his interests in litigation and to ask for mercy or special favors from a superior. But the form in which these interests are expressed is crucial: it is a context of complete deference and obedience to authority. The individual in Amhara culture has an inalienable right to present his claims, but no inalienable rights regarding the substance of his claims. The sole legitimate manner of interest articulation in Amhara culture has been the respectful petition of a man or spontaneously formed group of men before an authority.

This remains the dominant pattern today in the capital as in the provinces, with interesting implications for the political process. It accounts in part for the reluctance of the Amhara people to make use of the opportunities for interest articulation afforded by the electoral provisions of the new constitution. When faced with the prospect of electing parliamentary representatives in 1957 and 1961, most Amhara responded with indifference or cynicism. In some instances local officials actually had to force citizens to register to vote even though there was a plurality of candidates from whom they were free to choose. In few Amhara districts was the ballot understood as a possible vehicle through which to agitate in behalf of popular interests. Among those who did accept the new machinery the most common attitude was probably the very passive one expressed by a petty provincial governor who told me he would like to run for Parliament some time. When I asked why he wanted to run, and what he would do if elected, he replied: "I will go to the Government in Addis Ababa and tell them what the people of my district need. If they agree; they will give it to me; if not, they will not." In other words, being elected to Parliament meant being in a position to present a petition to the Emperor.

Despite the existence of Western-educated individuals who have promoted the idea of parliamentary representation in Ethiopia for more than sixty years, the idea runs so counter to the authoritarian cast of Amhara political culture that electoral procedures are simply not taken seriously. All serious articulation of interests has been in the form of petitions to His Majesty, either directly or through the mediation of a high-ranking official or member of the imperial family. An important implication of this is that the articulation of interests has been carried out in private through channels directly managed by the Emperor. The ban on the public articulation of interests has been virtually complete.

Those who have had recourse to these channels have for the most part been individuals, not groups. To a limited extent the leaders of the church and the military forces have represented institutional interest groups, but the Emperors intimate association with both institutions has meant that they have rarely stood apart and voiced demands autonomously. The chief exception to this was the Army's march on the palace in 1961 in demand for a pay raise (which they obtained). Spontaneous interest articulation in the form of riots and demonstrations has likewise been avoided, except for one or two polite demonstrations by students, because of the population's deep-seated respect and fear regarding authority as well as fairly effective security controls. Overt expression of the interests of regional or ethnic groups has also been rare. It appears only on the occasion of some acute problem, such as the local crisis over land rights in the Oromo Province of Wollega in 1962, which was solved typically by the sending of a delegation to the palace to petition and the royal appointment of a committee to produce some reconciliation. The establishment of associational interest groups, finally, has simply been forestalled for as long as it has been politically feasible to do so. Prior to the 1960 rebellion virtually the only formal associations permitted in the country were welfare organizations like the Y.M.C.A. and Red Cross and popular savings and welfare associations. Professional associations did not emerge until after the rebellion, and labor unions were suppressed until 1963.

In general the government's attitude toward the collective expansion of interests has been that conveyed by a government official when explaining, some years ago, why the students of a certain school who wished to voice their approval of a certain government policy were not being permitted to do so: "If they were allowed to express their agreement without being told to, they might sometime want to express their disagreement."[14] This attitude applies a fortiori to the process of interest aggregation. As Parliament enters its seventh year of deliberations under the new Constitution, political parties are still not permitted by the government. On the contrary, it has been the steadfast policy of the Emperor to forestall efforts toward the aggregated expression of interests in any form. Through techniques of *divide et impera*, frequent reshuffling of appointments, and systematic political surveillance, emerging coalitions of interests have typically been disintegrated well before they have reached a stage where positive political demands could be set forth.

The lack of organizations for the articulation and aggregation of interests in Ethiopia is the result not only of the authoritarian character of the regime, supported as this is by traditional Amhara attitudes toward authority. It also reflects the difficulty Ethiopians have in undertaking any sort of concerted action, particularly in the political sphere. Here again the Amhara conception of human nature is a factor of more than academic significance. The mutual distrust and lack of cooperation which inform the political climate of the country are directly related to a very low regard for man's capacity for solidarity and consensus—*saw yallam*. The idea that it is possible to transcend the prevailing atmosphere of anxiety and suspicion by trusting one another, by taking some risk based on a belief in human potentialities, has been slow to appear and extremely rare.

To say that the Emperor plays a key part in the performance of the functions of interest articulation and aggregation, then, is to say, perhaps somewhat poetically, that all serious expressions of interest have typically been brought under his direct purview sooner or later and co-determined by his intervention. The chief high-level organs of the government—the Crown Council, the Council of Ministers, and the Private Cabinet—may be seen as advisory councils assisting him in this as in other functions. When we speak of the Emperor's important role with regard to the functions of political communication and recruitment, on the other hand, no poetic license is involved.

Political information is transmitted to the government chiefly through a series of communications networks under the direct or indirect control of the Emperor: the formal intelligence networks, and informal networks operating through various officials who report to him more or less regularly. A further source of information consists of disclosures from various individual parties who hope to ingratiate themselves by reporting something incriminating about someone else.

Apart from these channels the central authority has relatively little access to information about current realities. The Emperor, though in a position of supreme power, has thus been at the mercy of those who control the communications channels to him. To a large extent he remains isolated from the real condition and aspirations of his people. It is possible to argue that the 1960 rebellion was as much as anything else the effect of a faulty communications system. Improvement of the channels for political communication has been at the forefront of the demands of the proponents of political modernization in Ethiopia, as illustrated by the following passage taken from a leaflet circulated by one underground agitational group in 1961: "The purpose of founding a government is to serve the people. To serve the people it is necessary to know the desires and ideas of the people . . . To know the thoughts of the people, it is necessary to give them freedom of thought, freedom of speech, and freedom of press. A people oppressed by spying and police is a slave; one may not truly call it a people. If the oppression becomes excessive, an explosion is inevitable. It is necessary for the people to have the power with which to control the government and the services they desire, and the opportunity to define the conditions of administration. Freedom of thought, speech, and press provides the means of gaining this opportunity."

The channels of political communication to the public are similarly circumscribed. The mass media are under the moral control of the government when not subjected to direct and unremitting censorship. They serve two purposes, neither of which has to do with the attempt to present objective, neutral, and thorough reporting on matters of domestic political interest. One is to produce propaganda, usually highly unsubtle, in support of the regime, a task that has been described by one of the employees of an Ethiopian newspaper as follows: "I am employed by the Government to help edit one of its papers and to write interpretive articles. My job is to commend the Government, and specifically the Emperor. My job is to inject this praise into every conceivable news item. But that is not all; I am also an advocate, a lawyer, for the Government. If, for example, a bad epidemic breaks out in the slums, and it comes about through the negligence of the Government's health services, then my job is to cover up this fact. But I go one step further, I will write how the Government had mobilized its forces to wipe out the epidemic, regardless of whether this is true or not. And then I praise the Emperor and His Government for their humanitarian action."

The other purpose served by the press has been to air some of the problems and frustrations of transitional Ethiopia through the medium of contributed articles and verse and editorial commentaries. Dealing with such questions as marriage among educated Ethiopians, the status of traditional medicine, the high cost of living, the immorality of modern life, and so on, these items skirt but do not penetrate directly political issues. When politically controversial matters have been touched on in the press, it has not been in the form of dispassionate or detailed analysis but through vague expressions of alienation or else ad hominem attacks, which are conveyed not openly but in the form of parables or secret messages, apprehended, for example, by reading the initial syllables of each line of a long poem. In recent years sober articles critical of the performance of some governmental ministry have appeared once in a while. But all such ventures are carried out at the author's and editor's risk: punishment from the palace—for example, loss of a week's salary—is readily imposed for any wanton display of critical sentiment.

It is obvious that the orientation toward authority which characterizes Amhara culture must preclude the development of an autonomous and differentiated medium of political communication. For, as we have seen, Amhara culture proscribes direct and honest public criticism of any authority. In authoritarian relationships—and again, all political interaction among the Amhara is contained within authoritarian relationships—there are only three alternatives: complete deference, acquiescence, and flattery; criticism by devious and covert means; or outright rebellion. Government and public will remain poorly informed about political realities until Ethiopian norms are changed to permit development of public discussion of controversial issues and a pattern of loyal opposition.

To deal "even cursorily with the function of political socialization and recruitment would entail entering into the complex question of stratification and mobility patterns in Ethiopia, which space does not permit."[15] Suffice it to observe that the Emperor personally has been the dominant agent of political recruitment since the time his power was secured, and that his appointments have been made primarily with an eye to maximizing loyalty and submissiveness and minimizing the chances for the coalescence of interests. This again represents the traditional orientation of authority figures in Amhara culture, the difference here being that Haile Selassie has for the first time in Ethiopian history been able to carry out this pattern fairly effectively throughout the whole empire.

IX.

As observed in the previous discussion of the Amhara approach to human nature, Amhara culture is not sympathetic to efforts to transform human society in accordance with abstract principles. On the contrary its fatalism, its patriarchalism, and its "realistic humanism" dispose its people to look askance at innovation. The basic outlook of the Amhara is thus one which is fundamentally incongruent with the ethos of dynamism inherent in the goal of political modernization.

On the other hand, we have also seen that the pre-eminent authority of the Emperor has provided a mechanism for the deliberate introduction of culture change. By virtue of this authority Haile Selassie has been able to effectuate a number of social and cultural changes in nearly every year of his reign. He has established a number of institutions without precedent in Ethiopian history, including a national parliament, an electoral system, military academies, technical schools, colleges, and a university—not to mention the written Constitution. He has, by direct proclamation, effected a number of specific changes in the customs of the country, including the formal abolition of slave trading and slavery, and modification of certain excesses with regard to traditional practices of mourning, arrest, and punishment. Through various indirect means he has promoted a number of other reforms, such as encouraging the preaching of sermons in church, removing some obstacles to ethnic and religious harmony, and eliminating archaic practices like the use of a drugged boy in cases of theft to identify the thief. Perhaps the greatest source of change for which he has been responsible has been importation of hundreds of European teachers and sending more than a thousand Ethiopians abroad for college and graduate study.

The consequence of the Amhara's ambivalent posture regarding change is that, while the initiation of change by imperial decree and recommendation is passively accepted, the desirability of change as a basic feature of contemporary life is not. With its penchant for equilibrium and its disdain for change stemming from non-authoritarian sources, Amhara culture supports no comparable mechanism for seeking to assimilate and plan for change. The Emperor, for his part, has insisted on the full prerogatives of his position and has thus tried to maintain a monopoly over the initiation of change and to retain control over its various ramifications. This has necessarily resulted in a crippling of energies, demoralization, and the obstruction of modernization.

Whether the rationalization and dynamism now sought by some educated Ethiopians can be attained by redefining the relevant beliefs and values of Amhara culture; or whether their goals will require more radical changes in political orientation, thus possibly endangering the stability of legitimate national authority; or whether the very goal of political modernization will be undermined by the persistence of traditional Amhara beliefs and values—these are the questions history now waits for Ethiopia to decide.

Notes

1 This point begs the question of the extent to which non-Amhara peoples in Ethiopia have suffered because of their subordinate status, a question concerning which the author does not possess reliable data.

2 This figure is based on a survey conducted by the author in 1959–1960.

3 Using somewhat different terms and evolving a richer framework of distinctions, Verba's concluding essay discusses some of the grounds of this relevance.

4 Such egalitarian sentiment as they have is manifest primarily in the notion that all men are to be judged impartially before God and in the (structurally unimportant) social form known as *mahebar*, a kind of religious fraternal association.

5 Cf. D. Levine, "On the Conception of Time and Space in the Amhara World View," *Atti del conveno international di studi etiopici*, Rome, 1960.

6 Cf. D. Levine, *Wax and Gold: Tradition and Innovation in Ethiopian Culture*, Chicago, University of Chicago Press, 1965, Chapter 7.

7 J. Spencer Trimingham, *Islam in Ethiopia*, London, Oxford University Press, 1953, p. 101.

8 Cited in L. Woolf , *Empire and Commerce in Africa*, New York: Macmillian, p. 145.

9 S. Chojnacki, "Some Notes on the History of the Ethiopian National Flag," *Journal of Ethiopian Studies*, Vol. I, No. 2, July 1963.

10 Harold Marcus, "A History of the Negotiations Concerning the Border between Ethiopian and British East Africa,"*Boston University Papers in African History*, Vol. II, 1964.

11 This is perhaps the place to refer, however briefly, to the largely unexplored problem area defined by the relationship between Amhara culture, as the dominant national culture, and the political cultures of other native traditions in Ethiopia. Since the Oromo constitute the largest ethnic group in the country, a word about Oromo political culture may be in order.

The classical Oromo social system is oriented around a system of temporally differentiated social classes, called *gadda*, which move through a series of ten periods, or grades, of eight years duration (cf. Asmarom Leggesse, "Class System based on Time," *Journal of Ethiopian Studies*, Vol. I, No. 2, July 1963, p. 2).

For present purposed what is relevant about this system is that it is highly "democratic," involving the periodic election of government authorities by the members of a *gadda* class w. The Oromo ethos moreover, is relatively egalitarian: relations between the father and the rest of the family tend to be friendly and informal, and provision is made for the incorporation of strangers into local communities.

In these respects nothing could be further apart than the political cultures of Amhara and Oromo. Yet the latter has had virtually no impact on the national political culture of Ethiopia. Amhara culture has worked rather—partly unwittingly, partly through conscious policy—to disintegrate the Oromo *gada* system. In so far as classical Oromo culture has survived at all in national politics, it may be reflected in the fact that, of the small percentage of Ethiopian who incline to a republican form of government, the Oromo appear to be overrepresented—an inclination also furthered by the fact that Oromo have most to gain from a political system based wholly on majority rule.

12 Trimingham, " *op.cit.*, p. 15.

13 "A Functional Approach to Comparative Politics," *The Politics of the Developing Area*, Gabriel A. Almond and James Coleman, eds. Princeton, Princeton University Press, 1960.

14 William Seed, "Ethiopia's Iron Curtain" (pamphlet issued under the name of the "Ethiopian Freedom Committee"), p. 32.

15 Cf. *Wax and Gold, op.cit.*, Chapter 5.

6

A Tigrean Legacy

The Kibre Negest as a National Script (1974)[*]

The medieval efflorescence of Amhara power and culture was predicated on a set of developments that took place long before the Amhara emerged as major actors on the Ethiopian scene. I refer to the role of Aksum, which served as a seedbed for the germination of elements which would later become firmly rooted in Amhara consciousness. After Aksum ceased to function as a political center these elements were transplanted to the Amhara homeland, where they flowered with unusual durability.

The achievements of Aksum can be identified as a specifically Tigrean contribution to Ethiopian nationhood, for present-day Tigreans are the direct descendants of the inhabitants of the Aksum plateau, and their language, Tigrinya, was already spoken in Aksum by the second half of the first millennium A.D. A major bequest of the ancestral Tigreans to Amhara culture was a national script. I use this ambiguous term advisedly, for they created a national script in three senses.

They developed the Ethiopic script, an indigenous form of writing that made possible the elaboration of a Great Tradition in Ethiopia and the formation of a stratum of literati.

They also created a national script in the dramaturgic sense. By this I refer to the set of motifs and directives that orient every societal community. Like the

---

* Originally published as Chapter 7 of *Greater Ethiopia: The Evolution of a Multiethnic Society* (Chicago, IL: University of Chicago Press, 2000 [1974]).

script of the play actor, the societal script provides a sense of the actor's identity, indications of significant past experiences, and guidelines for future actions.

Finally, as a major work in the Great Tradition and principal repository of the societal script, they created a particularly hallowed literary script, the *Kibre Negest.*

The *Kibre Negest*: A Reassessment

The *Kibre Negest* is often described as the foremost creation of Ethiopic literature. Its central narrative has held the imagination of northern Ethiopians for a thousand years. For centuries observers have commented on the extraordinary popularity of the *Kibre Negest* among Amhara and Tigreans. Abba Gregorios reported to Job Ludolf in the 1650s that the *Kibre Negest* was a work "of very great authority" among his countrymen, and somewhat more than a century later James Bruce noted that "its reputation in Abyssinia is immense." In the 1840s Rochet d'Hericourt observed that the legend of the Queen of Sheba, the central story of the work, "dominates the fastnesses of Ethiopia." The depiction of this legend in a conventionalized sequence of forty-four pictures, moreover, has long been one of the most widely enjoyed creations of Ethiopian painting.

It is surprising, then, that the question of the role of the *Kibre Negest* in Ethiopian culture has not been taken very seriously. One reason for this neglect may be its literary quality: to many readers the *Kibre Negest* has seemed little more than a hodgepodge. In this chapter I shall challenge that interpretation and argue that the *Kibre Negest* is a truly unified epic which has served a variety of important cultural functions, including the provision of a societal script for the Amhara-Tigrean peoples.

To be sure, the *Kibre Negest* is in many respects a composite work. The product of many hands, the final redaction was completed early in the fourteenth century by six Tigrean scribes. The principal redactor, a chief priest of Aksum named Yishaq, claims that he merely translated an Arabic version of the work into Ethiopic, although the text incorporates many oral and written traditions from Ethiopia as well as from the Near East. Quotations and allusions are drawn from a potpourri of identifiable sources: from thirty-one books of the Old Testament and twenty books of the New Testament; from Chaldean Targums, the Talmud and Midrashim, rabbinic commentaries, and the Antiquities of Josephus; from Koranic stories and commentaries; from Old and New Testament apocryphal writings, including the Syriac Book of the Bee, the Book of Adam, the Book of the Cave of Treasures, Wisdom of Solomon, Ascension of Isaiah, the Book of Enoch, Jubilees, the Legends of Mary, and the Testament of Reuben; from the writings of patristic authors including Origen, Cyril of Alexandria, Gregory of

Nyasa, Gregory of Nazianzus, Severus, and Epiphanias; and from other Ethiopic works including the Synaxarium and the Life of Hanna.[1]

Even when the content is original, the literary style of many passages of the *Kibre Negest* reveals its composite origin. As David Hubbard has shown in splendid detail, the style of the epic moves back and forth shamelessly among the styles of Old Testament wisdom writings, New Testament parables, rabbinic exegetical argumentation, Koranic lamentation, Koranic use of historical illustration, apocryphal biography, patristic homily, and patristic allegorical interpretation.

It is this composite character that has most impressed students of the *Kibre Negest* and has surfaced in general descriptions of it. Wallis Budge describes the *Kibre Negest* as "a great storehouse of legends and traditions," and Ullendorff calls it "a gigantic conflation of cycles of legends and tales."[2]

The *Kibre Negest*: Outline of Contents

I. Prologue — Chapters 1–18

- A. Question: Wherein lies the greatness of kings? — 2
- B. Sacred primacy of Tabernacle of Zion — 1, 10–11, 17–18
- C. Elect genealogy and God's covenant — 3–9, 12–16

II. Central Narrative: Book within a Book — 19–94

- A. Ethiopian monarchs connected with the chosen lineage — 21–43
    1. Visits of Tamrin the merchant and Makeda, Queen of Ethiopia, to King Solomon — 21–28
    2. Seduction of Makeda and birth of Menilek — 29–32
    3. Menilek acknowledged as Solomon's legitimate descendant — 33–34
- B. Moralizing glosses
    1. Polygamy attacked; Solomon's polygamy exonerated — 28B–29A
    2. Contra kings not of Israelite lineage — 348
    3. Proclamation of moral commandments by Zadok — 40–42.
    4. Pro authority of kings and clergy — 44
- C. Ethiopians take possession of the Tabernacle of Zion — 45–63
- D. Enhancement of status of Ethiopian kingdom — 63–83
    1. Decline and fall of Solomon — 63–67
    2. Prophecy of descent of Mary and Christ through Solomonic line — 68–71

3. Misguided reign of Solomon's second son and successor, Rehoboam — 70

4. Reign of Solomon's third son, Adrami, as king of "Rome" — 72–73

5. Semitic ancestry of other kings — 74–83

E. Moralizing gloss, criticism of the Jews — 69

F. Establishment of Menilek's kingdom — 64–94

G. Criticism of Christian heretics (Nestorians) — 93B

III. Epilogue — 95–117

A. Old Testament stories paralleling gospel events — 96–98

B. Defeat of Satan and omnipresence of God — 99–101

C. Coming of Christ and wickedness of Jews — 102, 106–11

D. Significance of the holy ark — I 03–5

E. Ultimate triumph of Ethiopia — 113–17

The result has appeared uneven and disjointed to most commentators. Rochet d'Héricourt considered its central narrative to be "confused, tangled, and devoid of interest."[3] Walter Plowden belittled the *Kibre Negest* as a "rubbish of invented tales, or imperfect and incoherent statements."[4] In more measured language a number of more scholarly readers have rendered similar judgments. Cerulli observes that the *Kibre Negest* consists of four different parts which are markedly unequal in artistic quality. Introducing the first publication of the complete text of the *Kibre Negest* in 1905, Carl Bezold held that "the question of the literary unity of the book . . . should be answered in the negative." Following Bezold, David Hubbard divides the book into three parts and argues that they were inserted at different periods. Hubbard also describes the first part as broken by interruptions and notes that the third part could readily be expunged.

The first cautious steps toward a reversal of Bezold's judgment were taken by Cerulli himself when he observed that a variety of inspirational subjects embodying varying degrees of expressive intensity may well serve the overriding objective of the work—that is, to exalt the Solomonid Dynasty. In alluding to this political motive Cerulli expresses what has become the prevailing view of the function of the *Kibre Negest*: that its chief purpose was to add legitimacy to the line of kings which gained ascendance with Yikunno Amlak in 1270. One need not accept this view, however, to see Cerulli's point and carry it further. A new appreciation of the *Kibre Negest* may be reached by looking not at the diversity of its contents but at its overall structure. In its inner form the *Kibre Negest* reveals a fully realized aesthetic unity.

Prologue, Narrative, and Epilogue

The general form of the *Kibre Negest* is that of a book within a book. Its central narrative, Chapters 19 through 94, is presented as a manuscript purported to have been discovered by an archbishop of "Rome" (Constantinople) in the Church of Saint Sophia. The narrative is flanked by a prologue of eighteen chapters and an epilogue of twenty-three chapters.

The prologue and epilogue consist, as it were, of a number of antiphonal statements between a chorus and a solo. The "chorus" takes the form of the "318 Orthodox Fathers," an allusion to the 318 bishops of the Council of Nicaea (A.D. 325). The solo speaker is named Gregory, a conflation of two historical personages: Gregory the Illuminator, who lived at the time of (but did not attend) the Nicene Council, and Gregory Thaumaturgus, who died half a century earlier. The bishop who is said to have discovered the manuscript of the central narrative is Domitius, who did attend the Nicene Council. The setting of the book thus may be dated in the fourth century A.D., and the actions of the book within the book take place more than twelve centuries earlier, about 960 to 930 B.C., during the reigns of Solomon and Rehoboam.

The issue which animates the work as a whole is raised near the very beginning, when Gregory says:

> When I was in the pit I pondered over this matter, and over the folly of the Kings of Armenia, and I said, In so far as I can conceive it, in what doth the greatness of kings consist? Is it in the multitude of soldiers, or in the splendour of worldly possession, or in the extent of rule over cities and towns? This was my thought each time of my prayer, and my thought stirred me again and again to meditate upon the greatness of kings.

The question is never answered head on. But the prologue indicates that the "greatness of kings" has to do with two things: possession of a sacred emblem—the Tabernacle of Zion—and connection with an elect genealogy, with whom God made a covenant. The entire prologue is concerned exclusively with these two motifs and the rest of the epic works out their implications and destinies.

The opening lines of the epic state forthrightly that these two themes are to be its central subject:

> The interpretation and explanation of the Three Hundred and Eighteen Orthodox Fathers concerning splendour, and greatness, and dignity, and *how God gave them to the children of Adam*, and especially concerning the greatness and splendour of *Zion*, the Tabernacle of the law of God, of which he Himself is the Maker and Fashioner, in the fortress of His holiness before all created things . . . [Emphasis mine]

The sacred primacy of the Tabernacle of Zion is celebrated in the first, middle, and closing chapters of the prologue. We are told that Zion "was the first" thing to be created by God; that it was the place where the Father, Son, and Holy Spirit agreed to create Adam; that the heavenly and spiritual Zion became incarnate in two respects, through the likeness of the Tabernacle which Moses made out of wood, and through the "Second Zion," Mary, mother of Christ.

The other chapters of the prologue describe the generations of the elect line, from Adam through Noah and Shem through Abraham to Jesse and David, and God's covenants with Noah, Abraham, and their descendants. God promises Abraham to "bring down the Tabernacle of My Covenant upon the earth . . . and it shall go round about with thy seed, and shall be salvation unto thy race." The prologue closes by joining the themes of Zion and the Chosen People even more closely:

> Unto David will I give seed in her [the Tabernacle]
> And upon the earth one who shall become king
> And moreover in the heavens one from his seed
> Shall reign in the flesh upon the throne of
> the Godhead.

The dynamic of the central narrative is thus established. If royal glory comes from descending in the line of King David and from possessing the Tabernacle of Zion, how can this glory be associated with the kings of Ethiopia?

The first objective is attained through the events described in Chapters 21 to 43, the second through those in Chapters 45 through 63. As Cerulli rightly observes, these two sections have the highest literary merit of the whole epic. They contain the heart of the plot and the most intense dramatic episodes.

The first episode begins with the visit of Tamrin, a wise merchant, to King Solomon. Overwhelmed by Solomon's wisdom, Tamrin returns to his queen, Makeda, the Queen of Sheba, and tells her "how Solomon administered just judgment, and how he spake with authority, and how he decided rightly in all the matters which he enquired into, and how he returned soft and gracious answers." Makeda at length makes the trip to Jerusalem herself and is similarly impressed. She decides to adopt Solomon's religion: no longer to worship the sun, but "the Creator of the sun, the God of Israel; [and the] Tabernacle of the God of Israel." Before leaving Solomon's court, Makeda agrees to dine with him, and then to spend the night at his palace provided that he swear not to take her by force. Solomon makes her swear a counter oath not to take by force any of his possessions. It is an oath she is forced to break when, parched with thirst after the highly spiced food Solomon deliberately had served her, she takes a goblet of water. Solomon thereby becomes freed from his oath and works his will with her. On returning to Ethiopia the queen gives birth to a son, who in the extant manuscripts is named variously as Beyne-Lekhem or lbna el-Hakim, but in oral versions of the story is always called Menilek. On reaching manhood Menilek journeys to Jerusalem, where he is recognized by his father and crowned as king of Ethiopia with the name David II.

In the second main episode, Menilek returns to Ethiopia with the firstborn sons of the nobles of Israel, including Azariah the son of Zadok the priest. Unable to tolerate the thought of being separated from the Tabernacle of Zion, Azariah replaces it with pieces of wood and spirits it away. Menilek, Azariah, and their companions, animals, and wagons are then raised above the ground and fly across the Red Sea back to Ethiopia before the theft of Zion is discovered and Solomon's men give chase.

Through Solomon's crafty seduction of Makeda and Menilek's clandestine abduction of the Ark of the Covenant, the Ethiopian king now has special claims to glory. These claims are enhanced in the succeeding section, Chapters 64 to 83, a collection of short narratives which relate: the corruption of Solomon by the daughter of Pharaoh and his subsequent downfall; a prophecy of the descent of Mary and Christ through the Solomonic line; the misguided reign of Solomon's second son and successor, Rehoboam; the reign of his third son, Adrami, as king of Rome [Constantinople]; and accounts of the Semitic ancestry of several other lines of royalty, including the kings of Medyam, Babylon, Persia, Moab, Amalek, and Philistia. The combined effect of these stories is to enhance the importance of Semitic ancestry for royalty. "For as God sware He gave ... an exalted throne and dominion to the seed of Shem" (Chapter 83)—a state which Ethiopia is about to achieve when Menilek returns and is crowned. Moreover, it implicitly celebrates the Ethiopian king over all the other Semitic kings, because Menilek is the firstborn of Solomon's three sons who become kings, and because the tales of nearly all the other kings involve wickedness or moral corruption. Only Adrami is presented in morally favorable light, enhanced by the prophecy of the coming of Christ in the immediately preceding chapter.

The final section (Chapters 84–94) of the book within a book describes the triumphant return of Menilek to Ethiopia, his mother's abdication, his coronation, and his institution of a new moral order. The Semitic line is now enthroned in Ethiopia, sharing glory with none but the descendants of Solomon who rule in Rome: "for the kings of Ethiopia and the kings of Rome were brethren and held the Christian faith" (Chapter 93). But the final glory must be reserved for Ethiopia, for we read that, 130 years after the time of Constantine, "Satan, who hath been the enemy of man from of old, rose up, and seduced the people of the country of Rome, and they corrupted the Faith of Christ, and they introduced heresy into the Church of God by the mouth of Nestorius." The manuscript ends with the established supremacy of the glory of the Ethiopian king, who promptly sets out to wage war, protected and blessed by possession of Zion, receiving tribute from the kings of Egypt, Medyam, and India—feared by all and fearing no one.

In Chapter 95, which begins the "epilogue," the word returns to the chorus of 318 bishops and Gregory. They heartily affirm the validity of the manuscript which has just ended. When that story begins, the Jews are the chosen people; when it ends, the mission has been transferred to Ethiopia. It is the task of the epilogue to celebrate that reversal: to add legitimacy to the story, to carry the reversal further, to infuse the whole conception with prophetic certainty and apocalyptic grandeur.

The reversal is accentuated in the epilogue by its focus on the coming of Christ and the salvation of Christians, on the one hand, and the wickedness of the Jews on the other. The warm sympathy for the Jews which marked the central narrative can now be discarded for the tables have been turned. The use of Old Testament prophecies as proof texts for the coming of Christ parallels the use of Solomonic ancestry to legitimate Ethiopian kings: Jewish symbols are used to discredit the Jews and glorify Ethiopians. The reversal is climaxed in the last two chapters, which allude to military expeditions against Jews. In those expeditions the kings of Ethiopia and "Rome" collaborate, an allusion to the sixth-century alliance between Kaleb of Ethiopia and Justin I of Byzantium. Even so, Rome's defection from the orthodox faith is also prophesied in the closing chapters, whereas Ethiopia by contrast "shall continue in the orthodox faith until the coming of our Lord." Gregory must finally conclude:

> Thus hath God made for the King of Ethiopia more glory, and grace, and majesty than for all the other kings of the earth because of the greatness of Zion, the Tabernacles of the Law of God, the heavenly Zion.

The *Kibre Negest* as a National Epic

We must conclude, then, that in spite of the great diversity of its material and the uneven quality of its parts, the overall structure of the *Kibre Negest* appears highly unified. All elements of the epic conspire toward a common end.

We may now ask, what is the cultural significance of this work? Is this coordination of literary elements mere propaganda, as Cerulli and others have suggested, a device to confirm the legitimacy of the usurping dynasty from Amhara? Is it so, as Conti-Rossini flatly asserts, that the *Kibre Negest* has no other purpose than that of demonstrating the usurpation of Yikunno Amlak to be nothing more than a just act of vindication?[5]

Evidence of many kinds contradicts that interpretation. For one thing, the date of the final redaction of the *Kibre Negest* is now believed to have been around 1320, half a century after the Solomonid usurpation, when the position of the Amhara dynasty was quite secure. More important, the redactors were not Amhara but Tigrean, and their patron was no Amhara ruler but a Tigrean lord named Ya'ibike Igzi. Far from being a devoted champion of the new dynasty, Ya'ibike Igzi attempted to rebel against the reigning Solomonid monarch, Amde Siyon, for which affront the king had him destroyed.

There are clear indications, moreover, that the central story of the *Kibre Negest* was current at least in oral tradition long before the Amhara usurpation. A passage in the history of the Coptic patriarch Philotheus shows that the Ethiopian legend ascribing the origin of Menilek I to the union of Solomon and the Queen of Sheba was known in Cairo as early as the tenth century. A work written in 1208 by an Armenian Christian records the belief that Abyssinians possessed the Ark of the Covenant and that the Queen of Sheba came to Solomon from Abyssinia. The allusion to Ethiopia's alliance with Byzantium in the epilogue convinced Budge and other scholars that much of the material of the *Kibre Negest* dates from a time when memories of this alliance were relatively fresh, around the year 600. In what is perhaps the most persuasive reconstruction of the origins of the *Kibre Negest* to date, moreover, Jean Doresse proposes that the Aksumites adopted the core ideas of the Solomonic saga from the Judaized legends of the South Arabian kingdom of Himyar in the course of their occupation of Yemen in the sixth century.

Historical evidence apart, the internal character of the work makes clear that much more is at stake here than the fortunes of a particular dynasty. On the contrary, I would argue that the *Kibre Negest* is more fruitfully viewed as a national epic, a work which in various ways embodies orientations developed by a stratum of Tigrean literati at a point when they had attained a working synthesis of diverse cultural ingredients and were ready to advance a firm conception of Ethiopian national character and purpose.

The *Kibre Negest* is a national epic in three respects. First, most simply and obviously, it contains a myth of the founding of the Ethiopian nation. It is thus a national epic in the conventional, dictionary sense: an imaginative work that embodies a conception of crucial formative events in the national history. As such it has aptly been compared with the Aeneid, another effort to glorify one nation's beginning by linking it to an earlier, prestigious nation's history and epic.

Second, it can be seen as expressing central psychological conflicts which members of the society typically experience in the course of growing up. This aspect of the work will be discussed in a separate publication.[6]

Third, it is the literary expression of what Talcott Parsons has referred to as a complex of constitutive symbolism and that is included in what I have referred to above as a societal script: a body of symbols that provides specialized cultural legitimation both for the societal enterprise as a whole and for privileged positions within the society.[7] To follow the inner logic of the epic from this perspective is to observe the dialectical resolution of the Tigrean struggle to create a viable national identity.

A Cultural Identity Struggle

Whatever the reasons may have been for Yishaq's disclaimer that he merely translated the *Kibre Negest* from an Arabic text into Ge'ez, the fact remains that the work itself is suffused with patriotic feelings and serves from first to last to glorify the land of Ethiopia and proclaim a proud Ethiopian identity. Several passages praise the country in a characteristically Ethiopian manner. The *Kibre Negest* repeatedly compares Ethiopia with Judah, a land flowing with milk and honey, a land of undisputed attractions; but whenever the comparison is made, Ethiopia appears the fairer. Thus, when asked to stay on and settle in Judah, the headmen of Tamrin the merchant reply:

> Our country is the better. The climate of our country is good, for it is without burning heat and fire, and the water of our country is good, and sweet, and floweth in rivers; moreover the tops of our mountains run with water. And we do not do as ye do in your country, that is to say, dig very deep wells in search of water, and we do not die through the heat of the sun; but even at noonday we hunt wild animals, namely, the wild buffaloes, and gazelles, and birds, and small animals. And in the winter God taketh heed unto us from year to the beginning of the course of the next. And in the springtime the people eat what they have trodden with the foot as in the land of Egypt, and as for our trees they produce good crops of fruit, and the wheat, and the barley, and all our fruits, and cattle are good and wonderful.

In a similar, but more poignant, situation, Solomon pleads with young Menilek to remain with him in Jerusalem. The reply could be that of a twentieth-century son of the Ethiopian soil, rejecting the fleshpots of Europe to return home to live out his bittersweet destiny:

> Though thou givest me dainty meats I do not love them, and they are not suitable for my body, but the meats whereby I grow and become strong are those that are gratifying to me. And although thy country pleaseth me even as doth a garden, yet is not my heart gratified therewith; the mountains of the land of my mother where I was born are far better in my sight.

And Menilek's chief companion on the return trip to Ethiopia, Azariah the priest, utters similarly appreciative words, words which Ethiopians could most naturally be expected to put in the mouth of this archetypical expatriate:

> We say that God hath chosen no country except ours, but now we see that the country of Ethiopia is better than the country of Judah. And from the time that we have arrived in your country everything that we have seen hath appeared good to us. Your waters are good and they are given without price, and you have air without fans, and wild honey is as plentiful as the dust of the marketplace, and cattle as the sand of the sea. And as for what we have seen there is nothing detestable, and there is nothing malign in what we hear, and in what we walk upon, and in what we touch, and in what we taste with our mouths.

The intensity of the protests suggests that the land of Judah had indeed exerted some attraction for Ethiopians. The issue, of course, is not the territory, with which Ethiopians probably had little acquaintance before the Diaspora, but Judaic culture, with which ancient Tigreans had a good deal of contact. In effect, the *Kibre Negest* is a record of the process of working out some of the mental conflicts engendered by that contact, a process that can profitably be analyzed in the terms of Anthony Wallace and Raymond Fogelson's seminal paper "The Identity Struggle."[8]

The identity struggle denotes a complex process in which one tries to maintain or restore a favorable self-image. This process consists of efforts to minimize the discrepancies between real and ideal identities and to maximize the distance between feared and real identities. These efforts take such forms as employing mechanisms of defense like denial, repression, projection, or rationalization; reconstituting the self through such devices as religious conversion, prophetic inspiration, or psychotherapy; or acting outwardly so as to change the kinds of communication one receives from significant others. Although these concepts were devised to deal with psychological processes within the individual, they apply to collective behavior as well. It may be postulated that a protracted identity struggle must have been set in motion by the sustained confrontation between the Northern Ethiopians and the intruding Oriental Semites. This would not have been so had the Ethiopians defined either themselves or the Semites as inferior people. Instead the ancient Tigreans conceived of themselves as superior people and at the same time perceived the Jews, Arabs, and Syrians as superior in certain respects. Impressed by aspects of Oriental Semitic culture, they may have associated the lighter skin color of its bearers with their achievements. Such a conflict demanded resolution.

Two passages in the *Kibre Negest* allude to these issues. Shortly after the headmen of Tamrin the merchant have eulogized the land of Ethiopia, they add the following qualification: "But there is one thing that ye have wherein ye are better than we are, namely wisdom, and because of it we are journeying to you." And just after Azariah the priest finishes his eulogy of Ethiopia he adds, "But there is one matter that we would mention: ye are black of face. I only mention this because I have seen it, and if God lighteth up your hearts there is nothing that can do you harm." This seems to imply that if God does not light up the hearts of the Ethiopians, their black skin puts them at a disadvantage.

These issues must have been posed time and again in the experience of the ancient Tigreans. Repeatedly they confronted aliens who impressed them because of certain cultural superiorities associated with a lighter skin color. It is possible that they adopted writing and religion from the Sabaeans; it is certain that they adopted many elements of Hellenistic, Judaic, and Syrian Christian cultures. Christianity may even have exacerbated a sensitivity to differences of skin color, for early church fathers were enamored of imagery that associated blackness with sinfulness. Gregory of Nyasa went so far as to say that Christ came into the world to make blacks white, and that in the Kingdom of Heaven Ethiopians become white. That such ideas were internalized by blacks is suggested by the remarks attributed to the ascetic Father Moses the Ethiopian, who derided himself as a "sooty-skinned black man" and once rebuked an archbishop for being white only outwardly but still black inwardly.[9]

Ethiopians could simultaneously acknowledge what they perceived as the superiority of an alien culture and assert their own indomitable sense of superiority by way of "creative incorporation." In the *Kibre Negest* this pattern is exemplified by the way the Tigrean literati dealt with a sequence of four identity conflicts. The first of these conflicts is triggered by the perception of Judaic religion as superior. This is symbolized in the *Kibre Negest* by the extent to which the Ark of Zion is glorified. The reaction of a proud people to this perception was one of anxiety about being inferior to the Jews with respect to religion. The narrative resolves this conflict by working out a new image of the Ethiopian self based on an identification with the intrusive culture. The Ethiopians can then say that, because they have abandoned their old beliefs and superstitious practices and have embraced the God of Israel and his commandments they are equivalent to the Jews.

Conversion to Judaism, however, produces an even more distressing identity conflict. It entails accepting beliefs about the descendants of Ham set forth in Genesis 9. The *Kibre Negest* makes it clear that Judaized Ethiopians must have chafed under the biblical curse placed upon them as Hamites. Thus an officer of King Solomon attempts to undermine young Menilek's commitment to his native land by reminding him that "when the sons of Noah—Shem, Ham, and Japhet—divided the world among them, they looked on thy country with wisdom and saw that, although it was spacious and broad, it was a land of whirlwind and burning heat, and therefore gave it to Canaan, the son of Ham, as a portion for himself and his seed forever." Another passage in the epic notes that "by the Will of God the whole of the kingdom of the world was given to the seed of Shem, and slavery to the seed of Ham."

Simple acceptance of Judaic beliefs would thus exclude the Ethiopians from the covenant with God and condemn them to the status of slaves. As this was intolerable, conversion was not enough. The Tigreans had to deny that they were the Hamites of the Old Testament. They did this by portraying their elite as having been descended from the elite of Judah, even as Menilek was descended from Solomon and David. They used this genealogy to replace an older Ethiopian tradition which held that the kings of Aksum were in fact descended from Ham—through Aethiopia and Aksumawi, his son and grandson! Having defined their rulers as Semites, the Tigrean scribes could now appropriate the divine covenant with the sons of Shem. This act is anticipated in the story of Solomon's dream in Chapter 30:

> And after he slept there appeared unto King Solomon (in a dream) a brilliant sun, and it came down from heaven and shed exceedingly great splendour over Israel. And when it had tarried there for a time it suddenly withdrew itself, and it flew away to the country of Ethiopia, and it shone there with exceedingly great brightness for ever, for it willed to dwell there.

The reversal of roles is actualized by the transfer of the Ark of Zion from Jerusalem to Ethiopia by Menilek's retainers. By this fateful deed the curse on the "Hamites" is lifted once and for all. The Ethiopians now become the chosen ones, while henceforth the Jews are to be excluded. When Menilek is told that the Ark now belongs to him and his people, he has an intense emotional reaction.

> He was perturbed, and laid both hands upon his breast, and he drew breath three times and said, "Hast thou in truth, O Lord, remembered us in Thy mercy, *the castaways, the people whom Thou hast rejected*, so that I may see Thy pure habitation, which is in heaven, the holy and heavenly Zion? ... He hath crowned us with His grace." [Emphasis mine]

This ascension to the Jewish role would have been sufficient to restore a favorable self-image for the Ethiopians had not another group of Semites convinced some Ethiopians of the superiority of the Christian religion. Although in the early centuries it may have been possible for some Christian communities to conceive of themselves as followers of a kind of reformed Judaism, over time political and psychological forces in the Christian world made it difficult to maintain a keen sense of identification with the Jews. At some point the Judaic component of Ethiopian identity had to be played down. This denigration could not be blatantly accomplished in the central narrative of the *Kibre Negest*, which after all was devoted primarily to the task of establishing that identity. So when the Jews are first chided, in Chapter 69, in the form of a prophecy by the angel Gabriel, they are not categorically condemned:

> But Israel will hate their Saviour, and will be envious of Him because He will work signs and miracles before them. And they will crucify Him, and will kill Him, and He shall rise up again and deliver them, for He is merciful to the penitent and *good to those who are His chosen ones*. And behold, I tell you plainly that *He will not leave in Sheol His kinsmen of Israel*. [Emphasis mine]

In the epilogue, however—once the new regime under Menilek has been firmly established and the Ethiopians stand in secure possession of the Ark and God's covenant—then a more scathing repudiation of the Jewish component of the new identity can be expressed. From the vantage point of Christian superiority, the verdict on the Jews in Chapter 115 is noticeably harsher:

> And the Jews shall weep and repent when it shall be useless to do so, and they shall pass into everlasting punishment: and with the Devil, their father who had directed them, and his demons who had led them astray, and with the wicked shall they be shut in. [Emphasis mine]

Having now established that their superiority over the Jews is based on their identity as Christians, the Ethiopians can deny their Jewish identification with clear conscience.

A final phase of the Ethiopian identity struggle is initiated by the consciousness that they are not the only Christian power in the world. As we have already noted, Byzantine Christian rulers attempted on several occasions in the fourth and sixth centuries to influence Aksumite policy. The Ethiopian Christians were doubtless aware that their theological doctrines had been repudiated by the Byzantine church at the Council of Chalcedon. These events may well have stimulated anxieties about whether Ethiopia was inferior to Byzantium. That issue was firmly settled, in Chapters 93 and 113 of the *Kibre Negest*, by accounts and prophecies which condemn the "Roman" Christians for having forsaken the orthodox faith and followed the heretical teachings of Nestorius. The Ethiopians thus emerge as the sole authentic bearers of Christianity, the only people in the world now favored by the God of Solomon.

The *Kibre Negest*, then, can be seen as a condensation of the complex identity struggles which the Tigrean elite experienced over a period of centuries. The confused and incoherent statements which earlier European commentators found in it were in fact the expression of the actual conflicts involved in this process. The conflicts in question were never resolved once and for all. But the *Kibre Negest* blended the diverse components of an Ethiopian self-image into a working synthesis that could define a national mission and legitimate the privileged positions of those responsible for bearing this mission.

Its appeal transcends the claims of any parochial loyalties in Ethiopia. It glorifies no tribe, no region, no linguistic group, but the Ethiopian nation under her monarch.

It declares this nation superior to all others—to the Persians, Moabites, and other alleged Semitic peoples, because of the corruption of their rulers and the fact that Menilek was the firstborn of Solomon's sons; to the Jews and other Christians; and a fortiori to all who were not of Semitic descent or Christians. It thus provides a mandate for the Ethiopian kingdom to expand its dominion in the name of the Lord of Hosts. The message is clear: no sooner is Menilek instated as king of Ethiopia (Chapter 92) than he embarks upon conquest (Chapter 94):

> And after three months they rose up to wage war from the city of the government. And the Levites carried the Tabernacle of the Law, together with the things that appertained to their office, and they marched along with great majesty . . . And the other mighty men of war of Israel marched on the right side of it and on the left, and close to it, and before it and behind it, and although they were beings made of dust they sang psalms and songs of the spirit like the heavenly hosts . . .
>
> And on the following morning they laid waste the district of Zawa with Hadiya, for enmity had existed between them from olden times; and they blotted out the people and slew them with the edge of the sword. Any they passed on from that place and encamped at Gerra, and here also they laid waste the city of vipers that had the faces of men, and the tails of asses attached to their loins.

This passage expresses the tremendous sense of mission with which the Solomonid expansion was charged. It contains a very contemporary reference indeed: Emperor Amde Siyon had attacked and conquered Hadiyya just a few years before the final redaction of the epic.

The *Kibre Negest* also highlights the special status of those entrusted to lead this mission. Chapter 44 gives specific advice about the deference expected toward kings: "It is not a seemly thing to revile the king, for he is the anointed of God. It is neither seemly nor good." If the king does well, God will favor him; if not, "retribution belongeth to God."

The royal authority, moreover, is to be confined to males. In two separate passages, Queen Makeda insists that women should never reign again in Ethiopia but only men.

In addition, the epic affirms that "the people must not revile the bishops and the priests, for they are the children of God and the men of His house." The priests have the duty to instruct men with wisdom and rebuke them for sins. The priests are also given a mandate to rebuke the king for any royal misconduct they have witnessed.

Indeed, the clerical mandate is spelled out in much detail. Polygamy is to be fought and monogamy upheld. The nakedness of close relatives is not to be uncovered. Sexual perversions are proscribed. The Ten Commandments are to be followed, as are the Judaic taboos on unclean foods. Pagan superstitions, signs, charms, and magic are to be abandoned. Judges are to refuse bribes and be righteous and impartial in judgment. Acts of kindness are to be shown toward neighbors and strangers.

Guided by the directives of this national script, the Amhara monarchs went forth to conquer other peoples and the clergy went forth to convert and reform them. Modeled on the drama of the kings of Israel, the script gave Old Testament themes a particularly prominent place. Hubbard has determined that there are five times as many Old Testament quotations and allusions in the *Kibre Negest* as New Testament ones. The names of the outstanding emperors of the period—Amde Siyon (Pillar of Zion), Dawit I (David), Yishaq (Isaac), and Zar'a Ya'qob (Seed of Jacob)—reflected an identification with ancient Israel. Authors of royal chronicles described kingly virtues in Old Testament terms: Amde Siyon, for example, was portrayed as "gentle and humble like Moses and David." After long controversy, the Ethiopians under Zar'a Ya'qob persuaded representatives of the Alexandrian Patriarchate to authorize their observance of the Jewish Sabbath in the Christian church. Long after all other Christians had rejected the Judaic concept of the covenant,[10] it was resurrected on the highland-plateau fastnesses of the Amhara. Theirs was the divinely ordained mission of a uniquely chosen people.

The Tigrean Contribution

If the principal beneficiaries of this covenant were the kings of Amhara, the fact remains that those who drafted its terms were Tigreans. If the story of the *Kibre Negest* has long dominated the fastnesses of Christian Ethiopia, it must also be noted that only in the northern part of Tigrinya-speaking territory does one find a cluster of places celebrated in local lore for having been associated with the legend of Makeda and Solomon. Near Adwa there is a place called Hinzat which is reputed to have been the location of Makeda's royal headquarters. On the outskirts of Aksum is a large reservoir, Mai Shum, where Makeda is said to have taken her baths. Farther north, on the Asmera Plateau, is a river named Mai Bela—"Fetch some water!"—where Makeda is believed to have stopped on her way back from Jerusalem and to have issued that order as she began the labor that issued in the birth of Menilek. A coffeehouse in Asmera now bears the name Mai Bela as well. The actual birthplace of Menilek is locally identified as a large piece of gneiss rock near the village of Adi Shemagali northwest of Asmera. Just west of Aksum are two large slabs of finished granite which are said to mark the site of Makeda's tomb. In the same region the ruins of an Aksumite building at the foot of Mount Zohodo are considered to be the tomb of Menilek I himself. Finally, the Old Church of Saint Mary in Aksum is believed to this day to contain the original Ark of the Covenant brought by Menilek I and Azariah from Jerusalem, locked within seven caskets inside the sanctuary.

Another set of local traditions in northern Tigray, moreover, relates to a comparably important primordial experience, the advent of the "Nine Saints." These were a group of Syrian missionaries who laid the foundations for the doctrinal and liturgical traditions of Ethiopian Monophysite Christianity. Settling in the Aksum Plateau toward the end of the fifth century, probably as refugees from the anti-Monophysite persecutions in the Byzantine Empire after the Council of Chalcedon, they established a number of monasteries and translated the Bible and other religious works into Ethiopic. Local lore in northern Tigray still celebrates the advent of these saints, with legends about the places visited by Abba Pentellewon and Abba Liqanos flourishing around Aksum and those concerning the activities of Abba Gerima and Abba Aregawi current in Adwa. Residents of Adwa even cherish the belief that Abba Gerima is alive in their vicinity today.

The ancient homeland of the Tigrean people thus possesses a particularly intimate relationship with the two central symbolic complexes that undergird the traditional Ethiopian political order: Solomonic genealogy and Monophysite Christian authority. Both of these complexes, as I have remarked elsewhere,[11] derive a peculiar force because they stem from outside the Ethiopian system. The legitimacy of the Ethiopian monarchy has traditionally been based on (1) the king's affiliation with a genealogy believed to descend from King Solomon of Jerusalem and (2) his anointment by an archbishop sent by the Monophysite patriarch at Alexandria. These traditions are reaffirmed in the 1955 Constitution of Ethiopia, which stipulates that the emperor must be a descendant of the line of Solomon and Sheba and profess the Monophysite faith and states that "by virtue of His Imperial Blood as well as by the anointing which He has received the person of the Emperor is sacred, His dignity is inviolable, and His power indisputable" (art. 2).

If the ultimate origin of these two long-lived legitimating principles lies outside the Ethiopian system, clearly their geographic point of entry has been the Aksum Plateau. To think that the political relevance of Aksum terminated with the downfall of the Aksumite dynasty is to overlook a fundamental feature of the evolution of the Ethiopian political system. It can be argued, rather, that it was precisely because Tigray lost political power that it was able to play a distinctive role in the evolution of a national society in Greater Ethiopia.

I began this chapter by suggesting that ancient Aksum can be viewed as a "seedbed" society. In *Societies: Evolutionary and Comparative Perspectives*, Talcott Parsons discusses some general characteristics of seedbed societies—those which are agents of cultural innovations that become very significant to societies of a different time and place. One of the points Parsons makes about seedbed societies is that before their cultural products could affect later distant societies they had to experience a loss of political independence and to transfer primary prestige to personalities who were not political powers but specialists in maintaining and developing distinctive cultural systems. This is exactly what occurred in northern Tigray. By the time Aksum's kings were overthrown, a stratum of monks had been securely established who were heirs to the prestige formerly associated with the Aksumite polity. They could more easily diffuse their ideas among peoples farther south who had had little or no contact with the Aksumite imperium, and the Amhara kings could more readily accept their moral authority and ideological formulations because Tigray was no longer a serious political competitor.

What parochial thrust the *Kibre Negest* had, then, was chiefly an effort to uphold the special place of Aksumite traditions in Ethiopian culture. In a colophon appended to some manuscript copies of the epic, Yishaq observed that the *Kibre Negest* was not translated into Ethiopic during the Zagwe Dynasty because those Agew-speaking Christians, "not being Israelites," would appear in its light to be illegitimate rulers. The subsequent usurpation by Yikunno Amlak and his descendants was therefore not only a victory for the Semitic-speaking Amhara; it was as much a vindication of the centrality of Aksumite traditions concerning Makeda and Solomon as a source of cultural legitimation for the monarchy. Tigreans and Amhara leaned on one another in a particularly effective way at that juncture, as they have done intermittently ever since.

Whatever the utility of the metaphor of Aksum as a seedbed society, the significance of Aksum as a source of legitimating imagery throughout the six centuries of Amhara rule after 1270 cannot be denied. Not only did the clergy of Aksum produce the script of the *Kibre Negest*, but the city itself became romanticized and revered throughout the Amhara kingdom. In writings often appended to the *Kibre Negest* Aksum was described as "royal throne of the kings of Zion, mother of all lands, pride of the entire universe, jewel of kings . . . She was the second Jerusalem. Because of her grandeur and her immense glory, all the kings are called Kings of Aksum, and the archbishops who came from Egypt are called archbishops of Aksum."[12] It was to the Church of Saint Mary of Zion in Aksum, the holiest place in Ethiopian Christendom, that the crowns of former emperors were customarily sent for preservation. In spite of the fact that the Amhara royal headquarters were usually located far from Tigray,

Amhara elite steadfastly believed that the proper place for the coronation of kings was Aksum. Although we have evidence in only four cases—Zar'a Ya'qob, Sertsa Dingil, Susneyos, and Iyasu I—of Amhara monarchs actually making the journey to Aksum for the ceremony, the symbolic importance of the idea is shown by the frequency and lavish care with which descriptions of the proper rites of coronation at Aksum appear in court chronicles and other Ethiopic writings over many centuries.[13]

During the last two centuries the Tigreans have also made direct political contributions of major importance in the effort to create a national society in Greater Ethiopia. In this chapter, however, I have been concerned to document their primary historical role, which has been the indirect one of providing some of the core symbolism that served to fashion, inspire, and legitimate the project of creating an Amhara imperium.

Notes

1 See David A. Hubbard, "The Literary Sources of the *Kebra Nagast*" (dissertation, University of Saint Andrews, 1956).

2 Budge, *The Queen of Sheba and Her Only Son Menyelek* (London,1922), p. vii,; Ullendorff, *The Ethiopians*, p. 144. Hubbard comments that as a repository of elements from many different literatures, the *Kibra Negest* "presents a literary reflection of the polychromic pattern of life which is Ethiopia" ("Literary Sources of the *Kebra Nagast*" p. 6).

3 *Voyage dans Ie Royaume de* Choa (Paris, 1841), 1: 204.

4 *Travels in Abyssinia* (London, 1868), p. 33.

5 *Storia d'Etiopia* (Milan, 1928), p. 319.

6 "Menilek and Oedipus: Further Observations on the Ethiopian National Epic, *Proceedings of the First United States Conference on Ethiopian Studies*, ed. Harold G. Marcus.

7 See *Societies: Evolutionary and Comparative Perspectives*, passim.

8 "The Identity Struggle," in *Intensive Family Therapy*, ed. Ivan Borzormenyi-Nagy and J.L. Framo (New York: Harper and Row, 1965). Wallace and Fogelson define identity as "any image, or set of images, either conscious or unconscious, which an individual has of himself." They conceive of a person's total identity as consisting of a number of analytically separable subsets of images. *Real identity* is a subset of images which the person believes, privately, to be a true present description of himself as he "really" is. *Ideal identity* is a subset of images which the person would like to be able to say was true but which he does not necessarily believe is true at present. *Feared identity* is a subset of images which the person would not like to have to say was true of himself at present and which he does not necessarily believe is true. *Claimed identity* is a subset of images which the person would like another party to believe is his real identity.

9 See Snowden, *Blacks in Antiquity*, Chapter 9.

10 For an illuminating analysis of this concept which throws light on the meaning of the Ethiopian case, see Delbert R. Hillers, *Covenant: The History of a Biblical Idea* (Baltimore: Johns Hopkins Press, 1969).

11 "Legitimacy in Ethiopia," paper presented at the 1964 meetings of the American Political Science Association (mimeographed, Department of Sociology, University of Chicago).

12 *Liber Axurnae*, ed. C. Conti Rossini (*Corpus Scriptorum Christianorum Orientalium*, scr. Aeth., ser. alt., 8; Paris, 1910), 67, 72 (text).

13 See Eike Haberland, "Die Fest-Inthronisation in Aksum," in *Untersuchungen*, pp. 90–103.

7

Menilek and Oedipus

Further Reflections on the Ethiopian National Epic (1973)[*]

The *Kibre Negest*, or "Glory of Kings," long has been regarded as the centerpiece of Ethiopic literature. Even so, questions concerning the literary character of the work and the needs it has fulfilled in Ethiopian society rarely have been accorded serious scholarly attention. In the course of a recent reexamination of the text of the *Kibre Negest* and of the historical context of its redaction, I sought to consider these questions directly and was led thereby to challenge some widely held views about the work.[1]

First, because of the diverse origins of its literary materials and the polymorphous nature of its constituent genres, the *Kibre Negest* commonly has been regarded as an aesthetic disaster. From the offhand remarks of commentators such as Rochet d'Héricourt, who found it "confused, tangled, and devoid of interest,"[2] and Walter Plowden, to whom it seemed "a rubbish of ... imperfect and incoherent statements,"[3] to the measured judgment of scholars such as Carl Bezold, who held that "the question of the literary unity of the book . . . should be answered in the negative,"[4] opinions of the literary character of the work typically have stressed its disunified nature. Examination of the overall *form* rather than of the contents of the *Kibre Negest*, however, shows that it exhibits an impressive structural unity and supports the contrary judgment of Eike Haberland that "everything ... is woven together here in an extraordinarily artful way."[5]

---

* Originally published in the *Proceedings of the First U.S. Conference on Ethiopian Studies*, ed. Harold Marcus (Lansing, MI: African Studies Center of Michigan State University, 1973), 11–23.

Second, because of the foreign origin of most of its literary sources and the fact that a colophon describes the *Kibre Negest* as having been translated from an Arabic version of a Coptic original, the *Kibre Negest* also has been regarded as a work of essentially foreign inspiration. Internal evidence of many kinds, however, indicates the propriety of viewing it as an essentially Ethiopian work, replete with indigenous themes and concerns.

Third, the purpose of the *Kibre Negest* commonly has been viewed as a narrowly political one, that of legitimating the overthrow of the Zagwe dynasty by the Amhara. Many writers uncritically have repeated Conti-Rossini's statement that the *Kibre Negest* "has no other purpose than that of demonstrating the usurpation of Yikunno Amlak to be nothing more than a just act of vindication."[6] Against this interpretation I would make two separate arguments. First, in so far as the *Kibre Negest* had a parochial thrust, it was not so much to exalt the Amhara as to reassert the importance of Aksumite traditions by a group of Tigrean literati. Second, there is a good deal of material in the *Kibre Negest* which contradicts the hypothesis that the work was written primarily to provide propaganda on behalf of parochial power interests.

All these lines of revision converge in the notion that the *Kibre Negest* is viewed most fruitfully as a *national epic*. This is so in three senses. It is a national epic in the conventional, dictionary meaning: an imaginative work that embodies a conception of crucial, formative events in the nation's history. In this context it aptly has been compared with the *Aeneid*, another effort to glorify one nation's beginning by linking it with an earlier, prestigious nation's history and Book.

It is a national epic in a sociocultural sense, a script containing what Talcott Parsons has called a body of constitutive symbolism: a complex of symbols that provides specialized cultural legitimation both for the society as a whole and for privileged positions within the society.[7] In this perspective, it can be argued, the *Kibre Negest* is the embodiment and outcome of a collective identity struggle carried out by a stratum of Tigrean literati at a point when they reached a working synthesis of diverse cultural ingredients and were ready to advance a firm conception of Ethiopian national character and purpose.

Finally, and in the sense that shall concern us here, the *Kibre Negest* is a national epic in that it expresses deep-lying psychological conflicts widely shared by members of Ethiopian society. It is a national saga for northern Ethiopians in the same way that Jacob Burckhardt linked the Oedipus saga with the ancient Greeks when he observed that every Greek had an Oedipus fiber which was capable of being directly touched and vibrated. Every Amhara-Tigrean, we may say, has had a Menilek fiber capable of being directly touched and vibrated. This article presents the results of some exploratory dissections aimed at exposing the properties of the Menilek fiber.

The *Kibre Negest* as an Oedipal Dream

Our inquiry proceeds from two methodological principles which have been solidly established by the psychoanalytic tradition. The first is the principle of over-determination, which states that every psychological event is determined by a plurality of causal factors. In other words, while it is legitimate to look for the political and cultural meanings of a myth like the *Kibre Negest,* as I have done in *Greater Ethiopia,* or for its cognitive and grammatical structure, as students of Claude Levi-Strauss are inclined to do, there is also some point in exploring the myth as an expression of unconscious emotional meanings that may be of some importance in the personal lives of its creators and audiences.

The second principle holds that in deciphering the unconscious emotional meanings of myths they can be analyzed as imaginative products comparable to dreams. The observation of numerous parallels between myths and dreams with respect to contents, form, and motivational elements led the pioneers of psychoanalytic inquiry, notably Sigmund Freud, Karl Abraham, and Otto Rank, to conclude that the myth justifiably could be interpreted as a "dream of the masses of the people." Our analysis of the *Kibre Negest* accordingly employs such tried and tested concepts of dream interpretation as condensation (interpreting a symbol as representing two or more distinct ideas), displacement (interpreting a symbol as standing for an apparently unrelated, more anxiety-arousing piece of imaginative material), and splitting (representing different aspects of the same person by different objects).

Viewed as an extended piece of dreamwork, the *Kibre Negest* readily divides into a sequence of seven episodes: the glorification of Solomon and Zion, the Ark of the Covenant (Chapters 1–28); Solomon's seduction of Makeda (Chapters 28–32); Menilek's confrontation with Solomon (Chapters 33–44); the theft of Zion (Chapters 45–62); the downfall of Solomon (Chapters 63–69); the fate of the other kings (Chapters 70–83); and the triumphant ascendance of Menilek (Chapters 84–95; 96–117).

Episode One: Initial Situation

The story begins with a series of passages which alternately glorify Solomon and Zion. Solomon is glorified indirectly at first, by narrations about his distinguished ancestors, from Noah and Shem and Abraham and Jacob through Judah and Jesse and David, a line blessed by a series of covenants .with God. Then Solomon himself is directly idealized, as a man exceedingly wise, powerful, competent, pious, and just, one who "administered just judgment, and. . . spake with authority, and. . . decided rightly in all the matters he enquired into; and he received information and imparted it twofold, and . . . all his handicraft and his works were performed with wisdom" (Chapter 23).

Similar adoration is expressed for Zion, the Ark of the Covenant: "It resembleth jasper, and the sparkling stone, and the topaz, and the hyacinthine stone, and crystal, and the light, and it catcheth the eye by force, and it astonisheth the mind and stupefieth it with wonder . . . . And it is a spiritual thing and is full of compassion; it is a heavenly thing and full of light; it is a thing of freedom and habitation of the Godhead" (Chapter 17).

INTERPRETATION. Solomon, of course, is the archetypical father figure. The glorification of Solomon's lineage and person represents an adoration of the dreamer's father.

Zion represents the dreamer's mother. The Ark of the Covenant is represented in churches throughout Christian Ethiopia by a hollow oblong box, a type of object that usually stands for the maternal womb in dream symbolism. One need not appeal to such generalizations for evidence that the Ark stands for a maternal figure, however. In the *Kibre Negest* the Ark is frequently referred to in feminine terms, as "Our Lady," for example. In some passages, it is explicitly likened to a maternal figure: "The heavenly Zion is to be regarded as the similitude of the Mother of the Redeemer, Mary" (Chapter 11), and "unto David will I give seed in her" (Chapter 18).

When the narrative begins, Zion appears as the legitimate possession of Solomon and as the source of his glory and happiness. Zion therefore represents certain aspects of the dreamer's mother in pure form, her qualities as a distant, idealized, ennobling, and legitimate possession of the father.

Episode Two: Solomon's Seduction of Makeda

After Makeda, Queen of Ethiopia, has journeyed to Jerusalem to partake of Solomon's wisdom, he desires to make love to her, but she begs off. They then swear an oath, whereby he promises not to take possession of her by force and she promises not to take anything in his house by force. After feeding her highly spiced food, Solomon has a goblet of water placed in her bedroom. When she rises in the night to take the water, Solomon defines Makeda's act as a breach of their oath (Makeda: "Is the oath broken by my drinking water?" Solomon: "Is there anything thou hast seen under the heavens that is better than water?") (Chapter 30). Having thus obtained release from his oath not to take possession of her, Solomon has intercourse with Makeda. The fruit of that act is Menilek, who is born after Makeda returns to Ethiopia.

INTERPRETATION. Makeda represents the dreamer's mother perceived as his own legitimate possession. In this episode she is portrayed as having been possessed by the father illegitimately. Solomon's promiscuity is noted and half-heartedly exculpated since he lived in a time before laws concerning monogamy had been established; but the allusion to his promiscuous behavior with women is accompanied by the observation that "those early peoples lived under the law of the flesh, for the grace of the Holy Spirit had not been given unto them" (Chapter 28).

What is more, Makeda comes to his court as a virgin, bound by Ethiopian laws which prescribe virginity for queens. Solomon's taking possession of Makeda is thus thrice illicit: because of his promiscuity, because of his violation of the norm of reginal virginity, and because of the reprehensible way in which he forces her to accede to his desires. This episode expresses the dreamer's feelings that the father has wronged the mother and that she does not really properly belong to him.

Episode Three: Menilek's Confrontation with Solomon

Upon reaching young manhood, Menilek says he wants to see his father. He journeys to Jerusalem where he is warmly received at Solomon's court. Solomon urges Menilek to stay on and succeed him as king of Israel, but Menilek demurs, stating that he prefers to go back to live near his mother.

Solomon finally accedes to Menilek's preference and arranges to have him crowned so that he can return as king of Ethiopia. He is anointed by Zadok the priest, proclaimed king with the throne name of David, and instructed by Zadok in the various commandments which he should uphold as king. Solomon also orders that the firstborn sons of the nobles of Israel should accompany his son David (Menilek) back to Ethiopia.

INTERPRETATION. The dreamer's ego, represented by Menilek, expresses a real feeling of affinity toward the father, wanting to be close to him (Solomon's invitation) and to be like him (assuming Solomon's father's name, incorporating his moral standards); but he also feels antagonism toward the father because he wants to possess the mother. He resolves the tension by rejecting the father as a person, but internalizing the father's ego ideal and super-ego, and by going off to live with the mother. The guilt aroused by his rejection of his father is alleviated somewhat by having all the firstborn sons of the nobles of Israel abandon their fathers as well.

Episode Four: The Theft of Zion

The firstborn sons who are to accompany Menilek to Ethiopia, led by Azariah, the son of Zadok the priest, form a plot to steal Zion from the Temple. They substitute a wooden frame for it and hide the real Ark among their possessions. The company is then blessed and departs, traveling in a magical manner three cubits above the waters of the Red Sea.

Following Menilek's exodus, the people of Jerusalem burst out in weeping because of the loss of the firstborn sons, and Solomon joins them: "Woe is me! For my glory hath departed . . . and my belly is burned up because this my son has departed, and the majesty of my city and the freemen, the children of my might, are removed" (Chapter 50). Then Solomon reconciles himself to this loss by citing several scriptural prophecies which justify it.

When Menilek's company reaches Gaza, the noble sons of Israel tell him the secret that they have taken possession of Zion, justifying their theft as reflecting the will of God. Menilek is elated. Meanwhile, Solomon and Zadok begin to have forebodings. Zadok is sent to the Temple, finds the Ark missing, and falls down "like a dead man." Upset by the news, Solomon sends men in pursuit, ordering them to bring Menilek back and slay the others, "for they are men of death and not of life" (Chapter 57). The pursuit is in vain, and Solomon and the elders of Israel are inconsolably upset. Eventually, however, they become reconciled to the event as one that must have been willed by God, and they resolve to continue to live in a righteous manner.

INTERPRETATION. If, as indicated above, Zion symbolizes the mother as the father's legitimate possession, the meaning of this episode is that the son has appropriated the father's wife. The objection that it was Azariah, not Menilek, who engineered the theft must evoke the standard psychoanalytic response: Whose dream is it? The act of appropriating the father's wife is fraught with such anxiety that the dreamer has another character, his peer, do the dirty work. His moral anxiety is further alleviated by the idea, twice repeated, that after all it was God's will that the theft be carried out.

Episode Five: The Downfall of Solomon

Solomon's spirits are revived when he considers that, although God saddened Israel by willing the theft of Zion, He would not break his earlier covenants and would again favor the people of Israel if they followed His commandments. Thereafter Solomon lives properly for eleven years, but "then his heart turned aside from the love of God, and he forgot his wisdom, through his excessive love of women" (Chapter 63). He becomes enamored of Makshara, the daughter of pharaoh.

Makshara and her servants worship idols, and Solomon comes to enjoy observing their services. When Makshara invites Solomon to join her in worship, Solomon refuses. Thereupon she provokes him, making herself especially attractive with perfumes and adornment but treating him haughtily, until in exasperation he agrees to do whatever she asks if she will only restore him to her favor. Makshara then ties a scarlet thread on the door of the house of her gods, places three locusts on the floor of the room, and asks Solomon to bend and seize the locusts without breaking the thread. In carrying out this request, Solomon unwittingly bows down to her gods. Not long after, he becomes sick and dies, having lived twenty years less than his father "because he was under the sway of women and worshipped idols."

INTERPRETATION. Menilek previously has wounded his father twice, first by rejecting his bid to stay and by taking with him the firstborn sons of Israel, then by stealing the Ark of the Covenant. Neither wound proved fatal: Zadok, who fell down as dead, again stood up, and Solomon's spirits revived both times. Now, again indirectly, the coup de grace is delivered. However, the dreamer is spared the guilt because it takes place after Menilek is gone from the scene and the deed is attributed to an alien woman, a projection which inspires a paragraph of invective against the nefarious seductions of women.

Makshara, Solomon's nemesis, is likened to Makeda, in that both are identified as of the Hamitic race. Makshara represents another aspect of the dreamer's mother, his perception of her as one who illicitly consorts with the father. In this episode, then, the dreamer gets even with the mother for her participation in the illicit acts of Episode Two and also rids himself of the father once and for all in a guilt-free manner.

Episode Six: The Fate of the Other Kings

Solomon's downfall is followed by what may seem a baffling digression, a series of short narratives concerning the other kings of the world: first Rehoboam, Solomon's successor as king of Judah, and Adrami, Solomon's third son and king of Rome, then the kings of many other lands. The overt point made in the epic in this section is that all these kings are, in one way or another, descendants of Shem. On the level of political culture, the point is to demonstrate the superiority of the Semitic race as source of all the rulers on earth.

INTERPRETATION. In the stories about all of these other kings, each is shown in some way to be flawed. Rehoboam and Adrami are not only *younger* sons of Solomon than Menilek, but Rehoboam becomes a foolish and tyrannical ruler, and Adrami's successors are tempted by the devil to embrace terrible heretical doctrines. The king of Medyam is associated with the greed of Esan, his forefathers; the king of Babylon is described as arrogant and an idol worshipper; the kings of Moab and Ammon are shown to be the offspring of incestuous unions; and the king of the Philistines is portrayed as a jealous, raving murderer. In this episode, then, the other kings are represented as Menilek's brothers, and he is shown to be morally superior to the lot.

Episode Seven: The Ascendance of Menilek

Makeda is described, for the first time, as a woman of extraordinary wisdom. Then she turns over the kingdom to Menilek. His kingdom is portrayed as that which has replaced Solomon's as the favored of God. The rest of the epic in various ways celebrates the glory of Menilek and the transfer of divine favor from Solomon's people to Menilek's.

INTERPRETATION. The wish is fulfilled. When the dream begins, the father is all-powerful and possesses the idealized mother. When it ends, the father has been destroyed, the son has replaced him and lives in possession of the father's wife (and free from the competition of his siblings). If the essential feature of an Oedipal dream consists of the expression of antagonism toward the father and desires to take possession of the mother, the *Kibre Negest* surely qualifies as an Oedipal dream.

The *Kibre Negest* as a Myth of the Birth of a Hero

In his classic study on *The Myth of the Birth of the Hero,* Otto Rank showed that in a number of respects concerning the birth and young manhood of legendary heroes, the Oedipus story reveals striking parallels with myths about heroic figures from many different cultures, including Sargon, Moses, Kama, Paris, Telephus, Gilgamesh, Cyrus, Romulus, Tristan, Siegfried, and others. Rank determined that the sagas of these heroes contain at a minimum the following common elements:

> (1) The hero is the son of most distinguished parents, usually the son of a king;
>
> (2) his origin is preceded by difficulties, such as secret intercourse of the parents due to external prohibitions or obstacles;
>
> (3) during or before the pregnancy there is a prophecy, in the form of a dream or oracle, cautioning against his birth and usually threatening danger to the father;

(4) as a rule he is surrendered to the water in a box and is then saved by animals or lowly people;

(5) after he is grown up, he finds his distinguished parents in a highly versatile fashion;

(6) he takes revenge on his father; and

(7) he achieves ranks and honors.[8]

All of these elements are represented in the *Kibre Negest* as well. Menilek is indeed the son of distinguished parents, the renowned king of Israel and the reigning sovereign of Ethiopia. His origin is preceded by the difficulties posed by the norm of reginal virginity and Makeda's strenuous opposition to Solomon's advances, an opposition that is overcome only by special machinations. Immediately after his seduction of Makeda, moreover, Solomon dreams of a bright sun that shines for a while over the land of Israel and then departs to hover over Ethiopia ever after. Following this he dreams of a second sun, brighter than the first, but the Israelites pay no heed to it and try to extinguish it. Solomon considers this dream a disturbing omen that God's favor will shift from his kingdom to that of Ethiopia.

The motif of abandoning the infant in the water Rank interprets as the reversal of a common childhood fantasy that involves a wish to repudiate the child's own father. The abandonment of the child by its parents in the myth, he suggests, is the equivalent of his repudiation or nonrecognition of them in the fantasy. In the *Kibre Negest* the theme of nonrecognition of the father that is presumed to underly the exposure motif is more directly expressed, for when Menilek grows up he does not know the identity of his father, and Makeda initially resists his efforts to learn it. In Episode Six, moreover, the motif recurs in a different form. The infant son of an Israelitic merchant living in Babylon is about to be exposed in a box in the river when the handmaiden who has been commanded by his mother to abandon him meets the handmaiden of the Queen of Babylon, similarly charged by the queen to expose her deformed, bird-like infant. The well-formed infant is then taken by the queen's handmaiden to the court and brought up as the king's son and successor.

The "versatile" nature of Menilek's quest to find his father is presented indirectly. Makeda warns Menilek that his father's country is far away and the road there very difficult; he is undaunted. At this point the narrative digresses to comment on the unusual qualities of young Menilek, noting, for example, that he was skilled in the manly arts of warfare, horsemanship, and hunting wild beasts. Shortly after this he is described to Solomon by spies as a marvelous figure: "He resembleth thee in noble carriage and in splendid form, and in stature and in goodly appearance ... His eyes are gladsome, like unto those of a man who hath drunk wine, his legs are graceful and slender, and the tower of his neck is like unto the tower of David thy father" (Chapter 34). After finding Solomon, Menilek takes his "revenge" on him in the manner outlined above. Finally, he achieves not only the kingship of Ethiopia but the distinction of being the exclusive bearer of the divine covenant which formerly had belonged to the kings of Israel.

The universality of this outline of events in the birth myths of heroes is taken by Rank to represent certain features of the universal experience of growing up. The key process in question is the detachment of the growing individual from the authority of the parents, the transition from a state of total dependence on and fusion with the parents to a state of independence and separation. In this process, the child invariably shifts from perceiving the parents as uniquely powerful and competent to being aware of their limitations and critical of their behavior. This is usually accompanied by a feeling of some neglect by the parents. In response to this feeling, many children come to have daydreams in which they imagine that the parents who are so imperfect and neglectful are not their real parents, but that they are actually the offspring of much better, nobler parents.

The "family romance of neurotics," as Freud called this archetypical fantasy, provides the core imaginative material which is elaborated in the hero myths. In conformity with the child's idealization of the parents in his earliest years, the hero myths begin with a depiction of ego's parents as particularly noble (1). This endeavor to replace the child's parents by more distinguished ones, Rank writes, "is merely the expression of the child's longing for the vanished happy time when his father still appeared to be the strongest and greatest man and the mother seemed the dearest and most beautiful woman."[9]

The boy's idealization of his father is disturbed, however, when he comes to feel jealousy and competition with the father for the tender love and devotion of the mother. This is often connected with the child's dim but growing awareness of sexual matters, which stimulates erotic fantasies in which the mother is frequently placed in illicit love affairs (2). The boy's feeling of antagonism toward the father, born of his growing impulse toward self-assertion, independence, and rivalry for his mother's attention, is then expressed in the motifs of the prophesied threat to the father (3), repudiation by nonrecognition of the father (4), self-assertive rescue (5), and revenge (6). The myth culminates with an expression of the triumphant vindication of the boy for whatever slights he believes he has experienced from his father (7).

The *Kibre Negest* and the Amhara-Tigrean Social Order

By likening the Menilek myth to that of Oedipus and others in the vast cycle of myths surveyed by Rank, we call attention to its general humanistic significance, as yet another expression of the universally experienced tensions inherent in the processes of individual maturation and generational succession. At the beginning of this article, however, I stressed that the *Kibre Negest* is a national epic, a document which gives expression to psychological conflicts that are particularly salient for members of Amhara-Tigrean society. The differences among various Oedipal myths are no less informative than their similarities, and the task of interpretation has only begun when one has identified the universal themes: the deepest and most revealing meanings of a myth are those most intimately tied to the particular features of its cultural and historical context.

If the general characteristic of an Oedipal myth is that it expresses the tensions involved in growing up within a family, the variations in Oedipal tales reflect the different types of adult social order and how they pattern the network of family relationships and the process of generational succession. Of the traditional Amhara-Tigrean system we can say, very briefly, that at all levels of the society, from the local household and seignory to the royal court, the dominant mode of social organization exhibits a pattern of patrimonial authority, including features such as the overarching status of and personal domination by an authoritative head; his assignment of different tasks to individuals ranked on the basis of age, sex, birth, loyalty, and other criteria; the support of retainers from the head's own tables or supply stores; and the performance of a diffuse array of managerial, judicial, political, and ritual functions by the head. The display of deference to the authoritative head of a household is the hallmark of this social order, and his directives are issued with the understanding that they will not be directly challenged, although in practice they are by no means always carried out.[10]

In the course of growing up in households of this sort, boys typically develop intensely ambivalent feelings of a determinate kind toward their fathers or father-surrogates. On the one hand, the father is the model of everything to which the boy aspires in life. His constant wish is to be like the father so that he can enjoy the status and perquisites which the father enjoys and can order others around as he has been ordered. On the other hand, he must feel betrayed for having had to shift from being a relatively indulged and affectionately treated infant and small child to being, from about the age of four onward, the target of an increasingly stern regime of parental discipline. He feels resentment toward the father for having suppressed, neglected, and ordered him about so much. Yet he is constrained, as much by his own hopes for future favors and inheritance as by the norms of the social order, from any overt expression of antagonism toward the father. So he shows respect; but, as a recent study of the Amhara family points out, it is a kind which the Amhara refer to as "fear respect," not "love respect."[11]

Symbolic narratives like the Oedipus myth have been said to "represent cultural models for coping with typical patterns of subjective stress involved in the orientations of individuals to problematic situations in their social and cultural orders."[12] The father-son relationship is the most poignant, problematic, and stressful relationship in Amhara-Tigrean society.[13] What kind of model for coping with this stress is provided by the *Kibre Negest*? In what manner is the filial antagonism expressed and resolved?

It does not take the form of the "primal horde" version of the Oedipal conflict, not a rejection of paternal authority in favor of a new democratic order based on a band of brothers. As in Amhara-Tigrean society, the relationship among brothers is competitive, not solidaristic. Menilek is portrayed as superior to all his brothers, the other rulers of the world. The father's type of political regime is left intact.

It is not expressed by a rebellion against the paternal personality in favor of a new individuality, the type of rebellion often found in families and myths of more differentiated societies. As Rank himself explicates this alternative so perceptively in his *Modern Education*, this kind of rebellion signifies a wish to keep the self from being submerged through too close an identification with the father, to avoid even becoming a future father. In every detail, however, Menilek is and wants to be like his father. He is portrayed as a mirror image of Solomon and is given the throne name of Solomon's own father, David, when he is anointed in Jerusalem.

It is not presented as a violation of the normative order represented by his father, not an anomic or liminal position in which the hero absorbs contradictory moral imperatives and thus places himself outside the moral order, as Terry Turner, in his brilliant reanalysis of the Oedipus myth, has shown to be the outcome embodied in Sophocles' version of the Oedipus myth. On the contrary, Menilek emerges as morally blameless, divinely favored, the perfect incarnation of the traditional moral order formerly upheld by his father.

What is striking about the *Kibre Negest* as an Oedipal myth is that the paternal principle is in no way challenged. Solomon is not assaulted, or overthrown, or criticized. Menilek embraces his father's political authority, his personal being, and his moral order. He becomes a ruler in Solomon's very image, with the sons of Solomon's nobles as his retainers, the son of Solomon's high priest as his high priest, and with a religion and moral code copied from that of his father. The principle of patrimonial authority is religiously upheld.

How, then, does the *Kibre Negest* provide a model for dealing with the negative feelings of sons toward fathers in Amhara-Tigrean society? By holding aloft the promise of succession. Eventually, the father will be forced to step down, the son will take his place, and he who was at the bottom of the hierarchy will be on top.

In the meantime, as a safety valve, it is possible to express antagonism indirectly, by deceit and by using third parties. A model is provided when the people of Jerusalem murmur against the king for having ordered them to send their firstborn sons along with Menilek. In private, they express resentment, although to his face they show acquiescence and support for the idea. (This episode is immediately followed by a moralizing gloss which affirms that "it is not a seemly thing to revile the king.") Menilek himself never directly attacks his father. This is done surreptitiously, and through third parties, using Azariah to appropriate Zion, the king's pride and joy, through a fake substitute, and Makshara to corrupt him through a subterfuge. But this mode of showing antagonism is all right, for did not the father-king himself point the way by initiating the whole sequence of fateful events with his deceitful mode of seducing Makeda?

As for the direct expression of aggression, that is to be limited to peers and outside groups, and it is notable that the first thing that Menilek does after becoming king in Ethiopia is to embark on a course of warfare against neighboring peoples.

The issue of succession is uppermost in the minds of sons in Amhara-Tigrean society. Their overriding concern is not: Shall I become like my father? Rather: How soon can I become like him? The matter is ambiguous, for the process of transition from senior to junior generations is not institutionalized, as it is in some other societies of Greater Ethiopia, such as those which have a gada type of generation-grading system or the halaqa type of assembly described by Dan Sperber. What is institutionalized is the principle of continuity of patrimonial authority.

In this situation, direct confrontation with an authority figure is out of the question; his status is supreme, his tenure of office indefinite. The alternatives are to obey, or to disobey deviously, or to obey and express negative feelings through third parties and in the indirect manner symbolized by the "wax and gold" type of communication,[14] or to deflect negative feelings against peers, outsiders, and domestic animals. By representing the way in which Oedipal tensions are handled within the Amhara-Tigrean order, the *Kibre Negest* thus has served to coordinate "the individual's subjective experience of conflict, tension, and diachronic change with the cultural vision of the synchronic order of the collective system," as Terry Turner has formulated the central preoccupation of traditional narrative forms.[15] It was a model for survival in a system of whose emperor it was promulgated, as recently as the Constitution of 1955, that by virtue of his descent from King Solomon as well as the anointing which he has received, "the person of the Emperor is sacred, His dignity is inviolable, and His power indisputable," and in which every household and seignory was ruled by an emperor figure.

Notes

1 Revised version of an article prepared for the First United States Conference on Ethiopian Studies, Michigan State University, May 4, 1973. I am grateful to Professor Victor Turner of the University of Chicago for his invitation to take part in a seminar on the comparative study of epics which stimulated the line of inquiry resulting in this article. The first part of that inquiry is presented as Chapter 7 of *Greater Ethiopia: The Evolution of a Multiethnic Society* (Chicago: University of Chicago Press, 1974). The introductory section of this article summarizes some of the conclusions of that chapter.

2 *Voyage dans Ie Royaume de Choa* (Paris: 1841), p. 204.

3 *Travels in Abyssinia* (London: 1868), p. 33.

4 "Kebra Nagast. Die Herrlichkeit der Könige," *Abhandlungen der königlich Bayerischen Akademie der Wissenschciften* (München), Phil. Class, vol. 23, Part I (1905) (Munich: 1909), p. xv.

5 *"Untersuchungen tun äthiopischen Königtum* (Wiesbaden: Franz Steiner Verlag, 1965), p. 32.

6 *Storia d'Etiopia* (Milan: 1928), p. 319.

7 See his *Societies: Comparative and Evolutionary Perspectives* (Englewood Cliffs: Prentice-Hall, 1966).

8 (New York: Random House, 1959), p. 65.

9 *Ibid.*, p. 71.

10 For documentation on this pattern see Donald N. Levine, "Ethiopia: Identity, Authority, and Realism," in *Political Culture and Political Development*, Pye and S. Verba, eds. (Princeton, N.J.: Princeton University Press, 1965); Allan Hoben, "Social Stratification in Traditional Amhara Society," in *Social Stratification in Africa*, A. Tuden and L. Plotnicov, eds. (New York: Free Press, 1970); Wolfgang Weissleder, "The Political Ecology of Amhara Domination" (unpubl. Ph.D. diss., University of Chicago, 1965); and Ronald Reminick, "The Manze Amhara of Ethiopia: a Study of Authority, Masculinity, and Sociality" (unpubl. Ph.D. diss., University of Chicago, 1973).

11 Reminick, "The Manze Amhara."

12 Terry Turner, "Oedipus: Time and Structure in Narrative Form," in *Forms of Symbolic Action*, Robert F. Spencer, ed. (Seattle and London: University of Washington Press, 1969), p.35.

13 See also Eike Haberland's observations on this point: "In spite of the strong respect which youth grants age and sons their fathers, it appears quite certain to Ethiopians that true love is only felt by fathers toward their sons, whereas the latter act in such a way as to become heirs as quickly as possible. This attitude is expressed in a story. . . which I heard from some Amhara. A father and son once went to battle together. In the evening both lay dead, their bodies, all hacked up, next to one another. The entrails of the father were distended toward the son's body, but the son's entrails pointed away from the father; thus was [the pathos of] fatherly love expressed even

after death." Haberland, *Untersuchungen*, p. 83.

14 See Donald N. Levine, *Wax and Gold: Tradition and Innovation in Ethiopian Culture* (Chicago: University of Chicago Press, 1965), Chapter 1.

15 Turner, "Oedipus," p. 67.

8

A Note on Ethiopia's Distinctive Religious Heritage (2007) *

When invited by the Ethiopian community of San Jose, California, to compose a short millennial piece celebrating something distinctive about Ethiopia's heritage, I decided for a variation on the theme of many of my previous writings, where I emphasize the multiethnic character of historic Ethiopia. This concerns the extent to which the various peoples of the Horn have come from common ancestors and intermingled in so many ways—through intermarriage, commerce, shared festivals, cultural borrowings, and common political aspirations and activities, most notably in the defense of Ethiopia against external invasions from the Turks, from the Sudanese, and on those two terrible occasions, from imperialist Italy.

In this piece I shall celebrate an aspect of Ethiopia's heritage that has rarely been accorded the attention it deserves. This concerns the character of her religious traditions. At least four features of religion in Ethiopia deserve special attention.

For one thing, Ethiopia became receptive to each of the three great Semitic world religions very early, earlier than nearly any other part of the world. Hebraic influence arrived at an extremely early period. This is attested by Hebraic words that were used in the translation of the New Testament into Ge'ez. Most

---

* Originally written for the Ethiopian community in San Jose, California on the occasion of the Ethiopian Millennium and later published in 2007 on the web forum of the Ethiopian Institute for Nonviolence Education and Peace Studies.

remarkably, the chief indigenous surviving Judaic community—that of the Beta Israel—knew only of Jewish holidays prior to exile of the Jews to Babylon in the 6th century B.C.E. The adoption of Christianity as the official religion in Aksum took place in the 4th century C.E., making Ethiopia, like Syria, Armenia, and Egypt, home to one of the oldest continuous Christian communities in the world. And she gave refuge to followers of the Prophet Mohammed before Islam was officially established, protecting them when the nascent faith was endangered, a gesture that inspired Mohammed to declare Ethiopia perennially exempt from any sort of jihadic intervention.

Because these religions arrived so early, they took shape in Ethiopian soil in a way that enabled them to grow side by side from the outset. They intertwined in many ways. None of them became used as the basis for any sort of rabid exclusionary project. Judaism in Ethiopia was always part of the Ethiopian national culture, not—until the past century—a force that led her followers to reject Ethiopia as their national homeland. Neither Christianity nor Islam was used historically as a basis for persecuting other populations or massacring dissidents, as happened so often with both of those religions in other countries. (Ahmad Gragn's jihad was instigated from outside Ethiopia by the Ottoman Turks. Emperor Yohannes's strict Christianizing policy reflected a national political fear of being invaded by Mahdist Muslims, who did invade and finally killed him. Popular prejudices against the Beta Israelis, often called *buda*, did not reflect a studied persecution of them by the Orthodox Church.) Beyond that, Ethiopians of different Semitic religions could and often did intermarry, often took part in one another's festivals, and shared certain special occasions together—most notably, the annual pilgrimage to the site of the Archangel Gabrael at Mount Kulubi.

Third, the relation to "pagan" Ethiopian religions was tolerant to a degree not shown much elsewhere—a subject that deserves a lot more study. Family resemblances between the properties of indigenous deity symbols, such as the Oromo *Waqa*, with the Semitic deities may have had some subliminal effect, even though resemblance of that name and other cognate names among peoples in the South—*Waq* (Afar, Somali, Burji, Konso, Dasensech, Gurage); *Wak* (Saho); *Wa'a* (Hadiyya); *Waga* (Gamu); *Waqaya* (Majangir); *Muqo* (Tsamako); and *Magano* (Sidamo)—with Amharic *wuqabi* (guardian angel) may reflect common sound and not linguistic kinship. To be sure, the Christian and Muslim missionaries pressured followers of indigenous faiths to embrace one of those Semitic religions. But there are many instances where indigenous religionists held joint celebrations with Christians and/or Muslims.

Finally, I would mention the depth of religious sentiment that marks so many Ethiopians. This trait came to the fore during the Derg period, when systematic efforts to eradicate religious traditions were met by increased observance, including a remarkable increase in the practice of fasting.

These elementary facts should be known by every single Ethiopian at home and abroad. One good way to celebrate Ethiopia's special millennium would be to promote awareness of these special features of her history and culture.

9

Greater Ethiopia Reconsidered (2014)*

In June 1992, when this article first took shape in Addis Ababa, Ethiopian society stood at a fateful crossroads. A year before, the Derg regime was displaced by insurgents. Derg officials, who in September 1974 had toppled the monarchical government by ousting Haile Selassie I, had aligned themselves with Marxist ideologies and ensured a rupture with the past through a massacre of dignitaries associated with the old regime. In the aftermath, the Derg regime effected revolutionary changes: massive redistribution of access to land use; legitimation of public use of languages other than the national language Amharic; legitimation of celebration of Islamic holidays; and making elementary education accessible across the nation.

Those changes also produced huge disruptions. Misguided collectivization policies had led to severe economic attrition, at the same time that 50% of the recurrent national budget went for military expenses. In 1987, Ethiopia's per capita income of US $130 made it the poorest country in the world for which World Bank figures were available. Chronic famine made Ethiopia dependent on external emergency relief. The country's skilled workforce hemorrhaged from the massive exodus of trained Ethiopians.

In the political sector, ethnic antagonisms and regional insurgencies flared up, while the government functioned without a constitution or other source of legitimacy. So in 1991, the new EPRDF regime had to provide quickly a system of stable national and local administrations. The problem was compounded

---

*. Newly revised and expanded, this article originally appeared in the *Ethiopian Review* 2 (8), August, 14-16, 1992.

by a complicated scheme of electoral politics and a hastily created system of decentralized governance, carried out by leaders and publics with little experience of democratic self-government.

Daunting as those economic and political problems may have been, the cultural dilemmas were no less formidable. Work of the late Shmuel Eisenstadt had sensitized me to the crucial need of rapidly modernizing societies to create new collective symbols for such societies. At a time when social scientists attended almost exclusively to problems of economic and political modernization, Eisenstadt insisted that collective identities "are not, as has so often been assumed in the relevant literature, epiphenomenal or secondary to power and economic forces and relations . . . [but] a basic component of social life."[1] And indeed, in the early 1990s, I argued that Ethiopia badly needed a refreshed set of ideas and symbols that could orient the population during the post-Marxist period.

A generation later, Ethiopia's political and economic systems had advanced considerably, while other problems had emerged. The government of Ethiopia has been relatively stable; political parties have been functioning; civil insurgencies have stopped; federal and local administrations have produced a huge growth of agricultural, health, and educational services. Nevertheless, Ethiopia sustained a costly war with Eritrea in the late 1990s, harsh violence followed the 2005 elections, and the press and dissident organizations continue to be intimidated. Similarly, the economy has grown a great deal, despite controversial official statistics and a surging inflation. In 2012 Ethiopia reportedly had a GDP real growth rate of 8.5%, ranking it 14th in the world for the fastest growing GDP.[2] Even so, chronic food insecurity and famine affect vast numbers of the population year after year.[3]

The cultural dilemma I identified in 1992 has been harder to come to terms with. While the economic and political challenges were conspicuous and impossible to ignore, questions of collective identity were rarely addressed. To gain some purchase on this elusive question, let us step back and place the whole matter in historical context.

Ethiopia's cultural dilemma of the 1990s could be likened to that of France in the 1820s, when Auguste Comte diagnosed French society as suffering from acute moral anarchy. The condition arose because beliefs that sustained the monarchy and the Catholic Church had been assaulted by a revolutionary ideology, which nonetheless failed to offer positive beliefs for reorganizing society in the post-revolutionary epoch. Comte held that the only way to secure such beliefs was for a group of scientific sociologists to fashion them. Since Comte's day, sociologists have fortunately become more modest. Rather than suggest what beliefs Ethiopians today should embrace, I shall point to problematic features of the situation and suggest resources to cope with it.

A condition of cultural identity crisis produces anxiety, which can impede the search for constructive solutions. It engenders a certain amount of magical thinking, including a search for salvationary figures. It is also likely to produce dualistic thinking, in which some people are identified as the "good guys" and others are vilified. In an effort to bring a constructive frame of mind to bear on this situation, I shall first provide some historic perspective, by reviewing earlier attempts to produce constitutive symbolism for Ethiopia, and then consider what resources my analyses in *Greater Ethiopia*[4] and beyond might contribute to the process today.

As *Greater Ethiopia* indicates, much symbolism that provided identity for Ethiopia up to the time of Menelik II was embodied in the its "national epic," the *Kibre Negest*. That epic celebrated the special character of the Ethiopian polity as a multiethnic community governed by a monarch whose legitimacy rested on legendary descent from King Solomon and a historic mission to champion the Ethiopian Orthodox Christian faith, Tewahedo. That symbolism served well for close to a thousand years, and energized the empire-building efforts of the 19th century. It was coupled with a belief in Ethiopia's superiority and self-sufficiency. The threat of European penetration, however, challenged the belief in Ethiopia's self-sufficiency and made Ethiopian leaders eager to incorporate features of European civilization.

The first efforts towards revising Ethiopia's national script thus concentrated on bringing Ethiopia abreast of modern technologies, out of fear that Ethiopia's very survival as an independent nation depended on adopting those features of European civilization. Many Ethiopian intellectuals viewed Japan as an exemplar for modernizing, since Japan shared many historical and cultural features with Ethiopia, and was the only other non-white nation to have defeated European forces around the turn of the century. For nearly four decades, Japan figured as the preeminent model in terms of which Ethiopia could energize its modernizing process. Expressions of the ideal of Japanization range from writings by Gabre Hywot Baikedagn in 1912 to statements by educators like Hakim Workeneh and Fitawrari Deresse in the 1920s and pronouncements by foreign minister Blatengetta Heruy Wolde-Selassie in the early 1930s.[5] Emperor Haile Selassie reportedly dreamed of Ethiopia as the Japan of Africa. The most dramatic manifestation of this outlook appeared in the Ethiopian Constitution of 1931, which proved to be a faithful copy of the Meiji Constitution of 1889. The dream was even revived in the postwar years by Education Minister Kebede Mikael, who published *Japan Endamen Salatanach* (*How Japan Modernized*) in 1953.

After World War II, however, Japan largely got displaced by England, Sweden, and the United States as models for Ethiopia's development.[6] The 1955 Constitution, for example, was modeled on that of England. Thousands of

Ethiopians went to Western Europe and the U. S. to study agriculture, business, engineering, law, medicine, and education in order to facilitate Ethiopia's transition into a modern society. They still did so, however, largely under the collective identity provided by the *Kibre Negest*.

By the late 1960s, during the international radicalization of studentry, the Soviet Union came to displace Western countries as the model for many Ethiopian intellectuals. The Russian example seemed more compelling than either Japan or the Western democracies: Russian modernizers not only had to contend with an ostensibly conservative monarchy and aristocracy but, unlike Japan, also had a deeply traditional Orthodox Christian church and an ethnically complex population. What is more, in identifying with its Marxist ideology, Ethiopian intellectuals could safely repudiate their own traditions at the same time as they affirmed Ethiopia's autonomy against so-called Western imperialist powers.[7] So, instead of an identity couched in terms of Ethiopia's historic identity as a proud independent kingdom charged with bearing the true Christian religion, *Tewahedo*, the collective self-image championed by the student radicals who oriented the Derg regime was that of an oppressive feudal monarchy that had "held Ethiopia back for 3,000 years." Not sustaining the complex educational system of the Church and conversion of the pagans but destruction of an oppressive and benighted system became their charge under this newly assumed collective identity.

Although one version of the Marxist worldview was displaced in 1991, another quickly took its place. The parallel with the Soviet Union continued, as both countries repudiated their repressive Stalinist regimes and faced an upsurge of pressures for self-determination from groups that had been dominated by the Ethiopian state. Those who advocated "emancipation" of indigenous nationalities from the grip of an encompassing imperial structure promoted a new collective identity, one which foregrounded Lenin's famous phrase about Tsarist Russia, and so defined Ethiopia as a "Prison House of Nationalities." Thus, they continued following the Soviet model just when the USSR was breaking up into increasingly fractious and hostile ethnic polities. Spokesmen for the ethnic and regional groups who wanted greater self-determination were happy with the new symbolism, but vast numbers of Ethiopians chafed at the dismissal of the image of historic Ethiopia as a valued multiethnic collectivity.

The explosive election of 2005 turned largely around that issue. I tried to minister to that collective trauma with a short piece that attracted several thousands of viewers, entitled "Two Tales of One City." The groundwork for that statement had been laid by my 1974 book, *Greater Ethiopia: The Evolution of a Multiethnic Society*, which was intended precisely to help Ethiopians devise fresh symbolic representations of multiethnic Ethiopia.[8] The book posed the following question, "Should the imperial expansion under Emperors Yohannes IV and Menelik II be viewed basically *as a subjugation of alien peoples or an in-gathering of peoples with deep historical affinities*?" I suggested that the realities underlying both images would somehow have to be taken into account as the current generation of Ethiopian intellectuals worked to shape their collective self-understanding. Peoples outside the northern highlands needed to have their traditions respected and their deprivations following the Menilek conquests acknowledged, at the same time that the historic Ethiopian state deserved appreciation for having introduced modern services for the entire population, put an end to slavery and the slave trade, and protected Ethiopia from being entirely colonized during the Scramble for Africa.

Above all, *Greater Ethiopia* argued, the sense in which the varied peoples of Ethiopia belong to a common culture area needed affirmation; the evidence of their deep affinities and age-old connections is simply overwhelming. In the light of that fact, I argued that Ethiopia's peoples are *enormously more similar and historically connected than the different nationalities that composed the Soviet Union. Greater Ethiopia* presented only a fraction of that evidence. Here I mention three of the pan-Ethiopian culture traits it lists, and consider their relevance to contemporary issues.

For one thing, all the historic peoples of the larger Ethiopian culture area subscribed to a belief in a supreme heavenly deity, and use similar words to represent this deity—most commonly, cognates of *waq*, which appear among the Afar, Saho, Somali, Oromo, Gurage, Hadiyya, Timbaro, Sidamo, Konso, Burji, Tsamako, Gamu, Dasenech, and Majangir; the root also appears in Amharic *wuqabi*, a person's divinely appointed guardian spirit. So one can view the peoples of Greater Ethiopia as monotheists, Semitic (Judaic, Christian, and Islamic) and local, who nevertheless share a number of other kinds of symbolism, like the special aura of respect for trees endowed with sacred significance. Certainly there has been, alongside of tensions, a great deal of intermixing of different Ethiopian religionists historically: Jews and Christians converted back and forth over the centuries, in ways unheard of elsewhere in the world; traditional Oromo rituals and Christian rituals were observed side by side at Zuquala; Muslims, Christians and Jews alike made the annual pilgrimage to Kulubi Gabriel; peoples of diverse backgrounds visited the shrine of Sheik Hussein.

Another pan-Ethiopian culture trait consists of a complex of beliefs, values, and observances related to the ideal of martial bravery, of *jegnet*. This, too, provides a basis on which Ethiopians of widely varying backgrounds can recognize and respect one another. For contemporary purposes, they may find it adaptive to transform that warrior ethic in ways parallel to the Japanese transformation of *bushido* into *budo*, from an ethic celebrating fierceness in martial combat to devotion to the welfare of all living creatures, even courage in the nonviolent assertion of civic ideals in the political arena.

One other pan-Ethiopian feature I'll mention is the love to travel. Settled or nomadic, nearly all Ethiopians are great travelers. To find new land, go on hunting or raiding expeditions, seek political fortune, escape enemies, study at a religious center, go on pilgrimages, visit distant relatives, or carry on trade, they have long been accustomed to moving from one part of the country to another. Such travel has frequently led to settlement in new places, as historical records and local traditions abundantly attest. This is why any policy that hardens ethnic or regional boundaries must definitely be regarded as un-Ethiopian!

No matter what the extent of pan-Ethiopian similarities, there is no gainsaying the fact that Ethiopia today is caught between pressures to affirm primordial entities and to embrace a new national symbolism. To some extent this expresses ethnic tensions generated under the Derg and its aftermath, reflecting the modernizing dynamic classically analyzed by Clifford Geertz as part of the "integrative revolution." The dynamics of modernization entail an inexorable increase of conflicts among groups organized by sentiments such as race, language, ethnicity, religion, or region in societies where such groups have traditionally lived side by side, since the spread of education makes those groups more aware of their identities and interests; increased power, prestige and wealth at the center gives them new ambitions; improved communications gives them an arena to compete in; and the increase of outside interventions makes local groups more sensitive to the identities of agents of the center who are regulating their lives in new ways.

Given that dynamic, it was only a matter of time before Christianity was disestablished as a state religion, and that communities that previously felt suppressed would welcome an opportunity to assert their traditions and claim a more equitable share of the nation's resources. In so doing, many fell into a polarizing trap, highlighted when anti-Amhara antagonism became fashionable under the EPRDF leadership, a sentiment that rested on counterfactual assumptions. For one thing, those called Amhara today do not constitute a single ethnic group but rather a language community composed of diverse ethnic groups that have adopted the Amharic language over the centuries. Indeed, the Amharic language, rather than being the tongue of an historically distinct ethnic group, appears to have emerged as a native lingua franca through a process of pidginization and creolization, such that it incorporated a good deal of Cushitic vocabulary and syntax as well as combined features distinctive of both the northern and southern branches of Ethiopian Semitic.

What is more, the representatives of "Amhara domination" who conquered and colonized the peoples of southern Ethiopia did not come from all parts of the Amharic-speaking territory, but primarily from Shoa province. Strictly speaking, one should really speak of a *Shoan dynasty* under Emperors Menilek and Haile Selassie rather than of Amhara hegemony, in the same way that other regional dynasties—in Tigray, Gonder, and Lasta—exerted imperial control at other times in the preceding millennium. Indeed, most Amhara areas received very little attention under the regime of the last Shoan emperor: the lion's share of Haile Selassie's beneficence went to urban centers—Addis Ababa, Asmara, Harar, Dire Dawa—while "Amhara" homelands like Gojjam, Begemidir, and Menz were neglected.

The forces that protected Ethiopia against the Italians included Ethiopians from many ethnic groups: Oromos, Gurages, Wolamos (Woleitas), Konta, Kulo, Limu, and Kaffa as well as Amhara and Tigreans. They were led by officers from many regions: Ras Alula and Ras Mengesha of Tigray, Dejazmatch Bahta of Akale Guzae, Wagshum Guangul of Lasta, Ras Mikael of Wallo, Ras Gobena and Dejazmatch Balcha of the Mecha Oromo as well as Ras Gebeyehu (who died fighting at Adua) and Ras Abate of Shoa. The coalition of forces that defeated the Italians was a powerful testimony to the symbolism of an independent multiethnic Ethiopian polity. Such a successful multiethnic coalition was not to be seen again until the concert of forces that brought down the oppressive regime of Mengistu Haile Mariam.

And today? The lack of a widely shared collective identity continues to foster demoralization throughout Ethiopia. None of the collective symbolism that seemed hegemonic over the past century—the Orthodox Christian monarchy, the model of Japan, the oppressive class structure, the prison house of nationalities—is viable. The country demands the rhetoric of an Auguste Comte.

Although there will be many who cling to one or another aspect of the former versions of collective identity,[9] the situation is ripe for voices working to refashion a fundamental principle of Ethiopian history into the idiom of modern pluralism. Just as over millennia Ethiopians shifted back and forth between the assertion of local interests, beliefs, and rights and the claims of an imperial center, so today Ethiopia can be affirmed as a historic civilization that has incorporated foreign influences selectively and makes room for multiple differences, in a population with many family resemblances and an ethos of dignity and self-respect. Perhaps Ethiopia's intellectuals and political leaders have only to acknowledge with gratitude what they already possess.

What seems clear is that a growing portion of the younger generation is ready to enjoy the colorful diversity of Ethiopia's numerous traditions in ways that embrace the symbolism of historic Ethiopia—through art, music, dance, and athletics. To watch a circus of ethnic groups each do their traditional dance and then weave themselves into a single pyramid with national colors, as I was privileged to do some years ago in Hawassa, is to sense the emergence of a collective identity well suited for the nation in a democratic, pluralistic era. And I expect that before long, a new generation of Ethiopian intellectuals and political statesmen will come forth with fresh ideas and arguments to solve that most challenging of human problems, to construct a narrative of the past and a script for the future that gives meaning and direction to the lives of their greater community.

Notes

1 S.N. Eisenstadt, *Comparative Civilizations and Multiple Modernities* (Leiden, Netherlands: Koninklijke Brill, 2003), 75.

2 The World Bank stated in 2013 that over the previous decade, Ethiopia's economy averaged growth of 10.6% per year, compared to the regional average of 4.9%.

3 A recent Oxfam database regarding how well fed the populations of different countries are lists Ethiopia as 123rd out of 125 nations.

4 *Greater Ethiopia: The Evolution of a Multiethnic Society* (Chicago, IL: University of Chicago Press, 2000 [1974]).

5 Bahru Zewde, *Pioneers Of Change In Ethiopia: Reformist Intellectuals of the Early Twentieth Century* (Eastern African Studies) (Athens, OH: Ohio University Press, 2002).

6 England was mainly responsible for ousting the invaders from Fascist Italy, with whom Japan became aligned in the Axis.

7 Donald Donham, *Marxist Modern: An Ethnographic History of the Ethiopian Revolution* (Berkeley, CA: University of California Press, 1999).

8 In the 1990s, the book attained some notice in Ethiopian public discourse, and two Ethiopians labored long and hard to produce a translation of it into Ethiopia's national language Amharic, *Tiliqua Etyopya* (Addis Ababa University Press, 2001). The primary translator was a distinguished public figure, the late Ato Million Miknik, who earlier had been the first Ethiopian to translate Shakespeare into Amharic. A professional linguist, Professor Hailu Fulass of the University of Maryland, assisted him.

9 For an examination of the plurality of identities embodied in different narratives among the Oromo, see Chapter 18.

Part II

HIGHER EDUCATION AND LITERATURE

IO

On General Education and the Ethiopian University (1961)*

In its *Survey of Higher Education in Ethiopia*, the University of Utah Survey Team has suggested that the attainment of an appropriate balance between specialized and general courses should be a task of high priority in curriculum development at the Haile Selassie I University. The following remarks are intended to support that suggestion, and in particular to call attention to the relevance of a properly constructed progress of general education to the broader goals on the University—sustained progress and national unity. They are further intended to suggest some of the principles which might inform such a progress.

In essence, the case for general education rests upon two fundamental truths. One is that enlightened performance in any field of specialized activity requires a breadth of perspective and flexibility of imagination that are best developed by an education in which the main fields of human knowledge are represented. The other is that a high level of cultured activity in any society depends on the cultivation in its educated classes of a general understanding and sense of responsibility for the main achievements of human civilization.

These two fundamental truths are more relevant than ever today, a time of avid specialization and cultural upheaval, for civilized men in all nations. With respect to the specific situation of contemporary Ethiopia, moreover, a

---

* Prepared as a memorandum for Dr. Harold Bentley, Acting President of Haile Selassie I University, in summer 1961. For more details on that episode, see footnote 1 to Chapter 23.

number of other considerations plead for the development of an appropriate curriculum of general education, mandatory for all undergraduate students at the University.

1. **The need for leadership.** For Ethiopia to participate fully in the general economic and social advances of the twentieth century, she must continue to develop people with technical proficiencies in a variety of fields. As the Chancellor said in his inaugural address, "In all countries of the modern world, special competence is required to deal with the advancement of agriculture, industry, commerce, and the civil service. That competence can be secured only through facilities which are provided in modern universities."

Those who are called on to exercise such competence in Ethiopia today, moreover, find that their skills must be employed in the most creative ways. They must blaze many trails. They must build new institutions. They must mediate, in countless particular encounters, the reconciliation of traditional practice and modern method. The capacity for leadership in such matters requires not only adequate specialized training, but also that broader understanding of work and life which is the aim of general education.

2. **The need for community.** For educated Ethiopians to exert effective leadership, they must be able to work in concert. Several factors have inhibited the solidarity and cooperation among the educated, however. One of these is that the secondary schools have followed such a variety of different patterns. Another is the fact that Ethiopian students who have been educated abroad have studied in so many different countries. Still another, of course, is increased specialization, the contemporary commonplace that practitioners in one field understand so very little of what those in other fields have on their minds.

There is thus no place in the educational system above the primary level where all those who are to become the future leaders of the country learn how to look at things in the light of a common educational background. The need for a common intellectual currency can to some extent be filled by requiring all undergraduates to pursue a minimum program of general education in common, as the Survey Team has recommended.

3. **The need for orientation.** Like the other modernizing societies of Africa and Asia, Ethiopia is beginning to undergo a cultural crisis due to the rapidity with which her traditions are being confronted with modern ideas and aspirations. The outcome tends to be acute disorientation and apathy, precisely among those whose talents are most needed for providing new kinds of orientation for the society. A suitable program of general education can help to provide the intellectual equipment with which the Ethiopian elite can react creatively rather than passively to the present cultural dilemma, and develop a culture that is both modern and Ethiopian.

4. **The need for fulfillment.** The life circumstances of the generation of Ethiopians are likely to be tragic to a high degree. Theirs is, as we just noted, a time of great cultural dislocation. It is also a time of social anachronism in which, as another observer has written, they are "condemned to experience the end of an era." Beyond this, it is bound to be progressively frustrating, since the modern economic aspirations which Ethiopians are coming to hold in increasing numbers, thanks to "the revolution of rising expectations," cannot possibly be satisfied in this century.

And yet modernization need not be exclusively colored by bewilderment and anguish. Many young Ethiopians have found in education the one fine and durable new meaning that the modern world, for all its turmoil, has to offer them. They have gone hungry and cold, as have students in Ethiopian church schools in the past, in order to remain in attendance at government elementary schools. Education could continue to be an important source of gratification in their later years, and for the rest of their lives, if it were possible to promote the appreciation of education as not only a means to progress, power, or a better job, but also as a source of some of man's greatest pleasures and of the joy of self-fulfillment.

In one of its senses, general education is also understood as "liberal education," a process in which one's faculties are cultivated for their own sake, and in which, as Newman expressed it, knowledge is acquired "which is durable, though nothing come of it, as being of itself a treasure." The provision of such liberal education for the students of Haile Selassie I University would help them to enjoy, and not just suffer, the challenging period of their history which lies ahead.

To construct a curriculum of general education that will minister to all these needs is no small task. Such questions as the timing of the general education courses, the degree to which they are to be integrated, the optimum balance between lectures and discussion periods, and between field coverage and concentration on principles and methods can only be resolved reasonably well through thoughtful planning and careful observation in practice. Conversations on these and related questions should be begun as soon as possible among Ethiopian educators and Americans who are experienced in dealing with problems of general education.

As one contribution to the development of the conversations, it is suggested here that the general education curriculum for Haile Selassie I University should be Ethiopian and African in flavor, Western in method, and universal in perspective.

1. **Ethiopian and African in flavor.** This refers to the need for making education relevant to the circumstances and background of the learner. The subject matter should draw to a large extent upon materials and

problems of Ethiopia and Africa. In a variety of fields—geology, botany, zoology, anthropology, economics, literature, music, etc.—materials describing Ethiopian and African phenomena should be selected and developed for the illustration of general concepts, and problems relating to their contemporary status should be included as subjects of analysis.

2. **Western in method.** This refers to the unique status of Western civilization as the matrix in which modern science and intellectual culture have developed. Cognitive standards evolved in Western civilization should be maintained both with regard to the evaluation of materials used in the curriculum and as ideals with which students should be encouraged to identify. To promote this, the need for a certain amount of special attention to the history of Western civilization and the character of Western institutions should be frankly admitted.

3. **Universal in perspective.** This refers to the need for combating the tendency, present in all nations and particularly so in rapidly developing ones, of becoming parochial in outlook as a consequence of efforts to maintain national self-esteem and solidarity. Fortunately, Ethiopia has both a long and proud history as a nation, and a distinguished record of participation in international organizations and commitment to the idea of world community. This should make it relatively easy, as well as highly appropriate, for her university to develop a curriculum that, while authentically Ethiopian and African, can be truly universal in its scope and point of view. This means that it would promote understanding of the international character of science, art, and philosophy; awareness of the dependence of intellectual culture on international communication; and a disposition to regard the experience of man in all times and places as a subject worthy of dispassionate consideration. Thus would the University contribute to the realization of those ideals so closely associated with the name of His Majesty The Chancellor—*Berhan'enna Salam*, Light and Peace.

II

Early Amharic Literature (1961)*

As in Czarist Russia, the encounter of a feudal-monarchical and Oriental Christian culture with the "civilized" West has formed the subject as well as the stimulus for much of contemporary Ethiopian literature. At each stage of its development, a polarization between more modernist and more traditionalist points of view is noticeable. Paralleling the Russian division of Westernizers and Slavophiles, the Ethiopian writers tend to say—by their form of writing if not in open argument—either that Ethiopia can only be saved by adopting the superior civilization of the West, or else that Ethiopia can move ahead only by reviving and cherishing its tradition

Because Ras Tafari (Haile Selassie's name before Coronation) sought to employ the new resource of printing as a means of educating the public, many of the titles published during the first period are simply instructional. The traditional culture was taught by translations and commentaries on Ge'ez texts, such as the teachings of St. John Chrysostom and the much-loved *Praises of Mary*, and the compilations of verses from the oral tradition. In the modernist vein there were tracts on subjects like Agriculture, Arithmetic, and Hygiene.

Yet there was creative literature too, and already in this first generation of Amharic authors two figures of some stature and individuality came to light—Heruy Wolde Selassie, a Shoan literatus who became director of the first printing press in Ethiopia, and Afeworq Gabre Yesus, a talented writer from Gojjam who spent many years abroad and first published in Italy. The achievement of these

* Originally presented to the Committee for the Comparative Study of New Nations at The University of Chicago on November 6, 1961. Previously unpublished.

two men was to provide new forms for the hallowed subject matter of Abyssinian writing, royal chronicles and religious examples.

In Heruy's short history of Yohannis IV and above all in Afeworq's *Life of Menelik II*, the dreary recitations of the traditional chronicles were replaced by a rich and colorful genre. Heruy and others also began to use European sources to assist the writing of longer histories, an effort that has been continued by others in the post-Liberation period. (Be it noted, however, that the conscientious examination of Ethiopian sources by an Ethiopian is a job that remains to be done.)

It was somewhat more of a departure to present religious themes in new literary forms, but the way had been prepared by the publication of *The Pilgrim's Progress* in Amharic by the Swedish Mission in Eritrea. Concerning the relevance of this—"...the first considerable work of European literature, apart from the Bible, to be translated into Amharic"—Stephen Wright has written:

> Bunyan's style and argument alike could not fail to make a strong appeal to the Ethiopian mind which...tending to regard art & religion as handmaids of religion, delights in parables and in stories of spiritual struggle typified by material trials. One of the most popular types of Ge'ez literature has always been the *gadl*, stories of the "strivings"—against temptations, persecutions, and so forth—of individual saints, the prose narrative being usually followed by a poem relevant to the subject. Bunyan's religious fantasy therefore pointed the way to an Amharic literary form at once original and imbued with elements deeply rooted in Ethiopian traditions. Consciously or unconsciously several authors have followed this indication.[1]

Both Heruy and Afeworq wrote allegories, and thereby established models which succeeding Ethiopian writers were to repeat *ad nauseum*. Indeed, the original title of Afeworq's novel *Tobia* has become the generic expression for Ethiopian fiction of any sort: *Libb Wallad Tarik*, or *Story Born of the Heart*, where "heart" is used in the Abyssinian sense as indicating the seat of the mental faculties. It is in this genre that Heruy and Afeworq's differential commitment to Abyssinian and Western culture become most apparent. The difference is manifest, not in any substantive disagreement, but in the manner in which they proceed.

Heruy's writing shows the marks of a well-schooled *debtera*. It abounds with allusions to Scripture, and runs in the figures and mannerisms of the traditional learning, even when he is presenting modern ideas to his countrymen. Abyssinian throughout, his tone is reserved, his outlook passive and fatalistic. For him the Western allegory, with its aura of mystery and ambiguity, provides a suitable new vessel for traditional modes of thinking. Here is part of the opening chapter of Heruy's first allegorical writing, *My Friendly Heart*—a title cast, appropriately enough, in the wax-and-gold form.

In the eighteenth year of my life I Left my family and set forth from home, accompanied only by my friend my heart [i.e., mind].

My idea was to travel about and see this world: East, West, North, and South. [In his preface Heruy explains that "East means the New Testament; West means the Old Testament; North means the Writings of the Doctors; South means Fiction; the world means the Books altogether."]

For my travels in the East I had a guide; for half my journey in the West I had a guide. But in the North and the South I was alone. That friend of mine my heart followed me carrying my provisions. Yet he sometimes left me and went along.

Shortly before arriving at a place called Investigation I came upon a tree. The shade of the tree was extremely pleasant. Many sorts of creatures were resting together in the shade: men, animals, wild beasts, and fowls. And I rested a short while in the shade. Psalm 145: 1–21.

As I rose from there that road guide approached me and asked: "Do you know the name of this tree?"

"O, my lord! The likes of this tree I have never seen, and I do not know its name," I said.

"Well, then, let me tell you," he said to me. "This tree is called God. But there is no man who knows the time of its blooming. And thus it was in the time of our fathers." …

I was greatly astonished, and what astonished me was this matter of its name. The names of the common and very well-known trees are: *Tenqway*, Maligner, Cynic, *Zar*, Pretending Nazarene, Pretending Hermit, Devil's Advocate, and Fortune Teller. The most beautiful and attractive of these, for the time being, is *Tenqway*. But its fruit is very bitter. A man who has tasted of its fruit will not find everlasting life.

After I had risen from under the tree and gone a long way, I stood in the East and turned around; and behold! That tree which I had seen appeared as three. Matthew 28: 19. Quickly I went around to the West. As I stood there and looked, it absolutely appeared as one. But when I brought out my glasses and looked again, bit by bit it appeared as three. Zeph. 1: 27.

…After a while I found some men who had come from the North: John Chrysostom; Cyril; Athanasius; and Gregory. I questioned them about the tree. They at once took me to their sitting room, named Explanation, and talked with me at length. In conclusion they said to me: "There is no one who has managed to penetrate this question of the tree. And you, do you not strive, saying 'I will study it and find out.' We, too, labored hard investigating this matter of the tree. But we saw only what you have seen and nothing else."[2]

This passage shows how readily Bunyanesque symbolism fits into Abyssinian thought patterns. There is a modernist touch in the implied criticism of old superstitions like those of the *tenqway* and *zar*; but the dominant note is the quiet Abyssinian fatalism about the futility of too much inquiry by man.

In Afeworq, on the other hand, we find a more ebullient spirit, whose Europeanization had gone deep enough to spur him to wholly new methods of writing. In *Tobia*, his only published work of fiction and the first Ethiopian novel, his aims are archaic: to create an apologetic myth of origin for Ethiopia, and to demonstrate that Christian fidelity is ultimately rewarded. But in doing so, the Afeworq succeeds in using the Amharic language for the first time in a truly lyrical way. His use of Christian allegory recalls the use of Crucifixion scenes by Renaissance painters, as an occasion for freely working with aesthetic materials.

Not the least of Afeworq's innovations was his inclusion of a romantic love motif in *Tobia*, albeit a somewhat muffled one—the heroine appears dressed as a young man most of the time. Eventually, however, we are treated to a striking description of her loveliness. Elsewhere, Afeworq's daring extends to the very un-Abyssinian use of erotic imagery, as in the passage, "The boundaries of earth were joined like lips of love."

The following excerpt from *Tobia* illustrates Afeworq's novel method of dealing with Abyssinian life in literature. The heroine's brother, Wahid, is seeking a job at the camp of a wealthy merchant:

> The butler noticed Wahid's style of dress, gentility, and manner of speaking, and he was an unlikely prospect; still, he must do his duty as butler by all comers; since he could not refuse to inform his master and since he knew of the master's need for loaders, he went in against his will and told him: "A fine young man asking to be a loader has come." On hearing that a fine young man had come, the master assailed the butler: "You tell me that a fine young man has come; have you ever seen me looking for a sickly one? Of sick ones I have more than enough in my own household!" With that he ran off ahead of the butler to find that young man. The butler was about to say, "But by 'fine young man' I mean to say one who doesn't appear suited for heavy work," but the master gave him no time and continued his steps. With the first words still hanging in his mouth the butler followed after.
>
> When the master reached the edge of the tent and looked every which way, there was no one other than a splendid youth, Wahid—no one suited for the work of tending pack animals. Then he turned to the guard and asked: "Where is the man who has come for loading?" Before the guard could answer Wahid raised his hand and said: "My lord, it is I; if you please, I have come to be your follower and your pack attendant; please grant it to me." The master looked Wahid over from the nails of his feet

> to the hair of his head; astonished, he began to mutter, "Indeed! A pack attendant like this! A loader of this sort! What the…" When Wahid saw that his application was being looked down on and that he was not being accepted, he said: "My lord, a lean but alert ox plows better than a fat and lazy one. Likewise, if you do not disapprove of me for my youth, loading will not be hard for me."
>
> When the wealthy merchant heard such words coming from this babe, from Wahid, he began to like his character and asked: "Why should you, the son of a fine man, step out of your rank and seek to do pack work? Your speech is refined, your dress comely; your deeds, your character, everything about you is lordly; how is it that you seek this sort of work for love of money?" Wahid listened quietly; when the master had finished, he said: "My lord, it is not because of greed for money; if you had heard of my grief and my losses you would not have judged against me." The master rose and said: "Well, Wahid, tell me; man judges by seeing the surface of things and cannot know what goes on within; so perhaps I erred unwittingly. Tell me (your story)."[3]

This passage contains a number of Abyssinian moments: the master's verbal aggression against his servant; the double interpretations of words ("fine young man"); the rhetorical use of proverbs; the upper class disdain for manual labor; the imagery of litigations ("Judged against me"); and the assumption that the inner truth is normally not known in interpersonal relations. Yet in this writing Abyssinian formality and studied ambiguity have given way to careful description and quick narrative. The genre is that of the realistic Western novel.

In the post-Liberation period this genre began to be taken for granted, as Western customs were increasingly imitated in many areas of life. It was by means of the novel, in fact, that the conflict between Abyssinian and Western culture was most frankly explored. The decade of the 1940s produced two outstanding novels of this sort: *Inde Wetatch Qeretch*, by Assefa Gabre Maryam, and *Araya*, by Girmatchew Tekla Hawaryat.

The two books have much in common. Their historical setting is the Fascist episode in Ethiopia. Both depict vividly the atrocities committed by the Italians and their Ethiopian mercenaries, and the hardships and heroism of the resistance fighters in the country. Both reveal faithfully and in some depth, the diverse perspectives of a wide variety of character. In both, the district of Tegulet (not far from Menz) alternated with Addis Ababa as the location for most of the action and is idealized as an embodiment of the best in Abyssinian culture.

It is more instructive to note wherein the two authors differ. Assefa, while supporting such importations as Western medicine, implies that Ethiopia's problem is the debasement of Abyssinian virtues through city vices like alcoholism and promiscuity which were encouraged by the advent of the

Italians. Girmatchew, while paying tribute to Abyssinian fortitude and family loyalty, urges that only a rapid replacement of old custom by Western know-how can save Ethiopia in the modern era.

The title of Assefa's book means *As She Went Forth She Remained.* That is, the heroine went forth from her rural hamlet when her husband left for the underground army and the Italians ravaged her country; after becoming the mistress of an Italian officer and later a prostitute in Addis Ababa, she refused to return to her husband and Abyssinian rural life following the Liberation. Her ending was tragic—death from illnesses due to alcoholism. That Ethiopia's ending will be tragic, too, if she takes the fatal step away from Abyssinian virtue, is the broader implication of the novel.

Assefa's traditionalism is reflected in the construction of *Inde Wetatch Qeretch.* The story is somewhat awkwardly put together; the author uses the Western novel, but is not yet fully at home in it. On the other hand the book is considerably enriched by a number of examples of the old oral genre: *shilela* war verse, rounds of poetic insults, and verses of mourning. At times, moreover, the Amharic prose rises to inspired eloquence, as in the following passage:

> "We Ethiopians have honored the laws of our religion and are proud to have observed them faithfully until now...If we do not have the arts of the machine, we do not lack the arts of kinship. This being out art, we bury our mortal neighbors according to the law. Without saying 'there is no gain in it for us', we go to far off places to mourn our dear ones. We honor the Sabbath. If we have, we love to give alms to the poor and to the sick. We receive guests with longing; with the eye of friendship, we accompany the traveler. As we gather to enjoy one another in days of happiness, so we console each other in time of difficulty. All this comprises the good arts found in our own civilization.
>
> One who wears what she herself has spun from her country's cotton, instead of silk cloth that comes from abroad, can be truly proud. Likewise, instead of decking oneself out with a foreign weapon brought from abroad, one can be proud to carry a spear he himself has forged. If we measure in terms of ability, we must give the highest grade of honor to those who fend for themselves."[4]

Araya is the name of the chief protagonist in Girmatchew's novel. The word literally means "example," and our hero is meant to illustrate the problems of one who has studied a long time in the West and come home to help modernize his country. Disturbed by the conservatism and lack of nationalism he finds in Ethiopia after fourteen years in France, Araya becomes frustrated beyond endurance by the meanness of Addis Ababa bureaucracy and retires to cultivate his own farmland. The Italian invasion appears to him as clearer evidence than ever that Ethiopia must hasten its modernization. He returns to government service after the war with the hopeful image of his infant son in mind.

Girmatchew's novel is smoothly constructed. The tone of the book, moreover, is palpably modern. The early chapters, consisting for the most part of conversations with various people whom Araya meets en route home from Paris, airs many of the political and ideological issues of the 1930s with notable intellectual clarity. Later on, the modernist's dilemma is presented with great poignancy, as in the following dialogue between Araya and an Abyssinian elder:

> —It is no more than a week since I returned from France where I went to study.
>
> —So! That is to say that you are a newcomer; by the way, what did you study there?
>
> —Agriculture.
>
> —Agriculture! What sort of education is that? Have we not known this and worked without going anywhere and without being taught by anybody? What sent you to a foreigner's country for this, my boy?
>
> —Agriculture is a broad subject, replied Araya without losing his patience. It is not just a matter of yoking oxen and steering the plow, as you believe. Let me tell you: the difficulty of Agriculture is greater, not less, than many technical subjects.
>
> —My brother, I do not understand all this you say to me. I myself am a farmer. I have a lot of land and know agricultural work through and through; I didn't have to go to school to learn this. In truth, I am astounded to hear you say that you have gone as far as Europe to study Agriculture… Cut it out, please! we have seen that your learning is good for nothing; all you know is to smoke tobacco and wear foreign coats; and to eat a lot (of salary); we have not seen you do anything! You don't even make matches or needle! On top of this, your pride is boundless! God save us![5]

From the mouths of younger men, too, comes a cry against the spoiled youth. It is one of the themes of Mengistu Lemma and Tadesse Liban, writers of the 1950 decade, both of whom have satirized the haughtiness and exaggerated worldliness of Western-educated Ethiopians. Here again, two points of view may be discerned. Tadesse's objections are more sentimental. In his story "Spoiled Fruit," a girl who returns from eight years abroad grieves her devoted mother by her estrangement, staying at a hotel instead of at home and wiping the spittle from her face with a handkerchief after her mother kisses her. The implied criticism stems from an identification with the traditional order. Mengistu, on the other hand, criticizes the Western-educated more in their own terms, suggesting that their vain and materialistic behavior represents an imperfect attainment of the higher ideals of Western civilization, and that their estrangement from old customs like hospitality and from the rural Abyssinian setting represents an impoverishment of their own spiritual life.

These two young authors are of interest for other reasons. They are in the forefront of the post-Liberation effort to introduce new literary forms. Amharic verse drama, for example, became fairly successful during this period, in productions like Girmatchew's *Tewodros*, Makonnen Endalkatchew's *The Voice of Blood*, and the polished works of Kebbede Mikael, Tadesse Liban and Mengistu Lemma were self-conscious pioneers who introduced, respectively, the Amharic short story and modern lyrical poems.[6]

More importantly still, these two writers, despite the contrast mentioned above, have in a sense transcended the traditionalist-modernist conflict. They have managed to tone down the partisan moralizing of so many earlier writings and, in subject matter as in style, to synthesize elements from both Abyssinian and Western traditions to good effect.

Tadesse is interested in seeing just what happens in this situation of culture conflict; what happens, for example, when an old-fashioned mother warns her son, a high school student, that a girl for whom he has a crush turns into a hyena at night? His feel for traditional modes of thinking and turns of phrase is complemented by a very Westernized style, featuring short declarative sentences and (sometimes questionable) rendering of English expressions in Amharic.

Mengistu has internalized the conflict, and thereby uses both Abyssinian and Western perspectives as ways of poking fun at each other. His style, moreover, represents a fascinating synthesis. Though he makes use of Western techniques of manipulating verse and stanza combinations, his most effective tools are Abyssinian ambiguity and plays on words. In one poem, for example, he talks about the way Abyssinian clothes are made without pockets while Western clothes have all manner of pockets; but the Amharic word for pockets is *kiss*, and the "golden" meaning of the poem is the absence of romantic kissing in Abyssinian custom.[7]

Thus, moving from the subtly contrasting approaches of Heruy Wolde Selassie and Afeworq Gabre Yesus, to the more explicitly tensioned post-Liberation works of Assefa Gabre Maryam and Girmatchew Tekla Hawaryat, to the uniquely synthesizing novels of Mengistu Lemma and Tadesse Liban in the 1950s, we discern a sequence of three distinct perspectives on the encounter between traditional culture and processes of modernization in Ethiopia today.

Notes

1 Stephen Wright, "Literature and the Fine Arts," in Talbot, *Haile Selassie I Silver Jubilee* (The Hague: Van Stockum & Zoon, 1955).

2 *Wedaje Libe* (Addis Ababa: Berhan'na Salam Press, 1923), pp. 6–10.

3 Afeworq also wrote two novels which were never published.

4 *Tobia* (Addis Ababa: Cooperative Education Press, 1958), pp. 4–5.

5 *Inde Wetatch Qeretch* (Addis Ababa: 1954 [written in 1949]), p. 125.

6 *Araya* (Asmaria: Silla Pietro, 1950), pp. 100–101.

7 Tadesse Liban, *Maskram* (Addis Ababa: Artistic Printing Press). Mengistu Lemma, *Ye-gitim Guba'e* (Addis Ababa: mimeographed, 1957–1958).

12

Wax-and-Gold Poetry (1965)*

The Amhara as a whole are not much given to aesthetic concerns. They are practical-minded peasants, austere religionists, and spirited warriors. Their interests and achievements as a nation are chiefly in the spheres of military activity and government. And yet, if we seek some theme with which to gain an entree into the spirit of their society and culture, we will do well to attend to the sphere of poetry. For it is a poetic phenomenon which constitutes both a key to the genius of Amhara culture and a highly distinctive Amhara contribution to Ethiopian culture.

Säm-enna-wärq ("wax and gold") is the formula used by the Amhara to symbolize their favorite form of verse. It is a form built of two semantic layers. The apparent, figurative meaning of the words is called "wax"; their more or less hidden actual significance is the "gold."

In its generic sense, the expression *säm-enna-wärq* refers to a number of poetic figures which embody this twofold meaning. The use of such figures distinguishes the Amhara equivalent of true poetry from ordinary verse, in which everyday language is merely embellished with rhyme and rhythm. In the genre known as *qenē*, the original and more elegant kind of *säm-enna-wärq* poetry, the lines are composed in Ge'ez and depend primarily on religious symbolism. But *säm-enna-wärq* constructions also appear in some types of secular verse in the vernacular Amharic and, indeed, at times inform Amharic conversation.

---

* Originally published as part of Chapter 1 "Introduction: Amhara Tradition and Ethiopia's Modernization" in *Wax and Gold: Tradition and Innovation in Ethiopian Culture* (Chicago, IL: University of Chicago Press, 1965), 5–10.

Masters of the art of *qenē* composition have analyzed these poetic figures into about a dozen different types.[1] *Säm-enna-wärq* in its more specific sense refers to one of these types of figures—the prototype of them all. It consists of an explicit comparison in which the subjects being compared—the wax and gold—are presented in apposition, while their predicates are rendered jointly by a single verb which carries both a wax and a gold meaning. (This terminology is derived from the work of the goldsmith, who constructs a clay mold around a form created in wax and then, draining the wax, pours the molten gold into that form.) So, for example, if the poet's aim is to praise a hero like Emperor Menelik, he creates a wax model, like "the lion," in terms of whose actions the gold, Menelik, is depicted: "The lion Menelik crushed the wolf Italy."[2]

Keeping this dual imagery consistent throughout the stanza is a primary rule of wax-and-gold composition. A poet who mixes his metaphors is sometimes rebuked with the epithet "hermaphrodite." The following example presents an Amharic couplet which properly embodies the *säm-enna-wärq* figure:

> *Etsa balas balto addām kanfareshe*
>
> *Madhānē alam lebē tasaqala-leshe.*

> Since Adam your lip did eat of that Tree
>
> The Savior my heart has been hung up for thee.

In this couplet the wax of Adam's sin and Christ's crucifixion in his behalf has been used as a form in which to pour a love message. A literal translation of the wax of the couplet is:

> Because Adam ate of the apple of the Tree of Knowledge
>
> The Savior of the World has been crucified for thee.

To savor the gold of the couplet fully, one must know that the verb meaning "was crucified," *tasaqala*, may also signify "is anxious to be near." So a literal translation of the gold would be:

> Because of your [tempting] lips
>
> My heart is anxious to be near thee.

In other more commonly used figures, the duplicity of the message becomes less explicit. In figures known as *hiber* and *merimer*, the wax and gold are combined in the same word or phrase instead of being put side by side. These figures thus correspond to the English pun. In verses which employ these figures the wax is often but a contrived and transparent excuse for getting to the real point, which appears only in the pun line. Such verses are highly prized, however, for the Amhara tends to regard the pun as a very high form of humor. Here are two examples of Amharic couplets based on simple puns:

(1) Ya-min tiqem tallā ya-min tiqem tajji

Tallat sishañu bunā adargaw enji.

Of what use is tallā, of what use is tajji?

When seeing an enemy off, serve him coffee.

(2) Yābbāt eddā la-lijj yebāl nabar dero:

Bāyāt eddā gabāhu ennē-mā zandero.

In olden times a father's debt was passed down to his son;

But here I have a debt today by grandfather begun.

The pun in the first example lies in the phrase *bunā adargaw* ("serve him coffee"), which by elision becomes *bun adargaw* ("reduce him to ashes"). In the second couplet the pun hinges on the word *bāyat*, which signifies "grandfather" but may also be understood to represent *bāyhuāt* ("because I saw her"). The gold meaning of this couplet is thus: It used to be said that one inherited the debt of one's father, but in my case it was the sight of her that put me into debt.

Ethiopic verse becomes most obscure in the figure known as *westa wayrā* ("inside of olive tree"). Here only the wax is given, and the listener must work to unearth the gold. Often this can be done only when the circumstances under which the verse was made up are known. The author of a *westa wayrā* often refuses to reveal anything that may help the listener to grasp its hidden meaning.

The expression *westa wayrā* alludes to the fact that the inner core of the olive tree is a hard substance encased by bark of a different color. The implication is that the inner sense of a *westa wayā* poem is concealed by a veneer which conveys a quite different sense and is difficult to penetrate. This figure is thus especially suitable for expressing insults in a safe way and for esoteric philosophical or religious messages. Here is an instance of the latter usage:

Ya-bāhetāwi lijj sifalleg le'ullennā

Ya-kristosn mesht talānt washama-nnā

Qetal betābalaw hono qarama-nnā.

The son of a hermit, high rank to display,

Made love with Christ's wife yesterday;

When she fed him leaves he wasted away

The surface meaning of this tercet describes an ambitious man who had relations with "Christ's wife" in order to raise his status, for in Ethiopia having relations with a woman of high rank is one way to gain prestige. Instead of advancing his position, however, this man lost all his power when the woman fed him (medicinal) leaves. The esoteric meaning, on the other hand, refers to the experience of a hermit. His "son" is intended to symbolize his hunger, and "Christ's wife" symbolizes fasting. The "inside" meaning, the gold, is therefore that the hermit's hunger is heightened by its relations with fasting, but it diminishes when he is fed leaves, the hallowed diet of a hermit.

The mode of the various poetic figures collectively designated as *säm-enna-wärq* is intellectual rather than sensuous. The chief delight of Ethiopic poetry is to attain a maximum of thought with a minimum of words. This effect is reached, as we have seen, through subtle allusions and plays on words. The point may be a serious moral comment, the understanding of which requires one to decipher hidden references to biblical passages or sacred legends; or it may be a jest about love based on a pornographic pun. In any case, the more ingeniously compact and obscure the construction of the verse, the more pleased will be the poet and his audience. Weighty (i.e., mysterious) verse is the ideal, for as the Amhara say, "weighty verse, like heavy clothing, warms the insides."

The creation of the wax and gold figures was an integral part of the development of *qenē*, the genre of verse composed to be sung at the conclusion of devotional services in the church. And *qenē* appears to be a specifically Amhara invention. Though exact documentation is not available on the matter, *qenē* appears to be one of the flowers of the literary renascence which took place during the centuries following the ascendance of the Solomonid Dynasty. The earliest specimens of *qenē* extant date back to the reign of Emperor Eskender (1478–94).[3] Ethiopian traditions trace the invention of *qenē* to the work of a man named Tāwanay, who is said to have lived in Gojjam in the fourteenth century.[4] The important schools of *qenē* have always been located in Amhara country, primarily at the monasteries of Wādelā in Lasta and Wāsharā and Gonj in Gojjam. While the choristers of Tigre have long since mastered the canons of *qenē* composition in Ge'ez, the use of wax and gold in the vernacular occurs much more often in Amharic than in Tigrinya. Indeed, wax and gold is so important in Amharic that some Amhara maintain that one does not properly speak the language unless he is well versed in the art of exploiting its numerous ambiguities. One of the more common indictments of Tigre character by Amhara is that the Tigre are "dry" (*daraq*); they say just what they feel and do not know how to be ambiguous. Conversely, many Tigre as well as other non-Amhara people in the empire complain about the excess of symbolism and subtlety in Amhara discourse.

Educated Amhara traditionalists extol wax and gold as a unique creation of their culture. One of them has written that *qenē* is as distinctive of Ethiopia's spiritual culture as *teff*, a species of grass grown as a cereal grain only in Ethiopia, is distinctive of her material culture.[5] They further maintain that Ge'ez *qenē* contains a unique kind of wisdom, dark and deep. Instruction in this occult art of verse composition has traditionally been regarded as propaedeutic to the study of religious texts. Partly this is because Ge'ez grammar, which must be known in order to understand these texts, is normally taught only in the schools of *qenē*. The more philosophical reason given, however, is that by affording exercise in fathoming secrets it "opens the mind" and thereby enhances the student's ability to approach the divine mysteries.

Important as such functions may be in the high culture of Ethiopia, wax and gold represents more than a principle of poetic composition and a method of spiritual gymnastics for a small class of literati. The ambiguity symbolized by the formula *Säm-enna-wärq* colors the entire fabric of traditional Amhara life. It patterns the speech and outlook of every Amhara. When he talks, his words often carry double-entendre as a matter of course; when he listens, he is ever on the lookout for latent meanings and hidden motives. As one of my Ethiopian colleagues has said: "Wax and gold is anything but a formula—it is a way of life."

In essence, wax and gold is simply a more refined and stylized manifestation of the Amhara's basic manner of communicating. This manner is indirect, often secretive. Amharic conversation is larded with vague remarks like *Min yeshāllāl?* ("What is better?") when the speaker has failed to indicate what is the issue at hand, or *Tādyās!*, an interjection which can mean almost anything. Often, when the speaker is then quizzed about the issue at hand, he will give an answer that does not reveal what is really on his mind at all, and even when he does, the person with whom he is talking is likely to interpret his response as a disguise.

Wax and gold embodies this fundamental indirection in speech by means of the studied use of ambiguity. Apart from its literary and religious manifestations, wax and gold appears in the common life of the traditional Amhara on a variety of occasions and serves a number of diverse functions

It provides the medium for an inexhaustible supply of humor, among a wry people who prefer the clever, double-edged remark to comic actions or incongruous situations. This includes the wit of daily life—the invention of puns and sly retorts, the telling and retelling of good anecdotes and famous lines—as well as the more formalized humor on festive occasions, where minstrels sing the *säm-enna-wärq* verses extemporized by the guests.

It provides a means for insulting one's fellows in a socially approved manner, in a culture which requires fastidious etiquette in social relations and punishes direct insults by heavy fines. *Säm-enna-wärq* insulting, too, has its more stylized expressions, as at the drink-house, where one may find persons competing in a prolonged exchange of more or less disguised insults, or in time of political or military conflict, when opposing lords were wont formerly to satirize one another with ambiguous couplets.

It provides a technique for defending the sphere of privacy against excessive intrusion, in a social order that thrives on rumor and gossip and puts most of its people at the mercy of superiors. While vague and evasive responses often suffice to dampen the enthusiasm of the tax collector or the curious neighbor, *säm-enna-wärq* constitutes another potent weapon of self-defense.

Finally, it provides the one outlet for criticism of authority figures in a society which strictly controls every kind of overt aggression toward authority, be it parental, religious, or political. Thus it has been a safety valve for certain social tensions, enabling, for example, witty individuals to satirize the monarch himself and still live to repeat the witticism—so long as its subject was himself duly appreciative of the cleverness of the lines.

Notes

1. Cf. Abbā Yā'qob Gabra Iyasus, *Matsehāfa Sawāsew Za-Ge'ez* (Asmara: Tipografia Francescana, 1920 E.C.*), pp. 288 ff.; Mars'ē Hāzan Walda Qirqos, *Yāmāriññā Sawāsew* (Addis Ababa: Artistic Press, 1948 E.C.), pp. 215–18; Alamāyhu Mogas, *Malkf'a Ityopyā* (Asmara: Kokaba Tsebāh Press, 1952 E.C.), pp. 10 ff. For an introduction to the European literature on *qenē*, cf. M. M. Moreno, *Raccolta di Qenē* (Rome: Tipografia del Senato, 1935); also Enrico Cerulli, *Storia della letteratura etiopica* (Milan: Nuova Accademia Editrice, 1956), pp. 154–56, 226–32.
2. Alamāyhu Mogas, op. cit., p. 12.
3. Cerulli, op. cit., p. 154.
4. Alamāyhu Mogas, *Sawāsew Ge'ez* (Addis Ababa: Tasfā Press, 1950 E.C.), p.117.
5. Alamāyhu Mogas, *Malk'a Ityopyā*, op. cit., p. 7.

13

Is Ethiopia Cutting Off Its Head Again? (1993) *

On a recent visit I asked a young Aksumite where he lived during the past decade. "Oh, I've been here in Aksum the whole time," he said, "under the Derg, during the time of freedom, and under the EPRDF."

In contrasting the EPRDF regime with the time of freedom, my Aksumite friend seemed to be saying what I have heard so often this past year. Even so it was startling to hear it right in the heart of Tigray! To him and to all who doubt that at least some elements of EPRDF are struggling to bring democracy to Ethiopia, I say: What about all the EPRDF fighters who gave their lives to liberate Ethiopia from the Derg? What about President Meles's expressed commitment to democratic process and to the rule of law? And what about the fact that Addis Ababa (if not the provinces) now supports dozens of new magazines and newspapers—not to mention the fact that criminal gangs no longer intimidate the capital and that low-level warfare no longer afflicts the countryside as it did only a year ago?

In spite of such facts, the perception still reigns that the EPRDF regime, as one Ethiopian puts it, "came to power through armed struggle and unfortunately it also wants to rule at the point of a gun." Perhaps nothing in recent months has given so much new life to this perception as the abrupt dismissal of more than forty faculty from Addis Ababa University. And perhaps nothing offers the EPRDF regime a better chance to show its true intentions about democracy and the rule of law than how it now handles the fallout from that action. If

* Published originally in *Ethiopian Review*, August 1993.

it does so honestly and courageously, it may yet offer a new round of hope to Ethiopians who are aching for peace, unity, and democracy in their beautiful but troubled land.

Crisis at the University

After the January 4 student demonstration at Addis Ababa University was suppressed, producing at least 85 hospitalized injuries and a still-unspecified number of fatalities, the University closed down for months. AAU President Alemayehu Teferra and two vice-presidents were detained (Dr. Alemayehu remains in prison as of this writing). Weeks went by; frustration among faculty and students mounted. In mid-March, some good news came—the University would reopen under the presidency of Dr. Duri Mohammed, the highly respected Minister of Planning—and all concerned breathed a sigh of relief.

Dr. Duri had won a reputation as a skillful administrator who helped rescue the University under the Derg. Trained in economics at Berkeley and Toronto, Dr. Duri was pursuing a successful career abroad when Colonel Mengistu asked him to reopen the University in 1975. As president he adhered to norms established during Dr. Aklilu Habte's tenure as president of Haile Selassie I University and quietly buried noxious orders from the Derg. Finding that he could not recruit academically qualified staff from the Soviet bloc, Dr. Duri upgraded faculty by training Ethiopian staff. He protected a number of colleagues from efforts to dismiss them on ideological grounds. Against Mengistu's wishes he supported elements of a graduate studies program through camouflaged budget lines. When the 1984 order for University personnel to wear khaki uniforms proved too much even for Dr. Duri, he went to the Economic Commission for Africa. As Minister of Planning, Dr. Duri is again positioned to help the University. In person he voices a commitment to the principle of academic freedom and a determination to provide the resources to make the University an internationally recognized center of academic excellence.

Thus it was an enormous shock to everyone when, a few weeks after the University reopened, Dr. Duri became the instrument of an action that threw it into a crisis from which it has not yet recovered. On Friday, April 9, AAU faculty received a letter of dubious legality requiring them to submit contract renewal letters by the following Monday. Far worse, forty members of the faculty received a different letter. Bearing Dr. Duri's stenciled signature, it informed them that they were summarily fired and must vacate their offices within three days. The community was stunned. Remaining faculty now find it hard to look Dr. Duri in the face. He no longer frequents his University office, conducting University business from the Ministry of Planning instead.

How EPRDF Justified the Dismissal Action

The decision to issue the dismissal orders was apparently favored at the highest levels of the Transitional Government. Reversing the promising development of the autumn semester when the University was drafting a charter that would have guaranteed it autonomy—a development which led people to hope that the gulf between regime and populace was finally being overcome—the TGE intervened with a heavy hand, replacing independents and academics on the University Board with political appointees and demanding the new faculty contracts. This enabled President Meles to say, in an ill-considered remark to a British journalist, that as employer of the faculty, he could fire anyone he wanted, even if it turned on a dislike of the color of their eyes.

The government's official explanation of the dismissal action depicted it as part of an aggressive campaign to upgrade academic standards. President Meles and others had become distressed by the poor quality of student work there compared to the way students performed prior to the Derg. That explanation raises more questions than it answers. Predictably, the dismissals lowered rather than raised the level of academic performance. Courses had to be suspended for lack of teachers. Student research projects were interrupted. Examinations had to be administered by people who had not taught the courses. An international conference on ethnic relations for which some forty scholars had prepared papers was abruptly canceled. Anxiety and frustration infected the academic atmosphere.

The government's action would have damaged the University even if the faculty in question were redundant and incompetent, but this was clearly not the case. Essential and not easily replaceable faculty were dismissed, including experienced faculty in engineering, medicine, economics, international relations, and linguistics—indeed, five of the University's only eleven full professors. The dismissees included Dr. Tamire Hawando, the University's only soil scientist; Dr. Admassu Gebeyehu, its only specialist in water resources; Ato Ayele Tarekegn, its only trained archaeologist; Dr. Makonnen Bishaw, its only medical anthropologist; and Dr. Taddesse Beyene, who managed the Permanent Secretariat for the International Conference on Ethiopian Studies.

What is more, most of these faculty held respected credentials in the academic world. To cite one case in point: on the dismissal of Professor Ayenew Ejigou, head of AAU's Statistics Department, the American Statistical Association issued a statement affirming that Professor Ejigou "has an international reputation as an outstanding scholar, based on his work on the relative risk of multiple matching, which has been a credit to Addis Ababa University." And the work of most of these reputable Ethiopian scholars was accomplished under the difficult conditions of the Derg period, when library holdings were impoverished and communications with Western countries impeded. Although the dismissed faculty had generally been critical of the Derg—and could, like so many others, have left the country to pursue their careers abroad—most chose to remain at the University to make their contributions at home during those trying years. Those who had left the country came home to serve their country at lower salaries than they were earning abroad.

Instead of improving AAU's academic quality, then, dismissing these Ethiopian faculty patently worsened it. No less disruptive was the procedure by which they were dismissed. Unbelievably, no deans or department chairs were consulted to evaluate them. The breach of contracts involved in the immediate dismissals violated the Higher Education Institutions Administration Proclamation (No. 109/1977) as well as a number of established University policies regarding contracts.

Actions against the faculty in question went well beyond breach of contract. Some have been stopped on the street, bodily searched, and otherwise harassed by armed and uniformed EPRDF soldiers. All have been denied rights of Ethiopian citizens by not being permitted to set foot on university grounds: newly installed campus police check the ID cards of all staff against the list of dismissed professors and turn away the latter at all University campuses. A few who somehow did enter in order to comply with the clearance instructions were temporarily detained and humiliated in front of their former students and colleagues. In some instances NGO's who sought to employ them have reportedly been questioned by security police. The Government also refused them permission to meet at the Chamber of Commerce hall to discuss a plan to form an educational and consultancy private enterprise.

The claim to be upgrading academic standards thus falls flat on its face. To their credit, none of the Government officials tried to justify the precipitous dismissals on anything other than political grounds. Dr. Duri maintains that the dismissed faculty were urging students to mobilize for political protest rather than attend classes. Another former AAU professor, Council of Representatives Vice President Fekadu Gedamu, maintains that riotous student demonstrations were imminent in a situation so precarious that the country could not tolerate them, and that the faculty in question were perceived as having incited students to riot.

None of these allegations has been substantiated with publicly available evidence. All evidence I have seen supports the notion that the dismissed faculty were exceptionally hard-working and conscientious. Even after dismissal some of them volunteered to help their remaining colleagues grade the heavy load of examinations. I have found no evidence of faculty dismissing classes or inciting students. Indeed, the only turbulent student behavior occurred after the faculty dismissals—a reaction to the dismissals and to continuing repressive action against students. What is more, well after the original dismissals and all hint of student unrest, on June 1 yet another faculty member was sacked (Fesseha Zewde of the History Department), thereby heightening the level of campus insecurity. One is left to wonder why this often pragmatic regime undertook such an egregiously self-defeating action.

Why They Did It

The most obvious explanation for the action taken against the faculty was that the Government acted out of excessive anxiety about possible demonstrations connected with the referendum in Eritrea in late April. Yet the character of the regime's intervention cannot be understood without considering how relations between the University community and the TGE had become polarized since the time of the Charter conference two years before.

In the face of determined efforts by the Transitional Government not merely to respect different ethnic groups but to divide Ethiopia up administratively and politically along ethnic lines, the University faculty and students constituted a conspicuous source of support for the unity of Ethiopia as a multiethnic society. President Meles and his colleagues have been keenly aware that some of these faculty members opposed what they consider his ethnically divisive initiatives as well as other measures, including the hasty implementation of a radical new plan to use local languages in elementary schools, and the resistance to opening up certain economic sectors to free enterprise. They are also aware that these faculty regard some of the changes introduced by the Transitional Government as illegitimate, since the charge of the transitional regime was not to implement new policies for the country but to prepare the way for a democratic constitution, and like so many Ethiopians they have questioned the legitimacy of redrawing provincial boundaries by the transitional regime.

What is more, the dismissed faculty are people of independent thought and character, men (and one woman) whose views cannot be bought. Whatever their substantive views, their independence of mind rankles some officials. Thus Dr. Befekadu Degefe, a dismissed professor of economics who was critical of the Derg and imprisoned by them, observes wryly that the same people who gave him trouble and labeled him anti-revolutionary under the Mengistu regime accuse him now of being against the Charter and against peace.

In return, President Meles feels that the University community has not sufficiently appreciated the sacrifices that he and his comrades have made for the country. Instead of staying at the University to complete his education as most Ethiopian students did, Meles left after his sophomore year and lived for the next decade-and-a-half under bitter conditions. He saw a great number of his friends killed in battle. Thus, while the dismissed faculty have resented Meles and his TPLF comrades for imposing their minority views on the country, he has resented them not only for resisting what he considers beneficial policies but for having sat out the Derg period in relative comfort at the University while the freedom-fighters were suffering in the field. President Meles doubtless senses that if he set foot on campus he would be greeted with disdain by the students, a bitter pill for a former student activist who has sacrificed much to benefit his countrymen—including those who now oppose him. Thus, hurt feelings on both sides have led to the polarization of the past two years, which was exacerbated by resentments and perhaps shame over the brutal attacks against students outside and even inside the university campus in January.

What It Signifies

Whatever complex of motives led to the dismissal of the 41 professors, that action has struck American and European observers as well as most Ethiopians with whom I've talked as reckless and destructive. The action violated established laws and the common norms of academic institutions. It inflicted much harm on the University and the country. It deprived the University of the contributions of many qualified and devoted teachers, and has prompted the best of the remaining faculty to have second thoughts about tying their futures to so precarious an institution. Foreign academics have been disgusted and discouraged from making future contributions, whereas much of the University's strength and attractiveness derives from its links with foreign universities, research institutes, and funding agencies. Secondary school students have also been demoralized. The word going around Addis Ababa now is: not to worry about the School Leaving Exams; why go to such a decimated university anyway?

On the harm to the country, let me quote some lines with which I concluded *Wax and Gold* nearly three decades ago: "The fate of Ethiopia one and two generations hence is linked more closely than members of large, industrialized societies can readily appreciate with a single small institution: the Haile Selassie I University." I stressed then that Ethiopia's university needed the benefits of "autonomy and insulation that can but further the patient development of Ethiopia's more sorely needed asset: cadres of individuals who can resist the facile slogans of the day and work to provide for Ethiopia's great transformation the benefits of enlightened aims and realistic practices." Although as an academic myself I could be accused of exaggerating the significance of an independent university, I still think a first-rate university can bring Ethiopia enormous benefits. Beside training badly-needed specialists in fields like engineering, medicine, law, and education, a first-rate university provides a protected space where fundamental questions can be examined in a disciplined and searching manner, thereby illuminating current problems and options and offering models of how to conduct debate constructively and with mutual respect.

A first-rate university is a delicate organism. It requires much care and sensitive handling. Faculty need to make long-term commitments and to feel secure about the future of their investments, just as peasants and businessmen need to feel secure about the harvest of their labors. The principle of academic autonomy is essential to ensure this. When Ethiopia's first university was being founded, this principle was put to test early on. In May 1961 I published an article critical of the regime of Emperor Haile Selassie just as the university was being founded. Although the emperor was furious about my article and even asked if the American government could put me in prison for writing it, he became persuaded by the Acting President, Dr. Harold Bentley, that an appointment for me under those circumstances would symbolize loud and clear his regime's commitment to a university where criticism would be tolerated and intellectual freedom guaranteed. As Chancellor of the new university, he therefore agreed to let university officials draw up a contract for my services. The Emperor also tolerated orderly demonstrations of students between 1964 and 1968.

Similarly, despite efforts to infiltrate the faculty in some departments and the noxious promotion of Marxist-Leninist ideology as official doctrine, the Derg by and large respected the boundaries of the University. Views critical of Derg policies got aired in the campus cafeteria. A group of University faculty proposed that the Derg voluntarily give up their power in April 1991 and were not put in jail. As one faculty member put it, "The Derg tried to influence things here and there, but never threatened to fire everybody." The EPRDF intervention thus represents a level of impairment of University autonomy that exceeds what had been practiced under the otherwise more repressive regimes of the Emperor and the Derg.

Even so, the EPRDF is not solely to blame for this sad turn of events.

The fact is that modern Ethiopia has yet to create an intellectual stratum independent from political control, such as existed in traditional Ethiopia with Christian and Jewish monks and Muslim clerics. Although a secular intellectual elite began to form in the early years of Haile Selassie's reign, most Ethiopian intellectuals were wiped out in the brutal retaliation for the attempt on Marshal Graziano's life in 1937. After the War Haile Selassie renewed efforts to bring modern education to the country but frowned on independent intellectual activity. Ethiopian intellectuals of the 1950s and 1960s felt too intimidated to organize significant public intellectual discourse. A modicum of academic freedom did get established in his university, but then Marxist ideologues and the Derg had no patience for intellectual independence.

To this deficit may be added certain features of the traditional culture which affect the quality of political interaction. I refer to the pronounced individualism of Amhara-Tigrean culture and its preference for litigation over dialogue—for casting discourse almost exclusively into a competitive if not combative mode. (*Chiqechiq* is a pretty good word for it!) In this mode it can be said that some faculty and students indulged in provocative behavior toward the EPRDF regime —denying them any shred of legitimacy and blaming them rather than the Derg for Eritrea's secession. Regarding the fateful demonstration in January, it appears that the students refused to apply for formal permission for their demonstration, and hurled ethnic taunts (and, some claim, physical objects) at the police which triggered the breakdown in discipline that led to the savage attacks against them.

The EPRDF shows much ambivalence regarding public criticism. President Meles tolerates critical questions in press conferences that would have been unthinkable under Haile Selassie or Mengistu, and permits a variety of critical newspapers and magazines. But some producers of independent publications continue to be harassed, such as the imprisoned editor of Mestewat magazine. And the one place that should be a haven for independent thought, the University, has been subjected to an array of intimidating tactics, such as expulsion of its student council representatives—including some who suffered torture under the Derg—as well as the faculty dismissal action in April.

The old familiar political culture that prevailed under Emperor Haile Selassie and under the Derg has gotten repeated—cycles of blame and counterblame in an atmosphere of intimidation, distrust, and fear. Since EPRDF has the guns and does not welcome opposing views, it is no wonder that many people are becoming depressed by the situation. In recent testimony before the House Foreign Relations Subcommittee on African Affairs, Marina Ottoway warned that if present trends continue, Ethiopia may "slip back into the pattern of armed opposition and terrorism on one side and brutal government repression on the other that were typical of the Mengistu era."

What Can Be Done About It

Several government officials with whom I spoke believe that dismissal of the University faculty was a mistake and that something should be done to rectify it. Dr. Duri does not rule out the possibility that mistakes were made, and claims to have mandated a committee to review the dismissal actions—although in June I could find no one on the faculty who knew anything about such a committee. Others have suggested that the dismissed faculty should bring a lawsuit against the university, noting that EPRDF has shown respect for independent judicial rulings—although the dismissed faculty have few resources with which to mount such an action and perhaps feel too intimidated by the government to try.

I have confidence in the capacity of Ethiopia's leaders and academics, with or without the assistance of external mediators, to come up with a constructive resolution of this situation if they possess the will to do so. At stake is not merely the careers of a few dozen faculty and the need to redress the severe injustice they have suffered. At stake is not even merely the future morale and quality of the University, important though that is. Rather, failure to rectify this action will tell the world that the EPRDF regime is dug into a policy of repression and, given the hypocrisy attendant on last June's elections, can no longer be given the benefit of more doubt about its commitment to move toward a genuinely open and democratic society under the rule of law. It will be sending a negative signal, loud and clear, both to democratic donor nations and to the tens of thousands of Ethiopian expatriates who still sit watching and waiting, in anxiety and frustration, as to whether they should throw their talents and resources into the rebuilding of Ethiopia or go their own way abroad and forget about it. This will give fuel to those dissidents who maintain that only military action of some sort can succeed in combating the dictatorial tendencies of the transitional regime.

On the other hand, judicious rectification of the faculty dismissal could turn into a signal of hope. It could indicate, not that the Transitional Government doesn't make mistakes—what regime doesn't?—but that it supports a process by which mistakes can be corrected through open discussion and due process. This would give heart to those numerous Ethiopians and foreigners who want nothing more than to see the reconstruction of Ethiopia succeed, so that scarce energies can be pooled into the mammoth tasks of rebuilding Ethiopia's impoverished infrastructures, conserving her environment, keeping population growth in pace with economic growth, healing the sick, confronting the AIDS epidemic, educating the young, cleaning the towns, and preserving deteriorating monuments. These are crucial moments in Ethiopia's history, and those in power have an awesome responsibility to make sure that the promise of a democratic and peaceful Ethiopia will not be betrayed yet again.

After a year in which the Derg had killed, imprisoned, or exiled so many of Ethiopia's best-educated citizens, Blair Thompson wrote a book entitled *Ethiopia: The Country that Cut off Its Head.* Can the TGE now restore the promise of Ethiopia's university by repairing its drastic action against intelligentsia who survived the anti-intellectual predations of the Derg? In so doing, it would embrace the great institutional challenge facing all nations emerging from dictatorial regimes—the formation of a genuine civil society.

14

Kwillo amekkiru we-ze-senay atsni'u (2004)*

Your Excellency President Girma,
Mr. President of the University of Addis Ababa,
Esteemed Colleagues of the University Faculty,
Members of the graduating class of 2004 and their families,
Honorable guests,

I am truly grateful for the opportunity to be here—again.

It was 45 years ago that my association with this institution started, when I taught a course at the old University College of Addis Ababa and organized what was probably the first interdisciplinary seminar on Ethiopian Studies in the world. One participant in that seminar was a young economic historian named Dr. Richard Pankhurst—Sir Richard, now, I am delighted to note. How wonderful that my esteemed colleague shares with me this honorific celebration.

And let me add how much I appreciate being a recipient of the honor that another old friend received here one year ago, the late Ato Kifle Wodajo. In preparing these remarks, I took a page from the talk he presented when awarded an honorary doctorate then. Ato Kifle defined the award, not so much for him personally, as an acknowledgment of contributions that his generation of Ethiopian diplomats and civil servants had made to the cause of African liberation and unity.

In that spirit, I should like to view my award as an acknowledgment of values that are embodied in my commitment to the academic calling and which

---

* Remarks on the occasion of receiving the award of Honorary Doctorate from Addis Ababa University, July 24, 2004.

were embodied in the foundation of this University in the 1960s. I refer above all to the value of excellence in the quest for truth and of the prerequisites for that quest: freedom of inquiry, freedom of teaching, freedom of speech, and freedom of publication.

The foundational years of AAU are truly inspiring, and worthy of special study. The same years that witnessed the upsurge of developments in Ethiopia's economy, human services, and international status that Kifle Wodajo's remarks recalled saw a generation of remarkable young Ethiopians work to build this fine institution. Happy to say, that work is receiving attention through a study carried out by the brother of Ato Kifle, Dr. Mulugeta Wodajo, one-time Dean of the Faculty of Education here and the first Ethiopian academic vice-president of this university.

A year or so before the University College was officially changed into Haile Selassie I University, I became keenly aware the special significance of establishing an independent institution of higher learning in this country. Accordingly, when that idea began to take shape, I accepted an offer to serve as assistant to the acting Vice-President, Harold Bentley. Before the project had a chance to break ground, however, Addis Ababa was wracked by an attempted coup d'état against the late Emperor.

The coup leaders, Germame Neway, and his brother General Mengistu Neway, were good friends of mine. Their action seemed to me ill-considered, because I felt that the country was not ready for such precipitous change. Even so, I did write something sympathetic to their action. One of the last persons to see Germame alive before he was captured and killed, I was riveted by his parting words to me: "Don, please tell our story to the world. Even if we are defeated and killed, at least a word of truth will have been spoken in this land of deception." And so, a few months later, I published an article in accord with Germame's testament to me, an article which the Emperor found so offensive that he wanted the U.S. Government to put me in prison. Vice-President Bentley dissuaded him with this memorable argument: "Your Majesty, think of yourself for a moment, not as head of the Ethiopian State, but as Chancellor of this new University. You want it to be internationally respected. For that, it must be able to guarantee academic freedom. What better proof of your intent could you demonstrate than to invite Dr. Levine to return to help build it?" The rhetoric was effective. Soon after, His Majesty approved the idea of inviting me to return. However, when it came time to secure a visa, the Embassy that I approached had received no authorization to do so—despite the fact that I had received a contract and several thousand dollars in advance to cover moving expenses. When I phoned Addis Ababa to inquire about this situation,

Dr. Bentley reported that his Majesty had said, "As University Chancellor, I still want him to come; but as Head of State, I do not."[1]

I relate this story to make two important points. For one thing, it demonstrates dramatically the contrast between the values of a University and the values of political authority. Although in principle the two institutions need not be in conflict, there often arise situations where they possess diverging interests: the quest for truth and the exercise of political power can indeed sometimes be in conflict. Even so, I would add that the quest for truth that the University champions is quite at odds with the expression of truth that Germame had in mind. The Neway brothers followed an age-old Ethiopian custom known as *meshefet*: to rebel against a ruler when one is radically displeased with him. The traditional options for public conduct in Ethiopia—as in many traditional societies—were either to comply with and defer to established authority, or to rebel by running off or violently challenging the rulers in question: either open combat, or clandestine discontent.

The modern university offers a third way. As I used to say to my Ethiopian friends in the 1960s, if only part of the courage required to take up arms and fight authorities were converted into non-violent public discourse about societal problems, Ethiopia would have the beginnings of truly productive and fruitful change. And the University had the potential to give citizens the discipline and the motivation to pursue the truth in a non-violent way. To be honest, this kind of action requires as much, if not more, courage than to shoot a rifle. It exemplifies the path defined by young Karl Marx in 1843 when, before he became a dogmatist, he called for unconstrained critical inquiry about everything and anything, uninhibited both in not being afraid of its own conclusions and in not fearing conflict with the powers that be.

This was the path charted by the founders of this University when they chose as its motto a phrase from another well-known writer, the Apostle Paul, a motto that—whether you know it or not—appears on the seal of this University, atop the entrance to Ras Makonnen Hall, and on each of the diplomas to the awarded today:

Kwillo amekkiru we-ze-senay atsni'u.

Investigate everything, and retain what is best.

This motto, selected by the first chairman of the University's Board of Governors, the noted scholar Blatta Marsie Hazen Wolde-Kirkos, inspires a commitment to searching inquiry and to evaluative discourse. To uphold such a commitment is relatively rare in human history. Most cultures impose strict limits on how far one can go in adhering to the injunction, *kwillo amekkiru*. It is the challenge and the glory of the modern university to uphold this value in as pure a form as possible.

Just as those who pursue the truth as a vocation need the support of Power, so does Power need an independent and open quest for truth. Even though the conclusions of such inquiry may at times be uncomfortable to the powers that be, in the modern world, surrounded as we are by unprecedented changes of enormous complexity, it stands to the advantage of these powers to support free inquiry and to be open to its honest conclusions. Failure to do so can result in calamities, based simply on ignorance and uninformed judgment.

For example, in the 1960s, the United States government committed itself to a horrible war in Southeast Asia from perceptions that were uninformed by sound understanding of Vietnamese realities. I shall never forget when the late Senator Robert Kennedy, speaking at a conference at the University of Chicago on Southeast Asia in 1966, confessed: "If only we in the government had known what you scholars knew all along, we never would have gotten into this horrible situation." More recently, the unilateral invasion of Iraq rested on views about the Middle East that most scholars of that region knew to be indefensible.

At certain points since the 1960s, groups of Ethiopians acted on notions that all disinterested scholars found unsupportable. Had the scholarly understandings been available to concerned parties, Ethiopians would have been able to avoid such errors as assuming that forced collectivization was a plausible road to economic development; that progress could only be won through terror and massacre; that the Eritrean region of Ethiopia had a long independent history, ignoring the fact that that territory was fully under the suzerainty of the Ethiopian emperor from at least the time of 'Amde Tsiyon through the Turkish invasions of the late 16th century; that a nation of Oromia had existed as an inclusive national polity, ignoring the substantial role that Oromo groups had played in building the Ethiopian nation since the 17th century; and that the regimes of Emperor's Menelik and Haile Sellassie were supported by Amhara plutocrats rather than by a of multiethnic Shoan elite, ruling over huge numbers of Amhara who were as impoverished as anyone in the country.

There have been and are today many Ethiopians, who, inside and outside the University, are fully committed to open inquiry and civil discourse. To name but a few among many, just bring to mind the character and achievements of such distinguished Ethiopian scholars as Professor Mesfin Wolde Maryam, Dr. Zewde Gabre Selassie, Dr. Getatchew Haile, Dr. Taye Wolde Semayat, and in memoriam, Dr. Asrat Woldeyes and Dr. Eshetu Chole.

It is through the scholarly integrity and dedication of scholars like these that hard intellectual work will be accomplished, resulting in ideas likely to help Ethiopia deal more effectively with such mammoth problems as poverty, overpopulation and urban congestion, famine, AIDS and other epidemics, destruction of the environment, decimation of animal populations, and loss of valuable cultural resources. These represent complex, difficult problems; simplistic formulas will not solve them. They require strong support for uninhibited quest for truth. One way of providing such support is to encourage a university faculty to be responsible for decisions affecting the academic side of the university's operations. Parliament has recently passed legislation that, while not granting the university autonomy, at least has the potential to open a path of movement in that direction.

A strong, secure, and courageous regime can accommodate novel insight and challenging truths. Your Prime Minister is a bold, determined, persevering veteran of the quest for what he believes to be the truth. He understands the difference between the courage of *wetadernet* and the courage of civil discourse, and the need for Ethiopia to move toward the latter. In that effort, to continue your valiant work toward a university that upholds the highest standard of teaching and research, I wish you Godspeed. And say, *Idem le-ras-adari* AAU—long live the autonomous University of Addis Ababa.

Notes

1 As those who personally knew him attested, the Emperor did not adhere to fixed policies but rather often followed the counsel of the last adviser to speak with him before a decision was to be made. It is likely that this pattern is reflected in the Emperor's last-minute change of mind concerning my appointment. For more on this, see Abebe Ambatchew, *A Glimpse of Greatness: Haile Selassie I: the Person* (Bloomington, IA: Trafford Publishing, 2008).

15

On Cultural Creativity in the Ethiopian Diaspora (2006)*

Since the time of the First International Conference of Ethiopian Studies held at the Accademia dei Lincei in Rome in 1959, the field of Ethiopian studies has expanded to incorporate a sizeable and more broadly interdisciplinary group of scholars. At the same time, however, Ethiopianist scholarly discourse has remained focused on homeland studies, despite the migration abroad of more than a million Ethiopians in the wake of the 1974 revolution and the subsequent settlement of Ethiopian diaspora communities around the world.

This volume of essays emerges from an invitational meeting of twelve scholars held in April, 2008, at Harvard University's Radcliffe Institute for Advanced Study. The presentations were united by a common topic: the exploration of processes of Ethiopian creativity in the diaspora from a cross-disciplinary perspective. I was delighted and honored to participate among this select group of colleagues, chosen for their long-established devotion to the difficult but enduring standards of the academic world. My task for the conference was to open up that dialogue with a series of questions pertaining to the central themes of the conference. The following reflections frame the purpose of our gathering as noted by its original title—"Beyond Creative Incorporation: On Cultural Innovation in the Ethiopian Diaspora." What is that all about?

---

* Originally published in *Diaspora: A Journal of Transnational Studies* Volume 15, Number 2/3, Fall/Winter 2006, pp. 215–220.

Creative Incorporation

On the face of it, nothing too startling. The phrase "creative incorporation" is drawn from a passage in my 1974 book *Greater Ethiopia: The Evolution of a Multiethnic Society* (2nd ed. 2000). The passage picks up on an idea adumbrated by the scholar who convened that first Convegno internazionale di studi etiopici, Enrico Cerulli. In all periods of their literary history, Cerulli notes, Ethiopians were influenced heavily by foreign writings—from Greek, Syrian, Arabic, and European sources. This extreme receptivity, however, did not take the form of simply passive, literal borrowing. Rather,

> One can say that it is precisely a typical Ethiopian tendency to collect the data of foreign cultural and literary experience and transform them, sooner or later, to such an extent that even translations in Ethiopic are not always translations, in our sense of the term; but they frequently contain additions, supplementary material, at times misrepresentations of the original, at other times simply the insertion of new materials in such quantity that the literal sense of the original is completely lost. (Cerulli 1956, 12–3)

And, Cerulli adds, once these materials from abroad were ingested and transformed, the resulting contents and styles quickly became canonized as part of a tenaciously conserved indigenous tradition.

I claimed that this pattern, which I termed creative incorporation, was manifest in other domains of Ethiopian culture. In the realm of art, for example, the traditional icon of King David playing his harp represents a transformation of a model found in an old Greek miniature, in which the personification of Melody in the Greek original was changed into an Ethiopian court attendant, the harp became the Ethiopian ten-stringed lyre, the bägänna, and the insignia of kingship became the Ethiopian umbrella and fly whisk (Heldman 1972, 82).

In the sphere of religion, creative incorporation was manifest in the ways in which the beliefs and symbols of Oriental Semitic faiths were accepted, ways "that permitted the continued belief in the sacral significance of stones, trees, waterplaces, and serpents and in the efficacy of rainmakers and the evil eye" (Levine 2000, 66). The Ethiopian pattern evinced in such phenomena, then, was interpreted as contrasting both with nativistic rejection and with slavish adherence to imported forms. Instead, it appeared to embody an effort by Ethiopian peoples to absorb only so much of the external elements as suited their purposes and thereby keep much of their cultural traditions in place.

What would it mean now for this pattern to be evinced among the bearers of Ethiopian culture in the diaspora countries? To forsake creative incorporation would mean total rejection of the ways of the host culture—hanging on for dear life to the old language, the old customs, the old liturgies, the old icons. And that is what a small minority has done, those who attempted to seclude themselves in same-country residences, especially immigrants of the older generation who departed at the beginning of the revolution. Dinaw Mengestu describes this group poignantly in his novel when he portrays a large apartment building near Washington, D.C., inhabited largely by Ethiopians who rarely speak English; whose hallways smell of *wat* [spicy Ethiopian stew], coffee, and incense; whose children keep only friendships sanctioned by their parents; and who sometimes "occupy entire floors...run like minor villages with children, grandparents, grandchildren, and in-laws all living within shouting distance of one another" (Mengestu 2007, 116).

On the other hand, those who want to live well in the new milieu sometimes run to the other opposite extreme, especially if they work in careers, from science to banking, where internalization of modern Western culture is indispensable. To what may be an extraordinary extent, however—especially when compared with many other African diasporas—the old pattern of creative incorporation seems to dominate. Ethiopians assimilate whatever of the host culture as they must to survive and then to become more generally modern, yet all the while maintaining traditional bonds and patterns. Even Ethiopians born and brought up in North America have begun as adults to revisit the homeland, to learn Ethiopian languages, and even to observe Ethiopian Orthodox Christian fasting regimes for the first time. For them and the culture-creators who express their sentiments, I suggest that their story is, to a large extent, simply another narrative of creative incorporation.

What then can it mean to say "beyond" creative incorporation? Do Ethiopians abroad, especially in North America, not absorb the new ways, to the extent that they must, and rework them to fit on a bedrock of traditional identity and symbolism? One difference from the historic pattern of creative incorporation seems indisputable. Rather than canonizing the newly incorporated styles, models, and genres into a hard-and-fast tradition, Ethiopians abroad today are caught up in the world civilization that places a premium on novelty, inventiveness, and continuous change. This seems to be particularly pronounced in the domains of popular music, modern painting, and literature—not to mention blogging. Beyond that, perhaps, there really is something else different at work here. But there remain several issues touched on in all essays that merit brief mention here.

The whole topic of creativity stands ripe for rethinking and I know of no attempts to clarify its several senses, as has been done so abundantly for the concept of culture. As a provisional semantic matrix I suggest the following.

1. Creativity has been associated with problem-solving, as in the work of John Dewey.

2. Creativity is commonly thought to consist of finding new ways of combining existing elements.

3. Creativity has been considered as a spontaneous expression of energies.

4. Creativity can also be viewed as the invention of novel forms.

If we convert the four views of creativity outlined above into a schema of different types, there is reason to suggest that different aspects of the diasporan situation can be seen to favor the emergence of each one of them. The settings in which they exist contain ingredients favorable to the creative solution of problems, to new combinations, to new energies, and to the creation of new forms.

The central experience of each immigrant group consists of unavoidable conflicts between their natal culture and social ties, and the different culture and social connections of their new home. This is of course particularly poignant for the first-generation immigrants. The noted film-maker Haile Gerima gave voice to this conflict in a recent interview regarding his new film "Teza," which he described as based on a recurring dream.

> The dream is basically about intellectual displacement. When I translated my dream it was about being displaced, unable to live up to your peasant life, your peasant family and at the same time reconcile (that) with your modern world. (Collett-White 2008)

This dilemma produces enormous adjustment problems that leave their mark unto the second and even third generations of immigrants. It is not a matter of indifference whether or not these adjustment problems are solved. They must be solved; the only question is how easily and how well.

One can say that solving those kinds of problems involves gestures of creativity in the sense of the combination of opposites. There are numerous ways in which this is done. One way is to adapt traditional forms to new circumstances, as for example when traditional Ethiopian melodies are played on Western instruments. Another is to create new forms in which old contents could be expressed, such as by using elements of Ethiopian faces or the Ethiopic syllabary in modern paintings. This combination of traditional elements with forms and ideas from another culture that seem important represents precisely the pattern of creative incorporation we considered at the outset. For example, instead of reproducing the traditional style of Ethiopian painting, or adhering mainly to modern Western genres, the semi-diasporan artist Fikru Haile-Mariam uses figures with faces and garments that hint of traditional styles while working them up into increasingly abstract configurations (see Chapter 14).

Perhaps the least-noticed dimension of creativity may be the spontaneous outpouring of new energies. Departure from the homeland invariably entails psychological reactions associated with the loss of objects to which persons have been attached (Weinstein and Platt 1973). The anxieties and strivings associated with object loss represent the psychoanalytic counterpart of what Dewey discusses when conceptualizing the release of impulse in the wake of a breach of habit (Dewey 1922), what Max Weber analyzed as a transition from tradition to charisma (Weber 1968), or what Victor Turner termed the move from structure to liminality (Turner 1969). That Ethiopians and others in the diaspora have become among our most creative citizens should be no surprise.

What distinguishes the Ethiopian case, I believe, is the special intensity that Ethiopians manifest in their attitude toward their homeland. There is a profound connection between being Ethiopian and feeling committed to the land wherein you grew. *Greater Ethiopia* mentioned the antiquity of this proclivity by citing some evidence for it in a chapter from the traditional Ethiopian source linking their history to the tale of King Solomon's liaison with the Queen of Sheba. When asked to stay on and settle in Judah, the headmen of Tamrin the merchant reply: "Our country is the better." And when Solomon pleads with young Menilek, the son of Solomon and the Queen, to remain with him in Jerusalem, the latter's reply "could be that of a 20th-century son of the Ethiopian soil, rejecting the fleshpots of Europe to return home to live out his bittersweet destiny":

> Though thou givest me dainty meats I do not love them, and they are not suitable for my body, but the meats whereby I grow and become strong are those that are gratifying to me. And although thy country pleaseth me even as a garden, yet is not my heart gratified therewith; the mountains of the land of my mother where I was born are far better in my sight. (Levine 2000, 102)

It is the dialectic between the deep ties to home and the challenges of diaspora culture across all domains of the Ethiopian experience that have catalyzed the creative responses of Diaspora Ethiopians examined in the volume that follows.

Bibliography

Cerulli, Enrico. *Storia della letteratura etiopica*. Milan, 1956.

Collett-White, Mike. "Ethiopian film explores nation's recent violent past." <http://africa.reuters.com/wire/news/usnL234537.html> 2 Sep 2008.

Dewey, John. [1922]1988. *Human Nature and Conduct*. New York: Holt.

Heldman, Marilyn, "Miniatures of the Gospels of Princess Zir Ganela." Ph.D. dissertation, Department of Art and Archaeology, Washington University. 1972.

Levine, Donald N. *Greater Ethiopia: The Evolution of a Multiethnic Society*. Chicago: The

University of Chicago Press. [1974] 2002.
______. "An Ethiopian Painter for the 21st Century." 2007
Turner, Victor. *The Ritual Process: Structure and Anti-Structure.* Aldine Transaction. 1969.
Weber, Max. *Economy and Society.* Ed. Guenther Roth and Klaus Wittich. Bedminster Press. 1968.
Weinstein, Fred and Gerald Platt. *Psychoanalytic Sociology*. Baltimore, Johns Hopkins University Press. 1973.

Part III
HISTORY

16

The Battle of Adwa as an Historic Event (1996)*

There are three reasons why we commonly refer to some happening as a historic event: either it occurs for the first time; it has significant consequences; or it is symbolically important. As a *first time event,* Emperor Menilek's cession of the Bogos highlands to Italy in 1889 has been described as historic, as the first time that an Ethiopian ruler ever voluntarily ceded territory to a foreign power. In the same vein, Abebe Bikila's victory in the marathon race in the 1960 Olympics at Rome was historic, as the first time that an Ethiopian won a gold medal.

We also designate events as historic when their *consequences significantly alter* the shape of subsequent *history*. The conversion of King Ezanas to Christianity in the middle of the fourth century was historic in this sense because it redirected Ethiopia's entire cultural development. Similarly, the protection given to disciples of the Prophet Muhammad by the Ethiopian king in the seventh century was a historic event. It led Muhammad to advise his followers to spare Ethiopia from the jihad of Islamic expansion that took place soon after. Likewise, the killing of Emperor Yohannes IV by Sudanese Mahdists in 1889 was historic because it opened the way to the ascendance of an emperor from Shoa.

Even when events have no significant direct consequences, we tend to call them historic when they *symbolize* important national or universal human ideals. The suicide of Emperor Tewodros II had little political consequence—his

---

* Originally published in *One House: The Battle of Adwa 1896*, edited by Pamela Brown and Fassil Yirgu (Chicago, IL: Nyala Publishing, 1996), 1-8.

rule was over, whether or not he was captured alive by the British—but it came to symbolize a sentiment of preferring death over demeaning captivity. The speech of Emperor Haile Selassie I to the League of Nations in 1937 is often called a historic address, even though it did nothing to change the course of history, because it came to symbolize the moral weakness of Western democracies in the face of fascist expansionism and the need for a stronger world organization empowered to provide collective security.

The Battle of Adwa in 1896 qualifies as an historic event in all three senses of the term. As a historic "first," it represented the first time since the beginning of European imperial expansion that a non-white nation had defeated a European power.

The Battle of Adwa in 1896 also had two fateful consequences—the preservation of Ethiopia's independence from Italian colonization, and the confirmation of Italy's control over the part of the country Italy had named Eritrea in 1890. Both consequences had repercussions throughout the twentieth century. Italy experienced her defeat at Adwa as intensely humiliating, and that humiliation became a national trauma which demagogic leaders strove to avenge. It also played no little part in motivating Italy's revanchist adventure in 1935. On the other hand, Italy's continued occupation of Eritrea gave her a convenient springboard from which to launch that invasion. A generation later, tensions stemming from the protracted division of historic Ethiopia into two parts—one under European governance, one under the Ethiopian Crown—culminated in a long civil war, and the eventual secession of Eritrea as an independent state in 1993.

In addition to these actual historic consequences, the Battle of Adwa was historic because it acquired symbolic significance of many kinds. (In some instances this symbolism itself came to exert a certain influence on the course of events.)

Adwa's Symbolism in Other Countries

In Europe, the short-term symbolic significance of the Ethiopian defeat of Italy in 1896 was that it served to initiate a process of rethinking the Europeans' image of Africa and Africans. During the nineteenth century Africa had come to be viewed in increasingly pejorative terms, as a continent of people so primitive they were fit only for European rule. Ethiopia did not escape such swipes. British officers called Ethiopia a nation of savages and Italian officials described it as "a nation of primitive tribesmen led by a barbarian." The British Foreign Office supported the provocative move of ceding Zula to Italy, expecting that Yohannes would protest by attacking them and then easily be punished for imagining that Ethiopians were equal to white men. Kaiser Wilhelm responded to Emperor Menilek's announcement of his accession to the throne with insulting language. The stunning victory at Adwa required Europeans to take Ethiopia and Africa more seriously. It not only initiated a decade of negotiations with European powers in which nine border treaties were signed, it made Europeans begin to reconsider their prejudices against Africans. It came to symbolize a rising awareness among Europeans of African political resources and yearnings and an increasing recognition of indigenous African cultural accomplishments.

In Japan, Ethiopia became appreciated as the first non-Caucasian power to defeat Europeans, an achievement the Japanese were to duplicate in warfare against Russia in 1904. This appreciation led to a sense of affinity that bore fruit for decades thereafter. Ethiopian intellectuals looked to Japan as a model for modernizing their ancient monarchy; the Meiji Constitution served as a model for the Ethiopian Constitution of 1931. When Italy invaded Ethiopia again in the mid-thirties, many Japanese citizens (if not the regime formally) expressed solidarity with Ethiopians, sending shipments of many thousands of swords to help Ethiopians in their plight.

In Africa, the Battle of Adwa inspired other kinds of symbolism. For a number of colonized Africans, the Ethiopian victory at Adwa symbolized the possibility of future emancipation. Black South Africans of the Ethiopian Church came to identify with the Christian kingdom in the Horn, a connection that led South African leader James Dwane to write Menilek for help in caring for the Christian communities of Egypt and Sudan. The victory at Adwa made Ethiopia visible as a beacon of African independence, a position that inspired figures like Nnamdi Azikiwe in Nigeria, Kwame Nkrumah in Ghana, and Jomo Kenyatta in Kenya in the early years of the African independence movement, as well as leaders in the West Indies like George Padmore and Marcus Garvey from Jamaica.

Adwa as a Symbol of Ethiopia's Tradition of Independence

Within Ethiopia itself, Adwa symbolized many things, some of which had positive consequences for her development while others did not. Internally as abroad, it symbolized Ethiopia's proud commitment to freedom from foreign domination. Of the many emblems of Ethiopia's historic independence, Adwa is perhaps the most visible and the most dramatic. The spirit of Ethiopia's defiant protection of their land from outsiders manifests itself in many forms. There is the apocryphal story of Emperor Theodore, who is said to have ordered the boots of some visitors washed before they embarked on a ship back to Europe, saying: "Far more precious than jewels is a single drop of Ethiopian soil." There was the refrain I used to hear young braves chant at festive times, jabbing *dula* sticks up and down as they danced and sang:

> *"Min alle Teqel, min alle?*
>
> *Agare le-sew, agare-le sew, al-setim ale"*

("What did *Teqel* [Haile Selassie's horse-name] say, what did he say?

I won't give my country to foreigners, that's what he said.")

With respect to Menilek's reputation, it partly overcame the resentments he had stirred up by ceding Bogos to Italy in exchange for help against his competitors in Tigray.

As a historic assertion of Ethiopia's independence, Adwa also reverberated with memories of Ethiopia's experience as a long-lived independent polity. Its symbolism thereby encompassed a layer of meaning that alluded to the historic depth of the Ethiopian nation. It revived memories of earlier achievements and yearnings.

At the same time, Adwa may have served to give Ethiopians a false sense of confidence about their position in the modern world. In showing themselves and the world that they could defeat a European invader with their own resources, the 1896 campaign may have led them to think that their traditional resources could be adequate in an era in which war would be waged with tanks and airplanes. It gave encouragement to isolationist and conservative strains that were deeply rooted in Ethiopian culture, strengthening the hand of those who would strive to keep Ethiopia from adopting techniques imported from the modern West—resistances with which both Menilek and Ras Tafari/Haile Selassie would have to contend.

Adwa as a Symbol of Multiethnic Cooperation

The symbolism of multiethnic collaboration evoked by the Battle of Adwa has been less visible than its role in symbolizing Ethiopia's tradition of independence. Yet in some ways the former was the most remarkable and meaningful aspect of the entire episode. Although members of different ethnic, religious, and regional groups had been interacting regularly in Ethiopia for more than 2,000 years—through trading, intermarriage, common ritual observances, pilgrimages, and political competition—from the perspective of Ethiopian history, Adwa offers the most dramatic instance of multiethnic collaboration before the 20th century. This is because it gave expression to a great outpouring of national patriotism, foreshadowing the great patriotic struggles of 1935–41. Even from the perspective of modern world history, Adwa represented a relatively rare struggle for national independence waged by a coalition of diverse ethnic groups.

Twenty-five years earlier, Adwa had been the scene of a protracted battle between Dejazmatch Kasa, who would become Emperor Yohannes IV, and the reigning emperor, Tekla-Giyorgis II, formerly Wag Shum Gobeze. What the 1871 Battle of Adwa symbolized was the age-old struggle among different regional and ethnic groups for dominance. Yohannes, like Tewodros II before him, came to the throne determined to reunify the empire, which had been fragmented following the invasion of Ahmad Gragn and subsequent divisive developments. Although Yohannes did not live to see it, the 1896 Battle of Adwa was a tribute to his vision and to the thoughtfulness and determination with which he sought to unify Ethiopia while respecting the local jurisdiction of regional kings and lords so long as they remained faithful to the national crown.

Those who would deny Ethiopia's long existence as a multiethnic society must be embarrassed by the facts of the Adwa experience. If the empire consisted of nothing but a congeries of separate tribal and regional groups, how then account for the courageous collaboration of 100,000 troops from dozens of ethnic groups from all parts of the country? How then explain the spirited national patriotism of such diverse leaders as Ras Alula, Ras Mengesha, and Ras Sibhat of Tigray, Dejazmatch Bahta of Akale Guzae, Wag Shum Guangul of Lasta, Ras Mikael of Wallo, Negus Takla-Haymanot of Gojjam, Ras Gobena and Dejazmatch Balcha of the Mecha Oromo, Ras Wele of the Yejju Oromo, Fitawrari Tekla of Wollega, Ras Makonnen of Harar, as well as Ras Gebeyehu (who died fighting at Adwa) and Ras Abate of Shoa?

Of course, deeply rooted antagonisms and persistent rivalries among different factions beset Ethiopia throughout the 19th century. And yet, as historian Sven Rubenson has written, "at the crucial moment, Menilek commanded the loyalty of every important chief in the country." The battle of Adwa became and remains the most outstanding symbol of what, a half-century later, a British colonel would describe as the "mysterious magnetism" that holds Ethiopia together.

17

Coming to America (1996)*

The story of the Ethiopian expatriate community in Chicago and beyond belongs to the larger story of the creation of the United States. For four centuries, successive waves of immigration from dozens of countries in Europe, Africa, and Asia have helped shape American society and provide it with continually renewed energies.

The earliest settlers came mainly from Britain, Holland, Germany, and France, in search of religious freedom or opportunities for exploration and trade. Once colonies were established, Europeans came simply to seek their fortunes in this new land, bringing or then importing indentured servants from England and slaves from Africa. After the importing of slaves was prohibited in the early 19th century, the immigrants came from Western Europe for some time, especially from England to find economic opportunities, from Germany to escape political repression, and from Ireland to flee poverty and famine. By mid-century, immigrants from China and Japan began coming to America's new Western frontier. At the century's end, most immigrants came from Southern and Eastern Europe, especially Italy and Poland. Huge numbers of Eastern European Jews joined the exodus, to escape murderous pogroms as well as poverty. Although immigration peaked around the turn of the century, waves of immigrants displaced by World War I, the Nazi persecutions, and World War II continued the cycle of coming to America.

---

* Originally published in *Meeting the Challenge: Building a Community Together* (Chicago, IL: Ethiopian Community Association of Chicago, 1996), 38–41. Originally prepared with the assistance of Sarah Busse, Department of Sociology, University of Chicago.

The last twenty-five years have seen an increase in the proportion of immigrants who came as political refugees. While immigrants still arrive from all parts of the globe, Southeast Asian refugees, especially from the war-torn countries of Cambodia and Vietnam, have been the most visible. The most recent arrivals include refugees from formerly communist countries, in search of both political freedom and economic stability. Although the Ethiopian immigrant community has arrived without much fanfare, its increase during the early Derg years was phenomenal. In 1974, I am told, Ethiopia had the smallest proportion of its citizens living abroad of any country in the world, while five years later, in 1979, it had the highest.

While over these centuries the physical process of "coming to America" has evolved from arduous long journeys to simple airplane trips, the psychological process of coming to America—that is, adjusting to American society—has changed no less dramatically. Changes in the ability of immigrants to adjust reflect two main factors: the reasons why they left their homeland, and the way they were received by the new environment

For what reasons do people leave their homelands? At the peak of immigration during the decades 1880–1910, most immigrants were drawn to America by their search for "a better life" than they could find at home. Millions were lured by the prospects of prosperity which was said to abound in the United States, harking to phrases like "there, the streets are paved with gold." These hyperbolic notions had some basis in fact. New industries required large supplies of labor. Immigrants had no trouble finding jobs in factories and on railroads. They were willing to work hard for little pay because it represented more than they could ever have imagined at home. Land and other material resources were just as plentiful as employment.

Immigrants who responded to such "pull" factors were for the most part voluntary migrants, those who chose to leave their homeland for the sake of economic opportunities. Some saved for years to make the journey possible; others were sponsored by family members who had gone before them. Coming through their own free choice, such immigrants were more likely to make the sacrifices, including their cultural habits, which were required at that time to make their "American dream" come true.

Pull factors continue to operate in bringing newcomers to America. Even though the age of rapid economic expansion has ended, making it difficult even for long-established Americans to find work or to make ends meet, the United States continues to be viewed as a land of economic opportunity by residents of many other countries.

Migration is spurred for different reasons when conditions in the home country are severe. Famines, chronic employment shortages, political or religious oppression, or wars or civil unrest often "push" dislocated, impoverished, or oppressed individuals from their homelands. In response to such push factors, people are not so much voluntarily coming to America as they are involuntarily leaving their homeland. They do so because America has historically been seen as a refuge for oppressed people. The motto inscribed on the Statue of Liberty—"Give me your huddled masses, yearning to be free"—publicly affirms a welcome to immigrants of all kinds.

Immigrants who left voluntarily had greater choice in the destination and time of their departure. They thus had more of a chance to prepare for life in the new country. Involuntary migrants, on the other hand, may have had little choice as to the time of their departure or their destination, giving them less opportunity to prepare for what lies ahead. What is more, those who come as refugees or other permanent involuntary immigrants generally seek to remain true to their native traditions and have no strong incentive to adopt American ways. Indeed, many are less anxious to join American society than they are desirous of returning to their homeland some day. This "sojourner mentality" makes them less likely to want to learn English and makes it more difficult for them to "come to America" in the sense of accepting idiosyncrasies of American society, things which voluntary migrants might more easily learn to deal with or even appreciate. This is often true even if they recognize that a return to their homeland is impossible, at least in their lifetime.

Forced to emigrate, refugees and other involuntary migrants tend to feel that although they may be taken from their homeland, their homeland can never be taken from them. Accordingly, they tend to create an island of familiar culture in a foreign cultural sea. To do this, immigrants typically gather in urban neighborhoods where others from their homeland have settled. Such neighborhoods are home to most new immigrants, whether they come voluntarily or involuntarily. Immigrants today often join together to form small businesses that appeal to customers in such ethnic enclaves. The ambitious among them may build these into large businesses or even move out of the ethnic neighborhood altogether. At the same time, those who wish to preserve their traditional ways might choose to stay in ethnic communities where their traditional ways are easier to maintain than when isolated from fellow ethnics.

Whether creating such a cultural "island" is possible depends not only on the desires of the migrants to create it and the resources they have to do so, but also on the environment in which they live. This environment has changed during the past century, from a demand for total assimilation to "American" ways to an acceptance of a pluralistic mixture of cultures.

At the turn of the century, when immigration from Eastern and Southern Europe was at its peak, most Americans embraced the notion of the "melting pot." This metaphor implied that the new country served as a crucible in which those of all ethnic backgrounds would be fused together to form a new American culture. In effect, newcomers of those years were expected to conform closely to the American culture established by long-term residents. Immigrants were expected not only to learn English, but also to acquire American habits as defined by those who had lived here for a generation or two. New immigrants were ridiculed into discarding their Old World ways and becoming more like those who had arrived earlier. This attitude instilled in an entire generation of immigrants striving to become just like other Americans a sense of shame regarding their own culture and language.

As a result of social pressures and their own desires, immigrants did not pass on their language and customs to their children. Second-and third-generation Italians, Irish, and Poles grew up with no knowledge of their parents' and grandparents' language and cultural heritage. A sense of unique cultural identity was something those early immigrants sought to lose as quickly as possible, because they recognized that "making it" in America meant giving up characteristics that made them seem "foreign."

Over the past few decades, America has learned to tolerate, or been forced to accept, many differences in lifestyle, language, and beliefs among its people. The Civil Rights movement of the 1960s and the feminist movement of the 1970s and 1980s forced Americans to reconsider traditionally disadvantaged groups whose needs and interests had been underrepresented, even silenced. Movements such as Black Power and La Rasa sent strong messages to African-American and Hispanic-American groups and individuals to take pride in their racial and cultural heritage. These "identity" movements stimulated other groups to reconsider their own ethnic heritage, giving rise to the formation of Italian-American, Irish-American, and similar ethnic "interest groups." Relatedly, Americans have recently witnessed the phenomenon of the "third-generation return," as grandchildren of immigrants discover and take pride in the heritage their grandparents were ashamed to transmit.

Due to such sweeping social changes, immigrants today face an environment radically different from that of a century ago. American society today is much more tolerant of diversity than before. Today, ethnic diversity is celebrated, multiculturalism is in style, and ethnic Americans tend increasingly to celebrate cultural heritages long buried by assimilationist trends. In fact, displaying unique cultural or ethnic characteristics has become an accepted, even encouraged, means of "being American." The United States is recognized as a country consisting of people from a variety of ethnic backgrounds, with a few, not all, characteristics in common. This pluralistic attitude is often compared to the image of a "salad bowl," a mixture in which, unlike the melting pot, each piece retains its distinctive form and flavor to produce a healthy collection of interests and backgrounds.

Although this acceptance comes at a time when the number of new immigrants is but a fraction of the number arriving in 1900, those who do come are given much more freedom, informally and officially, to retain their own distinctive cultural practices. Beyond learning some English, sending their children to school, and taking some form of employment, little else is required of immigrants, and they are required to relinquish few, if any, of their former habits and customs. In such an environment, it is clear that recent immigrants have it easier than their predecessors in not being forced to relinquish their past. Current newcomers are allowed to choose how much of their culture they want to preserve, and which "American" ways they want to adopt.

The contemporary situation, then, combines an increase in the number of immigrants who come more or less involuntarily, as political refugees, with an increased acceptance of the home cultures from which they come. Today's immigrants do not have to choose between social acceptance needed for economic survival and adherence to their traditional ways. Living in ethnic neighborhoods may even promote economic success. It certainly represents a fully accepted way of being American in our time. Today's immigrants thus arrive with a greater interest in retaining their home culture and enter an American society that shows enhanced appreciation of cultural diversity.

Accordingly, although today's immigrants may continue to feel some social pressure to conform to certain American habits of dress, food or behavior, and while they still face difficulties in maintaining their islands of ethnicity in a sea of "Americanisms," they should keep in mind how much less pressure exists today than a century before. The fact is that nowadays "coming to America," that is, learning to cope with a strange new world, is a good deal easier than for previous immigrants, because immigrants today enjoy a freedom to decide what traditional ways to maintain and what American ways to adopt.

In this more tolerant environment, recent immigrants are able to form stable, vibrant communities together with those who arrived earlier from their home country. Especially for refugees and other involuntary immigrants, these expatriate communities create a safe haven in which familiar habits and beliefs can be preserved. Such communities, however, do not preserve culture the way a museum would, as a static snapshot of one moment in time, but rather as a living, developing way of life. When a diasporic community retains a living culture, it then is in a position to be able to infuse new life back to the homeland, whose own traditions may face certain threats.

In this perspective, the Ethiopian community of North America faces a triple challenge. First, it needs to provide continuing assistance to new immigrants, especially those who may have been pushed to leave because of repressive conditions at home. On this front, the Ethiopian Community Association of Chicago has long played a conscientious and constructive role. Second, North America offers resources to sustain those aspects of its traditional culture that are being eroded at home due to ignorance, poverty, or reckless modernization. In this regard, such organizations as the Center for Ethiopian Arts and Culture, the Ethiopian Research Council, and the various Ethiopian magazines and publishing houses have made enormous contributions.

Finally, the Ethiopian and Eritrean expatriate communities face a special challenge in view of the tendencies toward ethnic and regional separatism that have threatened the integrity of their homeland. Indeed, in some quarters it has become fashionable to deny the very facts about the existence of the enduring multiethnic society that took shape in historic Ethiopia. In this country, at least, Ethiopians need not give in to the temptations of narrowly-based ethnic factionalism and can do much to preserve and restore the valuable traditions of their national culture.

18

Amhara (2003)*

The term Amhara (**አምሃራ, አምሓራ**) referred originally to a region of historic Ethiopia bounded on the west by the Abbay and its tributary the Bašəlo River; on the north by the regions of Angot and Lasta; on the east by the escarpment leading down to the Danakil Desert (Afar); and by the Wänčət River to the south (the southwest part of Wällo province). Typical high-plateau Ethiopia, it is filled with mountainous formations that break the terrain into highlands (*däga*), good for barley and sheep; midlands (*wäyna däga*), good for wheat and oats; and lowlands (*qwälla*), good for tef, goats, and vegetables.

The earliest references to the region appear in connection with the reign of a 9th century Aksumite king, Dəgnağan, who brought Christian missionaries to teach there (TadTChurch 35). Oral traditions of inhabitants of Amhara claim direct descent from ancient Aksum, and folk etymologies claim that the term Amhara means 'a free people'. Amhara people are mentioned early in the 12th century, as protagonists in armed conflict with the Warğih, a nomadic tribe to the east (Cerulli 1941:10,18).

The region came to national prominence by the late 13th century, when the Zagwe Dynasty was overthrown by a king from Amhara, Yəkuno Amlak, claiming Solomonic ancestry. During the 14th century his successors of the Solomonid dynasty became known as the "kings of Amhara" (Ge'ez **ንጉሠ አምሓራ** *nəguśä Amhara*). Even so, the Solomonid rulers did not establish Amhara as a fixed political center. Until they founded Gondär as a permanent capital in 1632, Amhara monarchs moved continuously from region to region, with

* Originally published in *Encyclopaedia Aethiopica* Volume 1, Institute of African and Ethiopian Studies, Hamburg University (Wiesbaden, Germany: Otto Harrassowitz KG, 2003).

especial fondness for the more southerly districts of Ifat, Shäwa, Däwaro, and Fätägar.

The regional name became attached to the South-Semitic language known as Amharic (Amarəñña), which emerged from a process of pidginization and creolization, combining Ethiopian Semitic with a large component of Cushitic vocabulary and syntax. The earliest extant Amharic text consists of songs of soldiers in praise of *Atse* Amdä Səyon (the so-called "Royal songs"). The language began to spread into adjacent areas, including Šäwa, Lasta, Bägemdər, and Goğğam, replacing Central Cushitic languages and other South Semitic languages like Gafat and Argobba. Its use as the language of the court and official documents after the 13th century aided its diffusion.

Within the broader territory of Amharic speakers, certain regions developed into autonomous political centres. Following the upheavals of the 16th century, the province of Bägemdər became home for the city of Gondär, royal capital for the Ethiopian polity from the 1630s to the mid-19th century. To the south, beyond Lake Tana, the great province of Goğğam developed a dynasty of rulers that often claimed the title of nəguś. The district of Mänz became the center for the development of a political dynasty culminating in nəguś Śahlä Səllase (1813–1847) and Emperor Menelik II (s. Levine 1965:30–38).

Over time the term Amhara came to be applied to a wider range of people, although the meanings of that appellation have varied. In some contexts it denotes a native Amharic speaker; in others, a Christian; in some instances, it has denoted a member of the ruling nobility (Chernetsov 1995). Most of those so labelled, however, have tended to identify themselves not as ethnic Amhara but as denizens of local regions—Goğğame, Gondäre, Mänze, and the like. Royal chronicles of the 14th–18th centuries consistently refer to Amhara only as a geographic region in Wällo, never as an ethnic name, and the same is true of Christian and Muslim annals up through the 19th century (Chernetsov 1995:20f.). Only in the last quarter of the 20th century has the term Amhara come to be a common ethnic appellation, comparable to the way in which Oromo has become generalized to cover peoples who long knew themselves primarily as Boorana (Boräna), Guğği, Mäčča, and the like. Even so, Amharic-speaking Šäwans still feel themselves closer to non-Amharic-speaking Šäwans than to Amharic-speakers from distant regions like Gondär, and there are few members of the Šäwan nobility who do not have Oromo genealogical links (Clapham 1969:81). Indeed, despite the recent ethnicization of political discourse, many if not most people considered "Amhara" continue to identify themselves primarily as "Ethiopians" beyond being residents of some local area (**አገር** agär).

Traditional Amhara social structure took the form of a peasant society. Agriculturalists subsist on the ox-drawn plough-cultivation (Plough) of cereal grains and herding of livestock. Their diet consists mainly of a "pancake" made of fermented batter of oats, wheat or, preferably, tef on which they place highly-spiced meat or vegetable sauces. They live in households that function as a unit of political economy, an *oikos*, rather than a kinship unit. Its members each carry out specific tasks assigned according to gender and other status markers, all under the authority of a single senior male. Each household lives in a compound containing a small number of round buildings built of wattle or stone, capped with conical thatched roofs. Homesteads usually are located on land worked by the peasant, though often a number of them group into hamlets (**መንደር** *mändär*, Levine 1965: 56–8).

Beyond that, Amhara households have been linked to one another along three separate axes. Economically, they are linked through weekly markets. Politically, they were linked traditionally by obligations to lords over seignories who held rights to tribute referred to as *gwəlt* (Crummey 2000), such that traditional Amhara society may be classed usefully as feudal (Hoben 1970:221). Since the bureaucratization of public administration following World War II, households have been subordinated to subdistrict, district, and provincial governors. Ecclesiastically, they have been linked through parishes (*Atbiya*), named after the sacred ark (*Tabot*) of its church, often coterminous with one or more local seignories. Traditionally, Amhara churches have been supported through *gwəlt* rights to usufruct and labour.

With respect to kinship, Amhara persons are linked through an ambilineal descent system. The Amhara rule of exogamy, prescribed in the *Fətha nägäśt*, requires that marriage partners not be closer than "seven houses" (**ሰባት ቤት** *säbat bet*); that is, not have a common great-great-great-grandparent. Kinship ties figure to some extent in connection with avenging murders, but primarily through determining the distribution of rights to the use of land (*Rəst*, Hoben 1973). Other forms of Amhara social relations include the daily coffee klatch (**ጥርትብ** *tərtəb*); monthly religious feasting associations (*Maḫbär*) in honour of a particular saint or angel; arrangements for reciprocal help in connection with farming, housebuilding and feasting; and voluntary dyadic personal relations including godparent-child, guarantor-guarantee and, pervasively, patron-client ties.

Most Ethiopians who consider themselves Amhara subscribe to the Ethiopian Orthodox Täwahədo faith, though Amharic-speakers in some regions are Muslim. The primary representative of this faith is the parish priest (**ካህን** *kahən*), who has exclusive access to the ark (*tabot*)—central devotional object of every church—and who celebrates the Mass. Usually a *qes*, essentially an "ordained farmer" (Weissleder 1974:70) whose marriage has been consecrated through the taking of communion (**ቍርባን** *qwərban*), the priest is assisted in church services by one or more acolytes (*Diyaqon*). In some instances, the ritual functions are performed by monks (መነኮሴ *mänäkwəse*), who renounce all worldly possessions to live a life of prayer and ecclesiastical service. Other religious functions are performed by men called *däbtära*, who serve as choristers and religious poets but also perform secular services as herbologists, scribes, and healers.

Many Orthodox religious centres are in Amhara regions. These include the island monastery of St. Stephen (Däbrä Hayq Əstifanos) at Lake Hayq, the first monastic centre in the historic Amhara region; Däbrä Libanos, the great monastery established in the 13th century by abunä Täklä Haymanot, at Sälale in western Šäwa; and Wašära Maryam and Gonğ, important centers for the teaching of the religious verse known as *qəne*, in Goğğam. Gondär came to flourish as a major centre for Ethiopian religious chant (*zema*) and dance (*maḫlet*), as well as the exegesis of the sacred texts. Monastic traditions linked with such centres preserved Ethiopic texts through the centuries and created a remarkable corpus of illuminated manuscripts.

Within Amhara aesthetic culture perhaps the most distinctive genre is a poetic form known as "wax and gold" (*Säm-enna-wärq*). Although this poetic figure refers primarily to religious constructions in Ge'ez, it is widely used by the Amhara in secular poesy as well as everyday conversation. "Wax and gold" verses are characteristically improvised by *azmari* as they play one-stringed violins called *mäsinqo*; their hidden meanings are usually political or erotic. Other forms of Amharic oral literature include *šəlläla*, a genre of boastful war chants that are partly intoned and partly shouted; and short rhymed proverbs (ተረት *tärät*) that express a wealth of folk wisdom.

Other traditional musical instruments include the *bägäna*, a box lyre with six strings plucked to create a deep-toned, slightly buzzing sound and played to accompany the Psalms of David or plaintive verses; wooden shepherd's flutes that pipe out brisk pentatonic melodies; trumpets associated with courtly and martial situations; and drums of many kinds.

Through their control of the political centre of Ethiopian society and through migrations, conquests, trading networks, and intermarriages, the Amhara have extended their language and many of their customs far beyond the borders of their primary home territory. This expansion has provided a glue to hold together the far-flung elements of the larger Ethiopian polity. This enabled the Ethiopian state to enter the process of modern nation-building in the 19th century and thereby maintain its independence against threats from Egypt and European colonial powers. It also aided such modernizing developments as ending the slave trade, installing new systems of communication and transportation, establishing schools and hospitals, and forming rationalized government institutions. At the same time, although the process of Amharization took place spontaneously for centuries, and has become a marker of full inclusion in the Ethiopian nation just as learning English has in the United States, it has led to resentments among members of some other ethnic groups—especially since World War II, when the government included Amharic as a requirement in the school curriculum. How these dynamics work out will do much to determine the future shape of the Ethiopian nation.

Bibliography

Enrico Cerulli, "Il sultanato dello Scioa nel secolo XIII", *RSE* 1, 1, 1941, 5–42;

Sevir Chernetsov, "On the Problem of Ethnogenesis of the Amhara", in: Rolf Gundlach – Manfred Kropp – Annalis Leibundgut (eds.), *Der Sudan in Vergangenheit und Gegenwart*, New York 1996 (Nordostafrikanisch-Westasiatische Studien 1), 17–35;

Christopher Clapham, *Haile Selassie's Government*, New York 1969;

Donald Crummey, *Land and Society in the Christian Kingdom of Ethiopia: From the Thirteenth to the Twentieth Century*, Urbana, Il – Oxford – Addis Ababa 2000 (Lit.);

Getatchew Haile, "Amharic Speakers and the Question of Nationalities," *Ethiopian Review, May 1992, 20–23;*

Allan Hoben, *Land Tenure among the Amhara of Ethiopia*, Chicago 1973;

Donald N. Levine, *Wax and Gold,* Chicago 1965 (Lit.); Id., "Ethiopia: Identity, Authority, and Realism", in: Lucian Pye – Sidney Verba (eds), *Political Culture and Political Development,* Princeton 1965, 245–81;

_______., *Greater Ethiopia: The Evolution of a Multiethnic Society,* Chicago 2000;

Simon David Messing, *Highland-Plateau Amhara of Ethiopia*, University of Pennsylvania 1957 [repr. and ed. by Marvin Lionel Bender, New Haven 1985]; TadTChurch;

Wolfgang Weissleder, "Amhara Marriage," *Canadian Review of Sociology and Anthropology*, 11, 1, 1974, 67–85.

19

Ethiopians in Israel (2006)*

For all the talk about ethnic self-determination in Ethiopia, almost no attention has been paid to the one and only ethnic group that actually seceded from Ethiopia—the Beta Israel, formerly called Falasha, whose entire population left the country. The story of their secession is full of drama, intrigue, suffering, and jubilation—and, like so much else about Ethiopia, fraught with misunderstandings.

One account of their exodus, which I once believed, was that their departure was instigated from outside pressures, most notably from the American Jewish community. Stephen Spector's meticulously researched *Operation Solomon* (2005) clarifies the matter decisively, locating the real impetus in the religious motives of the Beta Israel themselves. Spector and other sources demonstrate that during the mid-1970s, once Israel's two chief rabbis declared the Beta Israel authentic Jews, they experienced a heightened yearning to emigrate to the Land of Israel. How they strove to realize that yearning offers yet another testimony to the religiosity, hardiness, determination—and love of pilgrimage—that characterize Ethiopians of many regions.

Ethiopians of the North long regarded the Holy Land as an alluring beacon. Ethiopian Christians refer to themselves as *deqiqa Israel*, children of Israel; Ethiopians were among the earliest immigrant groups to settle in Jerusalem. Legend is that the Lalibela churches were constructed to enable Ethiopian Christians to have an awesome destination once the route to Jerusalem was

---

* Originally published in 2006 on the web forum of the Ethiopian Institute for Nonviolence Education and Peace Studies.

hampered by the Arab conquests. Years ago, I spoke with a group of resident monks in Jerusalem and asked if they did not miss their homeland: "*Sela-agaratchew nafqot albezabatchihum*?" "*Inday*!" they replied, "*izih new agaratchn*!" (What do you mean? Our homeland is right here!)

Visiting Jerusalem this year, however, I learned of two points at which Ethiopian Christians are vulnerable. One concerns the decision of authorities not to grant asylum to some seventy illegal Christian immigrants. They were detained in prison for two years until a court accepted the UNHCR judgment that their appeal for asylum based on fear of personal persecution in Ethiopia was not well founded. Under pressure from local Ethiopians, the Government of Israel stayed their deportation until the Canadian Embassy issued invitation letters for them to be interviewed.

More serious is the ongoing litigation over Ethiopia's age-old proprietary claims to a small enclave on the roof of the Church of the Holy Sepulcher, Deir es-Sultan (Eth. Debra Sultan). Thanks to their long presence in Jerusalem, from not long after their Christianization in the 4th century CE, Ethiopians acquired rights to some of Christianity's most sacred sites. These rights were attested repeatedly by European visitors through the Middle Ages, one reporting in the late 14th century that Ethiopians possessed four different chapels in the Church of the Holy Sepulcher. Even so, after Salahadin conquered Jerusalem in 1187 and assigned Ethiopia's rights to Egyptian Copts, those claims were contested repeatedly. Subsequent competition with diverse Christian nationals—Armenians, Greeks, and Copts—made it difficult for Ethiopians to hold on to those rights. Skirmishes with Egyptians during the two centuries after 1770 took away nearly all Ethiopian property. After the Six-Day War in June 1967, several Ethiopian monks who had to evacuate an old monastery near the Jordan River rejoined their compatriots at Deir es-Sultan just after it was evacuated by panicking Egyptian Coptic monks—all except the determined Coptic archbishop, who stayed on only to be manhandled by the tough Ethiopians. That was a retribution of sorts for the episode when Copts threw stones at the Ethiopian Easter celebration on the roof; Israeli authorities changed locks of the two chapels and handed Ethiopians the keys. Still, vicissitudes of relations among Egypt, Ethiopia, and Israel continue to jeopardize Ethiopian rights to the site; at the moment, the case is still before the Israeli High Court.

Most Ethiopians fail to grasp the significance of this monastery for their nation—so argues Daniel Alemu, a young Ethiopian scholar in Jerusalem. Yet if Badme is significant for Ethiopia, he says, Deir es-Sultan is far more integral to Ethiopian history and national identity. It also symbolizes the deep religiosity often attributed to Ethiopians of all faiths; only the unbounded devotion that Ethiopians have for this ancient holy site enables them to manifest the strength and tolerance needed to live for centuries under inhuman conditions in a collapsing monastery.

The attachment of Christian Ethiopians to the Holy Land pales next to that of their Beta Israel kinsmen. So deep was the Falashas' historic identification with their Hebraic roots that they created an annual holiday, *Sigd*, when they climb a mountain and recite the Ten Commandments in honor of Moses on Mt. Sinai. All the Ethiopian *olim* (immigrants) whom Spector interviewed mentioned this as their primary motive. He quotes an elderly *qes* (Jewish priest): "Our ancestors all hoped and prayed that they themselves would make it to Jerusalem. They did not make it. We are on the brink of reaching Zion." This evidence contradicts stories circulated in the West to arouse sympathy and donations, stories disconfirmed by those on the ground. Ethiopian officials, U.S. Government officials, and American relief agencies alike affirm that Falasha did not leave because of famine, warfare, disease, or persecution by Christians.

The dream of Zion drove Beta Israel to a via dolorosa into Sudan in the years after 1977 when the Derg halted emigration to Israel. Huge numbers made a long, dangerous trek across the desert, usually at night, in which thousands died dreadful deaths along the way. Once there, many more died in pestilential refugee compounds. Their tragic situation aroused people in Canada, the U.S. and Israel, after which outside support from North America and Israel became indispensable. Israeli Defense Forces began heroic efforts to locate and transport the survivors to Israel—efforts that culminated in Operation Moses of late 1984 when they brought some 6500 Falashas to Israel. When that was exposed in the Sudanese Press, it had to be discontinued. President Nimeiri was deposed, and the new regime imprisoned or executed Sudanese thought to have assisted those rescues.

Even after that, Israelis rescued a couple thousand more from Sudan. All told, some twenty thousand Beta Israel left Ethiopia by way of Sudan, of whom about four thousand perished before reaching their destination. By 1989, nearly half the recognized Falasha community had reached Israel. This fired a constant demand for family reunification, which led eventually to Israel's agreeing to let some 27,800 more Ethiopian come between 1990 and 1992. The American Association for Ethiopian Jews (AAEJ), fearing for the very survival of the remaining Falasha populace, brought them en masse to Addis Ababa. Many Ethiopian Christians pleaded with them not to leave, while others felt sympathy for their outpouring of collective devotion, including Berhanu Yiradu, who chaired a committee in Gonder working to expedite the movement to Addis; Dr. Girma Tolossa, who represented the Jewish Joint Distribution Committee in Addis; and an Ethiopian Christian priest who rented his large compound there to camp the Falasha migrants.

The climactic highlight was the remarkable Operation Solomon in which 14,300 Beta Israel were evacuated during a daring 36-hour airlift in late May 1991. A recent Jerusalem Post article includes Operation Solomon among the most memorable noble achievements in Israel's modern history, alongside the Six-Day War and the rescue at Entebbe.

Now amounting at 100,000 to two per cent of the Jewish population of Israel, Ethiopians comprise a larger percentage of the population there than of any other state outside of Ethiopia. Their adjustment problems have been amplified by having to leap from a rural subsistence lifestyle into that of modern cities as well as to learn a difficult new language and be absorbed in such large numbers in a short time. Much has been made of stories about their maladjustment: reported high rates of divorce, school dropouts, and suicide. For some, the cultural rift proved catastrophic. "On the day I set foot in Israel," one Ethiopian man said, "my life came to an end." A great deal of the Ethiopian Jewish community lives below the poverty line in depressed neighborhoods. A disproportionate number are unemployed, since they lack skills appropriate to work in a modern economy. Some claim to have been excluded from schools or jobs on racial grounds.

On the other hand, the Beta Israel of Ethiopia were treated with better accommodations and services than any other immigrant group in Israel's history. A recent survey showed that although their poverty level was higher than any other immigrant group, so was their level of satisfaction with life in the Promised Land. A decent number have made positive adjustments, becoming army officers, small businessmen, and successful candidates for city councils. Above all, from the viewpoint of the *olim*, coming to the Promised Land was the fulfillment of a culture's dream.

The situation is more ambiguous for several thousands of Christian Ethiopians who attempted to follow the trail of their Jewish countrymen. These are people who claim to be relatives of those already in Israel; the Hebrew name for them, *Falasmura*, signifies "Falashas who converted." Their case has been championed by the North American Conference on Ethiopian Jewry (NACOEJ), an organization that sprang up in the 1980s to assist the Falasha immigrants but was scarcely known in Israel before the completion of Operation Solomon in 1991. At that point the head of the Jewish Agency announced that the *aliyah* of Ethiopia's Jews had reached a successful completion. AAEJ, the chief charitable organization for the Falasha, closed down its American operation and all its work in Ethiopia. NACOEJ seized the opportunity to establish itself in Addis as advocate for those refused entry to the airplanes of Operation Solomon because they were known to be converts to Christianity—hence, according to the clear guidelines of the Law of Return, not eligible to come on *aliyah*.

After 1991 NACOEJ assumed jurisdiction over the 3000 or so *Falasmura* in Addis and sent agents to villages south of Gonder to recruit groups of Ethiopian Orthodox Christians who claimed that their ancestors had been Falashas. The new migrants needed little encouragement; they streamed torrentially into Addis Ababa, before long swelling the cumulative total of arrivals to 50,000. NACOEJ lobbies in Israel and in the States became influential; they enlist the support of the Black Caucus as well as the United Jewish Communities if Israel makes any move that seems detrimental to the "Jews" languishing in Ethiopia. Although the group has been thrown out of Ethiopia, it works behind the scenes to support those thousands of expectant Ethiopians who anticipate eventually being brought to Israel. Processing all those hopefuls and new immigrants has become what some call a racket. The large reservoir of potential immigrants get encouragement both from their relatives who are already in Israel and from the tireless efforts of a NACOEJ-affiliated Ethiopian, Avraham Beyene, whose organization, which seeks to bring all the *Falasmura* to Israel, is based in Jerusalem. Paradoxically, Ato Avraham's own Falasha ancestors were among those who early on converted to Christianity, and he, prior to his *aliyah*, had worked in Gonder under the auspices of the London Missionary Society for the Conversion of the Jews.

The Falasmura story threatens to override what was a narrative of triumph with a troubling denouement. Ethiopians who arrived since the early 1990s, despite their announced conversions to Judaism, keep distant from the Jewish life of the genuine Falasha community. They have become an increasing burden on the limited resources of the Israeli Government. They incite political opportunists to accuse the Government of racism by not admitting more Ethiopians, just as earlier ideologues accused Israel of racism by importing settlers from Africa.

The original Falasha exodus continues to have repercussions. Their departure had costs. It robbed Ethiopia of an important part of her history, a part to which recent scholarship has brought fresh attention. It deprived Israel of the only indigenous Jewish community left in the African Continent. It deprived Gonderes of close friends and neighbors. (Indeed, some Gonderes have come to feel guilty about how they mistreated the Falashas before their departure and wish to make amends by providing favorable conditions for their return.) And it stripped Falasha culture of its traditional moorings and accessories—ritual objects, prayerbooks, idiosyncratic monastic traditions.

On the other hand, Operations Moses and Solomon brought enormous joy to devoted Ethiopian Jews. Minashe Kimru, an elderly *qes*, exclaimed: "I feel happy like a lamb. . . . It is better to die as a free Jew than to continue living in exile in Ethiopia." The Operations saved a distinctive branch of Judaism for the world. Ethiopianist Chaim Rosen notes that "there are perhaps one hundred Falasha priests still functioning in Israel, with many followers, and determinedly passing their tradition down to their sons. So the unique Beta Israel religion remains alive in Israel, and has been preserved there perhaps even more than in it might have been in Ethiopia, where it could have faded away like the Qemant religion."

What is more, as I wrote in my *IJES* article, "Reconfiguring the Ethiopian Nation in a Global Era," Ethiopians in the Diaspora can and do continue to be an integral part of the Ethiopian nation. They engage from afar, through visits, the internet, sometimes by repatriation. I envisage channels through which Israeli Ethiopians can begin to connect back with the motherland, like other Diaspora Ethiopians who return for limited times or for good. Falashas are learning skills that can be put to good use in Ethiopia's development. They and fellow Israelis can harness the experience of Israelis in turning deserts into gardens, and fructify areas like the Ogaden and the their homelands in the northwest. The Ethiopian Government has broached the idea of offering fellowships at Ethiopian universities for Ethiopians in Israel. The prospect of giving Ethiopian Israelis a chance to renew ties to their other motherland offers opportunities for all concerned after the trials and tribulations of the past few decades.

20

Tigrayawinet (2006)*

Of the many strange elements in the current trial of political prisoners and journalists, the charge of genocide seems the most peculiar of all. Consider, for example, the idea of launching such a charge against Professor Mesfin Wolde Mariam—the man who, of all Ethiopians I know, owns the clearest lifelong record of standing for nonviolence. What is one to make of that?

For all the apparent irrationality of accusing Professor Mesfin and others of committing genocide (*zer matfat*) or even incitement to genocide, there are bound to be reasons for such an accusation. In searching for those reasons, one must be careful; so much of what passes for political discourse in Ethiopia consists of rumors and back-biting. For half a century I have witnessed constant imputing of far-fetched motives to political actors. "*Igele* is an opportunist," "*Igele* is really a spy for X"—you know what I mean. What facts can be fairly securely attested?

> 1. What is certain is that for many years, slurs and threats against Tigrayan Ethiopians have been fairly common, especially in the Amhara and Oromia regions, and that these escalated sharply in the aftermath of the 2005 elections.
>
> 2. It is also certain that CUD leaders carefully refrained from including any anti-ethnic language in all of their public documents. I could be proven wrong, but I doubt that any authentic documentation to the contrary will be produced in the trial proceedings.
>
> 3. Those who issued the anti-Tigrayan statements, then, were not the official party leaders now being accused, but ordinary civilians or, at most, rank-and-file party supporters. The CUD and other opposition leaders

* Originally published in 2006 on the web forum of the Ethiopian Institute for Nonviolence Education and Peace Studies.

actually exerted a moderating influence on those who wanted to express such feelings.

4. The resentments being voiced, finally, were not directed against ordinary Tigrayans. Rather, they expressed a long accumulation of resentments about governance under an overwhelmingly Tigrayan political elite. Those resentments became more open in the course of last year's political campaign and especially in its aftermath. In June, the sale of machetes surged in Addis and elsewhere; Tigrayan students in campuses in Addis, Alemayhu, and Awassa were armed and reportedly trained to "defend themselves."

5. By disseminating the allegation that those who vented those resentments were like the vengeful Interhamwe murderers, the government made tactical use of those expressed resentments. The government's allegation may in fact be responsible for inciting some of the surge in the procurement of weapons.

However, to repeat: the resentments were not directed against Tigrayan people as such. Numerous Tigrayans expressed resentments against the TPLF themselves; thousands of Tigrayans voted for the opposition candidates, and at least one Tigrayan and one spouse of a Tigrayan now sit in prison for allegedly supporting genocidal statements against Tigrayans. Those resentments were directed, rather, against the TPLF cadres, and that for two main reasons. One was in fact ethnic-political: the fact that the EPRDF administration has been directed by a small number of Ethiopians from a minority ethnic group, in violation of the regime's announced democratic aspirations.

The other was ideological: the fact that EPRDF had apparently betrayed Ethiopia's proud record as a historic nation and in so doing had stirred up ethnic tensions. Echoing the Eritrean fiction that "there was no country called Ethiopia before Minelik's rule," as a recent Sudan Tribune article puts it, one of their leaders even wrote under the TPLF seal that to say that Eritrea was historically been part of Ethiopia was "nothing more than a fairy tale [and that] Ethiopia as a country does not start from the civilization of Aksum." Accordingly, those who championed the symbolism of Ethiopian nationality they suspected of being "Amhara chauvinists."

The irony in all that must be stunning to anyone who knows the slightest bit about Ethiopia's history. If ever there was a seedbed of Ethiopian nationhood, it was Tigray. Tigray was the region that nurtured the core complex of Ethiopia as a multiethnic polity. The kingdom of Aksum was, Mani of Persia observed in the 280s CE, the third of the four great powers of the ancient world. As early as the 6th century CE the Roman Venantius associated Aksum with the country then known as Ethiopia. The Ethiopian power centered in Aksum controlled many tribes, and at its zenith reached across the Red Sea to Himyar as well as up to the citadel of Meroe in Nubia. Even after Aksum fell and the political center shifted southward, Tigray remained a vital part of Ethiopian nationhood. Tigrayan scribes reportedly redacted the *Kibre Negest* which provided a charter for Ethiopian nationhood. Emperors in principle returned to Aksum to be crowned; some of the most dramatic episodes in Ethiopic literature describe the visits of Iyasu I to Aksum in the 1690s. Ras Mikael Sehul of Tigray was the power behind the throne of the Gonderine court for many years. And it was a Tigrayan Emperor, Yohannes IV, who implemented the vision of *Atse* Tewodros in rebuilding a strong multiethnic polity, in a vigorous reign cut short by the vengeful spear of a scion of ancient Nubia fifteen hundred years later. The Raya region of Tigray, where Afar, Agau, Amhara, Oromo, and Tigrawi long lived together amicably, embodies Ethiopian mutliethnicity at its best.

Yohannes IV of Ethiopia would have been horrified by pronouncements of his descendants a century later who challenged the reality of Ethiopia's historic nationhood. Yohannes ridiculed the pretentious claims of Italian colonialists to the Red Sea Coast, affirming that it had always belonged to Ethiopia de jure, even during years when the Turks established beachheads there. He made common cause with "Amhara" Emperor Minelik in the effort to check the Italian encroachments. Yet the banner of Ethiopia as fiction guided the Tigrayan People's Liberation Front when they entered the capital in May 1991.

This dramatic reversal of Tigrayan sentiment, from champions of historic Ethiopia to debunkers of its reality—how did it come about? How did the TPLF warriors pursue the cause of partisan Tigrayawinet? How has the thinking of EPRDF leaders evolved since then? What options does that portend for Ethiopia's future? These questions will be addressed in Part II of this piece, which may shed additional light on the mystery of the genocide charge against the Kaliti detainees.

Tigrayawinet, Part II

Whence this dramatic reversal of Tigrayan sentiment, from champions of historic Ethiopia to debunkers of its reality? The story begins following the Liberation from Italian rule in 1942. The Tigrayan populace was stressed due to population pressures on increasingly infertile land. Nearly a third of Tigrayans migrated to other parts of the country. Their strained condition was severely exacerbated by impossibly heavy tax burdens, which the IEG refused to adjust. Indeed, the attitude of the central government seemed dismissive toward Tigray. It was clear that Shoa, the center of imperial rule since Minelik, and Eritrea, the returned province that Ethiopia sought to woo, were the major beneficiaries of the national budget. This grated on a people who had long played a central role in the Ethiopian political landscape.

These resentments boiled over in March 1943 when people from many parts of the province rose up in a rebellion (Tigr. *woyane*) against the Imperial Ethiopian Government that lasted for five months. In response, Emperor Haile Selassie I had RAF planes drop payloads of bombs against Tigrayan villagers (as he did when he was confronted with peasant uprisings in other parts of the country, such as Gojjam). That planted the seeds of a smouldering antagonism that was fueled when the Government's strict Amharization policy produced a ban against using the Tigrinya language in 1970.

It did not seem that things would improve under the Derg. Two days after they deposed the Emperor, a group of Tigrayans met in a cafe in Addis to plant the seeds of a Tigrayan opposition movement, taking the name Woyane—signifying a popular rebellion against outside oppression—as their logo. Derg policies reinforced their grievances. For example, the Derg forbade Tigrayans used to going to other parts of the country to work, a common basis for earning income that they would bring home to support their families and invest in their farms. This plunged Tigrayans ever more deeply into poverty and hopelessness, and gave the incipient TPLF movement important support from the very beginning.

"In my high school class in Agame," one TPLF veteran of the early 1980s told me, "80% of the students supported TPLF, the rest were for EPRP." This groundswell of sentiment led in two directions, however. One group (TPLF) wanted to press the claims of a greater Tigray (Tigray-Tigrini), uniting Tigrinya-speakers from Eritrea with the province. The other group organized itself politically and ideologically through the Marxist-Leninist League of Tigray. It conjoined the principle of class struggle with that of self-determination of nationalities. Like other radicals of the day, they appropriated the myth that Ethiopia was the invention of Minelik in order to legitimate the independence of Eritrea, and the principle of self-determination within Ethiopia.

This ethno-Marxist sentiment drove the most ambitious elements of the TPLF movement. It led those who took political control of the TPLF to turn against Tigrayan political elements who did not support Eritrean independence. Before long that led, evidence suggests, to a policy of liquidating those elements. Tigray became, survivors of those horrific years aver, a "killing field." According to many reports, which must be investigated further by future historians, Tigrayan civilians were slaughtered right and left—in many cases following gruesome torture, according to eye witnesses. Rumors of mass graves in the surroundings of Ghinem in Welkait Tsegede as well as in other parts of Tigray, if confirmed, would support such reports.

Like many idealistic youth of their generation, the Marxist-Leninist League of Tigray felt empowered by the seductive morsels of Marxian ideology—unaware of the wise pronouncements of the young Marx himself that Communism like other narrow doctrines was a dangerous "dogmatic abstraction." Coupled with the new dogmatic abstraction about Ethiopia as an invention of Minilek, it became a heady brew that induced the committed TPLF ethno-Marxists to murder great numbers of civilians and to perpetrate slanders against Amharas and Ethiopian patriots. One veteran of those killings confesses that when he told another, early in the fighting "the number of people we have killed thus far has reached 10,000," his comrade replied: "So what, Red China had to kill a million people in order to become victorious." Attitudes of that sort, be it noted, were shared by other Ethiopian revolutionaries of the time.

It is possible, then, that accusations of genocide against Mesfin Wolde Mariam and other defendants may reflect something else. *They may represent a wish to disavow the crimes against Tigrayans which the TPLF in its days of struggle felt it had to commit.* The current leadership has changed a good deal since those impassioned days. Prime Minister Meles Zenawi had strenuously disavowed the tenets of his early ideological commitments as early as 1990, arguing that what he wanted was a chance for the peoples of Ethiopia to decide their fate from the bottom up, not from the top down. The EPRDF has given up most of the doctrines of Leninism and insists that it wants to move Ethiopia in the direction of democratization. In recent months it has taken steps toward reforming parliamentary procedures, press legislation, and the Election Board. The nationalist sentiments evoked by the 1998–2000 campaign against Eritrea produced some recognition that *behere etyopiya* was not so fictitious after all. The old warriors may regret the misery they caused in their determined rise to power. They now insist that they want to get beyond a politics of violence.

There is much that they and the whole country can do to accomplish that. The Government commands the allegiance of cadres of Agazi troops—uncompassionate, socially isolated cadres who owe their existence to the TPLF, and who can be mobilized in an instant to inflict terrible cruelties behind the scenes. For the former TPLF leadership to embrace Ethiopian nationhood fully it will do well to insist on an impartial and transparent investigation of the actions of its security forces—at Dedessa, in Tigray, and in the streets and alleys of Addis Ababa. The current Government of Ethiopia demands that those currently indicted be held accountable for any crimes they committed by inciting illegal actions against the Ethiopian state, if such can be proven in court—even though, on the question of incitement to ethnic violence, it is doubtful that there can be credible evidence to convict the CUD leaders. Beyond that, the Government must also be vigilant in monitoring excesses of ethnic vilification. In Tigray since the election, a few people circulate the warning, "*Amharotch temelsu seltan intehizu iqetleke iyu naya'aharte sheate amat qalsi behama yiteref*"—"if the Amhara return to power, they will kill you all and your seventeen-year struggle will have been in vain." Surely that is something that can be discouraged.

Decades of suffering from destructive political conflicts can be ended, especially now that Ethiopia's security is threatened on all borders. It should now be possible again to view Adwa, not as a symbol of irrendentist particularism but once again as the triumph of multiethnic Ethiopianism, when 100,000 troops from dozens of ethnic groups fought together behind every important chief from all over the country—Ras Alula, Ras Mengesha, and Ras Sibhat of Tigray; Dejazmatch Bahta of Akale Guzae; Wag Shum Guangul of Lasta; Ras Mikael of Wallo; Negus Takla-Haymanot of Gojjam; Ras Gobena and Dejazmatch Balcha of the Mecha Oromo; Ras Wele of the Yejju Oromo; Fitawrari Tekla of Wollega; Ras Makonnen of Harar; as well as Ras Gebeyehu (who died fighting at Adwa) and Ras Abate of Shoa. Minister Fisseha Ashgedom, an early TPLF loyalist, talks proudly now of the role his grandfather Dejazmatch Tessema played in the battle of Adwa. The Adwa victory became and remains the most outstanding symbol of what, a half-century later, a British colonel would describe as the "mysterious magnetism" that holds Ethiopia together. This is a magnetism that will outlast the petty particularisms and personal ambitions that became so virulent under the ethno-Marxist ideologues of the 1970s and 1980s.

21

Two Tales of One City (2006)*

Commenting on the current political state of affairs, a knowledgeable journalist said to me in Addis: "People here have been attacking one another all year. But they never talk about things they are really mad about." His comment rang a bell. Don't we all know family members who quarrel about things that substitute for what they are really feeling hurt and angry about?

Time and again in October, Government and Opposition were on the verge of coming to an agreement that would have prevented the November violence and subsequent imprisonments. For a moment, if possible, let us set aside the question of who is to blame. Let us entertain the hypothesis that whatever the unprovoked harassment of CUD leaders by Government security personnel and whatever perceptions the Government had about insurrectionary ambitions of the opposition, there was something in the air that enabled the talks—for which the Prime Minister had at one point given assurance that everything was on the table—to break down. The parties had been talking about Parliamentary procedures, access to the Press, and the like. But what were the two sides really mad about?

Ever since the Derg was overthrown fifteen years ago, I have heard Ethiopians of different positions hurl insults at one another, accuse one another of the basest motives, and dig ever deeper the moats that distance them from one another. For fifteen years, I have wondered when the time would come that the underlying issues of their discontent might be addressed and resolved. Perhaps it took the killings and imprisonments of 2005 to force the issue, to get good Ethiopians of different persuasions to thinking in and about a new way.

---

* Originally published on the web forum of the *Ethiopian Review*, April 7, 2006.

That will take effort. To get beyond feeling aggrieved and injured, although grief and injury are abundant all around. To get beyond pouring blame on one another, although there are many things to blame. Perhaps the effort may involve realizing that what has been at stake all along has been two seemingly incompatible narratives about their country's history.

Narrative One:

1. Modern Ethiopia is an empire created by a hegemonic Amhara elite under Emperor Menelik II who conquered and dominated all of the historically separate and independent ethnic groups in the area.

2. It was dominated by a ruling class that had to be overthrown and prevented from regaining power or control of the land of peasants in the conquered territories.

3. The Derg was a ruthless, centrist regime that survived by terrorizing Ethiopian citizens.

4. TPLF troops, supported by EPLF, were the only viable opposition force to rebel against the Derg. For some seventeen years, they struggled as guerilla fighters and, after enormous sacrifice and suffering, succeeded in defeating the Derg and forcing its much-hated leader to flee.

5. Although they fought during those years under the banner of the Marxist-Leninist League of Tigray, they abandoned communist ideology as the Cold War came to an end and formally embraced liberal democracy.

6. They felt badly treated, after all that sacrifice and suffering, when their victorious entrance into the capital was met with hostility by those who sat out the Derg years in relative comfort.

7. Once in power, they proceeded to create a novel system of ethnic federalism to ensure dignity for all of Ethiopia's peoples and to prevent a resurgence of private plutocracy through continued state ownership of land and many industries.

8. To ensure the success of their program, they had to spread a network of EPRDF cadres across the country.

Narrative Two:

1. Modern Ethiopia is the outgrowth of a two-thousand-year-old polity rooted in Aksum. It became unified and remained independent thanks to the leadership of Emperors Tewodros II, Yohannes IV, and Menelik II.

2. It came to fruition under Emperor Haile Selassie I, who advanced national centralization, instituted ministries and standing armies and, though mostly

Shoan Amhara and surrounded by Shoan nobility, included Eritreans, Tigreans, Oromos, and others in the national elite he fostered.

3. The Derg was a ruthless communist regime that survived by terrorizing Ethiopian citizens.

4. TPLF troops, supported by EPLF, became the only viable opposition force to rebel against the Derg, although EDU and EPRP had been forces to contend with at one time. For some seventeen years, they struggled as guerilla fighters and, after enormous sacrifice and suffering, succeeded in defeating the Derg and forcing its much-hated leader to flee.

5. Although the TPLF leadership abandoned communist ideology as the Cold War came to an end and formally embraced liberal democracy, they never truly embraced the principles of liberal democracy.

6. Joy at the overthrow of the Derg was muted by apprehension about the revanchist tenor of TPLF anti-Amhara sentiments, their elevation of tribal ethnicity above Ethiopian nationhood, their Leninist political style, and their reluctance to de-collectivize land.

7. Once in power, EPRDF = TPLF excluded other ethnic groups from the center, imposed a system of ethnic federalism without broad national consensus, and continued state ownership of land and many industries. To defend these changes, they consistently harassed opposition parties, clamped down on a free press, and prevented an independent judiciary.

8. To ensure political control, they spread a network of EPRDF cadres across the country, who year after year abused the rights of civilians and did little to promote economic development.

These contrasting narratives bloomed fully in the months after May 1991. Beyond whatever strivings for power animated the leaders of the various parties in 2005, it was underlying antagonisms about these contrasting visions of the past and what they implied for Ethiopia's future that fueled an underground current of fire. The differences they embodied have never been addressed quietly and resolved amicably.

This way of framing the matter was suggested to me by a lecture given in Berlin by a seasoned scholar who discussed the essence of the Palestinian-Israeli conflict. He pointed out how chronic hostilities between Israelis and Palestinians flowed from contrasting narratives about their pasts. Jews live with a picture of their past that depicts them as perennial victims, deprived of their sacred land by ruthless Babylonian and Roman conquerors, abused by host societies for millennia thereafter, and subject to an effort at total annihilation so monstrous—*ha-shoah*, the Holocaust—that it gave rise to a new concept in human criminality, genocide. Palestinians live with a picture of their past that depicts them as resident in their land from time immemorial, proud caretakers of the holy places of Christianity and Islam, then confronted by a robust immigrant population that began with intrusive settlements and—through *al nakbah*, the Catastrophe—frightened many from their homes forever and eventually dominated them in their homeland territory. It would seem impossible for peoples with such incompatible stories ever to live together harmoniously—except, the lecturer pointed out, those narratives resembled the incompatible narratives that oriented France and Germany, now friendly neighbors, for a long time and impelled them into three horrible wars within one century.

To be sure, the centuries-old histories of Jews and Palestinians cannot really be said to have a counterpart in opposition between political parties who came into being les than two decades ago. And so, beyond the contrast of narratives, perhaps we must locate another factor. Perhaps it is what Dr. B. T. Constantinos, in a response to my article "Ethiopians in Prison,"[1] described suggestively by observing that:

> the Ethiopian political elite [has debated] problems of our democratization... largely within a particular tradition of political thought, argument and struggle that has origins in the radical student movement; in ideas of "national liberation," "class struggle," "national democratic revolution" spawned by that movement; and in the Marxist-Leninist tradition of political thought, discourse, and action that has been a decisive influence over the current political impasse. At a time when the tradition seems a spent force in much of the former second world, including post-Derg Ethiopia, a toned-down and somewhat reconstructed version of it seems to have gained a new lease on life among Ethiopia's political elite in the country and abroad.

Although Dr. Constantinos and I might disagree on details of that diagnosis, we probably agree on the hallmarks of that tradition: clever talk, arrogance, demonization of the other, presentation of preconditions in tight formulaic terms that are not amenable to alternative formulations and mediation (*shimgilna*), urbanite insurgency, and identification of one's position with the good and the will of the "people."

In this sense, then, the problem is not to move beyond Ethiopian traditions, but to restore the rich traditions of civility, forgiveness, neighborliness, and respect for one another that antedate the incivility of the Marxist tradition. For this purpose, Ethiopians could scarcely do better, for example, than return to the political culture embodied in that remarkable Ethiopian tradition, the *gumi gayo* of the Boran and Guji peoples, which opens each parliamentary debate with a caution not to look for the worst in what others have said in order to undermine their position and win an argument, but to look for the best they have to offer so as to find a common ground:

> *Dubbi qarumman dubbatani miti. Warri qaro qarumman laf keyyaddha.*
>
> This is not the place for clever talk. Clever people should leave their cleverness behind.

For today's political elite, that could mean listening to one another's narratives and perhaps even learning something.

22

Oromo Narratives (2007)*

Debates among Oromo citizens frequently turn about questions of identity and political action. In considering those questions, inquiries into views of the past may not be out of place. I support such inquiries on the basis of considerations spelled out in my book on the future of social theory, *Visions of the Sociological Tradition* (1995). Drawing on work by several social scientists, I argued there that narratives of the past held by human communities, no less than individual autobiographies, form an essential condition for constituting identity in the present and projecting meaningful action in the future. The point draws on a half century of discourse about the ways in which organizations of subjective meanings affect action, including the now classic text of Berger and Luckmann, which stresses the role of symbolic universes that locate all events "in a cohesive unity that includes past, present, and future" (1966, 103), and the seminal paper of psychologist Bertram Cohler (1982), which shows how narratives help persons make sense of their lives in times of change and how they revise earlier memories continually as a function of subsequent experience.

More concretely, at the communal level, French sociologist Maurice Halbwachs famously demonstrated, collective memories prove indispensable for the functioning of social groups of all kinds, for in recalling signal events of the past, they offer a focus for group solidarity, and during periods of routine activity they keep alive a group's connection to its ideals and symbols of identity. Group memories also function defensively, to justify claims and to valorize aggressive actions triggered by aspirations to pursue those claims. And just as

---

* Originally published in the *Journal of Oromo Studies* Volume 14, Number 2 (July 2007), pp. 43–63.

when actors grow and change, altered narratives about the self mediate changes of structure and commitment, so do alterations of collective autobiographies mediate changes in the lives of groups. One way to track the changes in the lives of communities, I argued in *Visions of the Sociological Tradition*, is to trace the sequence of narratives they tell about their own past as they evolve.

It is thus no accident that recent Ethiopian history has seen an outpouring of novel narratives in different communities. The massive introduction of Marxist ideas among educated Ethiopians in the 1960s engendered a number of new ways of telling the story of Ethiopia's past.[1] Such narratives need not be fully articulated or written down even; they may be vague and inchoate; but they play a necessary part in orienting Ethiopian actors, like any others, to a changing world. These new histories were most conspicuous—and consequential—in the case of Eritrean intellectuals, who developed a novel narrative of their past in the course of moving toward independence from Ethiopia, and by Tigrayan insurgents of the 1980s, whose distinctive narrative of Ethiopia's past helped to justify an ideology of ethnic federalism. In his perspicuous account of perspectival changes during the Derg years, Donald Donham notes that the effect of Derg policies was to alter the imaginations of Ethiopians—"their sense of their place in the world and the shape of their pasts and their futures." What is needed to follow these changes, he asserts, is "an ethnography of local historical imaginations" (Donham 1999, xviii).[2]

The comparison of collective narratives forms a theoretically fascinating subject for historical sociology. It can have practical benefits as well. On the one hand, by attending to the diverging narratives of groups in conflict, analysts can play a mediating role, by giving each group a sense that it is being heard and understood, and by helping ease the intensity of antagonisms through helping each group listen to the stories of the other. This was the use of narratives that I pursued in my little article, "Two Tales of One City" (2006a), in which I talked about the contrasting narratives of the polarized groups among Ethiopians following the post-election bedlam in 2005. On the other hand, the analyst may wish to reconstruct narratives in order to clarify options for the future, since visions of the future necessarily imply and flow from narratives of the past. That is the use of narratives I shall pursue in this paper. My aim here is to clarify Oromo options today by sketching in broad strokes some of the main types of narratives told by Oromos about themselves.

Although my analysis does not have the benefit of the fine-grained ethnographic reportage that Donham advocates, it may aid our understanding of these perspectives through a systematic articulation of their central assumptions and projections. I present these narrative perspectives in a form that sociologists refer to as "ideal types"—intellectual abstractions that rarely appear in pure form in reality but which are useful for teasing out the logic of various intellectual and normative positions.

I refer to these narrative types as the Traditionalist Narrative, the Colonialist Narrative, and the Ethiopianist Narrative. I do not attempt to provide a social location for the persons and groups subscribing more or less to each of these narratives. It should be noted, however, that the Oromo population I have in mind does not include the Oromos living in Kenya, but does include all the Ethiopian Oromos who live in the Diaspora and are thereby part of the reconfigured Ethiopian nation that I have depicted elsewhere (Levine 2004). As an approximation to those representing these ideal-typical narratives, I would suggest the names, respectively, of Gemetchu Megerssa, Asafa Jalata, and Fikre Tolossa.

Whatever form these Oromo narratives take, they presume a tradition of political culture that includes reference to common themes. These themes are common for being derived ultimately from the traditional institutions of the *gadaaqaaluu* system. Among Oromo groups that have diverged radically from the traditional culture, these themes have been altered to some extent. These groups would include the five Ghibe kingdoms of the southwest and the Leeqaa Neqamtee and Leeqaa Qellem kingdoms in Wallaga, which switched to a more traditional type of African monarchical system; those who converted recently to a radical Evangelical Christian belief system; and those who converted recently to a radical fundamentalist type of Islam. But the great majority of the Oromo in Ethiopia—those who did not convert to authoritarian political or religious systems—manifest each of the cultural themes, which I gloss below as egalitarian ethos, communal solidarity, democratic structures, separation of powers, and civility in deliberation.

Themes of Oromo Political Culture

Egalitarian Ethos

In nearly all areas of social relations, Oromo tradition deflates hierarchy in favor of egalitarian norms. Although differentials of rank and power exist throughout Oromo society, Oromo custom tends to minimize their significance. Delegated authority tends to be balanced by a countervailing authority held by others. Those who occupy prestigious positions tend to be regarded ambivalently, and are treated with humor if not ridicule. Thus, although the father in Oromo families plays the role of patriarchal figure, good-humored, bantering relationships with his wife and children offset the deference due him. Men with high status in local communities are not deferred to obsequiously or automatically, nor are they entitled to order anyone about other than their own wives and children. Among the Metcha, when neighbors meet to discuss problems of communal interest or settle disputes, they are guided by the notion of *qite*, an extension of the word for 'equal.' In the words of Herbert Lewis, *qite*

> stresses the ideal that when they come together, all the members of the group are equal. In fact, some men have more influence and esteem than others; they speak more, they direct the flow of the discussion, and their words count more heavily than those of others present. But the ideal does reflect important aspects of the reality: each member of the community is invited to and expected to take part in community affairs. (Lewis [1970]2000, 173)

The institutions of the *gadaa* system promoted an ethos of egalitarianism in many ways. By keeping adjacent generations at a distance from one another, *gadaa* protects the filial generation from excessive control by the paternal.

> As soon as the paternal *luba* class comes to power, their sons receive their own separate identity by being initiated and given names. As the paternal class goes through the grades of semiretirement, the filial class becomes more independent and better organized. By the time the filial generation is ready to assume power, the paternal class proceeds to a grade of full retirement. (Levine [1974] 2000, 138)

Gadaa also structures political relations in an anti-authoritarian direction. It does so through the regular circulation of elites, such that no ruling class is in power for more than eight years. The Tulema Oromo represent this in a traditional ceremony where the leader of the ruling class, after several years in office, climbs a platform of stones to proclaim the laws as usual only to be shouted down and ceremonially pushed off: a reminder that his rule is soon to end (Knutsson 1967, 174–5). Another respect in which powers are balanced appears in the positioning of moieties. Thus, the constitution of the Borana ruling council assures a painstaking balance of representatives from the two moieties. And throughout *gadaa* younger men, who on the basis of age alone should defer to older men, often hold more prestigious positions than their elders. In sum, Oromo customs see to it that no position of superiority puts a man beyond control or criticism from his fellows.

Communal Solidarity

The weaving of Oromo relations into so many corporate bodies—patrilineal families, local communities, age sets, generational classes—has traditionally had the effect of heightening the Oromos' sense of membership in solidary groups. The pursuit of individual interests among the Oromo has tended not to be obtained at the expense of their neighbors—as was the case typically in the North due to competition over land and for honorific appointments—and the satisfaction of personal success often redounds to the greater glory of their lineage.

As I noted in *Greater Ethiopia*, numerous observers describe a cooperative spirit in which most activities are carried out:

> Settlements are constructed and cattle are grazed and watered by members of the *olla* groups working in concert. Among the agricultural *Guji*, sowing and harvesting similarly are carried out on a communal, cooperative basis.
>
> Comparable cooperative patterns appear in Oromo military expeditions. The Oromo formed age regimens, or *chibra*, which collectively undertook to collect supplies for the campaign, elect leaders recruit scouts, and distribute booty. (Levine [1974]2000, 141)

A disposition toward social inclusiveness forms a corollary to the theme of solidarity. It has enabled Oromos who converted to Christianity and to Islam to live amiably together, even intermarry, among themselves and with those who adhere to traditional Oromo beliefs. This is manifest notably in the Oromo practice of incorporation through adoption (*guddiffachaa*). Over generations this practice enabled Oromos to integrate groups from other ethnies such as Konso and Wolleyta and assimilate immigrants, through their "genius for assimilation" (Hassen 1994, 21.)

Democratic Structures

Recent accounts of the *gadaa* assemblies by Asmarom Legesse (2000) and Marco Bassi (2005) identify several respects in which traditional Oromo institutions exhibit exemplary democratic procedures. Laws stand above all men—even the Abba Gadaa is subject to same punishments as other citizens if he transgresses. Historic precedent in both judicial and legislative matters is taken as exemplary model for future action. Despite this, laws are always considered man-made institutions, not god-given; therefore they are mutable, amendable, open to discussion and reevaluation. Accountability of leaders is paramount: constituents judge the competence of their leaders, and when found lacking leaders are subject to penalty.

In the *gadaa* system, hereditary and elected leaders serve complementary but separate roles. Leaders are elected for a single term of finite length, with the expectation that they will turn over the reigns of governance smoothly to a properly appointed successor cohort. A trial period between election and investiture, during which leaders are elected to lower office and promoted to higher office on confirmation of competence, ensures that no politician takes office on the basis of campaign bluster alone. Strict rules regarding representation maintain balanced opposition and distribution of power between moieties. A rule of staggered succession prevents transitional crises; discontinuity of authority subverts entrenchment of a single party, while oversight and counseling help prevent dilettantism and the errors of inexperience. Alternate age set groups form alliances with one another, transforming linear hierarchy into balanced opposition.

Separation of Powers

Traditional Oromo structures ensure that power can never be concentrated at a single spot. They embody a unique system of allocating political power equitably *across generations*: systematic allocation of responsibility to those in childhood, adulthood, and old age ensures access for all people and brings balance to the public realm.

Most tellingly, ritual and political spheres are maintained in a dynamic relationship of separation and interaction. The ritual sphere is headed by a *qaaluu*, who stays in office for life, whose office is hereditary, and who holds authority over one moiety, that is, only half of the tribe. Ritual participants are barred from carrying weapons and indeed wholly excluded from military deliberation. The political sphere is headed by an elected body, known as the *gadaa* class, strictly speaking. This class holds authority over the entire Borana population, yet holds office for eight years only. Participants in political ceremonies are required to bring weapons with them and take full responsibility for warfare.

Ritual and political elements commingle in varying degrees. The authority hierarchy between the Abba Gadaa and the Qaaluu varies according to the context of their interaction. The institutions themselves have spatial organizations that are separate from their functional roles: the Gadaa, for example, is a mobile institution, while the Qaaluu is traditionally sedentary.

Civility in Deliberation

To facilitate mutual respect in democratic deliberations, various customs encourage civility in public discourse. The opening language in the traditional *gadaa* assemblies encourages speakers to avoid provoking resentments and to promote peace (*nagaa*). Proverbial saying about right conduct enjoin participants not to be provocative or use the floor to upstage or "score points" against others. Speakers are expected not to make accusations or to show anger.[3] What is more, the pacing of decision-making in deliberative assemblies ensures that decisions to go on the warpath are not rash or hot-headed, and the fact that policy decisions are necessarily made with serious regard to precedent iterates the injunction to base deliberations on a highly respectful discursive field.

Views of the Oromo Past

Even apart from the need to fashion functional narratives in the present period, it was always of particular importance for Oromo males to possess a living sense of the past. Oromo tradition draws nourishment not only from Oromo language and culture, but also to a substantial extent on myths of origins, historical memories, and a vivid sense of the continuing impact of the past on present events and fortunes.

The Traditionalist Narrative

What I present as the Traditionalist narrative focuses on the sociocultural system embodied by the Oromo in their ancestral homeland in the south central part of present-day Ethiopia. The chief features of this system are well known and need not be repeated here.[4] Suffice it to say that this narrative hinges on a narrative that was embedded in its key institutions, the *gadaa* system of generational classes with a duration of eight years, the core symbolic status of the *qaaluu*, and an octennial general assembly, the *gumi gayo*, that constituted the ultimate authority for all groups represented in it.

The *gadaa* system was nourished by the recollection of genealogical lines involving multiples of eighty years, since each new ruling class was obliged to function with reference to its antecedent class, located a remove of two hemicycles of eight years each. Oromo time-keepers (*ayyantu*) and learned laymen have reckoned genealogical lineages with depths of up to four to five centuries. The centerpiece of these narratives concerns the sequence of leaders installed and the special laws proclaimed in *gadaa* assemblies every eight years for as far back as the best memories of the oldest elders can reconstruct. Associated with each of the ruling *luba* classes might be some special events, or laws that distinguished their regime.

The main channel that links present and past generations flows through a structure formed by the ties between the classes of fathers and sons across many generations. This structure—the *gogessa*, or patriclass—constitutes a collective entity worthy of special homage. The *gogessa* carries a significant shared past and bears a special historical destiny. The historical destiny of the *gogessa* is represented by the concept of *dachi*, "the mystical influence of history on the present course of events," as Asmarom Legesse described it in his first brilliant analysis of this complex system (Legesse 1973, 194). *Dachi* is transmitted either from specific ancestors or from an entire ancestral *gadaa* class to one of its successors. Indeed, one particular ancestral *gadaa* class—the one that was in power thirty-five *gadaa* periods, or 280 years, earlier—is thought to have a determining influence (*dachi*) upon the fate of its latterday successor.

The class currently in power is obliged to avoid the chief misfortunes which befell its ancestors or to repeat the outstanding successes. At the same time it is setting a precedent which will affect its patriclass descendants thirtysix *gada* generations in the future. (Levine [1974] 2000, 136)

As Legesse demonstrated, the operation of this system over time made it increasingly difficult to follow the norms that enabled it to function. Because of the two rules that governed recruitment into the *gadaa* classes—the rule of a forty-year interval between paternal and filial classes and the rule that no sons could be born before the man reached the fortieth year of the cycle—there was a cumulative tendency for the population to be distributed into classes occupying increasingly advanced grades in the *gadaa* cycle. This led both to the creation of age-homogeneous groups, the *hariyya*, needed to provide an ample supply of young warriors, and to the designation of new roles for the semi-retired grades, whereby they serve as ritual experts and "junior" councilors, a sort of cadre of *eminences grises.*

Such adaptations enabled the *gadaa* system to continue, in spite of internal strains it generated, among the Boran, the Guji, and the Wallaga Oromo. To my knowledge, there are no reliable studies about how changes of the past half-century have affected their historical outlook. Nevertheless, it will be articulated by any contemporary narrative recounted by an Oromo elder that presents Oromo tradition in some idealized form and represents the central features of contemporary Oromo life as so many efforts to preserve and sustain it. A Traditionalist narrative of that sort would recount the playing out of *gadaa* customary practices over generations, and would reconstruct the great Oromo expansions since the 16th century as driven by an injunction to go on *butta* (raiding wars) every eight years, which led to a series of conquests to the north, west, and east of their traditional homeland in and around the Bali region.

This narrative mode can be found as well among Oromo who have replaced traditional Oromo institutions and beliefs, referring to their paramount deity Waaqa as Allah or Egziabher instead. For many Muslim Oromo, the institutional pilgrimage every eight years to the great Qaaluu was replaced by the custom of annual pilgrimages in honor of the cult of Shaikh Hussein (Gnamo 1991). Certain Sharia laws could be enfolded as part of the Oromo legal complex known as *seera.* Even the founder of an Islamic Front for the Liberation of Oromia changed his name to Sheikh Jarraa, taking thereby the name that forms the basis of the traditional Oromo calendar, since the term *jaarraa* represents the ceremony that marks the end of the *gadaa* cycle, where the outgoing, *luba* class, passes power to the incoming *gadaa* class. And among Muslim Oromo the community of True Believers (*umma*) has been folded into the notion of the community of all Oromo (*oromumma*) (Gnamo 2002).

The Colonalist Narrative

While the Traditionalist celebrates the time-honored and continued functioning of whatever can be retrieved and protected of the sacred practices of the Oromo past, the Colonialist Narrative emphasizes the suppression of this past and the people who bore it. This narrative resembles what has been called a lachrymose narrative in accounts of Jewish history, one that makes episodes of victimization and suffering the benchmarks of their historical experience. As such it attends to a different order of facts than that of the Traditionalist narrative, which focuses rather on positive accomplishments.

The time frame of the Colonialist narrative is necessarily shorter, although its "prehistory" can be lengthy. The extreme version would hold that since time immemorial, the Oromo people inhabited vast areas of Ethiopia. From the sixteenth century onward, they migrated into north, east, and western parts of the country. In the course of the nineteenth century, however, the Oromo were overrun, their traditions suppressed, and their status reduced to that of serfs. They remained in this unrelieved suppressed status for the next hundred years. Despite the egalitarian pretensions of the regimes of the Derg and EPRDF, the Oromo to this day remain second-class citizens in a country of which they constitute the second largest if not the largest ethnic minority and have arguably become victims of a disproportionate percentage of human rights violations.

The benchmarks of this narrative would include the martial victories of Tewodros against the Oromo in the 1860s, the defeat of autonomous Oromo groups thanks to superior military technology acquired by Yohannes and Menelik from the British in the wake of efforts to curb Tewodros, and the consequent appropriation of vast Oromo lands by Amhara and Tigrayan *nefteññas* and the exploitation of Oromo who became tenants. They include the centralizing efforts of Haile Selassie who carried out an extensive program of Amharization, which led to such changes as the erasure of traditional Oromo names (Finfine to Addis Ababa, Bishoftu to Debra Zeit, and the like) and laws forbidding the use of Oromiffa in publications. An effort to redress these grievances was carried out with the Mecha-Tulema Association in the 1960s, but it was brutally suppressed.

The Ethiopianist Narrative

This narrative presumes a broader perspective both in time and in space than the first two. It views the emergence of distinctive Oromo language and culture through a multimillennial process of differentiation and interaction from a common Semito-Cushitic cultural matrix. More proximately, it views the Oromo expansions of the sixteenth century as advancing the process of building a modern multiethnic national state.

Thanks to their openness for adoption, assimilation, and intermarriage, Oromo settlers blended readily with the peoples living in the areas that they penetrated. Their characteristic openness and friendliness made it easy for newcomers to join their communities. They readily found ways of relating to peoples near whom they settled once the antagonisms of battle were temporarily or permanently set aside. Their penchant for affiliating with others disposed them to adopt the cultures of others as well as to share their own culture with outsiders. Oromos became Christians in the north and Muslims in the east; they established kingdoms in the southwest and farming communities in Shoa. It was thanks to their interaction with Amharic-speakers with whom they came in contact that Amharic, originally a purely Semitic language derived from Ge'ez, Tigrinya, Arabic, and Hebrew, came to incorporate significant East Cushitic linguistic elements—syntax, vocabularies, and idioms—from Oromiffa.

In the south, these intermixtures involved whole groups. Thus, Oromos who settled near Gurage adopted the *ensete* culture of their neighbors and came to be teased by other Oromo as "half-Gurage." The Otu branch of the Guji assimilated Sidamo culture so thoroughly that many came to speak only Sidaminya. On the other hand, the Guji Oromo readily incorporated groups of Sidamo and Wallayta people through the fiction of adoptive patrilineal affiliation. As Legesse summarizes this process,

> The Oromo seemed to assimilate the conquered populations as frequently as they were absorbed by them. In this process the [Oromiffa]-speaking region of central Ethiopia developed into a veritable cultural corridor. It opened up extensive cultural exchanges between societies, which would otherwise have remained isolated and atomistic. (1973, 9)

Beyond this steady stream of cultural intermixing with other peoples of Ethiopia, the Oromo moved to become significant actors at the national level. The Ethiopianist Narrative highlights the fact that Oromos penetrated the national political arena centered at the Imperial Court from the late 16th century onward. They served already in the army of Emperor Sertsa Dingil (1563–97) in his battles against the Turkish invader, and it was only with the help of his Oromo friends and followers that Susneyos recovered the throne in 1603 (Hassen

1994). And from the eighteenth century on, Abir notes, "they became enmeshed in the already intricate web of the country" (1968, 73).

Although the Oromo and Amhara interacted in many ways for generations, the process gathered momentum with the escape of future Emperor Bakaffa from the prison fortress at Wohni, from whence he went to live among the Yejju Oromo of Gojjam. Bakaffa grew up in accordance with the Oromo culture and became fluent in Oromiffa. As emperor (1721–30) he filled the court with his Oromo friends and soldiers, and sent Oromo fighters to rule over rebellious Amhara in Begemdir and Gojjam. His wife Empress Mentwab arranged for their son Emperor Iyasu II to marry an Oromo princess, Wubit (Wabi), daughter of the Wallo Oromo chief Amito. Their son, Iyoas, thereby became Ethiopia's first emperor with Oromo blood. Iyoas grew up speaking Oromiffa more fluently than Amharic. On reaching adulthood he assembled a Royal Guard consisting of three thousand Oromo soldiers and placed them under the command of his Oromo uncles Biralle and Lubo. Queen Wubit also appointed her brothers and other kinsmen to high positions throughout the empire.

When imperial power declined following Iyoas (during the Era of the Princes, *zemene mesafint*), power shifted to the Tigrean lord Ras Mikael Sehul; after Mikael's death, the power behind the throne was lodged in the court of a Yejju Oromo chieftain Ras Ali I, whose power derived from the support of Oromos in many provinces. W. Cornwallis Harris observed in 1840 that the Wallo Oromo "form the stoutest bulwark of the decayed empire" (1844, 354–5). Ras Ali's brother and then his nephew, Ras Gugsa, continued to form a strong political center, with the support of both Amhara and Oromo fighters. Later royal figures with Oromo blood included Negus Tekle Haymanot of Gojam, *Atse* Menelik II, Itege Taitu Betul, *Atse* Haile Selassie I, and Itege Mennen.

From intermarriage with royal lines, high honorific positions, and military appointments, the Oromo became central to the creation of the modern Ethiopian nation under Emperor Menelik. Menelik's historic encounter with invading Italians, just as Haile Selassie's four decades later, depended enormously on the hearty participation of Oromo generals and Oromo soldiers and supporters, including Ras Gobena, Ras Mekonnen Gugsa, Dejjach Balcha Safo, and Negus Mikael of Wallo. The fact that eminent Oromo figures like General Mulugeta Buli and Minister Yilma Deressa played such central roles in his regime was not anomalous or tokenism, but a natural expression of what had come be a multiethnic mix of the new ruling elite.

Options for the Future

As a result of the tumultuous changes that their country experienced over the past half century, all Ethiopians today confront a need to make decisions about the direction of their future political engagement. How they construe the past has implications for current and future political realities. For many, those decisions will be colored by an identity that is primarily Ethiopian, not ethnic. These citizens include the millions of Ethiopians who do not identify with any single ethnic identity because of their mixed parentage and/or because they have grown up with patriotic sentiments oriented toward strong national symbols.

The options of those whose self-concept is primarily ethnic are likely to reflect diverse narratives, as among the Maale studied by Donham. This is surely the case for Oromo people, given the complexity of their historical experience. I have tried here to describe ideal types of three narratives that apply to Oromo citizens. Awareness of the different paths embodied in the three narratives I have sketched may be useful in facilitating personal and communal deliberations. In making these choices, it may be of further value to consider the symbolic and normative implications of each one of those paths.

The Traditionalist Narrative identifies Oromo *culture-bearers as carrying a distinctive legacy of important sacred values*. It enjoins a course of action directed at sustaining and strengthening whatever can be preserved of the traditional institutions of the Oromo Gadaa system. Toward that end they should maintain a certain distance from the political center of the Ethiopian nation. They should do whatever can be done to resist the alienation of their land, and to promote the survival and rebirth of herds so important to their traditional lifestyle. The Traditionalist path could take a purely cultural form, with emphasis on the rituals associated with *qaaluu* and ceremonies that symbolize the continuing values of loyalty to *gogessa* and beyond that to the community of Oromo (*oromumma*). It could take political form, but that is only ambiguously Oromo. Their penchant, after all, although particularistic, is also to be inclusive; separatism would be one plausible path; but so would one in which the notion of adoption were pushed into a much wider context. As Gemetchu Megerssa reflects, Oromo tradition should "not only be viewed as part of a static traditional past, but rather as an area that is being continually and dynamically constructed by the wider experience that is part of the present" (Megerssa 1996, 98).

The Colonialist Narrative identifies the Oromo experience as essentially one of *victims of a century-and-a-half of unrelieved subjugation*. Unlike the Traditionalist Narrative, it encourages actions that engage fully in contest with the Ethiopian national center. At the very least, it promotes a struggle to ensure adequate representation in the Ethiopian Parliament and in the federal bureaucracy, and to maximize full and genuine autonomy for the Oromia region. In the words of one of its most eloquent proponents, it enjoins a "national liberation struggle [that] will continue between Oromia and Ethiopia until the Oromo nation freely decides its political future by uprooting Ethiopian settler colonialism" (Jalata 1993, 197).

The Ethiopianist Narrative identifies the Oromo *as participants in a five-century process in which diverse ethnies interacted to form a multiethnic national society.* In this view, differences among diverse Oromo groups are not to be suppressed or denied as compromising an integral Oromo nation, but as constituting strands of the tapestry of ethnies that constitute Ethiopia and the Horn. The opportunities for Oromo to contribute to the building of this nation have never been greater. In a period struggling to institutionalize pluralistic democracy and multicultural diversity, Oromo rhetoric and self-understanding should be revised to include appreciation of the many Oromo contributions to building the modern Ethiopian nation, and Oromo customs could be deliberately invoked and adopted to civilize the conduct of members of the national parliament and other deliberative bodies.

If something like this variety of narratives is acknowledged—and other narratives, which I have not articulated as such—the question remains: how are those committed to this array of narratives to relate to one another? In some contexts—Greeks versus Turks, Arabs versus Jews, Pakistanis versus Indians, and even, some might say, among extremist EPRDFers versus CUDers—differences of this sort have engendered mutual hatreds and uncompromising assertions of theirs being the only *right* point of view. But that is not the Oromo way to dealing with differences. Oromos generally insist on listening to each voice, to hearing everyone's story. As Gnamo wisely points out, "Oromo do have a centuries-long culture of tolerance and, as evidence, one can say that the Oromo do not have pejorative terms [such] as *aramane* (heathens) to qualify others" (2002, n.4).

Suppose Oromos listen to one another as participants in a *Gumi Gayo*. It might appear then that *each* of these narratives reflects the actual experience of important actors; that each retains important values; and that exclusive attention to just one neglects the values embodied in the others. If the airing of diverse narratives is carried out in that spirit, then perhaps Oromos can contribute not only constructively to the organization of discourse in Northeast Africa, but in an unparalleled way to contemporary efforts to organize dialogue in the global community.

Bibliography

Abbas Haji Gnamo. 1991. "Le rôle du culte de Chaikh Hussein dans l'Islam des Arsi, Ethiopie," *Islam et Sociétés au Sud du Sahara*, 5: 21–42.

________. 2002. «Islam, the Orthodox Church and Oromo nationalism (Ethiopia).» *Cahiers d'études africaines*, 165. *http:// etudesafricaines.revues.org/document137.html*

Abir, Mordechai. 1968. *Ethiopia: The Era of the Princes*. New York: Praeger.

Bassi, Marco. 2005. *Decisions in the Shade: Political and Juridical Processes among the Oromo-Borana*, trans. Cynthia Salvadori. Trenton, NJ: Red Sea Press.

Berger, Peter L. and Thomas Luckmann. 1966. *The Social Construction of Reality: A Treatise in the Sociology of Knowledge*. Garden City, New York: Anchor Books.

Cohler, Bertram J. 1982. "Personal Narrative and Life-Course." In vol.4 of *Life-Span Development and Behavior*, ed. Paul Bates and Orville Brim, 205–41. New York: Academic Press.

Donham, Donald L. 1999. *Marxist Modern: An Ethnographic History of the Ethiopian Revolution*. Berkeley: University of California Press.

Gudina, Merera. 2003. *Ethiopia: Competing Ethnic Nationalism and the Quest for Democracy, 1960–2000*. Netherlands: Shaker Publishing.

Harris, W.C. 1844. *The Highlands of Aethiopia*, 3 vols. London: Longman, Brown Green and Longmans.

Hassen, Mohammed. 1994. *The Oromo of Ethiopia: A History 1570–1860*. Trenton, NJ: Red Sea Press.

Jalata, Asafa. 1993. *Oromia and Ethiopia: State Formation and Ethnonational Conflict*, 1868–1992. Boulder: Lynne Rienner.

Knutsson, Karl E. 1967. *Authority and Change: A Study of the Kallu Institution among the Macha Galla of Ethiopia*. Göteborg: Etnografiska Museet.

Legesse, Asmarom. 1963. "Class Systems Based on Time." *Journal of Ethiopian Studies* 1(2),1–29.

________. 1973. *Gada: Three Approaches to the Study of African Society*. New York: Free Press.

________. 2000. *Oromo Democracy: An Indigenous African Political System*. Lawrenceville, NJ: Red Sea Press.

Levine, Donald N. 1965. *Wax and Gold: Tradition and Innovation in Ethiopian Culture*. Chicago: University of Chicago Press.

________. [1974] 2000. *Greater Ethiopia: The Evolution of a Multiethnic Society*. Chicago: University of Chicago Press.

________. 2004. "Reconfiguring the Ethiopian Nation in a Global Era." *International Journal of Ethiopian Studies* 1(2).

________. 2006a. "Two Tales of One City." Originally published in 2006 on the web forum of the Ethiopian Institute for Nonviolence Education and Peace Studies.

________. 2006b. "Tigrayawinet." Originally published in 2006 on the web forum of the Ethiopian Institute for Nonviolence Education and Peace Studies.

Lewis, Herb. [1970] 2000. "Wealth, Influence, and Prestige among the Shoa Galla," Pp.163–186 in *Social Stratification in Africa*, ed. Arthur Tuden and Leonard Plotnicov. New York: Free Press.

Megerssa, Gemetchu. 1996. "Oromumma: Tradition, Consciousness and Identity." Pp. 92–102 in *Being and Becoming Oromo*, Ed. P.T.W. Baxter, Jan Hultin and Alessandro Triulzi. Lawrenceville, NJ: Red Sea Press.

Tolossa, Fikre. 1997. "A Historical Explanation as to Why Members & Supporters of the TPLF are Ethnocentric." *Ethiopian Review*, Jan.–Feb. *http://www.ethiopic.com/Fikre1er.htm*

Trimingham, J. Spencer. 1965. *Islam in Ethiopia*. London: Frank Cass.

Notes

1 In the words of Merera Gudina, "History [had] to be re-written so that it would serve the political interests of the hitherto marginalized groups" (2003, 94).

2 Donham himself proposes a typology of divergent responses to modernist interventions: Traditionalist, Anti-Modernist, and Modernist. This typology bears a family resemblance to the five-fold typology that I proposed in *Wax and Gold*: the Traditionalist, the Modernist, the Skeptic, the Conciliatory, and the Pragmatist (Levine 1965, 12–13). It is even closer to the typology I shall present in this paper.

3 When tempers flared during a large public meeting of Diasporan Oromo in Minneapolis in 2006, the session chair called upon one of the elders to bless the assembly. The elder obliged, showering the assembly with a very long stream of benedictory oration, following which the debate resumed in a more even-tempered way.

4 For a summary of the system and related literature, see Levine [1974] 2000, 129–34.

23

Šum Šir (2011)*

The Amharic phrase *Šum šir* (ሹም ሽር) derives from the roots *šomä/mäšom* ('to appoint') and *šarä/mäšar* ('to demote'). This expression denotes a process of appointments to higher positions in the government (*Šum*), with the implication that every time someone is promoted, someone else must be removed from that position to make place for him. Although strictly speaking the announcement of a *Šum šir* episode designated the mere posting of a list of appointments, an underlying connotation was that those who had lost favor with the emperor were being demoted. Calling those so demoted the recipients of *šumät*, a promotion, had dual benefits: it enabled those demoted to save face, yet also preserved them in a pool of potential appointees whose loyalty could be counted on in the event of a more favorable appointment at a later time.

Although the expression was apparently known in earlier times, it became widely used only during the regime of *Atse* Haylä Səllase and, indeed, came to represent the quintessence of the political ethos of his regime. The emperor's political prowess rested on mastery of a nonviolent mode of political control over all his appointees, manifested through a variety of techniques including widespread surveillance, *divide et impera*, and patterns of forgiveness. *Šum šir* figured as perhaps the most dramatic and subtle of these. It meant that since those who are appointed are subject to possible demotion, they must be always on good behavior, for those demoted (or others) could come back to replace them. The feeling of uncertainty thus instilled becomes a motive of "good behaviour," which meant intense and unquestioning loyalty to the Emperor.

---

* Originally published in *Encyclopaedia Aethiopica* Volume 4, Institute of African and Ethiopian Studies, Hamburg University (Wiesbaden, Germany: Otto Harrassowitz KG, 2011).

Šum šir episodes fascinated the public, in part from what was often perceived as an unjust demotion, as in the cases of dedicated public servants such as Gärmame Nəway who was sent from the comforts of Addis Abäba to be governor of Wälamo and then of Ǧiǧiga in the late 1950s, and of Attorney General Bäräkät Ab Habtä Śəllase, who was exiled to be Mayor of Harär in the 1960s (Bereket Habte Selassie 2007). On the other hand, the adroitness with which the throne maneuvered these shifts aroused a certain admiration for the political skill they manifested.

Perhaps the most notorious case of *Šum šir* was that of *sähafe təɨ̓əzaz* Wäldä Giyorgis Wäldä Yohannəs, one of the most powerful men at court in the immediate postwar decade. When Haylä Śəllase I found his trusted courtier becoming too prominent and proactive, he banished him to a provincial home. The emperor's words on that occasion exemplify both his adroitness and the way in which he flaunted his will over that of the Ethiopian public:

> "Although We Ourselves told you that both your heart and feet have become increasingly distant, you do not seem to have given it much weight. You have ignored our repeated request to divulge what it was you promised to tell Us in London. You have neglected your work and your character has changed. Since this might be because of overwork, and in order that you might correct yourself, We have decided to transfer you to another post" (Bahru Zewde 2004:46).

With the introduction of more coercive forms of political control under the Provisional Military Administrative Council, the manipulation of political subjects by the centre became less subtle. Fear of demotion became replaced by fear of open harassment, threats, imprisonment, disappearances, and death. Yet the mindset that underlay the *Šum šir* syndrome has continued as has the more general underlying cultural disposition for indirect meanings exemplified by the poetic trope of *sämənna wärq*.

Bibliography

Bereket Habte Selassie, *The Crown and the Pen: The Memoirs of a Rebel* (Trenton, NJ, 2007), 227, 230.

Bahru Zewde, "The Fall of *Tsähafə Te'ezaz* Wäldä-Giyorgis: Reminiscences of the Victim", *Aethiopica* 7, 2004, 28–53.

Donald N. Levine, *Wax and Gold: Tradition and Innovation in Ethiopian Culture* (Chicago: University of Chicago Press, 1965), 187, 215.

Part IV

POLITICS

24

On the December 1960 Coup Attempt (1961)*

The public hanging of General Mengistu Neway in Addis Ababa on March 30 may seem to have brought to a close the unexpected episode in Ethiopian History that began with an unexpected coup d'état by the Imperial Bodyguard last December. The rebels have been identified as a perverse group of power-seekers. Emperor Haile Selassie's clemency has been manifest once more by his lenient treatment of rebel sympathizers. The Emperor's own modernization program has been resumed with new purpose, as appears from the appointment of several younger men to higher positions and his recent upbraiding of the bureaucrats for failing to carry out their responsibilities to the people. And so the West can breathe easily once again: all is well as usual in Ethiopia.

The West has long been more disposed to wax sentimental about Ethiopia than to grasp its reality. For Medieval and Renaissance Europe, Ethiopia was the land of "Prester John," a legendary bastion of Christianity in the Orient which European rulers eyed with fantasy as an ally against Mussalmans. Since the late Nineteenth Century, when she emerged the only native polity to survive the imperialists' scramble for Africa, Ethiopia has been a beacon for suppressed Negroes—in the United States, in the West Indies, and at the London School of Economics. Among Western Jews, Ethiopia has been romanticized as the home of Falashas, an obscure tribe of potters and metal smiths practicing a pre-Exilic form of Judaism. In recent decades Ethiopia, as Mussolini's victim, became a

* Published originally as "Haile Selassie's Ethiopia—Myth or Reality?" in *Africa Today*, Vol. 8, No. 5, May 1961. For part of the history behind this controversial piece, see Chapter 14.

crying symbol of innocence in the face of Fascist aggression and of the need for a world compact more serious than the League of Nations.

Haile Selassie I, Regent of Ethiopia after 1917 and Emperor since 1930, has inherited the awe and good will felt for his fabled kingdom by so many outsiders. His own reputation was elevated by the dramatic stand at Geneva, and has soared ever since thanks to a spate of Western writers who have gilded his regime and censorship system which assures that everything published in his country rings with eulogy. Thus he has become a legend himself—that of a wise ruler who knows how to combine social progress with political stability.

Incredible as it may seem, this image has scarcely been shaken by the revolutionary events of last December. Instead of attending at last to the realities of present-day Ethiopia, the Western press has allowed the rhetoric of the restored regime to revive our old credence in the myth of Haile Selassie. Perhaps we would not be so ready to do this if we could have heard General Mengistu's inspired reply to the judges who sentenced him to death: "I will not appeal your decision. You have already denied me justice by not letting me have proper defense in this trial. I have done what you say, but I am not guilty. Ethiopia has been standing still, while our African brothers are moving ahead in the struggle to overcome poverty. What I did was in the best interests of my country."

As all who knew him will attest, General Mengistu was no ideologist, but a *bon vivant.* The fact that *he* was led to sacrifice his easy life and enviable position and to betray the Emperor's trust in him should suggest to all concerned that there is a precious little progress *or* stability in the Empire of Ethiopia.

There is no doubt that Haile Selassie wants to go down in history as the builder of modern Ethiopia. Indeed, some of the most radical Ethiopians assert that he does not lack good intentions.

The tragedy is that he has been kept from realizing his progressive ideals by characteristics traditionally connected with the Ethiopian monarchy. Consistent with the traditional attitude that delegation of authority deprives the ruler of some measure of dignity, he has insisted on retaining the powers of an absolute despot. Similarly, believing that the welfare of the sovereign is more important than that of the people, he has diligently amassed a huge personal fortune. (Estimates which I have been unable to verify state that his assets exceed US $200,000,000, a large part of which has been taken from Ethiopia illegally and cached in Switzerland, Sweden, England, and the United States.) Finally, in keeping with the basic mistrust and ad hoc policy-making of Ethiopia's traditional rulers, he has failed to commit himself to a coherent program of national development. The result has been a compromise that has inspired no one but the court parasites: he has continued to behave much like his imperial forefathers while indulging at will in the oratory of modernization.

Perhaps in no other "under-developed" country have so much thought and energy gone into producing the *appearance* of progress. Embellishment of the capital city has epitomized this concern. Millions have been spent on broad boulevards to approach the palaces, while large numbers of diseased and unemployed still beg on the streets. A large commercial school was constructed on the airport road in order to confront the visitor at once with signs of civilization, against the advice of planners who rightly predicted that class work would be impaired by the sounds of heavy traffic. For the sake of Addis Ababa the provinces have been heavily taxed and left relatively undeveloped. Thirty-seven percent of the capital's children go to school, as compared with about four percent in the provinces. With regard to medical services, the discrepancy is many times greater (though in the last year the inauguration of a program of public health centers in some of the provinces is an encouraging step).

In nearly every area of Ethiopian public life, a progressive façade has been erected to cover the status quo. Land reform, which American and Yugoslav advisers agree to be the prerequisite for any significant increase in agricultural production, was achieved in September 1959 by a proclamation promising land to all who have none, but which in fact meant that some hundreds of peasants were permitted to borrow money from the Government to be paid back with interest after five years. Plans for industrial development were often announced on high, but foreign investors were given conditions which none but the most dim-witted would accept; the Emperor and his relatives buried fortunes abroad; and Ethiopian entrepreneurs were checked at every turn lest they become an independent bourgeois class. An elaborate exercise in popular elections took place in 1957, producing a house of representatives that has done little but what the emperor has ordered of it. A massive program to develop the arts got as far as the construction of the Haile Selassie I Theater, whose staff has had to limit its functions to the preparation of spurious folk-lore spectacles to impress foreign dignitaries.

Haile Selassie has often stated that the keystone of progress is education. He prides himself on retaining the portfolio of Minister of Education, and claims personal responsibility for the education of hundreds of young Ethiopians abroad. Yet these Western-educated Ethiopians have in effect been just another section of the façade. Personal loyalty, to the Emperor or one of his favorite ministers, has been the basis for government appointments. The office-holder who ventures to do something more efficiently or imaginatively—in short, to carry out his responsibility to the people—finds himself "promoted" to a lesser position. "The problem," said one official of the Ministry of ———, "is that we get punished for doing what in your country would bring rewards."

The returned students tried many ways of adjusting to this state of things. Some got used to the pace and intrigue of Ethiopian administration and worked as best they could: some withdrew to drink or orgies of chess-playing; some shed their schoolday principles to become informers and apologists for the regime. But the number of convinced dissidents grew steadily larger. "The Emperor will have to learn that our education is not a plaything he can turn on or off as he pleases," shouted one of them—when we were alone.

The frustration of the educated, however, comprise but one aspect of the opposition to Emperor Haile Selassie. Haile Selassie has never really been secure, in both senses of the world. The fact that he himself came to power following a coup and years of factional strife has left him with a constant pulse of anxiety. The monotonously repeated assertions of his legitimacy are so many attempts to make Ethiopians forget that his climb to power was at the expense of the then legitimate monarch, Lij Iyasu, and that with regard to genealogy other men had better claims to the throne.

Actually the chief criterion of succession in Ethiopia has usually been might, and the fear that others might be acquiring too much power has always troubled Haile Selassie more than his dubious origins. He never lacked grounds for such fears. Many battles had to be fought to suppress his enemies before he was crowned Emperor. The fascists released a number of his political prisoners, and the quick progress under their Occupation made some Ethiopians think Haile Selassie had not been doing all he could. His own flight from Ethiopia to appeal to the League of Nations—by Western standards, the only rational thing to do—was widely regarded by Ethiopians as a betrayal of his solemn obligations as warrior-king to fight to the finish. Even at the time of his "triumphant return" in 1941, when Haile Selassie was more popular than ever before or since, some of his own fellow Amharas waged a battle to prevent him from seizing power again.

The dozen or so revolts and projected coups which have threatened Haile Selassie since the Liberation have sprung from three main sources. Most visible have been the provincial revolts—Ethiopia's form of tribal conflict. In the 1940s two revolts were based in the western province of Gojjam and a serious one broke out in the northern province of Tigre. These were squelched by the Army, though the rebellious feelings of the people did not die. Several smaller incidents in the provinces consisted of the expression of tribal grievances by the suppressed Hamitic and Nilotic peoples in the southern half of the country, which the Amhara overlords were usually quick to muffle. One such incident, occurring about April 1960, involved the massacre of over a thousand Darasa tribesmen who had protested the dispossession of their land by the Emperor's daughter and some of her children.

A second type of dissidence has been of the palace revolution variety. Several ambitious individuals have hoped to seize power for their own purposes, but the centralization of power under Haile Selassie enabled him to check such plans before they began to materialize. The most famous scheme was that of Wolde Giorgis Wolde Yohannis, the Emperor's right-hand man until his demotion in 1955. Another notable case was the conspiracy led by then President of the Senate Negash Kebede, to assassinate Haile Selassie in the early 1950s. It is an irony of Ethiopian politics that this group was apprehended by a squad under the command of Mengistu Neway. (Many Ethiopians maintain, however, that the conspiracy was actually organized and financed by the Emperor himself—through Dejazmatch Geresu Duke, the "betrayer" of the group—in order to get rid of some influential people and also, by appearing to be threatened by Communist subversives, to gain greater bargaining power vis-à-vis the United States.)

With the return of foreign-educated Ethiopians from abroad a third type of dissidence began to grow. This was based more on ideological than on tribal or personal ambitions. These dissidents were moved by intense dissatisfaction with the widespread corruption and inefficiency in the government. They felt that if the Emperor had really wanted to improve things, he could have. Germame Neway, the civilian mastermind of the Bodyguard coup, was an outstanding example of this third sort of dissident.

After returning to the United States, where he studied political science at the University of Wisconsin and later Columbia, Germame was made Governor of Wollamo Sub-Province. This was the sort of post usually dreaded as exile by most urbanized Ethiopians, but Germame turned it into a day and night struggle to improve the living of his people. He set up scores of primary schools, built a number of bridges, and fought to bring justice to the peasantry there. Desta Fisseha, a wealthy Wollamo landowner, protested all this commotion and, through the customary channels of Palace intrigue, managed to have Germame transferred to another area, Jigjiga. In the new post Germame's reformist energies were cramped by the need to spend so many hours presiding over Somali litigation—he was often at court from early morning till late at night—and to attend to the security problems of that province lying on the Somali borders. But he spared no pains to listen carefully to all the disputes brought before him, and found time to have a hospital built nonetheless. Like most Amharans, Germame was quiet and well-mannered, giving no clue to the outsider that a storm of rebellion was brewing within.

If the façade of progress was built with empty words and hollow architecture, the façade of stability was achieved through the system of *shum-shir*, appoint-demote. This system consists of a constant shuffling of political appointments, whereby every Ethiopian official has been kept continually anxious about any appearance of disloyalty and so has been prevented from acquiring a significant following in any position. Haile Selassie's appointments were made in such a way that the officials in any ministry would be constantly spying on each other. For example, Abiye Abebe, the loyalist general who held down Asmara during the coup, and Tadesse Negash, one of the hostages slain by the rebels, had been lifelong friends. When they found themselves in the adjacent positions of Minister and Minister d'Etat of Justice, they began to inform on each other. "We have learned that the Emperor wants us to be enemies now," Tadesse once remarked.

The *shum-shir* system turned men's thoughts from social action to personal advancement. It virtually eliminated the possibility of sustained development since officials no sooner got acquainted with one post than they were transferred to another, and their budding programs were sabotaged by their successor. It intensified the atmosphere of mutual distrust that had been created by the ever-felt eyes of the Security Department and the personal networks of reactionaries like Makonnen Habtewold. The resulting suspicion choked all public discussion, smothered what intellectual interests had been cultivated abroad, and cramped the most innocent social relations. It was impossible to form groups of any sort—even a medical association, let alone an alliance of intelligentsia free to ponder their country's problems.

The engineers of the December uprising were thus forced to keep their plans strictly to themselves. Fearing to confer in advance with other dissident elements, they assumed that once the daring move was made the others would rally behind them. But the façade of stability was not yet ready to crack. In none of the dissident provinces was a finger lifted to support the coup. The educated civilians were afraid to show themselves until the new government proved itself a sure thing, though a group of college students did stage a demonstration in the final hours of the coup. Most important, despite widespread sympathy with the aims of the coup among the officers of the Army and Air Force, these forces did not come to terms with the Bodyguard, and ended by destroying the rebel government. Haile Selassie's masterful policy of *divide et impera* served him well in that fateful hour.

The December coup was bred of genuine domestic discontent, aggravated by the consciousness—after the big year of African independence—that the ancient symbol of African statehood had fallen well behind other countries on the continent in the race for modernization. It was triggered, after years of waiting, by the conviction that the old feudal-monarchical order could be changed only by some swiftly applied social remedies. The students who demonstrated sensed what it was all about; the placards they carried read "Liberty, Equality, Fraternity."

And though all these dreams were drowned in blood, one great accomplishment remains. A true word has been uttered in this land of deception.

Haile Selassie could get away with his policy of façade because Ethiopian custom envelops all human affairs in a thick mesh of equivocation. The traditional order admits only one kind of truth: loyalty to one's superior. Between father and son, ruler and ruled, there are no habits of honest communication. The alternatives are obedience and rebellion. The Bodyguard revolt has spoken aloud, by the loss of much life, what many Ethiopians have been aching to tell their ruler; it was probably the only way he could ever be told. The statement read by the (commonly misunderstood) Crown Prince when setting up the new government was indirect, but its meaning was unmistakable—to end the rule of the few for the few, and to make the monarchy an instrument for serving the people.

Can Haile Selassie listen? Can he yet make use of the great respect which the office of Emperor still holds in Ethiopia—which led the rebels to attempt a coup without resorting to assassination, to their great credit and their ultimate undoing—and push ahead on the imaginative program of real development? This is the question to which the blood of those who died in December demands answer.

One thing is certain: the Emperor cannot for long ignore this overwhelming question. Thanks to the heroic action of Germame, Mengistu, and their comrades, the facades are beginning to crumble. Many Ethiopians, who heretofore have been quietly obedient, from the Empress and the Crown Prince down to the common citizen, now venture to voice a degree of criticism. Some have even taken to swearing in the name of the martyred Mengistu instead of that of the Emperor.

No one at all acquainted with Ethiopia will pretend that Haile Selassie's task is easy, especially at this late date. Wealthy landlords, an obstructionist clergy, and those corrupt officials who survived the rebels' purge still hope to forestall change. The educated progressives often lack experience, daring, and careful knowledge of their country's problems. The Emperor, moreover, after having succeeded in bluffing his countrymen, then Europe and the United States, now manages to bluff even himself. Nevertheless, each day makes his alternatives more clear and ineluctable—either to launch at last an unambiguous program of modernization and liberalization, and perhaps redeem his place in history despite everything; or else to face the downfall of his throne and possibly the Congolization of Africa's oldest independent nation.

25

The Military in Ethiopian Politics (1966)*

Capabilities and Constraints

Stirred by the examples of Colonel Nasser and General Abboudin in the north, embarrassed by the comparatively high standard of living in African countries to the west and south, a small band of officers sought in the closing hours of 1960 to add Ethiopia to the growing list of developing nations in which military leaders have intervened to play a decisive role in national politics. The present study attempts to set that episode and its aftermath in a broader historical and institutional context, albeit in a brief and schematic fashion. It locates the novel position of the military in contemporary Ethiopia on a plane of continuity with the Abyssinian past, and in a field of opposing and concurring forces in the present. In so doing the present study may serve not only as an effort to clarify Ethiopian realities, but also as a contribution to the comparative effort to understand the dynamics of military involvement in politics.

The Ethiopian Military Organization

The Traditional Army

Warfare has been one of the most prominent activities in the Ethiopian kingdom since its founding. The ancient kingdom at Aksum sent out a number

* Originally published in *The Military Intervenes: Case Studies in Political Development*, edited by Henry Bienen (New York, NY: Russell Sage Foundation, 1966), 5–34.

of military expeditions in many directions—against African tribes to the north, west, and south, and twice across the Red Sea to conquer portions of Arabia. With the dissolution of the Aksumite polity around 800–1000 A.D., Ethiopian forces pushed south to invade territories of the Agau and related peoples. For two-and-a-half centuries after the ascendance of the Amhara dynasty, established by Yekuno Amlak in 1270, they carried on a long and largely successful series of campaigns against the petty Muslim states to the east. Although the *jihad* led by Ahmad Grāñ in 1527 wrought heavy destruction for many years, Ethiopian forces were routed in 1540 by an expedition of Portuguese matchlockmen and went on not only to defeat Grāñ's army but also to push back an invasion of Ottoman Turks in the north two decades later. During the three centuries which followed that victory, Ethiopian armies were preoccupied chiefly with battles against the Oromo, a large tribe of pastoralists who penetrated the country from the south after Grāñ's invasion. The nineteenth century also saw a half-hearted attempt to oppose the British expedition under Napier (1868); two victorious campaigns against invading Egyptian forces in the north and a series of battles with Sudanese dervishes led by Emperor Yohannes (1872–1889); the conquest of a number of tribes in the eastern, southern, and western regions of present-day Ethiopia under Menelik (ruler of Shoa, 1865–1889, emperor of Ethiopia, 1889–1913); and a brief period of warfare against the Italians, culminating in the decisive Battle of Adwa (1896).

In addition to this record of military campaigns against invaders and subject peoples Ethiopian history is marked by chronic internecine warfare. While this was most conspicuous during the century before the coronation of Theodore II (1855) in which the absence of strong central authority promoted a condition of extreme instability, the competition and rebellion of feudal lords and the chronic antagonism between peasants and regular soldiers made civil war among groups of Amhara and Tigreans themselves a regular feature of Abyssinian history.[1] The most cursory reading of Ethiopian history cannot but support the generalization made by Ludolphus, who wrote three centuries ago: "The (Abyssinians) are a Warlike People and continually exercis'd in War…neither is there any respit but what is caused by the Winter, at what time by reason of the Inundations of the Rivers, they are forced to be quiet."[2]

The prominence of warfare in Ethiopian history has been matched by the conspicuous place which military culture occupies in the overall pattern of Amhara-Tigre culture. Military virtues have ranked among the highest in the Abyssinian value system; military titles have been among the most prestigious in their social hierarchy; military symbolism has provided a medium for important national traditions and a focus for a good deal of national sentiment; military statuses and procedures have influenced patterns of social organization in many ways. Indeed, in the traditional Ethiopian system, the political involvement of the military is not a phenomenon that needs to be explained; on the contrary, any distinction between the two realms is difficult to make.

In perhaps the most dramatic manifestation of this permeation of Ethiopian culture by military themes, during most of the last millennium the political capital of Ethiopia frequently took the form of an army camp. It consisted of a vast array of tents, arranged in combat-ready formation with the Emperors tents in the center, flanked and guarded at the front and rear by officers of standard ranks with their entourages. The court would rest in one spot for a certain time until political or military considerations dictated a move or until the local supply of fire wood or food was exhausted. Then it would strike off for a new location where, on a sizable plain, a central (and often elevated) position would be staked off for the imperial tents. The rest of the population would quickly establish themselves in their accustomed positions relative to that of the emperor. The camp was so large, yet laid out so regularly, that despite its periodic movement from region to region, perceptible differences of dialect and vocabulary developed in different quarters of the mobile capital. In such a setting policies were forged, decrees promulgated, political intrigues hatched, and judicial verdicts pronounced. Even when Ethiopian emperors chose to reside for longer periods in more stable quarters, a military flavor was imparted to the capital. Military expeditions frequently originated there and high secular dignitaries bore such titles as General of the Right Flank, Commander of a Fort, and General of the Vanguard.

The armies which formed the matrix for this efflorescence of military culture in Ethiopia were not, as in Sparta, the product of careful organization and systematic development, but tended rather to be highly labile affairs. They were organized quickly, performed erratically, and dissolved in a moment. Their potency was due, not to the perfection of a specialized institution devoted to the art of warfare, but rather to the extent to which Ethiopian society as a whole was pervaded by military skills, virtues, and ambitions. For while the Ethiopian Army was neither trained nor disciplined, it could count on a number of cultural factors to produce an effective soldiery.

> (1) Observers of many centuries have commented on the extraordinary physical capacities of the Abyssinian people. As a rule thin, light, almost frail in appearance, the Abyssinian soldier is nevertheless noted for great endurance—he can climb mountains with ease, march rapidly for long distances under heavy pack with light rations, and can sleep on a rock.
>
> (2) Knowledge of how to use whatever weapons were available in a given century and region was widely diffused throughout the male population. Men saw and practiced arms from early childhood. Possession of arms of

some sort—formerly a spear, during the last century increasingly a rifle—has been considered a normal mark of manhood.

(3) A cult of masculinity was highly developed in Abyssinia and conceived specifically in terms of military prowess.[3] To be a man was to be a killer, tireless on the warpath and fearless in battle. The prospect of acquiring prestige through trophies collected from murdered enemies was a powerful incentive.

(4) The prospect of acquiring booty was another powerful incentive. The norms of combat in Abyssinia included wanton expropriation of conquered peoples. Cattle, grain, arms, and sometimes slaves were among the items to be gained.

(5) Success in military activity was the key route to social mobility. Outstanding achievement at arms brought a man honors, favors, and political appointments. Men with any ambition at all—and most had dreams of rising high at some time in their society, which provided some opportunity for and much talk about upward mobility—were thus motivated to seek occasions for combat.

(6) Personal loyalties, finally, played an important part in many cases—not the horizontal loyalty to comrades, which has been stressed in sociological studies of modern armies, but vertical loyalties to one's chief or patron.[4] Although service under a master was voluntary and was frequently discontinued when the leader's fortunes waned, so long as the leader was successful and reasonably effective in rewarding and supplying his followers—and in some cases even when he was not—a sense of being "his man" and wanting to be brave for him was another factor that motivated Abyssinians to do well in battle.

As this last consideration suggests, historical Ethiopian armies consisted of a number of individual leaders—the Emperor and the governors of provinces—and the fluctuating numbers of troops under their personal command. These troops were of three kinds. First, each "big man" had a standing corps of soldiers, armed retainers who lived near his quarters. Such men served their master for the security and comfort that came from living near a seat of power and at his expense. Second, there were men whose rights to the use of certain land entailed the obligation to serve some designated ruler for two or three months during the year—a kind of corvée labor in the form of military service. Third, there was the mass levy in time of emergency. Such troops were recruited by sending out a proclamation, and bringing to bear various formal and informal sanctions against those qualified males who failed to turn out. Delinquents in Menelik's day were punished by confiscation of goods, whipping, and imprisonment. One of his proclamations states that "if an eligible man remains at home, let him be called by the name of woman, and let his wife take possession of all his wealth and become head of the household."[5]

It was thus assumed in Abyssinia that every able-bodied adult male who did not belong to the clergy was willing and able to be an effective soldier. This assumption produced bewilderment and dismay when acted on in warfare against the Italians in 1935–1936, but until then it had been sound enough for Abyssinian purposes. The existence of a ready supply of capable soldiers enabled the traditional military system to function on a highly individualistic basis. Each soldier was responsible for procuring weapons, either from his own resources or through arrangements with his leader (although by the time of Menelik soldiers were typically issued rifles). He was expected to acquire the skills needed to use them on his own; there was no provision for collective training procedures of any sort. He was likewise expected to arrange his own logistics; he either walked to battle or else brought his own mule, arranged for his own sleeping quarters, brought his own food supply and supplemented it by preying on local peasants as he went, and brought along his wife or maidservant to prepare his food. Finally, each soldier was his own master in battle. The Abyssinian fighting unit was not the squad or platoon, but the individual combatant, who sized up the situation as he went along, chose his own time and place to close with the enemy, and chose the objects for his personal attack.[6]

Viewed as a collectivity, however, the traditional Abyssinian army appears to have been a comparatively unstable and inefficient organization. Troops moved into battle in a disorderly manner. They were not accustomed to persevering in battle; at the first sign of defeat, mass retreat was not unusual. When their leaders faltered, or failed to provide for them properly, or appeared to be heading for failure, Abyssinian soldiers often deserted en masse and went over to the other side. They were as quick to abandon the military role as they had been eager to assume it; barely had the din of battle ceased when they set about pursuing their favorite pursuits of civil litigation, plotting political intrigue, and caring for their home estates.

Even when fighting at their best, moreover, the Abyssinian soldiery did not form an efficient military force. Their standard tactics were to engage in massive sudden attacks in an effort to envelop and confound the enemy; the alternatives were victory or retreat. The more subtle maneuvers of guerrilla warfare and the taking of cover were tactics that conflicted with their ethic of impetuous, fearless aggression. Because of this "unreasoning offensive spirit," an Italian officer wrote in 1937, Ethiopian troops were easy to defeat by a disciplined modern army.[7] It was clear to Haile Selassie from the beginning of his reign that modern forms of organization as well as military technology were indispensable if Ethiopia were to continue to be a proud power.

Modernization of the Armed Forces

The modernization of Ethiopian military forces was prefigured by the Portuguese mission of the sixteenth century, which brought the first supply of firearms into the country and taught Abyssinian soldiers how to use the new weapons. While additional supplies of modern weapons filtered into the country during succeeding centuries substantial modernization of Ethiopian military technology did not occur until the late nineteenth century. The turning point was perhaps the defeat of the Egyptian forces by Yohannes: 20,000 Remington rifles were taken after the Battle of Gura (1876) alone. Subsequently, Menelik imported large quantities of rifles and ammunition and some artillery from France and Italy, an effort aided by the competition between these two powers to win his friendship. With the establishment of Italian and French ports on the Red Sea and Gulf of Aden, Menelik's needs for weaponry were filled by a lively arms trade. By the time of the Battle of Adwa in 1896 the armies of Menelik and his generals possessed an estimated 100,000 rifles and 40 cannon.[8] Menelik also employed French officers to train some of his personal troops.

A more serious attempt to impart modern military training to Ethiopian soldiers was carried out during the regency and reign of Haile Selassie, who sent a number of Ethiopian officers to the St. Cyr Military Academy in France in the 1920s. He also brought to Ethiopia in 1929 a military mission from Belgium that trained his Imperial Bodyguard for half a dozen years. Swiss and Belgian officers were sent to train the troops in his province of Hararge. In 1934 he established a Military Academy at Holeta, initially under Swedish management, 30 miles from Addis Ababa.

Haile Selassie's program of military modernization was barely launched, of course, before the Ethiopian Army was put to a shattering test. When the war with Italy broke out, only an insignificant number of Ethiopians could be said to have been modern soldiers commanded by trained officers. The vast majority of the troops were traditional soldiery, armed with spears or old-fashioned rifles and led by men who held their positions as old nobles or provincial governors rather than as professional officers. The modern ideas of strategy adopted by the Emperor at the instigation of European military advisers only confused and undermined the confidence of the old-time commanders and their armies.

By the time Ethiopian troops were fully defeated by the Italians in 1937, however, important lessons had been painfully learned. Ethiopian soldiers adapted themselves to guerilla techniques and, through constant harassment of Italian troops in well-chosen times and places, so undermined Italian morale that reconquest of the country was relatively speedy in 1941.[9] The need for modern training as well as weapons had been seen clearly by many men other than the small circle of European-oriented leaders at the top. After the liberation the government moved posthaste to replace the traditional system with a standing modern Army. The Emperor concentrated the responsibility for military activity in a national Ministry of War (later changed to Defense). The strength of the traditional war lords in the provinces had been greatly depleted by the losses of the war, and the Emperor effectively eliminated their potential for a comeback by depriving them of the right to appropriate local revenues, the foundation of their capacity to acquire soldiers in the past. The postwar development of the Ethiopian military forces may be traced in three stages, paralleling the three phases of political involvement by the military to be discussed in the next section.

I. ***1942–1950:*** The years following the liberation were marked by rapid development of modern-trained troops primarily under British auspices. Under a convention signed in 1942 the British agreed to provide at their own cost a mission "for the purpose of raising, organizing, and training the Ethiopian Army." They had begun such training in Khartoum in 1940, and proceeded to equip and instruct ten infantry battalions, a regiment of pack artillery, an armored car regiment, and engineer and signal services. The battalions thus readied were stationed at key points around the country and played an important role in maintaining internal security during the unstable decade which followed liberation. In addition, the Emperor revived and trained his Imperial Bodyguard under the command of Ethiopian officers who had attended the Holeta Academy before the war and matured during the campaign of liberation. As an indication of the seriousness with which the government took this military build-up, in addition to the resources contributed by the British, Ethiopian expenditures for the Ministry of War and Imperial Bodyguard alone—that is, excluding expenditures for police and other security services—amounted to 38 per cent of the total national budget in 1943–1944. The following year it dropped to about 25 per cent (although the absolute figures remained about the same) and remained approximately at that level the rest of the decade—in each year constituting the largest single item on the national budget.[10]

In addition to the forces trained by the British mission and those of the Emperor's Bodyguard, another army was set up in Ethiopia during this period. In order to absorb and disarm the relatively large numbers of armed patriot bands which were roaming the country as outlaws after the liberation, a loose Territorial Army was organized. In contrast to the new standing national forces, men entering this Army were not given rifles but rather were enlisted only if they already possessed rifles. This Territorial Army thus served to check postwar unemployment and brigandage. By the close of this period, most of its members had been absorbed into the regular Army or else into the newly formed National Police.

II. ***1951–1960:*** This period was marked by the replacement of British influence by a number of other foreign military missions, the expansion and diversification of the military forces, the introduction of substantial American aid, and the first participation of Ethiopian forces in an international military campaign.

The British mission began to withdraw during the late 1940s and left Ethiopia altogether in 1951. In an effort to reduce British influence in this area, the Ethiopian government had brought in Swedish military advisers and instructors as early as 1946. In 1953 a United States military assistance group came to Ethiopia to help train and equip various branches of the security forces. Swedish officers were brought to train the new Air Force, Norwegians for the fledgling Navy. Three cadet groups were taken successively through three-year training programs, in which Swedish officers also played a part. In 1958 a military mission from India came to set up and manage the new Military Academy at Harar. Israeli officers have also served as instructors in various sectors of the military establishment, and Japanese instructors were imported to train security personnel. Ethiopian officers were also sent abroad for training a variety of countries, including the United States, England, and Yugoslavia.

In 1951 the Kagnew Battalion, formed of crack troops selected from the Imperial Bodyguard, was sent to Korea to fight with the United Nations forces as part of the U.S. Seventh Division. Altogether, three battalions were sent prior to the cease-fire, a total of about 5,000 men; and additional battalions were stationed there following the truce. In appreciation of Ethiopia's contribution to the Korean campaign and in exchange for rights to set up a U.S. army base at Asmara, Ethiopia received a substantial amount of military assistance. The amount given to Ethiopia from 1950 to 1965 exceeds U.S. $91 million, approximately half of the amount of military aid given in all Africa during this period.

III. ***1961–1966:*** In the past half-dozen years no notable changes took place in the patterns of modernization, but Ethiopian troops were provided with three important occasions for active duty and thereby increased the general prominence of the professional Army in Ethiopian life. Ethiopia was among the first countries to send forces to the Congo; over 3,000 Ethiopian troops and half an air squadron participated in the United Nations military action there. Closer to home, skirmishes in the vicinity of the Somali border have occasioned a number of military reprisals and attacks, and the stationing of larger numbers of troops on the alert in the Ogaden. (The Somali danger also resulted in Ethiopia's first defense pact, with Kenya, in December, 1963.) Internally, the rebellion of the Imperial Bodyguard in December, 1960, led to an engagement in which the regular Army and the Air Force quashed the rebels after a day of heavy fighting. In the wake of this revolt, the officer corps of the Bodyguard was completely dismantled, and a new Imperial Bodyguard was reconstituted with fresh troops and officers from the Army and a new period of training under Indian officers.

The Military Today: Organization, Size, Recruitment, and Training

The Emperor remains the Commander-in-Chief of the Armed Forces of Ethiopia and intervenes authoritatively in all important decisions. Theoretically he is advised by a National Defense Council, about which little is known. Reporting directly to him are the Commander of the Imperial Bodyguard; the Minister of Interior, under whom are the Chief of Police and the Chief of Security; his own private intelligence networks; and the Minister of Defense. The latter commands the Chief of Staff, under whom are the Commanders of the Army, Navy, and Air Force; though in practice all of these officers also report directly to the Emperor.

The Imperial Bodyguard today consists of about 6,000 men, organized in 9 infantry battalions. The regular Army consists of about 24,000 men, including 23 infantry and 4 artillery battalions, an armored squadron, and an airborne rifle company. The Air Force numbers some 1,300 men, and includes a squadron of F-86 jet fighters, 5 T-33 jet trainers, and a transport squadron with DC-3's and C47's (all American made), as well as 18 piston-engined Swedish Saab-91 training craft and 2 squadrons of Saab-17 light bombers. The Navy has about 3,000 men, and includes 5 95-foot U.S. coastal patrol boats, 2 Yugoslav motor torpedo boats, and an eighteen-year-old reconverted seaplane tender outfitted as a patrol-boat tender, training vessel, and imperial flagship. There are approximately 30,000 men in the National Police force distributed throughout the country.[11] Since 1960 the Territorial Army has been reorganized. Little is known about it, though it is said to be concentrated in Shoa province at locations not too far from Addis Ababa.

Noncommissioned personnel have been recruited into the Ethiopian security forces on a purely voluntary basis, although unconfirmed rumors state that vagrants in the cities are sometimes conscripted into military service as they have been for service in the gold mines. They come primarily from three sources: patriots who fought in the underground during the Italian Occupation; rural youths who are dissatisfied with their lot and interested in the opportunities, adventure, and "manly" life of the soldier; and the unemployed of the cities, including numerous school dropouts.

The older generation of Army officers likewise enlisted voluntarily, as have most, if not all, of the Air Force cadets. The older officers include a small group who received some modern training before the Italian War; a group of officers of field-grade level who served with the patriot forces and are relatively untrained; and a group who were in exile with the Emperor during the Occupation and received some training at French or British hands during the war years. By contrast, the postwar cadres of officers in the Bodyguard, Navy, and (since 1957) Army have been recruited largely through conscription for lifetime service, an action which has frequently resulted in considerable bitterness over their being deprived of the possibility of civilian careers. These cadres have been handpicked from the cream of secondary school seniors and first-year college students.

In terms of ethnic composition, the enlisted men consist primarily of Amhara, with some Tigreans and a heavy admixture of Oromo. At the commissioned level, the proportion of Tigreans is higher and that of Oromo lower. A survey of the cadets in the Harar Military Academy in 1959–1960 revealed the following ethnic distribution: Amhara, 53 per cent; Tigrean, 26 per cent; Aderi (native of Harar) and Oromo, 8 per cent; no reply, 13 per cent. With respect to the socioeconomic class of their families, the same cadets responded as follows: upper class, 11 percent; middle class, 53 percent; "poor" or lower class, 21 per cent; peasant class, 3 per cent; no reply, 13 per cent.

Five schools are now devoted to the training of military personnel: the Infantry School at Holeta, the Air Force School at Debra Zeit, the Naval Cadets' School at Massawa, the Abba Dina Police College in Addis Ababa, and the Haile Selassie I Military Academy at Harar. All but the first of these are geared primarily to the training of commissioned officers, and accept only well-qualified secondary-school graduates in their programs. They are educational institutions in a broad sense, including in their curricula a variety of academic and practical subjects in addition to the strictly military and technical ones. The Abba Dina Police College, for example, which is in the process of expanding from a two-year to a three-year program, provides courses in law for its students, while cadets at the Harar Academy take courses in English literature. In addition to their substantive content, these training programs have three general educational objectives: the development of a loyalty to the nation that transcends loyalty to particular ethnic groups; the substitution of an ethic of professional competence for the old-fashioned military ethic of naive martial enthusiasm and wanton bravery; and the substitution of an ethic of professional duty for the old-fashioned ethic of political ambition through military service.

The Ethiopian Political System

Contemporary Political Structure

THE salient features of Ethiopia's political structure are generally well-known and need only be briefly reviewed here. Ethiopia is governed by a monarch whose theoretically absolute powers are legitimated both by ancient traditions and by a written Constitution (1955), which asserts that "By virtue of His Imperial Blood, as well as by the anointing which He has received, the person of the Emperor is sacred, His dignity is inviolable and His power is indisputable." Haile Selassie, the present incumbent, has worked steadfastly to consolidate and assert the full imperial power ever since his emergence on the national scene as Regent following a coup d'etat in 1916. In the prewar years, he attained this goal by building up his military strength to the point where he was stronger than any of the semi-autonomous feudal lords who might oppose him. Their power was decisively undercut in 1942, when the establishment of a national Ministry of Finance eliminated their rights to collect revenues, and when all provincial governmental functions were made subordinate to centralized Ministries of Interior and Justice. At the same time he constructed an elaborate edifice of national administration, including sixteen ministries; a number of independent agencies performing various developmental functions, like the Imperial Highway Authority and the Imperial Board of Telecommunications; and a number of coordinating bodies under the Council of Ministers, such as the National Coffee Board and the Economic and Technical Assistance Board.

Over all these administrative organs the Emperor's authority has remained supreme. While the burgeoning of this new governmental apparatus created new sources of power and hence potential opposition, the present Emperor has managed to secure the minimal loyalty of most members of the administration through a subtly graded system of economic and social rewards, and to forestall threatening coalescenses of interest through a multiplex surveillance network and a skillfully applied policy of *divide et impera.*

Haile Selassie has also established a Parliament in Ethiopia. The first Parliament, set up in 1931, consisted of a Senate whose members were appointed by the Emperor, and a Chamber of Deputies who were chosen by the nobility and local chiefs. Since the new Constitution of 1955, members of the Chamber of Deputies have been elected by universal suffrage; such elections were held in 1957, 1961, and 1965. The Parliament exists primarily as a deliberative body, since legislative power remains essentially in the hands of the Emperor. The Ethiopian Parliament convenes annually, but because the proceedings of

Parliament are not regularly covered by the Press or published entire in any form, it is difficult to determine exactly what happens in its deliberations.

The fourteen provincial governments are headed either by governor-generals, or by deputy governor-generals, appointed by the Emperor and receiving salaries through the Ministry of Interior. Under them are numerous district governors and subdistrict governors. All these officials are placed in lines of command emanating from the Emperor and the national Ministry of Interior, although in outlying districts the authority of Addis Ababa has not penetrated very deeply and these men are often members of local families long important in the area. This system of provincial administration is paralleled by a complex judicial system, which includes seven appellate levels culminating in the Emperor's private court. In addition, each provincial and subprovincial center includes a contingent from the National Police force.

Stability in the Present Regime

Although the present regime has attained a degree of autocratic control previously unknown in Ethiopian history, and although natural processes of social change at work in the country have introduced many new sources of tension, it has been characterized by a basic continuity and stability remarkable for a part of the world where convulsive change of government has been frequent in recent decades. As an indication of the magnitude of the present Emperor's political achievement consider that his predecessor, Lij Iyasu, had far better genealogical claims to the throne, but was overturned after only three years in the imperial office. Haile Selassie, however, has played the dominant role in shaping the fate of Ethiopia for virtually half a century now. In addition to his unusual manipulative talents, the durability of his regime may be attributed to the following factors.

(1) Sanctity of the Imperial office is an ancient theme in Abyssinian tradition. So long as the Emperor remains true to the Ethiopian Orthodox Church—it was Lij Iyasu's alleged conversion to Islam that hastened his downfall—he is endowed with a sacred aura that rests on three considerations: his membership in a royal line hallowed by alleged descent from King Solomon; his anointment at the hands of the archbishop of the Church; and his role as protector and defender of the Church.

(2) The centralization of military power in Addis Ababa before and after the Italian Occupation gave Haile Selassie the force with which to back up his claims to legitimate authority. The two dozen years of systematic acquisition and purchase of arms by Menelik after 1878 decisively shifted the balance of military power in the empire to the central province of Shoa. The modernization

of Haile Selassie's troops in the 1920s and early 1930s increased the extent of Shoan superiority, and the establishment of the British-trained regular Army following liberation, together with the reconstituted Bodyguard and National Police system definitively raised the might of Addis Ababa far above that which any potential provincial opponent could muster.

(3) The authoritarian ethos characteristic of Abyssinian culture has favored a state of mind which cheerfully relegates the responsibility for decisions concerning the public realm to the highest authorities, and which discourages the open expression of criticism of such authorities. This ethos is supported both by the Biblical notion that it is immoral to disobey one's superior and the secular argument that human affairs and social relations are headed for trouble in the absence of strong authoritarian leadership.[12] Thus, numerous Ethiopians who have had strong personal grievances against the Emperor or serious disagreements with some of his policies have refrained from criticizing him publicly in any way and have consistently shown him the greatest deference.

(4) The pursuit of interest on an individualistic basis has worked to support the present regime and Haile Selassie has deliberately sought to perpetuate it for that purpose. The traditional social system of Abyssinia encourages the pursuit of individual, not collective, ambition. It is lacking in mechanisms by which individuals can associate in the pursuit of collective interests. There are no fixed corporate structures, either in the kinship system or on a territorial or civic basis, which might channel the pursuit of common interests. There are almost no traditional patterns for cooperation beyond the reciprocal arrangements for attaining such restricted goals as the construction of a roof or the repair of a church.[13] The Abyssinians are sociologically unequipped for banding together to confront some authority with common demands. Their system promotes, rather, the pursuit of individual advantage by means of winning favor of some authority. Ethiopians today have therefore been almost—but not quite—as little disposed to insist on forming associations for the articulation and aggregation of interests as the Emperor has been disposed to permit the formation of such associations. Labor unions were not allowed in Ethiopia until 1963, professional associations have been discouraged, and political parties are still not permitted. The combination of repressive policies on the part of the government and the individualistic character of the populace has resulted in the absence of organized groups which could threaten the regime in anyway.

(5) The arrangement of marriages in order to promote political harmony has been a stabilizing technique used with great effectiveness throughout the present regime, beginning with Haile Selassie's own marriage to the daughter of an important Oromo chieftain before he came to power. Haile Selassie has

brought nearly all of the great, politically problematic families in the country into his fold by marrying one of their members to one of his children or relatives.

(6) The symbolic adequacy and instrumental effectiveness of Haile Selassie's regime must also be credited for contributing significantly to its durability. While all segments of the population know areas of frustration for which they hold him responsible, all of them are able to identify with him in some respect and to remember some of his policies from which they have benefited. While he has undermined the power of the old nobility, he gratifies them by retaining much of the old court symbolism and has rewarded many of them with appointments to the Senate and in the provincial administration. While he has undermined the power of the clergy to some extent and has been a primary agent of secularization in the country, he remains steadfast in his adherence to the basic traditions of the Orthodox Church, has won its independence from the partriarchate at Alexandria, and has handsomely rewarded the highest dignitaries of the Church. While he has antagonized the Abyssinian peasantry in various ways—by building up Addis Ababa at the expense of the provinces, by showing favoritism of various sorts, by maintaining what some feel to be a repressive political system, by introducing alien ways—he has won their everlasting gratitude by symbolizing the independence of Ethiopia from European rule, by freeing them from the traditional necessity of paying indefinite amounts of tribute corvée labor to exploitative local lords, and by bringing such benefits as roads and medical centers into some outlying regions. While he has kept the highest government officials in a state of anxiety and overdependence through the high-handed use of his authority, he has given them much of what prestige and income they possess and has increased the national prestige of Ethiopia so that they are benefited in many ways. While his behavior toward the modern-educated has often offended their dignity and while his policies have been (privately) criticized by them as illiberal and insufficiently progressive, he has also been identified as responsible for introducing modern education into Ethiopia and for giving them what facilities and rewards they now possess. Although to numerous ethnic and regional groups throughout the country he symbolizes the continuance of Shoan dominance under which many chafe, he gratifies them by virtue of the majesty of being an *Emperor* and by such improvements as increased security in the provinces and the rudimentary signs of better living standards. To all parts of the population, finally, his diplomatic success in capturing an important place in the leadership of the pan-African movement during the past decade has been a conspicuous source of support for the regime.

The Political Capability of the Military

Acutely aware of the age-old connection between military activity and political ambition in Ethiopia, Emperor Haile Selassie has taken pains to instill in his professional military forces the idea that they are to be guided solely by an ethic of duty and to refrain from getting involved in the political realm. The heading of every issue of the official Bodyguard newspaper has carried the injunction: "The soldier's work is to follow orders, not to engage in politics." The lesson was repeated at all levels: when General Mengistu Neway, the late Commander of the Imperial Bodyguard, was on a tour of the country with the Emperor in the 1950s, he was struck by the hunger and poverty of the people in a certain region and asked if something could not be done about it. The Emperor is said to have replied, "What's this? Meddling in politics? That is none of your business."

Significant as this question of the degree of *interest* in a political role may be, it does not afford so revealing a category for dealing with the political involvement of the military as does the category of political *capability*. For although interest may be high, the capability may be so low as to preclude the possibility of such involvement; conversely, even though such interest may be low, a military organization with a high degree of political capability may be pressured by societal strains and the flow of events into playing an important political role. In analyzing the elements of such capability, four variables seem to be of obvious significance: the economic and cultural resources of the military; their politically relevant value orientations; their position in the social structure; and the internal organization.

Economic and Cultural Resources

As we have seen, military expenditures have constituted the largest single item in the national budget ever since the liberation. During the past seven years expenses for the Armed Forces have averaged about 17 per cent of the budget. (Figures for the Police and security departments are not available.) In 1963 this amounted to approximately US $18 million. While not large in absolute terms, it represents the largest defense outlay of any country in Sub-Saharan Africa except South Africa and, in the past few years, Ghana and Nigeria.[14]

The income of the higher-ranking officers has been impressive by Ethiopian standards. They have received substantial salaries, free housing, free cars, and servants and retainers drawn from the ranks. In many cases their income is supplemented by rents from land holdings in the provinces and urban real estate, and at times by personal gifts presented directly by the Emperor. Many officers in the Air Force in particular have been recipients of royal gifts in the form of land and other privilege. Lower-ranking officers have complained of income insufficient to meet their minimal needs, and the low income of enlisted men has been a source of acute dissatisfaction for many years.

Collectively, the military possess a modest proportion of the country's modern facilities. They have their own engineers and roadbuilders, if not of the best quality; their own hospitals and doctors, if not the most effective. They operate at least three internal newspapers, and the Imperial Bodyguard operated a radio station in the 1950s until it was closed down because of political pressures.

The postwar generation of officers represents a significant proportion—probably no fewer than 10 to 12 per cent—of all Ethiopians who have received modern education beyond the level. Many of them pursue additional education on their own, those in Addis Ababa attending extension courses at the University.

Perhaps the most conspicuous cultural resource of the military is their primary role in the development of a secular national culture in postwar Ethiopia. Their soccer teams have helped to focus attention on national sports. Their Olympic champion Sergeant Abebe Bikila, two-time marathon winner, has been a major national hero and the focus of much national pride—and was the only Ethiopian other than the Emperor to be greeted by cheering crowds at the airport. In music, the military services have not only been the principal source of performing musicians in the modernizing sector—Army, Bodyguard, and Police have each maintained popular dance bands, and the Police have pioneered with a symphony orchestra—but have created distinctive Ethiopian tunes which have become popular with their countrymen. These and similar innovations have been fostered by their self-confident realization that in Ethiopia the military is the only institution that is simultaneously traditional, modern, and national; that they have a natural mission, as it were, to procreate the new national culture of modernizing Ethiopia.

Value Orientations

Although not much reliable information is available on the subject, it may be suggested with some confidence that, after national independence, technical modernization and social welfare are the primary values toward which most Ethiopian military officers are oriented. No longer are Ethiopian officers oriented in terms of defending the Church: religious issues have receded, and a good many military officers have became atheists, especially those trained under the Indian military mission. Nor are they likely to pursue partisan ethnic causes; a real and vital sense of common nationality is perhaps stronger among the military than elsewhere in the country. They favor technical modernization because their experience of modern technology has convinced them that it can only be useful for the nation, and those who have been abroad for training or active duty are particularly eager to have their country "catch up" with what they have seen elsewhere. They favor social welfare because most of them stem from humble families, and they feel a patriotic inclination to see the lot of their countrymen improved. Where they do not reject the authoritarian ethos of Abyssinia, they do reject the traditional pattern in which a privileged few live at the expense of a relatively impoverished many. Many of them have objected to what they considered the corruption of the present regime and its "parasites," and to the extent to which the Emperor was using his authority arbitrarily and unproductively. While most of them probably felt loyal to Haile Selassie in the years just after liberation, throughout the 1950s increasing numbers of officers were becoming alienated from his regime. To some extent this reflected grievances over salary on the part of lower-ranking officers and enlisted men; to same extent it meant a growing political consciousness. As one former officer of the Bodyguard recollected:

> Around the time of the Korean War a number of us officers in the Imperial Bodyguard began to talk about things that were bothering us. We observed the many oppressions in our country. We understood that it was not right for Ethiopians to live in subjugation under the power of one man. We saw that justice was destroyed and that everything was done by lies. Inspired by the spirit of nationalism, we therefore began to express opposition in conversations among ourselves.

Finally, most of them have not the slightest interest in an aggressive, expansionist nationalism, although some of the older officers have been advocates of a "preventive war" against Somalia. In recent years they have developed a keen interest in African politics and a sympathetic orientation toward the pan-African movement.

Position in Society

The status of the military in Abyssinian society was marked by three characteristics: lack of isolation of the military from civilian society; public appreciation of the values embodied by the military; public dislike of the predatory aspects of military behavior. In modified form, these characteristics are still in evidence today.

Although because of their special training centers and chains of command the military are today far more separated from the rest of society than before the war, they appear to remain in more intimate contact with civilian society than is true, say, of the American military. Most members of the forces stationed in Addis Ababa live, not in barracks, but in private quarters among the civilian populations. Military officers interact a good deal with civilians of high status at parties, dances, weddings, and funerals. Army officers are often related to civilian officials by blood or marriage. They mingle with civilian students at extension courses of the University. The postwar-trained officers typically retain contacts with their former fellow students from secondary school days.

With respect to their attitudes toward the military, the civilian part of the population is ambivalent The negative side of their attitude does not rest, as in some democratic societies, on an ideological distrust of the military because of their association with "militarism" and anti-democratic tendencies. On the contrary, at the ideological level Ethiopian society is, if anything, promilitary. Rather, the dislike of the military has to do with a sense of their being parasites on the people. Traditionally, this negative attitude arose as a reaction against the forces' quartering and pillage associated with soldiers on the warpath. Haile Selassie sought to overcome that opprobrium in the Italian campaign by insisting that civilians be reimbursed for anything that soldiers needed to take from them. It has a contemporary counterpart, however, in the idea that the military today are doing nothing to develop the country, that they just sit around and eat up the results of the hard work of others. The arrogant behavior of many veterans of the Korean campaign in the bars and cafés of Addis Ababa in the mid-1950s also exacerbated civilian feelings.

In two important respects, on the other hand, the military are objects of the highest admiration and appreciation. They are appreciated for defending the country's territorial integrity and political independence, matters about which Abyssinians feel very strongly. They represent, moreover, the style of life and the virtues connected with while masculinity, an ethic which remains of some importance in Ethiopian culture. The generally high esteem which the military enjoys because of these reasons, the appreciation of their contribution to the secular national culture, and the tradition of military involvement in politics suggests that the assumption of greater responsibility for national development by the military would not be regarded by the public as an unpleasant prospect, but might be welcomed as an opportunity for the military to stop sitting around and start doing something substantial for the country.

Some characteristics of the specific relations between the military and other elites in Ethiopian society can be noted. The regular clergy continue to have the same supportive attitude they have always had toward Ethiopian military endeavors. The two establishments are acknowledged partners in maintaining civil order. When the Army and Air Force were putting down the rebellion in 1960, one of their early actions was to drop leaflets containing a statement by the Archbishop that those who aided the rebels would be excommunicated. So long as there was broad agreement between the military and ecclesiastical leaders with respect to policies pursued, the support of the latter could probably be assumed and would be of some import. While most members of the Church hierarchy oppose many aspects of modernization, they have probably been most sympathetic to such modernization as has taken place under military auspices. In the event that the military becomes militantly secular, however, the Church might become alienated from them, a development that would, in turn, canalize opinion in crucial provinces against the military. Insofar as the Territorial Army is a force to reckon with, it can be considered much more closely tied to the traditional Church.

The civilian government officials live in a state of considerable anxiety over the prospect of being displaced by the military. One of the ministers most sensitive to this possibility, the late Makonnen Habtewold, was instrumental in having the Emperor make certain high level changes in military personnel and close down the Imperial Bodyguard radio station in the 1950s because he felt that the popularity of the Imperial Bodyguard and the stimulation of their political ambitions were reaching a dangerous point. Because of their fear of displacement, some of the civilian bureaucrats might be inclined to join with the church in the event of a Church-Army showdown.

The students and young intellectuals combine appreciation of the military's potential for modernizing the country with fear of the illiberal tendencies that might be associated with military rule. Most recently students have carried on a demonstration in Addis Ababa protesting "police brutality" in the suppression of an earlier student demonstration. But for the most part students and other youth appear sympathetic to the idea of universal military service, an idea currently promoted by some military men as a means of increasing civilian-military harmony.

Inner Solidarity

Aware of the relatively high esteem of the military in Ethiopia and of its potential, through possession of modern technology and aspirations as well as its monopoly of the means of violence, for radical intrusion into the political process, Haile Selassie has pursued a policy of checking, balancing, and dividing the Armed Forces internally since their establishment as a standing professional force. To the effect of his deliberately divisive policies must be added a number of tensions within the military which have emerged spontaneously.

Within the Army, the main axes of cleavage among the officers have been those dividing the postwar cadres from the older groups. These tensions have been partly those of a generational nature, partly reflections of ideological differences between the more progressive-minded of both groups and the conservatives among the older group. Differences in outlook stemming from the variety of national traditions—French, British, and American—which have influenced their training have compounded the cleavages to some extent. Finally, the alleged permeation of the military ranks with government informers, especially in recent years, has worked to sow widespread suspicion among the officers and to inhibit communication to a considerable extent.

Unlike the Army, the differences among officers in the Imperial Bodyguard were not so pronounced. The bulk of Bodyguard officers stemmed from the postwar period. They developed a morale and esprit, stimulated partly by their privileged training, uniforms, and other perquisites, including a handsome officers' club, which was a center for numerous cultural as well as social and athletic activities. These conditions led them to take a more sanguine view of the overall solidarity of the military than ever existed. In 1960, before the coup, a number of Bodyguard officers said in private conversation: "If and when the time for action comes, all of the Armed Forces will rise as one man."

The somewhat privileged status and perquisites of the Bodyguard had the additional effect, however, of arousing a good deal of envy among the Army officers. They were particularly envious because the officers and troops who went to Korea were nearly exclusively drawn from the Bodyguard ranks. Despite occasional friendships among individual officers from both forces, the relationship between Army and Bodyguard as a whole was colored by a significant amount of antagonism.

I do not have sufficient information to comment securely upon the internal solidarity of the Air Force, Navy, and Police, or of their relationships with the other Armed Forces. It is likely that morale is relatively high among the Air Force officers, since all of them represent the postwar generations and derive satisfactions and prestige from their familiarity with aeronautic technology. But the overarching reality in all these services is the fear of informants and mutual suspiciousness that decisively inhibits the development of the kind of solidarity that marked the Imperial Bodyguard in the 1950s.

Patterns and Sources of Political Involvement

Ethiopian military personnel have become directly involved in the input and output functions of government in four distinct ways in the postwar years: military personnel have been assigned to governmental positions; military activity has been a means of competing for power; one group among the military forces seized control of the government in a short-lived coup d'etat; and one group of the military created a precedent for public political expression in an unusual instance of institutional interest articulation. Broadly speaking, these types of involvement can be related to specific patterns of societal development and tension in the three periods following liberation which were described above.

1942–1950: Traditional Patterns of Political Involvement

The fusion of military and political roles was manifest in two ways in Abyssinian society. First, military activity was the key route to attain political power, both for the ambitious commoner or young man who sought to be rewarded by his lord with a political appointment of some sort, and for the ambitious lord whose fortunes vis-à-vis other lords depended to a large extent on the size and effectiveness of the army he could muster. Second, administrative, fiscal, and judicial functions were normally performed by men who were also military leaders and bore military titles.

With the reforms of 1942 Haile Selassie differentiated the two realms once and for all. Provincial lords were deprived of their private armies, and the civilian functions of government were bestowed upon specifically designated civilian officials just as the military functions devolved upon professional soldiers. But the transition was not completed overnight, and it is not difficult to discern in the new era what might be called modes of political involvement of the military that are cognate with the older patterns.

In 1943 a rebellion broke out in Tigre Province. The rebels blockaded the northern main road and stormed the provincial capital of Makalle. Battalions of the Territorial Army were sent up to no avail, and then two battalions of the British-trained regular Army were dispatched. The rebels were defeated after heavy fighting, and the bombing of the Makalle market by British planes. Earlier in the year, two Army battalions had been sent to contain hostilities in Hararge Province instigated by a group of Somalis. From the viewpoint of a modernized polity, these two incidents would be counted simply as instances of the normal military function of maintaining domestic security. But it had not been more than a dozen or so years earlier that the imperial forces were competing on a somewhat more equal basis with rebellious forces in the west and north. One scion of the old Tigre dynasty was associated, if only circumstantially, with the 1943 rebellion, and thus the military action against the Tigre rebels bears a sociological family resemblance to the old power struggles between an emperor and a dissident feudal lord. A more benign pattern of military involvement was that of appointing military personnel to governmental posts. By this is meant not merely that many of the postwar bureaucratic officials held the old military titles like *Dejazmatch* (Commander of the Gate) and *Balambaras* (Commander of a Fort). By 1942, these titles had become purely honorific, and the higher military ranks were represented by European terms. In addition to this traditionalistic usage, however, the Emperor appointed a number of men who were professional soldiers in the new Army to administrative posts in the government. This practice was continued through the 1950s. Among the most important appointments of this sort may be cited an acting Minister of Interior; the (late) minister of National Community Development, who had formerly been Commander of the Imperial Bodyguard; the Minister of Defense; and the governors of four of the largest and wealthiest provinces: Eritrea, Hararge, Kaffa, and Sidamo. Even though appointed to civilian posts, such men retained their professional military titles.

1951–1960: Modernizing Tensions and Political Involvement

The decade of the 1950s was marked by relative calm with respect to the provinces. Although tensions in Eritrea (which was federated with Ethiopia in 1952), the Somali area, and elsewhere existed below the surface, no attempt was made to gain power through provincial insurrection.

A new source of tension, however, appeared as a remit of the continuing education of groups of Ethiopian civilians and soldiers alike. They felt increasingly that Ethiopia's modernization was proceeding too slowly under the existing regime, that high government officials were using their offices for personal aggrandizement, and that the Emperor bore primary responsibility for both of these and other ills of the country. From about 1955 on, the idea of overthrowing his regime attracted a number of these modernizing Ethiopians, some of whom formed small conspiratorial groups in which military and civilian circles were linked. By the end of the decade, a fairly large circle representing a number of the most able and progressive military and civilian leaders had agreed that forcible overthrow of Haile Selassie would be too disruptive, but that they would wait until he passed from the scene naturally to remove the objectionable hangers-on of his regime and take the reins of government into their own hands. A small segment of this circle, notably the Commander of the Imperial Bodyguard and his civilian brother, became too impatient to follow that policy and decided to carry out a coup d'etat while the Emperor was out of the country on a state visit to Brazil. They were joined by the Chief of Security, who had himself been an officer of the Bodyguard previously. Their strategy was developed by a circle of about a dozen Bodyguard officers.[15]

Power was seized in the early hours of December 14, 1960, when after an initial roundup of the Crown Prince and other key dignitaries at the villa of the Empress, high government officials in Addis Ababa were summoned to Bodyguard Headquarters on the pretext that the Empress was seriously ill and were detained there under guard. Bodyguard soldiers seized control of communications and transportation lines, and established themselves at key points around Addis Ababa. The Chief of Police was quickly brought into the command circle, and the Police maintained order in the streets. At noon the titular head of the new government, the Crown Prince, read a message which proclaimed the end of "three thousand years" of oppression, ignorance, and poverty, and announced a policy of rapid modernization and political liberalization.

The Bodyguard leaders had instigated the coup on the blithe assumption that once the word was spoken, all patriotic forces would join hands to build the new society. They bad underestimated the extent to which Army-Bodyguard tensions bad been built up, the persisting adherence of the public to the old regime, and the degree to which Army commanders were disposed not to cooperate with the Bodyguard commander. Two key Army generals had escaped during the roundup of major political figures, however, and set up their own headquarters with the Army's First Division. Their group was joined by some highly influential civilians who had also eluded the rebels' net, notably the Vice-President of the Senate and the Patriarch of the Ethiopian Orthodox Church. The loyalist generals made contact with military commanders in provincial centers, mobilized additional troops and equipment from the provinces, and distributed counterrevolutionary leaflets to the populace of the capital. Negotiations between the two sides proved futile, and armed hostilities broke out on the afternoon of December 15. The Bodyguard forces were handicapped on several grounds: many of their troops were then stationed in the Congo; some officers deserted when it appeared that a bloodless coup was about to tum into civil war; some men deserted when they learned that they had been mobilized to overthrow the Emperor and not, as they had initially been told, to defend him; and their heaviest weaponry was light artillery. The Army had a potential of greatly superior numbers, as well as heavy artillery, a squadron of tanks, and the support of the air forces. The loyalist Army forces crushed the Bodyguard rebel forces after twenty-four hours of fighting, in which an estimated two thousand Ethiopians were killed or wounded. Meanwhile, the Emperor had flown back to Ethiopia, landing first in Asmara where his son-in-law, a brigadier-general, was provincial governor, and regained Addis Ababa on December 17.

1961–1966: Institutional Prominence and Political Involvement

The political position of the Army was decisively strengthened by its suppression of the attempted coup. Although the loyalist generals were subjected to virulent attacks in leaflets distributed by underground sympathizers with the coup, such dissidents were unable to sustain the momentum of the revolutionary moment. The Army emerged victorious over its old rival force, and self-important for having saved the Emperor's throne and demonstrating its vital role in preserving public order. Even many Ethiopians who shared the political aspirations of the leaders of the coup began to appreciate the prompt and resolute restoration, for it soon appeared quite certain that Army-Bodyguard solidarity in Addis Ababa would only have precipitated civil war on a national scale, since the Emperor would probably have reasserted his sovereignty through the forces commanded by his son-in-law in Eritrea.

Stimulated by this new prominence and sense of importance, the Armed Forces began to air grievances of their own which had long been suppressed. In the spring of 1961, in what was an unprecedented action, a large contingent of Army officers and men marched to the Palace and demanded a raise in pay. The Emperor had little choice but to acquiesce, and granted them what amounted to a budget increase of about Eth $2 million. About the same time, members of the Air Force went on strike for more pay. The Emperor tried to maintain control by assigning them to manual labor, but one group reportedly dug ditches at the Dire Dawa airport that hindered the traffic, and he was obliged to give them the salary increase after all.

The prominence of the Army has been strengthened by two other developments since 1960. Their participation in the United Nations military mission to the Congo, which involved a number of Army as well as Bodyguard men and officers, has brought them a good deal of prestige at home. Similarly, public appreciation of the military role has been enhanced by the security threat posed by Somali attacks and reprisals in the Ogaden. As a result, while military leaders may still be reluctant to seize control of the government while the Emperor remains in power, their political capability has been greatly increased.

Conclusion

The two decades following Ethiopia's liberation witnessed a systematic, continuous build-up of the national military forces. One segment of those forces—the elite Imperial Bodyguard—became conspicuous for its special recruitment, training, esprit, experience, solidarity, and modernizing momentum. Observers at the end of the 1950s tended to see in the Bodyguard the most hopeful force for progressive national development. Established specifically to protect the Emperor against coup attempts, the Bodyguard seemed nevertheless a plausible agency for introducing and supporting a more aggressively efficient and modernizing regime. Bodyguard officers themselves began to feel increasingly a sense of political mission. The stage seemed set for the enactment of that stirring modern myth: a group of educated and devoted military men take over, sweep away a regime of corrupt and inefficient civilians, and shock a country into new spurts of nation building and social progress.

Ex post facto interpretations tend to see the defeat of the Bodyguard's attempt at a coup d'etat as inevitable. Some of the participants themselves realized they had little chance, particularly after the first counter-revolutionary steps had been taken, but welcomed the chance to "speak the truth in the open" and set in motion the forces for more rapid change. They saw themselves as inaugurating a revolutionary tradition, much like the Russian officers of December, 1825, with whom they have often, and aptly, been compared.

While it is true that the actions of the Ethiopian Decembrists introduced some minor but significant changes in Ethiopia's political atmosphere, their experience has thrown some sobering light on the possible implications of military intervention in contemporary Ethiopia. Above all, the image of the military as a well-organized, highly unified force must be revised.

Rather than "rising as one man," as the Bodyguard officers idealistically expected, the Ethiopian military rose as twenty men, pursuing different lines of action for diverse ends. This is so for several reasons. First, as has been true throughout Ethiopian history, the military are not unified vis-à-vis civilian political leaders. High-ranking officers and civilian political leaders have much in common, are in close and frequent contact, and must be viewed ensemble as representing so many strands of individual interest and informal group affiliations. (This may have the long-term beneficial effect of minimizing civilian-military tensions and enabling the military to feel that they can be effective and express their patriotic aspirations without having to be in complete control of the government.)

Second, the top military leaders live in a precarious network of communications among themselves, and the attempt at intervention is fraught with the danger of misunderstandings. Such misunderstandings are characteristic of Ethiopian political style, a style marked by considerable ambiguity and reserve, and apparently played a crucial part in polarizing the Commander of the Imperial Bodyguard and his chief antagonist, the Chief of Staff of the Armed Forces, who prior to the coup had been fairly close friends.

Third, the coup drew attention to the differing orientations of various groups within the military. The modernizing thrust of the younger trained officers was opposed by historically rooted forces in the military loyal to the old regime: the conservative sentiments and personal loyalties of some of the older or more senior officers, the traditionality of the lower ranks,[16] and the spirit of vast numbers of men in the provinces who would seize arms and rise in a moment for a chance to engage in some old-time manly warfare on behalf of King and Church.

The suppression of the December, 1960, coup by the Army has given its leaders an increased sense of power and responsibility for the continuity of Ethiopian politics, and impressed upon the public the importance of the Army in calculations about Ethiopia's political future. The stability of Haile Selassie's regime has been based on the overarching authority of a single man. When he goes, a condition of relative instability is likely to follow. In to that vacuum, ready or not, the military will be drawn. Since Ethiopia has not yet developed highly differentiated political institutions, a military takeover would not constitute the dismantling of democratic forms to the extent that it has in some other countries. Even so, many Ethiopians, including a number of military men, seem eager to push for more democratic institutions, and the traditional closeness of military and political functions in Ethiopia might mean that the military could make a considerable contribution without having actually to control the Government. With respect to the resources at their command, their value orientations and trainings and the potential support of the public they are in a position to make a creditable contribution; but the disunity which continues to afflict them may limit their effectiveness for some time to come.

Notes

1 The Amhara and the Tigreans are the two ethno-linguistic groups whose joint culture is sometimes referred to as "Abyssinians." The Term "Abyssinia" will be used here in this technical sense when referring to Amhara-Tigre Society.

2 Ludolphus, Job, *A New History of Ethiopia*. Translated by J.P. Gent. 2d ed. London, 1684, p. 217.

3 Levine, Donald, "The Concept of Masculinity in Ethiopian Culture," *International Journal of Social Psychiatry*, vol. 12, 1966, pp.17–23.

4 Such horizontal loyalties have, however, been of importance in the military organization of the Oromo, whose traditional social organization is based on a system of age-graded classes.

5 Sambon, L., *L'esercito Abissino*. Rome, 1896, p.9.

6 Levine, Donald, *Wax and Gold: Tradition and Innovation in Ethiopian Culture*. University of Chicago Press, Chicago, 1965, pp. 262–263, 272–273.

7 Perham, Margery, *The Government of Ethiopia.* Oxford University Press, New York, 1948, p. 167.

8 Pankhurst, Richard, "Fire-arms in Ethiopian History," *Ethiopia Observer*, vol. 6, no. 2, 1962.

9 Marcus, Harold, "Insurgency and Counter-insurgency in Ethiopia, 1931–1941." Unpublished manuscript, Department of History, Howard University.

10 Perham, Margery. *op. cit.*, pp. 200–206.

11 Kitchen, Helen, editor, *A Handbook of African Affairs.* Frederick A. Praeger, New York, 1964, pp. 197–198.

12 Levine, Donald. "Ethiopia: Identity, Authority and Realism," in Pye, Lucian W., and S. Verba, editors, *Political Culture and Political Development*, Princeton University Press, Princeton, N.J., 1965.

13 There may be certain regional exceptions to this generalization—the Tigreans in the region of Wajirat are said to have a much more cooperative and community orientation, for example—and it certainly does not apply to many of the ethnic groups outside the sphere of Amhara-Tigre culture. The generalization may also be qualified by noting the existence of a voluntary fraternal association, the *mahebar,* in Amhara-Tigre society, an organization which has formed the model for a number of regional associations that have sprung up in Addis Ababa during the past decade.

14 Coward, H. R., *Military Technology in Developing Countries.* MIT Center for International Studies, Cambridge, Mass., 1964, p. 260.

15 See Greenfield, Richard, *Ethiopia: A New Political History,* Pall Mall Press, London, 1965, for a detailed account of the events of the coup.

16 Greefield observes that "the influence of tradition on the lower ranks is very strong and it is a moot point as to whether the soldiers would remain loyal to the military High Command if its authority were challenged by a senior member of the aristocracy or by the Patriarch," *Ibid.*, p. 456.

26

Concerning the Derg

Testimony for US Senate Subcommittee on African Affairs

A. Subcommittee on African Affairs of the Committee on Foreign Relations*

Domestic Ethiopian Developments (1976)

August 4, 1976

Washington, D.C.

SENATOR CLARK. I would suggest that we initiate the proceedings with a brief statement by each member of the panel and in turn to be followed by a general seminar discussion among the panel members and the members of the subcommittee. . . .

I think it has been decided that perhaps the appropriate way to proceed is to have Professor Levine and then Mr. Spencer and Mr. Korry. So we will go through the three statements and then spend the remainder of our morning in discussion.

Statement of Donald Levine, University of Chicago, IL

---

* Official Stenographic Transcript of Hearings before the Committee on Foreign Relations at the United States Senate in Washington, D.C. on August 4, 1976.

PROFESSOR LEVINE. The coup d'état by which the Dergue of the Armed Forces, Police and Territorial Army established itself on September 12th, 1974, followed eight months of widespread popular agitation against the Haile Selassie Government and some two decades of increasing dissatisfaction with the corruptness of his regime and the slow pace of modernization of Ethiopia.

In removing Haile Selassie, the Dergue thus represented a broadly based movement of public opinion. Contrary to predictions that the Emperor could not be removed from office while alive or that his overthrow would provoke mayhem, deposing him proved nearly effortless and the deed was greeted with a general sense of relief, determination to get the country moving, and immense pride that the "creeping revolution" which brought about his downfall had taken place without violence.

Today, nearly two years later, the revolutionary regime which initially enjoyed such widespread support appears to be every bit as unpopular as the Haile Selassie regime in its bleakest moments. . . . .

Lacking, moreover, any background of legitimacy comparable to that enjoyed by the monarchy, it has responded as vulnerable and insecure governments typically do: by a policy of terror, which has included mass arrests, bombing of civilian marketplaces, and summary execution of real or imagined enemies.

This condition injects great instability into the domestic situation of a longtime ally of the United States, at the same time that international tensions in Northeast Africa have reached unprecedented intensity.

How did the Dergue come into power? First, the agitations of a well organized and militant student movement had some real effect in diminishing popular support for the old regime in the late 1960s and early 1970s. That support plummeted in late 1973/early 1974, because Haile Selassie remained indifferent to the plight of hundreds of thousands suffering from famine and epidemics and ordered senior government officials to cover up the crisis; because of the abrupt manner in which he severed ties with Israel following the October 1973 War; and because he proved incapable of responding with firm actions in the face of popular unrest over inflation due to the OPEC oil price increases.

Second, a power vacuum was created by the absence of an organized political group that might assert authority given the extreme weakness of Haile Selassie's personal rule and the eruption of widespread popular demonstrations. I attribute the absence of a core of authoritative leaders to the following factors:

> The decimation of the first generation of modern-educated Ethiopians by the Italians in 1937;
>
> The dismantling of the next available cadre for constituting a modernizing elite—the Imperial Bodyguard officers—following their abortive coup in December 1960;
>
> Haile Selassie's refusal to permit the formation of political parties or associations, his discouragement of active leadership by anyone else under his regime, and his failure to designate a successor early or emphatically enough; and
>
> Deeply rooted patterns of suspicion and reciprocal distrust in Ethiopian political life.

Into this power vacuum, then, stepped the Dergue. They were a group of young, dedicated, patriotic soldiers, propelled into a position of political leadership at a time when their country was crying for justice and social change. Being, however, men of no political experience and little education, accustomed to accomplishing objectives through simple chains of command, fired by a simplistic populism, impatience, and thirst for revenge, they sought to impose massive changes instantly in a complex society with almost no planning or concern for repercussions.

For the most part, these repercussions have been tragic. To their credit, it must be said that the Dergue has removed from power a great number of corrupt and reactionary men; distributed land to great numbers of landless tillers in some Southern provinces; and accorded greater rights to some minority groups who previously felt like second-class citizens. In most other respects, however, their actions appear to me to have been highly destructive.

They have seriously weakened Ethiopia's economy, to the point that an acute housing shortage exists in the cities, and severe famines have been predicted for the coming year.

They have intensified the antagonisms among the major ethnic groups in the country, alienating the Tigrean people through their various actions against Eritrea, and stirring up the Oromo and some other Southern peoples to express hatred against the Amhara.

They have alienated virtually every constituency that might provide support for the authority of the official government: professionals, businessmen, workers, students, townsmen, and northern peasants (their strongest support being the peasants in some of the southern provinces); left, right, and center; civilians, and even many units within the Army itself.

They have weakened the authority of Addis Ababa in the provinces, to the point that banditry again flourishes and even slave-trading has reportedly reappeared in some outlying regions.

They have weakened the country's defense capability, since their energies have gone into attempting to govern and not into training soldiers, and the troops in some divisions are now reluctant to accept combat missions.

They have worsened Ethiopia's position in the international community.

Although the Dergue appears at present to be unpopular and inept, and faced by serious organized opposition both internally and at its borders, it seems likely that it will continue in power as the sequence of events tied to the coming independence of Djibouti unfolds. What problems does this pose for U.S. policy? I assume the United States has three major interests in that area: first, a diplomatic interest in preventing an escalation of Ethiopia's conflicts with Somalia and Eritrea to the point that warfare breaks out and the United States and the Soviet Union are drawn into an expanded confrontation there; second, a strategic interest in keeping the Bab el-Mandab, the port of Jibuti, and the Red Sea open to the free flow of international shipping; and third, a humanitarian interest in promoting economic welfare, human rights, and self-determination for all nations in the region.

Given these interests, and the problematic position of the Dergue, vis-à-vis the Ethiopian people and their neighbors, I fail to see how either a policy of unrestrained military aid to the Dergue or a complete cut-off of such aid can be justified.

Rather, some way must be found to express both our continuing interest in supporting the Government of Ethiopia and our concern that that government turn from policies of vengeance and terror to a policy that will enable the Ethiopian people to participate in shaping their destiny, and from a policy of simple nationalistic self-assertion to one that would support a multilateral, international effort to cope with the political tensions and economic problems of the whole region in Northeast Africa.

To those who may worry that this approach would involve unwarranted outside interference, let me report the following personal observations. When I was in Ethiopia in the late fifties, the complaint I heard most often was not that the U.S. interfered too much, but that they failed to use their immense influence to persuade the Haile Selassie Government to promote economic development and political liberalization.

During my recent visit to Ethiopia in April of this year, an Ethiopian who had worked ardently to topple the Haile Selassie regime said of its successor: "Uganda is lucky. They have only one Idi Amin. We have 100."

If American citizens and taxpayers would not want to aid the government of Amin, they will not, I believe, want to provide unrestricted aid to the Dergue if they knew the facts about it. Given that the present rulers of Ethiopia lack any kind of internal restraint, to provide restraint from the outside would be to respond to the deepest aspirations of the Ethiopian people.

SENATOR CLARK. Thank you very much. It is a very interesting statement.

[BRIEF RECESS.]

MR. LEVINE. [Responding to a question about cutting military aid to the Dergue Regime.] That is an extraordinarily complex question and I am still thinking it through myself. I will think out loud here for a minute with you on it.

I can think of two good reasons not to cut off military aid to Ethiopia. One is that this might signal to the Somalis and their Soviet and Arab backers that they could go ahead with whatever aggressive intentions they have in the Horn, which is likely to include the annexation of Djibouti and possibly constriction of shipping in the Red Sea.

Secondly, I think that there are many elements in Ethiopia, including within the Dergue, who for all the public display of attachment to the Communist bloc countries—one now sees in the ministries no longer European and Chinese publications, for example, and one sees the United States and European "imperialists" scored in the newspapers and only flattering stories about the bloc countries—for all of that, I think there remains an undercurrent of interest in retaining the friendship of the United States and at various levels.

I can think of some good reasons for cutting off that aid. As I indicated, the present regime is extremely unpopular, extremely repressive, and a policy of unrestricted aid today, as in the time of Emperor Haile Selassie, would signify a callous attitude toward human rights and basic human needs in Ethiopia. Even though one understands from Ambassador Korry and Ambassador Hummel that discrete pressures were placed on the former regime to be responsive to Ethiopia's problems, it still appeared to the public opinion bearers and makers under the old regime that the earlier statement was really operative: "Let the Emperor spend the money on gold Cadillacs or any other way he wants, as long as we have the Kagnew base."

So it looks today that there would be a repetition of that policy of unrestricted aid for a very repressive and unpopular regime and, as I have suggested, the continuation of that regime without restraints can only lead to the weakening of Ethiopia, to the fragmentation of the country, to the possible outbreak of civil war; perhaps the sooner it is replaced, the better.

So, as I have suggested, I think both of these extreme positions of abrupt cut off of aid or unrestricted aid have very serious arguments against them and some kind of a middle ground seems to me to be indicated.

SENATOR CLARK. What is the middle ground?

MR. LEVINE. That middle ground, I suggest, would consist in tying a reduced amount of military aid to pressures on the Derg to open up the political process, to reverse the direction of their activity which has been increasingly to isolate themselves from their constituency within the country, to perhaps permit the formation of political parties and to turn from a policy of vengeance and sloganized politicization to serious concern with economic development.

I realize this sounds quite idealistic, but I tend to believe that the only genuine solution in Northeast Africa is a preventive conference which would be multilateral, in which the Soviet Union, some other European powers, some Arab states, and all of the interested parties in Northeast Africa would convene and work out a more cooperative program for dealing with the political tensions and economic crises of the region.

SENATOR BIDEN. Professor, what realistic chance do you think there is that this middle ground of attempting to bring pressure by a reduction of aid would have an effect?

MR. LEVINE. I think that the Dergue basically considers itself quite dependent on continued United States aid. I do not think that the Russians are going to jump into that particular hole.

SENATOR BIDEN. Why?

MR. LEVINE. For two reasons: one, the Russians are already very well established in Somalia. As you know, they have engineered a huge military build-up in Somalia to the point where what was not too long ago a very inferior force is now considered by some to have parity and probably superiority over Ethiopia, and they have stationed Cuban units in Somalia.

So the Russians are very strongly allied with Somalia. They are also, through Syria, allied with the Eritrean Liberation Front. Finally, I think the Russians are aware of the problematic position of the Dergue and that it is not all that competent and reliable a partner to deal with.

So my guess is that the Dergue believe that for continued aid, they must keep coming to the United States; and that it is even conceivable that the Dergue might welcome some outside restraint. . . .

SENATOR CLARK. Yes. I want to hear Professor Levine and the Ambassador's answer. Go ahead.

MR. SPENCER. I will do it later.

MR. LEVINE. I would like to make a few points that bear on this question of Eritrea. First, there has been a lot of propaganda that has been misleading about the condition of Eritrea. Eritrea is not historically a distinct entity; historically and culturally it is part of greater Ethiopia.

It is an artifact of the uneven penetration of the Italian colonialism in Northeast Africa. So, one cannot claim on the basis of sentimental or historical ties that Eritrea has an historic right to self-determination.

The second point is that, again, contrary to propaganda which Muslim representatives of the ELF, the people who make contact with Syria and Libya, contrary to what they say, Eritrea is not 90 percent Muslim.

It is as Mr. Spencer has indicated, 50 percent Muslim, 50 percent Christian. The Muslim groups in the population inhabit the coastal regions, and they for the most part are nomads. The dominant highland population has overwhelmingly been the Christian, Tigrinya-speaking people, who are identical ethnically, linguistically, and culturally with their neighbors across the border. It is the same ethnic population.

SENATOR BIDEN. Do either of those distinct groups that you have pointed out in Eritrea, do either of them in your opinion wish continued association, to be included within Ethiopia, or do they both share a view that they would like to be out?

MR. LEVINE. At this point, I think they overwhelmingly share a view that they would like to be out.

SENATOR BIDEN. Both groups?

MR. LEVINE. Yes. I think that is counter to, as Mr. Spencer indicated, the condition that obtained as recently as 1952, when the overwhelming majority of the Christians and some of the Muslims wanted to be included with Ethiopia.

SENATOR BIDEN. Thank you.

MR. LEVINE. But if Eritrea becomes independent on the next day, the attempt to make Eritrea an Arab state will provoke a kind of civil war such as we have been seeing in Lebanon. I think there is no doubt about that.

SENATOR CLARK. I think the Ambassador wanted to comment.

MR. KORRY. I would endorse the point that Professor Levine just made; it is an area very much akin to Northern Ireland or Lebanon, that if you did create a vacuum, you would perhaps be guilty of participating in an unwanted, unwitting blood battle.

SENATOR BIDEN. It is the same rationale the British used for 300 years to keep Ireland under suppression.

MR. KORRY. I am talking about Northern Ireland.

SENATOR BIDEN. I understand Northern Ireland. I understand a lot about Ireland. That is the exact same rationale.

MR. KORRY. We are not in it though. The question is do you wish to set these forces loose? I don't know the answer. It is a Muslim-Christian issue. It is a bloody one. When they go at each other, it is very bloody. . . .

MR. LEVINE. The Dergue basically had little ideological orientation when they came to power. They were mainly soldiers; they had general enthusiasms and patriotism and populism; but very little ideological orientation.

That was injected into them by a few intellectuals around the University, and by the student movement, which was intensively Marxist oriented.

Again, if the Dergue came into a political vacuum when seizing power, they entered an intellectual vacuum as well, due to the Haile Selassie regime's prohibition that any of these issues be discussed publicly, and they have sort of let the intellectual vacuum be filled by militant Marxist slogans.

How deeply committed they are to Marxist-Leninism is something I am not sure about.

SENATOR CLARK. There is no indication I understand from your testimony, as I interpret it, that there is any attitude of friendship toward the West or toward the United States and toward the principles that we propound.

MR. LEVINE. That is correct. However, I had a conversation with one of the majors who was working with the Dergue when I was there recently. He said, "I hope that you will be an intermediary between our regime and the American people. You were able to support Yugoslavia, which was Communist, but which tried to be independent from the Soviet Union. This is the way in which we would like to see ourselves and have our relationship with the United States.". . .

SENATOR CLARK. I gather that from what the two of you have said, Professor Levine and Mr. Spencer, that the sole interest in the United States is in continuing to give military equipment and perhaps economic equipment, but there is no love lost for this country at all. Is that an accurate statement?

MR. LEVINE. I think that is accurate on the part of the Dergue themselves, not on the part of the number of civilian ministers, who have been working under the regime, however.

SENATOR CLARK. Senator Biden?

SENATOR BIDEN. How about the Israeli connection here? Do you gentlemen agree with the Ambassador's mention—without much detail, because I didn't give him much time—that it is somehow connected with the survival of Israel?

MR. LEVINE. I will make two brief points. One is the flow of shipping through the Red Sea and the Gulf of Agaba is crucial for Israel. The second is that Ethiopia is one of the few African countries in the United Nations which has a more moderate position toward Israel.

This is long-standing and I think will probably continue.

SENATOR BIDEN. Probably?

MR. LEVINE. Will probably continue.

SENATOR BIDEN. Including the present regime if the present regime continues?

MR. LEVINE. Yes. . . .

SENATOR CLARK. *[Raising the question of Eritrean secession.]* How feasible is this? I think I will call first upon Professor Levine to sort of lay out what his thinking is again, to summarize that, and then go to the other two panelists.

MR. LEVINE. I don't have a whole lot of thinking about it. The idea has been germinating as I have been working in the crucible of this question.

I don't think that any of the existing options that we have been thinking in terms of are going to lead us where we want to go.

I might, as a footnote on that related Eritrean question, say that even if one grants the indispensability of keeping Eritrea somehow connected with Ethiopia, military aid to the Dergue is by no means the clearest way to achieve that, that it is precisely the Dergue's military actions there that have driven Eritrea virtually to the point of no return.

The Second Division in Asmara is to some extent sitting in the barracks and no longer wanting to go on combat missions against the Eritrean troops.

So it seems to me some formula that transcends this deadlock absolutely is the only way out. I leave to the experts what the details of such a formula might be, but that is the general idea I would like to propose. . . .

SENATOR CLARK. [...] Let me ask each of you just very briefly—we have sort of done this in several other ways—to summarize in 30 seconds, if you can, why Ethiopia is important to the United States interest.

Mr. Korry?

MR. KORRY. I would say primarily because of its geopolitical situation in an area that is generally reffered to as the Red Sea Basin, but which encompasses all of the Arabian Peninsula, Egypt, and Israel, and is part of the Middle Eastern and Indian Ocean complex.

MR. LEVINE. I would second that. I think the Ethiopian connection with the whole Middle East crisis is very crucial. . . .

SENATOR CLARK. Do you see. . . I am going to keep asking until that second bell rings, which I think is a minute or two.

It seems to me your comments reflect a feeling that Somalia is really almost totally the tool of the Soviet Union, and that if they were to control what you call greater Somalia or even what they control now, that the Soviets would have a free hand to do almost anything they wanted to?

Is that an accurate representation of your view?

MR. SPENCER. I would say so. I would say with 2,000 advisers and technicians, that would be the case, plus their arms. The bases there.

SENATOR CLARK. Do you feel pretty much the same way, Dr. Levine.

MR. LEVINE. Yes.

MR. KORRY. I am in no position to judge today.

SENATOR CLARK. I think it has been very, very useful and very interesting, and very helpful to us. We are going to continue—we thank you very much—going to continue these hearings tomorrow at 10 o'clock, same place, same station.

We were very, very appreciative of having your ideas and your interpretations. Needless to say, we are going to continue to get additional feelings and interpretations as these hearings proceed.

Thank you again. The hearings are adjourned.

B. Subcommittee on African Affairs of the Committee on Foreign Relations*

Domestic Ethiopian Developments (1976)

Thursday, August 5, 1976

Washington, D.C.

MR. LEVINE. I won't repeat what is in my written statement, and I won't make a long opening statement. I prefer to respond to your questions. Let me elaborate on one or two points that have come up in the discussion thus far.

First, one general characteristic of the present situation in Ethiopia is that it is in a highly disintegrative phase and it is not at all clear to me that when the egg is broken that all the pieces are going to come back together again very easily.

Although I would agree with my colleague, Professor Farer, that it is very difficult to know what the demonstration effect of Eritrean Independence may be on other African countries, it seems to me clear that it will have repercussions within Ethiopia, leading most likely to a move on the part of Tigray Province, which is filled with secessionist strivings at the moment, to try to break away, to encourage perhaps parts, if not all, of the Oromo people to break away and certainly to encourage the Ogaden Somalis to break away.

I think if the independence of Eritrea is inevitable—I am not sure that it is—that certainly presents a grim prospect for the future of any kind of viable Ethiopian nation.

A few more points concerning the internal disintegration of Ethiopia: I think any post-Haile Selassie regime would be faced by some degree of disintegration, though I would like to remind you that when the Dergue came into power, there was an enormous national consensus behind their toppling of Haile Selassie and their announced goals. I think the goals of the Dergue are one which Congress and the United States public could certainly approve of.

The problem is that they went ahead, implementing these goals without any concern for developing a constituency. They thought that the slogans were

* Official Stenographic Transcript of Hearings before the Committee on Foreign Relations at the United States Senate in Washington, D.C. on August 5, 1976.

sufficient and in the process of moving pell-mell toward the accomplishment of these goals, they alienated one section after another of a potentially sympathetic public.

They alienated the bureaucrats who at this point are more concerned with accusing one another and covering up any expression of independent thoughts they might have. They alienated the workers by imprisoning their leaders and firing point blank into crowds of demonstrating workers and killing them.

They alienated the students who were enthusiastic about their development programs by sending them out with little preparation and inadequate controls so that in the northern regions the students antagonized the peasantry who in many instances killed the students which, in turn, provoked retaliation from the government. In the south, they mobilized the peasants against existing authority structures which, in turn, provoked retaliations against students.

Even within the army, I think they have alienated a great deal of their own natural potential support. It is my understanding that the Second Division in Asmara is quite alienated from the Dergue at this point. There have been calls for Major Mengistu from his own unit in Harar to return, which he has ignored.

The Dergue, when it was forming, maintained regular contact with its home base units through intermediate committees; after it seized power, it abolished these committees. So, the Dergue has simply increasingly isolated itself from the great bulk of the Ethiopian public.

I want to stress this present political situation as part of the reality to which we must be oriented in thinking about these policy questions.

SENATOR CLARK. I think what I would like to do is just ask you first, Dr. Levine, five or six or seven questions that I think can be answered rather quickly, and I think will be important to have on the record. I will ask the other two witnesses to feel free to discuss this as well; just on some of the internal or the domestic situation in Ethiopia, then I would like to return for most of our period on this discussion of independent Eritrea, how that affects Israel, which is an issue that came up yesterday that Dr. Farer raised.

There are some other things, particularly about Somalia and its position and its relationship to the Soviet Union and to the United States; the strategic interests of the Red Sea area, particularly anything that might develop in Eritrea, Djibouti and some of those questions.

First I wondered, Dr. Levine and others of you—as I said, just pitch in here if you have something to add or a question—what do governmental opinion-makers, if that isn't too much of an American political phrase, really feel about our association with the Dergue? Do you have any feel for that at all?

One fear is, of course, that with the lack of success that they seem to have had, at any rate it is your contention and I think the contention of most authorities that the Dergue started with great popularity, and it seems to have lost most of that popularity now. I would think that our government is associated with it insofar as we give military or economic aid.

What is the view toward our association with that government? Are they happy with it, critical of it, feel that we are helping to sustain it, or seen as an ally who are keeping the Somalis away or helping to fight the Eritrean war? What is the view of non-governmental opinion-makers toward the United States association with the Dergue?

MR. LEVINE. I don't think we have very much hard evidence on that. I think that would differ from group to group. I would hazard the generalization that the dominant attitude is that the United States again, as under Haile Selassie, has the Dergue as a client and should use that client relationship to impose some kind of restraint on the Dergue in its repressive policy.

SENATOR CLARK. That would be a natural desire of many of these people?

MR. LEVINE. Right. There is the Ethiopian People's Revolutionary Party which—even more vehemently then the Dergue—attacks all imperialist, feudalist forces in the world and should they come to power, it seems to me that they would be much less likely than the Dergue to want to cultivate any friendly relations with the United States.

SENATOR CLARK. I guess I am particularly interested in whether we are suffering from this association in terms of Ethiopian public opinion.

MR. LEVINE. I think we are. I think insofar as the Dergue is viewed as an American client, and I think it is, and it is viewed as highly repressive, then we are, I think, suffering. . . .

MR. LEVINE. In addition to the Ethiopian People's Revolutionary Party, there is another underground party which is pro-West, the Ethiopian Democratic Union, which has its headquarters in London and has a fair amount of sympathy in the northern provinces.

If the Dergue continues to be unpopular and if the EDU succeeds in mobilizing enough support in the Northern provinces and enough support in Addis Ababa, one of the conceivable future developments at some point is that they would come to power; and they are certainly critical of support that the U.S. gives to the Dergue.

SENATOR CLARK. Let's look at the Dergue itself for a moment. Is the prevailing element there which several of you have described as being rather pro—it is a hard phrase to use—pro-Communist, pro-Soviet, leftist, whatever—is that prevailing view, in your judgment, something that barely prevails, or are there all kinds of different political views within the Dergue?

Do you see the kind of diversity within the Dergue apparently that you would have seen in the Revolutionary Council of Portugal, for example, where the military leaders came to power and you had everything from sort of the left Maoist to the rather conservative people on the other side?

Are these military leaders, military political leaders, really very divided within the Dergue as far as you can tell? Are there some who are very pro-Mao, some very pro-Soviet, some very pro-Chinese? What is the make-up of the Dergue as best you can see it?

We will start with you, Dr. Levine.

MR. LEVINE. I think there is a division within the Dergue. I think there has been sort of oscillation back and forth between those who are primarily ideological Communists and pro-Soviet and those who are basically what one might call Ethiopian nationalists.

I would say that almost any regime in the future is going to be oriented in a socialist kind of direction and that certainly no future regime is going to try to restore the previous system. All elements agree that the land should be redistributed, that there should be more social justice, and so forth.

Within that general consensus there are and have been different orientations. The tragic shoot-out in November 1974 reflected a major split within the Dergue. General Aman wanted to pursue a more moderate policy; he advocated a more conciliatory approach to Eritrea and wanted to follow legal procedures in dealing with the imprisoned officials.

That was an important part of the reason that he was executed and with him the 59 other officials. So, I think these differences persist. I think the recent execution of Major Sisay was a reflection of that. Just what the count is, I don't have any figures. . . .

SENATOR CLARK. I want to come back to Sisay's death in a moment. I think you wanted to comment, Dr. Levine.

MR. LEVINE. I wanted to clarify the point I made which I think was not entirely accurately represented.

SENATOR CLARK. Which was what?

MR. LEVINE. About the division within the Dergue; that is, it is quite likely that there are no members of the Dergue who are Soviet agents in the sense that they would put Russion interests ahead of Ethiopia's interests. I still think it is useful to try to understand the difference between those who are guided by a very thorough commitment to Marxist ideology as the way in which they define the realities of Ethiopia, and those who are more pragmatic—when I say nationalist, I mean more pragmatic—with respect to Ethiopian development issues. I think that division has been persistent. Mr. Spencer referred to Haile Fida and the Politburo. These are groups of highly ideologized people who, I would argue, grossly misconceived aspects of the Ethiopian land tenure situation on the basis of these doctrines and not on the basis of any kind of attention to Ethiopian realities. . . .

SENATOR CLARK. Again, I don't want to spend a lot of time on each of these questions. I think we want to get to some of the broader issues. Just briefly, what do each of your see as the significance of Major Sisay's execution? You sort of explained that already, Dr. Spencer. You see it as a distinct indication of a very pro-Soviet trend in the Dergue. . . .

SENATOR CLARK. Dr. Levine?

MR. LEVINE. I would add to that, that there is a problem in the Dergue having to do with the level at which problems are discussed and analyzed. The rank and file of the Dergue are young officers and noncommissioned officers who had relatively little education. Their approach is often very simplistic. When you have someone who intellectually is more outstanding and commands respect by virtue of the clarity with which he grasps complex issues, this rankles.

I have some reason to believe that it was due to this kind of personal competition that Sisay, whatever his views, became unacceptable to the Dergue: he somewhat transcended their collective level of mediocrity. . . .

SENATOR CLARK. Do you feel this regime of the Dergue has been a constant violator of what most of us would consider to be the basic human rights?

MR. FARER. In Eritrea, there is no question but those violations of human rights were going on before the Dergue came to power. In Eritrea, you had a series of My Lais. My Lais are normal in Eritrea.

SENATOR CLARK. What about Ethiopia? I shouldn't put it that way. Outside of Eritrea, within Ethiopia.

MR. FARER. I don't know about torture, but the other main elements, it seems to me, as what I define as fundamental human rights would be summary execution. So, I would say yes.

MR. LEVINE. We have had summary execution; we have had arrests without cause. We have had people detained without giving any reason.

In most cases these prisoners have never been brought to court; in a number of cases they have been brought to court, cleared, and then put back in prison and are still there. We have had indiscriminate firings into groups of demonstrators; we have had bombings of civilian marketplaces.

I think that the record of the Dergue, from the day they stepped into power to today, is one of a very clear and consistent violation of human rights. . . .

SENATOR CLARK. Dr. Levine, what is your answer to that? Why should the United States, facing a very anti-American [regime], one that is so freely violating human rights, why should we be its strongest supporter, perhaps its sole supporter? I don't know.

MR. LEVINE. I think there is a paradox at the heart of my position, which Senator Biden brought out nicely yesterday, that we support this regime—even militarily—in order, hopefully, to have some leverage over its use of its military might.

I don't have great faith in that formula. But I see that as the only justification, both in terms of providing some minimal threshold of respect for human rights within Ethiopia and to move the Dergue to realize that a military solution in Eritrea is absolutely out of the question, that the only solution there can be political settlement, which means a less militaristic policy toward Eritrea as well.

SENATOR CLARK. Do you believe that our government is using its military assistance and economic assistance to bring about this kind of leverage?

MR. LEVINE. I have seen some evidence that we have in the past. I understand that we temporarily withheld military assistance following the November 1974 executions, that there have been some effects in this direction that have been salutary.

It seems to me that we must, if we continue to aid Ethiopia, we must do this more actively, much more emphatically, much more consistently.

SENATOR CLARK. As a condition of aid?

MR. LEVINE. Yes. . . .

SENATOR CLARK. Without getting into the Eritrean independence question, which we are going to get into very soon, what is your feeling? I don't throw this question to you with any idea that it is a simple answer.

As I say, Congress has dealt with it very unsuccessfully. What about this question? Ethiopia is apparently, according to your testimony, a good example of what gross violations of human rights. Do we talk about that or do we cut of military aid? What do we do? Dr. Levine?

MR. LEVINE. I am not sure that the difference between our opinions is as great as it initially appeared because I am also talking about using assistance as a lever. I do not think that we should continue to provide assistance without that effort. Whether it takes the form of getting credibility by saying we are going to cut off assistance until we see evidence that changes have been made—that might be the most effective approach.

I certainly think, as I said yesterday, that a policy of unrestricted aid really can't be justified.

SENATOR CLARK. In other words, it would be your feeling that if our leverage does not work and the Dergue continues to exercise gross violations of human rights, in spite of our efforts to end it, you would cut off aid?

MR. LEVINE. I would be very sympathetic to that.

SENATOR CLARK. Very sympathetic to cutting off aid, you are not sure?

MR. LEVINE. Because it is tied also with the Eritrean question. . . .

SENATOR CLARK. Let's get to these other questions.

I think that Dr. Farer threw out a rather interesting comment about his feeling, I guess, of the world and this nation, that we are perhaps as well off or perhaps better off to see an independent Eritrea. Quite aside from the Israeli question for the moment, how do the others of you feel about the view that he has put forward? Dr. Levine?

MR. LEVINE. As I said, I think that the most serious repercussion would be in the rest of Ethiopia, that it would open the door to a balkanization of Ethiopia.

It might, I don't know what the current status is in the O.A.U. of these issues; it might fuel the ambitions of the other elements in Africa, who want to redraw some state boundaries, and that is certainly the present danger elsewhere in Africa.

SENATOR CLARK. Of course, Dr. Farer challenged that thesis, too, in his statement, but you still tend to believe it would encourage others?

MR. LEVINE. I think what Dr. Farer said was that we don't know, and we don't know for sure, but it certainly is something that I think other African leaders, including, I might mention, President Nimeiri of Sudan, are very concerned about, despite the fact that Sudan permits arms traffic to flow through Sudan to Eritrea.

Nimeiri, in Sudan, is very concerned that Eritrea not be independent because then the question of splitting up the Sudan would come up.

SENATOR CLARK. Why the collaboration with the two movements for independence in the Sudan?

MR. LEVINE. I think that he is sympathetic with Eritrean demands for greater autonomy, for greater rights, and the pressures within the Arab world to support the ELF, but I think he is in a bind on that question, and he has indicated his willingness in the past and would like in the future to serve as a mediator between Eritrea and Ethiopia, to bring about a political settlement which would assure greater autonomy within Eritrea, perhaps within some Federal formula, but not complete independence. . . .

SENATOR CLARK. [. . .] I understand one of the members of the panel wanted to try to say something additional about the Christian leadership, about the Eritrean movement.

MR. LEVINE. Whether the Christians now represent a nominal majority in the ELF and PLF movements in Eritrea, the fact is that the muscle behind this entire movement has come from Libya and Syria, that the ELP troops are currently being trained in South Yemen, that many of the Christian Eritreans are basically very Marxist and Soviet-oriented, and therefore it is misleading to think that a nominal majority of the Christians means that if Eritrea becomes independent, then Syria, South Yemen, and Libya wouldn't make a serious effort to dominate Eritrean policies.

The almost predictable response to that, it seems to me, would be fairly shortly a rebellion by the Christian elements in Eritrea so that a situation such as we have been witnessing in Lebanon is bound to erupt.

It might, however, be in the interest of a group of countries, including Egypt, Sudan, and Saudi Arabia to forestall that kind of a take-over by the more radical Arab group.

So they might conceivably be interested in supporting mediation that would lead to a Federal kind of formula. . . .

SENATOR CLARK. [Presumed question under discussion: do the Israelis think it in their national interest to secure Ethiopian control of the Red Sea straits?] Dr. Levine?

MR. LEVINE. I would second, support everything that Mr. Spencer has said. I do believe that even if theoretically Dr. Farer has a point here, the fact is that Israeli strategists view Ethiopian control of Eritrea and those islands as indispensable to the free flow of traffic, both to Israel and Western Europe and the United States.

SENATOR CLARK. They perceive it that way?

MR. LEVINE. Yes.

SENATOR CLARK. Do you perceive it that way?

MR. LEVINE. Mr. Spencer is more of an expert and his arguments seem to me compelling; but another factor is that Israel would perceive this as an extremely destabilizing development if Ethiopia were to succumb to it. . . .

SENATOR CLARK. [Will Eritrean independence result] in a bloody war?

MR. LEVINE. I am sorry, Senator. I really don't feel I have enough information to comment on that. I would, if I might, reserve my last sentence to comment on something which I feel in Dr. Farer's remarks was a very upsetting idea and that is that the United States should in any form countenance, in clear contravention to the principles of the United Nations Charter and the O.A.U., the balkanization of Ethiopia, the movement toward a separate Eritrean-Tigrean nation, which could not help but provoke a civil war which I can't believe wouldn't have international repercussions.

SENATOR CLARK. That is a violation of the U.N. Charter, you say?

MR. LEVINE. The dismemberment of a sovereign state by outside support.

27

On the Eritrean Referendum (1993)*

I.

I support the referendum in Eritrea, even though as a general rule the practice of settling questions of membership in a political community by democratic vote must be considered the height of folly. History and theory alike teach that to give constituent members of a state the right of self-determination up to and including secession is to promote chaos and court disaster. Consider the implications of enabling any group in a political community that wants to claim separate status to do so: ensuing instability would lead to the progressive unraveling of authority and threaten the ability of any constituted state to operate democratically. The secession of the southern states after only seventy years of membership in the federal union was a case in point: it provoked the bloodiest war in American history, because citizens of the northern states understandably believed in the inviolability of the compact that sealed that union.

Many if not most Ethiopians in and out of Eritrea continue to feel some sense of connectedness. The decision about Eritrea's status arguably belongs not to the Eritreans alone but to all of the people of historic Ethiopia, including the hundreds of thousands of Eritreans long resident throughout Ethiopia. What is more, although Eritreans have suffered much over the past three decades, especially during the Derg regime, it was after all Eritreans who initiated the combat with their armed insurgencies—started by small bands of dissidents lacking popular support. The objectives that they sought, short of secession, could have been obtained by other means. The aspirations of all Eritreans but

* Originally published in *Ethiopian Review*, April 1993, pp. 36–39.

for a few extremists could have been satisfied through negotiations. Remember that in spite of Haile Selassie's mismanagement of the Federation and the brutal search and destroy tactics against insurgents in the early 1970s, some 20,000 to 30,000 Eritrean citizens rallied in October 1974 to support a peaceful settlement, and the 19-point plan of General Aman Andom offered a workable basis for such a settlement.

Having said that, I must concede that the exceptional developments that took place after 1974 justify an exception to this general rule. Hardliners on both sides forestalled efforts toward reconciliation, leading on the Derg side to the assassination of General Aman and an uncompromising militaristic policy toward Eritrea. In consequence, many thousands of Eritreans fought and suffered for the right to determine their future, and they did finally prevail on the battlefield. What is more, immediate secession after the overthrow of the Derg would have been enormously disruptive for the entire region, and it was constructive to arrange for the decision to be made by Eritrean citizens in a peaceful and orderly manner. Given that, it was good the referendum was delayed for two years, since so important and complex a decision requires much time to think through. It might have been better to have waited even longer, since it takes time to organize and communicate facts and considerations about the advantages and disadvantages of each option. One can only hope that the deliberations and voting take place with a minimum of harassment and intimidation.

II.

I find four reasons that would justify Eritreans' voting to remain with Ethiopia. First, both populations represent the same mix of peoples and have peen part and parcel of the same extended cultural community for more than two thousand years, as my book *Greater Ethiopia: The Evolution of a Multiethnic Society* makes abundantly clear. The Aksumite realm straddled the present-day Eritrean border. Afaris and Saho, Tigrawis and Jabartis, Christians and Muslims, are the same on either side of that border.. The Bilin are first cousins to the Qemant. Rases and troops from presentday Eritrea fought alongside Ethiopians from many other regions in the Battle of Adwa. The modernization of Asmara was paid for in part by taxes from the peasants and merchants of Ethiopia.

Second, Eritrea was conquered by Italians, not by Ethiopians. The participation of Eritreans in the Ethiopian state was not coerced. Not only did they form part and parcel of the Aksumite polity and its successors, but a plurality of Eritreans indicated their wished to federate with Ethiopia after World War II, and the move to make Eritrea a province of Ethiopia in the 1960s was actually initiated by the Eritrean Parliament—however much they may have regretted that initiative later—in order to secure certain benefits they did not have without being a full-fledged member of the Ethiopian state.

Third, after the overthrow of Emperor Haile Selassie there was a moment when General Aman's leadership might have healed the entire country and led it toward an era of justice and economic progress. Those who assassinated him and introduced the Derg brought enormous misery to Eritrean Ethiopians and non-Eritrean Ethiopians alike. Mengistu Haile Mariam not only bombed Eritrean villages mercilessly; he also inflicted the Red Terror, forced collectivization, inhumane relocations, and economic misery on non-Eritrean Ethiopians as well. It is not from the Ethiopian people that Eritrea should separate but from the Derg—which they already have.

Fourth, this is an era when progressive peoples are cooperating on a larger scale. On the other hand, it is also an era of decentralization and devolvement of powers, and if they do not separate, the Eritreans should certainly be granted more autonomy than they had since the 1960s.

III.

It is always hard to forecast human events, although in the 1960s my publications predicted the emergence of a military regime in Ethiopia. Of one thing one can be certain: the formation of a separate state for Eritrean Ethiopians will be a profoundly traumatic experience for non-Eritrean Ethiopians. It may lead to social disruptions and economic privations that will make the rest of Ethiopia negatively disposed to its northern neighbor for some time to come. Trade barriers will have negative economic consequences for both sides. It will probably be followed by the outbreak of internal political tensions within Eritrea and/or a more repressive regime there, which will make it difficult for Eritrea to do what is essential for long-term stability in the region: to reach out in a friendly and collaborative spirit. I hope I am proven wrong and that, if separation does occur, a process of healing and cooperation can be set in motion before long.

IV.

Ethiopian elites traditionally have been more disposed to engage in politics and warfare than in economic development. Yet the country cries out to eradicate poverty and disease. The Horn of Africa stands at a crossroads—to go the way of Yugoslavia or the way of the European community. One road leads to the fueling of narrow political ambitions, national divisiveness, and wasted resources. The other leads to political cooperation and economic progress. The parochial choice has been followed in Somalia over the past two years with results everyone knows.

28

Will the Real Spirit of Adwa Please Stand Up? (1995)*

During a visit to Ethiopia in April 1976, I went to a jewelry shop on Churchill Road to buy gold earrings for my wife. The proprietor told me there were none to be had, for the *negus* had taken all the gold. I said I thought the revolution had gotten rid of the *negus*. "*Simu bitcha lewete*," he quickly replied—"only the name changed."

This bit of popular comment deserves consideration. Of course, the personalities and politics of Emperor Haile Selassie I and Colonel Mengistu Haile Mariam—and now President Meles Zenawi—are immensely different. Their deeds must be judged very, very differently—as current trials of the Derg regime will rightly emphasize. But something may be gained by considering certain similarities among them.

What do Haile Selassie I, Mengistu Haile Mariam, and Meles Zenawi have in common? They all came to power by the forceful overthrow of the previous regime. They all possessed an ideal vision of Ethiopia's development. They have all ruled in a dictatorial manner. Each accomplished certain valued reforms, but each also brought Ethiopia severe new problems. And each has been the target of a dangerous game we may call "Blame the Negus."

---

* Originally published in the *Ethiopian Register* 2 (3), April, 1995, pp. 16–23.

Blame the Negus

There is an old human, all-too-human, recipe for dealing with problems. That is to identify an agent responsible for the problem and then try to eliminate that agent. Consider the practice of *zar* healers. They link an affliction with possession by a *zar* spirit, then heal the patient by weakening the hold of that spirit. In the political realm, this recipe takes the form of explaining a social ill, not as the result of a complex of factors, but as due to the malevolence or incompetence of a single ruler. The solution is easy: depose the ruler, and all will be better.

This practice is probably found in most societies, especially during times of stress. In the United States, presidents are sometimes blamed for problems for which they cannot realistically be made responsible and which they have almost no power to repair. In some African societies, if the rains don't come, the king is toppled. In Ethiopian history, I know at least one instance of this: a ruler of Menz, Akawa, son of Negasse Kristos Werede Qal, was reportedly deposed by the *mekwannint* early in the 18th century when he was blamed for a period of drought and famine.

Ethiopia suffers from a complex of crises—economic, ecological, medical, political, and cultural. Most of these crises stem from processes that go back a century or more. Yet there is a tendency to blame most if not all of these ills on the current ruler and to assume that getting him out will automatically improve things. This reminds me of conversations I had with educated Ethiopians around 1960. I expressed puzzlement then that they were not organizing discussions about political reform and how to prepare for what might follow the regime of Haile Selassie. "I'm waiting until the government changes," was a common a reply, as I reported in *Wax and Gold*. "Things can only get better." "You don't know what you're talking about," I responded. I wish I had not been right. The same thing happened during the time of the Derg. "Just get Mengistu out and things will have to get better." One hears the same refrain today. *Simu bitcha lewete.*

Of problems for which the current regime is most loudly blamed, two stand out. One is the failure to establish multi-party democracy and civil liberties. The other is the increase in hostilities among ethnic groups. There can be no doubt that policies of the Transitional Government under Meles Zenawi have abetted these developments. However, to cope with them properly requires a broader perspective, which I hope these remarks may convey.

The Roots of Ethnic Tensions

I need not document the deterioration of relations among ethnic groups in Ethiopia. Interethnic hostilities have reached a level that those of us who remember the harmony among Ethiopians of the postwar years find hard to recognize. In a recent communication, one Ethiopian bemoaned such tensions in the following words:

> "When I read about boycotting Eritrean/Tigrean/Oromo/Amhara . . . etc. businesses or restaurants, I almost burst into tears. First of all, I didn't know the existence of Eritrean/Tigrean/Oromo/Amhara/Gurage . . . etc. restaurants. The only restaurant I knew was the Ethiopian restaurant. Whenever I ate a very delicious Kitfo, I just said I ate it from the Ethiopian restaurant. Whenever I ate a very delicious Ayib & Irgo, I just said I ate it from the Ethiopian restaurant. Whenever I ate a very delicious Doro Wat I just said I ate it from the Ethiopian restaurant. Whenever I ate a nice Ambasha and Pastal-Furno, I just said I ate it from the Ethiopian restaurant. So I burst into tears because we went backward by at least 500 years when we started debating whether we eat Kitfo, Doro Wat, Ayib & Irgo, Ambasha and Pastal-Furno. I wept because the different European countries are forming a united community while our country Ethiopia is on the verge of disintegration. Who put us in all this mess?"

It may be comforting to blame all these developments on the Meles regime, but to do so overlooks some critical points. Such tensions reflect, not a sudden explosion of ethnicity, but a process of national fragmentation going back three decades. It was in 1962 that a major challenge to the Ethiopian center began to brew with the formation of an insurgent liberation front in Eritrea. It was in 1966 that the Metcha-Tulema Development Association began to stake out claims for the Oromo, after which their suppression by the government led to an insurgency in northern Bali. Nor were these events purely rural. Growing tensions were manifest, for example, by serious fights between Tigrean and Oromo students at the Wingate School in the late 1960s, and an Oromo nationalist publication was circulated clandestinely in Addis Ababa in 1971.

With the overthrow of the monarchy, things quickly worsened. Nearly every political faction that took part in the postrevolutionary skirmishing made appeals to a principle of self-determination of nationalities. Except for the Ethiopian Democratic Union, Christopher Clapham writes, all of the factions went a long way toward conceding a right of secession, including the presumably centrist EPRP (Ethiopian Peoples Revolutionary Party) and even the Seded party to which Mengistu Haile-Mariam belonged. A natural outcome of this sympathy for the self-determination of nationalities was the eventual organization of insurgent opposition groups along ethnic lines. When a coalition of these ethnically-defined insurgent groups overthrew the Derg, can it have been surprising that the consequence would be to expand the scope for the assertion of ethnic allegiances and identities? The TPLF must be seen more as a symptom than as cause of the problem. What can we say about the underlying cause of the problem?

I suggest that the problem stems from three factors that work to intensify ethnic tensions in any society: an administratively strengthened center, a geopolitically weakened center, and a culturally depleted center.

Throughout Ethiopia's history there have been tensions between the national center and diverse regional and ethnic groups. Yet the bureaucratic centralization of the postwar years was bound to exacerbate these tensions at the same time that it created elements of enhanced national unity. In a classic analysis of this problem in the developing states of Africa and Asia first published in 1963, Clifford Geertz described this transformation toward greater national unity as an "integrative revolution," a change that necessarily involved an intensification of loyalties along lines of ethnicity, clanship, language, locality, race, religion, and/or tradition. More recently, several nations of Europe and North America witnessed comparable developments in waves of what has been called "ethnonationalism."

As Geertz analyzed the matter, peoples in modernizing societies are animated by two powerful, thoroughly interdependent, yet distinct and often actually opposed motives—the desire to be recognized as a responsible person whose wishes, acts, hopes, and opinions matter, and the desire to build an efficient, dynamic modern state. The first aim is to be noticed. It is a search for identity, coupled with a demand that the identity be publicly acknowledged—a social assertion of the self as being somebody in the world. The other aim is a demand for progress: a rising standard of living, more effective political order, greater social justice, and heightened international visibility. As the second aim is pursued—as national governments become more effective in pursuing collective aims—the tension increases, because people's sense of self remains so much bound up with attachments based on identities that are not national in scope. To subordinate these familiar identifications in favor of commitment to an overarching and often alien civil order is to risk a loss of definition as an autonomous person, either through absorption into a culturally undifferentiated mass or, what is even worse, through domination by some other rival ethnic, racial or linguistic community that is able to imbue that order with the temper of its own personality.

Political modernization quickens sentiments like ethnicity, then, because it involves new extensions of central political institutions into personal lives at many points. Through such structures as nationally organized schools, judicial systems, media broadcasts, taxation, road construction, land-development programs, and electoral campaigns, persons whose lives had been circumscribed by local customs and authorities become ambivalently linked to a national center. They want the benefits this center provides but not at the cost of humiliating subordination. Those who enter the modern sector through education enter an arena of intensified competition for jobs, authority, and status. Those who stay in the traditional sectors often become more identified with local ways in response to threats to their traditional status and ways of living. All these forces produce greater visibility of ethnic identities, along with more competition and tensions among ethnic groups that formerly got along quietly with one another. It is a time when long-submerged peoples slowly warm to their own self-discovery and begin to recall or imagine a shared past filled with glories, often even to engender resentments against a dominant power that seems responsible for their unrequited dreams and current humiliations.

Although Ethiopia had the advantage of existing as a multiethnic polity for two thousand years, it could not remain immune to this dynamic forever. Primordial assertions germinated during the last years of Haile Selassie and sprouted under the Derg. These trends were intensified by two other factors. One was Ethiopia's declining geopolitical status. Sociologists like Randall Collins have argued that ethnic groups tend to assimilate the language and culture of a dominant ethnic group during times when a nation or empire is enjoying political and military success, while a process of ethnic separatism sets in at times when a state becomes geopolitically weak. The latter process, "Balkanization," occurred classically during the 19th century when, due to the weakening of the Austrian and Turkish regimes, anti-Austrian and anti-Turkish sentiments provided major points of reference for unleashing political activism among the peoples of the Balkan peninsula.

Following World War II, both the United States and Ethiopia were enjoying a good deal of international prestige. (The story of Ethiopia's international prestige in the postwar years was told eloquently by Professor John Spencer in *Ethiopian Register*, November 1994, p. 25.) In both countries, various groups tended to accept the dominant culture associated with the national center, through processes of Americanization and Amharization, respectively. In the 1960s, the U. S. troubles in Vietnam diminished the prestige of the center and sub-national identities came to be asserted more aggressively. A comparable development took place in Ethiopia with the loss of Ethiopia's strategic importance due to the obsolescence of the Kagnew Station in Eritrea, which led to diminished support from the United States.

More important, I think, was the threat to the center posed by internal cultural difficulties. I refer to problems posed by the decline in authority of the

Solomonid ideology as a basis for legitimating the national center. As I argued in *Greater Ethiopia*, the *Kibre Negest* provided Ethiopia with a remarkable national script, a basis for establishing and restoring a multiethnic polity that endured for a nearly a millennium. Yet the time arrived when it could no longer serve as a script for a modern Ethiopian nation, both because of its sacralization of imperial authority and because its affinity with the Christian tradition rendered the inclusion of the many non-Christian groups in Ethiopia difficult. Ethiopian intellectuals who searched for a new cultural script thought they had found it in Marxism, rather than in the vision of a liberal democracy that acknowledged both the rights of all citizens and the values of all her constituent cultural traditions. The absence of the liberal alternative helped legitimate the atrocities of the Mengistu regime. (I feared such a horrible future might be in store for the country when a young Ethiopian intellectual, years before the Derg came to power, told me that he and his friends were admiring the model of the Soviet Union. When I reminded him that the Soviet Union killed off 20 million people in pursuing the communist revolution, he replied that they did not think killing off 10% of Ethiopia's population would be too high a price to pay for social progress.) When the shortcomings of Marxism became apparent, what was left? Since insurgent opponents of the Derg had failed to organize around a persuasively articulated vision of their country as a historic multiethnic nation based on liberty and justice, ethnic identity seemed the most promising principle for organizing a political future. From Marxism they salvaged only the Stalinist principle (which of course was never respected in the USSR) of self-determination up to secession. This was not a mere invention of Meles Zenawi of Adwa. Reliable sources have told me that the Oromo Liberation Front leadership made this tenet a precondition of participation in the Charter conference. The new ideology of Ethiopia was to consist of an aggregation of numerous ethnic liberation movements.

Amhara Oppression: Myth and Reality

In order to promote this ideology, its supporters had to find an oppressor from whom the various ethnic groups had to be liberated from, and they found it in the image of the wicked Amhara. There was just enough truth in this image to make it plausible and attractive to many Ethiopians. It is true that part of the cement used to build a modernizing Ethiopian nation was the use of Amharic as a national language. Never mind that Amharic historically grew through the interaction of many ethnic groups, as an amalgam of diverse tongues from many language families—North Ethiosemitic, South Ethiosemitic, Central Cushitic, and Eastern Cushitic—and that it provided a valuable lingua franca that enabled Ethiopians from diverse backgrounds to communicate with one another. The fact is that some people found it oppressive to have to use Amharic in schools and in courts, and perhaps even more resented having familiar place-names changed into Amharic. It is also the case that the Amhara elite, despite its own ethnically-mixed genealogies, tended to depreciate the customs and manners of Ethiopians from other ethnic groups. And it is surely the case that many Amhara soldiers and officials were rewarded by grants of land in southern parts of the country where the indigenous peoples were expropriated and often treated abusively.

All this must be said and understood. Yet to say this is not to tell the whole story. It overlooks the fact, attested by all knowledgeable scholars, that the so-called Amhara elite of the Ethiopian state was robustly multiethnic for many centuries. In particular, one should note the prominence of Oromo in the royal court at Gonder in the 18th century, when Emperor Bakaffa employed Oromo soldiers as palace officers, Iyasu II married an Oromo woman from Wello, and his son Iyoas I insisted on speaking Oromiffa at the court. Perhaps better known is the fact that Tigreans play a crucial role in Abyssinian national politics over the centuries, including such figures as Ras Mikael Sehul, a major figure during the Zemena Mesafint; the Tigrean Emperor Yohannes who ruled the empire from in the 1870s and 1880s; and figures like Ras Alula, Ras Mengesha, Dejazmatch Bahta (of Akale Guzae), and other Tigreans who helped preserve Ethiopia's independence in the fighting before and at the Battle of Adwa, along with Oromo officers like Ras Gobena and Dejazmatch Balcha.

The image of the Amhara oppressor also overlooks the contributions of Amhara rulership to the well-being of other Ethiopian peoples. For the conquests carried out under Menilek—largely, but not wholly, by Amhara, for Tigreans, Oromos, and others also took part—also prepared the way for the unification of the country and led to such reforms as the outlawing of the slave trade, the construction of roads and telecommunications, the introduction of schools, the use of a common currency, the provision of medical centers, and the pacification of a country where inter-group warfare had been common.

To be honest, this image also overlooks even harsher realities. For one thing, the fact remains that 95% of the Amhara people have lived under such oppressive political and economic conditions that it is hard to say who was most oppressed. What is more, the image overlooks the oppressive practices of other ethnic groups toward Amhara and toward one another. Tigreans, Oromos, and others took slaves. Adalis and Oromos wrought destruction, not only of people but also of beautiful churches and rare manuscripts, and the severity of Oromo incursions led the Hararis to build their famous wall.

Finally, the image of Amhara ethnic oppression overlooks the fact of Ethiopia as a historic multiethnic society, united by ties of intermarriage, trade, migration, multiethnic religions, ceremonies, and pilgrimages—a major lesson of my book, *Greater Ethiopia: The Evolution of a Multiethnic Society.*

Many Ethiopians are aware of all this. That is why Ethiopians from so many ethnic backgrounds find it so galling to find their nation's political discourse preempted by talk of ethnic liberationism. They cherish the historic reality of Ethiopia as a genuinely multiethnic society. They fear the mobilization of ethnic hatreds that made a corpse of Yugoslavia and killed thousands in former Soviet republics like Moldova, Georgia, Azerbaijan, and Tajikistan and, closer to home, in Rwanda. They dream of a future where Ethiopia's transformation to a modern, pluralistic democracy can be completed. Yet the regime in power seems to be throttling efforts to move in that direction.

The Hope for Freedom

In most states, including Eritrea now, national governments use their repressive powers, if at all, to prevent expressions of ethnic separatism. Ethiopia occupies the strange position of doing the reverse. Official policy has been to foment ethnic allegiances and to downplay the symbolism of Ethiopian nationhood. In fact, however, the EPRDF has worked behind the scenes to control expressions of ethnic political solidarity, such that certain Oromo, Amhara, Tigrean, Argobba, Wolleita, and other ethnically-based parties as well as centrist groups like EDAC have been harassed to the point of incapacitation. EPRDF repressiveness has been carried out under the umbrella of a rhetoric of pluralistic democracy and freedom of expression. That is what has made it so difficult for superficially-informed European and American observers to catch on to what has happened in the past few years. My own inclination, returning to Ethiopia in 1992 for the first time in sixteen years, was to believe the new claims about political democracy. But when a taxi-driver described what was going on as mere window dressing—"*wushet*-democracy," he called it—I began to pay closer attention to the flow of stories about harassment, imprisonments, disappearances, and political killings. So I was not too surprised about what happened when, a year later, the Vice President of the Council boasted to me of Ethiopia's new freedom of press. He cited as case in point the publication of a cartoon showing President Meles watering two plants, Ethiopian and Eritrean. A few hours later, I learned that the publisher of the newspaper in question had "disappeared"—and weeks later was discovered in a prison cell. Since then, as several human rights organizations have documented, several dozens of independent journalists have been imprisoned or sentenced large fines arbitrarily.

Despite this continuing record of human rights violations and suppression of political parties by the EPRDF, it is hard to deny that Ethiopia now enjoys more political freedom than it ever has. There is low-grade terror but it is surely not the terror of the Derg. That is why it may now be possible for concerned Ethiopians to move forward in a vigorous way to secure their long-awaited liberal democratic revolution. For this to take place, two notions need to be clarified—the idea that Ethiopia is not ready for freedom, and that freedom can only be secured through violence.

It has long been a piece of conventional wisdom among social scientists that political democracy could not established in just any kind of society. The prerequisites for democracy were held to be a relatively high level of economic development. Therefore, the conventional wisdom held, if you really want to promote political freedom, the best thing to do is to promote economic development first and democracy will be sure to follow. This understanding has now been successfully challenged by sociologist Orlando Patterson, author of *Freedom in Western Culture* and now at work on its sequel, *Freedom in the Modern World*. Professor Patterson's work supports the proposition that political democracy and civil freedom do not depend on high levels of socio-economic development. Some relatively poor countries, like India, enjoy a high level of freedom, while several highly-developed countries, like Singapore and South Korea, have quite repressive regimes. What is more, Patterson's analysis shows that it is precisely the less-developed countries like Ethiopia where freedom can be fairly quickly introduced. Countries like Guyana, Nicaragua, South Africa and, most recently, Haiti represent cases where outside pressure has brought about fairly rapid transformations in the direction of freedom, whereas countries that are more highly developed economically, like Singapore and South Korea, can better resist such pressure.

The second idea is that the only way to achieve political freedom is through armed insurrection. I sympathize with those whose impatience with the hypocrisies and apparent national betrayals by the present regime—its imposition of an unpopular constitution, its damage to precious national institutions like Addis Ababa University and the Ethiopian Airlines, its curtailment of labor unions and the press, its record of unlawful incarcerations and tortures—would lead them to advocate yet another round of violence in Ethiopia. There would seem to be no other way to get the Meles regime to become more inclusive and to back up its verbal commitment to democracy with actual support. Yet it remains questionable whether genuine democracy and national harmony can result from violence and doubtful whether the welfare of Ethiopia's people can be advanced by further warfare. The successes of non-violent struggles in this century should be given careful study. Until just a few years ago, who ever would have thought that South Africa could have been transformed without a blood bath? I have no doubt that the breakthrough toward freedom can be achieved by combining the possibilities for change through non-violent struggle within the country with renewed efforts to secure pressure from donor governments on the outside. In any case, *simply toppling another negus will not suffice*. Freedom will never be handed over on a platter. If Ethiopians want freedom, they must pursue it vigorously and steadfastly, with a positive vision, with selfless leaders, and with sophisticated organization.

Challenges to the Ethiopian Community

Perhaps the most encouraging fact about the official promotion of politicized ethnicity is the extent to which Ethiopians from all parts of the country have said *imbi*. No, they have said, we do not want to be categorized that way; we are and want to be Ethiopians. Thus far, those holding such sentiments have been frustrated by the lack of opportunities to give expression to their feelings of national patriotism. My sense is that the time is ripe for a series of efforts on many fronts to counteract both the ethnically divisive tendencies of the society and the regime and to weaken the hold of the repressive forces centered in the TGE.

The trick is to turn the negative posture of mere oppositionism into a positive effort to construct a new Ethiopia in accord with a view of national unity and justice. Outside of direct political action, there are a number of ways that Ethiopian citizens can neutralize the tendencies toward Balkanization. (1) They can become active in organizations based on multiethnic coalitions, organizations devoted to dealing with global economic, social, and cultural matters. (2) They can become active in institutions that are "group-blind," such as the Red Cross and Human Rights organizations. (3) In all organizations in which they participate, they can promote distributive justice, working to ensure minimally representative access to public resources for all ethnic groups. (4) They can accentuate conflicts that crosscut ethnicity by reflecting cleavages along other lines, such as region, religion, ideology, or occupation. (5) They can work to promote new cultural constructions of a multiethnic national identity appropriate to a postmonarchical, post-Leninist society. Imagine what could be done by propagating a vision of the future that integrates, rather than repudiates, the positive achievements of the past, including the magnificent Oromo capacity for democratic political organization and the historic Amhara-Tigrean creation of a multiethnic polity, the industry of Gurage and Beta Israel, the artistry of Harar and Dorze.

As for political activity, I can think of nothing better to suggest than the formation of a genuinely inclusive national democratic unity party. This should rally, not just those who already possess a strong Ethiopian consciousness, but can reach out to those who are ethnically identified—people who could be persuaded to relinquish old ethnic resentments and pride on behalf of common creative solutions to Ethiopia's pressing economic, educational, health, and ecological problems. These people should be helped to see that without some relaxation of the kinds of ties typically cultivated in groups based on ethnicity, it is impossible to establish binding notions of political and civil rights. General slogans, however positive, are not enough. A national unity party should begin the long process of developing a genuine platform, a set of principles they want to implement, a set of concrete changes that they want to see introduced.

A democratic unity movement could have supporters in the expatriate community who work on their behalf. In the United States, they can continue to work through the political process to exert pressure on the United State Government. They can also provide moral support to an Ethiopian democratic national movement at home, including advising them in tactics on the ground that might help reorient U. S. Government policy.

To voice such a proposal may be to court ridicule. How can Ethiopians possibly get along with one another long enough to develop such a movement? Is it not more fun to engage in the familiar pastimes of backbiting and name-calling ("adventurers," "chauvinists," "ethnocrats," "incompetents," "sellouts," etc.)—the unholy trinity of *mesedadeb, metemamet,* and *chiqachiq*? My response is: once Ethiopia's disintegration has been forestalled, there will be plenty of time for all that. Right now, *the imminent prospect of further drastic disintegration calls for a serious collective response.* Now is the time for Ethiopians of all walks of life simply to turn their backs to the things that divide them and to face together the great challenges they confront as a nation. Perhaps it is time for the solidarity and courage that went into fighting the Battle of Adwa to become transformed into the solidarity and courage it takes to sustain a non-violent political process. Is it out of the question that all of the pro-unity and pro-democracy forces might come together and form an alliance at this point? Perhaps it is time at last for all Ethiopians to stretch out their hands—to embrace one another and to reclaim their historic heritage.

29

More People More Hunger

*Sew Beza Ye-Rehab Neger Beza (2006)**

> Famine is a visible horror. . . . Witness the agony, degradation, hopelessness and silent anger on the dismal and skeletal faces. . . faith for survival while in the agony of slow and grinding teeth of famine. . .the slender and uncontrollable hope for miraculous succour in the face of pious indifference. . . . Nothing else manifests man's inhumanity to man more than famine. —Mesfin Wolde Mariam

Traveling north to Aksum and Adwa and south to Awassa I was struck by two things, the wan landscape and the swarms of people. The Awassa road, not so long ago lined with trees, appears bare savannah now. Formerly tiny towns had turned into sprawling urban centers. It made me think.

On return I studied up on food insecurity in a course on World Hunger co-taught with biologist Jocelyn Malamy. This made me more aware than ever of the close ties among population growth, deforestation, and food insecurity—and gave me a sense of responsibility to share that awareness with any reader who would engage the issue. Conveniently, one of my readers did so. Consider the response sent by Ato Zinah Minyehal:

Professor Levine,

> Why is population increase for Ethiopia such a concern? There are many countries with higher density of population than Ethiopia. Ethiopia's problem is the dysfunctional political system, not the population. When

* Originally published in 2006 on the web forum of the Ethiopian Institute for Nonviolence Education and Peace Studies.

> democracy takes hold, the country will certainly prosper. I strongly disagree with the premise that population growth is a problem by itself. . .

Ato Zinah's point of view represents the views of many Ethiopians I know. But I disagree, and in response, let me share some uncomfortable facts.

Some 85% of Ethiopia's people still live in the rural sector. By itself, population growth automatically increases food insecurity among them. Can there be any doubt that malnutrition, hunger, and famine comprise a major challenge to Ethiopia in its foreseeable future? To take the most extreme of these afflictions: although famines have been reported in Ethiopia for nearly as long as we have records, averaging one famine every fifteen to twenty years between 1500 and 1940, in the last fifty years famines have occurred with increasing severity and frequency, averaging one every seven years. Recall: 1959; 1973–4; 1985; 1995; 2003; 2006.

Poverty is a major cause of these famines. At times when production is ruined from natural hazards—drought, locusts, excessive rainfall—impoverished farmers and pastoralists have no reserves and no cash with which to secure food. As Mesfin Wolde Mariam demonstrated in *Rural Vulnerability to Famine in Ethiopia*, subsistence rather than commercial farming is the condition of famine in rural Ethiopia. Given that rural Ethiopians live in a subsistence economy, it follows that rapid population growth renders them more vulnerable to hunger, disease, and famine. Two million more infants per year means two million more mouths to feed, two million more children to school in a severely impoverished system. Increased family size means decreased size of food portions and declining nutrition. Malnutrition has already reached the point, UNICEF reports, where 47% of children under five are underweight, and more than half are stunted. Chronic hunger and intermittent famines require substantial relief aid. That heavily burdens the state, donors, and NGOs, diverting resources that might otherwise go to education, health, reforestation, crop improvement, soil restoration, water-harvesting technology, agricultural research, and improved farming technology.

Larger families diminish agricultural output, since all land that is physically cultivable is now cultivated. Larger families result in smaller farming plots, which means less food production per family for each new generation. Land units formerly measured by the gash are now measured in hectares. Land use demands created by larger families cause subsistence farmers to overuse their land, thereby ceasing crop rotation and degrading the soil. Over four per cent of the country's arable land has already lost its ability to support crops, according to Ethiopian environmental scientists.

Increased population also exacerbates one of Ethiopia's most alarming, if largely ignored, problems—deforestation. More rural people require more land for farming and grazing and more timber for construction and firewood. Over the past thirty years, population pressures have led to a 70% reduction in forestland in Ethiopia. This leaves only 3% of the country's forests still standing in a land where some 4/5 of the people depend entirely on wood for essential energy needs. What is more, deforestation wrecks havoc on the quality of topsoil. Lack of trees to facilitate the underground collection of water produces rock-hard soil, which does not absorb rain and instead promotes crop-destroying floods. Floods also sweep away the nutrient-rich topsoil, leaving farmers with a dry and infertile substratum. The soil degradation due to erosion issues in massive drops in food production. High population densities also cause degradation of water resources. Such dynamics appear to some extent in countries all over the world.

Demographers project an increase of 2.6 billion people by 2050 living on roughly the same amount of arable land. But the cycle of poverty, hunger, and disease in which millions of Ethiopians are trapped makes these factors affect Ethiopia to an extreme degree. And they threaten to grow worse, much worse, if present population trends persist. Consider projections provided by Daniel Assefa of the Ethiopian Economics Association in his penetrating analysis of the dimensions and impacts of Ethiopia's demographic explosion. He calculates that Ethiopia's current Total Fertility Rate (TFR = births per woman per lifetime) of 5.9 would produce a total population of about 325 million by the year 2050. This means that an area of farmland that hosted about 44 persons in 1995 and about 65 today would have to supply food for 300. Keeping to its current exceptionally high birth rate means nothing but catastrophe in Ethiopia's future. At that rate, in ten years the population of childbearing age will have increased to the point that huge continuing population increases will be inevitable.

And yet, solutions to this crisis are not overwhelmingly difficult. Education is a major key, especially for women. Keeping girls in school longer will postpone the age at which they begin to bear children. Education empowers them to consider the advantages of smaller families and to learn about family planning. In addition, raising the age at which girls become sexually active lowers their vulnerability to HIV/AIDS infection and helps them withstand the pressure to enter the growing prostitution industry. To be sure, additional schooling is expensive and not quickly instituted. Family planning services delivered efficiently to all women of reproductive health and in particular to those who are married would likely have a powerful effect in a fairly short time.

In his report on population and environment in Ethiopia published by the Woodrow Wilson International Center for Scholars, Sahlu Haile rightly affirms that no population program has succeeded without strong and proactive support from national governments. Whatever the political system, this critical area can be dealt with. For example, Iran is viewed as a success story for reducing population growth dramatically by means that are universally applicable. In the decade after 1976, Iran's population increased by 50 percent; at that rate of growth Iran's population would have reached 108 million by 2006. But through a variety of methods—dropping maternity benefits for couples with more than three children, requiring men and women to attend classes about contraception before obtaining a marriage license, and making both condoms and contraceptive pills widely available, even giving away condoms at health clinics—the government of Iran managed to check population growth to reach only 71 million this year. Iran's TFR started at Ethiopia's current level of around 6, and then dropped to below 2!

Ethiopia's government has done relatively little to deliver the message about family planning. Although some of her ministers realize the importance of this problem, the government has addressed it so ineffectually that dramatic changes are needed to deliver incentives to engage in family planning. Ato Daniel would expand the circle of agents to include private groups, NGOs, and the public at large as well as government agencies. To that, Dr. Ghelawdewos Araia has written in *Combating Future Famines in Ethiopia*, the conquest of famine in Ethiopia is a "mammoth historical task," requiring action on many fronts, and should not be left to the homeland authorities alone: "The Ethiopian intellectual and professional in the Diaspora must be willing to contribute."

Population growth and environmental degradation present the two most critical challenges that face this generation of Ethiopians. They constitute a common ground on which all Ethiopians can congregate. This common purpose can best be served by a robustly democratizing process, which supports a framework within which differences can be resolved nonviolently; which supports media that can freely report successes and shortcomings of initiatives; and which enhances communication that can facilitate all development undertakings.

Of course, many factors beside population growth contribute to chronic hunger and vulnerability to famine. But that is a big one. Can it be controlled? Only if more Ethiopians become concerned, and if all concerned demonstrate a commitment to "deny famine a future in Ethiopia" in Dr. Gheladawdewos's stirring phrase. And, may I add, if we move to take action before it is too late.

30

Ethiopia's Missed Chances: 1960, 1974, 1991, 1998, 2005, and Now (2007) *

Not since the 16th Century has Ethiopia experienced changes so convulsive as in the past fifty years. The 16th century changes were instigated by the Ottoman Empire under Sultan Suleiman, who gave arms and soldiers to satellite state Adal under Ahmad Grañ. Grañ assassinated the rightful Harari ruler Sultan Abu Beker Mohammed and abrogated the Islamic doctrine that Ethiopia was a righteous land to be spared jihad. His attacks destroyed vast stretches of highland Ethiopia and created a vacuum that invited Oromo peoples to conquer vast parts of the country, initiating the chronically contested multiethnic rulership of the Ethiopian state. Turks later invaded Ethiopia directly and wrested away Ethiopia's historic coastal strip, paving the way for conflict three centuries later. 20th-century turbulence likewise was due to invasions from outside: first Sudan, then Italy—twice. These invasions pushed Ethiopia toward deliberate programs of internal change, what sociologists call "defensive modernization." One way or another, however, a push toward modernization was inevitable, given the

---

* Originally presented at the Fourth International Conference on Ethiopian Development Studies, Western Michigan University, Kalamazoo, Michigan: August 3–4, 2007. Originally published in 2007 on the web forum of the Ethiopian Institute for Nonviolence Education and Peace Studies.

steady engulfment of a global civilization. What was not inevitable was how Ethiopia faced the challenges of becoming modern.

Parameters of Modernization

When we think about roads to modernity we often invoke the trope of revolution. We link the modern world with the revolutions in America and France, Russia and China—what Eisenstadt (2006) calls the "Great 'Classical Revolutions.'" Or we associate to generic transformations that use the same label—the Industrial Revolution and the Democratic Revolution. Social scientists may associate to phrases recognized from the work of penetrating originary theorists, terms such as the Managerial Revolution (Burnham, 1941), the Integrative Revolution (Geertz, 1963), the Academic Revolution (Jencks and Riesman, 1969), the Participatory Revolution (Huntington, 1974), and the Disciplinary Revolution (Gorski, 1993).

Whatever 'revolution' is taken to signify, the term often connotes *changes of form that combine abruptness and violence.* We tend to suppose that modernization requires societies to suffer a set of wrenching events, in which one complex of deep structures must necessarily be eradicated in favor of another. Lenin's famous phrase puts the matter with crude succinctness: "You can't make an omelet without breaking a few eggs." But surely the subject demands a more differentiating perspective.

I approach this grand theme from a lifetime of study of the seminal figures of modern social science, each of whom penetrated a central feature of the modern order. Some analyze modernity in terms of the division of labor, specialization, and increased productivity (Smith, Marx, Durkheim); some see political centralization, mobilization, and nation building (Tocqueville, Elias); some stress increasing equality and the extension of rights (Hegel, Tocqueville, von Stein). Others stress the advancement of objectified knowledge and scientifically educated elites (Comte, Weber, Dewey) or the creation of world-shaping ideologies (Pareto, Eisenstadt); still others, in terms of changes in the condition of persons, for example, as becoming more disciplined (Weber, Freud, Elias) or more individuated (Durkheim, Simmel) or more flexible (Simmel, Riesman, Lerner). My recent work seeks dialogue among these authors by connecting the phenomena they discuss in terms of six major categories: specialization, individualization, social equalization, political unification, cultural rationalization, and personal discipline. I have also sought to specify the costs and dissatisfactions associated with modernization as well as its benefits (Levine 2005, 2006).

Figure 1: Modernity, Revolution, and their Effects

Process	DIFFERENTIATION		DEMOCRATIZATION		RATIONALIZATION	
	Specialization	Individuation	Unification	Equalization	Cultural	Personal
Revolution	Industrial	Urban-Commercial	Integrative	Social	Academic	Disciplinary
Benefits	Commerce, goods	Freedom	Efficacy	Justice	Knowledge	Civility
Disadvantages	Personal atrophy; Social deficits	Hyper-specialization; Alienation; Consumerism	Repressive centralization; Violence	Mediocrity	"Tragedy of culture"; Jacobin barbarities	Psychic repression

The transformations analyzed by these authors often appear to occur suddenly. I prefer to view those changes as the acceleration, albeit at times at breakneck speed, of large-scale processes that evolved over centuries. As Donald Donham suggests in his perspicuous account of modernization among the Maale of Debub Kilil, regarding "the question of modernity . . . a long, vernacular conversation has gone on for centuries among ordinary men and women the world over" (1999, 180). In contrast to earlier epochs, these processes have often been greeted with enthusiasm for the sheer fact of their novelty, whereas the word 'modern,' historians of ideas tell us, had previously evoked negative associations. But whether or not those rapidly unfolding processes entail *abruptness of change is a variable*, not an inexorable feature of the dynamics of modernization, an understanding that informed my work in *Wax and Gold* (1965).

So, relatedly, is the question of whether or not modernization necessarily entails violence. Although the hegemony of "revolutionary" ideologies seems to rationalize—idealize, even—the use of violence in producing some of the changes associated with the modern order, *it has never been shown that any of these changes could not have come about in nonviolent ways.* Indeed, one of the greatest theorists of modernity, Alexis de Tocqueville, demonstrated that after all the bloodletting of the French revolution, what emerged was essentially a set of changes that had already been quite firmly in place under the *ancien regime* ([1856] 1955).[1]

We would do well, then, to conceptualize modernization in ways that accommodate variations in whether, how, and how well the challenge to make certain modernizing changes is met. To deal with this variable, I propose now the notion of *structural opening*—a moment of fluidity in which actors imagine and deal with the array of options that every situation presents. Every opening harbors possibilities for change and action that are more or less constructive, more or less beneficial. It requires disinterested analysis to identify and clarify the options available in a situation, in order to enable actors to transcend the inertia and passions of the moment and thereby avert possibly disastrous results.

Within this perspective I shall review openings for Ethiopia that appeared over the past half century, openings which in each case found key players moving in suboptimal directions. I invite you to reflect upon five such opportunities that arguably were mishandled, as these became manifest in (1) the abortive coup of December 1960; (2) the ferment of 1974; (3) the regime change of 1991; (4) the Eritrean war of 1998; and (5) the May 2005 national election.

Base Line 1957

It must be hard for Ethiopians today to grasp the confidence about Ethiopia's future that prevailed in 1957.[2] Half a century ago, one could imagine that Ethiopia's future would be benign. Consider what had been accomplished. Regional warlords had given way to a standing national army, one trained to handle modern technology. Central ministries dealt with justice and tax collection. The slave trade was ended (1923!). Internal customs barriers that impeded the flow of domestic trade were removed. Ethiopia had a written constitution, a fledgling national parliament, a central bank, and a national currency. The country had built networks of schools and medical facilities; industrial plants in textiles, cement, sugar, and electric power; and modern media of transport and communication. The modernizing sector pulsated with the energies of foreign-educated young people and graduates of Ethiopia's new colleges.[3] Things appeared so good that by 1960, when the march of African colonies toward independence raised concerns about their viability, it seemed that Ethiopia, thanks to its long history, might offer a model, averting the internal conflicts that threatened so many of the new states.

Ensuing decades dimmed such hope. The December 1960 coup attempt valorized a pattern of murder to effect social change, and cost an opportunity to move toward consensual liberalization. The Derg takeover of 1974 escalated violence against dissident domestic groups and against Eritrea and reversed promising lines of economic development. The regime change of 1991 was met with an escalation of ethnic tensions and new forms of internal suppression. The war with Eritrea destroyed countless lives, resources, and development opportunities. The aftermath of the May 2005 elections plucked disaster out of the jaws of triumph, yielding a fresh polarization of political attitudes.

How can Ethiopia reverse this pattern of missed opportunities? I propose now to revisit those junctures with an eye to raising questions about what might be done to enact more benign solutions in the future. Let us ask: what structural openings had emerged in each case, and what forces drove the country toward those less constructive solutions?

Five Missed Chances

1960: Year of Ferment

1960 saw sixteen African countries achieve independence.[4] With Ethiopia no longer almost the only independent sub-Saharan country, educated Ethiopians chafed that under European powers, other countries had acquired economic and education systems that outshone their own. As one Ethiopian told me, "Our problem is that we never 'suffered under colonialism.'" Impatience with Ethiopia's slow pace, outmoded hierarchical structure, and conservative folkways grew, especially among Ethiopians returning from education abroad.

It was clear to me in 1960 that some of them yearned to engage in progressive forums of some sort, but were fearful of doing so. One complained, "Our culture praises *gwebeznet* (courage). Why have we become so afraid of speaking out?" What options were there? Progressives could have formed a political party. To be sure, they might have landed in jail, since the regime objected to parties and frowned on all voluntary associations and free publications. Still, they might have created a journal under the umbrella of enhancing civic education. They might have formed discussion groups; some did, but in secret—even the alumni association of Haile Selassie I Secondary School was clandestine.

The alternative was to change regimes by peaceful means. This route was accepted initially by Germame Neway, a US-educated returnee eager for change. As provincial administrator in Walayta, he enacted reforms to ease the burden of tenant farmers—with innovations that earned him a transfer to Jijjiga, where he worked to integrate Somali Ethiopians more effectively by offering them schools, clinics, and roads. In Bahru Zewde's words, Germame converted these "exile posts into stations experimenting in equitable administration" (Zewde 1991, 213).

Meeting official resistance, he enlisted his brother General Mengistu Neway, who commanded the Imperial Bodyguard, into a conspiracy that attempted a coup d'état on December 14. They did so while the emperor was in Brazil, hoping he would stay there in peaceable retirement.[5] General Mengistu had refused overtures by his brother to use violence and counted on support from other military commanders. As one Bodyguard officer boasted to me a month before the coup, "When a signal for change is given, *be-and innenesalan*, we shall rise as one." That was the preference of those who marched from Arat Kilo to the Piazza, with placards that proclaimed, "*Ityopiya le-hulatchn be-selamawi lewet*—Ethiopia for all of us through peaceful change." [Figure 2]. This option, also, was not taken. Failed communication between Bodyguard and other military units led to a counter-offensive; army and air force troops defeated the rebels.

A third option might have been for the rebel leaders, once defeated, either to give themselves up[6] or to flee and issue statements from hiding. Instead, prior to leaving the Grand Palace where the ministers and other high-ranking figures were held, Germame and others machine-gunned the hostages in cold blood.

The coup's failure promoted the consolidation of imperial power, leading the emperor to focus on "rewarding those who had defended his throne, not in trying to solve the problems indicated" by their protest (Zewde 1991, 214). This produced continuing efforts to quell dissent and to spread the hegemony of Shoan Amhara rule. It led to efforts to marginalize the main other languages—Tigrinya, officially suppressed in 1970, and Oromiffa. It also led to annexing the federated province of Eritrea, in ways that undermined Eritrea's more liberal democratic achievements—multiple political parties and a free press, which the British protectorate had encouraged. In sum, the failure of Ethiopians to pursue constructive options in 1960 sowed seeds of all the later disturbances: the violence of the Derg, and the alienation of Tigrinya-speakers, Oromo-speakers, and progressive Eritreans.

1974: Revolutionary Breakthrough

The year 1974 created a large opening for structural change at the country's political center. On the one hand, Haile Selassie's waning abilities to govern as before became glaringly apparent. On the other hand, unprecedentedly, diverse groups mounted a series of protests airing a variety of grievances. This led to efforts to achieve the unlikely: a wholly peaceful change of political structure. "*Ityopiya tikdem/yala mimin dem*"—"Let Ethiopia progress/Without any bloodshed"—became the popular slogan of that heady time.

On the surface, this almost seemed plausible. A new cabinet was formed under conservative Endelkatchew Makonnen, later under the more popular liberal aristocrat, Mikael Imru. A blue-ribbon committee, respected by a wide range of civilian and military elements, drafted a progressive constitution, described as "years ahead of its time in terms of Ethiopia's social and economic development" (Marina and David Ottoway 1978, 41). Another committee was set up to investigate whether or not figures from the ancien regime suspected for wrongdoing were legally liable. Following the emperor's deposition on September 14, the popular General Andom was selected to head the military committee that had become the de facto governing power of the nation. Andom, an Eritrean himself, was well positioned to heal the country's major festering wound: the rebellion of dissident groups in Eritrea.

The non-violent option was not taken. Already in February an engine of potential violence was forming when a cabal of junior officers organized an Armed Forces Coordinating Committee, called the Derg. As this committee moved increasingly to attain control, senior officers, civilian leaders, labor unions, and friendly foreign governments all stood by. One of its members, a misfit from Harar named Major Mengistu Haile Mariam, came to dominate the Derg. On November 23, Mengistu engineered a murderous attack on General Andom and then summarily shot 59 former imperial officials. That night, Paul Henze wrote, "the Ethiopian revolution turned bloody. Blood never ceased to flow for the next 17 years" (Henze 2000, 289).

Mengistu's coup became aligned with some groups of communist intellectuals who supported his efforts to impose a Leninist-style revolution from above. They proceeded to confiscate budding enterprises, nationalize all land, herd farmers onto unproductive collective farms, and force tens of thousands of people into resettlement sites. Their heavy-handed policies and violent tactics provoked reactions in many parts of the country; the Derg period was marked by insurgencies and severe famine. Their uncompromising military action against Eritrea finally turned that ancient part of the Ethiopian homeland toward secession.

1991: A Multiethnic Polity

1991 offered a reprieve from the Derg and yet another opportunity for non-violent change.[7] The May regime change was painless enough: Mengistu fled to Zimbabwe, senior Derg officials were imprisoned, and EPRDF established control with hardly a shot fired. The turnover was soon followed by a national conference, which established a Transitional Government. A year later, the country's first multi-party elections were held. Dozens if not hundreds of publications sprang up overnight. A new Constitution was ratified in 1995.

Before long, however, the EPRDF ascendancy mired the country into yet another period of internal discord. Viewed by some chiefly as a takeover of revanchist Tigrean rebels, the EPRDF victory unleashed a storm of protest at the Embassy of the United States, blamed for facilitating the transition. The removal of Shoan Amhara from power coupled with virulent anti-Amhara attitudes in many TPLF leaders stirred waves of Amhara chauvinistic response. The Oromo Liberation Front, central to the new regime's commitment to ethnic regional autonomy, was not satisfied and refused to lay down arms. A similar attitude was taken by remnants of the EPRP group of radicals who had opposed both the Derg and the TPLF. The emphasis on ethnicity as an absolute value, manifest in the EPRDF's commitment to ethnic federalism, traumatized those who considered themselves to be above and beyond tribal allegiances. Reacting to these dismissive attitudes and to implement their own distinctive revolutionary doctrines, the EPRDF became repressive against independent journalists and individuals oriented to forms of protest other than what the regime favored.

1998: Competition without Fratricide

After Eritrea became independent in 1993, official relations between the two countries remained cordial, the Eritrean leader espousing fraternity between the two countries and promoting mutual trade and cooperation. Issues regarding trade imbalance and currency restrictions, and Ethiopia's lingering grief over the loss of the Red Sea ports, began to sour those relations. Since certain boundaries had never been demarcated, this situation might have occasioned an appeal for mediation by an international body.

Instead, when Eritreans who entered the town of Badme in May 1998 were met with gunfire from Ethiopian militia, massive military operations between the two states ensued quickly. Within two years, virulent warfare produced an estimated 100,000 casualties and some 400,000 refugees. Both countries employed cluster bombs. In June 1998 Eritrea launched air-delivered CB-500 cluster munitions against the Mekele airport, two of which struck a school and residential area resulting in civilian deaths, wounds, and suffering, and similar hits caused dozens of deaths and injuries in the town of Adigrat. In May 2000 Ethiopia bombed two camps of internally displaced persons with BL-755 cluster munitions and hit civilian airports in Asmara as well.[8] The cost of the war for the world's two poorest countries was enormous, and led to further destabilizations in subsequent troubles in Somalia.[9]

2005: Democratizing Breakthrough

The first years of the 21st century found Ethiopia beginning to hit its stride. The economy grew, repressiveness abated. In 2004, for the first time since coming to power, Prime Minister Meles Zenawi was removed from Reporters Without Borders' annual list of "Enemies of the Free Press." The government decided to make the 2005 election a surge toward political pluralism. Opposition parties for the first time had access to the media, and televised debates between representatives from opposing parties were aired. The elections were monitored by international bodies, including representatives from the European Union and the Carter Center, who called the elections fair in many respects yet noted serious irregularities before and after the election day. The election outcome saw opposition groups leap from 15 to 180 members of parliament and sweep into control over the city of Addis Ababa.

Ensuing post-election complications offered two options. One was to abide by existing National Election Board procedures and accept their verdict regarding disputed contests. Repeat elections in several of them actually resulted in switches of parliamentary seats in both directions. A second option, after the CUD party caucused and decided that its members would not enter the Parliament, was a negotiation with the government that went on for several days in late October.

Instead of either of these denouements, Ethiopia experienced fresh outbreaks of violence and stirrings of hatred. Compounding the June killings, the November demonstrations led to numerous deaths, bringing the total fatalities to 193 (as a Commission report confirmed). Tens of thousands were carted off to prison. More than one hundred dissident political party officials, civil society leaders, and independent journalists were incarcerated. Their long detention during court procedures judged to be flawed exacerbated animosities between the two sides. Resulting polarization weakened the new government's claim to legitimacy and damaged its efficacy.

The points just covered are summarized schematically in Figure 2.

Figure 2: Issues and Openings

DATE	Developmental Issue	Missed Constructive Opportunity	What Happened
1960	Hunger for accelerated economic development and democratization	1. Nonviolent advocacy of reforms 2. Successful nonviolent coup 3. Failed coup without assassinations	1. Nothing 2. Impulsive coup attempt 3. Cold-blooded assassinations
1974–5	Social class egalitarianism	Differentiated land reforms	Stalinist collectivization
1991	Ethnic egalitarianism	Multiculturalist recognition	Imposed ethnic federalism polarization
1998–2000	Geopolitical boundary problem	International adjudication	Destructive "border war"
2005	Pluralist political democratization	Adjudicated multiparty election outcome	Incendiary reactions; numerous deaths, casualties, incarcerations

An Ambiguous Balance Sheet

Before proceeding further, I want to emphasize two points. For one thing, probably no society has ever responded to all its challenges in the most constructive and beneficial way possible. Beyond that, we must of course acknowledge that although Ethiopia took many damaging missteps in the past half-century, the country accomplished a great deal of progress on the always-difficult paths toward modernization.

In response to the abortive coup of December 1960, the Emperor made a few progressive ministerial appointments, notably Yilma Deressa who transformed budget and appropriation procedures in the Ministry of Finance (Clapham 1969). Ethiopia's first university (Haile Selassie I University, now Addis Ababa University) was established and quickly flourished. The economy developed steadily, with stable currency and a solid financial position. Haile Selassie reached his pinnacle as an African and world leader. Ethiopia's prominence in African affairs was marked by the establishment in 1963 of Addis Ababa as home to the Organization of African Unity and the UN Economic Commission for Africa. Ethiopia stayed on course while much of the rest of Africa deteriorated.

However heavy-handed and destructive, the Derg reforms valorized the public use of languages other than Amharic—notably Tigrinya and Oromiffa—and religions other than Christianity—notably, Islam. Although the quality of education deteriorated, the Derg increased school enrollment dramatically; during the Derg's first decade the number of students in government schools rose from about 800,000 to nearly 3,100,000 and the number of students in higher education likewise quadrupled (Clapham 1988, 150). They started the Workers' Party of Ethiopia in 1984—the first political party in the country's history—and established the *kebele* system still used to organize neighborhoods.

The TPLF victory rid the country of an oppressive dictatorship and such damaging policies as collectivization of agriculture and forced resettlement of hundreds of thousands. TPLF maintained the value of Ethiopia's currency against all odds: Ethiopia may be the only country to emerge from an authoritarian regime and economic collapse without suffering from serious inflation. TPLF also gave unprecedented levels of political autonomy to peoples in the southern parts of the country. The EPRDF government has presided over a growing economy, expanding construction of modern buildings and roads, and opening hydroelectric plants that doubled the country's energy supply.

For the border war with Eritrea, to be sure, it is almost impossible to find any positive achievement. By contrast, the 2005 elections achieved a great deal. They opened up electoral competition to an array of national political parties and offered them unprecedented access to the media—a major milestone in Ethiopia's journey toward political modernity. The disasters of the Derg period and the repressions of EPRDF can also be "credited" with driving hundreds of thousands to emigrate. That created a large diaspora of modern-educated Ethiopians whose continuing devotion to their homeland makes them part of the new Ethiopian nation—which consists, I noted elsewhere, of three parts: *ye-bét agar, ye-wutch agar*, and *ye-cyber agar* (Levine 2004)—and which positions them to make major contributions to Ethiopia's development (as this very conference demonstrates).

These and other positive accomplishments must be kept in mind. Nevertheless, they came at far too steep a cost. To sum up what of all of us must be feeling about these decades, I say: *Ethiopia, you deserved better*! And it is in the hope that whatever produced such dire outcomes might be minimized in the future that I inquire into what factors were responsible for those missed opportunities.

An Ethiopian Dilemma

I employ this phrase, an association to Gunnar Myrdal's *An American Dilemma*, to suggest how attempting an objective analysis might contribute to analyzing problematic situations.[10] Let us review those episodes to see if we can discern patterns evident in all of them.

Wax and Gold: A Culture of Distrust

Two of those factors, I suggest, represent customs that were adaptive in pre-modern periods but have become dysfunctional in the present. One is a deep-seated habit of suspiciousness and distrust in social relations. The prevalence of this tendency was thematized in the title of my first book, *Wax and Gold*. For a social order in which so much hinged on the securing of rights to use land, an ethos of manipulative tactical scheming proved advantageous. For a political order in which power and status hinged on strict deference to superordinate patrons, the open voicing of critical sentiments was intolerable; they had to be expressed in some clever surreptitious manner. That order made it hard to generate trust, and disposed people to be always on the lookout for hidden motives and deceptive maneuverings.

When one examines the episodes I have been describing, this trait is hard to miss.

In 1960, endemic suspiciousness and distrust colored the entire social fabric, preventing even those who thought themselves friends from discussing grievances and aspirations openly. This mindset kept them from any proactive para-political initiatives. The coup leaders and the generals who opposed them were presumptive friends, but held back from sharing ideas about the need for change and in the end battled against each other. When General Merid of the loyalist forces visited General Mengistu in the hospital before he was hanged, the latter reportedly told him: "I thought you would understand."[11]

The Crown accentuated the pervasive distrust. Following the coup attempt as before, the Palace discouraged transparency in public communications. After Eritrea was annexed, a number of high school students from Dessie wanted to come to the Palace to express their appreciation of the Emperor's bold move. He forbade their visit, reportedly saying, "If they come now to say they approve of my policy, what is to prevent them from coming in the future to say they disapprove?" This fear of open public discourse lay behind the Emperor's misguided policy of suppressing political parties and the free press in Asmara. It even led to the suppression of Tigrinya in 1970, a grievous error, especially in view of Paul Henze's observation that "Amharic is firmly established as the national language with English in second place. . . . What this goes to prove is that the Imperial regime could have safely afforded to be much more open-minded about language questions than it was" (2007, 214).

The 1974 demonstrations represented a big shift in the openness of public protest. Even so, what proved to be the central political dynamic was kept clandestine and murky for nearly a year after the initial protests of February. How the Derg was organized and where it was heading remained secret. Rumor remained the prime medium of public communication.

Nearly universal relief over the dissolution of the Derg in 1991 gave way to mutual suspicions and incriminations. Although Oromo Liberation Front leaders gained a great deal in negotiations over the new order, they feared laying down their arms following the EPRDF ascendancy. Remnants of the EPRP remained armed. Above all, although serious substantive differences arose between Ethiopian patriotic nationalists and TPLF proponents of ethnic federalism, these differences were compounded by distortions that stemmed from deep suspicions about one another's motives. The TPLF leaders accused the nationalists of being Amhara chauvinists, even though they included numerous non-Amhara people and for the most part Amhara Ethiopians whose allegiance was primarily to Ethiopia as a multiethnic nation.[12] The nationalists accused the TPLF leaders of being agents of their Eritrean comrades in EPLF, even though TPLF and EPLF had been enemies during much of the previous decade and seeds of future animosity were not hard to discern below the surface. These seeds sprouted in 1998, when distrust between brothers yielded to lethal attacks.

The tragic dénouement of summer 2005 represented nothing so much as a flagrant manifestation of the archaic pattern of distrust. The regime acted on the suspicion that the opposition was deliberately stirring up anti-Tigrayan hostilities when the CUD leadership explicitly discouraged their followers from doing anything of the sort. They also ran with the idea purveyed in a tract by Negede Gobeze that the opposition should mobilize the populace in an effort to overthrow the regime through a kind of Orange Revolution, when in fact the opposition wanted nothing more than an exact count to be respected. Based on the regime's initial hasty declaration of martial law on Election Day and premature announcement of victory, the opposition went on to distrust nearly every post-election action of the regime. They studiously maintained that a complete victory had been stolen from them, even though some foreign analysts—even those antagonistic to the regime, like Siegfried Pausewang (2006)—questioned the claim that the CUD might have won the election. The regime's hyper-vigilance in the wake of their suspicions led them to provocative incidents and well-documented excessive violence against demonstrators in June and November of that year. The latter confrontations, with fatalities on both sides but overwhelming brute violence from government security troops, might have been averted had last-minute daily negotiations at the end of October succeeded. Although an exact account of what happened there must await future historians, it is my understanding that those negotiations, too, broke down on the basis of mutual suspicions.

Wendinet Idealized: A Culture of Martial Honor

The other dysfunctional tendency exhibited in Ethiopia's series of missed chances reflects the prevalence of what I have elsewhere described as a "masculinity ethic and the spirit of warriorhood."[13] I refer here to the traditional code of *wendinet*, masculinity, which prescribes a courageous disposition to fight enemies. Related to this is a sensitivity to personal slights and a commitment to *man yebiltal*—'who in the world is superior to me?'[14] The importance of this value in a society whose politics was dominated by warfare is self-evident.

The *wendinet* factor played a big role in the missed chances I have been describing. It was manifest in the last-minute decision of the coup leaders to assassinate their hostages in the Green Room of the Old Palace. Indeed, Germame egged on his more amiable brother; when Captain Dereje Haile Mariam approached the palace calling Mengistu to surrender, Gemame shouted at him, "Out of my way, woman of a brother!" and shot the captain dead (Greenfield 1969, 429). It underlies a kind of subliminal admiration for the 'tough guy' rebel who shoots his way into power, like Kassa Haylu on his way to becoming Emperor Tewodros, or Mengistu Haile Mariam on his ruthless route to supreme power in the Derg. It informs the passionate heroism of those who endured more than a decade of hardship existence as guerilla insurgents.[15]

The combination of distrust and *wendinet* has probably impeded Ethiopia's capacity to take advantage of structural openings as much as anything. It casts political options within a schema of "*metazez* or *meshefet*," obey or rebel. The compulsion to obey superiors means that any stirring of dissent must either be suppressed or expressed in devious ways. The ideal of *wendinet* means that if the dissent becomes too intense, the way to express it is to rebel against the leader and to charge off from afar.

The Seduction of Revolutionary Ideologies

In addition to old patterns that impede optimal courses of action, one can identify a third factor of a radically contrasting sort. This is the proclivity to emulate foreign patterns to a degree that does not fit Ethiopia's own historic and current realities. This factor reflects the doctrinaire quality of the modernizing ideologies with which Ethiopian political leaders identified.

Like his peers, Germame Neway returned from study abroad fired with an ardor to accelerate the pace of building schools and factories and to improve the life of peasants. Like many Western-educated radicals, he assumed that the populace was similarly disgruntled and ready for massive change. This assumption proved erroneous. In words which I am told Ras Imru spoke about him, "*Germame ye-ityopia hizb gemet alaweqem*"—"Germane did not understand the limitations of the Ethiopian people." This was to be a top-down quasi-revolutionary movement, which ran counter to the persisting deference of the people to the authority of the throne, the church, and the aristocracy, all of whom finally opposed the coup. Accordingly, the coup leaders actually mobilized troops on the grounds that Haile Selassie's position was being attacked and so they needed to defend him! The intensity of Germame's commitment to revolutionary change found expression, finally, in his order to assassinate the hostages.

By the end of the 1960s, Ethiopian students at home and abroad were seduced by the radicalization of students in many countries. They began to identify with the tenets of Marxism-Leninism and with Russia and China as models of modernization. This had two deleterious consequences. For one thing, it inclined them to find the truth about Ethiopia's situation in the intellectual abstractions of the Marxist tradition. It also inclined them to adopt the Manichean perspective of committed Marxists, using the idiom of Marx's vitriolic attacks on social classes and an inclination to demonize the other. These tendencies have haunted all further Ethiopian political conduct, issuing in the violent "anti-feudal" enactments of the Derg; the "anti-Amhara" and radical "ethnic-liberationist" enactments TPLF; and the virulent mutual incriminations of Ethiopia and Eritrea in 1998, and between the EPRDF and CUD in 2005.

All these phenomena evince a lack of connectedness to Ethiopian realities on the ground, a lack of respect for the common sense of the Ethiopian people, and a departure from traditional Ethiopian customs of tolerance and everyday morality. That Ethiopia was in for a long, horrible time under the influence of these attitudes was brought home to me when a talented and well-meaning Ethiopian graduate student said to me in the early 1970s, "What Ethiopia needs to do is what Russia did." When I told him that the consequence of the communist policies under Lenin and Stalin resulted in the deaths of about ten percent of the Russian people, he paused only briefly and said, "Well, Ethiopia has 30 million people right now. The death of three million would not be too high a price to pay for progress."

Ethiopia's dilemma of the past two years reflects the persistence of doctrinaire positions and polarizing sentiments on both sides.

The points just made can be seen schematically in Figure 3.

Figure 3: Three Factors Leading to Sub-Optimal Outcomes

DATE	Traditional Distrust Factor	Traditional Martial Ethic	Alien Factors
1960	1. Distrust and fear within civilian elite 2. Suspiciousness within military elite	Commitment to violence as a means of political change	Modernization ideologies
1974–5	Distrust of democratic process	Rulership succession through martial combat	Marxist-Leninist-Maoist ideologies
1991	Distrust of democratic process	Continued resort to arms	Stalinist ideology of "self-determination of nationalities"
1998–2000	Intense mutual suspicion	Martial pride and drive for revenge	Arabist support for Eritrean insurgency
2005	Intense mutual suspicion and mutual demonization	Fight against the system, rather than within the system	Tenacity of radical polarizing ideology

And now to this point, I have sketched a series of openings presented, opportunities missed and advances made. Today's Ethiopia has taken unmistakable steps toward many of its modernizing goals—bureaucratized administration, codified legal systems, commercial facilities, modern technologies, academic institutions, scientific research, multicultural equity, transportation and communication, and political integration. A plethora of tasks remain, not least to address the increase in chronic poverty outlined by Abu Girma Moges (2007). In pursuing these tasks, new tensions might provoke further violence and suboptimal solutions.

Enhancing Functionality Through Trust and Civic Courage

The diagnosis I have offered suggests ways that may enable Ethiopians to move forward without repeating the costly mistakes of the last half-century.

This would mean to deal with the symptoms of chronic suspiciousness and distrust, compulsive combativeness, and inattention to Ethiopia's own traditions and resources. The solution, in each case, involves staying rooted in Ethiopia's traditions while adapting creatively to present needs and modern realities, a solution that involves *structural differentiation*.

Regarding the first factor, it means preserving the wax-and-gold complex where it still belongs—in religious *qene*, in secular poems, and in social banter—and replacing it in the area of public discourse with more straightforward, transparent communication.

Regarding the second, it means preserving the warrior ethos when security situations require, but keeping it out of politics and cultivating civic courage to replace martial courage in the latter realm.

The fusion of these two traits produces what I am calling the "*metazez* or *meshefet*" complex—either obey and express dissent ambiguously, or exit the system and rebel. Let me relate two personal experiences that may drive this point home.

At 11:30 am on Friday, December 18, 1960, I was the last person to speak with Germame Neway before he returned to the palace for that fateful shootout. His final words to me were as follows. "Even if our cause is lost and I am killed," he said, "we have at least spoken the truth in this land of deception." Over the years I have thought about his words, and have come to see more significance in them: in this land of deception, the only way one can speak the truth is through violent rebellion. *Metazez* or *meshefet*.

Forty-five years later, a kindred thought was voiced by a prominent Ethiopian-American who wrote me in the wake of my efforts to foster dialogue among polarized Ethiopians in 2006: "Ethiopia will never make any progress unless we learn to fight as hard within the system as we do against the system." And now listen to this: when I asked him if I might use his name when citing this inspiring statement, he said, "Oh no, I don't dare to do that."

In a searching analysis prepared for this conference, Salaam Yitbarek (2007) outlines a complex of related Ethiopian traits. He identifies these as personalization of issues, parochialism, mutual suspicion and mutual distrust, paranoia, lack of empathy and empathetic understanding, character assassination, lack of openness, holding grudges, and envy. Most of these traits which I have described over many decades (see especially 1965a, 1965b, and 1995). Importantly, Ato Salaam offers an incentive to move beyond these impediments by noting that to overcome them is to do something to create more social capital.

Enhancing Functionality Through Self-Understanding and Self-Appreciation

The third factor that has derailed Ethiopia's efforts to modernize, an ungrounded attachment to alien ideas, can also be addressed through a sort of structural differentiation. How can Ethiopian intellectuals incorporate ideas from abroad into a grounded sense of evolving realities? How can they move from ideological fixities to pragmatic solutions?

One piece of this answer lies all around you: engaging devoted scholars to address current issues and to communicate with one another in forums and media that enhance the chances of sensible interventions to promote capacity-building. This effort should also include serious investigation of resources that Ethiopian traditions may contain. Although modernization imperatives remain stronger than ever, it must no longer be understood in terms of uncritical imitation of forms from other places. In recent scholarly work this way of thinking about modernity has been foregrounded by Prof. Shmuel Eisenstadt and colleagues, under the banner of what they call "multiple modernities."

At a more modest level, I propose here the metaphor and the reality of the lesson of the eucalyptus tree. Emperor Menelik II sought to solve Ethiopia's reforestation problems by importing eucalyptus from Australia. It is telling that the Amharic phrase for this tree became *bahr zaf*, "the tree from across the sea" (*bahr*). Eucalyptus has been used ever since as an easy source of wood for cooking and construction. The problem is, eucalyptus trees are invasive, destroying other plants with their rapid growth. Moreover, they are extremely 'thirsty' and dry up rivers and wells. Their dangers became so evident early on that Emperor Menelik issued a decree for them be uprooted and replaced with mulberry trees; this was never enforced. In the meantime, over the past half-century, Ethiopia's level of forestation dropped precipitously.[16]

Is it not time to stop planting the *bahr zaf* and start planting indigenous trees that are fast-growing, hardy, and environmentally friendly—as knowledgeable local environmentalists like those associated with Lem Ethiopia have long advocated? Some of these species have been neglected so long that they are now even threatened. These include the *weyra* (olive trees), the juniper, the *tiqur inchet*, and the *Igenica Abysinica* (*kosso*). What could be a more felicitous way to celebrate the new millennium than to encourage every citizen of Ethiopia who lives in a suitable place to plant one of these indigenous trees?

Beyond that: what could be more suitable now than to encourage all Ethiopian leaders to discard attitudes imported uncritically from abroad and make use of indigenous customs friendly to the societal environment. One of these is age-old patterns of inter-group toleration, as manifest, for example, in the multiethnic and multireligious pilgrimages such as at Zuqwala and Qulubi Gabrael. Another is the near-sacred right of peasants to own their own land. Another is the resort to mediation by "elders," *shimgelina*, as a means of conflict resolution. For another, what could be more beneficial than to incorporate and expand the customs of Oromo assemblies, the *gumi gayo*, which open with calls for mutual respect and involve so many felicitous procedures for attaining group harmony? And let us not forget the striking tradition of forgiveness, which, as Charles Schaefer (2006) tellingly documents, Ethiopian rulers so often employed as a way of restoring social equilibrium and discouraging impulses to revenge. For one memorable instance of this, recall the gesture of Ras Tafari who, following his defeat of thousands of Negus Mikael's followers after the battle of Segele, performed "a remarkable act of clemency," declaring "We are all Ethiopians" (Marcus 1987, 24).

Recovering such traditions yields the additional benefit of moral inspiration. This theme was replayed recently by Jonathan Lear in *Radical Hope: Ethics in the Face of Cultural Devastation*, which tackles the haunting existential question of what a people is to do once their traditional culture has become obsolete. For Lear, the solution "would require finding something in one's own culture or tradition that would enable one to draw new meaning from old definitions that are no longer appropriate." Lear was talking about the Crow Indians of North America, whose great chief Plenty-Coups describes the erosion of Crow culture in the late 1920s by saying: "When the buffalo went away the hearts of my people fell to the ground, and they could not lift them up again. After this nothing happened." Karl E. Knutsson reported a similar sentiment in his study of the Macaa Oromo:

> When gada was destroyed . . .the bull refused to mount the cow. . . the crops that were cultivated no longer grew, and the oxen refused to fatten. . . There were no longer any real elders, and few children were born. . . . When the gada customs were destroyed, everything else was also destroyed. . . the man who had formerly respected truth and justice abandoned them. (Knutsson 1967, 180)

All over Ethiopia, as throughout the world, global modernization entails obsolescence of certain cultural forms. Their loss has been linked with contemporary ills such as vulnerability to demagogues, crime, suicide, substance abuse, and fundamentalism. Ethiopian tradition offers a multitude of resources on which to draw in inspiring a new courage to hope.

A Missing Revolution

Returning to the paradigm of modernization processes touched on at the beginning, it is clear that Ethiopia has gone some distance on dimensions of increasing equality and extensions of rights; political centralization, mobilization, and nation-building; specialization and increased productivity; and the creation of scientifically-educated elites (although a good portion of the latter live in the Diaspora).

In one domain classically associated with modernization, Ethiopia has yet to make a signal advance. That concerns the process of rationalizing personal conduct in everyday life, a process so fundamental to modernity that it has acquired its own name as "the disciplinary revolution" (Gorski 1993). This involves a complex of traits including a commitment to an ethic of hard work, punctuality, reliability, responsibility, and a sense of vocation. The importance of this dimension in transforming the economies of Western Europe and North America was established in the classic work of Max Weber, who associated it with the new ethical habits introduced with the Protestant Reformation. In other countries, it has been associated with different cultural patterns: in Japan, with an ethic inspired by the samurai code of duty to the collectivity (Bellah 1957), in Russia and China with work ethics associated with communist ideologies.

What could possibly serve as the Ethiopian equivalent of the "Protestant Ethic"?—a question, interestingly, that was posed in a letter sent me on the eve of my first voyage to Ethiopia in 1957, by the late distinguished psychologist Erik Erikson. The chief message of both of my books on Ethiopia was to envision a future built confidently on enduring features of Ethiopia's past. To begin with, it is heartening to note that some of the traditional religions are beginning to adjust themselves to novel challenges and reach out to young people, who are desperately in need of moral guidance. The schools of course have a crucial role to play in moral socialization. Across the board, enhanced economic opportunities are essential for young people to have futures to look forward to. But to engage Ethiopians in ways that mobilize their energies on behalf of self-discipline and striving for excellence requires something more. It requires an overarching vision of the good life in which those traits find meaning. I am doubtful that this can occur if the largest frame of reference is that of tribal loyalty. It requires something of transcendent significance. It would be hard to find something more compelling than a renewed vision of Greater Ethiopia as home to a diversity of citizens enjoying basic rights in an age-old and continuing multiethnic society.

Bibliography

Bellah, Robert. 1957. *Tokugawa Religion: The Values of Pre-Industrial Japan*. Boston: Beacon Press.

Burnham, James. 1941. *The Managerial Revolution*. New York: John Day Co.

Chole, Eshetu. 1992. "Ethiopia at the Crossroads." Published online at www.eeaecon.org/pubs.

Clapham, Christopher. 1969. *Haile-Selassie's Government*. New York: Praeger.

__________. 1988. *Transformation and Continuity in Revolutionary Ethiopia*. Cambridge: Cambridge University Press.

Eisenstadt, S.N. 2006. *The Great Revolutions and the Civilizations of Modernity*. Leiden: Koninklijke Brill.

Geertz, Clifford. 1963. "The Integrative Revolution: Primordial Sentiments and Civil Politics in the New States." Pp. 105–157 in *Old Societies and New States*, ed. Clifford Geertz. New York: Free Press.

Gorski, Philip. 1993. "The Protestant Ethic Revisited. Disciplinary Revolution in Holland and Prussia." *American Journal of Sociology*, 99:2, 265–316.

Greenfield, Richard. 1965. *Ethiopia: a New Political History*. London: Pall Mall Press.

Henze, Paul B. 2000. *Layers of Time*. London: Hurst & Company.

________. 2007. *Ethiopia in Mengistu's Final Years, I: The Derg in Decline*. Addis Ababa: Shama.

Huntington, S.P. 1974. "Postindustrial Politics: How Benign Will It Be?" *Comparative Politics* 6, 163–191.

Jencks, Christopher and Riesman, David. 1969. *The Academic Revolution*. Garden City, NY: Doubleday.

Kaase, Max. 1984. "The Challenge of the 'Participitory Revolution' in Pluralist Democracies." *International Political Science Review* 5: 299.

Levine, Donald N. 1965a. *Wax and Gold: Tradition and Innovation in Ethiopian Culture*. Chicago: University of Chicago Press. Phoenix Paperback, with a new preface by the author, 1972. Reprinted by Tsehai Publishers, 2007.

________. 1965b. "Ethiopia: Identity, Authority, and Realism," pp. 245–81 in *Political Culture and Political Development*, eds. Lucien Pye and Sidney Verba. Princeton: Princeton University Press.

________. 1966. "The Concept of Masculinity in Ethiopian Culture," *International Journal of Social Psychiatry* 12 (1), 17–23.

________. 1968. "The Military in Ethiopian Politics," pp. 5–34 in *The Military Intervenes: Case Studies in Political Development*, ed. Henry Bienen. New York: Russell Sage.

________. 1974 [2000]. *Greater Ethiopia: The Evolution of a Multiethnic Society*. Chicago: University of Chicago Press. 2nd ed., with a new preface, 2000. Amharic translation, *Tiliqua Etyopya*, Addis Ababa University Press, 2001.

________. 1981. "Sociology's Quest for the Classics: The Case of Simmel." Pp. 60–80 in *The Future of the Sociological Classics*, ed. Buford Rhea. London: Allen and Unwin.

________. 1991. "Simmel as Educator: On Individuality and Modern Culture." *Theory, Culture and Society* 8(3), 99–117.

________. 1995. "Will the Real Spirit of Adwa Please Stand Up?" *Ethiopian Register* 2 (3), April, 16–23.

________. 2004. "Reconfiguring the Ethiopian Nation in a Global Era." *International Journal of Ethiopian Studies* 2004 Vol. 1, No. 2., 1–15.

________. 2005. "Modernity and Its Endless Discontents." Pp. 148–68 in *After Parsons: A Theory of Social Action for the Twenty-First Century*, ed. R. C. Fox, V. M. Lidz, and H. J. Bershady. New York: Russell Sage.

________. 2006a. "Two Tales of One City." Published online at www.eineps.org/forum.

________. 2006b. *Powers of the Mind: The Reinvention of Liberal Learning in America*. Chicago: University of Chicago Press.

Marcus, Harold G. 1987. *Haile Sellassie I: The Formative Years, 1892–1936*. Berkeley: University of California Press.

Moges, Abu Girma. 2007. "The Political Economy of Policy Reduction Policies in Ethiopia." Paper prepared for presentation at 4th International Conference of Ethiopian Development Studies, Western Michigan University, Kalamazoo, MI.

Ottaway, Marina and David. 1978. *Ethiopia: Empire in Revolution*. New York: Africana Publishing Co.

Pausewang, Siegfried. 2006. "The Oromo and the CUD." Paper prepared for presentation at Oromo Society of America Annual Conference, University of Minnesota, Minneapolis, MN.

Schaefer, Charles. 2006. "Reexamining the Ethiopian Historical Record on the Continuum between Vengeance and Forgiveness." Unpublished.

Tadesse, Medhane. 1999. *The Eritrean-Ethiopian War: Retrospect and Prospects*. Addis Ababa: Mega Printing Enterprise.

Tocqueville, Alexis de. (1856)1955. *The Old Regime and the French Revolution*, trans. Stuart Gilbert. Garden City, NY: Doubleday.

Yitbarek, Salaam. 2007. "A Problem of Social Capital and Cultural Norms?" Paper prepared for presentation at 4th International Conference of Ethiopian Development Studies, Western Michigan University, Kalamazoo, MI.

Zewde, Bahru. 1991. *A History of Modern Ethiopia 1855–1974*. Addis Ababa: Addis Ababa University Press.

Notes

1 Even more challenging to the notion that modernization requires abrupt, violent shifts from one state to another, I would stress, as did Max Weber and Georg Simmel preeminently, that *the diverse currents of the modernization process do not all flow in the same direction*. Although at times they support one another—as in Weber's famous argument that the modern commercial order requires the institutions of a stable legal system—at times they also run counter to one another. This can be seen, for example, in Weber's implication that the bureaucrats' obligation to "follow the rules" contradicts the wish to achieve goals in the most efficient matter; in Simmel's analysis of the contradiction between the modern promotion of individuality and precisely its opposite, the need to conform to objectified structures; or in Luhmann's argument that different institutions of the modern world carry opposing values and languages.

2 The Emperor's Silver Jubilee in 1955 had inaugurated the Ethiopian National Theater and a constitution allowed the lower house of Parliament to become an elected body. The First Five-Year Plan (1957–61) envisioned a strengthened

infrastructure, particularly in transportation, construction, and communications. It proposed an indigenous cadre of skilled and semiskilled personnel to work in processing industries, in order to reduce Ethiopia's dependence on imports, and to promoting commercial agricultural ventures. The emperor maintained contact with his people by traveling around the country; wherever he went, people cheered his presence with *ililtas* and a sense that the Head of State was a *gêta* to whom one could ultimately cry *Abêt*!

3 Agricultural Colleges at Alemayhu and Jimma, the University College of Addis Ababa at Arat Kilo and the Health College at Gonder with its pioneering model of teams of medical officers, community nurses, and sanitary engineers.

4 Cameroon, Togo, Mali, Senegal, Madagascar, Democratic Republic of Congo, Somalia, Benin, Niger, Burkina Faso, Cote d'lvoire, Chad, Central African Republic, Congo, Gabon, Nigeria and Mauritania.

5 Colonel Sadat's book describing how King Farouk had been deposed by sending him away from Egypt on his yacht reportedly impressed them (Greenfield 1965, 381).

6 A leaflet issued by the chief of staff to encourage civilians to capture the fleeing rebels stated: "People who seek to establish a truth should not run away" (Greenfield 1965, 434).

7 It was with a sense of the importance of seizing this opportunity that the late Eshetu Chole wrote his challenging paper, "Ethiopia at the Crossroads" from 1992, published online at www.eeaecon.org/pubs.

8 "Fatal Footprint: The Global Human Impact of Cluster Munitions." Handicap International Report, November 2006; published online at http://www.handicap-international.org.uk//files/Fatal%20Footprint%20FINAL.pdf

9 One account concludes: "The Eritrean-Tigrayan elite has been bent on exporting conflicts and engaged in a self-destructive mission in the whole region" (Tadesse 1999, 190).

10 The phrase "An Ethiopian Dilemma" alludes to the first talk I gave to an Ethiopian audience regarding problems of their future. This was at the May 1961 Washington DC conference of ESANA, the Ethiopian Students Association of North America. The talk began with a preemptive move to disarm those who might object to my presuming to say something useful to Ethiopians with the attitude "Ferinji, min yaweqal?" What can a ferinji possibly understand about us? I referred then to the contribution of a Swedish sociologist, Gunnar Myrdal, whose work brought fresh understanding to the United States public about its simmering crisis of race relations.

11 According to Greenfield, "an ambiguous reply he made early in 1960 to a remark of Mengistu's and the fact that Merid's grandfather, Dejazmatch Mangasha, had been out of favour with Haile Sellassie, led Mengistu to assume—mistakenly as it turned out—that Merid would support an attempted coup" (Greenfield 1965, 378). And Merid himself, shortly before dying a few years later, reportedly expressed remorse over his suppression of the Mengistu coup, saying "I regret nothing so much in my life."

12 For an interpretation of the differing narratives that underlay this mutual distrust, see Levine 2006.

13 This, too, was something described in *Wax and Gold* and related publications of the time (1965b, 1966, 1968) as well as in later publications (1974, 2005).

14 Saving face is important in all cultures, but in those permeated by martial values it ranks high and valorizes extreme reactions.

15 Meles Zenawi confessed in a Tigrinya publication that he had felt at his best when fighting in the bush, and the standoff in 2005 arguably owes something to a determined pride in not giving in to the other.

16 This is so even if the reported figures of 35% dropping to 2.5% are exaggerated. What is clear is that erosion due to the decline of woodland has been responsible for flooding and impoverished topsoil, and this at a time when the loss of good soil no longer benefits Egypt but clogs up her dams with silt.

31

The Promise of Ethiopia:

*Public Action; Civic Forgiveness; Creative Power (2008)**

Beset on all sides by states riven with strife, political crisis, and human misery, Ethiopia stands at a crossroads. Will she join the company of those troubled states through an escalation of internal strife and repression compounded by increasing levels of chronic poverty, disease, and hunger?—or will she step forward to be the exemplar for Africa her friends and admirers have long hoped she would become once again?

In a pair of talks last year I discussed five missed opportunities for constructive, peaceful change over the past half century: the failed coup d'état of December 1960, the stolen peaceful revolution of 1974, the contested liberation of 1991, the gratuitous war of 1998, and the broken promise of multi-party elections in 2005.[1] This millennial year offers a good time for all Ethiopians, including those Ethiopians who call themselves Eritreans, to ask how that pattern of missed

---

* Presented originally at the conference "Fostering Shared Core National Values: Expanding Common Political Space in the New Ethiopian Millennium," organized by InterAfricaGroup, United Nations Conference Center, Addis Ababa, Ethiopia, January 15, 2008. Helpful inputs along the way were provided by Alula Pankhurst, Bereket Habte Selassie, Chaim Rosen, Charles Schaefer, Daniel Abebe, Getatchew Haile, Mehari Maru, Shawel Betru, Solomon Gashaw, and Dan Slater. Published originally in *International Journal of Ethiopian Studies*, Vol. 3, No. 2 (Winter / Spring 2008), pp.103-122.

opportunities might be transcended by drawing on traditions of constructive decision-making that are deeply rooted in Ethiopian culture.

Need for a Public

The Inter Africa Group's (IAG) mission statement and objective reads as follows and note what words jump out:

Mission: To enhance democratization and good governance in Ethiopia by facilitating **public** participation in policy making and ensuring **public** access to *government* information.

Objective: The program aims to build **public** influence on *government* policy and **public** access to *government* through policy dialogue, research and advocacy to enhance *government* awareness and understanding of **public** needs, aspirations and views on *government* policy.

In those sentences the words "government" and "public" each appear five times. The former word, Amharic *mengist*, is a very old hereabouts and familiar to every Ethiopian citizen. On the other hand, the word "public" is fairly new, and I doubt if it can be rendered in Amharic at all.[2]

That is not surprising. The idea of a public is relatively new in world history, even though it was embodied in the *poleis* of ancient Greece and had some currency in Roman times with the notion of *res publica*. Yet the idea of the public has become a major concern in some of the milestones of contemporary political thought.

One way to account for this is to note that processes often linked under the rubric of modernization—the expansion of cities, markets, polities, technology, and media—have bridged historic gaps between centers of societies and their "peripheral" populations. Consider, for example, the huge distance between historic Ethiopia's political center, the imperial court, and its far-flung peoples. Local rule counted for far more than that of the center in routine directives—*ke-negus/ ye-agar balambaras*. It took a long course of *dej tinat* to approach a regional ras, let alone the *negusa negast*.

As modernization processes enveloped Western Europe and North America, and eventually the globe, those distances shrank. It became easier to mobilize people with demands from and to the societal center. This shift came to a head with the French Revolution, where popular mobs coalesced to make demands of and eventually overthrow the monarchy. Heightened popular demands through the 19th century prompted observers like Gustav le Bon to analyze "The Crowd" as a novel social form. Unruly crowd behavior led many to fear the phenomenon of mob action. Against that fear, sociologist Robert Park ([1904] 1972) contrasted the mob with a different form of collective behavior which, following his mentor John Dewey, he called the Public. In the Crowd, Park wrote, a large group of people become as one, responding to a given object with the same value and passions. In the Public, by contrast, members of a group focus on the same object, but respond to it differently; they bring different ideas and values to the discussion of common issues.[3] Dewey himself went on, in *The Public and Its Problems* (1927), to analyze conditions that give rise to a public. Dewey sees this happening when citizens develop a shared interest in solving problems and then deliberate in order to find legislation to solve those problems.

Does Ethiopia need an informed national public? Do its citizens find common cause in wanting to address such issues as: growing rates of poverty and malnutrition; epidemics of AIDS and other diseases; massive deforestation; threatening population growth; land tenure; under-education of females; electoral reform; addiction to foreign aid; and the like? If so, then Dewey may be a good consultant. What is essential to forming a public, Dewey claimed, is "improvement of the methods and conditions of debate, discussion, and persuasion" ([1927] 1984, 365). And because he believed that the knowledge needed in political solutions to problems had to be generated by the interaction of citizens, elites, and experts, through the mediation and facilitation of journalism, *then not just the government is held accountable, but the citizens, experts, and media professionals must be held accountable as well.* With a well-formed and active public, it should no longer be possible to blame everything good or everything bad that happens on a single, exaggeratedly potent leader.

To say that modern societies need to form active and enlightened publics is not to say that it is easy to create them. Indeed, some of the most trenchant theorists of the public, like Walter Lippman and Morris Janowitz, have highlighted poignantly the difficulties of sustaining them. For Lippman, the fact that most citizens lack the competence and the will to participate in the political process means that the notion of a public competent to direct public affairs represents a "false ideal." However precarious this ideal, it has continued to inspire most theorists of democracy, who follow Dewey's notion that, however difficult, democracies could form a 'Great Community,' consisting of a number of publics, which could become educated about issues, make judgments, and pose solutions to societal problems.[4] This tradition of thought was summarized ably just a few months ago by Nancy Fraser, who defined the public sphere as having two dimensions: a space where public discussion "is supposed to discredit views that cannot withstand critical scrutiny and to assure the legitimacy of those who do" and "a vehicle for marshaling public opinion as a political force [in order] to hold officials accountable and assure that actions of the state express the will of the citizenry" (2007, 7).[5]

In Ethiopia, this notion of an active societal public must contend with centuries-old habits of deference to authority. Historically, affairs at the center were handled by central authorities who did not need to consult with subjects and nor could even communicate with them readily. Overthrowing the monarchy changed this situation—but for the worse. The Derg opened channels of communication with the peripheries but used them to command, not listen to, an increasingly mobilized citizenry. The present regime took steps to improve the situation through a more open if still tightly-controlled press and multiple party system. This process advanced notably during 2004, but so reversed itself in the aftermath of the May 2005 election that the Committee to Protect Journalists named Ethiopia as the "world's worst backslider on press freedom."

Nevertheless, the 2005 election amounted to a huge step forward. For one thing, it occasioned open debates among spokesmen for plural political parties, which betokened a courageous display of genuine public actions on all sides. At the same time, it occasioned an unprecedented spontaneous entrance of masses into a political arena. To be sure, no one knew quite how to handle what turned into crowd behaviors. Serious mistakes were made on all sides—which suggested to some observers that Ethiopia was "not ready for democracy."

But is that really so? Dewey argues that local communities are essential building blocks for a democratic public, places where people engage issues of communal concern and thus gain practice in ways of communicating that form a great community. He finds the template for American democracy to be the town meetings of New England. In that perspective, one could say that Ethiopia is exceptionally well endowed for forming a national public. Nearly all local traditions in the Greater Ethiopian culture area exhibit some form of public action, through which persons display habits of communal concern, mutual respect, effective conflict resolution, and public problem-solving. Their levels of communal responsibility and civility of conduct might put to shame many modern urbanized Ethiopians, at home and in the Diaspora—not to mention members of the United States Congress. The rancorous polarizations of the past fifteen years, especially following the 2005 elections, have kept such capacities from coming to the fore. Let us consider a sample of these local traditions.

Local Traditions of Public Communication

Consider the Qemant, who maintain formal councils of elders. Presided over by an *alaqa* who is elected yearly, these councils deal with judicial and administrative problems. The Qemant also have ad hoc informal councils formed at the request of two litigants, who personally choose five to seven council members and a leader. In addition, they form numerous ad hoc subcouncils, which allow nearly every Qemant male to participate sometime during his life in the government of his community (Gamst 1969, 58).

Consider Tigray and Tigrinya-speaking Eritrea, home of customs like the *baito*. a village meeting chaired by elected elders in an open court wherein people can argue their points openly about village matters, and the *debter,* a written agreement akin to a constitution, which everyone agrees to uphold as the law of the village.

Consider the Gurage, who organize councils at two levels: the clan council, which works to resolve local disputes according to established norms, and a pan-tribal council known as *yejoka*, which administer customary law through moral suasion and ritual sanctions, and can enact new laws. The *yejoka* is animated by the principle of *ang*, justice, a sense that proper compensation will be made when a person's rights are infringed and enjoins an even-handed apportionment of whatever resources are at hand (Shack 1966, 157–65).

Consider the Sidama, who employ two kinds of public forums for adjudicating disputes, a council of clan leaders, called *Gudamaalee* ("place of justice"), and neighborhood councils of elders. The elders councils handle such issues as personal quarrels, disputes over land boundaries, cases of theft, and cattle destroying crops. The council of clan leaders deals with disputes between clans (and also homicide). Gudumaalee refers to a place where the councilors sit on the ground, without chair or bench, under one of the trees. Elders who might come from different villages to attend hearings sit circling the council members. Any passer-by except women can watch and engage the process. Councils pass decisions after free and open debate not only between disputants and witnesses, but also by all discussants who are present at the session. Hearings normally conclude with compromise and reconciliation, which prevents lasting enmity between disputants and their families (Alula and Getachew 2008).

Consider the Konso councils of elders, *hiyoda*, whose members debate issues of public concern and act as a court of justice, and can call on a warrior grade—the Hrela—to enforce their decisions and arrest criminals (Hallpike 1972, 68). Each Konso town ward elects a councilor. The only hereditary official, the *ballabat*, although from an eminent priestly family, still can be ousted if citizens do not like him. Each town also has a body of men who are peacemakers, the *Apa Dawras*, who rush between quarreling factions and throw down their staves of office on the ground to separate them, since staves are thought to have mystical powers and anyone who steps over them might incur death (72).

Konso articulate the value of bringing issues into the open for public vetting. They place a premium on what they call *dehamda*, discussion. Only in nonviolent discussion, they say, can citizens manifest *dugada*, truth. At public gatherings they uphold norms aimed at unruly neighbors and exhort everyone to behave properly. In the face of human tendencies to be self-serving and dishonest they proclaim *afa pisa olini dagini*, when "all voices are heard together," as a guiding ideal of social relations (132).

Perhaps the most fully developed of Ethiopia's proto-democratic local traditions appears in Oromo culture—in customs preserved, preeminently, among the Borana and the Guji. At one level they surface in talk about local issues, like access to water from wells. Boran take their cows for water every couple of days, and an office-holder, the Aba Harega, draws up a schedule for visits to the well. If someone needs water from a well owned by another clan, he appeals to the clan owners who hold a meeting to decide if he may use it. Since mud wells need constant repair, all clan members are expected to help keep them up. Whoever fails to help must slaughter a cow for the others, or he will not be permitted to use the well. Social cohesion that forms around the wells provides a cushion for dealing with conflictual issues. More generally, in the words of a Borana man: "If there is a problem we investigate it with the help of the traditional judges: the elders. We all come to the shadow of the tree to discuss the problem. Anyone in the community can voice their opinions and problems are discussed until we resolve them."

This approach to dealing with problems is amplified at the octennial parliamentary meetings of all clans known as the *Gumi Gayo*, the Great Gathering. These gatherings embody the Oromo conviction that laws stand above all men. Precedent in judicial and legislative matters is taken seriously, but laws are open to change and amendment. Constituents routinely judge the competence of their leaders. Leaders are elected for a single term of finite length, expecting that they will turn over the reigns of governance smoothly to a properly appointed successor cohort. A trial period between election and investiture, during which leaders are elected to lower office and promoted to higher office once their competence is confirmed, ensures that no politician takes office on the basis of campaign bluster alone. A rule of staggered succession prevents transitional crises; discontinuity of authority makes it hard for any group to get entrenched, while oversight and counseling reduce dilettantism and errors from inexperience.

At these large assemblies, Borana rules and regulations are reiterated and possibly changed, and leaders of the tribe for the next eight years are elected. Those assemblies exemplify public discussion at its best. To facilitate mutual respect in democratic deliberations, various customs encourage civility in public discourse. Sessions begin with invocations that promote peace (*nagaa*); they encourage speakers to avoid provoking resentments or use the floor to upstage or "score points" against others. Speakers are not to make accusations or to show anger. What is more, the pace of decision-making and the expectation of paying serious regard to precedent ensures that weighty decisions, like going on the warpath, are not made rashly.

So, if one heeds John Dewey's claim that the roots of democratic publics lie in local communities—places where people can engage issues of public concern in mutually respectful ways and so lay the groundwork for webs of communication that form a larger public—then Ethiopia is well on the way. The question is then: how can these local communities be interconnected so their habits of public deliberation can rise into a national conversation?

Ethiopia does not start from scratch. Ethnic groups of the larger Ethiopian culture area have been interconnected in numerous ways for centuries, as I demonstrated in *Greater Ethiopia: The Evolution of a Multiethnic Society*. They have been connected through markets and the exchange of services, through extensive systems of Christian and Islamic religious institutions, through intermarriage and adoptive practices like the *gudifacha*, through interreligious celebrations and common pilgrimages, through widespread migrations and the like. Indeed, it is because I feared that this historical intermingling would be curtailed that I have expressed concerns about certain consequences of the system of ethnic federalism, insofar as it tends to reinforce exclusive tribal identities without affording adequate space for other subnational, national, and global identities.

Beyond that, Amhara-Tigrayan traditions led the way to national community by establishing a multiethnic polity at least two millennia old. Although Amhara-Tigrayan traditions do not include deliberative settings like the Gumi Gayo, they encompass customs that figure as ingredients for communal action. I shall mention four of them: *chelot*, *mahiber*, religious protests, and *zemetcha*—each of which represents an ingredient that could be reconfigured in the process of creating a national public.

Chelot, the traditional form of dispute adjudication above the informal reconciliation by elders, brought persons into a civil scenario where they would litigate about such matters as rights to land use, inheritance, alleged theft, and insults. It was customary for every Abyssinian male to show a minimum of competence in litigating and, when a dispute became heated, to reach for the nearest elder to sit and hear their claims and render some resolution.[6] The institution of *chelot* ranged from the impromptu court under a tree to formal hearings before a nobleman to the highest court of all, that of the emperor.

Whereas Abyssinians entered *chelot* on behalf of personal interests pursued in a public space, they formed organizations known as *mahiber* and *iddir* for communal ends. Each *mahiber* was dedicated to a particular saint and on the monthly saint's day its members congregate in one another's homes. At times *mahiber* undertake communal projects, such as helping a family that lost one of its members. *Mahiber* often function as mutual assistance groups, whose members contribute a fixed monthly fee that helps cover expenses related to weddings, funerals, births, and illness. More recently, another group known as *iddir* has evolved, specifically for the purpose of offsetting costs and handling arrangements for funerals, and other special expenses. The *iddir* have grown into models of secular democratic conduct, often having "elected" officials and even written bylaws. And *mahiber* subsequently become vehicles for urban associations at home and abroad that render assistance to their home *agar*.

A third proto-public element, I suggest, appears in instances when spiritual figures spoke out against the immoral behavior of rulers. Thanks to the autonomy of ecclesiastical institutions, traditional church education could inculcate moral instruction that stood independent of the vicissitudes of political pressure (Messay 2006). Records of religiously-grounded moral protests appears as early as the first Ethiopic written documents. In the reign of Emperor Yishaq (1414–29) some two dozen judges protested against his cruel treatment of the Beta Israel, for which they were dismissed from office. In some cases critics paid with their lives. Abuna Takla Hawaryat wanted to present a protest directly to Emperor Zar'a Ya'qob (1434–68), voicing his objection to the brutal treatment of civilians by the king's soldiers. Denied an audience, he asked a courtier to deliver his message to the king who, wrathful over such criticism, confronted him at once and ordered him sent to jail, where he died (Getatchew1994: 98, 108). In other cases protests bore fruit, resulting even in the overthrowing of emperors, as when Susneyos was deposed for converting to Catholicism.

Finally, consider the role of the warrior and the military campaign, or *zemetcha*. Although moved by an individualistic ethic to some extent, Abyssinian soldiers were quick to heed calls of lords and kings to defend their *agar* up to and including that of their national homeland. Their determination was manifest in numerous campaigns against invaders. Rousing battle chants known as *shillela* changed the posture of warriors from that of anonymous foot-soldiers to protagonists in a public cause. Although at times the *shillela* became competitive contests in which two or more warriors took turns affirming their commitment to martial courage and engagement, the verbal artistry of the one who chanted out the *shillela* serve to articulate the sentiments of the collectivity of soldiers. The high point of Ethiopian *zemetcha* was surely the battle of Adwa, which in a sense figured as the first major manifestation of a pan-ethnic national public in modern Ethiopian history (Levine 1996).

Conditions for a GREATER Public

What might be helpful in converting such resources into a genuinely effective national public in Ethiopia? For one set of such ideas I turn to a challenging work by the eminent political philosopher Hannah Arendt, *The Human Condition* (1958). Although its point of departure is more existential than practical, the book complements Dewey's view of the public as an agency for addressing common problems by seeing it as a site for meaningful *action*, a public space where others can witness and give meaning to one's actions. Politics, she holds, provides an arena where persons can disclose themselves through free speech and persuasion—and thereby encounter one another as members of a community.

Like Dewey, Arendt finds a public sphere essential for attaining societal power. And power arises when humans act together, and when words and deeds join together: "where words are not empty and deeds not brutal, where words are not used to veil intentions but to disclose realities, and deeds are not used to violate and destroy but to establish relations and create new realities" (Arendt 1958, 178–9). Since tyrannical regimes spring from a condition of *isolation*, which engenders a sense of impotence and futility among the rulers as well as the ruled, they have little creative power. In this perspective, the Amharic saying—*Dir biyabir Anbessa yassir*—represents not the mere massing of people but their active participation in a community of mutual understanding.

To manifest a public and the power it generates is no simple matter. For Arendt, public action involves some five ingredients. These are 1) courage; 2) common objects; 3) diverse perspectives; 4) forgiveness; and 5) promise.

Courage—In Arendt's perspective, the private and sheltered world of the household serves survival needs mainly. It takes a certain amount of courage to leave the household for some enterprise on behalf of the common weal. For this reason Classic Greek authors tended to name courage as the preeminent political virtue (33). Arendt goes further. She claims that courage is already present in leaving one's private hiding place and showing who one is, in disclosing one's mind and exposing one's self (166).[7]

Common objects—Even if persons venture forth to speak in public, a true public forms only when a plurality of actors hold some object in common. A common world cannot survive the destruction of this shared object. This can happen under conditions of extreme isolation, where nobody can agree with anybody else, as often occurs in tyrannies; but also under conditions of mass hysteria, where diverse people behave as a single unit, each imitating his neighbor.

Diverse perspectives—So a public realm requires not only the same object, it requires that its participants feel free to and have the opportunity to express their own views in an open public space. As Arendt summarizes this condition: "The end of the common world has come when it is seen only under one aspect and is permitted to present itself in only one perspective" (53). This point recapitulates an essential notion of the public forwarded by Park and Dewey.

Forgiveness—Besides courage, common objects, and diversity, Arendt specifies two more elements relevant to forming a public: Forgiveness and Promise. Forgiveness is essential because we all make mistakes. All deeds take place in a context of other actors, each of whom can have a reaction that in turn initiates multiple responses from others. It is impossible to predict for sure the consequences of one's actions. What is more, once an action has taken place, it is irreversible. This produces a predicament: unpredictability means that one could not have known exactly what one was doing, irreversibility means that one can never undo what one has done. So we are all of us bound to make mistakes that cannot be undone: *Ke-sew sihetet/ Ke-beret zeget/ Aytefam*. The only escape from this predicament is forgiveness. Since forgiving and acting are tied so tightly, a public cannot long survive without expressions of forgiveness on all sides.

Promise—Unpredictability stems not only from the unbounded consequences due to the reactions of other free actors, but also from unreliability, since other actors may or may not do what they are expected to do. Against this endemic unpredictability of actions people can have resource to a distinctively human faculty, the power of making promises. To make a promise is to make the future a little more predictable. Think of the institution of the *wass*.

Resources for a National Public

Turning again to the Amhara-Tigrayan traditions, which are responsible for Ethiopia's long existence as a multiethnic polity, one finds a store of elements that could be conjoined to form a public at the national level as well. Imagine combining the forthrightness of public debate in *chelot*, of communal engagement as in the *mahiber*, of critical engagement as with the moral protesters, and of courageous enlistment on behalf of communal defense as in the *zemetcha*. This sense of taking an active part in Ethiopia's national public certainly was manifest in the conduct of Ethiopians in the remarkable turn-out for the elections of May 2005.

What concrete steps might Ethiopians take to activate a national public? First they need *access* to public media; then they need to *participate* in networks of communication; then they have to identify and articulate and prioritize public *needs*; and then they need to exert *influence* on legislative and implementation processes.

The technology for mass communication is at hand. Ethiopians already have considerable experience as receivers. A task force concerned with enlarging the public sphere might well investigate ways and means of refining that technology.

The next step would be to expand the circle of users and to instill higher standards of responsibility and a larger scope of imagination in using the media. There is much to be gained by scrupulous adherence to the evolving liberalized Press Law and by using the media, as Lippman urged, both to call attention to emerging issues and to transmit pertinent facts from policy-makers and from experts. In particular, all concerned could strive to give more publicity to national issues through local media—local radios have proven particularly useful elsewhere in Africa—and to cultivate national attention to local issues.[8]

As for engaging in public discourse and action, Ethiopia has only to retrieve and expand elements of its traditions that correspond to the principles enunciated by Arendt. Let us examine them one by one.

Common object—As often noted, Ethiopia is privileged in relation to the rest of sub-Saharan Africa by virtue of standing as an ancient multiethnic polity that maintained independence during the European Scramble for Africa. The symbol of Ethiopia has been a recurrent object of attention for millennia. Indigenous inscriptions naming Ethiopia go back to the 4th century CE. External attention included numerous references to the Ethiopian kingdom in early Persian, Christian, and Muslim sources, and by the use of Ethiopia as a symbol to inspire African leaders in their quest for independence and African Americans in their struggles for equal rights. This symbolism has constituted the kind of shared object that Arendt finds crucial for the formation of publics.

I fear that fewer Ethiopians than ever are aware of these facts. The obsession with Westernized modernization that gripped the country in the post-War decades precluded a decent respect for the warning issued by Aleqa Asres in 1945:

> A youth who does not know about his or her history is like a person who drinks alcohol without putting food in his stomach. These students will get drunk quickly and will be bitter towards their own people. For Ethiopia's problem, they will seek foreign (alien) solutions because they wouldn't know that the solution is in their own backyard. As a consequence, they themselves become the problem. (cited Aleme 2008).

Ethiopian students, like so many others in Africa, became far more acquainted with Western history and institutions than with their own, leading to a denigration of their nation as backward. Under the Derg an entire generation was taught in school that everything in Ethiopia's past was bad, just like under the Maoist regime in China. And then, during the heyday of ethnocentric self-affirmations that began in the late 1960s, the symbolism of national identity itself came under attack. A rash of liberationist groups began to espouse ethnocentric ideologies. Revisionist historians associated with the EPLF, TPLF, EPRP, and OLF composed narratives that omitted the achievements of historic Ethiopia.

The current regime began by equating Ethiopian nationalism with chauvinism and gave ethnic identity a privileged status over a common over-arching collective identity. Ethiopia came to be defined as nothing more than an assemblage of separate "nations" and "nationalities." The adoption of an ethnic federalist system, however well-intentioned and whatever short-term gains it affords, created a risk that younger generations may no longer identify with historic Ethiopia but with their artificially circumscribed ethnic boundaries alone. What is more, heightened ethnocentrism inhibits civil discourse across *kilil* boundaries and accentuates a political consciousness that to some extent runs counter to our globalized world. The very word *kilil,* unlike *kifle agar*, connotes separateness, being fenced apart.

The noted political scientist Dankwart Rustow, in a classic paper (1970), demonstrated that the only precondition for democracy is the experience of national unity. If there were one grand effort that might promote an Ethiopian national public, it might be to revive and disseminate the authentic narratives about Ethiopia's past, her present claims for attention, and her future promise—including a narrative that does justice to the past of regions that came to be called Eritrea and that were entirely part of Ethiopian life right up to 1896, and to assimilationist measures that neglected or suppressed important regional and ethnic claims.

Diverse Perspectives—The toleration, indeed welcoming, of diverse perspectives essential to a functioning public can draw on numerous exemplars from Ethiopia's traditions. Habits of wholly confrontational discourse are recent, the products of alienation from Ethiopia's own civilized traditions. What would it be like to show dramatizations of *mwoget* at *chelot*, in which divergent claims are aired respectfully before a judge or elder, and the latter articulates the claims on both sides and renders a reasoned judgment? What would it be like to show dramatizations of the proceedings of an Oromo *gumi gayo*, where participants are advised to listen respectfully to one another, and peaceful resolutions of heated disputes unfold in a civil manner? It might be instructive for urbanized Ethiopians to see how their rural countrymen can disagree, deliberate, forgive, and recognize that *chiq-a-chiq, mesedadeb*, and violence are by no means the primary ways in which Ethiopians customarily resolve disputes.

Courage—To speak of courage in an Ethiopian context is like bringing coals to Newcastle. Yet however valiant the Ethiopian *wetadar,* that is not the kind of courage needed for forming today's public. First, however, it might be useful to acknowledge and own the fierce masculinity ethic that persists among virtually all ethnic groups in Ethiopia (Levine 2001, 2004).

Ethiopian males pride themselves on their toughness. They point with pride to the remarkable achievement of a common soldier of the old Imperial Bodyguard, Abebe Bikila who, running barefoot and without athletic training, unexpectedly won the marathon race in the World Olympics at Rome in 1960 and again in Tokyo in 1964—inspiring generations of Ethiopian athletes to follow his example, down to our own Haile Gebre-Selassie. The Western world took sharp notice of the performance of Ethiopian troops, in United Nations expeditions in Korea and in the Congo, where their capacity for enduring hardships and their flashes of exceptional valor impressed many observers. The world was stunned by how the Ethiopian forces held back invading Italians in 1896, and forty years later when, despite military defeat, the story was one of heroic defense, in which Ethiopians armed with spears and rifles fought against a war machine that included airplanes and poison gas; and many of whom continued, after defeat, an underground resistance throughout the enemy Occupation (Levine 1966).

The *zemetcha* are populated by warriors of this sort, those who display, as an Italian observer once wrote, an "unreasoning offensive spirit." Their combination of courage, stamina, and zeal has been manifest historically in two directions. They fought on behalf of and under the command of legitimate authorities, be it the *ras* and the *negus* of the Amhara-Tigrayan peoples or the *abba gada* and *abba dula* of the Oromo. On the other hand, when a warrior could no longer abide the authority he fell under, he had the option of *meshefet.* To rebel and take to the bush was also a kind of cultural ideal in traditional Ethiopia. Stories of successful rebels were told and retold—of the likes of Dejazmatch (later Ras) Woldemikael of Hamasien, whose rebellious spirit was celebrated by popular song, "*Imbi ale Woldu, imbi ale!*" (Wolde refused, he just said 'No'!), or the *shifta* Kassa Haylu, who fought his way to power on the way to becoming Emperor Tewodros. The *meshefet* template came to be applied by ideological oppositional groups, from *Tateq* (gird for battle) and *Tigil* (fight) of radical youth movements to liberation fronts under the Derg.

However adaptive the *meshefet* pattern was earlier, when outlets for civil opposition under the old hierarchical system did not exist, it obstructs the formation of a civil public. So, in fact, does the idealization of martial aggressiveness. While a public requires divergent opinions, those opinions must be expressed verbally. It involves, to cite the title of a dissertation about local politics in the town of Adwa, "Warring with Words" (Rosen 1974). As one expatriate wrote me, "Ethiopia will never progress until we learn to fight as hard within the system as we do against the system." It may take more courage in some quarters just to say that openly than to take up arms in the field.

The challenge of civic courage offers a wide field for experimentation. In courts, it could appear in new forms of what lawyers call "judicial daring." In universities, it could appear in efforts to break through the clouds of fear that impede open discourse, such as were revealed in a recent report from the flagship university at Mekelle (Salisbury 2008). Those who speak out would need to be aware and confident of their constitutional rights as citizens and the protection of a legally supported independent press.

Forgiveness—Any nation that lives through traumatic conflicts needs to experience forgiveness. Aggrieved parties tend to bask in their sense of victimization, aggressors to fortify themselves with self-righteous arrogance. Such dynamics escalated in Ethiopia in recent decades, as revolutionaries on all sides adopted the demonizing rhetoric of the Marxist canon, which compounded traditional habits of personalizing disputes about issues. Young people today may be puzzled and disturbed by those polarizing charges and counter-charges; they need to learn about traditional thoughtways that take a more accepting view of human aggression (Levine 1965), and of customs of forgiveness that imbue Ethiopia's cultural fabric.[9]

Ethiopia's rulers often followed victory over an enemy by some gesture of forgiveness, if only to restore social equilibrium and discourage impulses to revenge.[10] The monasteries of highland Ethiopia, travelers noted, did much to mold the peace-making process. The judges and kings of Israel were their models. Samuel Gobat observed, "The Abyssinians are very easily provoked to anger; but they are as easily reconciled to each other" (Gobat 1834, 358). Emperor Tewodros, crazed with vengeance late in life, was observed early in his reign to have "exercised the utmost clemency towards the vanquished, treating them rather as his friends than his enemies" (Dufton 1867). Emperor Yohannes made peace with Menelik after defeating the latter. Emperor Menelik personally put butter on the wound of Negus Tekle Haymanot of Gojjam after crushing the latter's rebellion. Ras Tafari Makonnen, after defeating thousands of Negus Mikael's rebels at the battle of Segele, performed what Harold Marcus describes as "a remarkable act of clemency," when he renounced vengeance and declared "We are all Ethiopians" (Marcus 1987, 24). On return from exile in 1941, Haile Selassie forbade vengeance against Italians remaining in the country, and showed clemency toward Ethiopian collaborators.

The Ethiopian penchant for forgiveness can be traced to religious traditions. Although information about the non-Semitic religions remains scant, we know that forgiveness figures importantly in the Abrahamic religions, all three of which have deep roots in Ethiopian culture. Judaism requires individuals to acknowledge their sins and ask for forgiveness. *Teshuvah*, repentance, becomes particularly salient during the ten days of personal penitence leading to pleas for communal forgiveness on Yom Kippur, the Day of Atonement.[11] Rabbinic traditions identify five elements of repentance—recognition of one's sins as sins (*hakarát ha-chét*), remorse (*charatá*), desisting from sin (*azivát ha-chét*), restitution where possible (*peira'ón*), and confession (*vidúi*); each is required for forgiveness by others and by God. Ethiopia's Jews, the Beta Israel (also known as Falasha), incorporate repentance in their prayers, indeed reciting every evening a prayer in which they ask for forgiveness for their sins. They also observe the equivalent of Yom Kippur, which they call Astaserayo, meaning "forgiveness of sins."[12]

Both sides of this process, Repentance and Forgiveness, are stressed in Christianity and Islam no less. The Gospels of Matthew and Luke contain the Prayer that presents the matter with memorable brevity: "Forgive us our sins, as we forgive those who sin against us." St. Mark puts it graphically: "When you stand praying, if you hold anything against anyone, forgive him, so that your Father in heaven may forgive you your sins" (Mark 11:25). And the Passion of St. Luke expresses the forgiveness of *selicha* with unforgettable poignancy: "Father, forgive them; for they know not what they do" (Luke 23:34).

The Islamic canon parallels the Jewish requirements for being forgiven: acknowledge the offense, promise not to repeat it, make amends, ask pardon of the offended party, and ask God for forgiveness. The Qur'an describes believers as persons who forgive when angered as well as who avoid vice. Common Muslim prayers contain phrases such as *Astaghfiru-Allah*, "I ask forgiveness from Allah." Several passages in the Qur'an repeat this theme: "Keep to forgiveness, and enjoin kindness" (Qur'an 7:199–200). "If one is patient in adversity and forgives—this, behold, is indeed something to set one's heart upon" (42:43).

The Ethiopian disposition toward forgiveness may be dimmed but it is not forgotten. Listen to these words from a letter written to me spontaneously by a young friend:

> I lost my father . . . in 1970 in a war [for which] he was never trained. My father was a very diligent farmer . . . He decided to fight because as an Ethiopian man he was not meant to flee with mothers and children. We went to a refugee camp in Dire Dawa. I was at the verge of death because of an epidemic in the camp. . . . Hence, I was raised hating Somalia, especially Siad Bare. As I grew up I realized that my past should never spoil my future. I forgave . . . all parties to my losses.
>
> There is a lot of grudge in Ethiopia but we have to discuss it in good spirit [realizing] that we all are human beings with a real chance of learning

> from our mistakes. [Ethiopians tend to presume that] Governments leaders know everything and that their mistakes are always intentional. We forget that we are all just humans.

Recently we saw a shining instance of Ethiopian forgiveness. Imprisoned politicians, some of whom may have encouraged some of their supporters to engage in actions that could be construed as illegal—including violent actions against Ethiopian policemen and innocent civilians—apologized for that mistake and asked for forgiveness. In response, the President of Ethiopia pardoned them and released them from prison. Those gestures brought a sigh of relief to countless Ethiopians and progress toward a national public.

And now, consider how much greater the relief—and how much progress toward a vigorous public might be made—if converse gestures were expressed. What an empowering step for Ethiopia if something like the following would be said:

> In June and November 2005, in the course of protecting public security, agents of the Federal Republic of Ethiopia killed many innocent Ethiopian civilians. For those actions and any others that resemble them, we who support the EPRDF are deeply sorry. We ask our fellow Ethiopians for forgiveness for those terrible deeds. We ask the Government to take steps to prevent such actions in the future and to send belated messages of regret to the people of Ethiopia.

Responsibility for such actions in a democracy extends to others beyond government officials. However, any official government pronouncement of that sort, far from being viewed as a sign of weakness, might restore confidence in those who support the current regime and reactivate a sense that all Ethiopians are members of a single public community.[13] It could open the door to an evolving program of restorative justice, which would include the admission of past wrongs by all political forces, including official acknowledgement of past misdeeds without naming individual perpetrators, but mentioning victims in general.

Most Ethiopians can probably claim to have been aggrieved from one side or another. The aggrieved usually want to hold on to their grudges, blaming others and seeking vengeance instead of rapprochement. In a country where nearly everyone counts as *ye-tewegga*, what is to happen? In response to that question, I have composed a little *gitim*:

"Ye-wegga biresa	"While the attacker may forget
Ye-tewegga ayresa"	The attacked one forgets not"
Endetebale irgit new;	Is an old saying, to be sure;
Ine gin yemilew:	But I would like to say:

Yiqirta kalgebba	Without bringing in forgiveness
Selamim aygebba.	There can never be peace.

IN SUM: All sides need some space in which to vent their hurt and anger over what they believe others have done; in which to be heard; and in which to listen to all of the others.

The Promise of Ethiopia

Promise—To her discourse on the importance of forgiveness, Hannah Arendt juxtaposes the idea of promise. Her argument, again, is that the unpredictability of all courses of action creates uncertainty and confusion, which can be relieved by promising actions to which pertinent stakeholders will subscribe. To promise something in an uncharted future amounts to offering promise for the future. Ethiopians know the double meanings of *tesfa*. They need hope today as much as they need *berberé*. All Ethiopians—from *ye-bét agar, ye-wutch agar*, and *ye-cyber-agar*[14]—want promises about the country's future in order to revitalize their commitments.

The traditional pattern has been to wait for such pronouncements from a central authority. Putting all this weight on a single figure leads both to undue idealization and to undue demonization.[15] The Prime Minister should be commended for urging his countrymen to come forth and participate openly in a national discourse. Even though some who have done so may have paid a large price, that has surely not been true for all. What might happen if a large number of Ethiopian citizens took him seriously?

This *could* happen, *qas be-qas*, if more public-minded organizations issued statements in a Deweyan mode: identifying issues, formulating problems, assessing resources, examining options. They could do so through existing media; they could start a print, radio, or TV forum of their own. To catch attention they could employ colorful means, like the young players of the Awassa OneLove Theatre, who capture attention for their message about AIDS-prevention through a circus with awesome gymnastics. They could do something dramatic like the residents of Adwa in 1947, when they petitioned the Emperor about the oppressive rule of their *awraja gej*, then tied some meat to a copy of the petition and placed it to attract an eagle, for it to swoop down and carry the petition to God Almighty—"*coppia le-semay*," they called it (Rosen 1974).

Whatever tactics are chosen, the priority for a working public must be a commitment to identifying problems and nonviolent solutions. Moving beyond blame and self-pity, public-minded citizens can look to openings and collaborative initiatives. The experience of sustained public questioning and deliberation could have a transforming effect on Ethiopia. It will be thrilling to see it happening again at the national level—as it has so often before at local levels in Ethiopia's rich history.

Notes

[1] See Chapter 30.

[2] The closest word may be *hizb*, people, which could designate 'public' in the sense of a collective object, but does not quite connote the collective subject associated with the concept of public.

[3] Park's colleague, George Herbert Mead, analyzed the psychological underpinnings of that contrast. Against the state of fusion of the individual 'I' with the group 'Me' he posed the kinds of rational discussions that take place in scientific discourse and relatedly in democratic groups. Illustrating the point by referring to examples from topics such as public health to municipal management, Mead argued that both the ethical ends and the means to attain them are "subject to restatement and reconstruction" by the "intelligent method of science" (Mead 1923, 237).

[4] In any case, both Dewey and Lippman held that the problems of modern society are so complex that they require the inputs and directives of specially trained persons needed to provide expert opinions on a wide range of issues.

[5] In this seminal piece, Fraser goes on to argue that the time has come for conceptualizing the public in ways that transcend the purely national boundaries in which it has hitherto been framed. That raises another set of considerations for future thought about Ethiopia and the Horn of Africa.

[6] In a retrospective, Blatten-Geta Mahteme-Selassie Wolde-Maskal (1970) describes the expectation that all Ethiopians were taught to plead cases clearly and skillfully in a court of law.

[7] In an apt comment on this point, Andreas Eshete observes that even within the household some forms of courage may be manifest.

[8] Alula Pankhurst provided this apt suggestion in his discussion of the presented paper. On the enormous potential of local radio in promoting public discourse, see the case of Sierra Leone described in Common Ground 2007.

[9] In a valuable paper, Charles Schaefer voiced this point eloquently: "Vengeance marks the politics of the Horn of Africa today; however, that was not always the case. History indicates that the ability to forgive characterized time-honored methods to resolve disputes and end wars. These methods were indigenously concocted and applied; moreover, they appear to have resonated with the population. What is puzzling is the extent to which these traditional methods based on forgiveness have been forgotten in Ethiopia and Eritrea today." 2006, 1.

[10] Barry Schwartz (1978) has analyzed the general sociological significance of this dynamic.

[11] Judaism requires a person on the day before Yom Kippur to ask forgiveness from those he has offended; those who have been asked are then obligated to show forgiveness.

[12] A former Beta Israel Qes wrote, "every Beta Israel has to look inward towards his own soul and self. It is the day when he/she admits to his or her sins and atones for

them" (Yayeh 1995, 89).

[13] What is more, such a gesture might raise the position of Ethiopia in the international community, since something like that is almost never done. To be sure, the governments of Japan, of Belgium, and of the Sudan have failed to do so, although Germany, Italy, Libya, and South Africa and others have, not to mention the State of Georgia which took the unprecedented step of passing legislation to convey its regret over the institution of slavery.

[14] This draws on distinctions made in my article, "Reconfiguring the Ethiopian Nation in a Global Era." *International Journal of Ethiopian Studies* 2004 Vol. 1, No. 2.

[15] See Levine 1995.

Bibliography

Aleme Tadesse. 2008. "Ethiopia—The end of the student movement 1960–2008." http://nazret.com/blog/index.php?blog=15&title=ethiopia_the_end_of_the_student_movement_2008&more=1&c=1&tb=1&pb=1

Alula Pankhurst and Getachew Assefa. 2008. *Ethiopia at a Justice Crossroads: The challenge of Customary Dispute Resolution.* Addis Ababa: French Centre of Ethiopian Studies.

Arendt, Hannah. 1959. *The Human Condition.* Chicago: University of Chicago Press.

Asmarom Legesse. 2000. *Oromo Democracy: An Indigenous African Political System.* Lawrenceville, NJ: Red Sea Press.

Blumenthal, David R. 1996. "Repentance and Forgiveness." *Crosscurrents.* http://www.crosscurrents.org/blumenthal.htm

Common Ground. 2007. *Search for Common Ground: Elections Special—Sierra Leone.* (September). www.sfcg.org

Dewey, John. [1927] 1984. *The Public and Its Problems.* New York: Holt. Reprinted in The Later Works, 1925–1927, vol. 2

Dufton, Henry. 1867. *Narrative of a Journey through Abyssinian 1862–3.*

Gamst, Frederick. 1969. *The Qemant: A Pagan-Hebraic Peasantry of Ethiopia.*

Getatchew Haile. 1994. "Martyrdom of Abunä Täklä Hawareyat of Shoa and the Translation of his Relics," Pp. 93–113 in *Etiopia e Oltre. Studi in onore di Lanfranco Ricci.* Napoli.

Hallpike, Christopher. 1972. *The Konso of Ethiopia: A Study of the Values of a Cushitic People.* Oxford: Clarendon Press.

Levine, Donald N. 1965. "Ethiopia: Identity, Authority, and Realism," in *Political Culture and Political Development*, ed. Lucien Pye and Sidney Verba (Princeton University Press), 245–81.

———. [1974] 2000. *Greater Ethiopia: The Evolution of a Multiethnic Society*. Chicago: University of Chicago Press. 2nd ed., with a new preface, 2000. Amharic translation, *Tiliqwa Ityopya*, Addis Ababa University Press, 2001.

———. 1995. "Will the Real Spirit of Adwa Please Stand Up?" *Ethiopian Register* 2 (3), 16–23.

———. 1996. "The Battle of Adwa as a 'Historic' Event," in *One House: The Battle of Adwa 1896,* ed. Pamela Brown and Fassil Yirgu (Chicago: Nyala), 1–8.

———. 2004. "Reconfiguring the Ethiopian Nation in a Global Era." *International Journal of Ethiopian Studies* 2004 Vol. 1, No. 2.

———. 2005. "The Masculinity Ethic and the Spirit of Warriorhood in Ethiopian and Japanese Cultures." *International Journal of Ethiopian studies* 2, No. 1.

———. 2007. "Oromo Narratives." *Journal of Oromo Studies* 14. No 2, 43–63.

Mahteme-Selassie Wolde-Maskal. 1970. "Portrait Retrospectif d'un Gentilhomme Ethiopien." *Proceedings of the Third International Conference of Ethiopian Studies.* Addis Ababa: Institute of Ethiopian Studies, Haile Selassie I University.

Mead, G. H. 1923. "Scientific Method and the Moral Sciences. *Intern. Journal of Ethics* 35:229–47.

Messay Kebede. 2006. "The Roots and Fallouts of Haile Selassie's Educational Policy." UNESCO Forum Occasional Paper Series Paper no. 10.

Rosen, Charles B. 1974. Warring with words: patterns of political activity in a northern Ethiopian town." Unpublished dissertation, Department of Anthropology, University of Chicago.

Rustow, Dankwart. 1970. "Transitions to Democracy: Toward a Dynamic Model." *Comparative Politics*. Vol. 2, No. 3.

Salisbury, Abigail. 2008. "Linking Rights and Foreign Aid for Ethiopia: The Case of HR 2003." http://jurist.law.pitt.edu/forumy/2008/01/linking-rights-and-foreign-aid-for.php

Schaefer, Charles. 2006. "Reexamining the Ethiopian Historical Record on the Continuum between Vengeance and Forgiveness." *Proceedings of the 15th International Conference on Ethiopian Studies*, ed. Siegbert Uhlig. Wiesbaden: Harrassowitz. 348–55.

Schwartz, Barry. 1978. "Vengeance and Forgiveness: The Uses of Beneficence in Social Control." *The School Review*, Vol. 86, No. 4, 655–68.

Part V

COMPARATIVE AND GLOBAL

32

Ambiguity and Modernity (1985)*

Ambiguous modes of expression are rooted in the very nature of language and thought. Although linguists disagree about whether some natural languages harbor more ambiguity than others, no linguist disputes the point that ambiguity is an inherent property of all natural languages.

Language generates ambiguity, first, because lexical elements tend to be imprecise. A single word or phrase may carry a number of meanings (polysemy); differently spelled words may sound alike (homophony); words that differ in derivation, meaning, or even pronunciation may be spelled the same way or represented by the same ideographic character (homography).[1] Sentences with univocal lexical forms, moreover, may yet be ambiguous because of confusion about how they are to be punctuated. In addition, even when a sentence contains but a single lexical and grammatical structure, it can still be insufficiently specified for purposes of clear communication—for example, "he hit the man with the stick" or "she is a Chinese art expert"—instances of what linguists gloss as 'grammatical homonyms' or 'structural ambiguity.' Aristotle's *De sophisticis elenchis* indicated the grounds for all this long since: "For names are finite and so is the sum-total of formulae, while things are infinite in number. Inevitably, then, the same formula and a single name have a number of meanings."

Another source of ambiguity in language is the tendency for words to acquire associations. Even words that are highly univocal in what they denote inevitably accumulate a wealth of connotations. Commonplace words like 'window' or

---

* Originally published in *Flight from Ambiguity: Essays in Social and Cultural Theory* (Chicago, IL: University of Chicago Press, 1985).

'bridge' are rich with personal and collective meanings of this sort. Rilke's ninth Duino Elegy alludes plaintively to this:

> Are we perhaps here, only to say: House.
> Bridge. Fountain. Gate. Jug. Fruit tree. Window.—
> at most: Pillar. Tower.... But to say them, mind you,
> *so* to say them, as the things within themselves never
> could have intended.

The human mind, moreover, inclines to exploit the possibilities for ambiguous expression which are inherent in language. We feel compelled to produce constructions such as metaphor, allegory, pun, irony, and paradox in order to express feelings and articulate realities which are too subtle for straightforward univocal representation. Although sober philosophers once taught that metaphoric constructions are idiosyncratic if not pathological forms of language use, now they affirm that metaphor permeates normal everyday language, thought, and action.

Cultures differ with regard to the scope they allow for the exercise of those ambiguities which inhere in speech and thought. To be sure, every culture insists on certain areas of univocal precision, according to the practical exigencies of the people who speak its language. Arabic, for example, is famous for the variety of terms it provides for designating different kinds of camels. But apart from such practical necessities, there is a wide range of variability in attitude toward the use of ambiguities generally. At the extremes, one type of culture puts a premium on the use of ambiguities in conversation and literary forms generally, while the other type disparages the use of ambiguities at all levels of communication.

Ambiguity in Premodern Cultures

The movement against ambiguity led by Western intellectuals since the 17th century figures as a unique development in world history. There is nothing like it in any premodern culture known to me.

Studies of the traditional cultures of Asia and Africa reveal time and again cases where ambiguous modes of expression are at the very least benignly tolerated. Indeed, most if not all, of the literate civilizations have considered the cultivation of ambiguous locution to be a wonderful art. Generations of Westerners have been struck, for example, by the privileged position of ambiguous expressions in the civilization of China. With a lexicon built so largely of concrete, multipurpose terms, the Chinese language is ill-suited to making sharp distinctions and analytic abstractions, and Chinese speakers like to evoke the multiple meanings associated with concrete images. Traditional Chinese produced an ornate literary style that blends a complex variety of suggestive images and creates subtle nuances through historical allusions. Mastery of such a style became one of the specially prized arts of classical China. In highly stylized contests Chinese courtiers vied with one another in palavers by inventing verses or singing songs that were filled with "diplomatic double meanings" (Granet 1958, 292–94). Despite enormous differences between them, both Confucianism and Taoism were rioted for disseminating precepts open to multiple interpretations.

Many of the linguistic customs of China are found in Japan as well. The love for evocative concrete terms reached its pinnacle in the highly prized forms of condensed poetry known as *tanka* and, especially, *haiku*. As with Chinese, Japanese language use promoted ambiguity by constructing sentences in which the subject was often omitted. In addition, Japanese added the distinctive particle, *tenioha*, which expresses delicate shades of emotion and thereby suggests rich overtones of meaning. Japanese Buddhists continued the ambiguous and obscure interpretations of Buddhist texts that evolved in China, and Zen teaching perfected the art of ambiguous response: a question like "What is the essence of Zen Buddhism?" would elicit such answers as "The wind blows and the sun heats" or "An oak tree in the garden."

Hindu traditions cultivated a garden of ambiguities with different cognitive equipment. Instead of idealizing concrete objects with their multiple associations, Hindu thought was inclined to regard concrete objects as less real than many abstract ideas, and to see particulars as illusory manifestations of universals. Paradigmatic for the polysemy this gives rise to the Hindu notion of *atman* refers both to the individual ego and the Universal Self. It has been a Hindu goal to erase the distinctions between self and others, and to attain truth, *satya*, by negating all forms of conceptual discriminations.

Because of this fondness for the abstract, one scholar has written:

> The Indians tend to pay more attention to the unknown and the undefined.... This attraction for the unknown resulted in a fondness for concealing even the obvious; their way of thinking tended to prefer the dark and obscure over that which was clear. (Nakamura 1960, 31)

Such an orientation underlies the Indian fondness for riddles and the profusion of allegorical expressions in the Upanishads and other writings. Even when Indian philosophers pursue their arguments in accord with the rules of logic, they prefer to make use of riddles and allegories.

In that remarkable outlier of Indian civilization, traditional Java, Clifford Geertz found a number of patterns that evince a studied cultivation of ambiguous expressions. In the *prijaji* or gentry culture of Java, the term *alus* signifies a person who speaks flawless high Javanese, and *alus refers* as well to a clever poetic conceit. Similarly, the term *rasa* is used to refer to a general principle of life-whatever lives has *rasa*, and whatever has *rasa* lives—yet again "*rasa* is applied to the words in a letter, in a poem, or even in a speech, to indicate the between-the-lines 'looking north and hitting south' type of allusive suggestion that is so important in Javanese communication" (Geertz 1960, 238). For the Javanese gentry, communication that is open and to the point comes across as rude, and *prijaji* etiquette prescribes that personal transactions be carried out by means of a long series of courtesy forms and complex indirections.

Jacques Berque (1961) has attempted to interpret those "chaotic inflections" of Arabic discourse that appear in the Arabs' penchant for metaphors, allegories, associations by resemblance and contiguity, and dissemblance, as in expressions of rage that merely signify alibis or gestures of appeasement that are pure camouflage. He views them in the context of a deep tension in Islamic culture between the ideal of unity and the reality of historical diversities, much as Nakamura connects the Hindu love of allegory to a tension between particular and universal. Berque relates that tension to the fascination with which Muslim literati examine the ambiguities of Arabic and, in particular, to their penchant for distinguishing between the figurative and the deeper, actual meanings of Koranic passages.

In one African variant of Islamic culture, that of the Somali nation, a love for ambiguity appears particularly notable in the political sphere. David Laitin reports that the Somali boast that *af somaaliga wa mergi*, "the Somali language is sinuous," because it permits words to take on novel shapes that accommodate a richness of metaphors and poetic allusions. Political arguments and diplomatic messages take the form of alliterative poems, mastery of which is a key to prestige and power. These poems typically begin with long, vague, circumlocutory preludes, introducing the theme at hand, which is then couched in allegory. Of these poems, Laitin writes:

> A poetic message can be deliberately misinterpreted by the receiver, without his appearing to be stupid. Therefore, the person for whom the message was intended is never put in a position where he has to answer yes or no, or where he has to make a quick decision. He is able to go into further allegory, circling around the issue in other ways, to prevent direct confrontation. (1977, 39)

The classical traditions of Western civilization appear scarcely less hospitable to ambiguous expressions. The Jews created a Book whose sparse detail has been a standing invitation for evocative interpretations. Generations of Talmudic scholars and then Kabbalists spent lives in savoring the wisdom and the mysteries of polysemous words and phrases. Jesus and his followers loved to represent spiritual truths in terms of familiar worldly images and events. Christian preachers over the centuries have delighted in unraveling the strands of thought entwined in his parables. Medieval dramatists and Renaissance poets proclaimed moral truths through elaborate allegories. The Platonic tradition made much of the multiple meanings of words, both in their dual capacity as referents to sensible and ideal objects and as signs whose meanings shift in the course of dialectical inquiry. Ciceronian rhetoric made much of the paradox as a device for startling and persuading one's audience, and figures of all sorts were celebrated in handbooks of classical rhetoric. These were all manifestations of those modes of expression and thought that writers like Locke and Condorcet sought to combat in prescribing a curriculum that excluded the classics.

The fact that ambiguity was cultivated in so many forms in so many traditional cultures suggests that ambiguous expressions serve a number of social and cultural purposes. These purposes should be examined before one endorses without reservation the modern project of eradicating ambiguity. To facilitate such an examination, I should like to compare two cases that represent sharply contrasting attitudes toward ambiguity; the culture of the Amhara of Ethiopia and that of the United States of America.

Ambiguity in Amhara and American Cultures

Within the universe of traditional cultures where we have seen ambiguity as such is probably never the object of focused aversion, Amhara culture presents a case where the love of ambiguity appears particularly pronounced. This is so much the case that one is considered a master of spoken Amharic only when one's speech is leavened with ambiguous nuances as a matter of course. Even among other peoples in Ethiopia the Amhara have been noted for extremes of symbolism and subtlety in their everyday talk.[2]

The Amhara's basic manner of communicating is indirect, often secretive. Amharic conversation abounds with general, evasive remarks, like *Mĭn yeshallāl*? ("What is better?") when the speaker has failed to indicate what issue he is referring to, or *Setagn*! ("Give me!") when the speaker fails to specify what it is he wants. When the speaker then is quizzed about the issue at hand or the object he desires, his reply still may not reveal what is really on his mind; and if it does, his interlocutor will likely as not interpret that response as a disguise.

This pattern of indirection in speech governs Ethiopian literature. The written literature of Ethiopia is suffused with parable and protracted symbolism. In what is perhaps the most characteristic expression of the Amhara genius, moreover—a genre of oral literature known as 'wax and gold'—the studied use of ambiguity plays a central part.

Wax and gold (*säm-enna-wärq*) is the formula with which the Amhara symbolize their favorite form of verse. The form consists of two semantic layers.

The apparent, superficial meaning of the words is called "wax" (*sam*); their hidden, deeper significance is the "gold" (*warq*).

In its generic sense, the expression *säm-enna-wärq* refers to a number of poetic figures which embody this duplicity of meaning. The use of such figures distinguishes the Amhara equivalent of true poetry from the ordinary verse in which everyday language is merely embellished with rhyme and rhythm. In the genre known as *qen*, the original and most elegant kind of *säm-enna-wärq* poetry, the lines are composed in Ge'ez (the ancient and liturgical language of Ethiopia) and depend primarily on religious symbolism. But *säm-enna-wärq* constructions also appear in many types of secular verse in. the vernacular Amharic and, indeed, frequently inform ordinary Amharic discourse.

Masters of the art of *qene* composition have analyzed these poetic figures into about a dozen different types. *Säm-enna-wärq* in its more specific sense refers to one of these figures—the prototype of them all. It consists of an explicit comparison in which the subjects being compared—the "wax" and the "gold"—are presented in apposition, while their predicates are rendered jointly, by a single verb which carried both a "wax" and a "gold" meaning. This terminology stems from the art of the goldsmith, who constructs a clay mold around a form created in wax and then, after melting and draining off the wax, pours the molten gold into that form. So, for example, if the poet's aim is to praise a hero like Emperor Menelik, he creates a "wax" model, like "the lion," in terms of whose actions the "gold," Menelik, is depicted: "The lion crushed the wolf Italy."

The following Amharic couplet exemplifies the *säm-enna-wärq* figure:

Etsa balas balto addam kanfareshe

Madhane alam lebbe tasaqqala-lleshe.

Since Adam your lip did eat of that Tree

The Savior my heart has been hung up for thee.

In this secular couplet the "wax" of Adam's sin and Christ's crucifixion in his behalf has been used as a mold in which to pour a love message. A literal translation of the "wax" of the couplet is:

Because Adam ate of the apple from the Tree of Knowledge

The Savior of the World has been crucified for thee.

To appreciate the "gold" of the couplet, one must know that the verb meaning "was crucified," tasaqqala, may also mean "is infatuated with." A literal translation of the "gold" content would be:

Because of your (tempting) lips

My heart is infatuated with thee.

In other figures, the duplicity of the message is rendered less explicit. In figures known as *hĭber* and *merĭmer*, the "wax" and "gold" are combined in the same word or phrase instead of being put side by side. These figures thus correspond to the English pun. For example:

Ābbāt-ennā innātesh sigā naw irmātchaw

Ānjat tabayāllash āntchi-mmā lijātchaw.

Your father and your mother have vowed to keep from meat

But you, their very daughter, innards do you eat.

"To eat someone's entrails" is an Amharic idiom which means "to capture his heart." The hidden meaning of the couplet is thus: "You made me love you."

Ethiopic verse becomes most obscure in the figure known as *wesṭa wayrā*, "inside of olive tree." Here only the "wax" is given, and the listener must work to unearth the "gold." Often this can be done only when the circumstances under which the verse was made up are known. At times the author of a *wesṭa wayrā* verse may even refuse to reveal anything that would help the listener grasp its hidden meaning.

The expression *wesṭa wayrā* alludes to the fact that the inside of the olive tree is of a different color from its bark. The implication is that the inner sense of a *wesṭa wayrā* poem is concealed by a veneer which conveys a quite different sense. For example:

Ya-bāhetāwi lij sifalleg le'llennā
Ya-kristosen mesht telānt washama-nnā
Qeṭal betābalaw hono qarrama-nnā.

The son of a hermit, high rank to display,
Made love with Christ's wife yesterday;
When she fed him leaves he wasted away.

The surface meaning of this tercet describes an ambitious man who had relations with the "wife of Christ" in order to raise his status, for in Ethiopia having relations with a woman of high rank is one way to gain prestige. Instead of advancing his position, however, this man lost all his power when the woman fed him (medicinal) leaves.

The esoteric meaning, the "gold," on the other hand, refers to the experience of a hermit. His "son" is intended to symbolize his hunger, and "Christ's wife" symbolizes fasting. The "inside" interpretation, then, is that the hermit's hunger is heightened by its relation with fasting, but it diminishes when he is fed leaves, the hallowed diet of a hermit.

The ambiguity symbolized by the formula "wax and gold" colors the entire fabric of Amhara life. It patterns the speech and outlook of every Amhara. When he talks, his words carry *double entendre* as a matter of course; when he listens, he is ever on the lookout for latent meanings and hidden motives. As an Ethiopian anthropologist once told me, wax and gold is far more than a poetic formula; it is the Amhara "way of life."

The American way of life, by contrast, affords little room for the cultivation of ambiguity. The dominant American temper calls for clear and direct communication. It expresses itself in such common injunctions as "Say what you mean," "Don't beat around the bush," and "Get to the point." A Nigerian novelist summed up his impressions of the American style after living more than twenty years in the United States as follows: "Americans tend to be direct and literal rather than allusive and figurative, stark rather than subtle. They are happier dealing with statistics than with nuances" (Echewa 1982, 13).

Intellectual discussions in the United States commonly reflect the assumption that the meaning of a word must be precisely determined before it can be used seriously. The dominant philosophical orientations are given to insisting on the univocal definition of terms. Few American thinkers would be disposed to challenge Abraham Kaplan's straightforward judgment: "Ambiguity is the common cold of the pathology of language" (Kooij 1971, 1).

Poetry, the last refuge of ambiguity, has received relatively little attention in American culture. The poetry that is commonly prized is likely as not to be of a fairly literal sort; and the American way of understanding a poem is often that of translating the "meaning" of the poem into univocal prose.

To lampoon public figures for their alleged equivocation has long been a favored American pastime. George Washington became a culture hero to a large extent because of the perception that he studiously avoided misrepresentations of any sort. A 19th century American patriot, General John Wilcott Phelps, expressed a characteristic attitude in writings that praised the candor and openness of Americans, and scored the machinations of secret societies as a threat to republican institutions:

> When men resort to the use of ambiguous expressions, vague similes, parallels, signs, symbols, grips, etc., it is reasonable to infer that they have some object in view that will not bear the light. The borrowing of the livery of the devil, to serve Heaven in, will ever excite suspicion, and impair the confidence of men in each other. Honest intentions should receive honest modes of expression. (1873, 219)

The Function of Ambiguity and Univocality

These opposed attitudes toward ambiguity reflect contrasting patterns in Amhara and American value systems and social institutions. The shape of those patterns and affinities becomes evident when we examine the properties of ambiguous expressions and the diverse purposes they serve.

Comments by Amhara who have thought about the matter provide a useful starting point for identifying those purposes. *Wesṭa wayrā*, the most obscure of the wax-and-gold figures, they tell us, is ideally suited both for expressing deep philosophical insights and for insulting one's enemies with impunity. In other words, ambiguous discourse functions generally as a preferred medium either for revealing realities or for obfuscating them. These functions may be divided further according to whether the realities in question are those of the external world or those of the communicating subject.

When ambiguous locutions are used to represent external realities, their properties of evocativeness serve a distinctively illuminative function. When ambiguity is used to represent the inner realities of a subject, its property of allusiveness serves an expressive function. When ambiguity is used to conceal the beliefs and intentions of a subject, its property of opaqueness serves a protective function. When ambiguity works to obfuscate external realities, its property of vagueness serves a socially binding function.

Ambiguity as a Medium of Enlightenment

In the cultures of India and China, as Max Weber observed, knowledge is highly respected, not in the sense of knowing the things of this world—the everyday events of nature and of social life, and the laws that govern them—but as philosophical knowledge of the meaning of life and of the world (1958c, 330). The same holds true for Ethiopia. In all these cultures, as in so many phases of Western culture, it has been felt that this sort of knowledge finds its natural medium in some sort of ambiguity, whether the form be spiritual parable, philosophic paradox, lofty allegory, subtle symbolism, or "wax and gold."

The prestige of wax and gold among the Amhara is attributed in part to what is considered its philosophic value. Amhara traditionalists extol wax and gold as a unique creation of their culture. One of them has written that *qene* is as distinctive of Ethiopia's spiritual culture as *teff* (a species of grass grown as a cereal grain only in Ethiopia) is distinctive of her material culture (Moges 1956, 117).

They further maintain that Ge'ez *qene* contains a uniquely profound sort of wisdom. Instruction in this occult art of verse composition has traditionally been regarded as propaedeutic to the study of religious texts. This is partly because

Ge'ez grammar, which must be known in order to understand these texts, is normally taught only in the schools of *qene*. The more philosophic reason given, however, is that by affording exercise in fathoming secrets it opens the mind" and thereby enhances the student's ability to approach the divine mysteries.

What is the basis of this virtually universal appeal of the ambiguous? It is, first, that we experience reality as complex, full of overtones and cross-currents which razor-sharp univocal statements do not capture, whereas ambiguous expressions favor the representation of this richness of reality in an economical way. It is, moreover, that when we confront words which first mean one thing, and then mean something else, we feel that we are moving from appearance to reality; we experience a progression from a mediocre truth to a higher, or deeper, truth. It is, finally, that encounter with the ambiguous creates an inner confusion, a tension which is relieved when the two meanings are synthesized or when the deeper meaning has been secured.

A more inclusive sense of reality, a sense of mystery, and the experience of oneness that accompanies release of tension—these are the attributes of mysticism. Ambiguity is par excellence the handmaid of mysticism, a type of cognitive orientation primarily concerned with the meaning of life and of the world.

The connection between ambiguity and mysticism is the obverse of the connection between univocality and rationalized science. What we may call the mystical approach differs from the scientific approach in at least two fundamental respects. The truth sought by mysticism is not knowable or communicable by conventional methods. It is not susceptible to formulation in precise propositions, and often—as was maintained by many Asian sages—it can best be communicated by silence. At the most, it can only be alluded to by ambiguous formulations. For science, on the other hand, the mysterious and incommunicable realities of life are relegated to a residual category outside its purview. Scientific truth is restricted to what can be formulated in clear definitions and precise propositions.

Another difference between mysticism and "scientism" concerns their opposing relations to the natural world. Mysticism involves a kind of surrender to the universe, an intimate participation in the oneness of reality, whether this reality be located in a realm of miracle and fantasy, as in India, or in surrounding nature and the events of daily life, as in China, or wherever. Science in both its ratiocinative and its empirical dimensions, involves opposition between the knower and the known, some sort of confrontation in which the attempt is made to make subjective knowledge conform to external reality. Whether its aim be purely cognitive or utilitarian the scientific approach works to dominate reality, while mysticism aims toward fusion with some transcendental reality or else a state of harmonious oneness with the universe.[3]

If ambiguity is favored by those oriented intellectually to savoring the mysteries of life and pragmatically to a state of harmonious fusion, then one strand of the Amhara-America contrast is at once illuminated. The foundations of American religious culture were laid by those who subscribed to the Protestant turning from otherworldly orientations, a development so vividly portrayed by Max Weber. Within Puritanism, moreover, they subscribed overwhelmingly to its ascetic rather than mystical branches. The latter was precluded not only by the establishment of ascetic Covenant Puritanism as the mainstream version of Puritanism in America by the 1640s, but also by the need to adopt a strenuous this-worldly discipline to build and maintain frontier settlements. Mystical modes of piety could scarcely be tolerated where Indians, famine, climate, and wilderness provided unfamiliar enemies to battle against. The persisting exigencies of a frontier mentality were conducive to making the impulse to mastery over nature a core motif of American culture. Indeed, the Impulse to dominate nature developed in the United States to a degree the world had never before experienced. I would argue, then, that a strong practical orientation to dominate nature and an intellectual orientation toward gaining cognitive mastery over the world contributed to the American aversion toward ambiguity.

In Ethiopia, on the other hand, a strict conservatism that eschews any departure from inherited techniques and a passive fatalism that declares man's efforts to better himself futile precluded the development of a highly instrumental orientation toward the world. Intellect was applied instrumentally to worldly matters only to the extent required by a subsistence standard of living and a minimum of social order. Beyond that, the Amhara mind devoted itself chiefly to contemplating the mysteries of life—and enjoying the subtleties of social intercourse.

Ambiguity and Expressiveness

Univocal verbal communication is designed to be affectively neutral. It aims for the precise representation of fact, technique, or expectation. Univocality works to strip language of its expressive overtones and suggestive allusions.

Ambiguous communication, by contrast, can provide a superb means for conveying affect. By alluding to shared experiences and sentiments verbal associations can express and evoke a wealth of affective responses. The exploitation of ambiguity through wit and jokes can convey a wide array of feelings. The clandestine ambiguities of ironic messages have the capacity to transmit sentiments of enormous power.

Puritanical, utilitarian, commercial, legalistic, and, more recently, bureaucratic and scientific pressures have dried out many of the springs of affectivity in American social intercourse. They have promoted an asceticism in language that in many spheres comes close to defining the indulgence of verbal nuance as a forbidden pleasure.

Traditional Amhara culture exhibits none of those pressures that in the United States have worked to reduce the expression of affect in human communication. Although the Amhara maintain a posture of dignified reserve in most of their social interactions, the subtle expression of affect appears prominently in their social intercourse. Utilitarian or strictly cognitive considerations rarely dominate attention so much that ambiguity is out of place. Whether in the religious constructions of the literati, the political innuendos of lords, the clever repartee of litigants, the improvizations of minstrels, or the banter of soldiers and peasants, "wax and gold" provides a commonly used medium of entertainment. The enjoyment of verbal ambiguities plays a significant role in conversations and stories.

Ambiguity as a Medium of Self-Protection

Univocal expressions enable, if not force, speakers or writers to communicate openly and clearly, and to hold back nothing of their intentions. Ambiguous expressions have the contrary property of enabling their users to conceal, more or less deeply, what is really on their minds. Such concealment may be in the passive vein of withholding information for the sake of privacy or secrecy, or in the more active mode of seeking to deceive others for the sake of tact or some defensive strategy.

One might expect, therefore, to find a marked aversion to ambiguity in societies or groups that place a high value on openness as opposed to secrecy. Secrecy is favored in societies organized on a strongly hierarchical basis. Sharply stratified societies make considerable use of secrecy-elites in order to maintain their privileged status through possession of esoteric knowledge, non-elites in order to defend themselves against intrusive encroachments. Egalitarian societies have an affinity for the value of openness and publicity.

Because of the strongly egalitarian cast of American society, secrecy has typically played a very small part. As Edward Shils has observed, "The United States has been committed to the principle of publicity since its origin" (1956, 37). Communication among Americans is characteristically direct and open. In this century, at least, the thin bastions of privacy have been invaded to the extent that people tend to feel entitled to know what is on everyone else's mind. Americans resent esoteric knowledge of any sort as symptomatic of "undemocratic" snobbishness.

This attitude has been linked to a distinctively American emphasis on univocality in the movement to codify the law. While the tradition of common law inherited from England did not place much weight on clarity and univocality—Blackstone delighted in ambiguity and loved the "mysterious science" of the law—the Jacksonian democrats who sponsored codification saw beneath ambiguity arbitrariness and behind arbitrariness, aristocratic privilege.

Amhara society, by contrast, has been described by all observers as pervaded by a hierarchical ethos, one in which even servants are proud to have servants and where the desire for a title of some sort figures as one of the greatest social passions. And Amhara social structure represents what could be described as an ideal type of "secretogenic" social structure. The nobility have traditionally gained or lost position through notoriously secret intrigues. Literati have maintained their superiority in good part through their monopoly of esoteric knowledge (including the knowledge of how to write). The peasantry have resorted to secrecy, and equivocal and evasive communication, in order to defend themselves against exploitation.

Among the Amhara, accordingly, everyone is assumed to be harboring secrets. The Amhara define a close friend as "someone with whom one can share secrets." The popularity of wax-and-gold locutions becomes yet more understandable. Indeed, the word *mistir*, often used to designate the "gold" meaning of an obscure stanza, is in fact the Amharic word for "secret."

One might also expect to find an aversion to ambiguity related to sentiments that favor the value of impersonal honesty, as opposed to deception. The extent to which deception is tolerated or even appreciated in societies or groups reflects, I believe, the degree to which universalistic standards are institutionalized. The modern Western notion of truth, along with sincerity and univocality, is a rare sociological flower. The medieval ideal of truth was not truth as we know it, in the sense of being in accord with impersonal and objective standards, but was construed as personal fealty: "being true" to one's lord or companion. Where particularistic standards are paramount, there is no obligation for anyone to be honest for the sake of honesty, and accordingly no generalized sanction against deception or equivocation as such.

In American society, universally valid moral precepts have taken precedence over particularistic obligations. This means that cognitive standards have precedence over appreciative standards, and that in turn entails a concern for intellectual integrity. The American ethos does in fact idealize intellectual integrity and, closely related to that, unequivocal communication. This appears, for example, in popular legends about George Washington and Abraham Lincoln that portray their exemplary honesty, and in such maxims as "Honesty is the best policy" and the nearly sacred sense of obligation to honor the terms of any "deal."

Among the Amhara, where particularistic standards dominate, integrity as an abstract ideal plays a lesser role. Amhara culture consequently encourages deceptive modes of communication. Political figures are celebrated not because they "cannot tell a lie," but for their shrewdness and wit in deceiving opponents. One of the most notable Amhara culture heroes, the nineteenth-century literatus Aleqa Gabra Hanna, achieved anecdotal fame precisely for his adroit use of deceptive wax-and-gold equivocations, whether for the sake of personal gain, to insult others slyly with impunity, to criticize authorities, or simply to display his virtuosity as a wit.

Deception shades readily into tact and etiquette in personal relations, and these values seem especially prominent in societies or groups where particularistic standards are combined with a hierarchical ethos. Particularism implies that consideration of impersonal honesty must be subordinated to the aesthetics of a personal relationship, and emphasis on hierarchy means that persons are to be treated according to what fits their status, not according to what they have or have not accomplished. For these reasons too ambiguity serves the Amhara well, enabling him to express compliments he does not mean, and avoid direct utterances that might injure the sentiments of others. The contrast with the direct, outspoken, unmannered but honest American could scarcely be more striking.

Ambiguity and Vagueness

Univocal communication has the properties not only of being literal, affectively neutral, and public, it is also precise. Ambiguous expressions, by contrast, can be vague. And vagueness in social intercourse is depreciated when it is important that norms, roles, and beliefs be defined specifically.

Role specificity of an extreme degree has developed in the United States since the middle of the nineteenth century, as a result of extensive occupational specialization and the rationalization of activities in most spheres of life. Job descriptions have come to enumerate in unambiguous terms the duties and facilities appropriate to each office. This simply accentuates a pattern common to all industrialized societies, which rely on a methodical division of the integrated activities of continuously operating offices, on clearly defined spheres of competence, and on a precise enumeration of official responsibilities and prerogatives.

Amhara social organization, by contrast, exhibits a great deal of functional diffuseness. Kinship, political, and religious roles carry multiple functions. The boundaries of responsibilities and prerogatives associated with them are not clearly defined, and there is considerable overlapping among roles. This pattern of diffuseness encourages the vagueness of ambiguity in communication. For example, the term for father, *abbat*, applies equally to one's natural father, guardian father, political lord, religious confessor, and king.

This kind of vagueness, and the social diffuseness it subserves, may be seen to have a kind of socially binding function. That is particularly important in societies of small scale where people carry out their lives with a relatively small number of face-to-face consociates. By contrast, the compartmentalization promoted by functionally specific relationships serves in societies of larger scale and more complex organization to promote the improved performance of specialized roles.

David Laitin's analysis of ambiguity in Somali makes a kindred point about the effect of ambiguous locutions in avoiding political confrontations. In traditional Somali political culture debate usually takes the form of highly metaphorical arguments preceded by long circumlocutory introductions. As Laitin sees it, these poetic forms serve a very important function in Somali politics; they allow for sufficient public ambiguity concerning the issue at hand as to allow the person who cannot get his way to leave without losing face. In a small scale society, this is most important, because it is very difficult for a clansman to avoid seeing members of his political contract group all the time (1977, 207).

It is probably impossible for politics to be carried out in any community without the use of ambiguous language. The American system of political parties has long been celebrated for providing an agency through which varieties of special and divisive interests might be aggregated behind relatively vague party orientations.[4] Yet a countercurrent of confrontational politics has been prominent in American political history, and the recent emergence of a politics that defers to groups advocating single, special causes does seem to reflect a deep American commitment to specific, unambiguous claims. This reflects yet another dimension along which American patterns contrast with Amhara culture, where the public articulation of specific interests has never been favored and the art of politics is overwhelmingly an art of confrontational maneuver.

The distinctions I have been making are represented schematically in Figures 1 and 2.

Figure 1: The Function of Ambiguous Discourse

	EXTERNAL REALITIES	INTERNAL REALITIES
Cultural functions	Enlightenment through intuited indeterminacy (mysticism)	Expressivity through evocative allusions (metaphor)
Social functions	Bonding through diffuseness (solidaristic symbolization)	Self-protection through opaqueness (secrecy, deception)

Figure 2: The Functions of Univocal Discourse

	EXTERNAL REALITIES	INTERNAL REALITIES
Cultural functions	Cognitive mastery through determinateness (Secular science)	Disciplined expression through literalness
Social functions	Discrimination through specificity (Specification of claims)	Self-disclosure through transparency (publicity, honesty)

Ambiguity and Modernity

I have argued that a predilection for ambiguity appears in most traditional cultures but that in Amhara culture the penchant is manifest to an extraordinary extent. Conversely, I believe that a flight from ambiguity characterizes the culture of most modern societies but that in the United States this tendency has been manifest to an exceptional degree.

The several strands of aversion to ambiguity in the United States recall the special role played by Puritanism in the shaping of American culture. Puritanism worked in many ways to combat the uses of ambiguity. Newtonian science, the great fountainhead of univocality among Enlightenment intellectuals, found support and legitimation in the Puritan ethos, as Merton and others have shown. Puritanism turned the mind from otherworldly orientations and from mysticism, the natural haven for ambiguous thoughtways, to the utilitarian application of intellect to the problems of this world. It discouraged aesthetic pleasures, including the enjoyment of ambiguous figures in repartee. In place of the latter it favored plain talk. Puritanism stressed the moral imperative of honesty and the political imperative of publicity, values that came to be cherished to a remarkable degree in American society.

Apart from what may be considered the distinctive coloring of American culture by the Puritan ethic and by such other factors as the exigencies of frontier settlement and an insistent populism, the fate of ambiguity in the United States probably reflects above all the fact that the institutions and ideals of modern culture are seriously dependent on unambiguous modes of expression. Modern science, technology, commerce, occupational specialization, bureaucratic management, and the formal rationalization of legal procedures and much else are all unthinkable without resources for clear and distinct communication. Insofar as ambiguous patterns are prominent in traditional cultures like that of Ethiopia, they must present an obstacle to the modernizing aspirations of their new elites.

During my sojourn in Ethiopia in the late 1950s I found that tension between traditional proclivities for ambiguity and modern demands for univocality had indeed surfaced as a troublesome issue. I found modern-educated Ethiopians anxious to secure greater clarity in the way that administrative responsibilities were specified. I found an undercurrent of chafing at the devious, equivocal talk that seemed de rigueur for political action of any sort. I found a special sensitivity to cognitive standards and honesty flowing from a certain embarrassment about traditional patterns of deceptiveness. That this issue was on the minds of Ethiopian youth seemed to be indicated by responses to a questionnaire I administered to seven hundred secondary and college students in 1959: when asked to identify the best character trait of all, by far the largest number indicated "honesty"—a conspicuous departure from traditional norms—and a number mentioned "honesty" when asked to name what they would most like their children to have that they did not themselves have.

Regarding the use of the Amharic language itself, I found that many Ethiopians who spoke Amharic regularly at home, and enjoyed the ambiguities of wax-and-gold expressions, often preferred to speak English at work, to avoid what some complained of as the excessive and burdensome subtleties of Amharic. Comparable contrasts have been noted elsewhere; one observer who had access to cabinet meetings in Tanzania noted that the use of English facilitated clear, precise decisions, whereas when the officials spoke Swahili, with its expansive, often imprecise, style of exposition, they often reached less clear decisions.

Also commonly, I found journalists and writers attempting to adapt Amharic to a modern idiom, "honest, straightforward, sensible, grammatical, and plain." Again, changes of this sort have been reported for a number of other modernizing societies, such as Japan, where increasingly strict and precise modes of expression have been grafted onto the traditional, highly ambiguous, Japanese style (Nakamura 1960, 484).

In short, something akin to what I described as the flight from ambiguity seems no less essential to modern societies than the institutions of money and banks, electronic communications, written legal codes, and highway systems. Such a change, however can be viewed in either of the two ways that any aspect of modernization can be conceived: as a substitutive *replacement* for an outmoded pattern, or as a newly specialized *addition* to a previously less differentiated pattern.

Many of the seminal statements about modernization have viewed it as a process of evolutionary or progressive supersession. Comte viewed theological and metaphysical orientations as archaic forms that would be wholly replaced by the patterns of positive science. Marx imagined that capitalist forms of ownership and production would be wholly replaced by socialized forms. Weber seemed to suggest that traditional forms of authority would be wholly replaced by rational-legal forms, and some followers of Parsons have taken him to imply that particularistic-ascriptive patterns would be superseded by universalistic and achievement patterns in modern societies.[5]

My own view is that the question whether any kind of social change takes the form of A followed by B, or of A followed by a + b, in which the original pattern differentiates into a continuing feature and a contrasting emergent feature, can only be answered empirically. But I think one is justified in taking a skeptical stance toward proponents of some novel form who claim that their new creation has come to replace any prior dispensations, even though belief in the absolute virtue of a new approach often figures in the motivation to pursue it.

In the case of ambiguity, there can be no doubt that the institutions of modern society and culture require an enormous increase in the resources of univocal communication. As our examination of the American case has intimated, univocal discourse serves functions that are indispensable to any high-tech society. Univocal discourse advances our capabilities for gaining cognitive mastery of the world, both by the determinateness that it lends to the representation of external phenomena d the control over internal sentiments by which it disciplines verbal communications. Univocal discourse also provides resources essential to life in complex societies by facilitating the precise designation of specific rights and responsibilities and by constituting a symbolic coinage of the realm—unequivocally understood tokens and measures that are available to a wide public.

On the other hand, if univocality is essential to modernity, ambiguity is no less so. Just as, contrary to the projections of a Comte, a Marx, or a Weber, there remains an important role to be played by theological and metaphysical thinking in regimes dominated by positive science, for private ownership and production in the most socialized of economies, and for primordial ties and traditions of ritual despite a hegemony of rationalized institutions, so, contrary to the projections of a Condorcet, there remain spheres of representation and expression that are best served by the re sources of ambiguous language. These spheres include, on the side of interiority, the need for expressivity under a regime of computerese and other formal rationalities, and the need to protect privacy in a world of extended central controls. In the domain of external realities, moreover, these include the need for mediating the experience of community in a society built of highly specialized units, and the persisting need, in a culture informed by disenchanted representations of the external world, for symbolic forms that mediate the experience of transcendent unities.

A theme central to critiques of modern culture in recent decades has been the danger to our humanity posed by the ascendance of a monolithic idiom of language use. Richard Weaver scored this development by bemoaning the triumph of "journalese," characterized by "words of flat signification...and with none of the broadly ruminative phrases which have the power to inspire speculation." As Weaver further observed:

> The essential sterility of such a style is one of the surest signs we have that modern man is being desiccated. For the 'modern' style is at once brash and timid; brash enough to break old patterns without thinking, and timid before the tremendous evocative and constructive powers immanent in language. (1958, 77)

George Orwell could think of no more horrifying denouement for modern man than a language constituted by words to which one and only one specific meaning was permitted. In the last few decades, moreover, the formal rationalities of bureaucratic organization, on the one hand, and high-tech computerism, on the other, have amplified the extension of univocalese to a degree that even the humane mind of a Weaver or the fevered imagination of an Orwell could scarcely conjecture. If the ambition of modern culture to create a fuller life for human beings is to retain full credibility, it must unleash the tremendous evocative and expressive powers immanent in language no less than its capabilities for precise and disinterested representation.

The extension of centralized political control and political technology are fatefully consequential not only for our habits of language use, they make possible an extraordinary degree of surveillance and control over personal lives. In the modern societies where this kind of threat has been realized in its most malignant form, the totalitarian societies of Eastern Europe, the ambiguities of oral wit and certain literary genres have provided desperately embraced safety valves. The productions of Polish playwrights, Romanian novelists, and Russian poets have been widely celebrated for facilitating the assertion of personal autonomy under conditions of stark political repression. The much milder version of repressiveness that obtains in modern democratic polities may be countered tonically by comparable ambiguous forms, forms that express the plaint of modern souls against the DO NOT FOLD, MUTILATE, OR SPINDLE mentality.

However much the bureaucratic administration of modern society relies on univocal messages, moreover, modern political communities remain unthinkable without the sinews of ambiguous language. This is true, to begin with, for the fundamental process of modernization itself. The problems of "cultural management" faced by the developing nations have been dealt with only by an almost deliberate effort to exploit the ambiguity of traditional symbols. Time and again the historical record demonstrates the futility of attempting the revolutionary implementation of a clear and distinct ideal in human society. No matter how bold and sweeping the program, traditional patterns persist tenaciously. The only real alternatives are whether they are to be maintained in isolation from the modern culture or whether traditional and modern patterns can be successfully fused to produce a novel synthesis. To my knowledge no one has refuted Almond's (1960) argument that the latter alternative contributes significantly to political stability over time. For that to take place, however, traditional symbols have had to be interpreted with sufficient ambiguity to permit their fusion with modern ones.

The contribution of ambiguity to the process of political modernization is but a special case of the crucial role of ambiguity in the life of all modern political systems. The formal rationalization of law, far from putting an end to ambiguity, has rendered its uses more indispensable than ever. The codification of legal norms, through case law, statutory law, and constitutional law alike, simply provides a complex of verbal formulations that need continuously to be interpreted and reinterpreted. In the words of Edward Levi, "It is only folklore which holds that a statute if clearly written can be completely unambiguous and applied as intended to a specific case" (1948, 6).

The benefits of the inherently ambiguous character of legal rules are twofold. The ambiguity of the categories used in the legal process permits the infusion of new ideas, and thus enables societal regulations to adapt to an inexorably changing environment. And it permits the engagement of parties who submit contending interpretations of legal notions to participate, through the open forum of the court, in the continuous reestablishment of a rule of law that stands as their common property and their warrant of real community. In Levi's analysis,

> If a rule had to be clear before it could be imposed, society would be impossible. The mechanism [of legal reasoning] accepts the differences of views and the ambiguities of words. It provides for the participation of the community in resolving the ambiguity by providing a forum for the discussion of policy in the gap of ambiguity. (1948, 1)

It is not only through the language of the law that ambiguity serves to promote community. In the modern world this takes place preeminently through a style of political language that Murray Edelman describes as "hortatory language." This is a mode of language use in which commonplace terms, like 'justice,' 'freedom,' and 'public interest,' are invoked to elicit the support of particular audiences for certain policies. Edelman finds this style distinctively significant for modern political practice because of the modern emphasis on participation and rationality. "In spite of the almost total ambiguity of the terms employed," he writes, and "regardless of the specific issue discussed, the employment of this language style is accepted as evidence that the public has an important stake and role in political decisions and that reason and the citing of relevant information is the road to discovering the nature of the stake" (1964, 135). Even in a language style that puts a premium on univocal talk, the language of bargaining, Edelman suggests that ambiguity has a role to play, both by permitting a degree of feinting and feeling out of positions in the early stages of negotiation, and by providing a means of getting agreement on unambiguous central issues.

In many ways, then—by enhancing adaptiveness to change, by facilitating negotiation, by mobilizing constituencies for support and for action, by inviting participation in the definition of communal beliefs, by permitting different elements of the polity to share each other's response precisely in situations where conflict would otherwise occur, by providing symbols that are constitutive of the identities of communities of many kinds—ambiguous talk makes modern politics possible. It does so by tempering the assertion of particular interests and parochial understandings with symbols whose common use, in the face of diverse interpretations, provides a mooring for social solidarity and a continuing invitation to engage in communal discourse. And that continuing invitation, finally, engages us as well in quests for meanings that transcend whatever univocal determinations we have achieved at any moment. In the words of my epigraph, "We proceed as if we were faced with a choice between the univocal and the ambiguous, and we come to the discovery . . .that the univocal has its foundations and consequences in ambiguities" (McKeon 1964, 243). Indeed.

Notes

1 Yuen Ren Chao estimates that about 15 percent of the characters in a running Chinese text have alternate pronunciations, usually associated with differences in meaning and function (1959, 3).

2 The following paragraphs incorporate material published previously in my *Wax and Gold* (1965).

3 This contrast as recently received an important elaboration by Fritiof Capra (1984). Science, writes Capra, "aims for clear definitions and unambiguous connections, and therefore, it abstracts language further by limiting the meaning of its words and by standardizing its structure in accordance with the rules of logic." Mystics, by contrast, "well aware of the fact that all verbal descriptions of reality are inaccurate and incomplete [strive for] a direct experience of reality [that] transcends the realm of thought and language" (19, 29).

4 In recent studies of the "art of ambiguity" practiced by politicians (which he, however, finds harmful to electoral democracy) Page (1978) has argued that political candidates have deliberate recourse to ambiguous talk, not in response to their perception of the interests pursued by rational actors but as a way to exert strategic control over the types of information and campaign issues they wish to bring before the public.

5 Mayhew has produced an important critical revision of this Parsonian implication in his "Ascription in Modern Society" (1968).

Bibliography

Almond, Gabriel. 1960. "A Functional Approach to Comparative Politics." *The Politics of the Developing Areas*. Princeton, NJ.: Princeton University Press.

Chap, Yuen Ren. 1959. "Ambiguity in Chinese." In *Studia Serica Bernhard Karlgren Dedicata*, ed. S. Egerod and E. Glahn, 1–13. Copenhagen: Munksgaard.

Capra, Fritjof. 1984. *The Tao of Physics*. Rev. ed. New York: Bantam Books.

Berque, Jacques. 1961. "Expression et signification dans la vie arabe." *L'homme* 1 (2):50–67.

Echewa, T. Obinkaram. 1982. "A Nigerian Looks at America." *Newsweek*, July 5:13.

Edelman, Murray. 1964. *The Symbolic Uses of Politics*. Urbana: University of Illinois Press.

Geertz, Clifford 1960. *The Religion of Java*. Glencoe, IL: Free Press

Granet, Marcel. 1958. *Chinese Civilization*. New York: World.

Kooij, J.G. 1961. *Ambiguity in Natural Language*. Amsterdam: North-Holland.

Laitin, David. 1977. *Politics, Language, and Thought*. Chicago: University of Chicago Press.

Levi, Edward H. 1948. *An Introduction to Legal Reasoning*. Chicago: University of Chicago Press.

Mayhew, Leon. 1968, "Ascriptions in Modern Society." *Sociological Inquiry* 34: 105–20.

Moges, Alemayhu. 1956. *Sewāsew Ge'ez*. Addis Ababa: Tasfā Press.

McKeon, Richard. 1961. "The Flight from Certainty and the Quest for Precision." *Review of Metaphysics* 18: 234–53.

Nakamura, H. 1960. *The Ways of Thinking of Eastern Peoples*. Japanese National Commission for UNESCO.

Phelps, General John Wolcott. 1873. *Secret Societies, Ancient and Modern*. Chicago.

Shils, Edward. 1956. *The Torment of Secrecy*. Glencoe, Ill.: Free Press.

Weaver, Richard. 1958. "Individuality and Modernity." In *Essays on Individuality*, ed. Felix Morley, 63–81. Philadelphia: University of Pennsylvania Press.

Weber, Max. 1958c. *The Religion of India*, trans. H. H. Gerth and Don Martindale. Glencoe, Ill.: Free Press.

33

Ethiopia and Japan in Comparative Civilizational Perspective (1997)*

Although Ethiopia and Japan appear disparate, depth-historical analysis reveals striking similarities across four epochs. An epoch of genesis and classical synthesis, ca 600 BCE to mid-7C CE, displays migrations across narrow waterways, prehistoric centers, burial megaliths, worship of nature/heavenly bodies, leading to strong kingdoms (4C CE), conversions to world religions, episodes of return colonization, then (6–7C) spread of those religions and related architecture. Epoch II, mid-7C through 15C, opens with civil warfare, abandonment of classic capitals; by 12C, new centers arise inland (Zagwe, Kamakura), leading to geopolitical expansion, burgeoning national sentiment, and (in 14–15C) efflorescence of religious/aesthetic culture.

Epoch III displays external warfare, then Portuguese Jesuits in mid-16C. Expulsion of Catholics (early 17C) precipitates isolation for two centuries—time for political realignments, magnificent castle towns, new decentralizations. Finally, 19C European incursions disrupt isolation and force modernization.

---

* Originally presented at the 13th International Conference of Ethiopian Studies, Kyoto, December 12-17, 1997. Published in *Passages: Interdisciplinary Journal of Global Studies* 3 (1), 1-32.

Pressures from Egypt, Sudan, Europe incite nation-building in Ethiopia; Anglo-American ships unleash modernization in Japan. Ancient myths of sacred emperors revive to advance modern nation-building, including victories against Italy and Russia ca 1900. Constitutions of 1889 (Meiji) and 1931 (Haile Selassie) pronounce emperor "sacred and inviolable."

Comparable formal features of the two civilizations include:

(1) receptive insularity

(2) idealized alien culture

(3) sacralizing homeland

(4) cultural parochialization

(5) religious pluralism

(6) political decentralization

(7) warrior ethos

(8) value patterns of hierarchical particularism

Differences highlighted against this ground of commonalities may explain the two countries' radically divergent modernizing experiences. Salient factors include:

(1) geographic conditions favoring trade

(2) use of monetary currency

(3) urbanization

(4) ethnic homogeneity

(5) centuries of domestic peace

(6) differentiation of political structures

(7) legitimation of trade and a commercial class

(8) valorization of craft ethic

(9) collectivism/individualism pattern variable

At first blush, it is hard to imagine two societies more dissimilar than Japan and Ethiopia. Consider their religious traditions. With most of its historic peoples adhering to Judaism, Christianity, and Islam, Ethiopia presents an exemplar par excellence of Semitic religiosity, marked by moral subordination to a commanding supernatural deity—as is its largest indigenous tradition, that of the Oromo. In sharp contrast, Japanese religiosity, which draws from an even more diverse range of traditions—Shinto, Buddhism, neo-Confucianism, and Taoism—has been oriented in ways that sacralize the natural world.

Or consider their economies. With 7% of its labor force in agriculture, Japan ranks among the wealthiest countries in the world; Ethiopia, with a labor force

80% in agriculture, remains one of the poorest. Japan reports a literacy rate of 100%; Ethiopia's populace is largely illiterate (10% literacy in 1976, about 36% two decades later). Japan's population enjoys exceptional health, registering life expectancies of 77 (male)/83 (female) and an infant mortality rate of 4 per 1,000, and supporting one physician per 566 persons; Ethiopians still suffer a number of chronic epidemics, register life expectancies of 46 (male)/48 (female) and an infant mortality rate of 123 per 1,000, and get by with no more than one physician for 60,000 people.

Or consider their political records. Japan shows continuous political stability over the past half century. During the same period, Ethiopia witnessed numerous revolts and attempted coups; a rash of civil wars, leading in the case of Eritrea to outright secession; two forcible changes of regime; and, at present, a regime held illegitimate by some sectors of the population and by a vocal expatriate community. Japan has maintained a civil society that permits a wide range of free political and cultural expression, whereas Ethiopia holds more independent journalists in prison than any country outside of China and Turkey.

Their records in the international arena show comparably dramatic contrasts. Japan's invasions of Manchuria and China in the 1930s helped trigger World War II and led to severe cruelties toward the peoples of East Asia, including China, Korea, Burma, and the Philippines. By contrast, Ethiopia in the 1930s was a victim of unprovoked invasion by Fascist Italy, pursued through a war machine that rained poisoned gas upon peasants armed with spears. In the postwar era, Japan tended to abstain from international efforts to stem Communist expansion and maintain world peace, whereas Ethiopia, earlier casualty of a dysfunctional system of collective security, played a gallant role in United Nations military actions in Korea and the Congo and, through actions of both Emperor Haile Selassie and her current Prime Minister, performed statesmanlike services in mediating major conflicts in Nigeria, Morocco, Somalia, and the Sudan.

Given such contrasts, a thesis about basic similarities between the two nations would appear fanciful. To note, for example, that Showan Emperor Haile Selassie I (1931–74) was reckoned the 126th monarch of a continuous Solomonid dynasty while Showa Emperor Hirohito (1926–89) was reckoned the 124th monarch of the continuous Jimmu dynasty must seem part coincidence, part pun. Yet even those who link a thesis about parallels between Ethiopia and Japan to the fevered imagination of a comparative sociologist might pause before this fact: earlier in the present century, writers in both countries expressed acute awareness of their mutual affinities (Zewde 1990). Thus, an issue of The Japanese Weekly Chronicle in 1933 celebrated "the spiritual affinity between Japan and Abyssinia,"[1] while in Ethiopia, pre-war Foreign Minister Blattengeta

Heruy Walde Selassie (in Medhara Berhan Hagara Japan [The Japanese Nation, Source of Light]) and post-war Minister of Education Kebbedde Michael (in Japan Indemin Seletenech [How Japan Modernized]) described striking similarities between the two countries. Scarcely noticed among those similarities was the fact that Ethiopia and Japan were the only non-European countries to defeat modern European imperialists (Ethiopia against Italy in 1896, Japan against Russia in 1905). Prior to that, moreover, they had distinguished themselves by withstanding other imperial powers: Japan against Mongols in the 1280s, Ethiopia against Ottoman Turks in the 1580s. Both countries welcomed intercourse with the Portuguese early in the 16th century, whom they then extruded abruptly early in the following century.

Behind those stunning coincidences, I shall now argue, lay societal developments that exhibit strikingly similar trajectories across two-and-a-half millennia, and civilizational forms that are in important respects identical. Appreciation of those similarities may led to hypotheses about patterns of civilizational dynamics more generally as well as provide some considerations to qualify claims of absolute uniqueness. Against those similarities, moreover, factors that led to such discrepant experiences of modernization come to be seen with increased clarity and security.

A. Historical profiles

The many connotations of the concept of civilization include the notion of a society extended in time and space. Although the spatial extensions of Ethiopia and Japan are not nearly so vast as those of the commonly cited cases of Chinese, South Asian, Islamic, and Hellenic civilizations, their extension in time is remarkable. Both societies bear marks of continuous development over more than 2,500 years. To represent those developments in summary fashion I have divided them into four periods, which are represented schematically in Figure 1.

Figure 1: Developmental Profiles of Ethiopian and Japanese Civilizations

PERIOD	HISTORICAL EPISODES	ETHIOPIA	JAPAN
I. 7C BCE to 8C BCE GENESIS AND CLASSICAL SYNTHESIS	Immigrants cross channels, upgrade agriculture, mix with indigenous peoples	Semites from SW Arabia invade indigenous nilotes and Cushites, 1st Millenium BCE	Yayoi from Korea invade indigenous Ainu and Jomon, 4C BCE
	Prehistoric kingdoms established, ca 7–5C BCE	Pre-Aksumite kingdoms at Yeha and Azbi, ca 7–5 BCE	Mythic Jimmu dynasty at Nara, ca 7–5C BCE
	Historic Kingdoms flourish 1–7C CE Burial megaliths for chieftains Conquest of nearby peninsula	Agazyan kingdom at Aksum, 1–7C CE Giant obelisks at Aksum SW Arabia occupied, 3–4C & 520–575 CE	Yamato dynasty, 4–7C CE Giant mounds (kofun) at Yamato, 3–6C Korea occupied, 360–562; final rout, 668
	Early nature religions, supplemented through imported world religion, 4–7C	Nature spirits, sun, moon, Venus Christianity enters with conversion of Ezana, 356; diffused by Kaleb and Syrian missionaries, 6C	Nature spirits, sun-goddess; Buddhism enters from Korea, 538; diffused via Prince Shotoku, early 7C
	Classical religious architecture	Debra Damo monastery, 6C Rockhewn churches throughout Tigray	Horyuji monastery, 7C Nara temples, Daibutsu, 8C

PERIOD	HISTORICAL EPISODES	ETHIOPIA	JAPAN
III. 16C mid-19C INTER-NATIONAL TENSIONS AND NATIONAL ISOLATION	Protracted warfare, internal and external	Adali jihad, 1527–43 Oromo incursions, 1527–1600 Defeat of Ottoman Turks, 1580s	Wars of unification, 1568–1603 Hideyoshi invades Korea and China, 1590–1600
	Portuguese Jesuits introduce European culture; alien religion engenders civil strife, expulsion of Jesuits, 16–17C	Portuguese Jesuits arrive (Alvarez mission), 1520 Emp. Susneyos converts, 1622 Aggressive Mendez mission arrives, 1622 Jesuits are expelled, 1632	Jesuit mission arrives, 1549 Daimyo of Kyushu converts to Catholicism, 1563 Hideyoshi Edict curtails work of Jesuits, 1587 Christian missionaries are expelled, 1624–1639
	2 1/4 centuries of national isolation, 1620s–1850s	1632–1850s	1614–1850s
	Stable capital; construction of major castles	Gonder flourishes, castles are built by successive emperors, 1632–1755	Osaka and other sites are established as castle towns, 16C
	Rule by feudal lords, with emperor a background figurehead	*Zemena mesafint*, ca 1750–1850	Tokugawa Shogunate, 1603–1868

IV. mid-19C to mid-20C	Incursions by European powers	British at Magdala, 1868	Americans at Uraga, 1853; British bombardments, 1863–4
EUROPEAN INCURSIONS AND IMPERIAL MODERNIZATION	Classic notion of sacral monarchy restored	Tewodros II, 1855–68; Yohannes IV, 1871–89; Sahle Maryam restores Solomonid symbolism as Menelik II, 1889	Restoration of Meiji emperor, 1868
	First defeat of European powers	Dogali, 1887; Adwa, 1896	Russo-Japanese War, 1904–5
	Constitution promulgated, defining emperor as "sacred and inviolable"	1931	1889
	Reign of last traditional emperor		Hirohito, 1926–89 ("124th monarch of Jimmu dynasty")

Period I: Genesis and Classical Synthesis

The prehistories of both nations are conspicuously obscure. In both cases, they have left exquisite pottery: recently-discovered ceramic pots of pre-Aksumites, long-celebrated pottery from Jomon culture. Both prehistories involve the migration of technologically advanced people across waterways—the Yayoi from Korea, Sabaeans from Southwest Arabia—over unknown centuries of the first millennium BCE. Improved agriculture, including irrigation, supported a regime of sacred chieftains, who established cities that were at once political capitals, sacred sites, and commercial centers. They also produced enormous burial structures—obelisks at Aksum, kofun at Yamato. Their religions were oriented to the worship of natural spirits and heavenly bodies.

The period from mid-4C to mid-6C CE formed a turning point in both civilizations. It saw the consolidation of strong kingdoms and initial conversions to a world religion—Christianity and Buddhism, respectively. Growing strength of the kingdoms was accompanied by episodes of return colonization. Aksumite expeditions to South Arabia date from early 3C, and King Kaleb colonized the Yemen for two decades in the sixth century. Japan occupied, by some accounts, three Korean provinces from mid-4C to mid-6C.

The classical period reached a climax with new impetus toward the diffusion of the world religions in the 6th century. Ethiopia experienced major liturgical innovations and missionary activity carried out by a number of Syrian monks, followed by the creation of enduring valuable religious architecture: the Debra Damo monastery and rock-hewn churches throughout Tigray (Plant 1985). In Japan there were numerous missions to and from Buddhist centers in China, leading to the construction of the Horyuji monastery, numerous Buddhist temples, and the great Daibutsu sculpture at Nara.

Period II: Turmoil, Translocation, and Medieval Synthesis

From about the middle of the seventh century, both societies saw increased skirmishing among rival groups which, for different reasons, had the effect of leading to the abandonment of the classic capitals. Expansions of Arabs, Bejas, and Agews crippled Aksum as a commercial center and led to her destruction in late 10C. Sectarian factionalism at Nara induced Kammu in late 8C to abandon Nara as the imperial capital, and eventually to establish the new capital at Kyoto.

In both places, the societal centers moved inland, away from the shores closest to the points of entry for the migrations and influences from abroad. In Ethiopia this movement pushed southward, leading to the Zagwe Dynasty at Wag and Lasta in 12–13C, then further south to Shoa in 1270. In Japan the movement was generally eastward; although Kyoto stood in the same region as Nara, by the twelfth century the great eastern plain of Kanto had begun to compete with the classical core area of the Kinai Plain, which was located closer to the Korea Strait.

These inland movements were accompanied by a number of indigenizing cultural changes. The elaborate stylized forms of the classical period gave way to earlier traditions more attuned to nature. In Ethiopia, rectangular stone constructions of churches in the north became cylindrical churches with thatched roofs further south. After the Japanese court ended all official communications with the faltering Tang Chinese empire in 894, its culture also became inward-looking. Ornate Chinese styles gave way to the Heian style of palace architecture that used unpainted wood and thatched roofs, and a "Yamato" style of painting came to feature local scenes and incidents. Vernacular languages developed out of the classical forms. Ancestral Ethiopic (Ge'ez) produced Tigrinya and Amharic; ancestral Japanese evolved into modern Japanese and Okinawan.

Developments in the interiors issued in climaxes of political control and cultural efflorescence. In Ethiopia we find a formidable expansion of the Solomonid polity under Emperors Amde Tseyon and Zar'a Ya'qob. We also find the expansion of religious culture through the disciples of charismatic monks like Tekla Haymanot and Ewostatewos, and a new and expanding cultural role played by monasteries generally. Religious and political energies blended in the production of hagiographic chronicles of kings and saints, and a national epic, the *Kibre Negest*. In the 14–15C came the flowering of esoteric poetry and what are generally regarded as the finest works of Ethiopian painting in the form of miniatures in illustrated manuscripts.

Japan experienced a comparable medieval synthesis. This was based on the political consolidations under the Kamakura Shogunate (1185–1333) and the repulsion of an attempted invasion by Mongol forces in the 1280s, which did much to stir up national sentiment. That period was also a high point for the growth of Buddhist sects in provincial monasteries, including Lotus, True Pure Land, and Zen. The founder of Lotus, Nichiren (13C), aroused large followings with his transposition of Buddhism into a fiercely nationalistic key. The later Ashikaga Period (mid-14C to mid-16C) was a time of intense economic and cultural growth during which a number of aesthetic genres underwent notable development, including the formalized tea ceremony, no dramas, ikebana (the art of flower arranging), and what are considered to be the greatest schools of Japanese painting.

Period III: International Tensions and National Isolation

For both civilizations, the sixteenth century marked a crucial turning point. The scale of warfare was magnified as both empires found themselves embattled within and without. The Ethiopian kingdom was attacked in 1527 by Adali subjects from the east, on a jihad that had local roots but was inspired and equipped by the Ottoman Turks. After barely surviving that assault, the kingdom was engaged in decades of struggles sparked by the momentous expansion of Oromo tribes from the south. During a resurgent interval, the monarchy under Sarsa Dengel (r.1563–1597) checked the territorial ambitions of the Turks along the Eritrean coast. In Japan, a century of protracted feudal skirmishings—the period of "Warring States"—led to the massive centralizing military campaigns of Nobunaga (d. 1582) and his successors. Under Hideyoshi (r. 1582–98), Japan attempted to conquer China by mounting two mammoth (but unsuccessful) invasions of Korea in the 1590s.

More consequential for their longer-term histories, the sixteenth century marked the beginning of a shift of Ethiopia's and Japan's external focus from their classical sources of stimulation in Semitic and Chinese civilizations to the encounter with European civilization. Navigators from Portugal, who reached both shores at about the same time in the early 1540s, were the prime initiators of this encounter. The Portuguese brought such benefits—military and diplomatic assistance to Ethiopia, trade links to Japan, firearms to both[4]—that they were welcomed in both lands, and Portuguese and then Spanish Jesuit missionaries converted significant sectors of their elites to Catholicism.

By the end of the century they had won sufficient converts among the high and mighty, and alienated other elite elements, that intense civil strife ensued. This eventuated in a backlash against European Christians and their abrupt expulsion. Efforts to suppress Christianity in Japan began with Hideyoshi's edict of 1587 and culminated with the expulsion of the Spanish in 1624 and the Portuguese in 1639. After Emperor Susneyos decided his conversion to Catholicism was disastrous for the country, he abdicated in 1632, whereupon Fasilidas expelled the Jesuits.

These episodes with the Jesuits precipitated a revulsion against Europeans and national policies of isolation and turning inward that persisted for more than two centuries. Although their isolation deprived them of the stimulation and technical advances they would have enjoyed by remaining in contact with the outward world, it gave them opportunities to develop their own political institutions and resources. The dynasty of emperors from Fasilidas through Iyasu II created the first stationary political capital in Ethiopia since Aksum; the dynasty of shoguns founded by Tokugawa Ieyasu constructed a new imperial bureaucracy and consolidated a stable class structure. The new dynasts flaunted their national political muscle from magnificent castle towns, at Gonder, and at Azuchi, Momoyana, and Osaka.

Period IV: European Incursions and Imperial Modernization

The centuries of national isolation were interrupted by dramatic episodes that signaled a need to contend with expansionist foreign powers. In Ethiopia the pressures of Mahdist expansionism from Egypt and Sudan and of British, French, and Italian colonialism incited the nation-building efforts of 19C emperors Tewodros II, Yohannes IV, and Menelik II. The cannon at Uraga Bay unleashed a burst of nationalist activity in Japan that included restoration of the Meiji monarchy. In both cases, ancient myths of sacred emperors were revitalized as a way to inspire efforts needed to build a modern nation, and both nations enshrined the symbolism of their ancient sacral monarchy in their modernizing constitutions.[4]

So mobilized, both peoples mounted major efforts to defend themselves against encroachments from European powers. These resulted in the defeat of Italian forces by Ras Alula at Dogali in 1887 and by Emperor Menilek's armies at Adwa in 1896, and in the defeat of Russian forces, after two years of intense combat by Emperor Meiji's troops, in 1905. Their military prowess made Ethiopia and Japan the first two non-European powers to negotiate treaties with European nations at the turn of the century. The internal history of both societies since the late 19C includes numerous efforts to promote modernization from above that were legitimated by the imperial throne.

Compressing this brief summary, one can weave key developments of each period into a single narrative. Both Ethiopia and Japan began their civilizational growth by grafting an idealized external culture onto a proud indigenous base. Over centuries the resulting culture diffused inland over far-flung areas through the institutions of a sacralized monarchy and religious traditions that buttressed those institutions. In the sixteenth century they again found external challenges, and briefly shifted attention from their classical roots to a newly expanding Europe. After some initial conversions to European Christian faith, their elites evinced nativistic reactions. Ensuing centuries of isolation gave them space to build up internal political might along traditional feudal lines. When at last they could ignore the threats of foreign expansion no longer, they looked toward European models in determined efforts to modernize, while restoring an archaic notion of imperial grandeur.

B. Civilizational form

In addition to comparing their patterns of historical development, one can also think about civilizations by considering certain formal properties they exhibit across their innumerable changes. To do this is to think of a civilization, as Robert Redfield once put it, "as having a form that remains the same while the content, institutions, usages, beliefs change" (Redfield 1962, 373). In comparing the civilizations of Ethiopia and Japan, I find a common form that exhibits a complex of geopolitical and cultural features. These I propose to gloss as receptive insularity; idealization of alien culture; sacralization of an imperial homeland; parochialization; religious pluralism; political decentralization; a hegemonic warrior ethos; and hierarchical particularism.

1. Receptive Insularity

Begin with geography. Japan comprises a set of large islands and countless small ones; Ethiopia is a virtual island: a large land mass bordered nearly one third by water, and otherwise ringed by forbidding deserts, lowlands, and mountainous escarpments. Both territories exerted an attraction on outsiders; both contain temperate climates, fertile areas, and sticky borders, in that people tend to stay once they have made it in.

This is true for movements of culture as for movements of peoples. Observers of both civilizations emphasize the extent to which each was eager to import alien cultural elements and then to appropriate them in their home idiom through processes of "Ethiopianization" and "Japanization." In *Storia della letteratura etiopica* (1956), Enrico Cerulli described this trait by noting that throughout their history, Ethiopian authors were influenced by foreign writings —by Greek, Syrian, Arabic, and European sources—to an exceptional degree, but in a way that never took the form of passive, literal borrowing:

> Rather, one can say that it is precisely a typical Ethiopian tendency to collect the data of foreign cultural and literary experience and transform them, sooner or later, to such an extent that even translations in Ethiopic are not always translations, in our sense of the term; but they frequently contain additions, supplementary material, at times misrepresentations of the original, at other times simply the insertion of new materials in such a quantity that the literal sense of the original is completely lost. (Cerulli 1956, 12–13).

A pattern of indigenizing incorporation has also been described for painting, music, agriculture, and religion, where

> "Ethiopian responses reveal a recurrent pattern that indicates neither nativistic rejection nor slavish adherence to imported forms, but a disposition to react to the stimulations of exogenous models by developing and then rigidly preserving distinctly Ethiopian versions" (Levine 1974, 65).

A comparable pattern of importation and indigenization has been ascribed to Japanese culture by many observers. It was manifest over centuries by the deliberate importation from China of forms of writing, architecture, technology, religious belief, and ethical doctrines, which in turn underwent a special coloration in being fashioned to suit the themes of Japanese experience. This reshaping into a Japanese idiom affects virtually everything that has been imported, from Chinese Buddhism to American baseball. Referring to the extensive incorporation of external influences—"ideas, artifacts, technologies, styles of dress"—into Japanese culture, Shmuel Eisenstadt contends that the process of Japanization "entailed, not just the addition of local color, but the transformation of their basic conceptions in line with the basic premises of Japanese civilization" (Eisenstadt 1996, 303–4). This was manifest, for example, in the transformation of the Chinese notion of the emperor as standing under the Mandate of Heaven to the Japanese notion of tenno, a heavenly ruler not accountable t o any transcendent authority. Similarly, in his noted novel Silence (1969), Shusaku Endo describes the early Japanese appropriation of Christianity as confounding the Latin term Deus with the Japanese Dainichi—Great Sun; somewhat mordantly, Endo employs the metaphor of a mud swamp for the Japanese pattern of receptive insularity.

2. *Idealized alien culture*

The receptivity of these two geopolitical islands to foreign cultures displayed a special intensity and poignancy in relation to two major civilizational centers—Solomonic Israel and T'ang China. The path laid by prestigious Sabaean culture-bearers was followed by waves of later immigrants who converted inhabitants of the Aksumite realm to Judaeo-Christianity, later to Islam. In this process, Jerusalem became idealized as the ancestral center whence originated the two major sources of royal legitimacy, descendance from the line of King Solomon and possession of the Ark of the Covenant from the temple at Jerusalem. This momentous cultural transfiguration was embodied in the *Kibre Negest*, a text incorporating many oral and written traditions from Ethiopia and the Near East, which was redacted by Tigrean scribes in the 14th century.[4] The idealization of Semitic culture anchored at Jerusalem appears as the generative assumption of the *Kibre Negest*. It appears in total acceptance of the belief in the divine dispensation accorded to the Solomonic lineage and the Christian mission, and extends to denigration of dark skin color and of the lineage descended from Ham (Levine 1974, 103 ff).

During the same centuries that would lead to the compilation of an Ethiopian epic extolling Semitic symbols, Japan's elite was drawn toward what they perceived as the superior Chinese civilization. As Ethiopia had imported a Semitic script from Arabia Felix, Japan imported ideographic writing from China. From the sixth century on, Japanese kings sent emissaries to China in a determined effort to enhance their power and prestige. The Yamato court adopted the Chinese calendar, reorganized court ranks and etiquette in accordance with Chinese models, created a system of highways, began to compile official chronicles, and erected Buddhist temples. Prince Shotoku (573–621), in particular, sent many students to learn Buddhism and Confucianism, and promulgated a Seventeen Article Constitution based largely on Han Confucianism. Shotoku's respect for Chinese culture was so immense that he suppressed any reference to traditional Japanese religious practices or to the Japanese principle of hereditary succession in his Constitution.

3. *Sacralized homeland*

Although Ethiopia and Japan idealized the foreign sources of Great Traditions which they sought to incorporate, they counterposed to that idealization a strong feeling of national pride and a keen sense of being hallowed as a chosen nation. They accomplished this by creating a divine emperor and by identifying the inhabitant of that office with the sacred mission of his nation, which gave them sufficient self-confidence later to disavow their earlier sources of foreign inspiration.

In Ethiopia, this involved a reversal of values through which Ethiopia came to be defined as a Chosen Nation that had taken the place of the Chosen People of Israel. The *Kibre Negest* did this, first, by representing Menilek as the first-born of Solomon's sons, then by having Menilek and his retainers steal the Ark of the Covenant from Solomon's temple in Jerusalem and spirit it back to the region of Aksum. The transfer of God's favor to Ethiopia was sealed by their reception of the Christian faith, and finally by condemning the "Roman" Christians for having forsaken the orthodox faith by following the heretical teachings of Nestorius. This signified Ethiopia's emergence as the sole authentic bearer of Christianity, home of the only people in the world thereafter favored by the God of Solomon.

In Japan, a comparable tension was already hinted at in the reign of Prince Shotoku, in letters he sent to the Sui court that seemed to assert a status equal to that of the Chinese sovereign.[5] As in Ethiopia, the crucial factor in elevating Japan above its idealized source of legitimacy was to claim a special divine status for the country's emperor by tracing his lineage to a uniquely sacralized apex. This stemmed from indigenous beliefs associated with what came to be called Shintoism, especially the notion that the Japanese emperor was descended from Amaterasu, the Sun Goddess. The charisma thus associated with the Japanese emperor became constitutive of the privileged status of the Japanese people. As one of the leaders of the 18C Shinto revival, Motoori Norinaga, reaffirmed: "The Sun Goddess is a universal deity as well as a national one, but she has shown special favor to the Japanese and guides them to a special destiny" (Tsunoda et al. II, 15). (There is solar symbolism in the Ethiopian lore, too, for the *Kibre Negest* marks the shift of divine favor from the Jews to the Ethiopians by a dream of Solomon in which the sun flies away from Israel to shine brightly ever after over the land of Ethiopia.)

Throughout the past millennium, the emperors, however powerless, never ceased to be the ultimate legitimators of the sacralized political order. Rases and shoguns, however ambitious, could never be invested with the powers and symbols of a legitimate monarch. Although Hideyoshi and Tewodros came from peasant stock, they both sought to legitimate themselves by associating themselves with imperial symbolism. The latent symbolic significance of the emperor made it possible for the imperial symbol to be drastically reconfigured in the Meiji period as the central symbol of the new political regime (Eisenstadt 1996, 249), as happened to a large extent during the reigns of Menelik II and Haile Selassie I.

In both countries, the feeling of being part of a chosen nation has been reinforced at the local level by the dispersal of symbolism that embodies their chosenness. Most Abyssinian homes belonged to a parish which contains a tabot, a replica of the Ark of the Covenant allegedly brought to the land from Jerusalem. Similarly, many Japanese homes in the Edo period came to possess a piece of the shrine of the Sun Goddess at Ise, thus honoring the divine ancestry of the emperor. The sense of being especially chosen referred to land and language as well as to the image of an age-old divine monarchy. Both Ethiopians and Japanese tend to revere their scenic landscapes as exceptionally precious and their national languages as bearing some transcendent imprint.

4. *Parochialization*

Central to the civilizations of Ethiopia and Japan alike, then, is a collective self-image that rests on a perch facing in two directions, outward toward an idealized foreign culture and inward to a sacralized imperial homeland. One may gain further insight into this combination of outward idealization and self-idealization by considering the formulations of S. N. Eisenstadt in his magisterial Japanese Civilization (1996). Eisenstadt views Japan in a perspective framed by the conception of Axial civilizations—those civilizations within which emerged new types of ontological visions involving conceptions of a basic tension between transcendental and mundane orders (ancient Israel and later second-Temple Judaism and Christianity; ancient Greece; Zoroastrian Iran; early Imperial China; Hinduism and Buddhism; and, later, Islam). This leads him to construe Japan as "the only non- Axial civilization that maintained . . . a history of its own, without being in some way marginalized by the Axial civilizations . . . with which it was in continuous contact" (14). Moreover, unlike other non- Axial civilizations, Japan evolved an elaborate "wisdom literature" and sophisticated philosophical and aesthetic discourse. The uniqueness of Japanese civilization, he suggests, reflects its pervasive "de-Axialization." Although Japanese elites imported the Axial traditions of Buddhism and Confucianism, they transformed them in ways that weakened their critical impact on the mundane order. This transformation "was a double-pronged one, manifest, on the cultural and ideological level, in the weakening of transcendental and universalistic orientations and their channeling into an immanentist, particularistic, primordial direction and, on the organizational level, in the relatively low institutional autonomy of the major Confucian schools and scholars and of the Buddhist's sects' leaders and seers, who remained embedded in the prevailing social settings and networks—be they familial, regional, or political" (259–60).

The key moment in Eisenstadt's interpretation would seem to be the shift of sacralization from transcendent principles to the glorification of Japan itself. More generally, this can be construed as a process of parochialization. This process has other manifestations. Historically, Japan has been content to hold on to its indigenized versions of universalistic ideologies such as Buddhism,

Confucianism, and various Western ideologies without attempting to re-export them. Prior to its expansionist counteroffensive against the West earlier in this century, Japan showed no missionary impulse. And although Japan has continually been oriented to other, broader civilizations, it has never considered itself to be part of a broader civilizational universe (Eisenstadt 1996, 304, 308).

Although one must be careful to avoid distortions when fitting the facts of Ethiopia's civilization into this mold, to the extent that resemblances can be identified, they are illuminating. It is perhaps most accurate to say that Ethiopian civilization tilted heavily in the direction of Japan's parochialization, even if it did not lean quite so far as Japan did. It is true that Ethiopian Orthodox Church was formally under the jurisdiction of the Alexandrian Patriarchate for sixteen centuries (ca 360 CE to 1960); that Ethiopian Christians and Jews alike oriented themselves to what they understood as their ancestral homeland in the Holy Land; and that Ethiopian delegates were welcomed at the Council of Florence in 1441. That said, it is also true that a primary orientation of most Ethiopian elites has been to the suzerainty of their divine emperor, and that no Ethiopian emperor could have been overthrown before 1974, as occurred repeatedly in China or Europe, by an appeal to universalistic principles. The rebellions against Emperors Susneyos and Lij Iyasu were cases in point, since the charges against them were that they were threatening the national polity by affiliating too brazenly with religionists from outside lands.

Again, apart from the brief excursion into Yemen at the behest of the Byzantine King Justin, the enlargement of their territory by conquest of adjacent areas, and the exceptional proselytizing of Emperor Yohannes IV, Ethiopian kings were not disposed to engage in missionary activity on behalf of their parochialized faith. One cannot imagine Ethiopian kings, no matter how powerful, organizing something on the order of a European Crusade or an Islamic jihad. The latter-day diffusion of Ethiopian themes in Jamaica through the Rastafarian movement was a source of embarrassment for Ethiopians. Finally, although Aksumite Ethiopia did indeed figure as an active part of a broader civilizational universe, following the Arab expansions of the 7C which cut her off from much of the outside world Ethiopia became peripheral to the Judaic and Christian ecumenes—as, later, her converts to Islam became peripheral to the Islamic ecumene.

In the encounter with modernity, finally, neither civilization sought to legitimate its reluctant embrace in universalistic terms. The Meiji insistence on progress and on learning from the West, like that of Emperors Menilek and Haile Selassie, appealed to needs to defend their country against foreign imperialisms and to cope with the more successful nations of Europe, not to a discourse that affirmed the general, universalistic values of modern culture.

5. *Religious pluralism*

One consequence of softening the demands of an axial doctrine has been a relatively permissive attitude toward different faiths. Although all historic religions can be said to involve combinations of cultural traits, there seems to be a distinctive type of syncretic pattern in Ethiopia and Japan that marks their religious experience off from comparable experiences elsewhere, especially in Europe and much of the Islamic world. I shall gloss it as pluralism, to emphasize a certain degree of acceptance and interconnection of distinct religious traditions rather than their syncretic combination in a single faith.

In both countries, this pluralistic acceptance extends to ancient local traditions as well as to world religions, although the former is more pronounced in Japan and the latter in Ethiopia. In Japan, devotion to spirits known as kami reflects an ancestral worship of things of nature that became codified as Shinto. Local kami have been worshipped for protection and have formed a basis for communal identities. They have entered into the national political culture by the myth of Jimmu, a divine warrior. This myth makes subsequent Japanese emperors descendants of the kami whose shrine is at Ise, Sun Goddess Amaterasu. Side by side with these beliefs has been the observance of many forms of Buddhism. The two traditions have not been synthesized, but have functioned in a complementary way, for example, with Shinto rituals being observed for birth and wedding ceremonies and Buddhist rituals at death.

Perhaps the most striking feature of Ethiopian religious pluralism has been the extent to which the different Semitic religions, so often at war with one another in most other countries, have been practiced in ways that have not been absolutely exclusive. Ethiopian Christianity not only incorporates a number of ancient Judaic features but also enjoyed many centuries of intercourse with Hebraized religionists, like the Felashas and the Qemant. The former, it now seems clear, incorporated Christian liturgy and monastic practices in the course of constituting their distinctive tradition (Shelemay 1986). Indeed, over time there have been numerous conversions in both directions between Christians and Jews (Pankhurst 1992). Relations with Islam began on a cordial foot, with Mohammed reportedly telling his followers of the friendliness of the Abyssinian kingdom; despite severe political hostilities in 16C and more recent times, Muslim traditions have also enjoyed phases of toleration and mutuality. Symbolic of their close relations is the existence of ceremonies and pilgrimages where members of all three religions participate, such as the annual pilgrimage to honor Saint Gabriel at Kulubi.

In addition, Ethiopian national culture continues to draw on pre-Christian local traditions, as in the sacralization of natural phenomena like mountains and trees, and the association of chiefly power with the symbolism of lions and honeybees. The constitution of Christian Ethiopian communal identities in terms of the local tabot has some resemblance to the Japanese association of local identities with their kami. And there is more than a little resemblance between their respective customs of carrying about portable shrines: parading with the colorfully-attended tabot on Ethiopian Orthodox holidays and celebrating the brilliantly-decorated makoshi during matsuri festivals. Indeed, a number of ceremonies and pilgrimages find practitioners of traditional Oromo religion, Christianity, and Islam participating jointly or taking turns. Thus, the Faraqasa pilgrimage draws heavily on Islamic traditions, yet includes elements of Christian and local Oromo symbolism (Pankhurst 1994).

6. Decentralization of control

Beyond the fact of their insularity, Ethiopia and Japan further exhibit geographical similarities in the character of their terrain. Both countries possess forbiddingly mountainous topographies, often described as the Alps of Africa and Asia. Their mountains formed borders among numerous localities, affording them distinctive identities as provinces or feudal domains. The political histories of both countries have accordingly been stories of continuous oscillation between efforts to centralize and centrifugal forces that isolated local domains. At the extreme, this issued in periods of feudal organization where the hold of an imperial center was extremely attenuated. Even at its strongest, however, the Ethiopian monarchy always characterized itself as negusa negest—King of Kings—indicating that in principle the rulers of provincial regions had some sort of claim to special authority. This devolution of authority reproduced itself at successive lower levels. Folk wisdom on the process found expression in the words of an Amharic proverb, "Ka-Gonder negus/ yagar ambaras"—"the petty district chief [is obeyed] more that the Gonder King" (Levine 1965, 156). When Emperor Menilek embarked on far-reaching imperial expansion that more than tripled the size of the territory under the authority of the Ethiopian state, he was perfectly content to recognize the jurisdiction of local chiefs and kings so long as they submitted to his overarching authority.

The pattern of decentralizing control figures as one of the most frequently noted themes in analyses of Japanese society. It was manifest in the unique baku-han system of the Tokugawa political system, whereby authority was wielded by regional administrators, the daimyo, despite a unified national authority under the shogun. Ruth Benedict (1946) describes this pattern more generally as a parcelization of obligations into separate spheres of activity. Thomas Rohlen (1989) represents it as a devolution of political authority, involving delegated trust, to various peripheral domains. Eisenstadt (1996) represents it in various ways, including flexibility of movement among different social contexts, extensions of trust, and a striking capacity to incorporate protest and oppositional demands. For both countries, a disposition to tolerate political decentralization evinces an elective affinity for the pattern of religious pluralization.

The necessity of decentralization has favored the longevity of a type of social system that has often been described as feudal in character. Analysts have estimated the duration of feudalism in both societies at more than a thousand years (Reischauer 1950, Levine 1965). In thinking of Japan, the definition of feudalism that John Hall formulated with an eye to Japan holds equally well for Ethiopia:

> Feudalism is . . . a condition of society in which there is at all levels a fusion of the civil, military, and judicial elements of government into a single authority. This fusion of public and private functions being achieved in the person of the locally powerful military figure, it is also natural that military practices and values become predominant in the total society. (Hall 1970, 77)

7. *Warrior ethos*

The ascendance of powerful warrior-lords and their retainers made martial values dominant in both civilizations during the past millennium, and military prowess was long the royal road to prestige and legitimacy. This was not just a matter of according high prestige to military men; it involved the diffusion of martial attitudes, virtues, and ambitions throughout the population.

This came about through very different routes. In Ethiopia, it meant the diffusion of combative dispositions and abilities throughout the population. This feature so impressed the first European practitioner of Ethiopian Studies, Job Ludolphus, that he described Ethiopians as "a Warlike People and continually exercis'd in War . . . except in Winter, at what time by reason of the Inundation of the Rivers, they are forc'd to be quiet" (Ludolphus 1684, 217). It meant that every able-bodied male who was not a clergyman was assumed ready to engage in battle at a moment's notice—armed, skilled, supplied, and transported, all through his own devices. It meant that boys were encouraged to be combative and that as men they were disposed to be fearless in combat.[6] It even meant that, for most of the past millennium, the royal capital took the form of an army camp—"a vast array of tents, arranged in combat-ready formation with the Emperor's tents in the center, flanked and guarded at the front and rear by officers of standard ranks with their entourages" (Levine 1968, 7).

In Japan, the hegemony of martial values derived not from universal combat-readiness but from the way in which a military class, the samurai, came to set the tone of the national culture over the past millennium. This class emerged in the late Heian Period as a group of military specialists positioned to serve the court nobility. In time they acquired power in their own right by establishing domination over agricultural land and building their own hierarchical political organizations, culminating in a semicentral regime, the shogunate, in the late 12C. The samurai political organization rested on the formation of strong emotional bonds between military masters and vassals upheld by a strict code of honor (Ikegami 1995). In the Tokugawa Period this code was elaborated into a formal code of martial ethics known as Bushido (the Way of the Warrior). The code enjoined such virtues as loyalty, politeness, diligence, frugality, and a constant sense of readiness to die. At this time, the bushi class became more segregated than ever, since membership in it was hereditary and only those within it were entitled to bear arms. On the other hand, the ethos of this class became hegemonic in the society. In contrast to China of the time, the Japanese insisted on retaining a martial spirit as part of the mark of a gentlemen (Hall 1970, 82). During the Tokugawa period, it has been said, the samurai ethic came close to being the national ethic, for even the merchant class had become "Bushido-ized" (Bellah 1957, 98).

One of the marks of the warrior ethos in both cultures was a disposition to value ascetic hardiness. This is manifest, for example, in the Ethiopian ideal of gwebeznet, a symbol for masculine aggressiveness and hardiness. This virtue has traditionally been instilled by encouraging boys to return insult or injury with sticks and stones, rewarding temper tantrums, and associating proper masculinity with the ability to walk barefoot, go long without food, or eat hot peppers (Levine 1966). In consequence, Ethiopian soldiers have been noted for great endurance—they climb mountains with ease, march rapidly for distances under heavy pack with light rations, and sleep on a rock. In Japan, similar virtues were the pride of the samurai class, who prided themselves on undergoing great hardships without complaint—for example by undergoing a week of arduous training outside each year in the dead of winter (kangeiko).

Another mark of the warrior ethos has been a pronounced concern about honor and a sensitivity to insult that numerous observers have found in the psychological profile of both peoples. This sensitivity probably also reflects the tension between the idealization of outsiders and self-idealization noted above.

One can also associate the prominent place of martial values in both cultures with certain aesthetic dispositions. There may be an elective affinity between the lifestyle of the warrior and an interest in expressive genres that are terse in form and wryly fatalistic in content. Beyond that, both cultures involve a mixture of emotional inhibition, strict control, and a reliance on ambiguous modes of expression that would appear to conjoin a martial ethos with what may be described as a pervasive pattern of hierarchical particularism.

8. Hierarchical particularism

A number of the features noted above and many others reflect a complex of value orientations that Robert Bellah (1957) began to analyze under the rubric of "particularistic performance" values. Particularism refer to a primary emphasis in social relations on evaluative criteria grounded on personal relations rather than universalistic standards. Kin relations comprise the locus classicus of particularism. In Japan, the family is overshadowed by larger groupings, especially the han or fiefdom, but han as well as other institutions outside the family are permeated by kinship symbolism. The same can be said of extrafamilial institutions in Ethiopia. Performance values stress the achievement of goals rather than the possession of certain qualities. In Japan, Bellah argues, there appears to be no quality or status, which, once possessed, is self-validating; rather, persons in all spheres are judged by the contribution they make to achieving the goals of the system in question. The same holds for traditional Ethiopia, where peasants were judged by their abilities in farming, litigation, and following local customs, and rulers were judged by their martial prowess and ability as governors.

I wish to extend this analysis by adding, to the pattern variables of particularism-universalism and quality-performance, a pattern variable which I employed in analyzing the traditional Abyssinian social system: hierarchalism-egalitarianism (Levine 1974). This variable concerns the extent to which a society values differences in status and relationships that involve ruling over others. Here both Ethiopia and Japan stand at the end of the continuum where all social relations are cast into superior-inferior levels, and vocabulary and gestures that register different levels of deference are highly differentiated and prominent. Although both societies honor universalism, qualities, and egalitarianism to a limited extent in certain contexts, it is clear that they place overwhelming emphasis on particularism, performance, and hierarchalism. This is to say that the archetypal social form in both societies is the patron-client relation, in which patrons are owed total allegiance and deference, while clients are supported so long as they performs in ways that enhance the patron's well-being. This pattern is not the only one that can be combined with an emphasis on martial values, but it is constitutive for martial societies that are organized as feudal systems. Allegiance to the emperor becomes a template for all other relations, but one's highest level of allegiance is due to one's local lord.

The pattern of hierarchical particularism links a number of the civilizational features already identified—in particular, features of parochialization, religious pluralism, political decentralization, and ambiguity in expressive culture, as well as systems of cultural features not yet mentioned. The primacy of particularism sets an automatic limit on the extent to which beliefs and actions can be subordinated to universalistic doctrines and standards. It provides the spiritual energy behind processes of de-Axialization that Eisenstadt has analyzed so incisively. It limits the level of universalistic regulation of moral and philosophical doctrines, thereby facilitating the kind of accommodation of differing religious traditions so conspicuous in both countries. The combination of particularism with performance and hierarchical values supports the devolution of authority onto local authorities, such that generalized criteria of service to their society at large, as evolved in China or Western Europe, can never replace patron-client connections. They translate the notion of truth into the personalistic notion of being true to one's liege, such that the deference owed to superiors in both cultures makes it important t o suppress negative feelings and to present a deceptive, congenial response on the surface.

Indeed, both countries evince an aesthetic based on suppression of affect, rigid control, and cultivation of ambiguity. This pattern appears in Abyssinian art and architecture, which reveal highly controlled repetition of geometric motifs. It is also evident in the trope of *semm'nna warq*, wax and gold, which has been favored as a way to represent the contrast between a concrete public image and a concealed private meaning. "Wax and gold" symbolizes the configuration behind the Abyssinian's predilection both for ambiguous verse couplets and for indirection in interpersonal communications (Levine 1965). All genres of Japanese art evince a tightly controlled mastery of form. In Japan the notions of tatemae and honne (public and private), and its older parallel dichotomy, omote and ura (front and back), signify important distinctions between what one reveals to others and what one keeps to oneself, a mode so constitutive of normal intercourse that outsiders tend to experience it as exasperating deception (Doi 1986). In poetry the use of a concrete image to evoke deep meanings and unspoken feelings is fundamental to the samurai aesthetic, and was articulated in the aesthetic principle of yugen, the mystery behind appearances.

The pattern of hierarchical particularism, finally, generates a mode of cultural transmission in which devotion to a particular teacher becomes a paramount consideration. This appeared in Abyssinia in the special attachments to the masters of diverse schools of liturgical song and religious poetry and, to a greater extent in Japan, in fealty to senseis who impart distinctive ways of fighting, meditating, serving tea, or arranging flowers.

9. *Weak public domain*

One of the most illuminating dimensions of Eisenstadt's analysis of Japanese civilization concerns his treatment of features of the political system that have been continually reproduced over the centuries, albeit in changing concrete forms. Persisting into the contemporary era, these include traits that disposed a constitutional-democratic system to function in a highly restrictive and repressive manner, including bureaucratic censorship; a weak system of judicial review; weak protection of human rights; and behind these, a set of decision-making processes that are diffuse and secretive, rendering it difficult to pinpoint a locus of responsibility for decisions—developments that have led some to describe the modern political system of Japan as a "pseudo-democracy" (Eisenstadt 1996, 75; Herzog, 1993).

Throughout the Meiji regime, which mediated the transition to a modern political order, public space and discourse continued to be monopolized by the government and the bureaucracy as representatives of the national community, the kokutai, legitimized by the emperor. This meant that the state was conflated with civil society, which prevented the formation of a public arena that could be autonomous from the state yet enjoy access to it.

Although Ethiopia did not develop a widely-shared conception of a national community comparable to that of the kokutai, as I mention below, Eisenstadt's account of Japanese political customs could have just as well have been written about Ethiopia. In both systems, during the crucial modernizing decades under Meiji and Haile Selassie, a continual tendency to conflate the public domain with that of the state disabled any tendencies toward open, principled political discourse. It was due to this conflation of state and civil society with the national community, Eisenstadt and others have argued, that produced so weak a civil society and led to what has been described as a pseudo-democracy.

Although Ethiopia did not achieve a constitutional democracy under Haile Selassie, it did secure a revised constitution in 1955 that provided for a system of parliamentary elections. Even so, under Haile Selassie it proved nearly impossible for participants in a civil society to form professional associations, let alone political parties. It was this difficulty, arguably, that created the vacuum into which the Derg marched during the declining months of the late emperor's regime. Under the Derg, of course, this pattern of central control of all manner of associations was enormously amplified. The pattern persists, albeit in less brazen and conspicuous form, under the current regime, whose leaders publicly advocate a strong opposition—but only after they have armed themselves handsomely, disarmed the opposition, and used their superior might to harass and discredit potential opponents. It is not surprising that one hears references to Ethiopia's current system as a pseudo-democracy (*wushetdemocracie*) even more frequently than in Japan. What is rarely appreciated is how deeply the system that leads to this repressiveness has been rooted in civilizational conditions which, like those in Japan, have a long prehistory—and which, as with Japan, figured in earlier successes in which both countries withstood European imperialisms.

C. Historic differences between the two civilizations

Faced with the profound and extensive similarities between Ethiopia and Japan outlined above, one naturally wonders how they could have negotiated the challenges of modernization so very differently. Yet precisely their extensive base of historic similarities throws into relief the factors that caused Japan to modernize so swiftly and Ethiopia so haltingly. An efficient way to identify those factors might be to ask: what accounts for the fact that in Japan, unlike Ethiopia, an extensive commercial class and a disciplined work force were securely in place when the two countries faced a need to modernize in the course of the 19th century? I shall mention nine such factors.

1. Geographic conditions favorable to trade

Although both countries were mountainous, Ethiopia's mountains were more severe. Japanese travelers could take advantage of the vast plains of Honshu, on which good roads were built during the Heian period. By the 17C a system of five major highways, the Gokaido, radiated out from Edo to connect with the highways of central and western Japan established earlier, thereby creating a national system of good roads. Ethiopia's trails could not even accommodate wheels, and travel by foot or mule was impeded for months during the annual rainy season. Not until the Italian Occupation of the 1930s did Ethiopia secure a minimal system of national highways.

With respect to transportation abroad, Ethiopia's single sea coast made it vulnerable. The 7C Arab expansion closed off the Red Sea littoral and drove a wedge between Ethiopia and Mediterranean Europe that had been essential for Aksumite trade. Although moving its center toward the interior meant a radical diminution of foreign trade for Ethiopia, in Japan moving away from the Korea Strait simply meant moving toward other ports (Hakata, Mura, Sakai, Kamakura). Both of these geographic advantages, which brought with them transportation systems for the roads and waterways and skilled merchant seamen, enabled a continuous development of domestic and foreign trade in Japan.

2. Continuous use of monetary currency

Monetary currency was widely used in both countries during the classical period. Some five hundred different mintings in gold, silver, and bronze were made in Ethiopia between 3C and 10C.[7] For reasons that have never been fully explained—but surely including the cutting off of Red Sea trade due to Islamic expansion, and protracted internal warfare—the use of monetized coins came to an end with the fall of Aksum and the move to the interior. Early in the 19C Maria Theresa Thalers came into use, but Ethiopians continued to resist the use of coinage until well into the 20C. Not until the 1920s did the peasantry and traditional elites come to accept coins at their face value. For nearly a millennium up to the eve of Ethiopia's drive to modernize, then, trade beyond barter relied largely on imperfect media like salt bars, cloth, iron bars, and, later, rifle cartridges—a condition that posed an enormous impediment to the development of capitalist enterprise there (Schaefer 1990).

Japanese trade, however, had the advantage of monetized currency throughout its history. By the Tokugawa period monetary currency was used on a national scale. Although the Japanese government was not yet minting coins again in 17C, imported Chinese currency was widely circulated, and unminted gold and silver were used by weight. Cash currency facilitated the expansion of moneylending, credit arrangements, and the one-price system, all of which were highly developed in the Edo period. It promoted the extension of trust throughout the country, a condition that is essential for the capital-intensive development Japan enjoyed and that was so muted in Ethiopia.

3. *Urbanization*

Except for the Gonderine period, Ethiopia's emperors ruled from mobile capitals for most of her history after the fall of Aksum. Except for Islamic Harar, no cities emerged to serve religious or commercial needs. Trading went on at local markets that were usually held on a weekly basis, although some larger markets were held on a daily basis. Japanese rulers, however, generally resided in urban centers. From an early period, political capitals like Nara, Kyoto, and Kamakura as well as port towns like Hamata and Osaka provided opportunities for lively commercial activity. On the eve of the Tokugawa Shogunate there occurred an enormous boost in urban development. The three decades after 1580, when the largest daimyos settled down to consolidate their resources and regimes, has been described as a period of urban construction without parallel in world history (Hall 1970, 157). By 1800, there existed a great department store in Edo (modern Tokyo) which employed over a thousand persons, and cities provided an ample supply of formally free labor available for employment in enterprises of many kinds.

4. *Ethnic homogeneity*

A prime factor affecting the birth of a secure national market in the two countries was the level of ethnic heterogeneity. Although Japan had to contend with provincial parochialisms that impeded trade at times, she had only one sizeable ethnic minority, the Ainu. Consequently, Japan never experienced destructive warfare among groups organized on ethnic and religious lines, and was able to orient nearly the entire population to the symbolism of a Japanese nation with relatively little difficulty. By contrast, Ethiopia's more severe mountainous terrain favored the separation of habitational enclaves that promoted processes of ethnic and linguistic differentiation. Consequently, the Greater Ethiopia culture area included dozens of diverse ethnic groups, most of whose members probably possessed little or no attachment to the symbolism of the Ethiopian polity. Although trading patterns among them were often of very long standing, the formation of a national market was impeded by traditions of mutual distrust, not to mention the periodic warfare that was so destructive of economic resources.

5. Centuries of domestic peace

Building on the favorable infrastructure of roads, merchant marine, currency, cities, and a nationwide ethnolinguistic community, economic development in Japan expanded enormously during the Ashikaga Period, thanks to a close, mutually supportive association between feudal lords and the merchant class. The destructive domestic warfare that occurred during the century of "Warring States" known as Sengoku (1467–1568) came to an end through the actions of the three great reunifiers: Oda Nobunaga, Toyotomi Hideyoshi, and Tokugawa Ieyasu. The Tokugawa Shogunate, or Edo period (1600–1868) provided more than two centuries of Tahei, the "great peace," giving Japan an extraordinary opportunity to develop its economic resources.

Ethiopia had a nearly identical set of geopolitical developments—a period of the princes (the Zemene Mesafint, 1755–1855), followed by three great reunifiers: Tewodros II, Yohannes IV, and Menelik II. In Ethiopia, however, these developments took place three centuries later, and were not finished when Ethiopia faced the challenge of economic modernization. The centuries Japan could use to reach a point of takeoff for full-speed economic growth were spent on protracted internal conflicts in Ethiopia.

6. Differentiation of political structures

Japan enjoyed two further structural advantages that favored the stabilization of a national market. One was the separation of the figure of the emperor from the role of the supreme political ruler, a development that was anticipated not long after the Heian period and fully consolidated during the Tokugawa Shogunate. The symbolism of the sacred throne provided some unifying cement in the country even when political differences and competing military ambitions were in play. In Ethiopia, except for the relatively short period of the Zemene

Mesafint, emperors were also supreme political rulers, such that disaffection with their policies always posed a threat to the unity of the state.

Japan's other structural advantage was the development of a somewhat rationalized bureaucratic administration during the Shogunate. The Tokugawa peace turned the caste of military lords into a stratum of civil administrators. The level of centralization achieved by the Shogunate favored the promulgation of numerous legal regulations for them to administer. Ethiopia had to wait until the reign of Haile Selassie for a national bureaucratic administration to emerge.

7. Legitimation of trade and a commercial class

The emphasis on virtues such as courage, self-discipline, and loyalty under feudal regimes typically entails the depreciation of commercial activity for being animated by selfishness, greed, and laxity. This was true in both countries during the medieval period. In Ethiopia, trade was left largely to outsiders such as Arabs and Armenians or to members of lower-status ethnic groups. In Japan, however, development of an indigenous merchant class, the chonin, was favored by the lack of ethnic differentiation and by the emergence of ideas and attitudes that valorized commerce. Thus, the popular Buddhist sect Jodo Shinshu developed a number of formulations that made the work of merchants righteous by defining their business as "Bodhisattva deeds," and the widely influential teachings of Ishida Baigan decried those who spread hateful sayings about merchants and insisted that the work of merchants was comparable to that of the samurai (Bellah 1957, 120, 158).

8. Valorization of craft ethic

Substantial economic modernization, we have known since Max Weber, has involved some sort of cultural support for disciplined manual labor. This entails clothing mundane work with ethical significance such that it can be viewed as an admirable calling. Absent that, manual work will be viewed as drudgery if not demeaning. In traditional Ethiopia, the notion of calling was attached to four roles only: rulers, warriors, clergy, and peasants. If the activity of merchants was morally disfavored, that of artisans was often despised. It was relegated to pariah groups that were treated as outcastes. The work of tanners, potters, smiths, and weavers—however essential their products—was typically looked down on and frequently despised; this was especially often the case for leather workers (Levine 1974).

Although the Japanese too have denigrated certain kinds of labor, most notably in tenacious attitudes toward the outcast burakumin who work as butchers and tanners, they nevertheless underwent a major change over the past several centuries whereby the work of artisans came to be endowed with the same religious valorization as has the labor of those who followed the Protestant ethic in Western Europe. Bellah (1957) describes a number of religious movements that sanctified hard work, frugality, and mundane production—ethical values that may have been directly initially to peasants but that accompanied them as they streamed into the cities to become artisans throughout the Tokugawa centuries. In a widely recognized formulation of Ishida Baigan, not just the samurai are retainers, but the farmers are "retainers" of the countryside while artisans and merchants are "retainers " of the city streets. Besides Shingaku, the popular ethical movement that Baigan founded, other traditions drawing on Buddhist and Confucian ideas, such as Jodo Shinshu and Hotoku, stressed diligence in production and economy in expenditure. Instead of opposing the status honor of warlords to morally suspect activities of merchants and artisans, they drew on the palette of samurai values to depict mundane daily labor in a radiant light.

9. Collectivism versus individualism

Bellah likened Japanese religious ideas that turned mundane labor into a sacred obligation to the Protestant idea of this worldly calling depicted by Weber. In addition, however, he emphasized a different kind of value, one that was not prominent in the Protestant tradition. This is the value of selfless devotion to the collectivity and its goals. Bellah finds this value embodied in the Japanese disposition to promote loyalty to various corporate groups: to the family, to the fiefdom, and to the nation. The transference of the imagery and sentiments of family loyalty to the nation informed the notion of kokutai, "national body," a concept of the state in which religious, political, and familistic ideas were indissolubly merged (Bellah 1957, 98–106).

In *Greater Ethiopia* I designated this value orientation as "collectivism," in pointed contrast with the pattern found in Abyssinian, or Amhara-Tigrean, society, which I glossed as "individualism."[8] If traditional Abyssinia and Japan share the values of particularism, performance, and hierarchicalism, they diverge markedly on this pattern variable. Attitudes toward litigation and toward outlaws illustrate that difference conspicuously. Ethiopians tend to maximize the opportunity for self-assertion through litigious disputes; the Japanese go out of their way to avoid confrontation and open conflict. Ethiopians admired the shifta, the lone individual who rebels from his lord and takes to the bush; such a career might lead ultimately to the throne, as it did for Tewodros II. By contrast the ronin, unattached samurai who wandered about without a political home, were scarcely culture heroes in Japan. Under Tokugawa law, the smallest unit of society was the family (ie)—the individual as such did not exist—and it was a matter of honor to keep one's family name unblemished. In Abyssinia, there were no family names. Rules of ambilineal descent gave individuals rights through both parental lines, man and women alike were expected to promote their own interests, prudently but aggressively.

The Meiji Restoration, and the miracle of Japan's economic modernization more generally, owed much to the confluence of a solidaristic ethic, one that enjoins selfless work on behalf of collectivities, with an ethic of disciplined labor in this world, and to government actions that fostered economic growth by moral exhortation as well as through technical information and entrepreneurial incentives. Economic modernization in Japan, Bellah persuasively argues, stemmed not so much from the industrious strivings of individual entrepreneurs as from the corporate strivings of families, companies, and patriots. In Western Europe and the United States, an ambitious individualism could drive the engine of economic development because it was so thoroughly harnessed to an ethic of universalistic achievement criteria. In Ethiopia, however, hierarchical individualism was tied to particularistic values and to a martial ethic that extolled hardiness and courage more than self-discipline and frugality. Ethiopian religionists and moralists never made the leap from their notion of the Warrior's Way to an ethic that praised diligence in all forms of homely everyday labor. Abyssinian individualism was tied to strivings to please a superior patron, and the highest worldly honors accrued to those who literally fought their way to the top.

Even today, the modal Ethiopian disposition is probably to promote oneself politically by finding a suitable patron, in a way that looks down on activities like commerce and craft or industrial labor, and with little sense of corporate loyalty of any sort. The current Prime Minister has, like a number of his predecessors, literally shot his way into power, and has publicly boasted of the significance of his guerrilla days in the bush as the schooling of choice for his political career and vocation.[9] At the same time that well-to-do Japanese citizens appear to be chafing under the conformist pressures of a national culture that subordinates individual expression to the demands of hierarchy, performance, and group solidarity, Ethiopians are experiencing frustration over their inability to subordinate individualistic ambitions to the welfare of larger communities, and by a slow pace of economic growth that seems due to a paucity of motivation for rigorous entrepreneurial commitment and regular industrial work. How hauntingly similar, those two civilizations, and yet—how striking the contrast between those two different worlds.

Bibliography

Bellah, Robert. 1957. *Tokugawa Religion*. Boston: Beacon Press.

Benedict, Ruth. 1946. *The Chrysanthemum and the Sword: Patterns of Japanese Culture*. Boston: Houghton Mifflin.

Cerulli, Enrico. 1956. *Storia della letteratura etiopica*. Milan.

Doi, Takeo. 1986. *The Anatomy of Self*, trans. Mark A. Harbison. Tokyo: Kodansha International.

Eisenstadt, S.N. 1996. *Japanese Civilization: A Comparative View*. Chicago: University of Chicago Press.

Endo, Shusaku. 1969. *Silence*, trans. William Johnston. New York: Taplinger.

Ikegami, Eiko. 1995. *The Taming of the Samurai*. Cambridge, MA: Harvard University Press.

Hall, John W. 1970. *Japan From Prehistory to Modern Times*. New York: Dell.

Herzog, Peter J. 1993. *Japan's Pseudo-Democracy*. New York: New York University Press.

Levine, Donald N. 1965. *Wax and Gold: Tradition and Innovation in Ethiopian Culture*. Chicago: University of Chicago Press.

_______. 1966. "The Concept of Masculinity in Ethiopian Culture," *The International Journal of Social Psychiatry* XII, 1, 17–23

_______. 1968. "The Military in Ethiopian Politics: Capabilities and Constraints," in Henry Bienen, ed., *The Military Intervenes: Case Studies in Political Development*: 5–34. New York: Russell Sage.

_______. 1974. *Greater Ethiopia: The Evolution of a Multiethnic Society*. Chicago: University of Chicago Press.

Ludolphus, Job. 1684. *A New History of Ethiopia*, trans. J.P. Gent, 2nd ed. London.

Munro-Hay, Stuart. 1991. *Aksum: An African Civilization of Late Antiquity*. Edinburgh: Edinburgh University Press.

Pankhurst, Alula. 1994. "Reflections on Pilgrimages in Ethiopia." in Harold Marcus, ed., *Papers of the 12th International Conference of Ethiopian Studies II*, 933–953 Lawrenceville: The Red Sea Press.

Pankhurst, Richard. 1992. "The Felashas in their Ethiopian Setting," *Ethiopian Review* June 1992: 23–25.

Perham, Margery. 1948. *The Government of Ethiopia*. New York: Oxford University Press.

Plant, Ruth. 1985. *Architecture of the Tigre*, Ethiopia. Worcester, UK: Ravens.

Redfield, Robert. 1962. *Human Nature and the Study of Society: The Papers of Robert Redfield*. Ed. Margaret Park Redfield. Chicago: University of Chicago Press.

Reischauer, Edwin O. 1956. "Japanese Feudalism," in Rushton Coulborn, ed., *Feudalism in History*: 26–48. Princeton: Princeton University Press.

Rohlen, Thomas P. 1989. "Order in Japanese Society: Attachment, Authority, and Routine," *Journal of Japanese Studies* 15: 5–40.

Schaefer, Charles. 1990. "Enclavistic Capitalism in Ethiopia, 1906–1936: A Study of Currency, Banking, and Informal Credit Networks." Ph.D. dissertation, The University of Chicago.

Shelemay, Kay Kaufman. 1986. *Music, Ritual, and Falasha History*. East Lansing, Mich.: African Studies Center, Michigan State University.

Tamrat, Taddesse. 1972. *Church and State in Ethiopia 1270–1527*. Oxford: Oxford University Press.

Tsunoda, Ryusaku, et al. 1958. *Sources of Japanese Tradition* (2 vols.) New York: Columbia University Press.

Zewde, Bahru. 1990. "The Concept of Japan in the Intellectual History of Modern Ethiopia," *Proceedings of the Fifth Seminar of the Department of History* (Debre Zeit, 30 June–3 July 1989). Addis Ababa: Addis Ababa University Press.

Notes

1 Such perceptions of affinity fed the pronounced sense of solidarity with Ethiopia expressed by the Japanese public following Italy's invasion of Ethiopia in 1935—evident, for example, in the decision of the Osaka Chamber of Commerce to provide straw sandals to Ethiopians to protect their feet against poison gas, in the dispatch of 1,200 Japanese swords to Ethiopia to assist in the war effort, and in the applications of Japanese volunteers to join the Ethiopian Army that flooded the Ethiopian consulate in Tokyo (Zewde 1990).

2 The very year that firearms entered Japan, 1543, was the year that Portuguese firearms were used to kill Ahmad Gragn and thus reverse Christian Ethiopia's faltering military fortunes.

3 The Meiji Constitution of 1889 designated the person of the emperor as "sacred and inviolable," language that, along with many other passages, was incorporated into Ethiopia's first Constitution in 1931. In Ethiopia as in Japan, the emperor thus came to be conceived, at one and the same time, as "1) a constitutional monarch, head of an authoritarian state established by a constitution granted by the emperor, not demanded by the people; 2) supreme authority over the armed forces, independent from control of the cabinet; and 3) a monarch of divine right" (Eisenstadt 1996, 35).

4 This text was translated and published in by E. A. Wallis Budge, as The Queen of Sheba and her only Son Menyelek (1922). For further discussion of its provenance and contents, see Levine 1974, Chapter 7.

5 For example, one Shotoku letter bore the superscription, "The Son of Heaven of the Land of the Rising Sun to the Son of Heaven of the Land of the Setting Sun." This quite displeased the Sui emperor (Tsunoda et al. 1958; I, 37).

6 It was due to their "unreasoning offensive spirit," an Italian officer wrote in 1937, that Ethiopian troops were easy to defeat by a disciplined modern army (Perham 1948, 167).

7 Indeed, coins minted at Aksum were found as far afield as Egypt, Persia, and India (Schaefer 1990, 24).

8 I contrasted this pattern with that of the other most extensive population in historic Ethiopia, the Oromo, who tend to exhibit a pattern of egalitarian collectivism.

9 In an interview in a Tigrinya-language Eritrean quarterly, the Prime Minister expressed his conviction that "To me quality of life means to be part of an armed struggle . . . I don't think that there is a better life than the life of a combatant. If I were not a combatant I don't think I would have been a happy person." (Hwyet 11, May 1997)

34

Masculinity and Warriorhood in Ethiopia and Japan (2002)*

In modern social science, the notion that human behavior has instinctual bases has been downplayed. Over the past century, anthropologists and sociologists have marched under the banners of Sumner's dictum that "the folkways can make anything right," Dewey's advice that there are "no separate instincts," and Benedict's formula that cultures pattern behavior.

In one area, however, some resonance to the notion that genes affect destiny has persisted: the phenomenon of human aggression. To William James's suspicion before World War I that "our ancestors have bred pugnacity into our bone and marrow, and thousands of years of peace won't breed it out of us" (James 1910, 314) Freud added his theory, in the inter-war years, that humans are animated by an inexorable stream of destructive energy fueled by a Death Instinct. The thesis of innate aggressiveness was advanced, and linked to gender, with the work of ethologists Konrad Lorenz (1966) and Nicholas Tinbergen (1968), who analyzed the adaptive significance of aggression among human males. Revising Freudian instinct theory from such an ethological perspective, psychoanalyst John Bowlby argued that:

---

* Originally presented at Research Committee on Armed Forces and Conflict Resolution, Session 4: The Military and Masculinity, World Congress of Sociology, Brisbane, Australia, July 8, 2002. Published in *International Journal of Ethiopian Studies*, Vol. 2, No. 1 (2005).

> Virtually every species of animal shares its habitat with a number of potentially very dangerous predators and, to survive, needs to be equipped with behavioural systems resulting in protection. . . . When members of the group are threatened, the mature males, whether monkeys or men, combine to drive off the predator whilst the females and immatures retire. (Bowlby 1969)

More recently, comparative primate studies have marshaled robust evidence to show that the human genome resembles most closely that of the chimpanzee, and the latest research on chimpanzees shows an unmistakable proclivity for violence by males against males of other groups (Wrangham and Peterson 1996). In addition, genetic research has begun to zero in on the chromosome that may account for such aggressivity. For example, on chromosome #17, there is a coding region which affects the distribution of serotonin throughout the body, and the extent of that distribution in turn affects the disposition to commit violent actions (Ridley 2000, 168).

Be all that as it may, the fact remains that as with any other such genetically-based traits, cultures shape inborn dispositions variously; in the felicitous words of a dictum pronounced, I think, by P. B. Bedawar, "Instinct proposes . . . culture disposes." Even if humans possess a genetically-based behavioral system that tends toward physical aggression, cultural systems process that disposition in various ways—by glorifying it, polishing it, or suppressing it. They determine whether or not and how aggressive inclinations get molded into an ideal of what it means to be a "real man." In many cultures, the ideal of virtuous manhood stands to impose over aggressiveness strict control, which thereby becomes subordinated to a more pacific model of what it means to be a mature human being and citizen. In the ancient Hellenic period, for example, the virtue of a man, arηtη andros, was equated with the capacity to manage one's household and the affairs of the city well. When a man's personal obligations conflicted with his civic obligations, it was simply a mark of manliness (andreios) to resist the requirements of the law (Adkins 1960, 226–322). Within the Jewish tradition, being a real man was associated with the assumption of full moral responsibility, either in the mode of altruistic generosity symbolized by the Yiddish term Mensch or in the mode of manly self-control sometimes described as the mark of modern Jewish manliness at the turn of the last century (Boyarin 1997). Closer to this mode of manly self-control, Alexis de Tocqueville described Americans as tending to esteem "all those quiet virtues which tend to regularity in the body social and which favor trade" (Tocqueville 2000, 621). Insofar as the American conception of honor includes the virtue of courage, it does not have to do with martial valor. Rather, the type of manly courage best known and best appreciated is that which makes a man brave the fury of the ocean to reach port more quickly, and face without complaint the privations of life in the wilds and that solitude which is harder to bear than any privations, the courage which makes a man almost insensible to the loss of a fortune laboriously acquired and prompts him instantly to fresh exertions to gain another. (622)

Not surprisingly, however, Tocqueville contrasts this ethos with that of a feudal aristocracy "born of war and for war," in which "nothing was more important to it than military courage. It was therefore natural to glorify courage above all other virtues" (618). Indeed, societies in which warriorhood figures prominently tend to feature combative excellence in their ideal of masculinity and to give it a high place in their scheme of values. This was surely the case in the Archaic Age of Greece, when the most powerful words of commendation used of a man, ἀγαθός and ἀρετή, signified above all military prowess and the skills that promote success and war (Adkins 1960, 31–32).

Martial Values in Ethiopia and Japan

This pattern was also conspicuously evident in two of the oldest continuous national societies, Ethiopia and Japan, where, for most of the past millennium, there existed expectations of continuous readiness for martial combat. In both countries, military prowess offered a royal road to prestige and legitimacy, and in both the ascendance of powerful warrior-lords and their retainers lifted martial values to a dominant position. It was these two nations alone that successfully defied European imperial ambitions: Ethiopia over Italy in 1896, Japan over Russia in 1904.

In both nations, esteem for warriorhood was not just a matter of according high prestige to military men; it involved the diffusion of martial attitudes, virtues, and ambitions throughout the population. That diffusion came about through very different routes. In Ethiopia, it took the form of promoting widely the inculcation of combative dispositions. This feature so impressed the first European scholar of Ethiopian civilization, Job Ludolphus, that he described Ethiopians as "a Warlike People and continually exercis'd in War . . . except in Winter, at what time by reason of the Inundation of the Rivers, they are forc'd to be quiet" (Ludolphus 1684, 217). It meant that every able-bodied male who was not a clergyman was assumed to be ready to engage in battle at a moment's notice—armed, skilled, supplied, and transported, all through his own devices. It meant that boys were encouraged to be combative and that as men they were disposed to be fearless in combat. It even meant that, for most of the past millennium, the royal capital took the form of an army camp—"a vast array of tents, arranged in combat-ready formation with the Emperor's tents in the center, flanked and guarded at the front and rear by officers of standard ranks with their entourages" (Levine 1968, 7). As a result of the prominence of warfare in Ethiopian history, military virtues have ranked among the highest in the Abyssinian value system; military titles have been among the most prestigious in their social hierarchy; military symbolism has provided a medium for important national traditions and a focus for a good deal of national sentiment; and military statuses and procedures have influenced patterns of social organization in many ways (Levine 1968, 6).

In Japan, the hegemony of martial values derived not from universal combat-readiness but from the way in which a military stratum, the *samurai*, came to set the tone of the national culture. This class emerged in the late Heian Period (10–12 C) as a group of military specialists positioned to serve the court nobility. In time they acquired power in their own right by establishing domination over agricultural land and building their own hierarchical political organizations, culminating in a semicentral regime, the shogunate, in the late 12C. The samurai political organization rested on the formation of strong emotional bonds between military masters and vassals upheld by a strict code of honor (Ikegami 1995). In the Tokugawa Period this code was elaborated into a formal code of martial ethics known as *Bushido* (the Way of the Warrior). The code enjoined such virtues as loyalty, politeness, diligence, frugality, and a constant sense of readiness to die. At this time, the *bushi* class became more segregated than ever, since membership in it was hereditary and only those within it were entitled to bear arms. On the other hand, the ethos of this class became hegemonic in the society. In contrast to China of the time, the Japanese insisted on retaining a martial spirit as part of the mark of a gentleman (Hall 1970, 82). During the Tokugawa period, it has been said, the *samurai* ethic came close to being the national ethic, for even the merchant class had become "*Bushido*-ized" (Bellah 1957, 98).

One of the marks of the warrior ethos in both cultures was a disposition to value ascetic hardiness. This is manifest, for example, in the Ethiopian ideal of *gwäbäznet*, a symbol for masculine aggressiveness and hardiness. In consequence, Ethiopian soldiers have been noted for great endurance—they climb mountains with ease, march rapidly for distances under heavy pack with light rations, and sleep on a rock. In Japan, similar virtues were the pride of the samurai class, who prided themselves on undergoing great hardships without complaint—for example by undergoing a week of arduous training outside each year in the dead of winter (*kangeiko*).

Another mark of the warrior ethos has been a pronounced concern about honor and a sensitivity to insult that numerous observers have found in the psychological profile of both peoples. In Ethiopia, insults traditionally formed reason enough for violent retribution, and continued into the modern era as grounds for instigating legal proceedings. In Japan, a cult of honor became the subject of extensive elaboration, leading samurai to cultivate an extreme sensitivity to insult (Ikegami, 1995). Countless legends idealize the person who secures delicious revenge against someone who impugns his honor.

Finally, although Ethiopia and Japan have traditionally held esteemed the just warrior, in both cultures there existed a type of antinomian hero who carried masculine aggressivity to a high pitch. In Ethiopia this took the form of the *shifta* (from *shefete*, to rebel), a retainer who rebelled against his chief and withdrew, often hiding in the hills, to fend as an outlaw (Levine 1965, 243–4). In modern times, this word has in fact acquired the primary meaning of a bandit. Many stories depict the shifta in idealized terms. The first modern nation-building emperor, Tewodros II (1855–68), famously began his climb to power as a *shifta*.

The Japanese counterpart of the *shifta* was the *ronin*, a samurai who left his lord or never subordinated himself to a lord. Here, too, heroic performances by *ronin* form the stuff of legends. And in modern times, the status of outlaw strong man has been taken by the *yakuza*, the bold gangster. In a playful form of this status, Japanese young males in the 1970 and 1980s took up a semi-delinquent lifestyle called Yankee and, combined with prowess on motorcycle, formed *bosozoku* ("violent driving tribe") gangs in major cities where their ultramasculinity could be flaunted (Sato 1991).

The Ethiopian Masculinity Ideal: Aggressivity Unbound

Although both Ethiopians and Japanese construed the ideal of masculinity in ways that provided a strong impetus to warriorhood, one can also identify characteristic differences in how these play out in Ethiopia and Japan. In presenting this analysis, I shall also comment on distinctive institutions that represent a counterbalance to male aggressivity.

In describing the Ethiopian pattern, I shall rely initially on what for most of the past millennium has been the politically and culturally dominant group, the Amhara, and the terms of their language Amharic.[2] The Amharic term for male, *wänd*, not only indicates gender (e.g., *wänd lijj*, "male child"), but also connotes strong emotional approval. To say of someone, *Essu wänd näw*, "He is a male," is to state more than biological fact; it is a eulogy of virtue, analogous to the American expression, "He's a real man." However, unlike the American concept, *wänd-nät* does not connote manly maturity and the assumption of adult moral responsibilities. In Amharic, this notion is signified by the term for middle-aged man (*mulu säw*). The term *wänd* may refer to any age and has nothing to do with moral maturation. Nor does it connote male prowess in heterosexual affairs, for the Amhara attach no particular to the expression of heterosexual sentiment or the enjoyment of sexuality. In fact, a puritanical attitude toward sexuality in the public realm has the effect of keeping such matters from becoming the object of spoken concern at all; for an Amhara male to boast of his heterosexual achievements would be considered shameful.

The traditional Amhara ideal of masculinity refers primarily to aggressive capacity. The Amhara male likes to boast over his ferocity, his bravery in killing an enemy or a wild beast. Amhara culture provided genres of oral literature for such impassioned boasting, employed before and after military expeditions as well as for entertainment on festive occasions. In the second place, *wänd-nät* connotes the ability to make little of physical hardship—to live for a long time in the wild, to walk all day long with no food. In short, for traditional Amhara the virtues of the male are the virtues of the soldier.

The Amharic word which represents the virtues of the soldier is *gwäbäz*. *Gwäbäz* may be translated as "brave," as "hardy," or simply as "outstanding." One of the goals in the socialization of boys was to teach them to be *gwäbäz*. This is done in a variety of ways. Amhara boys are early taught to defend themselves with sticks and stones against any outsider who happens to injure or insult them. Tiny boys are trained in mock battles with members of their family. Temper tantrums are regarded positively by the child's parents as a sign that he is *gwäbäz*. The norms of violent revenge when someone has taken one's land, harmed one's relative, had relations with one's wife, or spoken a grievous insult are taught to growing boys. Boys of about twelve were wont to prove their virility by scarring their arms with red-hot embers. The Amhara youth develops skill in improvising *shilläla*, the strident verse that is declaimed in order to inflame the blood of the warrior; and he commits to memory verses which glorify the *gwäbäz* warrior and the act of killing (Levine 1966, 18–19).

Warriorhood takes different forms among the two major cultural traditions in Ethiopia, the Amhara-Tigrean and the Oromo or Galla,[3] as we shall see below. In both cultures, however, the secular identity associated with being a male is tied closely to a man's capacity for combat. Both Amhara-Tigrean and Oromo cultures extol courage the virtues of aggressive masculinity and martial courage in particular. In both societies, boys are trained to be fearless fighters. Men who slay dangerous animals or human enemies are lavishly honored. Special boasting chants are declaimed to shame cowards and incite the brave. Amhara and Oromo verses of this sort often share a close resemblance.[4]

This has the effect of informing warriorhood in both traditions with a spirit of enormous daring, bordering at times on foolhardiness. In the modern period, this meant that Ethiopians with arms inferior to the Italians were able to inflict a crushing defeat on that invading force at the Battle of Adwa in 1896. Their spirit was embodied in the refusal of some Ethiopian soldiers to get down in trenches; they insisted in fighting out in the open, as befits a real *wänd*. This meant that Ethiopian men were disposed to fight again in 1935 with spears and limited weapons against an Italian enemy now equipped with planes and poison gas.[5] It was later reflected in the extraordinary performance of the battalion of Ethiopian troops sent to Korea to fight with the United Nations forces in 1951, a performance that earned them the reputation of being perhaps the most effective military unit of the entire U.N. contingent.

The Japanese Masculinity Ideal: Aggressivity Bound

Although the ideal of courage figures prominently in the Japanese ethic of masculinity, that ethic has come to depart from a notion of raw aggressivity. The Japanese have traditionally referred to those who behave with untamed violence, not as real men, but as barbarians or wild beasts. The attitude toward a man who manifests physical strength alone is just as negative as that toward an effete courtier. Rather, the fully realized masculine character—*otoko no otoko*, a "man's man"—modifies raw, self-asserting physical prowess in a number of ways.

To be sure, the earliest professional warriors, of the 8th and 9th centuries, who may represent a distinctive ethnic group who were originally hunters, appeared extreme in their raw violence. However, by the middle ages and continuously thereafter, samurai violence was progressively domesticated, as Eiko Ikegami's *The Taming of the Samurai* (1995) demonstrates so elegantly.

The conduct of the samurai and of those who emulate the samurai model came to exemplify a quality called *shibui*. As Lebra describes it,

> The concept of *shibui* implies an outlook which is practical, devoid of frills, and unassuming, one which acts as circumstances require, simply and without fuss. In baseball, neither the spectacular homerun batter nor the brilliant infielder can really become valuable players unless they acquire this *shibui* quality. Unless the spectacular and the brilliant include in themselves this element of the *shibui*, the technique can never really be called mature. The ever-available ability to go concisely and simply to the heart of what is required . . . the pursuit of high efficiency, shorn of excessive individual technique, neither flashy nor yet dull (Lebra 1976, 20).

In addition, Lebra writes, manlike behaviors include suppression of the emotions. It is important to be free from lingering attachments, so that one does not hesitate for a second to kick one's wife out if something is found wrong with her. Real men should also not talk too much. One of the best-known commercial catchphrases in recent years is: "*Otoko wa damatte Sapporo biru*" ("Men silently drink Sapporo beer"), uttered by Toshiro Mifune, the John Wayne of Japan (80, 18, 78).

Beyond such qualities of personal comportment, certain cultural accomplishments formed part of the repertoire of the Japanese male ideal. Japanese samurai were expected to show proficiency, not only in the arts of war (*bu*), but in a number of non-martial spheres that linked with the neo-Confucian notion of personal culture (*bun*). This linkage was represented by an ideal that joined them by means of a compound phrase, *bu-bun*. Proficient calligraphy was the main one. The embodiment of *bu-bun* involved practice with the pen and brush in a manner that evinced unself-conscious and fearless directness. A secondary art was the composition of highly stylized verse, most notably haiku.

As samurai culture evolved, it also came to experience the martial code in a context formed by overarching ideals of loyalty and devotion to corporate groups. This progressed from impassioned martial loyalty to the household (*ie*) of one's lord, to a sense of loyalty to the samurai status group and its code of honor, to political loyalty to the head of the state (Ikegami 1995). Such loyalty was no less important than courage in defining the ethic of the full Japanese male. Well-known stories describe Japanese retainers undergoing enormous pain and other deprivations to serve their lords, not to mention the countless episodes of *seppuku* (suicide by disembowelment). This ideal of manly courage pertained to the peasants as well as to the *samurai*. A famous tale of peasant protest concerns a 17C villager named Sakura Sogoro who, at the cost of being crucified, brazenly presented a petition from his neighbors to the *shogun* in the tip of a six-foot-long bamboo pole. The traditional text about this episode concludes, "Truly if you are a warrior, you ought to leave behind a glorious reputation because your name is written down in the records for all posterity" (Walthall 1991, 75).

The sacrifice of personal comfort on behalf of corporate goals and organization fed into the Japanese penchant for collective discipline. Before WWII at least, regimentalized patterns of collective action were instilled in Japanese schools.

In warfare, these ideals promoted distinctive patterns of conduct. The implications of these ideals for patterns of martial conduct were twofold. On the one hand, the notion of subordination of the individual promoted deeds of suicidal daring, most notably in the kamikaze pilots. On the other hand, the ideal of cultivated warriorhood, *bu-bun*, meant that combativeness was traditionally restrained by norms of exaggerated gentlemanly decorum. Even so, a turbulent self-assertiveness that constituted what Ikegami has called "honorific individualism" fueled their dispositions to serve.

Ethiopian and Japanese Warriorhood in Social Context

Within Ethiopia, however, how the masculinity ideal played out in warfare was further determined by the context of social structure. This variable led to marked differences between the two major ethnic protagonists of modern Ethiopian history, the Amhara-Tigreans, often known as Habesha or Abyssinians, and the Oromo, formerly known as Galla.[6]

The Abyssinian military ethic took the form of a cult of the hero. Personal bravery—not discipline, training, honor, or self-sacrificing loyalty—was the paramount virtue in Abyssinian warfare. The *gwäbäz* warrior was rewarded by his chief, praised by the minstrel, and esteemed by the populace. His bravery was ranked according to the fearfulness of the enemy vanquished. Thus, in Menelik's day the fanciest headdress was given to a noble who killed one of the fierce Danakil, a less fancy headdress being awarded the killer of the tough Raya Oromo. Such actions constituted the one area in which personal boasting was permitted and, in fact, institutionalized in the genre known as *fukara*.

We are indebted to Arnauld d'Abbadie for a firsthand account of the effect of this cult of the individual hero on the orientation of the Abyssinian warrior, in a passage worth citing at length:

> The type of combat which [the Abyssinian] prefers over all others—because it gives him the most freedom to expand his personality—is that where, due to insufficiency of terrain or other circumstances, the chiefs can engage only a part of their forces. . . . Joyously he throws off his toga to clad himself in some military ornament. . . . He loves . . . to know, finally, that on the hills, behind their drummers who beat out the charge in place, the two rival chiefs and the two armies are following him with their eyes, and that he may at one moment or another, return to his lord and, hurling before him some trophy, tell him, at the end of his war chant: "There! This is what I know how to do!" (Abbadie 1868, 313)

The military organization of the Amhara was highly individualistic. Unlike traditional Oromo, the Amhara did not provide for the collective training of their warriors. Each man was left to learn how to fight by himself and to provide his own equipment. A man could become a "career" soldier when he came of age simply by purchasing a shield; or he might prevail upon an established lord to arm him temporarily, with the promise of returning equipment should he leave that lord's service. Similarly, there were no collective provisions for the supply of troops. Each man was left to fend for himself, drawing upon the supply of grain he brought along and whatever booty he could acquire on the warpath; the preparation of his food was left to the wife or servant who accompanied him to battle.

The conduct of a military operation exhibited a minimum of external constraint and discipline. Chains of command existed with respect to the general direction of troop movements, and the camping pattern was highly structured. But the marching and fighting unit seems to have been, for all practical purposes, the individual soldier and his retainers. Battles were not fought in a disciplined manner; the outcome depended on the sheer number of troops, their state of morale, and the chance of catching the enemy off guard. Except for the large-scale deployment of troops in accord with the customary tactic of envelopment, there was little expectation of subordinating the impulses of individual soldiers to the needs of a "team"; the prevailing military ethic stressed rather the heroism of the individual soldier and his drive to bring back a cache of booty and trophies (Levine 1965, 262–3).

This pattern contrasted with the pattern exhibited by Oromo warriors. The Oromo went to war, not as proud and self-sufficient individuals, but as members of named collectivities. Raiding and military expeditions were executed by members of the same age set, or *hariyya*. Formed by boys in their late teens by wandering from camp to camp, the age sets were deployed in organized divisions called *chibra*, which collected supplies for the campaign, elected regimental leaders, recruited scouts, and distributed booty. The *chibra* served as fighting units and followed carefully planned battlefield strategy. Where Amhara males fought as individual soldiers, expected to provide their own supplies and capture personal booty, the Oromo derived support, resources, guidance, and morale from their age-mate comrades. Oromo proverbs celebrate the efficacy of massed collective action in waging war.

Beyond that, Oromo were bound to one another deeply through a number of social classes that went through a system of grades generally lasting eight years, a system known as *gäda*. Often misconstrued as an age-class system, *gäda* was actually a system based on generational position, in which sons of whatever age entered the system precisely five grades after their fathers. Each *gäda* class took a turn at serving as the governing class of a particular Oromo society, during which it made the decisions as to when and where military expeditions should be launched as well as when ritual ceremonies should be performed. Oromo males traditionally felt strong ties not only to the general class which they joined but also to a transgenerational solidarity, the *gogessa*, consisting of the classes of their father, their son, their son's sons, and so on. The decisions of a particular ruling class thus had historic implications. The class in power felt obliged not only to avoid the chief misfortunes that befell its ancestors and to repeat its signal successes, but also to set precedents that would benefit its descendants many generations in the future (Legesse, 1973).

Oromo traditionally observed an injunction to undertake a ritual killing expedition every eight years. The *gäda* class that undertook the expedition fought not only for itself but also to live up to the reputation of its ancestral *gogessa* classes. In contrast to the repertoire of Abyssinian martial chants, which exclusively glorify the boasting man's own exploits, Oromo also possessed a distinctive genre of boasting songs known as *farsa*, which celebrate the deeds of famous ancestors. The *farsa* are sung to glorify Oromo solidary groups—clans, lineages, age sets, or *gogessa*.

One other important difference should be mentioned, the religious dimension. Although Abyssinian culture put a premium on associating masculinity with aggressive prowess, it nevertheless placed great emphasis on the curbing of aggression through religious teachings and practices. An extensive regime of fasting in Abyssinian Christianity is held to curb man's natural sinful aggressive inclinations. A substantial proportion of the populace—a 17C visitor estimated as high as one-third (Lobo 1984, 178)—have been monks and clergy, and so ineligible to take up arms. Piety in many forms stood to curb the tendency to violence. Among the Oromo, warfare itself was integrated into their religious system. A religious ritual known as *butta* entailed the execution of raiding and killing expeditions every eight years.

The structuration of masculinity and warriorhood in Japan represented a kind of middle ground between Abyssinian individualism and Oromo collectivism, and also between their respective forms of religiosity. As with Abyssinian Christianity, Japanese Buddhists promoted an ultimate ethic of nonviolence, and supported monastic roles on its behalf. On the other hand, Buddhist temples were among the staunchest bastions of armed defense during the medieval period. Some forms of Buddhism preached the oneness of death and life, and did not regard death as a source of impurity (as did native Shinto). The samurai drew eagerly on Buddhism as a resource to steel themselves against fear of death.

Institutionally, Japanese warriordom was centered in a complex of patron-client ties, as was the case in Abyssinia. In contrast to the Amhara pattern, however, Japanese patron-client ties were embedded in a named collectivity to which deep loyalty was expected: the household (*ie*) of a lord. This nexus enmeshed the warrior in a corporate grouping, which reinforced a disposition to self-sacrifice on its behalf. Even so, the striving for aggressive self-assertion continued to permeate the samurai outlook. The result, Ikegami notes, was "two coexisting modes of aspiration in the Japanese elite . . . competitive individuality on the one hand and orderly conformity on the other" (1995, 335).

Historic Consequences

Differences in the ways in which the traditional cultures of Japan and Ethiopia construe the masculinity ethos in the service of warriorhood represent instructive exemplifications of how "culture disposes" what male gender-linked instincts of aggressivity propose. Beyond that, these phenomena may be seen to have had important historic consequences.

To begin with, differences in the spirit of warfare between Abyssinian and Oromo had, I have argued, important consequences for the making of the modern Ethiopian state. In the course of the Oromo expansions of the 16th and 17th centuries, their advances were rarely checked by Abyssinian troops. This remarkable fact was noted by our most valuable contemporary source, an Amhara monk named Bahrey who wrote a *History of the Galla* in the 1590s. "How is it," Bahrey wondered, "that the Galla defeat us, though we are numerous and well supplied with arms?" (cited Levine 2000, 89)

In accounting for the Oromo victories, I have relied on a clue provided by a statement attributed to Bahrey's contemporary, Emperor Särtsä Dingil, who reportedly ascribed the Oromo conquests to their firm determination on going into battle to either conquer or die, and the routs and defeats of the Amhara to the exact opposite disposition. In explaining this difference, I have argued that although both cultures placed enormous emphasis on fearless masculine combativeness, they differed in the extent to which those motivations were activated.

The Amhara pattern of hierarchical individualism had the effect of making the motivation of individual soldiers contingent on the particular reward structure of a given campaign. Amhara troops fought for personal gain from booty and to be acknowledged and rewarded by their superiors. The presence of the king or lord on the battlefield typically made a great difference in how bravely Amhara soldiers were inclined to fight. If the relevant lord was killed, or if there was no chance of his learning about a soldier's bravery, the latter was likely to feel that there was not much point in fighting. If their lord was defeated in battle, Amhara soldiers often shifted allegiances and went over to another side. If the gains possible from any battle situation seemed too small, they felt no moral compulsion to continue the fight.

In the Oromo case, by contrast, several factors made the activation of their military ethic less contingent on the particularities of the battle situation. For one thing, killing a man was intrinsically an important accomplishment for any Oromo male who wanted to live a self-respecting life. It enhanced his chances of securing a wife or wives, and not to be married at the appropriate time was considered quite shameful. It gave him the self-esteem associated with wearing the victorious warrior's hairstyle. Beyond that, the Oromo warriors' engagement drew considerable support, we have seen, from the social structures in which it was organized. Consequently, he was inspired to contribute to the corporate success of his fighting division, and to play his part in the drama of Oromo history, as well as to appear a fully competent male in the eyes of his home community. Since he thereby had a set of motivations for battle that were continuously operative and not contingent on the circumstances of the particular battle, the Oromo warrior needed no lord to inspire and reward his particular exploits in battle.

The upshot was that the Oromo not only overran a vast territory inhabited by Amhara and other ethnies, but made their way to the center of the historic kingdom. Their accommodation with indigenous groups with which they came to mingle, and their integration to the national center by intermarriage and vassalage constituted the central dynamic of the emergence of the modern Ethiopian nation (Levine 2000). In particular, they soon came to provide troops for the Ethiopian Crown. Quick to appreciate their valor, Särtsä Dingil, for example, deployed Oromo warriors as early as 1580 in missions to defeat rebels aligning themselves with Turks on the Red Sea Coast, and also to in expeditions against the Falasha and other Oromo tribes (Conti Rossini, 1907).

This pattern made it possible for Oromo troops in substantial numbers to fight alongside Amhara-Tigreans under Emperor Menelik II, who quadrupled the size of the Ethiopian empire, and led a multiethnic army to defeat the Italians in 1896. In Japan, the samurai ethos likewise played a double role in creating the modern nation-state. Their ethic of shaping conduct through rigorous discipline and subordinating individuals to collective interests worked wonders when transferred to nation-building under the Meiji restoration and economic transformation thereafter. The transference of absolute martial loyalty from one's immediate lord to the imperial head of the Meiji state furthered mightily the establishment of a powerful modern nation, one which at Port Arthur in 1904 became the first Asian country to defeat a European army.

With that achievement, Japan joined Ethiopia to become the only other non-European country to defeat a European army in the final era of imperial expansion. Recognizing this affinity, a number of Japanese citizens showed enormous sympathy with the Ethiopians when they were invaded in 1935, even to the extent of sending them a shipload of swords. Differences in their social structural and other cultural patterns, however, meant that the application of martial dispositions to economic life enabled the Japanese to modernize far more rapidly in both economic and political domains (Levine 2001).

Bibliography

D'Abbadie, Arnauld. 1868. *Douze ans de séjour dans la Haute-Éthiopie*. Paris.

Adkins, Arthur W. H. 1960. *Merit and Responsibility: A Study in Greek Values*. Oxford: Clarendon Press.

Bellah, Robert. 1957. *Tokugawa Religion.* Boston: Beacon Press.

Bowlby, John. 1969. *Attachment*. NY: Basic Books.

Boyarin, Daniel. 1997. *Unheroic Conduct: The Rise of Heterosexuality and the Invention of the Jewish Man*. Berkeley: University of California Press.

Conti Rossini, Carlo, ed. 1907. Historia Regis Sarsa Dengel (Malak Sagad). Paris.

Hall, John W. 1970. *Japan From Prehistory to Modern Times.* New York: Dell.

Herzfeld, Michael. 1985. *The Poetics of Manhood: Contest and Identity in a Cretan Mountain Village.* Princeton: Princeton University Press.

Ikegami, Eiko. 1995. *The Taming of the Samurai.* Cambridge, MA: Harvard University Press.

James, William. 1910. "The Moral Equivalent of War." In *Essays on Faith and Morals*, 311–28.

Lebra, T.S. 1976. *Japanese Patterns of Behavior.* Honolulu: University of Hawaii Press.

Legesse, Asmarom. 1973. *Gada: Three Approaches to the Study of African Society*. New York: Free Press, 1973.

Levine, Donald N. 1965. *Wax and Gold: Tradition and Innovation in Ethiopian Culture*. Chicago: University of Chicago Press.

____________. 1966. "The Concept of Masculinity in Ethiopian Culture." *The International Journal of Social Psychiatry* 12:1, 17–23.

____________. 1968. "The Military in Ethiopian Politics: Capabilities and Constraints." In Henry Bienen, ed., *The Military Intervenes: Case Studies in Political Development*, 5–34. New York: Russell Sage Foundation.

____________. 2000. *Greater Ethiopia: The Evolution of a Multiethnic Society*. Second edition. Chicago: University of Chicago Press.

____________. 2001. "Ethiopia and Japan in Comparative Civilizational Perspective." *Passages* 3:1, 1–31.

____________. In press. "Amhara." *Encyclopaedia Aethiopica.*

Lobo, Jerónimo. 1984. *The Itinerario of Jerónimo Lobo*. London: Hakluyt.

Lorenz, Konrad. 1966. *On Aggression.* New York: Harcourt, Brace and World.

Ludolphus, Job. 1684. *A New History of Ethiopia.* Translated by J.P. Gent. London.

Mead, Margaret. 1937. *Cooperation and Conflict among Primitive Peoples*. New York, NY: McGraw-Hill.

Morgenthau, Hans. 1960. *Politics Among Nations*, 3rd ed. New York: Knopf.

Perham, Marjorie. 1948. *The Government of Ethiopia.* London: Faber and Faber.

Portal, Gerald H. 1892. *My Mission to Abyssinia*. New York: Negro Universities Press.

Ridley, Matt. 2000. *Genome: The Autobiography of a Species in 23 Chapters*. New York: Harper Collins.

Sato, Ikuya. 1991. *Kamikaze Biker: Parody and Anomy in Affluent Japan*. University of Chicago Press.

Simmel, Georg. 1903/4. "The Sociology of Conflict," trans. Albion W. Small. *American Journal of Sociology 9*, 1903/4, 490–525, 672–89, 798–811.

_____. (1908) 1955. *Conflict*, trans. Kurt H. Wolff. Glencoe, Ill.: Free Press.

Tinbergen, N. 1968. "On War and Peace in Animals and Man: An ethologist's approach to the biology of aggression," *Science 160*, 1411–18.

Tocqueville, Alexis de. (1835) 2000. *Democracy in America*. New York: Perennial Classics.

Walthall, Anne, ed. 1991. *Peasant Uprisings in Japan: A Critical Anthology of Peasant Histories.* Chicago: University of Chicago Press.

Wrangham, Richard, and Dale Peterson. 1996. *Demonic Males: Apes and the Origins of Human Violence*. New York: Houghton Mifflin.

Zivkovic, Marko. 2002. "Noble Criminals, Highlanders and Cryptomatriarchy: Poetics of Masculinity in Serbia (and how to get at it)." Paper presented at conference on *Balkan Masculinities*, University College London, 7–8 June 2002.

Notes

1 Reconfigured in an aesthetic mode, this antinomian undertone to masculinity persists in present-day Crete. According to Michael Herzfeld, in *Poetics of Manhood*, the Cretan village ethos foregrounds a studied skill in playing at being a man, through deeds that strikingly speak for themselves; in any domain such performative excellence "can gain from judicious rule breaking, since this foregrounds the performer's skill at

manipulating the conventions" (Herzfeld 1985, 25).

2 Strictly speaking, although the Amharic language was the national political language of Ethiopia from the thirteenth century at least, the term Amhara denoted a local geographic region, and was not extended to the vast population of Amharic speakers until the second half of the twentieth century. See Levine, in press.

3 Similar to the way in which "Amhara" was extended to represent a much broader population that its original local referent, the term "Oromo" has come to designate the entire population of those who speak dialects of the language called afan Oromo, formerly known as Gallinya. Even today, a group believed to represent the purest form of traditional Oromo culture refuse to refer to themselves as Oromo, but as Boran. It has therefore been difficult to adopt a tern that can be used consistently.

4 **Amhara:**

Shellelew shellelew – War cries, war cries!
Mindenew shellelew – Of what use is boasting and challenging
Baddisu gorade – Unless you decorate your new sword
Demun telamesew – With his blood!

Oromo:

Sala buttan dakkutti sala – The sword's edge on the [shepherd's] apron is shameful
Chirriqun durba sala – To spit on a girl is shameful
Sala lama batani – After bringing the two edges [of a spear]
Lama bachifatani – After ordering two [edges of a spear] to be brought
Dirarra diessun Sala – The flight from men [enemies] is shameful (Levine 2000, 152–3)

5 It was due to their "unreasoning offensive spirit," an Italian officer wrote in 1937, that Ethiopian troops were easy to defeat by a disciplined modern army (Perham 1948, 167).

6 In present day Ethiopia, the term Oromo has become standard for referring to all of the peoples formerly designated as Oromo in the Ethiopian chronicles. Even so, some "Oromo" groups today still do not use that term for themselves. I shall use both terms loosely, depending on the context. Interaction between the Oromo and the Amhara-Tigreans from the sixteenth century on, I have argued, formed a central dynamic in the evolution of the modern Ethiopian nation-state (Levine 1974).

35

Ethiopia, Japan, and Jamaica

*A Century of Globally Linked Modernizations (2005)**

Modernization studies focus on bounded societies, ignoring interactions like those found among Japan, Ethiopia, and Jamaica. Prodded to modernize by foreign warships, Japan pursued unification, bureaucratization, codification, and military centralization. Following attacks from Sudan, Ethiopia undertook modernizations in which Japan and the Meiji Constitution became exemplars. Ethiopia became a model for African nations and diasporas, inspiring Rastafarianism in Jamaica. Rasta culture transformed from a religion of the oppressed to a worldwide force crystallized in Bob Marley's music, offering Japanese youth a vehicle for individualism in the 1980s. These interconnections came full circle in 2005 when dreadlocked pilgrims from Japan attended the Marley festival in Addis Ababa.

Accounts of modernization generally take the national society as the central unit of analysis. To be sure, most of the nineteenth-century theorists of modernization tended to hold an abstract, global imaginary in mind. This was true of Comte and Hegel, Marx and Engels, Spencer and Tönnies, and

---

* This is a revised version of a paper originally presented at the 37th World Congress of the International Institute of Sociology, Stockholm, Sweden, Regular Session: "Comparative Modernization Studies in the Globalized World," July 9, 2005. Ellwood B. Carter, Jr. and Benjamin Cornwell provided valuable research support.

others. This perspective has been resurrected with increasing frequency in recent decades through the work of scholars like Talcott Parsons, Roland Robertson, Immanuel Wallerstein, and Saskia Sassen.

For most of the twentieth century, however, the dominant unit of analysis for modernization studies has been the nation. Whether the analytic focus was on social stratification, education, political organization, ethnic relations, language, banking systems, jural codes, or military capabilities, the empirical focus was circumscribed by the accepted boundaries of each nation-state. One thinks of Japan (Bellah 1957), Turkey (Lewis 1961) India (Rudolph and Rudolph, 1967), Ethiopia (Levine 1965), Lebanon (Binder, ed., 1966), Brazil (Ribeiro 1995), and the like.

Comparative work has simply grafted this perspective onto studies of a number of national societies. This was true of in-depth analyses of a small number of cases, like Geertz's work on state-building in Asia and Africa (1963), Ward and Rustow's volume on political modernization in Japan and Turkey (1964), Wallerstein on Ghana and the Ivory Coast (1964), and books by Reinhard Bendix on authority in industry (1963) and on nation-building and citizenship (1996). It was also true of studies that used data from numerous nations, like the survey analyses produced by Alex Inkeles (1998) and Ronald Inglehart (1997).

This paper employs a different perspective, one that treats modernization not within the contours of a particular national society, singular or plural, or that adopts an increasingly familiar perspective of the world society. It focuses, rather, on lines of modernizing influence that flow from one country to another. This approach attempts to do justice to the point made by Bjœrn Wittrock, who observes: "The formation of modernity in the late eighteenth and early nineteenth centuries is the first major period of cultural crystallization when transformations in different parts of the world are directly interconnected" (2000, 58; emphasis mine). I shall illustrate Wittrock's point by discussing three apparently unrelated countries in three different continents—Japan, Ethiopia, and Jamaica.

To begin with, let me introduce a paradigm of modernization, viewing it as a complex world historical development consisting of "breakthrough" processes in several separate but interrelated dimensions. These include specialization, individuation, unification, equalization, cultural rationalization, and personal rationalization. These processes have been associated with what have often been called a number of "revolutions" as shown in Figure 1. My assumption is that once the modernity dynamic gets started in a particular society, for endogenous or exogenous reasons, there is a need, if not pressure, to secure resources to abet other revolutions, that can often be imported or modeled on breakthroughs achieved in other societies. That is the dynamic to be illustrated now in considering the linkages among Japan, Ethiopia, and Jamaica.

Figure 1: Modernity Revolutions and Their Effects[2]

	DIFFERENTIATION		DEMOCRATIZATION		RATIONALIZATION	
Process	Specialization	Individuation	Unification	Equalization	Cultural	Personal
Revolution	Industrial	Urban-Commercial	Integrative	Social	Academic	Disciplinary
Benefits	Commerce, goods	Freedom	Efficacy	Justice	Knowledge	Civility
Disadvantages	Personal atrophy; Social deficits	Hyper-specialization; alienation; consumerism	Repressive centralization; Violence	Mediocrity	"Tragedy of culture"; Jacobinism	Psychic repression

Japan's Breakthrough to a Modern Polity

Pressures toward modernization began to percolate in Japan by the advent of the nineteenth century. An expanding economy began to weaken the patrimonial system of the Tokugawa shogunate, when family rank largely determined the makeup of the administrative hierarchy. Exposure to mathematics and business by members of lower classes prepared them for bureaucratic offices better than the Confucian classics absorbed by the upper classes. Increasing financial difficulties of the samurai opened the door to the purchase of status by low-class vassals. But these changes allowed only a "modernization by stealth and by loopholes" (Inoki 1964, 286).

All that changed abruptly in 1853, when Commodore Matthew Perry guided American warships into Uraga. The Japanese were stunned by those steam-powered ships and intimidated by their armaments. Shogun Tokugawa Iesada (1824–1858) had little choice but to accept a treaty that provided for friendly trade with the United States.

Immediately upon this "opening" of Japan to the West, it became clear that future challenges would require a system that could harness and, indeed, cultivate all available talent. The administration began to recruit staff on the basis of merit rather than patronage, a shift that also entailed substituting loyalty to one's lord with loyalty to the emperor, who became increasingly affirmed as a symbol of the entire country.

With the ascendance of Emperor Meiji in 1868, Japan's government embarked explicitly on a program of economic, political, and cultural modernization. The young emperor signed a Five Charter Oath that proclaimed the goals of this modernizing program. It sought to dissolve the old feudal system by broadening the scope of political participation, abolished restrictions on occupational mobility, standardized legal codes and procedures, worked to fuse loyalty with talent in building economic and military structures that could rival those of the West, and established universal education. This involved consolidating provincial governments into a centralized apparatus, coupled with efforts to model the military after France and England, including conscription and a robust reserve force (Hackett 1964). These drastic and surprisingly rapid reforms in turn created needs for financial consolidation and tax revenue, increased exporting activity, and an administrative structure to supporting it.

Japan as a Model for Ethiopia

Like Japan, Ethiopia was propelled toward modernization by attacks from outside powers. Ethiopia's effort, too, took off in the 1850s, when Emperor Theodore II made a determined effort to mobilize Ethiopian forces in the face of attacks from Sudan. Although he hoped to secure assistance from England, his relations with that country soured in a way that led to a massive invasion by British troops in 1868. The British also contributed modern arms to Theodore's Ethiopian enemies in the northern province of Tigray, a move that encouraged Tigrean Emperor Yohannes IV (1871–89) to equip himself further with modern arms in battles against invading Mahdi troops from Sudan. The succeeding emperor, Menelik II (1889–1913), became the first Ethiopian ruler to pursue a broad-gauged program of modernization. He drew on a number of European resources, including a Swiss advisor who played a crucial role. Under Menelik, Ethiopia acquired the first rudiments of a railway system, postal system, modern school system, and cabinet of ministers.

Menelik's most serious foreign threat was Italy, which acquired the Eritrean coast from Turkey and then launched a campaign to colonize inland as far as possible. The Italian venture was halted decisively by the Battle of Adwa in 1896, in which Ethiopia became the first non-white country to defeat a European colonial power. This victory put Ethiopia on the map, and within a few years dozen European countries had established diplomatic missions in the new capital of Addis Ababa.

Not long after, Japan became the second such non-white country in its defeat of Russia in the 1904–05 war. In so doing, Japan achieved even more international attention. Both countries became aware of themselves as staunchly independent nations with a venerable political history and a traditional society organized around the institutions of an ancient sacral monarchy. In the early years of the twentieth century, writers in both countries expressed awareness of their mutual affinities (Zewde 1990). This awareness continued for decades; an issue of *The Japanese Weekly Chronicle* in 1933 celebrated "the spiritual affinity between Japan and Abyssinia,"[3] while in Ethiopia, pre-war Foreign Minister Blattengeta Heruy Walde Sellasie (in *Medhara Berhan Hagara Japan* [*The Japanese Nation, Source of Light*]) and post-war Minister of Education Kebbedde Michael (in *Japan Indemin Seletenech* [*How Japan Modernized*]) described striking similarities between the two countries.[4]

If Ethiopia's survival in the twentieth century depended on military equipment and training which it acquired from Europe, it needed no less the institutions of a modern political system that had some affinity with its distinctive political traditions. This made Japan an obvious model to imitate. Ethiopian intellectuals became known as "Japanizers." They worked to advance connections between the two states in order to facilitate this transformation. The process reached a kind of climax with the promulgation of Ethiopia's first constitution in 1931, which incorporated directly many passages from the Meiji Constitution of 1889. These included the description of the person of the emperor as "sacred and inviolable," and a jural conception of the emperor as, at one and the same time: "1) a constitutional monarch, head of an authoritarian state established by a constitution granted by the emperor, not demanded by the people; 2) supreme authority over the armed forces, independent from control of the cabinet; and 3) a monarch of divine right" (Eisenstadt 1996, 35).

Ethiopia as Inspiration for Self-affirmation among Jamaican Blacks

Japan and Ethiopia were both non-Western countries with traditions of national independence tied to the institutions of a sacral monarchy. Provoked by modernized European states, they strove to secure modern, centralized armies, which in turn entailed constitutional restructuring to legitimate a strong central authority and adumbrate a more rational political bureaucracy. Their examples in turn inspired peoples still under colonial or caste-like rule to aspire for self-determination, another lynchpin of the modern agenda. In this process, the example of Ethiopia had far-reaching effects.

From the time of the Adwa victory onward, an image of Ethiopia the Independent was cherished increasingly by colonized Africans and repressed Afro-Americans. In 1892, the efforts of some Bantu Christian leaders to emancipate themselves from the authority of European missions led to the formation of an independent Black South African denomination named the Ethiopian church. For secular leaders of colonial Africa, moreover, the image of independent Ethiopia offered a constant source of inspiration. The threat to this symbol posed by the Italian revanchist invasion so upset Kwame Nkrumah, he recalls in his Autobiography, that he became motivated to work for the day when he might play a part in bringing an end to so wicked a system as colonialism. Jomo Kenyatta spoke for many Africans when he envisioned Ethiopia's response to the invasion: "Ethiopia, with her Emperor leading, relies on her soldiers, her courage, her traditions. There will be no concession; Ethiopia will fight, as she always has fought, to preserve her independence against this encroachment of Imperialism." Together with J. B. Danquah of the Gold Coast, Mohammed Said of Somaliland, George Padmore of Jamaica, and others, Kenyatta formed a group that came to provide leadership for the African liberation movement, the International African Friends of Abyssinia.

Similar stirrings across the Atlantic drew strength from the independent kingdom of Ethiopia. A key figure in this movement was Marcus Mosiah Garvey (1887–1940), who formed the Universal Negro Improvement Association in the1920s with the goal of uniting black people with their African homeland. After traveling in the United Stated and Great Britain, Garvey returned to Jamaica to spread his views among the black working class. He assured his followers that the hour of Africa's redemption was nearby and told blacks to watch for the crowning of a king in Africa for evidence of their coming redemption. When Prince Ras Tafari Makonnen was crowned as emperor of Ethiopia in 1930, taking thrown name of Haile Selassie (Power of the Trinity), the Rastafarian movement began officially. Inspired by what they viewed as a monumental event that marked the fulfillment of Garvey's prophecy, Rastafarians formed a number of different groups, all of which worshipped Haile Selassie as the sole divinity and proclaimed their faith as a basis for collective self-determination. The Jamaican Rastas embraced Ethiopian symbolism with gusto, employing those symbols—the lion, the drum, the chalice, and the flag of red, green, and yellow stripes—to express their resistance to a white minority government (Carter 2005).

The Rastafarian movement went through four stages. In the 1930s, it manifested itself as a religion, providing solace and inspiration to suppressed blacks, giving them a sense of pride and hope for freedom through repatriation to Africa. During and after the war, when Jamaica's economy deteriorated dramatically, black workers were plagued by malnutrition and poor wages, and the Rastafarian movement became politicized; their leaders intensified opposition to the colonial state by defying the police and organizing illegal street marches. In the 50s and early 60s, Rastas turned from political action toward private withdrawal, concentrating on meditation and self-medication through their omnipresent marijuana. Because of their lower-class manners, marginal status, and unkempt appearance, Rastas were violently repressed by edgy Jamaican police. In the 1970s Rastafarianism underwent yet another transformation. It became more of a positive cultural force, contributing to Jamaican art and music, especially reggae. One outstanding reggae musician, Bob Marley, came to symbolize Rasta beliefs and values. Reggae became the Rastaman's living Bible as well as a bully pulpit and a forum for artistic expression. Bob Marley's popularity ensured a diverse audience for Rasta messages and concepts, and diffused Rastafarian symbols worldwide.

Jamaican Rastas as Inspiration for Japanese Moderns

Of all instances of cultural diffusion in the last century, that of Jamaican culture to Japan would seem the least likely. Two more dissimilar cultures and lifestyles are hard to imagine. The Japanese aesthetic seems the very antipode of Rastaman, based as it is on suppression of affect, rigid control, and symbolic subtleties. The fervent religious belief displayed by reggae musicians lies outside the experience of the largely non-religious Japanese (Carter 2005). There is powerful religiosity and little subtlety in the lyrics of Bob Marley:

> We sick an' tired of-a your *ism-skism game—
>
> Dyin' 'n' goin' to heaven in-a Jesus' name, Lord.
>
> We know when we understand:
>
> Almighty God is a living man.
>
> You can fool some people sometimes,
>
> But you can't fool all the people all the time.
>
> So now we see the light (What you gonna do?),
>
> We gonna stand up for our rights! (Yeah, yeah, yeah!)

In spite of this, or perhaps because of it, Jamaica Rasta served as the medium for the appropriation of Ethiopia-derivative elements into modern Japanese culture. Visits by Marley and other reggae musicians to Japan in the 1970s exported the stimulus. Japanese youth resonated to the rebellious message and pounding rhythms of reggae and the vague mysticism of Rastafarianism. Thousands of young people attended Marley's concerts in Japan and identified with him, his message, his lifestyle, and his look. In the 1980s homegrown Japanese reggae took root and flourished. The appeal of Rasta culture may be illuminated by referring to the schema of modernization processed noted above. While Japan made large strides in the areas of political unification, occupational specialization, and cultural rationalization, and personal discipline, it lagged behind in the areas of social egalitarianism and individualism.

Although the Meiji reforms erased the ascriptive inequalities of shogunate feudalism, they accentuated an attachment to Japanese ethnicity as privileged. This included both the well-known prejudices against foreigners (*gaijin*) and against local minority groups, Ainu and Koreans. On the other hand, in the post-Meiji drive to absorb modern culture from abroad, the Japanese developed a highly selective orientation to the outside world. Their concept for such cultural importation, *kokusaika*, is elitist, connoting identification with the major industrialized nations. Japanese Rastas, by contrast, exhibit a kind of egalitarian internationalism. They do not approach Jamaicans with the attitude of 19C white missionaries who looked down on the black and brown inhabitants of the globe. Rather they seem to believe that, in some ways, Jamaican Rastas have found a way of life that is *superior* to modern Japan.

This lifestyle ministers to other needs that appear to have been lacking in Japan's modernizing culture. Perhaps reggae's most direct and immediate appeal was what it offered on behalf of individualism, especially in the sense of self-expression. Reggae provides a means for Japanese youth to resist the "straightjacket society" in which they live, where their life plans are already determined by the time they reach thirteen years. Although Rasta culture originated as a medium for collective self-affirmation for oppressed people, it took on the colorations of its engendering milieu and became a popular vehicle for defiant expressiveness—in clothes, hairstyles, marijuana use and, above all, music. In the words of one young Japanese, "We're always told to be a good child, a good student, but still we don't know how to be ourselves. Reggae is helping us to do that" (More, 3).

It is not only the modernist value of individualism that supports such yearnings, it is also a rebellion against certain modernizing traits themselves. One of those, labeled 'personal rationalization' above, concerns the heightened forms of personal discipline required by industrial forms of production, bureaucratic management, and modern urban living. All known instances of modernization thus entail new types of socialization that produce these heightened forms of discipline and self-discipline. Processes that have been analyzed, variously, by Max Weber on the ascetic dimensions of capitalist entrepreneurship and bureaucracy, Norbert Elias on *The Civilizing Process*, and Georg Simmel on the modern metropolis, they amount to what has been called a Disciplinary Revolution (Gorski 1993).

In reaction to these disciplinary pressures, a common phenomenon of the modern order is the eruption of what may be called protest individuality—a feature of the counterculture that is also an essential ingredient of modernity[5] Two other features of modern countercultures likewise appear in the Japanese resonance with Rastaman. One is the yearning for the world we have lost, sometimes glossed as neotribalism or the search for *Gemeinschaft*. As close observers have noted, in its affinity with traditional village *matsuri* festivals and the *bon odori* festival music, Reggae offers contemporary Japanese a taste of the simpler lifestyle and values of earlier Japanese life (Collinwood and Kusatsu 1988, 3; More).

In sum: the identification of Jamaicans with Haile Selassie I has radically transfigured core symbols of traditional Ethiopian culture. Jamaican Rastas produced a new subculture that offers young Japanese moderns the elements of a nonwhite protest against dominant features of modernity. In its emphases on expressivity and on egalitarianism, and its idealization of pre-modern lifestyles, Jamaicans created a nonwhite version of the counterculture that has been co-constitutive of modernity ever since Rousseau and the various movements of European romanticism of the early 19C.

Conclusion

The custom of conceiving of social phenomena as concrete bounded entities has formed the basis of innumerable valuable analyses and insight. This tendency has, however, tended to obscure the very real connections among different groups, near and far. In an earlier work (Levine 2000) I demonstrated how the image of historic Ethiopia as consisting of a number of discrete ethnic groups needed to be supplemented by awareness of the numerous ways in which those groups had been interlinked over millennia—through trade, combat, migration, intermarriages, functional exchanges, and joint ceremonies and pilgrimages. A tenacious penchant for thinking of contemporary nations and civilizations in that manner has similarly obscured the innumerable forms of interaction among them. The histories of Japan, Ethiopia, and Jamaica can each be told without any reference to the facts recounted in this paper. And thereby, some of the most interesting facts about modernization process in the twentieth century would not be known. And one would be hard-pressed to make sense of the fact that at a memorial celebration in Addis Ababa, Ethiopia, honoring the sixtieth anniversary of Bob Marley's birth in February 2005, the visitors included dreadlocked pilgrims from Jamaica and Japan.

Bibliography

Carter, Jr., Ellwood B. 2005. "Rasta in Japan—Who Knew?" Department of Sociology,University of Chicago.

Collinwood, X. and Kusatsu, Osamu. 1988. "Japanese Rastafarians."

Gorski, Philip. 1993. "The Protestant Ethic Revisited: Disciplinary Revolution in Holland and Prussia." *American Journal of Sociology*, 99:2 (Sept.), 265–316.

Hackett, Roger F. 1964. "The Military: Japan," in Political Modernization in Japan and Turkey, edited by Robert E. Ward and Dankwart A. Rustow. Princeton:

Princeton University Press, 328–51.
Inoki, Masamichi. 1964. "The Civil Bureaucracy: Japan," in *Political Modernization in Japan and Turkey*, edited by Robert E. Ward and Dankwart A. Rustow. Princeton: Princeton University Press, 283–300.
King, Stephen A. "International Reggae, Democratic Socialism and the Secularization of the Rastafarian Movement, 1972–1980." *Popular Music and Society* 22: 39–60.
Levine, Donald N. 1991. "Simmel as Educator: On Individuality and Modern Culture," *Theory, Culture and Society* 8, 99–117.
______. 1996. "The Battle of Adwa as a 'Historic' Event," In *One House: the Battle of Adwa in 1896*, ed. Pamela Brown and Fassil Yirgu (Chicago: Nyala Publishing), 1–8.
______. 2000. *Greater Ethiopia: The Evolution of a Multiethnic Society*. 2nd ed. Chicago: University of Chicago Press.
______. 2001. "Ethiopia and Japan in Comparative Civilizational Perspective." *Passages: Interdisciplinary Journal of Global Studies* 3 (1), 1–32.
More, Blake. "Jamming in Jah Pan." Available online: www.snakelyone.com/jahpan.htm
Redington, Norman Hugh. 1995. "A Sketch of Rastafari History." Available online: www.nomadfx.com/old/rasta1.html
Ribeiro, Darcy. 1995. *O Povo Brasileirio: A Formação e o Sentido do Brasil*.
Zewde, Bahru. 1990. "The Concept of Japanization in the Intellectual History of Modern Ethiopia," in Bahru Zewde et al., eds., *Proceedings of Fifth Seminar of the Department of History*. Addis Ababa: Addis Ababa University.

Notes

1 This is a revised version of a paper originally presented at the 37th World Congress of the International Institute of Sociology, Stockholm, Sweden, Regular Session: "Comparative Modernization Studies in the Globalized World," July 9, 2005. Ellwood B. Carter, Jr. and Benjamin Cornwell provided valuable research support.

2 This figure is adapted from Figure 2 of *Powers of the Mind: The Reinvention of Liberal Learning in America* (University of Chicago Press 2006).

3 Such perceptions of affinity fed the pronounced sense of solidarity with Ethiopia expressed by the Japanese public following Italy's invasion of Ethiopia in 1935—evident, for example, in the decision of the Osaka Chamber of Commerce to provide straw sandals to Ethiopians to protect their feet against poison gas, in the dispatch of 1,200 Japanese swords to Ethiopia to assist in the war effort, and in the applications of Japanese volunteers to join the Ethiopian Army that flooded the Ethiopian consulate in Tokyo (Zewde 1990).

4 Scarcely noticed among those similarities was not only the fact that Ethiopia and Japan were the only non-European countries to defeat modern European imperialists but even that earlier in history, both nations had distinguished themselves by withstanding other imperial powers: Japan against Mongols in the 1280s, Ethiopia against Ottoman Turks in the 1580s, and both had welcomed intercourse with the Portuguese early in the 16th century, whom they then extruded abruptly early in the following century.

5 Whatever feature one may select as a hallmark of modernity, one need not look

far to identify its opposite. That is why, following Simmel, I have long argued that the most prominent defining feature of modernity may be its tendency to amplify opposed characteristics (Levine 1991). An increase in popular mobilization for war is accompanied by an increase in organized pacifism. Increased central authority stimulates heightened assertion of sub-national identities. Increased mobility and equality of opportunity generate new forms of inequality. And increased levels of self-discipline are linked with increased pressures for self-expression.

36

Ethiopian Nationhood in a Global Era (2011)*

Conventional theories trace nationalism to modern Western Europe, usually following the French Revolution. However, markers of nationalism used by most scholars are attested by evidence of Ethiopia's nationhood as early as sixth century C.E. This requires revisions in both conventional notions of nationhood and views of those who find Ethiopianness a recent invention. Moreover, the experience of Ethiopians in their recent Diaspora warrants rethinking the very notions of nationhood. Continuing ties of Ethiopian expatriates with their homeland and communication through electronic media manifest a new configuration of Ethiopia's nationhood, consisting now of three confluent parts: *bet-agar* (homeland); *wutch-agar* (diaspora); and *sayber-agar* (cyberspace).

Renewed scholarly attention to nationhood and nationalism in the 1980s produced an array of interpretations. Some analysts viewed nationalism as a political ideology that galvanized a social movement (Breuilly 1982). Some saw it as a cultural glue for the new kind of society associated with industrialism—one driven by economic and scientific growth, impersonal, and built with mutually substitutable, atomized individuals (Gellner 1983). Others took nationalism to be a symbolic form created to replace discredited religions, a symbolism, dispensed through printed media, projecting "imagined communities" of nations through

---

* An early draft of this paper was presented at the Fifteenth International Conference of Ethiopian Studies, Hamburg University, July 2003, and published in the *International Journal of Ethiopian Studies* I No.2 (2004), pp. 1-15, with the title "Reconfiguring the Ethiopian Nation in a Global Era." Adam Mohr assisted with the original draft. Alemayehu F. Weldemariam contributed to the present enlarged and updated version published in *Análise Social*, vol. XLVI (199), 2011, 311-327.

which a sense of immortality could be evoked and with which otherwise anonymous individuals could identify (Anderson 1983). Hobsbawm and Tanger (1983, 1990) defined it as an historically novel form, ministering to doctrinal needs so intense that rising elites felt compelled even to invent an ancient past through which they could claim historical continuity.

However diverse their viewpoints, these authors shared one problematic assumption. They assumed that nationalism is an essentially modern Western phenomenon, a byproduct of, if not midwife to, the democratic and industrial revolutions of the late eighteenth century. They adhered not only to Elie Kedourie's benchmark formulation of nationalism as a *doctrine* — a doctrine which holds that humanity is naturally divided into nations, that nations are known by certain characteristics that can be ascertained, and that the only legitimate type of government is national self-government. They also followed his firm dating of the phenomenon: it was "invented in Europe at the beginning of the nineteenth century" (Kedourie [1960] 1994: 1). Craig Calhoun's more recent disquisition emphatically concurs: "nationalism is one of the definitive features of the modern era" (Calhoun 1997: 12). They assume this, Philip Gorski (2000) has shown, in spite of the extensive use of "nation" and kindred terms in classical Greek and Latin and older European vernaculars, and despite the appearance of medieval and early modern nationalisms—facts they discount by claiming that such traces of national consciousness simply do not amount to full-blown modern nationalism.

To be sure, a few scholarly outliers have arisen to challenge the consensual "modernist" view of nationalism as a relatively recent invention. Liah Greenfield's magisterial five-nation overview (1992) disputes the claim that nationalism originated with the French Revolution and locates its birthplace in Reformation England more than two centuries earlier. Gorski likewise places the birthdate of nationalist identities and ideologies in the early modern period, but emphasizes the Netherlands as birthplace of a truly modern form of nationalism. Yet even these revisionists seem content to keep the birth-place of nationalism in Western Europe in the post-medieval period. They ignore the fact that countries like Japan and Ethiopia had developed nationalist cultures as early as a millennium before their putative origins in Western Europe (Levine 2007).

Ethiopia's Status as an Historic Nation

This is particularly ironic in the light of Gorski's analysis, which posits a form he calls "Hebraic nationalism" as archetype for modern forms of nationalism. Gorski points to numerous moments during the Dutch Revolt against Spain when Hebraic imagery figured prominently—celebrations of

William the Orange in 1577 with tableaux that depicted David and Goliath, Moses, and Joseph; commemorative coins that showed an angel driving Sennach'erib from Jerusalem; official proclamations that commonly invoked the God of the Old Testament. Deployed to serve a liberation movement, such symbolism transcended cleavages of class, confession, and region on behalf of a burgeoning nationalism. It went on to facilitate that national formation through analogies with the biblical Covenant, which committed them to observe and enforce God's laws throughout the covenanted nation. Beyond that, in the post-1648 period two new discourses emerged. One lauded the House of Orange dynasty as an instrument of God, incarnating special gifts passed from father to son. The other appeared as a populist discourse, connoting the equivalence of such phrases as "God's People," the "Chosen people," and the "Netherlandish people." All this leads Gorski to posit a "Mosaic Moment" in early North Atlantic nationalism, a Moment that figured in England also, explosively during the Civil War and, in different garb, during the Restoration (Gorski 2000).

About a millennium before these Old Testament morality plays were dramatized in the Netherlands and England, a comparable configuration took shape in Northeast Africa. In the *Kibre Negest* (KN), a text aptly referred to as Ethiopia's national epic (Levine [1974] 2000), the portrait of an early Hebraic nationalism was made with extravagant, gaudy strokes. All the themes that Gorski found in sixteenth and seventeenth centuries Netherlands appear there in vivid colors: a founding monarch presented as the son of King Solomon, named David in the KN; Exodic transport of an endangered Hebraic elite by miraculous passage above the Red Sea; inheritance of a Holy Ark of the Covenant; a monarchy sacralized both by Solomonic genealogy and divine anointment; and a People enjoined to witness, protect, and advance the divine Christian mission which, by virtue of the Hebrews' failure to follow Christ, had devolved upon the blessed Ethiopians. No Mosaic moment this, but a Mosaic Momentous.

Archaically *pre-national*, then? Consider what criteria the modernist scholars of nationalism have posited as defining the *sine qua non* of true nationhood in the effort to distinguish what they call pre-national from truly national formations. They stipulate that true nationalism involves a political doctrine or ideology (Kedourie [1960] 1994; Gellner 1983); they refer to a special cognitive notion—"nation" = "people" = "state" (Hobsbawm 1990)—or discursive formation (Calhoun 1997); they emphasize a social scope that includes the entire nation as a unit (Weber 1976); they stress the element of political mobilization (Breuilly 1982). Heeding these criteria and thus pointing to (1) the Dutch reference to theirs as a nation among nations; (2) their early equation of nation with people; (3) the exposure to nationalist discourse and symbols throughout Dutch society, and (4) the resort to nationalist political mobilization, Gorski handily demonstrates that early modern Netherlands evinced all four of these ingredients.[1]

As far as the limited documentary evidence allows us to understand, so did historic Ethiopia. A prime text for this claim, the *Kebra Negast* stands for nothing if not the image of the Ethiopian nation as belonging to a world of distinct nations among which it stands out by virtue of possessing a special mission. The bulk of the epic contrasts the nation of Israel with that of Ethiopia, mentioning Egypt along the way, and it concludes by naming several others—Rome, Armenia, and Nagran—and asserting the primacy of Ethiopia as God's favored among the nations. One remarkable feature of this epic is its consistent reference to Ethiopia as a sovereign, inclusive polity, ignoring the numerous ethnic divides within historic Ethiopia. Although mentioning various provinces within the country, it names them only as geographical markers. Their unification under the sovereign state is manifest in passages like, "And all the provinces of Ethiopia rejoiced, for Zion sent forth a light like that of the sun into the darkness wheresoever she came" (Budge 1922: 84).

With respect to cognitive categories, the KN assumes the equivalence of land = people = nation = polity. Thus, it speaks of the rejoicing which took place in *bihere Ityoppiya*, a phrase that connotes land, country, and people alike. And when David, the Ethiopian son of King Solomon, returns to Ethiopia with the Ark of Zion, he is welcomed joyously by the "*seb'a Ityoppiya*," the people of Ethiopia, a phrase connoting the overarching nation.[2] Among other older records that instantiate the equation of people with nation, *hezba Iteyoppeya* is found in a document from the time of Na'od (ca. 1500).[3]

These symbols were spread throughout Ethiopian society by virtue of an extraordinary system of national communication that was provided by the Ethiopian national Church. Churches and monasteries throughout the country embodied a nationwide system of communication. Liturgically, it was unified by the classical Ethiopic language, Ge'ez, much as medieval Europeans speaking different languages were unified by Latin. Their texts likewise made mention of Ethiopia, especially the phrases from the Old and New Testaments that the Septuagint translated with that term.

Finally, from earliest times, the symbolism of Ethiopian statehood could mobilize members of diverse ethnic groups and regions on behalf of their national homeland. Although we have no evidence of the composition of the forces that accompanied King Caleb's expedition to Southwest Arabia in the sixth century, it is hard to imagine that they were not from a variety of regions and ethnic groups. But we do have evidence about the mobilization of forces on behalf of the national expansion under the Solomonid emperors of thirteenth to fifteenth centuries and of the mobilization against the Turks in the sixteenth century. This proud tradition was then fatefully drawn on to mobilize tens of thousands of troops in wars against Sudanese and then Italian invaders in the late nineteenth century.

Ethiopia's Nationhood in the Twentieth Century

In the wake of Ethiopia's victory against Italy in the battle of Adwa in 1896, her nationhood was fortified by a series of changes: a national system of secular schools; a national bank and postal system; a national network of roads; a standing national army; an effective and prestigious national airline; and a number of cultural forms that gave expression to a modern Ethiopian national culture in such areas as athletics, literature, music, and the visual arts. Through these changes and the majesty of two powerful emperors, Ethiopia was well on the way to becoming a successful, independent nation-state in the twentieth century. Ethiopia proudly took its place among other sovereign states by joining the League of Nations in 1923. It played a prominent role in the United Nations as a founding member and a staunch supporter of UN collective security and other UN missions. Thanks to her historic role as a symbol of African freedom and the mediations of its skillful emperor, the regime became recognized as a major player during the decade of African independence of the 1960s. Addis Ababa was host for the United Nations Economic Commission for Africa. What is more, at two critical junctures, in 1960 and in 1974, the regime came close to becoming a constitutional monarchy, in which case there was every reason to expect its continued growth as a modernizing polity, in which democratic rights would have been extended, and a greater openness to civic participation by diverse religious and ethnic groups would have been accepted.

That this did not happen was due to a number of factors. First and foremost, the ageing emperor failed to take steps to ensure an appropriate process of succession. His retention of absolute power until the last moment left a vacuum which the most aggressive political forces would fill. Relatedly, educated Ethiopians failed to develop the lineaments of a movement, let alone a political party, in which the seedlings of liberal democracy might germinate. Instead, the active political space was monopolized by radical Marxist ideologues (Balsvik 1979; Kebede 2008).

This occurred in conjunction with a number of threats to Ethiopia's status as an historic nation—threats that stemmed both from tribalist movements and Marxist ideologues. The former represented an upsurge of particularistic demands of the sort that appear in all modernizing countries as states become more centralized and resourceful, and as citizens with local and ethnic identities seek a more effective voice (Geertz 1963). The latter reflected the slogan of "self-determination of nationalities" imported from Soviet ideological mentors (Levine 2000: XIV).

Accordingly, when Ethiopia's 2000-year-old monarchy was overthrown in September 1974, a tortuous period of revolutionary violence, political repression, chronic civil war, and ethnic fragmentation ensued, culminating in the 1990s in a new regime that initially rejected the notion of an age-old nation of Ethiopia altogether.

"Nationhood" in Contemporary Social Science

During the period when Ethiopia's nationhood was being challenged on the ground, academic critics were raising questions about the very notion of the nationally-circumscribed society as the foundational unit in sociological analysis.[4] They pointed to the rising salience of international and supranational forms (Levine 1995, 1996). They took note of economic globalization as a process that transcended national sovereignty and territoriality, and required a shift toward "transnational analysis" (Sassen 1996). They highlighted the salience of transnational connections in the process of modernization (Levine 2006). At meetings of the World Congress of Sociology in July 2002, one of the hot ideas in circulation concerned the obsolescence of the nation-state as a central unit for sociological analysis, and the theme of "sociology without society" was being taken up as a banner behind which to secure a putative emancipation from all previous sociology.[5]

In the spirit of such revisionist notions about the concept of nationhood, it was not only students of Western history who slighted the story of Ethiopia's precocious achievement of nationhood, it was post-modern Ethiopians and their sympathizers no less. Inasmuch as scholars of nationhood had already begun to dispute the salience of well-formed nations prior to the modern period, when the regime shift of 1991 catapulted into power an elite with a dim view of historic Ethiopia, apologists for the dismemberment of Africa's oldest independent nation could wear the mantle of academic respectability for some patently counter-factual reconstructions. Books with titles like *The Invention of Ethiopia* (Holcomb and Ibssa,1990) and *Imagining Ethiopia* (Sorenson 1993) could then brazenly claim that the Ethiopian nation-state was an invention of late nineteenth century imperialism.

Forming a Diaspora

Ethiopia's political upheavals in the 1970s added her to the list of countries suffering a massive hemorrhage of population through migration. In 1974

Ethiopia had the distinction of having the smallest proportion of its population living abroad of any country in the world. The traumatic dislocations of the Derg regime made it the nation with the *highest* proportion of its citizens living abroad just five years later. The World Refugee Surveys show a high of 1.9 million total refugees in 1981 from Ethiopia. Figures for 1983 report some 1,215,000 Ethiopian refugees in Northeast Africa (Somalia, Djibouti, Kenya, and Sudan), more than 10,000 in the Middle East (Saudi Arabia, UAR, and Egypt), tens of thousands in Europe, especially England, Germany, Italy, the Netherlands, and Sweden, and about 10,000 in the United States. For most of the 1980s, Ethiopia was one of the top three contributors of refugees in the world.[6]

Following the collapse of the Derg in May 1991, a large number of Ethiopian refugees returned. The Ethiopian population virtually disappeared in Somalia and the Arab countries, and dwindled in Djibouti, while the UN High Commission for Refugees repatriated 83,000 from Sudan and 80,000 from Kenya. Even so, in 1993 Ethiopia still had the sixth highest number of the world's refugees. New waves of emigration kept the refugee populations in Kenya at 26,500 and in Sudan at 173,200. Massive airlifts helped bring tens of thousands of Ethiopian immigrants to Israel, where the total population of Ethiopian-Israelis now numbers more than 90,000. Substantial increases of Ethiopian immigrants appeared in England, Germany, and Canada.

Soaring above all others, the number of Ethiopian immigrants to the United States rose to more than 100,000. This represents a long-term cumulative trend, starting with groups of university students who became stranded after the Derg revolution and ended up staying, often sending for their families. The immigrant stream grew from a few hundred per year in the 1970s, to about 2,000–3,000 per year in the 1980s, and 4,000–5,000 per year in the 1990s. The current Ethiopian population in the United States has been estimated approaching half a million.

Like other immigrant groups in the United States, the Ethiopians found ways to keep in touch with one another and reproduce their home customs. They settled in the same neighborhoods—the Uptown area in Chicago; Arlington, Adams Morgan, and Silver Spring in the District of Columbia area; in Los Angeles, a section of the city recently publicized as "Little Ethiopia." They established community newspapers, national magazines, and radio programs. Through these and other media, including even an "Ethiopian Yellow Pages" (in the Washington, D.C. area), they informed their fellow immigrants about Ethiopian and Ethiopian-friendly businesses. In many cities, they formed self-help organizations to minister to the adjustment needs of their compatriots. These community associations provided a wide range of services to assist new immigrants, improve the life chances of existing immigrants, and provide language study for the younger generation. For example, services of the

Ethiopian Community Mutual Association of Seattle, Washington, include case management and advocacy for Ethiopian expatriates, job placement, language training (Amharic and English), translation and interpretation, and citizenship classes. The association also organizes sports activities, after-school tutoring, and parenting classes.

Over time, the services became increasingly sophisticated. The Ethiopian Community Association of Chicago (ECAC) established a Computer Training Center; equipped with state-of-the-art facilities, the program includes career counseling and job placement services, and resettlement from many countries. Moreover, unlike immigrant populations of previous generations, the Ethiopian Diaspora took shape at a time when the melting-pot ideal had given way to a norm of respecting the identity and cultures of incoming populations. Ethnic diversity was coming to be celebrated, multiculturalism was in style, and ethnic Americans tended increasingly to cherish cultural heritages long buried by assimilationist trends. Immigrants were quick to establish restaurants serving traditional Ethiopian cuisine, in a (mostly) authentic manner. In many cities community associations organized celebrations of *Enquatatash*, the Ethiopian New Year. In Chicago, the ECAC organized an annual Ethiopia Day at the Civic Center, with live performances of Ethiopian music and dance. Indeed, some Ethiopian ethnic, regional, and religious groups created centers of their own: Oromo associations, a Gondere association, even a restaurant specializing in Gurage cuisine, a Kitfo Megab Bayt, in Washington, D.C.

A major bulwark of Ethiopian traditions in the Diaspora has been the formation of numerous Ethiopian houses of worship, mostly Ethiopian Orthodox churches and some mosques and Protestant churches. Ethiopian Orthodox Churches located across the United States include St. Michael's Ethiopian Church in Las Vegas, Debre Medhanit Medhane-Alem Cathedral in Columbus, Ohio, and three churches dedicated to Saint Mary in Los Angeles.

Depending on the size of the local Diaspora, similar institutions sprang up in Ethiopian communities elsewhere. One finds, for example, Ethiopian restaurants in Tokyo and Paris; a Medhane-Alem Church in Stockholm and a Debre-Tsion Kidist Mariam Church in London; and a number of active community associations in Israel which offer programs on parenting, civic skills, Ethiopian traditional music, and *shemgelena* (mediation by elders). In Germany, Diaspora organizations span a wide spectrum, from churches and humanitarian agencies to women's groups and community support organizations.

Such developments serve to maintain a sense of national identity and pride in Ethiopian culture. To be sure, the level and quality of interest in homeland culture becomes increasingly problematic with the second generation. In Israel, for example, observers have noted a certain dropping of Ethiopian cultural practices among youth, often for symbols associated with African Americans and Rastafarians—even among youngsters who may not know who the historic Ras Tafari was. Even so, many younger Ethiopians abroad have become active in attempting to reappropriate their homeland culture and in supporting political and civic actions to help its development. That has had an impact on the reconfiguration of Ethiopian nationhood.

An association called the Ethiopian Global Initiative seeks to network Ethiopian students and young professionals from many countries who believe that founded social entrepreneurship would transform Ethiopia.

Diaspora Connections with the Homeland

What is more, in contrast to the mass emigrations of previous generations, the migration of Ethiopians coincided with the onset of extraordinary technologies of transportation and communication. Settling into their "Diaspora," most Ethiopians have not turned their back on their homeland but have used these technologies to set up unprecedented networks of communication, among themselves, and with their homeland. One way they have done this is to maintain continuous communication with family and friends at home of a sort that would have been unthinkable before these newer technologies. Ethiopians now walk down the streets of Addis Ababa with cell phones, speaking to kith and kin who live abroad. Easier travel connections bring emigrants home for holidays, weddings, and ordinary visits. They send packages and monetary gifts.

Some groups get actively involved with development projects at home. One effort sought to collect 30,000 books to send to school libraries in the home country. The Gonder Development Association builds schools and hospitals in the Begemdir region. Ethiopians in Israel recently formed a kind of Peace Corps of volunteers to carry professional services back to their homeland. A potent group, the Ethiopian Physicians of North American Health Professionals Association, regularly sends teams of doctors, dentists, nurses, and pharmacists who volunteer one to two weeks each year working in Ethiopian hospitals and clinics.[7]

Since the fall of the Derg, many Ethiopians abroad have participated in business ventures with homeland partners. One particularly well-developed trade route of these "transnational entrepreneurs" involves Ethiopians in Israel who travel home to procure goods—such as *gesho* to make *talla*, Ethiopian barley beer, and *tef*, the preferred grain for making *enjera*, the daily pancake-bread—and bring them back for their nostalgic compatriots (Rosen 2001).[8]

Media for making and maintaining these kinds of business connections are growing rapidly. These include annual conferences of Ethiopian American investors, and an Ethiopia Investor newsletter providing information about Ethiopian exports and agencies that facilitate transnational commerce.

Continued involvement with the Ethiopian Church keeps Diaspora Ethiopian Orthodox Christians attuned to ecclesiastical affairs in the homeland since, unlike nearly all other Christian religions, Ethiopian Orthodoxy is closely tied to the home nation-state. This political issue has been conspicuous in the past few decades, with the changes of regime: Abuna Tewofilos, who was deposed and then assassinated by the Derg, was replaced with Abuna Tekla Haymanot and then Abba Merkorios, who was in turn deposed by the EPRDF regime and replaced with Abuna Paulos. In the United States, at least, almost no churches accept the authority of the current official patriarch; some look to Abba Merkorios, and many are independent.

More generally, the flowering of Ethiopian national culture in the past generation has to be seen as a continuous homeland-Diaspora phenomenon. Audiences in both domains are galvanized by vocalists such as the late revered Tilahun Gessesse and renowned jazz instrumentalist Mulatu Astatke and younger vocalists like Aster Aweke and Teddy Afro. Combined Beta Israeli and Israeli musicians have jointly produced popular CDs. Film makers Haile Gerima and Yemane Dempsey attract equally enthusiastic audiences in Addis Ababa and Washington DC. Ethiopian painters, mindful of one another's work, flourish in both venues; for example, Fikru Hailemariam lives and maintains studios six months a year each in Addis and Paris (Levine 2008). Fresh cultural creation in the Diaspora reached such proportions that an international conference on the subject was convened at Radcliffe/Harvard in 2008 (Shelemay and Kaplan 2011 [2006]).

Party politics has offered a dramatic manifestation of Diaspora involvement with home events. Public demonstrations have been organized in England and the United States to protest policy and personnel matters that emigrants find offensive. Diaspora communities have participated vigorously in the organization of dissident political parties, several of which work in tandem with homeland counterparts.[9]

Relations between Ethiopian government officials and members ofDiaspora communities have suffered from enduring currents of political distrust, but intermittently they have reached out to one another. From time to time, government officials have gone abroad to encourage support through overseas "nationals." Such moments instantiate the concept of the "deterritorialized nation-state," in which boundaries are defined socially rather than geographically (Basch *et al.* 1994; Glick Schiller and Fouron 1998). Diaspora Ethiopians thereby continue to be engaged by raising funds, organizing demonstrations, and launching advocacy and lobbying campaigns. Altogether, pan-Ethiopian nationalism, unbounded by its borders, manifests itself in this global era in what has been called "long-distance nationalism," or the persistent claim to a national identity by people residing away from their homeland (Anderson 1992; Glick Schiller and Fouron 2001). In sum, transnational migration, rather than weakening the sense of pan-Ethiopian national identity, has actually strengthened it by creating a new incarnation of this identity in the form of long-distance pan-Ethiopian nationalism.

The Virtual Nation

The swift growth of information technology engineered a public space for the participation of nationals, both at home and abroad, in their homeland affairs. More particularly, such innovations made active civic engagement by Diaspora Ethiopians possible. Continuing engagement of Diaspora Ethiopians, in both their vibrant communities abroad and in interactions with their homeland, redefines the locus and scope of Ethiopian nationhood. What is more, in the global high-tech era, Ethiopian nationality asserts itself in a third arena space: cyberspace. Sassen has theorized this arena as follows:

> Cyberspace is, perhaps ironically, a far more concrete space for social struggles than that of the national political system. It becomes a place where non-formal political actors can be part of the political scene in a way that is much more difficult in national institutional channels. Nationally politics needs to run through existing formal systems: whether the electoral political system or the judiciary (taking state agencies to court). Non-formal political actors are rendered invisible in the space of national politics. Cyberspace can accommodate a broad range of social struggles and facilitate the emergence of new types of political subjects that do not have to go through the formal political system. [Sassen 2003: 13]

Cyberspace has produced remarkable new forms of civic participation. Digital networks have created virtual neighborhoods, bounded no longer by territory, but by access to requisite software and hardware. Due to the paucity in Ethiopia of the software and hardware on which these networks are based, they are dominated by Diaspora communities, but they include serious participants from the home country who provide information for which the emigrants hunger. One major category of these media consists of news-centered websites. (See Appendix, Figure 2, for a partial listing of these sites.) Other networks, known generically as "countrynets," primarily facilitate discussion of Ethiopian politics and culture. These include the EthioForum network, a network sponsored by CyberEthiopia known as Warka, and the Ethiopian Email Distribution Network (EEDN), which purports to offer "a home away from home" and adopts the byline "One Country, One People, One Flag". EEDN offers a forum for Ethiopians in many countries—recent messages have come from Ethiopians in Zimbabwe, Italy, Sweden, and England—as well as some at home. Like Burundinet, a countrynet for Burundi that has been analyzed in depth (Kadende-Kaiser 1998, 2000), EEDN offers a medium for negotiating national and subnational identities, striving to overcome subnational claims to citizenship and rebuild a fragmented national community from afar. Its threads, which often draw as many as 25 different respondents, have included such topics as securing the release of political prisoners; ways to harness Ethiopia's water power for development; what to do about the hated ethnic ID cards; the belief that "God selected Ethiopians as his chosen people"; and historical origins of the name Oromo. The constant growth of electronic networks and websites revivifies Ethiopian national identity and appears as a force in the creation of Ethiopia's collective future.

The medium of "paltalks" has come to play a role in Ethiopian homeland affairs. Besides offering discussion platforms, paltalks afford Ethiopians a way to circumvent government restrictions on information access though programs that supplement chat service with text, audio, and video capabilities. A single paltalk chat room supports up to 500 participants; when a room is full, participants can enter another room, with no limit on the number of new rooms that can be formed. The May 2010 general elections formed a hot issue for thousands of Ethiopian paltalk users, who joined chat rooms to replay jammed media programs such as DW and VOA and discuss the electoral process.

Ethiopian Nationhood Reconfigured

Just as the historic realities of long-established nations like Ethiopia pose a challenge to conventional ideas about modern nationhood, so the contemporary Ethiopian experience reinforces pressures to rethink conventional notions of national boundaries. The nation whose conquest and dispersal across the world two millennia ago gave rise to the term diaspora seemed anomalous up to the past century, when a home territory with well-defined and secure boundaries seemed the only way to construe nationhood. The Jewish case now seems normative for many countries, whose boundaries, like that of ancient Israel, have expanded to involve a level of co-determination that previously could not have been imagined. The globalizing tendencies favored by electronic media and easy transportation will continue not only to promote subnational and supranational communities, but will also play a major role in strengthening the age-old nation of Ethiopia.

Appendix

Country	Categories	Ca. 1973	Ca. 1983	Ca. 1993	Ca. 2003
USA	Total Immigrants Refugees	149 (1973) 2 582 (1979) 2 476 (1979)	9 761 (1983) 9 655 (1983)	96 000 (1998) 16 684 (1993)	86 000 (2001) 11 536 (2001)
Canada	Total Immigrants Refugees			12 100 (1991) 7 786 (1994)	14 455 (1996) 2 034 (2001)
UK	Refugees		909 (1988)	5 026 (1993)	5 100 (2001)
Germany	Total Immigrants			20 631 (1995)	15 305 (2000)
Sweden	Refugees			8 452 (1991)	681 (2001)
Netherlands	Total Immigrants Refugees			6 438 (1996) 2 645 (1995)	7 149 (2002) 1 776 (2001)
Australia	Total Immigrants			1 341 (1991)	3 544 (2001)
Other Europe	Refugees	218 (1980)	597 (1983)	1 159 (1997)	2 141 (2001)
Somalia	Refugees	1 175 000 (1979)	700 000 (1983)	399 (1993)	567 (2001)
Sudan	Refugees	46 300 (1973) 311 200 (1979)	484 000 (1983)	173 200 (1993)	16 120 (2001)
Djibouti	Refugees	28 800 (1979)	29 170 (1983)	16 383 (1993)	1 428 (2001)
Kenya	Refugees	1 170 (1979)	1 670 (1983)	26 466 (1993)	13 541 (2001)
Middle East	Refugees	840 (1979)	9 360 (1983)	969 (1993)	1 582 (2001)

Periodicals

1. www.aigaforum.com
2. www.tigraionline.com
3. www.ethiomedia.com
4. www.addisvoice.com
5. www.nazret.com
6. www.tecolahagos.com
7. www.addisnegeronline.com
8. www.ethiopianreporter.com
9. www.allafrica.com/ethiopia
10. www.cyberethiopia.com
11. www.asmarino.com(Eritrean)
12. www.awate.com(Eritrean)
13. www.ethiopiadaily.com
14. www.deki-alula.com
15. www.addisfortune.com
16. www.jimmatimes.com
17. www.walta-info.com
18. www.capitalethiopia.com

19. www.ethiopiazare.com
20. Tadias
21. Ethio-American

Blogs

1. www.ecadforum.com
2. www.hmbasha.net
3. www.arefe.wordpress.com (Addis Journal)
4. www.smgebru.blogspot.com
5. www.alemayehufentaw.blogspot.com (Rasselas Review)
6. www.awate.com (Eritrean)

Entertainment Websites

1. www.hagerfikerradio.com
2. www.addiszefen.com
3. www.addislive.com
4. www.paltalk.com — Several hundred paltalk rooms include *Ethiopians* Forum For Political Civility, *Ethiopian* Review, Ethio-Civility, Lesane *Ethiopia*, Geza Tegaru, Assimba, *Ethiopian* Current Affairs discussion Forum (ECADF), and International *Ethiopian* Women's Organization (IEWO)
5. www.seleda.com — Posted articles written by Ethiopians covering various themes; humorous, including a "top-ten list"

Informative Websites

1. www.ethniopiannationalcongress.org (information civic education projects)
2. www.ethioguide.com — Ethiopian news, cultural information, history, health, links to religious sites (including a few EOC church pages)
3. www.ethioyellowpages.com — Similar to print version of Ethiopian Yellow Pages, but less detailed; run from Beverly Hills, CA; links to Ethiopian restaurants and markets in U.S. cities, Europe, Ethiopia
4. www.imperialethiopia.org — Official site of Imperial Crown Council of Ethiopia with links to Dynasty, History, Church, and Charitable Work done by Monarchy and related organizations
5. www.ethioworld.com — Business news; online shopping and travel with some news as well as discussion forum
6. www.oromoliberationfront.com — Official political OLF site
7. www.ethio.com — News, Ethiopia information (history, currency exchange, weather), can subscribe to Ethiolist (to directly receive Ethiopia-related news and information at email account)

Web Hosting Sites

1. www.ethiopiaonline.net — Lists online newspapers and magazines

2. www.ethioguide.com — Lists Ethiopian news websites

3. Several hundred paltalk rooms include *Ethiopians* Forum for Political Civility, *Ethiopian Review*, Ethio Civility, Lesane *Ethiopia*, Geza Tegaru, Assimba, *Ethiopian* Current Affairs discussion Forum (ECADF), and International *Ethiopian* Women's Organization (IEWO).

Bibliography

Albrow, M. (1997), *The Global Age: State and Society Beyond Modernity*, Stanford, CA, Stanford University Press.

Anderson, B. (1983), *Imagined Communities: Reflections on the Origin and Spread of Nationalism*, London, Verso.

Anderson, B. (1992), *Long-Distance Nationalism: World Capitalism and the Rise of Identity Politics*, Amsterdam, Center for Asian Studies.

Balsvik, R. (1979), *Haile Selassie's Students: Rise of Social and Political Consciousness*, PhD diss., Norway, University of Trømso.

Basch, L., Glick Schiller, N. and Szanton-Blanc, C. (1994), *Nations Unbound: Transnational Projects, Postcolonial Predicaments, and Deterritorialized Nation-States.* New York, Gordon and Breach.

Breuilly, J. (1982), *Nationalism and the State*, Chicago, University of Chicago Press.

Budge, Sir E., and Wallis, A. (ed.) (1922), *The Queen of Sheba and Her Only Son Menyelek [Kebra Nagast]*, London.

Calhoun, C. (1997), *Nationalism*, Minneapolis, University of Minnesota Press.

Caquot, A. (1961), "Les actes d'Ezra de Gunda-Gunde, Gadla Abuna Ezra". *Annales d'Ethiopie*, 4, p. 86.

Geertz, C. (1963), "The integrative revolution". In *The Interpretations of Cultures*, New York, Basic Books, pp. 255–310.

Gellner, E. (1983), *Nations and Nationalism*, Ithaca, N.Y., Cornell University Press.

Glick Schiller, N. and Georges, F. (1998), "Transnational lives and national identities: The identity politics of Haitian immigrants". *In* M. P. Smith and L. E. Guarnizo (eds), *Transnationalism from Below*, New Brunswick, N.J., Transaction Publishers, pp. 130–161.

Glick Schiller, N. and Georges F. (2001), *Georges Woke Up Laughing: Long Distance Nationalism and the Search for Home*, Durham, Duke University Press.

Gorski, P. (2000), "The mosaic moment: an early modernist critique of modernist theories of nationalism". *American Journal of Sociology*, 105 (5), pp. 1428–1468.

Greenfield, L. (1992), *Nationalism: Five Roads to Modernity*, Cambridge and London, Harvard University Press.

Hobsbawm, E., and Terence, T. (1983), *The Invention of Tradition*, Cambridge, Cambridge University Press.

Hobsbawm, E. (1990), *Nations and Nationalism since 1780*, Cambridge, Cambridge UniversityPress.

Holcomb, B., and Sisai, I. (1990), *The Invention of Ethiopia*, Trenton, N.J., Red Sea Press.

Kadende-kaiser, R. M. (2000), "Interpreting language and cultural discourse: internet communication among Burundians in the Diaspora". *Africa Today*, 47 (2), pp. 120–148.

Kebede, M. (2008), *Radicalism and Cultural Dislocation in Ethiopia, 1960–1974*, Rochester, N.Y., University of Rochester Press.

Kedourie, E. (1994 [1960], *Nationalism*, Oxford, Blackwell.

Levine, D. N. (2000 [1974]), *Greater Ethiopia: The Evolution of a Multiethnic Society*, 2nd ed., Chicago and London, University of Chicago Press.

Levine, D. N. (1995), *Visions of the Sociological Tradition*, Chicago, IL, University of Chicago Press.

Levine, D. N. (1996), "Sociology and the nation-state in an era of shifting boundaries". *Sociological Inquiry*, 66 (3), pp. 253–266.

Levine, D. N. (2004), "Beyond the nation-state: multiple openings for sociological discourse". In E. Ben-Rafael (ed.), *Comparing Modern Civilizations: Pluralism versus Homogeneity*, Boston, Brill.

Levine, D. N. (2007), "Ethiopia, Japan, and Jamaica: A century of globally linked modernizations". *International Journal of Ethiopian Studies*, 3 (1), pp. 18–28.

Levine, D. N. (2008), "An Ethiopian painter for the 21st century". [Fikru Gebre Mariam]. Published in *Tadias* and in *The Ethiopian-American.*

Portes, A., William, J. H., and Eduardo Guarnizo, L. (2002), "Transnational entrepreneurs: an alternative form of immigrant economic adaptation". *American Sociological Review*67 (2), pp. 278–298.

Rosen, H. (2001), *Hedgehogs and Foxes among the Ethiopian Olim in Kiryat Malachi: Economic, Social and Political Dynamics and Developments*, State of Israel, Ministry of Immigrant Absorption, Planning and Research Division.

Sassen, S. (1996), *Losing Control of Sovereignty in an Age of Globalization*, New York, Columbia University Press.

Sassen, S. (2003), "Globalization or denationalization?". *Review of International Political Economy*, 10 (1), pp. 1–22.

Shelemay, K. K. and Steven Kaplan N. (2006), "Introduction. Creating the Ethiopian Diaspora". *Diaspora, A Journal of Transnational Studies*, 15 (2–3), pp. 191–213.

Sorenson, J. (1993), *Imagining Ethiopia*, New Brunswick, N.J., Rutgers University Press.

Stehr, N. (2001), *The Fragility of Modern Societies: Knowledge and Risk in the Information Age*, London, Sage Publications Ltd.

Weber, E. (1976), *Peasants into Frenchmen: The Modernization of Rural France, 1870–1914*, Stanford, Stanford University Press.

Wimmer, A., and Glick Schiller, N. (2002), "Methodological nationalism and beyond: nation- state building, migration and the social sciences". *Global Networks*, 4, pp. 301–333.

Notes

1 The only feature that is missing here is what Kedourie stresses as romantic nationalism: an amalgam of post-Kantian self-determination, Fichtean glorification of the state, and Herderian enthusiasm for cultural diversity and language. But then, by this criterion, Kedourie considers neither England nor the United States to exhibit genuine nationalism.

2 These phrases appear in Chapters 85 and 55, respectively. Thanks to Dr. Getatchew Haile for confirming this interpretation of the significance and for the reference that follows.

3 See Andre Caquot, (1961, p. 86, lines 14–15): "tselleyu kama inekwen

te'eyyerta la-hezba Iteyoppeya" ("Pray lest we be a mockery for the people of Ethiopia"). Caquot's French, p. 11:, lines 21–22: "Priez afin que nous ne devenions pas la risée des peuples d'Éthiopie."

4 To be sure, long before the rise of these objections to using the trope of *society qua nation* as an authoritative notion for sociological inquiry, the sociological tradition included several strands of work that transcend this analytic focus. These include the Simmelian notion of interaction among parties at any level; the Weberian idea of "society" as a mere object of orientation constructed by actors; Parson's conception of the system of modern societies; and the multidisciplinary perspective of civilizational analysis all perspectives that informed the lifework of one of the foremost sociologists of the late twentieth century, the late Shmuel N. Eisenstadt (Levine 2004).

5 The list goes on. Martin Albrow argued that the Modern epoch has ended and we have entered *The Global Age (*1997*)*. Nico Stehr rejected the continuing identification of modern society with the nation-state as an obsolescent ideological and epistemological residue of the nineteenth century origins of social science discourse (2001, pp. 9–11). Andreas Wimmer and Nina Glick Schiller faulted "methodological nationalism" for stifling social theory: "The social sciences have become obsessed with describing processes within nation-state boundaries as contrasted with those outside and have correspondingly lost sight of the connections between such nationally defined territories" (2002, p. 307). Some even argued that the age of sociology was over altogether, inasmuch as its essential heuristic unit, the national society, is now obsolete. This thesis informed Immanuel Wallerstein's widely discussed 1997 presidential letter to the International Sociological Association, which decried sociological investigation of national societies on grounds that only an interdisciplinary and evolutionary framework made sense for the social sciences.

6 For most of the migration data, we are indebted to Sanyu Mojola, based on information kindly supplied by Bela Hovy at UN High Commission for Refugees. See Table 1.

7 <http://www.enahpa.org>.

8 For a discussion of this as a more general phenomenon, see Portes *et al.* (2002).

9 As is often the case with modern Diaspora communities, Ethiopian Diasporas in North America have been particularly active in "homeland politics." One reason is that the Ethiopian Diaspora in the U.S., like much of the Ethiopian homeland public, believes that the U.S., through the London Peace Conference in 1991, helped bring EPRDF to power and consequently have looked to the U.S. Government to help bring the derailed democratization process back onto track. Their distinctive political engagement was manifest in a nearly successful advocacy for passage of a bill known as The Ethiopia Freedom, Democracy and Human Rights Advancement Act of 2006 (HR 2003) by the House of Representatives in October 2007, through lobbying campaigns spearheaded by the Ethiopian American Civic Advocacy. Among 131 opposition party leaders, journalists, and civil society persons who were on trial for alleged constitutional coup attempts and incitement to genocide in the wake of the May 2005 elections, several were Ethiopians in the Diaspora in the U.S., including journalists working for the Voice of America (VOA).

37

A Revised Analytical Approach to the Evolution of Ethiopian Civilization (2012)*

Assumptions of the Revised Theory of Societal Evolution

The theory of sociocultural evolution provides a framework for describing certain empirical regularities in the sequence of complexity observed in human societies, and conjectures mechanisms behind those regularities. The three authors on whom I drew in earlier efforts in this vein—Talcott Parsons, Shmuel Eisenstadt, and Robert Bellah—share the following assumptions.[1,2]

(1) In his revised conception of sociocultural evolution, Parsons like others refuted the earlier notion that human societal and cultural evolution proceeds in a single straight line. Rather, he stressed that societal evolution was neither a continuous nor a simple linear process (Parsons 1966: 26), even though he held that early primitive society had a single origin and, following Weber, that the modern type of society had a single evolutionary origin (1971b: 109). Relatedly, he went on to hold that there have been *multiple* origins of evolutionary shifts, and that lines of evolution involved *branching*, which could manifest considerable

---

* Originally published in the *International Journal of Ethiopian Studies*, Volume VI, Number 1&2 (2012), pp. 29-70.This paper has benefited from the helpful comments and assistance of Robert Bellah, Andrew DeCort, Jacob Foster, Getatchew Haile, and Victor Lidz.

variability of content (1977: 231). What is more, a revised approach to societal evolution takes note of a considerable amount of inter-societal transfers, such as stimulus diffusion and defensive borrowings, as well as regressions to less complex stages.

(2) Even so, Parsons stressed that any evolutionary perspective implies a criterion of evolutionary direction. Bellah described this direction as "a process of increasing differentiation and complexity of organization that endows the organism, social system, or whatever the unit in question may be with greater capacity to adapt to its environment" ([1964] 1970:21). Parsons similarly identified "the directional factor as an increase in generalized adaptive capacity" (1966: 26) and went on to identify four main processes of evolutionary change: differentiation, inclusion, and value generalization in addition to adaptive upgrading. Interacting together, these four processes "constitute 'progressive' evolution to higher system levels" (1971: 26).

(3) In reformulating evolutionary theory Parsons maintained the notion of different "stages" of evolutionary development. He stated that although "we do not conceive societal evolution to be either a continuous or a simple linear process . . . we can distinguish between broad levels of advancement without overlooking the considerable variability found in each" (1966: 26). Broadly speaking, he distinguished three evolutionary levels—identified by the scope of their generalized adaptive capacity. These levels he designated as primitive, intermediate, and modern. This schema organized a pair of short books in the late 1960s (1966; 1971), republished in a single volume in 1977.[3]

(4) None of these theorists held that their revised perspectives on evolution entail a normative endorsement. They adhered to a biological criterion of increased adaptive capacity, understanding that such capacities could be used for good or for evil—although the notion of evil may not ever have figured explicitly in their discourse. This position provides a counter to objections to any sort of evolutionary perspective in the name of a cultural relativism that embraces the peculiar notion that in all respects every culture possesses the same value as any other. Beyond that, however, I wish to add a more serious proposition: that *every stage of sociocultural evolution involves existential losses as well as adaptive gains.* At every rung of the evolutionary ladder, I shall suggest, one could write a plaintive tract entitled *"The World We Have Lost."*

Stages of Sociocultural Evolution

The evolutionary framework presented by Parsons and Lidz projects a schema of six stages of sociocultural evolution: early primitive and advanced primitive; archaic and historic; early modern and late modern. Bellah's newest formulation (2011) transmutes this into four stages: tribal, archaic, axial, and modern. I follow Parsons and Lidz in identifying a significant contrast between what they call early and advanced primitive stages. However, I propose to replace their term 'primitive,' and Bellah's 'tribal,' on grounds that both terms carry pejorative overtones and do not connote anything about the features of the societies they classify. Making them more descriptive helps indicate something of the directionality of the evolutionary process. Accordingly, I use the term 'kinship' to replace the category of 'early primitive,' and 'communal' to replace 'advanced primitive.' Conversely, I follow Bellah in using the term 'Axial' for Historic, and a single category for Modern. The schema I follow, then, consists of: Kinship; Communal; Archaic; Axial; and Modern.

Kinship societies

"Primitive society," the broad category that Parsons uses for all societies without written language, designates types of social order organized essentially through kinship ties and otherwise showing minimal structural differentiation. Within this broad category, neo-evolutionary theory has done relatively little to track different degrees of evolutionary complexity. The coast is clear for social anthropologists to produce a more differentiated classificatory system of developmental stages within this category, a task I found important to engage as I revisited the range of Ethiopian cases discussed below.

The category of kinship societies includes systems ranging from networks of nuclear family homesteads to those with local chieftains and even kings commanding vast lineages. Although this type of society can become large, its leaders function within the idiom of kinship and mobilize resources through lineage channels. Beyond the most elementary level of kinship crystallization, lineages accrue functions that facilitate higher degrees of connectivity. Such connectivity becomes stabilized through society-wide complexes of religious symbolism. For Parsons as for other scholars, the prime exemplars of this category are the societies of aboriginal Australia in which "the whole society constitutes a single affinal collectivity composed of descent groups allied through the marriages of their members" (Parsons 1966: 36; 1977: 32). Key features of religion there include intimate relation between the mythical world and actual world. As Robert Redfield put it: the "primitive worldview" involves little separation among God, Man, and Nature (1953: Chapter 4). Early stages of human culture exhibit a belief in spirits who do not control the world and are not worshipped, but simply exercise supernatural influence over people (Bellah [1964] 1970: 25–9).

Communal societies

At the stage Parsons placed at a second evolutionary level—"advanced primitive"—some lineages distinguish themselves by controlling special resources and/or by adopting specialized political, military, and/or religious functions. Stratification makes possible the centralization of societal responsibility. At the same time, certain resources are tied no longer to kinship but are organized through crosscutting social forms such as age groups and local territory. That development produces a kind of collectivity that can confer higher status on more favored kinship groups and gain strength through symbols of a supra-lineage collective identity. In communal societies, *territory* and *trans-kinship* symbolism become a more salient basis for collective identity than kinship[4]; location becomes a ground for rights to property; in some societies, age groups become an organizational form that crosscuts kinship and fortifies the sense of belonging to a supra-lineal community.[5]

In this stage, political and religious roles become differentiated. Mythical beings become viewed as definite objects, as gods. They are conceived as actively, sometimes willfully, controlling the natural world. As such, humans must deal with them in a definite, purposive way.

Archaic societies[6]

Development of written language maintained by an upper class marks a watershed which separates primitive societies from an "intermediate" level of evolutionary development, which Parsons divides into two sub-stages: "archaic" societies and "historic empires." In archaic societies, knowledge of writing belongs only to specialists: a literate priesthood which maintains a stable tradition, and craftsmen able to keep records, thereby enabling extended political control through an administrative apparatus. A literate priesthood also makes it possible to construct a distinct cultural system, including a cosmological religious belief system, independent of the social system. The belief system consists of esoteric knowledge interpreted for the society by temple priesthoods with their cults. Archaic societies differentiate a four-class system, consisting of a political elite—a king, his notables, and attendants; a religious elite; peasants; and a stratum of service-providers: craftsmen, merchants, and slaves.

Archaic societies institutionalize separate political and religious structures, but maintain close linkage between the two domains. They are headed by a powerful monarch whose charisma reflects a fusion of religious legitimation and politico-military strength. Whereas ritual in pre-archaic societies involves communal experience, "in stark contrast, ritual in archaic societies focuses above all on one person, the divine or quasi-divine king, and only few people, priests or members of the royal lineage, participate" (Bellah 2005: 69). Their religions involve what has been described as "a grandiose cosmology elaborated in myths by literate priest-intellectuals" (Lidz and Parsons 1972: 125). Their religious beliefs consist essentially of narrative myths (Bellah 2011).

Archaic societies tend to generate urban centers, for both religious and political functions. Their cities also support regular markets for agricultural and handicraft products, provision for mercantile credit, and means to accumulate huge amounts of wealth and labor services (125). Societies at this stage include many peoples of ancient Asia, the Middle East, and much of Africa, Polynesia, and pre-Columbian Latin America. In ancient Egypt, the pharaonic fusion of religious and political domains involved conceiving the ruler as himself a divine being. In Mesopotamia it took the form of requiring religious legitimation by one or more gods, reinforced by annual ceremonies that refreshed the king's solidarity with divine forces.

Axial stage societies

Parsons designates as "historic empires" or "historic civilizations" the final stage prior to the evolutionary breakthrough that ushers in the system of modern societies; Bellah refers to the attendant sacred symbol systems as "historic religions." This is the pre-modern stage familiar to humanists, historians, social scientists and, more generally, to scholars in the areas of Civilizational Studies. Sociologists know such societies mainly through Max Weber's comparative studies of world religions and subsequently through the ideas of Karl Jaspers and Shmuel Eisenstadt on Axial Civilizations.[7]

The central advance at this stage consists of a continued differentiation in two directions: between religious and political institutions and, within the former, between attitudes toward the everyday world and a transcendental sphere. The evolutionary breakthrough associated with Axial Civilizations involves the identification of a radically different realm of reality, which devalues the given empirical cosmos. In Bellah's early formulation, historic religions identify humans no longer by clan or ethnic group or the particular god they serve (archaic) but rather as beings capable of salvation. In this worldview, religion functions not to promote normal human ends, but to compensate for an essentially sinful, disobedient, or otherwise imperfect human nature. At the same time, this shift broadens the reference of the constitutive symbolism of collectivities (Bellah, 1970: 32–33). Similarly, Eisenstadt lists the constitutive features of Axial worldviews as 1) an ontological distinction between higher and lower levels of reality, 2) a normative subordination of the lower to the higher, and 3)a broadening of social horizons (2011: 203).

In the Parsonian schema, the historic stage develops when archaic societies become transformed through the spread of literacy to the entire ruling class, and thereby the growth of a stratum of literati that is separate and distinct from the stratum of political rulership. Bellah locates the axial development in the move beyond "mythic" thinking to what he calls "theory," and what others call reflexive or second-order thinking. The process of radical differentiation whereby cultural systems become separated from the societal matrix that gave birth to them spells the end of divine kingship. It makes the bearers of transcendent values autonomous vis-à-vis the political authority, and enables them to exert a directing and controlling influence back onto the social systems. Monarchs themselves no longer *embody* transcendence, but must rather be *directed* by the ideas and values codified in transcendent belief systems. A religious hierarchy emerges that exists parallel to and in partial independence from the political hierarchy. Their privileged connection with the transcendent order gives religious literati a dimension of moral authority that supersedes that of the king and his noblemen. Such strata are illustrated in China by the scholar-gentry class; by the twice-born Brahmans in India; by the prophets of ancient Israel; and by the '*ulamā* in Islam. In Rome, this stratum consisted of the senatorial class, whose charisma drew from the legal system anchored in the Stoic conception of a Law of Nature.

Modern society

The modern type of social system originated in the 17th century in Northwest Europe. The hallmarks of this new stage included the development of a generalized legal order and the institutionalization of the authority of secular offices. This went hand in hand with the crystallization of new collective identities, organized no longer through clans, or tribes, or royal domains, but through broader communities defined by national boundaries and legislative jurisdictions. Value generalization proceeded through the state rather than through ethnic or religious parameters.

The turn to earthly political communities invested the kingdom of man with fresh significance. As Weber famously argued, starting with Luther the Protestant Reformation pioneered this transition by endowing lay persons with the capacity to gain unmediated salvation. It thereby sacralized right action in this world, eventually legitimating proactive engagement rather than a dutiful passive acceptance of the world. The Reformation also contributed to the weakening of the four-class systems of peasant societies and its replacement by a more flexible multi-centered mode of social organization based more on contract and voluntary association, changes that implanted conditions favorable to commerce and democratization and therewith to the revolution of the productive powers of industry.

A more developed form of this societal type has emerged since the 19th century. To broach the nature of this "late-modern" type is to enter a maelstrom of views in multiple lines of discourse. Each major social theorist has focused one or another of the evolutionary directions that reached self-sustaining power in late modernity: Smith on adaptive upgrading; Marx, Simmel, and Durkheim on differentiation; Comte and Tocqueville on inclusion; Weber and Parsons on value generalization.[8] Bellah has described the religious dimension of late modernity.[9] And some now propound the idea of a single modern world societal system to be glossed as Global Civilization, thereby replacing separate historic civilizations (Wilkinson 2007).

Enter Ethiopia

How might understanding of Ethiopia's complex history and diverse sociocultural systems benefit from applying the conceptual framework just outlined? To begin with, consider two common views which it stands to supplement. The first was suggested by the eminent Ethiopianist Carlo Conti-Rossini, who described large parts of Ethiopia as *tutta un museo* (simply a museum) (1929: 37): the view of Ethiopia as a country of extraordinary ethnic diversity. A second view, popularized by Ethiopian activists of the 1970s, envisaged Ethiopia in terms made famous by Lenin for pre-revolutionary Russia, as a "prison house of nationalities"—a view that all ethnic groups in Ethiopia were equivalent politically and that all but one of them had been repressed by the hegemony of a single group, the Amhara. In a way, the Ethiopian Constitution of 1995 embodied both perspectives, declaring the country simply an aggregation of "Nations, Nationalities, and Peoples" each of which possesses "a right to self-determination up to and including secession."

The ethnic assemblage model

A cursory visit to the vast culture area of what I have glossed as Greater Ethiopia can evoke the first view. One encounters peoples exhibiting a catalogue of languages, livelihoods, terrains, life styles, and religions.[10] Superficially self-evident, this view neglects two massive facts, both discussed in *Greater Ethiopia* as well. One is to view Ethiopia merely as a collection of distinct ethnies overlooks the descent of her peoples from two main demographic stocks and the vast number of cultural elements that they share.[11] A second is that the diverse ethnies of what I have called Greater Ethiopia never lived as unchanging separate collectivities with impermeable boundaries. Rather, they developed continuously over the centuries. Many merged with one another and quite a few disappeared.[12] What is more, they have constantly connected with one another through migration, warfare, trade, shared religion, pilgrimages, intermarriage, and the provision of complementary services. Reliable data on ethnically mixed families do not exist, but crude estimates range from 20% to as many as 40%.[13]

The prison house model

The prison house metaphor represents what has long been perceived as reality for many of Ethiopia's peoples: a sense of being second-class citizens or worse in a state dominated by one ethnic group with its hegemonic language.[14] On the other hand, consider its limitations.

Problematic notions about popular sentiments

No study was ever undertaken to determine how the different ethnies in Ethiopia actually felt under the Haile Selassie regime. During the 1950s and 1960s, when ethnographers had free rein to document the lives of dozen of Ethiopian ethnic groups, the sense of living in something like a prison-house was never mentioned. The late Paul Henze recalled showing slides of happy people in the countryside to incredulous students in Addis Ababa whose ideology bred the conviction that those people had to be miserable.[15]

Historic myopia

Far from the multiethnic Ethiopian state being the late 19C creation of an Amhara elite, as Prison House model proponents suggest, the Ethiopian state is of ancient origin and was *multiethnic* for most of its history. Known in antiquity first as the land of the Ag'azi, at some early point—probably as early as the 5th century CE—it became known as Ethiopia. The state was tied closely with the Ethiopian Orthodox Church, which was maintained by a network of holy men from Tigrinya, Agawinya, and Amharic-speaking regions far to the South. Ethiopian church documents from the 15C refer to adherents from distant disparate groups such as the Sidamo, Welayta, Bosha, and Bahiya (Getatchew, tr. 2004: 46). Only the coalition of battalions from numerous regions and ethnic groups made possible the landmark defeat of Italian colonialist forces at the famous battle of Adwa in 1896.[16]

Simplifications about the Amhara ethnie

Historically there was no ethnie known as Amhara, in the current sense of designating a single ethnic group that encompassed most of four large pre-1991 provinces. That name referred, historically, to a small enclave in southwest Wollo

(Levine 2003). In the more contemporary sense of the term, the ruling elite under Haile Selassie was predominantly but by no means exclusively Amhara. The emperor himself was generally known to be of mixed blood, and his Empress Menen was descended from Oromo royalty. Through intermarriage and political appointments, Haile Selassie included a number of Tigrayans and Oromo into a national elite. On the other hand, nobles from Amhara regions outside of the province of Shoa were routinely neglected.

Simplifications about Amharic

Amharic became used as a national language around the 13C. This practice was continued even by Tigrinya-speaking Emperor Johannes IV, who led a program of enforced Amharization in the 1880s. On this vexed question, two further points deserve consideration. For one thing, Amharic is not, strictly speaking, an *ethnic* language. What is more, the language itself emerged as a pidgin amalgam of local dialects, and has long been used in many areas as a lingua franca (Levine [1974] 2000). And although some populations have found it frustrating to need to speak Amharic for official purposes, just as some immigrant groups in the United States find it frustrating to have to use English, many groups—like those living the linguistic Babel area of the southwest—benefited from using that lingua franca at the market and elsewhere.

What is more, making Amharic the official national language did not in and of itself preclude using widely-spoken local languages. A policy of suppressing publications in some of those languages under Haile Selassie arguably sprang from the Emperor's deep personal and political insecurities, and from a perceived need to provide some social glue to hold the country together. That policy was and is widely considered to be a grave tactical error on the part of his regime.

The *expanded* multiethnic empire under Menelik was built upon conquest. Most but by no means all of the conquerors were lords and soldiers from Amhara, but not a few stemmed from Tigray and Oromo regions. As Merera Gudina aptly observes, it is an "irony of Oromo history. . . that they were part of the conquerors as well as the conquered" (2006: 125). This expansion can be viewed as a normal part of the state-building process, as happened earlier, for example, in France, Japan, Vietnam, and Italy. The rough-handed conduct of Ethiopia's largely Amhara political elite also produced numerous benefits for the entire population. They defended Ethiopians from repeated invasions from Turkey and the Sudan, and fought twice against Italian colonialists. They provided an appellate level of justice, expressed poignantly in the Amharic dictum: "*Negus kelêla, le-man 'abêt' yilllal?*" ("Without a king, to whom shall one shout for justice?"). Emperors Menilek and Haile Selassie I put an end to human sacrifice, the slave trade, slavery, and civil war, and introduced such elements of modernization as secular schools, hospitals, banking, printed currency, telecommunications, and modern transportation.

An evolutionary perspective, however, needs to retain and illuminate insights from the two other models. It can do so, first, by showing how a particular evolutionary stage can be maintained over long periods, thus accounting for the stability of the multiple distinct formations within Greater Ethiopia. And it can throw light on how those boundaries became broached by the ever-expanding outreach of the most evolutionarily advanced society, one that reached the stage of becoming a historic empire.

Greater Ethiopia in Evolutionary Perspective Revisited

Ethiopia seems a particularly apt place in which to apply an evolutionary perspective. Paleoanthropologists have now established the claim that the human species began its evolutionary career in the Ethiopian area. The skeleton of *Ardipithecus ramidus* ("Ardi"), unearthed in the Middle Awash Valley of Ethiopia and estimated at 4.4 million years, represents the oldest known human ancestor with a fairly complete skeleton. The second oldest fossil skeleton, also discovered in the Awash region, was the famous Lucy (*Australopithecus afarensis*), who was estimated to have lived 3.2 million years ago.

Kinship societies

Over hundreds of millennia, there evolved in Ethiopia elements of kinship systems, language, technology, and religion, which scholars have associated with the earliest human groups. One can only conjecture about the processes that led to the creation of such traits. At any rate, Greater Ethiopia does include a number of relatively undifferentiated societies, which appear to be organized almost solely on the basis of kinship connections.

In the 20th century, one society that appears to exist at the least complex stage is the **Majangir** of Western Ethiopia. Now under the administrative control of the Federal Democratic Republic of Ethiopia in the Gambela Region, the Majang people still follow ancient ways. They employ simple agricultural techniques, cultivating fields that are periodically opened through slash-and-burn cultivation, using hands and knives, to grow maize, sorghum, and sesame. Their social order consists of nuclear families set in homesteads, a unit they term *wai.*[17] Although residence is patrilocal, patrilineal kin clusters are inhibited by the mobility of Majang homesteads in their constant search for fresh arable lands (Stauder 1971: 155). Progressively larger groupings are indicated by categories that connote neighborhood ("people of the same coffee"), settlement ("the same fields"), and community ("the same beer"). These categories, however, serve purely to identify current connections; their memberships fluctuate according to the movements of the populations; in no way do those categories designate collectivities in any meaningful or functional sense.

Majangir have no separate political or religious roles. They possess no symbols for objectified supernatural figures. They do, however, believe in random spirits, known as *wakayo*, who bring misfortune or injury to moral offenders. The *wakayo* find expressions of human violence especially objectionable and regard them as personal offenses. The *wakayo* are channeled by shamanic persons known as *tapat*, who exert religious and political influence informally. A *tapat* is expected to be fair, strong, generous, and wise, and effective in rituals that placate the *wakayo*. The area inhabited by the constituents of a given *tapat* is thought of as his own particular ritual territory. A person becomes a *tapat* by establishing his or her own base of followers. The position is not hereditary; upon the death of a powerful tapat the population of his followers will scatter. The *tapa* enjoy benefits such as prestige and the privilege of marrying several wives.

All other societies within Ethiopia manifest greater complexity. Among these, the **Qemant**—one of the surviving small groups of Agaw peoples—would represent the next order of complexity, still within a kinship framework.[18] The Qemant rely on patriclans not only to guide them into eligible marriage matches but also to perform distinct functions, both ritual and political. Councils of elders drawn from particular lineages make policy for the larger settlements and select persons for the role of *wambar*, the "arch-politicoreligious leader" of the Qemant. The *wambar* officiates at major ceremonies where priests perform rituals essential for the society's wellbeing. He executes prayers to regulate weather, cure disease, alleviate misfortune, dispel wild beasts, punish sinners, and pray for dead souls to assure their entry into heaven (Gamst 1969: 29, 39–40). He rules over two orders of priests, each drawn respectively from a senior and a junior moiety. Other politico-religious positions include a dispute mediator, a majordomo for religious ceremonies, and a steward who presides over distribution of the sacred beer at ceremonies.

Qemant religious symbolism includes a pantheon of sacred figures, most traceable to traditions that antedate admixtures of a few Hebraic elements. They include a sky god, *mezgana*; personal spirits—*zar* and others; genii loci; sky spirits, minor deities often thought of as culture heroes; and certain trees and animals. The Qemant have attempted to keep their religious beliefs and practices as secret as they can, to maintain their internal identity against the outside world.

The Qemant resolve administrative and judicial matters by councils of Elders, democratic assemblies composed of prestigious males who are "old enough to have grey hairs" (58). Formal councils meet monthly, informal councils convene whenever invited to adjudicate disputes by litigants. In addition to his priestly duties, the *wambar* has the final authority on all judicial and administrative questions. In addition to this elementary political-religious division of labor, the Qemant exhibit an elementary occupational division of labor by allocating to a specific caste, the *arabinya*, the task of curing leather.

The **Gurage** present a slightly more differentiated system within the set of Ethiopian kinship societies. Gurage patriclans, known as *bét* (house), comprise corporate bodies that select village heads who make policy and allocate rights to land. In addition, a differentiated set of religious officials serve both to valorize and counterbalance the authority of the political officials. The reality and symbolism of clanship permeate the sociocultural system of the Gurage. The whole population commonly calls itself *Yä säbat bét Gurage*—the Gurage of Seven Clans (literally, Houses). The Gurage political system never approximated to a centralized form headed by a king, but rested rather on a system of non-totemic, exogamous patriclans, with chieftainship was vested in one maximal lineage of each clan and the office inherited within that patrilineal. Gurage live in agnatic homesteads organized in villages. Patrilineally selected village heads make policy decisions regarding rights to land and "act in conjunction with other village heads in a system of alliances to form the basis of intervillage politics" (Shack 1966: 91–3, 105, 144–6, 149).

Similarly, Gurage religion is tied to clans. In the words of ethnographer William Shack, ritual relations "intrinsic to the ideology of Yä säbat bet Gurage [are] the organizing mechanism of the Gurage social system. The organization of ritual ties corresponds with that of clanship ties. . . Both can be translated into the idioms of kinship and genealogical relations" (179). Maximal lineage heads serve as custodians of sacred shrines, the foci of Gurage rituals. The Gurage pantheon consists of ancestral heroes and a trio of deities—a High god Yəgzär, a Thunder god Bwäzä, and the God of war, Waq. The deities are commonly extolled in praise songs which are composed and sung by the common people, not ritual specialists, whose role is minimal and limited to serving as intermediaries between the natural and supernatural worlds at annual festivals (Shack and Marcos 1974; Shack 1966, 178). The only functional domain beyond that organized by kinship consists of occupational craftsmen. While Gurage subsist on the basis of the hoe cultivation of ensete plants, they employ a division of labor involving three different caste groups: woodworkers (fuga), tanners (gezha), and smiths (nefwra).

Slightly more differentiated yet are the neighboring Sidamo. Like the three foregoing societies, the Sidamo have patriclans (gurri) and subclans (bosello), which regulate exogamy and allocate property rights. The clans also form the basis for a differentiated political sector with two components. The primary one, a Council of Clan Leaders, called Gudamaalee ("place of justice"), deals with disputes among clans, and also with weighty crimes like homicide. The term Gudamaalee signifies a place where councilors sit on the ground, without chair or bench, under a special tree. The other forum, Councils of Elders, get elected in neighborhoods of patrilineally based homesteads. These councils handle personal quarrels, allocate land and settle disputes over boundaries, theft, and crop-destroying cattle. These institutions do not set up rigid boundaries. Elders who might come from different villages to attend hearings sit circling the council members. Any passers-by, except women, can watch and engage in the process. Councils pass decisions after free and open debate not only between disputants and witnesses, but also by all discussants who are present at the session. Hearings normally conclude with compromise and reconciliation, which prevents lasting enmity between disputants and their families (Pankhurst and Assefa 2008).

The Sidamo have a minimal religious pantheon. Their religious symbolism centers on a sky god, Magana, believed to have let down the first Sidamo men from the sky on a rope. The sun and moon comprise his eyes. Another deity, Batto, is considered the creator of the earth. Magana's intervention can be invoked by clan chiefs. They do, however, make use of two kinds of special ritual functionaries. The chief ritual expert (*qullu*) communicates with the supreme being Magana, often through the intermediation of hyenas and serpents. The Python, thought to be an incarnation of a divine being, is an object of worship and is reared in the huts and fed on meat (Cerulli 1956: 129).

Table 1. Degrees of Differentiation in Ethiopian Kinship Societies

Domains of differentiation	**MAJANGIR**	**QEMANT**	**GURAGE**	**SIDAMO**
Regulation of marriage	Named patriclans regulate exogamy	Named patriclans regulate exogamy	Named patriclans regulate exogamy	Named patriclans regulate exogamy
Rules of Inheritance	None	Ambilineal inheritance	Patrineally determined rights to land	Patrlineal authorities decide on land rights

Differentiated religious symbolism	Random spirits only (wakayo)	Sky god, Mezgana; personal spirits—Zar and others; genii loci; sky spirits; certain trees and animals	Pantheon of both gods (high god Yəgzär, thunder god Bwäzä, god of war Waq) and ancestor heroes	Sky god Magana; earth god Battta; hyenas and pythons
Special ritual functions	None	prayers for communal wellbeing, entry of souls into heaven	supplication rituals at annual festivals	chiefs actively invoke intervention of sky god Magana
Territory as relevant to social organization	general patrilocal residence but not in clusters	general patrilocal residence, in dispersed homestead cluster	general patrilocal residence, in agnatic homesteads organized in villages	villages of nuclear family households related patrilineally (kača)
Differentiated religious Functionaries	Tapat only	Leader, wambar; priestly hierarchy of two tiers drawn from senior/junior moieties; ceremonial roles	religious officials validate and counterbalance political leaders	professional diviners (količa) capable of communicating with shatāni spirits
Differentiated political Structures	None	councils of elders come from high-status lineages	patrilineally determined village heads make policy decisions	two kinds of public forums settle disputes: 1) a Council of Clan Leaders, deals with disputes among clans and homicide; 2) neighborhood Councils of Elders
Specialized occupational castes	None	Tanners (Arabinya)	woodworkers (Fuga) tanners (Gezha); smiths (Nefwra)	potters (Adicho), tanners (Awacho), smiths (Tunicho)
Cross-cutting age groups	None	None	None	age grades organize men in categories of "young"/ "old" by which they get assigned to political, military, and ritual roles

1-nominal lineages
2-functional lineages
3-differentiations beyond lineages

In addition, professional diviners (*količa*) have the ability to communicate with spirits, which bring afflictions to individuals (Hamer and Hamer 1966: 395, 406). The Sidamo have a special veneration for Mount Bensa and the River Logida, to which only the elders (*jarsa*) may go in pilgrimage.

Like Gurage, the Sidamo employ a set of caste workers who carry out certain occupational specialties: potters (*adicho*), tanners (*awacho*), and smiths (*tunicho*). What distinguishes the Sidamo from the societies considered thus far is a loose system of age grades, the structural point of departure for reaching the next level of complexity. Even so, the Sidamo age-grade system embodies minimal functional differentiation. It plays no role in marriage and the establishing of families, nor does it have members advance through a series of classes with differential rights and obligations. The generational differences it defines are not thought of as being cyclical. Rather, its function seems simply to be the organization of Sidamo men into clearly defined categories of "old" and "young," with attendant "ascription of political, judicial, military and ritual roles" (Hamer and Hamer 1966: 55). Table 1 represents grades of differentiation among these societies.

Communal societies

At what we designate as a second stage of evolutionary development, kinship rights and obligations become supplemented and to a notable extent transcended by other social structural principles, and by more inclusive boundaries and more generalized values. In this category I would place the Dassanetch,[19] the Dorze, the Konso, and the Boran Oromo.

The **Dassanetch** share several features of the more differentiated kinship societies just described: ranked patriclans regulating exogamy, division into moieties of unequal status, and belief in a sky god. What differentiates the Dassanetch, and the other societies to be described below, are structural features that cut across the boundaries of actual kinship units.

For the Dassanetch, this means primarily a complex system of age-grades and age-sets. All Dassanetch men are divided between two alternate-generational age groups (*haariyam*), the *Badiet* and the *Gerge*, each of which is endogamous (limiting inter-generational competition for women). These groupings in turn overlay a system of generation-sets that is "organizationally coherent, generates strong feelings of solidarity, serves as the main social framework for ceremonies and is the central political institution of each tribal section" (Almagor 1978: 23–4). Each generation-set consists of age-sets of co-initiates within the same four-year span, which are sequentially ordered within the generation-set. These age-sets rarely assemble, but a man depends for political support and economic cooperation upon his generation-set. It is the cross-lineal generation-sets, not clans, that direct officiation in the most important ritual in Dassanetch life, the '*dimi* ceremony. The '*dimi* ritual functions to "induce fertility in a man's daughters" and must be conducted before they begin to menstruate, lest a curse befall the family and they be ostracized. The ritual is also an important stage in the life of the man for whose daughters it is being conducted: "After the 'dimi, a man is spoken of as a big man (*maa gudo*) and on his death he will be buried inside his cattle pen" (Houtteman 2011, 185).

In contrast to the Ethiopian Kinship Societies described above, in Dassanetch culture the language of kinship has been abstracted from actual relationships of consanguinity and affinity. Members of the same clan do not necessarily consider themselves to be kinsmen, or even descended from the same ancestor. Dassanetch clans are not localized, lack a genealogical structure, and control no resources of their own. Dassanetch who share the same or similar cattle brands reckon themselves as sharing common descent. Importantly, clans and sub-clans are ranked according to the sequence in which their ancestors are thought to have been absorbed into the Dassanetch ethnie. They give symbolic expression to this belief in collective circumcision ceremonies. Circumcised in the order that their clan ancestors were absorbed, they "*become Dassanetch*" in the same order as did their respective clans. Thus abstracted from actual kin relations, the idiom of clanship thus permits a greater range of inclusiveness, permitting the ready assimilation of immigrant groups. This idiom thus facilitates movement between sections and their integration into broader networks of exchange and reciprocity along pseudo-kinship lines.

The **Dorze** system adds complexity to this configuration with a more differentiated political structure. In addition to maintaining a system of named patriclans that regulate exogamy, within which lineages may be ranked according to relative "seniority" in various domains, they maintain a generalized principle of relative seniority (*baira*) and generational transition structures "all practically or conceptually asymmetrical relationships between: people, class, districts, ethnic groups, and even animal species, plants, and natural phenomena" (Sperber 1975: 210). Claims to *baira*-ship become a shared idiom of political, ritual, and territorial competition, which occasionally extends even beyond the Dorze collectivity. Thus, they even cherish "a myth which explains that the Gamu [of which the Dorze are one] are *baira* to the Amhara, and why the latter nevertheless have fared better" (211). Importantly, the dual ideology of seniority and transition structures the political organization of district and sub-district assemblies. It is these territorial units, not lineages that form the basic corporate units of Dorze society. They are governed by assemblies that are led ritually by an appointed dignitary, the *halak'a*. These may convene a larger regional assembly presided over by a hereditary king (*ka'o*).

Table 2: Degrees of Differentiation in Ethiopian Communal Societies

Domains of Differentiation	**Dassanetch***	**Dorze****	**Konso*****	**Boran*****
Regulation of marriage	Named patriclans regulate exogamy	Named patriclans regulate exogamy	Named patriclans regulate exogamy	Named patriclans regulate exogamy
Differentiated religious symbolism	Supreme male sky god (Waag). 3 kinds of ancestor spirits	Supreme male sky god (Waag). Genii loci	Supreme male sky god (Waag). Genii loci	Supreme male sky god (Waag).
Special rituals	'Dimi fertility ritual	Rituals under trees, sometimes with animal sacrifice, for birth of sons, health, harvests	Rituals for rain, health, longevity, virility, peace	Rites of passage between gada age classes and hariyya age sets; fatherhood ceremony
Differentiated religious functionaries	Elders of senior generation (jelaba)—after initiation and election—perform both religious and political functions.	Regional (district-level) religious officials (demutsa), perform strictly ritual functions, including taboos (woga) arbitration.	Three types of priests: regional (suaita), lineage, and guardians of sacred places (mora). Regional priest promote moral unity.	Each moiety headed by ritual leader (qallu), who mediates conflicts and anoints political leaders.
Differentiated political structures		District assemblies led by appointed leaders (halak'a), unite in regional assemblies led by hereditary king (ka'o), who represents region (dere) in inter-dere linkages.	Town councils of elders (hiyoda) elected by wards mediate disputes, assess taxes Warrior age sets (Hrela) perform policing and some judicial functions.	Ruling age class based on generational position headed by abba boku passes laws. Warrior age sets headed by abba dula raid and fight.
Stratification/ Lineal hierarchy	Clans ranked in order of absorption into Dassanetch ethnie.	Relative seniority (baira) of certain lineages is claimed over others along a variety of axes (ritual, territorial, political, etc.).	Lineages no longer provide the major social organizational principle.	Rotating age classes constituted status hierarchy.

Specialized occupational castes	None	Tanners (Degala), Potters (Mana)	Smiths, Weavers, Potters, Tanners (Hauda)	Hunters (Watta)
Cross-cutting age groups	Initiation sets form alternate generational endogamous age groups (haariyam).	No age grade system, but general principle of seniority and generational transition culminating in kingship.	Generation grades, which however do not transcend/unite town identities.	Gada system of double age classes with specialized functions.
Territory in regards to social organization	Rights in common territory based on tribal section.	Dorze territory divided into 14 districts subsumed into two basic east/west regions.	Territory divided into three regions, each with autonomous towns divided into wards. No corporate property of the lineage.	Expansive areas bounded by subordination to single juridical and ritual system.

*Three Lines of differentiation
**Four Lines of differentiation
***Five Lines of differentiation

Even more than Dorze, the **Konso** moved beyond kinship as a dominant organizing principle. Traditional Konso society comprised a number of autonomous towns. These are large, densely settled populations, averaging about 1,500 persons each. They form in areas atop hills, surrounded by defensive stone walls. Each town consists of two or more homestead groups: *ganda*, or wards, and are administered by elected councils of elders. Konso towns are grouped into regions for ritual purposes. Ritual affiliations are organized in complex forms through a distinctive system of age grades that incorporates lineages. Their religious beliefs include the notion of a supreme deity, W*aga*, the source of rain and of justice—interrelated functions, since *Waga* withholds rain from towns guilty of too much internal quarrelling. *Waga* is thought to have laid down a benign moral order that is perennially reinforced by the teachings of elders and priests. This is not a transcendent, world-judging jurisdiction but, regarding the realms of God, Earth, and the Wild: "These three realms so deeply interpenetrate one another that it is meaningless . . . to talk of their religion on the one hand their society on the other" (Hallpike 1972: 328).

The Konso stage of differentiation exhibits clear adaptive advantages. It supports resources for internal defense, and for communal undertakings such as the construction of terraces for farming and other cooperative activities. The territorial organization facilitates a high degree of communal harmony.

Nevertheless certain crucial adaptive advantages are precluded by the absence of authority structures that transcend the towns. Although they possess cross-town ritual alliances, they lack comparable structures that could provide political integration. As a result, there was historically a good deal of warfare among the towns, and never any mobilization of the entire Konso population. Accordingly, while reputedly formidable warriors, the Konso were no match for the Ethiopian State when it moved to conquer them in 1897.

The **Boran** constitute the core tribe of what became the vast nation of **Oromo** peoples. As with Majangir, Boran households are normally nuclear family units. Due to polygyny, Boran males often reside in a number of households. The household is the site of basic activities, with women responsible for building huts, fetching water from wells, preparation and distribution of food, and making milk containers and leather garments. Men build kraals and fences, carve wooden utensils, water and milk cattle, and provide defense. Clusters of households form neighborhood groups known as *olla*, responsible for local cooperative activities as needed: building fences and kraals, watering cattle, growing crops. Like the Konso, the more encompassing social organization of Boran comes from two sources. One consists of a complex of nested descent groups of decreasing genealogical depth. These include the two pan-tribal moieties and numerous sub-moieties, clans, and major, minor, and minimal lineages. The other Boran structure comprises a "*gada*" double complex of classes. (1) A "*luba*" set of classes, based on generational position, comprises a system of ten grades, each of eight years duration, such that after forty years, the sons enter in a cycle that parallels the grades of their fathers. Each *luba* class has a particular function: boys of the second and third classes have separate herding responsibilities; men of the fourth join prescribed war parties. Class V undertakes martial or cattle-raiding expeditions. After men serve as political and ritual leaders in grade VI, they become elder statesmen and religious experts as *yuba* in grades seven to ten, then retire in grade XI to bestow refuge and blessings. (2) The other, "*hariyya*" set of classes consists of age groups. Boys in their late teens form *hariyya* and recruit regiments of other boys in the same age group, which traditionally served to carry out raids and military expeditions.

Each Borana moiety is headed by a *qallu*, who represents the chief Oromo deity known as *Waka* or *Waaq*. *Waaq* is viewed a supreme sky god, who creates and regulates the existence of all animate, inanimate, and nature objects and places them in a balanced cosmic order. Waaq has jurisdiction over omnipresent spirits called *ayyaana*, which exist in every person and thing in the universe. Through the *ayyaana*, Waaq exists in everything and everything exists in It.[20]

As with the Konso, traditional Oromo culture worked to maintain harmony within a moral community. For the Oromo, however, instead of locating their moral communities within walled towns, they located it in vast areas bonded by subordination to a single juridical and ritual system. In consequence, their traditional system included features that enabled them to secure a higher level of adaptive capacity than the Konso and, indeed, for some breakaway segments to reach the archaic stage of evolution. Even so, no pan-Oromo system of governance held together its diverse lineages when they began to bifurcate. Accordingly, Oromo history involved a great deal of intertribal warfare.[21]

Archaic Societies in Ethiopia

Jimma Abba Jifar

Before proceeding to the analysis of the famous kingdom of Aksum, let us consider the emergence of an Archaic Kingdom so recent that we can reconstruct its evolution before our eyes, as it were: the Oromo kingdom of Jimma Abba Jifar. In the course of the continuing expansion of the Oromo peoples from the 17th century onward, one branch, the Matcha, moved west to conquer large swaths of territory occupied by many ethnic groups speaking languages of the Omotic family. When they reached the region of the Gibe River, a tributary of the Omo River, in the early 19C, they instituted changes that led to an unprecedented centralization of their governance structure. Often explained as a result of "imitating" other nearby kingdoms, this change evidently occurred through endogenous processes. The shift went furthest in the Oromo kingdom of Jimma, which crystallized under a charismatic monarch. This process, one could say, meant shifting from one evolutionary stage to another.

As Oromo migrants came to the Jimma area, they divided into distinct, mutually hostile groups, connected only through a loose confederation. For a while, their representatives met in the traditional manner and made laws, *sera tuma*, under the leadership of an *abba boku* ("father of the sceptre") whose authority lasted for the customary eight years (Lewis 2001: 27, 39). Over time, one group began to extend its domain and conquered most of the other small groups. This consolidation was brought to a head by a powerful figure named Sanna, who transfigured his status as elected war leader (*abba dula*) under the *gada* system to become an absolute king. Following Sanna's conquest of the entire region, he took his battle "horse name" of Abba Jifar as a royal name, and in 1830 proceeded to designate the kingdom as Jimma Abba Jifar.

Although King Abba Jifar I (1830–55) never attained the full trappings of sacred royalty as in neighboring Kaffa and elsewhere in Africa, he did display a gold ring as insignia of royalty. Of his most noted successor, King Abba Jifar II (ruled 1878–1932), it was said that he was carried around by two servants who never permitted his feet to touch the ground. Rather than remain bound by norms and rituals associated with the *gada* system, on taking the throne Abba Jifar II shed Oromo religious traditions and embraced Islam as an ideology that could strengthen the unity of his people and support the idea of an absolute king (Hassen 1994: 157–8). After declaring Islam the religion of the court, he imported a number of Muslim teachers to establish madrasas and spread the new religion, a project that had been initiated by a predecessor king, his brother Abba Bok'a (1859–62).

The potent position of Abba Jifar II enabled him to stand free of obligations to lineage groups. He could appoint whomever he wanted to political positions and not have to contend with lineages having political leaders (Lewis 2001: 127). The political edifice he built included a bureaucracy with a prime minister, a minister of war, and a group of senior counselors. He appointed governors and lieutenant governors for each of the sixty provinces, who were assisted by heralds or couriers. As his chief ethno-historian has written:

> The governing of Jimma Abba Jifar was accomplished through appointed officials—not through hereditary chiefs or representatives of tribal or descent groups. Below the king were hundreds of officials in a great many categories: governors, market judges, border guards, tax collectors, couriers, military officers, overseers of artisan labor, jailers, palace officials, and many others. Although the jurisdiction of each official was not always tightly defined, the principle was that different officers were required to carry out or oversee different activities. (Lewis 2001: 80)

By consolidating power the Jimma king warded off the encroachments of ambitious governors and tribal leaders. He divided Jimma into sixty provinces, thereby limiting the power of any one provincial authority. He appointed administrators to positions in unfamiliar provinces, thus limiting the possibility that a province might become loyal to the minister rather than to the king. Furthermore, the King made sure to appoint followers loyal to him, largely blood relatives and royal favorites among the nobles.

The King also acquired powers over the Jimma economy, including rights to territories, slaves, and specific commodities. He gained possession of most of the Jimma territory and rights to dispose of all unclaimed or barren land in the area. When his armies conquered a population, he had rights to enslave the captives. Local informants reported that Abba Jifar II owned some 10,000 slaves (Lewis 2001: 66). He also possessed the authority to confiscate the property of those who did not fulfill their duties to the kingdom and to seize elephant tusks, hides, and horns of all kinds. Finally, he controlled trade routes and areas designated as markets. In the place of fractious local governors, the King's minister, the Negadra, provided a uniform system of regulating trade. He levied tolls and tariffs, organized the layout of markets, and maintained infrastructure. Crimes or disputes that took place in the market came under royal rather than local jurisdiction (93–97).

As the monarchy evolved, it acquired a monopoly over military forces—a process that came to a head under Abba Jifar II. Centralized standing forces hunted bandits and fought wars. District governors were expected to police their lands, but could not retain more than a dozen armed men. Posts along Jimma's borders were constructed and defended by men under the royal command (Lewis 2001: 101–04).

In just a few generations, then, the Boran Oromo sociocultural order became transformed from a Communal to an Archaic stage of sociocultural evolution and soon after, with the importation of Islam, proceeded to acquire some elements of an Axial society.

Sultanate of Afar

The Oromo kingdom at Jimma survived as an independent polity within the Ethiopian Empire until the death of Abba Jifar II in 1932, thanks to the king's acceptance of subordination to Emperors Menilek and Haile Selassie. On the other side of the empire, the Afar monarchy survived until the present.[20]

The Afar Sultanate (also known as the Aussa Sultanate) emerged in 1734 following a series of translocations of the historic Sultanate of Adal. First mentioned in the Chronicle of 14C Emperor Amda Seyon, the Adal Sultanate consisted of a number of ethnic groups, primarily Somalis and Afaris, both of which, like the Oromo, lived largely as pastoralists and spoke languages belonging to the East Cushitic branch of the Afroasiatic language family. Formed by descendants of Arab traders who migrated down the Red Sea Coast following the Muslim conquest of Egypt, at its height the Adal Sultanate controlled much of what today is labeled Somalia, Ethiopia, Djibouti, and Eritrea. It established towns and maintained a lively trade—in slaves, ivory, and other commodities—with Arabian markets and remote Asian ports. Historic cities in the region, such as Berbera, Zeila, and Harar, flourished with mosques, shrines, courtyard houses, and cisterns during the kingdom's Golden Age. Fighting numerous battles with the Amhara kings, Adali sultans moved their capital inland toward Ethiopian territory, settling at Harar in the early 16C. From there its charismatic leader, known as Ahmad Gragn, launched a devastating jihad against Christian Ethiopia, aided by cannons and soldiers from the Ottoman Turks.

Given their formation during the flourishing centuries of Islamic Civilization, the Adal Sultanates must be regarded as Axial outposts from the start. And not such remote outposts: through proximity to Arabia, they imported a rich mix of Islamic elements, including scholars and dervishes. Harar went on to be a major center of Islamic learning and came to be regarded as the fourth holiest city in Islam.

Even so, although the Adal and Afar rulers considered themselves defenders of the Faith, they were unconstrained by spiritual authorities represented elsewhere by caliphates and imamates (Arjomand 2011). Outside of Harar, moreover, Islam tended to effect only a superficial veneer over deeply-rooted pre-Abrahamic practices in the region. Like other Ethiopian ethnies descended from Cushitic peoples, the Afar localize spirits on mountains, make offerings to sycamore trees, and wear amulets made of skin (Trimingham 1952). The persistence of these and other pre-Axial elements made them fit in with the Christian Ethiopian civilizational pattern which, we shall now see, developed a comparably distinctive blend of Archaic and Axial tendencies.

Archaic Aksum

The ancient Ag'azi people who lived in the far north of the Ethiopian highlands gave rise to the first Archaic Society we know of in Ethiopia. Their transformation to the archaic stage was pivotal in mediating Ethiopia's eventual evolution into a modern type of society.

From an early site in a place known as Yeha, they shifted by the early centuries CE to the city of Aksum.[23] In the early centuries CE, the Agaziyan exhibited key hallmarks of the Archaic stage as Parsons construes it: craft literacy and deified royalty. Literacy would have been confined to priests and those who kept royal records and administrative accounts.[24] In addition, the Ag'aziyan had an all-powerful ruler who embodied the intimate tie between religious and political domains. The Ag'azi kings were sacralized by viewing them as descendants of gods—in particular, of the god of war Mahrem (Greek Ares). The king's politico-military prowess was symbolized by the imperial title *negusa negest*, king of kings. Inscriptions with his title usually included a list of names of the peoples whom he had conquered and who paid tribute to him. The fusion of his political-military and religious roles can be seen in the famous inscriptions regarding King Ezana (320s to c.360CE), which describe him as "Aeizanas, king of the Aksumites, Himyarites and Raeidan, the Ethiopians, the Sabaeans and Silei, Tiamo and the Beja and Kasu, king of kings, son of the invincible god Ares" (Munro-Hay 1991: 225).

The fusion of religious, political, and martial values gave the Ag'azi monarch enormous charisma. Beginning with King Endubis in the second century CE, he was celebrated by having his picture on coins. He was glorified by the erection of huge obelisks used to mark graves. At what was probably the apex of Aksumite glory, the reign of Kaleb, the royal residence consisted of a four-tower palace decorated with bronze statues of unicorns. Kaleb was honored by victory monuments in the form of enormous granite thrones.

It has long been thought that the society that emerged with the establishment of the Solomonic Dynasty in Shoa in 13C represented simply an extension of what was established at Aksum and continued at Lalibela. Nevertheless, I argue, Ethiopia's medieval empire was not just centered in a different part of the country, it constituted *a different type of society*—one that had attained higher levels of differentiation, inclusion, value generalization, and general adaptive capacity. This was precisely because of what Parsons identified as the hallmarks of historic empires. In contrast to what might have been possible under the kings of Aksum, the differentiation of an autonomous stratum of literati made it possible for monks to diffuse the Ethiopian national religious system far and wide. They were able to "broadcast" their ideas, as Parsons suggestively terms it. The expansion of literacy made it possible to extend administrative control to the far reaches of the empire. This would include detailed records of land grants that greatly facilitated administration.[25]

They could also develop a literary tradition that underlay a more inclusive collective identity. This came to a head with two major texts, the *Kibre Negest* of the 13th century and the later *Fetha Negest*. The *Kibre Negest*—the Honor of Kings—sought explicitly to provide a coherent narrative for the legitimization of royalty. The emperor of Ethiopia drew honor, not from divine lineage, but because he descended from divinely favored human ancestor, King Solomon. The shift of that divine favor from Israel to Ethiopia, moreover, involved a thoroughly human action: the clandestine removal of the Ark of the Covenant from Jerusalem to Ethiopia. In addition, the *Kibre Negest* expanded the scope of the constitutive symbolism of the Ethiopian collectivity. The polity was no longer tied to a specific place, Aksum, but to the entire Empire with its ever-shifting boundaries; nor to a specific ethnie, but to the multiethnic panorama that was historic Ethiopia (Levine [1974] 2000: 92–112).[26]

The *Fetha Negest* (Laws of the Kings) consisted of a compilation of religious and civil laws redacted probably in the 16th century. Unlike the *Kibre Negest*, the *Fetha Negest* was not an indigenous Ethiopian composition, but rather a translation of a 13th-century text composed by an Egyptian Christian jurist. Quickly it assumed the authority of an antique text, and was adopted by the educated elite as the supreme law of the land. As late as Ethiopia's revised Penal Code in 1957 and the Civil Code of 1960, legislators deferred to the *Fetha Negest* as the ancient and venerable Law of the Land (Tzadua 2005). By virtue of the traditional educational system, in which the elite were schooled in the classical Ge'ez language, the vast territory under the reign of the emperors of Ethiopia was to some extent connected by virtue of having this common authoritative legal referent.

Enter Axiality

What made it possible for the Ethiopian king to shed his character as a divine figure and subordinate himself to a set of symbols that transcended his earthly authority? The matter may be elucidated, first, by comparing the king of Aksum with two other divine monarchs, those of ancient Egypt and of historic Japan, and by considering features of the Judaeo-Christian religion, which the Ethiopian elite imported.

One key variable, I suggest, concerns *what constituted the order of divinity with which the king was supposed to be imbued.* In Egypt, the kingship not only formed an essential aspect of the sacred order, but also constituted a crucial link in the continuity of all meaningful phenomena. As offspring of Re, the sun god, the pharaoh was symbolically connected to the general procreative order of animal life and to nature's cyclical processes—the planting and harvesting of crops and the Nile's annual flooding. He thereby functioned to regulate the cosmic order of human affairs and even of organic and inorganic nature, and did so through a large core of priestly officials to whom he imparted his divinely ascribed charismatic powers (Parsons 1966: 54–62). It was thus impossible for the pharaonic system to accommodate a split between political and religious domains that would have been necessary for it to have evolved to the level of an axial civilization.

In Japan, the breakthrough to such a bifurcated order never happened either. The Japanese emperor was always thought of as a divine being; his status, *tenno*, signifies "heavenly emperor." Like pharaoh, he was descended from the ultimate source of living things, deities who procreated the islands of Japan as well as its imperial lineage. The emperors of Japan were believed descendants of the earliest divine being, Izanagi no Mikoto (Exalted Male) and Amataseru, the sun goddess.[27] What *tenno* symbolized, however, was not the entire cosmic order as did pharaoh, but the state of Japan and the unity of the Japanese people. Accordingly, sacral places—like Mount Fuji—came to symbolize the Japanese nation. That "sacred particularity," as Japan's worldview has been called, made it virtually impossible to separate the religious from the political systems in Japan. The more universalistic notions of transcendence that came to Japan through Confucianism and Buddhism were fatefully subordinated to the sacred particularity of Japan's "liturgical, sacral, primordial, 'natural' collectivity [which] ultimately prevailed—albeit in continuously reconstructed forms." In contrast to the Chinese emperor, therefore, he could never be overthrown by appeals to transcendent values (Eisenstadt 1997: 250–1).

In contrast, by virtue of linking the Aksumite king's divinity with the god of war—rather than with the source of all life as in Egypt and Japan—it proved less problematic in the long run to circumscribe royal authority. Initially the king simply figured as a politico-military ruler under the aegis of Christianity, not unlike Constantine I. The Aksumite monarchs could maintain their Archaic status as divinely charged warriors even while embracing the powerful new Judaeo-Christian God. Accordingly, even two centuries after King Ezana's conversion, royal thrones could still bear metal statues dedicated to pre-Christian deities such as Astar, Beher, Midr, and Mahrem, the god of war. Enrico Cerulli caught this adaptation deftly, when he remarked on the cautious and ambiguous language with which Emperor Ezana recorded his conversion: Ezana referred to his new deity not as "God of the Christians" but with the old pagan symbolism, "God of the Heaven" and "God of the Earth," and praised his new God in words previously used to describe the pagan Mahrem, "Who has not been conquered by enemies" (Cerulli 1956: 17–21; Levine 1965: 16). Ezana could thereby lord it over his subjects absolutely, simply issuing gold coins with a cross instead of a crescent, the symbol of the Sabaean Moon Goddess. Although neither he nor his successors could imagine imbuing a representative of that God with the moral authority to constrain a Christian monarch, such as Henry IV, to bow down before a representative of the Church, his conversion to Christianity planted a seed from which stirrings in that direction might eventually sprout.

Additional light on the Ethiopian case may be thrown by the concluding chapter of Parsons's brief reconstruction of the theory of societal evolution, "The 'Seedbed' Societies: Israel and Greece."[28] There he outlines a societal type which produces innovations significant for societies not their direct sequels, due to "a basic loss of political independence, and the transfer of primary prestige within the relevant populations to elements which were not carriers of primary political responsibility at the societal level, but specialists in the maintenance and development of the distinctive cultural systems themselves" (Parsons 1966: 96). This pattern characterized ancient Israel and Greece. The Israelites' conception of Yahweh emphasized the absolute sovereignty of God in ways that accentuated the chasm between the divine and the human, making it out of the question for any human king to claim any semblance of divinity. Although early on Israel resembled its neighbors in having an "Oriental monarchy" associated with a quasi-tribal sacrificial cult centered on the Temple, the Babylonian captivity and the subsequent destruction of the Temple eliminated the cult and left Judaism with the Law as the exclusive medium of contact with the transcendent deity. The Prophetic movement sharpened the significance of the law as distinct from the value of political autonomy. That lent special salience to literacy and disciplined knowledge of the law which, given the relatively egalitarian character of the society, placed a premium on securing knowledge of basic religious documents. Israel became one of the first societies to develop extensive literacy among all its responsible adult male members. The loss of political independence left the

Jews with a divinely mandated code borne by literati independent of a concrete political community.

Ancient Greece consisted of a number of independent city-states, or *poleis*. The several *poleis* were linked through a common literary heritage centered on texts by Homer and Hesiod. Since Greek religion was polytheistic, it was exempted from subordination to the will of a single transcendent deity; since it was pan-Hellenic, Greek culture transcended the authority of any single political community. Its focus came to be centered on a transcendent normative order—not that of divinely decreed laws, but of an order that philosophers like Plato and Aristotle came to articulate as an order of nature. Rather than placing divinity at so exalted a level it could be regarded as author of transcendent decrees, the Greeks brought gods down to their own level and made both gods and human subject to a binding order of nature that was normative (Parsons 1977: 110). The independence of the Athenian polis and of other Greek city-states of its time was ended by the Macedonian conquests of the 330s BCE, such that the philosophers no longer held the status and responsibility they enjoyed in an independent polis. Eventually, the intellectual center for Hellenic philosophy and science moved to Alexandria.

Emerging from both Jewish and Greek culture, then, were scholar classes—the rabbis and the philosophers—who due to external conquests could no longer affiliate with political structures of the sort that had been in place among pre-Exilic Hebrews and 5th century Greeks. In other societal contexts, however, those literati could become anchorage points for their relatively independent cultural traditions (Parsons 1966: 108). And the traditions they carried subordinated norms based on kinship, ethnicity, place, and language to norms of a proto-universalistic character.

In all essentials, the Ag'azi case fits this profile of Seedbed Societies. Like Jerusalem and Athens, Aksum suffered invasions that eclipsed its potential continued evolutionary development. Although no historical documents have survived to throw light on the five centuries after its decline around the 8th Century CE, architectural evidence and liturgical traditions identify the Zagwe Kingdom at Lalibela as a lineal successor to Aksum. The Zagwe kings were accorded supernatural powers. Given the massive power involved in the construction of the monolithic cathedrals, they must have commanded vast human and material resources. Zagwe churches show continuity with both the designs of the Aksum stelae and numerous rock-hewn churches across Tigray province. These retained the old rectangular construction, which would be abandoned for circular churches in the historic empire.

By contrast, the Ethiopian Empire centered in the Shoan region to the south can be said to have represented a kind of evolutionary jump. What triggered that leap was another intervention from the outside, the arrival in the late 6th century, of nine Monophysite monks, previously known as Syrians, but now thought to have come from other quarters as well, including Cappadocia, Armenia, Constantinople, and even Rome. Hagiographies of these "Nine Saints" celebrate their exceptional self-denial, courage, and perseverance (Henze 2000: 38). The *Tsadiqan* abandoned the attractions of the capital city to establish churches and monasteries in the countryside. These include a monastery atop a high hill—Debra Damo, accessible only by rope—and several other monasteries in Tigray.

The monastic missionaries provided a cultural repertoire on which Christian Ethiopia would draw for a millennium and a half. They codified the ritual. They created a system of pentatonic modes for liturgical music. They translated the Bible and other sacred texts. They initiated the system of monastic orders, based on the rule of the 4th century St. Pachomius from Egypt. They planted the roots of Monophysite doctrine so deeply that it would withstand the strenuous effort of delegations of Catholic missionaries a millennium later.

By the time of the Zagwe dynasty (ca 1150–1270) seeds were ready to sprout in the fertile soil of a distant region. This happened thanks to the creation of a class of literati who carried the seeds of Judaeo-Christian culture into the Ethiopian interior until the state could be reborn on a different level of societal complexity. By the 13th century those seeds had been broadcast to venerable monastic centers in Amhara and Shoa, Debra Istefanos and Debra Libanos, respectively. And the exceptional proselytizing teacher who founded Debra Libanos, Abuna Tekla Haymanot, came to be revered throughout historic Ethiopia, possibly more than any king. The independent authority of the clergy became deeply institutionalized, empowering them to criticize secular rulers at all levels through moral exhortation and threats of excommunication. By the 14C four monastic movements had arisen, in different times and locales, each possessing distinctive ritual practices and theological tenets, yet all of them, so Steven Kaplan writes, "were characterized by an initial period of anti-monarchical activity during which their members defied and denied the authority of the Solomonic kings." As monk and as ascetic, Kaplan continues, "the holy man expressed his rejection of the passing world of wealth, power and kinship. Rather, he sought to achieve a new and independent existence outside the customary rights and obligations of secular society" (Kaplan 1985: 236–7).

Although Arab conquests along the Red Sea and internal campaigns that racked the city between the 8th and 10th centuries ended the position of Aksum as center of the Ethiopian polity, the place continued to command a role in the imagination of Christian Ethiopia. Just as Jewish Diasporans never forgot Jerusalem, and Europeans never ceased to revere Athens, so Aksum remained an object of devotion throughout Ethiopian history. Not only did those who compiled the *Kibre Negest* claim to be from Aksum, the city itself became romanticized. In writings appended to the *Kibre Negest* Aksum was described as "royal throne of the kings of Zion, mother of all lands, pride of the entire universe, jewel of kings. . . . She was the second Jerusalem. Because of her grandeur and her immense glory, all the kings are called Kings of Aksum, and the archbishops who came from Egypt are called archbishops of Aksum." The holiest place in Ethiopian Christendom, the Church of Saint Mary of Zion in Aksum, received crowns of former emperors. Although the headquarters of Shoan and Gonderine royalty usually stood far from Tigray, Ethiopia's Christian elite regarded Aksum as the right place for the coronation of kings. Royal chronicles record at least four Amhara monarchs—Zera Ya'qob (1434–68), Sersa Dingil (1563–97), Susneyos (1607–32), and Iyasu I (1682–1705)—journeying to Aksum for the ceremony, and describe the rites of coronation in lavish detail (Levine [1974] 2000: 111–2).

Thanks to this continued remembrance of the Ag'azi center of Aksum, Ethiopia could develop a sense of national community that transcended the limitations of monoethnic nations elsewhere in the world.[29] Creating a supraethnic nation coupled with a code of law and a judicial system that spanned the vast country left Ethiopia poised to enter the world of modern nations. The reign of Emperor Haile Selassie facilitated that entrance in many ways, and Ethiopia's two subsequent regimes, whatever their noted shortcomings, advanced it further.

Ethiopia and Japan Reconsidered

Nevertheless, the history of Ethiopia's imperial system reminds us of what Eisenstadt has consistently underscored: the inexorable tensions between the claims of axial ideals and the political dynamics related to their implementation. Although the above analysis notes ways in which Ethiopia's imperial system diverged from that of Japan, a closer look at Ethiopian history reveals that, for all of Ethiopia's affinity with Axial moments, its historical experience resembles the Japanese case more than that of European Christian countries—in ways that have had serious implications for her development as a modern nation.

The primordial sacralization of the Japanese emperor was challenged repeatedly from the 8C onwards by universalistic traditions imported from China. These included strong currents of Confucian teaching and several schools of Mahayana Buddhism. Their ethical doctrines could be tolerated so long as centralized instruments of political control had not developed. However, with the ascendance of strong centralizing political leaders in the late 16C—Oda Nobunaga, Toyotomi Hideyoshi, and Tokugawa Ieyasu— that came to an end. Nobunaga (d. 1582) set the stage by utterly destroying the independent power of the Buddhist organizations, including burning the great temple on Mt. Hiei and slaughtering all its inhabitants, after which the era of "kingly law and Buddhist law" was over (Bellah 2003, 19).

As on so many other counts, the parallels with Ethiopia are striking.[30] The achievement of revered 9C Buddhist monk Kukai resonates with that of 13C Abuna Tekla Haymanot, "Planter of the Faith." After centuries of gestation, Ethiopia's Monophysite Christians gave rise to a number of monastic movements, paralleling the schools of Buddhism. And then, as in Japan, the political ambitions of strong centralizing leaders could no longer tolerate their defiance even as they came increasingly to rely on the Christian clergy as agents of control over far-flung conquered territories.

This dynamic unfolded as the centralizing program initiated by Amde Siyon (1314–44) culminated in the climactic leadership of Emperor Zar'a Yaqob (1434–68). The royal dynamic involved two strategies, the carrot of cooptation and the stick of repression through exile and physical persecution. Amde Seyon instituted the office of the *Aqabe Sa'at*, "Guardian of the Hours," a title conferred on an abbot who was charged both with the responsibility of offering verdicts in religious matters and keeping the calendar of the ruler. This position became the second or third highest ecclesiastic position in the land, and was retained through the regime of Haile Selassie ending in 1974. Through this close proximity to the throne and generous gifts of land and sacred objects, Ethiopian monarchs assured themselves of effective ecclesiastical support. On the other hand, just as Japanese rulers came to reject the radical implications of the Chinese notion of monarchy, so Ethiopian kings came to reject the Judaeo-Christian doctrine promulgated in the *Kibre Negest*, that it was the province of priests to rebuke the king for his immoral deeds. Those who gave a show of independence from the king, by rebuking him for polygamy as with Amde Seyon, or for refusing to prostrate themselves before him, as with the monks who followed St. Istefanos, were exiled, imprisoned, flogged, or assassinated. The terrible persecution of the Stefanite monks by Zar'a Yaqob quite parallels the persecution of Buddhist monks by Nobunaga a century later.

With the effective suppression of independent voices espousing Axial values, the Ethiopian monarchy approximated the Archaic model of the *tenno*. Subordination to universalistic standards was precluded by the particularistic cast of its supporting ideology, which made Ethiopia, as successor to ancient Israel, the sole authentic bearer of divine, now Christian, favor. After Zara Ya'iqob, the clergy almost never exerted critical moral judgments over the conduct of rulers, whose chief thought on reaching the throne was how to secure legitimacy through claiming lineal descendance from King Solomon. They supported the Church, sometimes lavishly, yet always in ways that ensured reciprocal ecclesiastical support of the throne. Resistance or opposition to royal policy was almost never tolerated.

Bearers of the transcendent values of Orthodox Christianity fare no better at the cultural than at the institutional level. They did not quite reach the stage of what Bellah calls *theory*, a conscious reflection on the principles of cosmic coherence and right action. They remained attached at the pre-Axial cognitive stage: mythic thinking. That is why the greatest part of the substantial body of Ethiopic literature consists of narratives: the chronicles of kings and the lives of saints (Haile 1993).[31]

Emperor Tewodros II in the mid-19C was famous for his use of force both in promoting Christianity—he ordered the conversion of Wollo Oromo, Felasha, Agaw, and Wayto—and in controlling it, by reducing the property held by churches and even imprisoning the Coptic Patriarch from Alexandria. Following him, Emperor Yohannes IV reportedly claimed he needed an actual copy of the text celebrating the Solomonic genealogy, the *Kibre Negest*, in order to rule effectively, and his successor reached back to that epic for the throne name of the legendary son of King Solomon, calling himself Menelik II. The antique aura of Solomonic legitimacy figured prominently in the reign of Haile Selassie (1930–74), who saw to it that both the Constitutions he gave to the Ethiopian people enshrined this feature. The 1955 Constitution stipulates that by virtue of his descent from King Solomon as well as the anointing he received, "the person of the Emperor is sacred, His dignity is inviolable, and His power indisputable."

In sum, as in Japan, both Christian and Islamic Ethiopia experienced "the deep implication of persisting strains of non-Axial culture with continual reformulated structures of power determined to prevent the full institutionalization of Axial premises" (Bellah 2003: 59).

Enter Modernity

Haile Selassie I mediated the transformation of Ethiopia's historic patrimonial empire into an early modern bureaucratic nation-state (Perham 1969; Clapham 1969; Levine[1974] 2000; Marcus 1987). In so doing, he famously followed an old Ethiopian pattern of selective importation of external cultural complexes, taking care to prevent this flow of influence from being circumscribed to any single channel. Up to a point, that worked successfully in the old pharaonic model. Yet as his subjects became educated in the ways of modern Western institutions, they came increasingly to chafe under his intense sacralized patrimonial control (1965).

The abolition of the monarchy in 1974 removed the emperor but not the imperial system. Where Bellah, like Eisenstadt, finds the Archaic pattern sounding tenaciously, like a cantus firmus, beneath the vicissitudes of Japanese history, so the Archaic pattern, albeit moderated intermittently by Axial ideals, continues to manifest itself under the rule of the post-monarchical revolutionary democratic regimes. Ethiopia's post-monarchical rulers are *Republicans on the Throne*, as Tekalign Gedamu (2011) puts it so evocatively. The change of players on the throne makes little difference to the underlying script.[32] As Ethiopian monarchs cherished the conceit that the entire land of their country belongs to the ruler, when the Derg regime came to power in 1974 they lost little time in nationalizing all rural property, a condition that prevails to this day. Where aspiring valiants gained position by becoming retainers of patrimonial lords, farmers and university students gain benefits by deferring to agents of the ruling party. As the Meiji "Revolution" of 1868 can be seen as a drama wherein political forces on the losing side in 1600 finally managed to oust the Tokugawa House and accede to supreme control themselves (Bellah 2003: 31), so the Tigrayan revolution of 1991 can be seen as a return to hegemonic power by northern forces who lost out in the 13th century. Where monks who voiced opposition to the king were exiled or punished, political dissidents often face threats of imprisonment or pressures that impel them to flee the country. In an order in which "every household and seignory was ruled by an emperor figure" (Levine 1975), authority commonly reflects a line of command all the way to the peak. Conversely, as subordinates defer instinctively to those above, all the way to the top, so it remains difficult within bureaucracies and businesses to find persons willing to assume responsibility. Political allegiances continue to form within particularistic networks, and political parties based on theoretical differences gain little traction.

Rulers and ruled alike thus find themselves in a situation that frustrates their shared aspirations, since all Ethiopians see benefits in achieving a society freed from the age-old afflictions of war, pestilence, and famine. Need it be said that a neo-Archaic system can mobilize enormous resources on behalf of such goals, not to mention public works, economic development, modern technologies, and the like—which the current regime has expanded enormously? Nevertheless, these are goals that most social scientists find best promoted by open regimes beholden to just laws universally applied.[33] The disjunction between these archaic patterns and the norms associated with modernity produces a great deal of disaffection and unprincipled opportunism.

For all the parallels between the political histories of the two countries, one major respect in which Ethiopia differed from Japan was in the presence of numerous ethnies representing earlier evolutionary grades. In this respect, Ethiopia resembles China and India more than Japan in having numerous primordial populations, which could not be integrated adequately through the cultural patterns defined as ideal by the elite traditions. This was due to the geographically protected indigenous traditional cultures, their internal vitality, and the expansion of Ethiopia's Islamic culture centered at Harar. Haile Selassie's regime fell short by paying insufficient attention to, and often deliberately stifling, the expressive needs of peoples who were not native Amharic-speakers or Christians—a vast problem that the short reign of the pro-Muslim Regent Lij Iyasu (1913–16) had hoped to address preemptively. That integrative failure, however, was crucially fateful. It affected the succeeding half-century no less than his failure to take adequate steps for succession. As Parsons observed, residual problems of exclusion from the societal community inexorably generate—in Ethiopia as in the United States—ethnic or other particularistic revolts, based to some extent on objectively incorrect charges concerning the condition of the country's economy, polity, and moral order (Parsons 1977: 19; see also Geertz 1963 [1973]). When the post-Derg Tigrayan Peoples Liberation Front came to power in 1991, the new rulers found the issue of inclusiveness of primordial collectivities in the societal community of Ethiopia so pressing that it overrode the importance of sustaining a viable societal community at the national level.[34]

In their urgent drives toward "development," however, Ethiopia's governments of the past four decades have not respected and protected these distinctive cultures. They have uprooted local communities on behalf of forced villagization. They erect dams that endanger entire traditional cultures. They displace communities by selling their land to foreign investors No national vision has room for seeing what could be drawn from traditions representing diverse evolutionary grades to enrich a national repertoire in search of ways to approximate the democratic ethos of political Modernity. Although the policy of ethnic federalism built into the 1995 Constitution seemed to acknowledge appreciation of ethnic diversity, it could not define the nation as a whole whose parts might contribute differentially to an integrated system.[35]

Much of the country's tortuous vicissitudes of the past four decades might have been avoided had a perspective more in line with some sort of evolutionary reconstruction been adopted. Although conflicts inherent in evolutionary transformations rarely take place without serious costs, less destructive modes of evolutionary advance were possible without the rhetoric that guided virtually all the progressive groups of the 1960s and 1970s, who viewed remnants of Ethiopia's patrimonial empire as having comprised an evil despotic system that "held Ethiopia back for three thousand years" and then as a prison house of nationalities whose right to self-determination up to secession was the paramount developmental need of the country. This rhetoric forced Ethiopia to forego liberal progressive alternatives which some of her most educated citizens had espoused in 1960, 1974, and 1992 (Levine 2007). In 1974 I voiced a hope that such diversity might to some degree be protected as a humanly valuable representation of different stages of sociocultural evolution.[36]

Beyond that, the concluding portions of Bellah's analysis regarding the drive toward modernization in both Japan and the United States warrant careful attention. Nearly a decade ago he cautioned that, inasmuch as biological and cultural evolution are deeply connected, new dangers have arisen regarding the role of culture in steering us in today's world. Speaking of the commitment of societies like Japan and the United States to relentless economic expansion, he cautioned that

> Expansion seems destined to lead to global self-destruction unless there is some critical redirection in the not too distant future. . . . Both societies need to consider the judgments that axial traditions have made concerning self-aggrandizing human action and whether their own lack of axial reference points are part of their present predicament. (2003: 61)

Several traditions in Ethiopia offer resources for moving toward a more open society. In her Communal Societies, in particular, conventions regarding peaceable conflict resolution, democratic deliberation, and selection and term limits of political rulers are often exemplary.[37] Throughout Amhara-Tigrayan society, moreover, there was historically a deeply rooted disposition to listen carefully to opposing arguments in court and hope for wise decisions. And the axial traditions that encouraged renunciation of the world on behalf on transcendent ideals never completely died out, despite the best efforts of despotic regimes to extinguish them.[38] The motto of Ethiopia's flagship university, Addis Ababa University, remains a Ge'ez phrase from the Bible: "Kwillo amekkiru we-ze-senay atsni'u"—"search all sources and select the best," a dictum pertinent to all universalistic investigative inquiries (Levine 2004a). Indeed, all Ethiopian religions associated with Axial breakthroughs—Judaism, Christianity, and Islam—and also many local religions, like those devoted to Waaka, cherish symbolism that exhorts people to live in harmony and mutual respect. All these can be drawn on to promote the habits and institutions needed to transcend the limits of persisting elements from the Archaic past by containing Ethiopia's drives and frustrations within an encompassing moral fabric.

Core Assumptions Revisited

The dichotomy between Tradition and Modernity has long directed the thinking of commentators on the societies of Africa and Asia. Indeed, it was foregrounded in my first book on Ethiopia, *Wax and Gold: Tradition and Innovation in Ethiopian Culture* (1965), which began by describing a stark opposition between the two sociocultural universes in general and in Ethiopia in particular. Under a major heading, Tradition and Modernity, I wrote: "In considering the encounter between traditional and modern culture patterns currently experienced in acute form in most nations of the world, one may discern, at a high level of abstraction, these five positions: (1) the Traditionalist; (2) the Modernist; (3) the Skeptic; (4) the Conciliatory; and (5) the Pragmatist" (1965, 11).

Even as I published those formulations, I was starting to feel uneasy about maintaining so stark a dichotomy. For one thing, I grew aware of the absurdity of implying that any modern institution could exist without its own "traditions", a point elaborated inter alia by one of my mentors, Edward Shils (1981). What is more, the dichotomy conflates all pre-modern orders so roughly as to be useless. I came to reflect on the lack of realism in depictions of any tradition as a fixed, uniform set of symbols, when I recalled, for example, lively disputes among traditional Amhara peasants regarding just what certain rites consisted of or how they should be performed. This led me to publish a revisionist essay, "The Flexibility of Traditional Cultures," just a few years later ([1968] 1985). And what the present analysis demonstrates vividly is the importance of holding in mind the radical contrasts among the diverse orders of pre-modern sociocultural systems.

Relatedly, the dichotomy of center/periphery conflates all the societal formations outside of an imperial or now national center, without acknowledging the existence of significant centers in subnational collectivities. Although awareness of such a configuration went without saying when one attended to the historic empires, including the historic Empire of Ethiopia whose sovereign was labeled Negusa Negest, "King of Kings," this point implies a need for caution when employing the center/periphery dichotomy uncritically in any complex system.

Other revisionist thinking, guided less by regional study than by theoretic reflection, has led me to emphasize the contradictory features of the Modern culture pattern, both by highlighting the contradictory directions of rationalization identified in the work of Max Weber (Levine 1985, Chapter 7) and, more generally, by elaborating the insight of Georg Simmel that an essential feature of Modernity is its amplification of opposed tendencies in all areas. Even before the current reversal of optimism about progress in the face of doomsday visions of endless warfare and ecological catastrophe, it was becoming important to engage more honestly with what I termed "Modernity and Its Endless Discontents," a phrase that highlights the negative features of modernity not as accidental annoyances but as its inexorable constituents (Levine 1995, 306–16; 2003; 2005, 25–35). Projecting this sort of assessment backwards, one finds my idea of the contemporary relevance of Ethiopia's persisting pre-Archaic cultures foreshadowed in something like Habermas's calculus that the evolutionary advance in Archaic levels of domination "has to be considered retrogressive in comparison with the less significant social inequalities permitted by the kinship system" (Habermas 1979, 173). More positively, a number of features of the pre-Archaic cultures in Ethiopia can be searched for embodiments of forms and values of direct relevance in modernity, such as the fluid formation of voluntary groups among the Majangir, the sensible deliberations of local public meetings among the Sidamo, and the creative institution of democratic procedures among the Boran.

In pointing to the relevance of the democratic customs of Ethiopia's pre-Archaic cultures for nourishing a contemporary democratic ethos, the present chapter takes a small step in advancing this work of revision. More generally, I hope that it may open the door to future inquiries that can reveal systematically how *each evolutionary grade includes features that are both positively and negatively adaptive as well as homes for features that carry both positive and negative ethical value.* What is more, this study suggests the possibility that societies other than Ethiopia contain formations at diverse evolutionary stages.[39] Stated more boldly: examine *any* society with an eye to discovering customs and institutions that represent a diversity of evolutionary grades and values.

Notes

1 In *Greater Ethiopia: The Evolution of a Multiethnic Society* ([1974] 2000) I drew on Eisenstadt's *The Political Systems of Empires* (1963) as well as Parsons's notion of "seedbed societies" (1977). Revisiting the latter notion, my paper "Aksum as a Seedbed Society" ([2006] 2010) applied ideas of Bellah (1964), Parsons (1977), and Eisenstadt (1982) to a more delimited nexus in Ethiopian history.

2 Although in 1937 Parsons himself had dismissed the idea of societal evolution—an idea that remains anathema to many social scientists—he sought three decades later to reclaim it in ways that avoided objectionable features of the earlier idea. Parsons's changed comments about Herbert Spencer represents this shift dramatically. His first book scored Spencer and others for espousing an untenable doctrine of evolutionary progress—for being "believers" in the "god" Evolution (Parsons 1937: 3–4). A generation later he introduced the reprint of a volume by Spencer by observing that "very much of the framework of a satisfactory sociological scheme was already present in Spencer's thinking" (1961: x).

3 In the course of working out these new formulations, Parsons was influenced heavily by an early draft of the seminal paper by Robert Bellah, "Religious Evolution," published eventually in 1964. In fleshing out his evolving conception, he was assisted by Victor M. Lidz. Lidz also did most of the work for the under-appreciated companion volume, *Readings on Premodern Societies* (1976). Bellah's new *Religion in Human Evolution* (2011) provides the most comprehensive realization of this conception to date. Eisenstadt remained more circumspect about identifying evolutionary stages, but in practice did much to contrast patrimonial and bureaucratic empires, and pre-Axial and post-Axial civilizations.

4 "The societal collectivity becomes ... an ethnic group maintaining jurisdiction over a territorial area ... Advanced primitive societies are characterized by stratification

and by some kind of central political organization based on secure territorial boundaries" (Parsons 1977: 42, 44).

5 As it turns out, Eisenstadt's first major monograph (1956) offered the first general theoretic interpretation of the structural significance of age groups as providing a mechanism for transforming social organization beyond family and kinship in the direction of universalistic integrative principles.

6 To be descriptive, I would prefer the term 'Patrimonial-Mythic' societies—but the term is too complex and I do not want to challenge what is already a fairly widely used term.

7 The classic sources include Weber 1921; Jaspers 1949; and Eisenstadt 1963. See also Eisenstadt 1982.

8 See Levine 1995, 2005b, 2006 for systematic explications of this argument.

9 "The fundamental symbolization of modern man and his situation is that of a dynamic multidimensional self capable, within limits, of continual self-transformation and capable, again within limits, of remaking the world, including the very symbolic forms with which he deals with the world" (1970: 42).

10 A comprehensive catalogue of that sort was first compiled as the Appendix to *Greater Ethiopia* ([1974] 2002).

11 As a pertinent case in point: the attentive reader of what follows may note that all of the eight Ethiopian traditions discussed in some details—those of the Majangir, Qemant, Gurage, Sidamo, Dasenetch, Konso, Oromo, and Amhara-Tigrayan—contain cognate words that represent some sort of spiritual entity—respectively, *wakayo, mezgana, waq, waga, waag, waaq*, and *wuqabi* (Levine [1974] 2000: 60). The case for shared cultural elements in Ethiopia was reemphasized recently by Tekalign Gedamu (2011: 402–9, 427).

12 Ethnic groups from the historical records that no longer exist include the Janjero, Gafat, Gagra, Harla, and many others.

13 Chafing under the 1992 requirement to declare ethnic identity for purposes of voting and gaining ID cards, numerous Ethiopians have begun to champion the idea of the category of "ethnic Ethiopians."

14 This model encompasses what Merera Gudina has glossed as two different, but closely related narrative perspectives: "national oppression" and "colonial" (Gudina 2006: 120–26).

15 "'What did you do to make them laugh when you photographed them,'" one said. I replied I did nothing except talk to them. On the whole, I added, I had found Ethiopians a rather happy people. The student scowled, reflected a moment, then declared, 'You may be right. They look happy. But they shouldn't be' (Henze 1977: 19). This is not the place to explore further the disastrous consequences of the adherence of many Ethiopian intellectuals to an ideology that, as one knowledgeable Ethiopian writer describes it, "has turned out to be triply fraudulent ... [with promises that] have turned out to be as hauntingly empty as abandoned prehistoric caves" (Gedamu 2011: 342).

16 This point was emphasized by Addis Ababa president Andreas Eshete, in the documentary film *Adwa*, when he observed that forces heeded the call of Emperor Menilek from all over Ethiopia, including peoples who had been conquered by him not long before!

17 As they themselves describe it:

> A young man marries a girl, and after he has paid the bridewealth she comes to live with him. He makes fields for her and she cooks him porridge. They have their own homestead (*wai*). They have children. The children grow up, the boys help their father make fields for their mother and sisters, and the girls help their mother cook for their father and brothers. A man and wife and their children live at one homestead. Eventually a man's children marry. His daughters leave to go with their husbands, who must pay bridewealth to the girls' parents and brothers. But a man's sons marry wives who come to live with them. Each new wife must have her own homestead of huts and fields made for her by her husband, for whom she cooks meals. He and their children live at her homestead. They live near his parents and brothers. (Stauder 1971: 53–4)

18 Besides the Qemant these include the Awi of Gojjam, the Beta Israel (Falasha) of Begemdir, the Bilin of Eritrea, the Kunfel of Begemdir, and the Xamir of Wollo (Levine [1974]2000, 189).

19 Alternately transliterated as Dasanetch, Daasanech, and Dhaasanac.

20 In one formulation, Oromo beliefs are embodied in a tricolor emblem with white, red, and black hues. The white is the past, the ancestors, the bones, the ashes... . The red is the present, the living, the here and now. Red is flesh. Red is the blood that rushes through our veins... .The black is the future. ... the unknown and the unknowable. Black is the spirit, the soul." In weaving together these three colors Waaq conjoins past, present and future: bones, flesh, and soul. Absent balance between female and male, young and old, spiritual and physical power, society collapses. Waaq's peace and order is *safuu*. If the balance is disturbed, *safuu* is lost, which betokens a loss of seera Waaq (Waaq's law and order). That produces chaos and disaster. http://meta-religion.com/World_Religions/Other_religions/oromo_religion.htm

21 In the course of those external campaigns, the Oromo moved in diverse directions, often assimilating with the peoples whom they conquered or settled near. Through this long-term secular process, Asmarom Legesse and I came to think, the Oromo created multi-dimensional cross-ethnic connections that provided a sort of glue that held together much of the expanding Empire of Greater Ethiopia (Levine [1974] 2000).

22 Not without recurrent fateful struggles. The efforts of revered Sultan Ali Mira Hanfare (1921—2011) to maintain autonomy within Ethiopia's centralizing nation-state ran head on against efforts of Haile Selassie and the two succeeding regimes to quash that autonomy.

23 As Getatchew Haile explains, what has been conventionally called an Aksumite Kingdom should more properly be referred to by the indigenous names, Ambehere Aga'azi, the country of Ag'azi. N. d.

24 Those who wrote the epigraphic inscriptions often did so in three languages—Ge'ez, Sabaean, and Greek. As early as the first century CE, we have reason to believe that King Zoskales was acquainted with Greek literature, and that his courtiers included Greeks and Hellenized Egyptians (Tamrat 1972: 22).

25 And provide a historiographical treasure for future scholars (Crummey 2000).

26 The *Kibre Negest* assumes the equivalence of land = people = nation = polity,

using phrases like *bihere Ityoppiya* and *seb'a Ityoppiya* as terms that connote land, people, and country alike (Levine 2004a: 363). For an important new interpretation of the origins of the *Kibre Negest*, see Getatchew Haile 2009.

27 Until Japan's defeat in World War II, children were taught that they would go blind if they looked directly in the face of their divine emperor; photographs of him in houses were covered so that he could not be seen directly.

28 In the slightly revised version of this essay, which Parsons issued in a volume that also included its sequel, *The System of Modern Societies*, he omitted the seedbed metaphor. The volume editor, Jackson Toby, retained it, however, in the accompanying introduction. I prefer it for its evocative quality, rather than the more literally descriptive phrase Parsons used later, "cultural legacy for later societies" (Parsons 1976: 99).

29 Her precocious achievement in nation building has escaped the notice of scholars who treat nationalism as a quintessentially modern political movement, albeit one that first appeared in Western Europe as early as 19C if not as early as 17C. Philip Gorski, who has perhaps gone furthest of any scholar in documenting the earliest appearance of modern nationalism—16C Netherlands—ignores the fact that countries like Japan and Ethiopia had adumbrated nationalist cultures centuries before their putative origins in Western Europe (Gorski 2000). This is ironic in that Gorski's analysis posits a form he calls "Hebraic nationalism" as archetype for modern forms of nationalism, quite cognate with what Ethiopians accomplished with the *Kibre Negest* (Levine 2004: 2).

30 In "Ethiopian and Japan in Comparative Civilizational Perspective" ([1998] 2001), I enumerated dozens of such parallels.

31 The one apparently glaring exception turns out to prove the rule. This is an ostensibly 17C manuscript known as *Hatata Zara Ya'iqob*, *The Investigations of Zara Ya'iqob*, hailed by some Ethiopian intellectuals as evidence that their culture has created an indigenous text of philosophic argument. However, as the work of Eugen Mittwoch (1934) and others long since demonstrated, this text proves to be a forgery, created in the early 19C by a Franciscan missionary fearful of expressing his own philosophic doubts openly.

32 A pertinent episode I often tell concerns my experience in 1976 when visiting a jewelry shop in Addis Ababa in search of gold earrings for my wife. When the shopkeeper said that he had no gold, since the *negus* (king) had taken it all, I replied, "But I thought that there was no longer any *negus* (since the monarchy has been overthrown two years before). To which he replied: *Simu bitcha lewete, yaw new*; "the name alone has changed, it's the same old thing."

33 To cite one pertinent voice, the prominent Ethiopian economist, Dr. Costantinos Berhe Tesfu, recently stressed that modern economies will thrive in the long run only if legal systems change so that most of the people feel that the law is on their side (2012).

34 In vain, the late Dr. Eshetu Chole warned that efforts to redress previous regimes of discrimination and neglect of diversity should not be accomplished at the expense of unifying national legacies (1992).

35 It did, however, make provision for the validity of traditional legal norms that did not contradict the national laws.

36 My 1974 vision: "An internally specialized central sector may provide security and relief from natural disasters for the entire populations while a number of groups

with little internal differentiation ... [embodying] qualities of expressiveness, security, communality, and egalitarianism ... [might] provide specialized agricultural products and crafts as well as living exemplars of kinds of human experience and values which may give deep satisfaction to modernized Ethiopians" ([1974] 2000: 183).

37 On this, see *Oromo Democracy*, by Asmarom Legesse (2006). More general surveys of such resources can be found in Pankhurst and Assefa (2008) and Levine (2008).

38 Space does not permit discussion of those heroic martyrs who walked to their death singing the tune of Axial ideals. To name only two, recall Ethiopian Orthodox Patriarch Abuna Petros, executed in July 1936 for failing to stop his incitement to resistance to Italian occupation, exclaiming "The cry of my countrymen who died due to your nerve-gas and terror machinery will never allow my conscience to accept your ultimatum. How can I see my God if I give a blind eye to such a crime?" And recall Reverend Gudina Tumsa, general secretary of the Ethiopian Evangelical Church Mekane Yesus, a follower of Reinhold Niebuhr and a deeply originary African theologian. Rev. Gudina refused to abandon his ministry when offered a chance to escape certain death by the Derg regime, adhering to his central mission: "People are tormented with fear of spirits and they want to accept the new religion of love and justice." For a searching inquiry into how present-day religionists might draw inspiration from figures like the 15C Saint Istefanos and his followers, see Mennasemay Maimire 2010.

39 In a sense, an effort that adumbrates what I am proposing here was carried out in the classic work of Robert Redfield, *The Folk Culture of Yucatan*. The point has come increasingly to the fore in the work of Robert Bellah. See Bellah 2012.

Bibliography

Almagor, Uri. 1978. *Pastoral Partners: Affinity and Bond Partnership among the Dassanetch of South-West Ethiopia*. Manchester: Manchester University Press.

Arjomand, Said Amir. 2010. "Legitimacy and political organisation: caliphs, kings and regimes." *Cambridge History of Islam* 4.

Bellah, Robert N. 1964. "Religious Evolution." *American Sociological Review*, 29: 358–74. Reprinted in *Beyond Belief: essays on Religion in a Post-Traditional World*. New York: Harper and Row. 1970.

______. 2011. *Religion in Human Evolution*.

______. 2012. "The Heritage of the Axial Age: Resource or Burden?" In *The Axial Age and Its Consequences*, ed. Bellah, Robert N. and Hans Joas. Cambridge, Mass.: Harvard University Press.

Cerulli, Enrico. 1956. *Storia della letterature etiopica*. Milan: Nuova Accademia Editrice.

Cerulli, Ernesta. 1956. *Peoples of South-West Ethiopia and its Borderland*. London: International African Institute.

Chole, Eshetu. 1992. "Ethiopia at the Crossroads." Published online at www.eeaecon.org/pubs.

Clapham, Christopher. 1969. Haile Selassie's Government. NY: Frederick A. Praeger.

Conti-Rossini, Carlo. 1928. *Storia d'Etiopia*. Milan: Lucini.

Crummey, Donald. 2000. *Land and Society in the Christian Kingdom of Ethiopia: From the Thirteenth to the Twentieth Century*. Urbana, IL: University of Illinois Press.

Eisenstadt, S. N. 1963. *The Political Systems of Empires.* London-New York: Transaction Publishers.

______. 1982. "The Axial Age: The Emergence of Transcendental Visions and the Rise of Clerics." In: *Eisenstadt, S.N., Comparative Civilizations & Multiple Modernities* Vol 1, 2003, Leiden, Netherlands: Brill. 195–217.

______. 1996. *Japanese Civilization: A Comparative View.* Chicago: University of Chicago Press.

______. 2011. "The Axial conundrum: between transcendental visions and vicissitudes of their institutionalizations: constructive and destructive possibilities. *Análise Social* 41, 2. August: 201–17.

Gamst, Frederick C. 1969. *The Qemant: A Pagan-Hebraic Peasantry of Ethiopia.* New York: Holt, Reinhart and Winston.

Gedamu, Tekalign. 2011. *Republicans on the Throne.* Los Angeles, CA: Tsehai Publishers.

Geertz, Clifford. 1973. *The Interpretation of Cultures.* New York: Basic.

Gorski, Phillip. 2000. "The Mosaic Moment: An Early Modernist Critique of Modernist Theories of Nationalism." *American Journal of Sociology* 105, 5: 1428–68.

Habermas, Jurgen. 1979. "Toward a Reconstruction of Historical Materialism," in *Communication and the Evolution of Society*. Boston: Beacon.

Haile, Getatchew. 1993. "Ethiopic Literature." African Zion. New Haven: Yale University Press, 47–56.

______. 2009. "The KN Revisited." In *Oriens Chistianus* 93: 127–34.

______. 2011. "Thinking of Geʽez Literature." Unpublished.

Hallpike, C.R. 1972. *The Konso of Ethiopia: A Study of the Values of a Cushitic People*. London: The Clarendon Press.

Hamer, John H. 1970. "Sidamo Generational Class Cycles: A Political Gerontocracy." Africa 40 no. 1, 50–70.

Hamer, John H. and Irene Hamer. 1966. "Spirit Possession and Its Socio-Psychological Implications among the Sidamo of Ethiopia." Ethnology 5 no. 4, 392–408.

Hassen, Mohammed. 1994. *The Oromo of Ethiopia: A History 1570–1860*. Trenton, NJ: Red Sea Press.

Henze, Paul. 1977. *Ethiopian Journeys*. London: Ernest Benn.

______. 2000. *Layers of Time: A History of Ethiopia*. New York: Palgrave Macmillan.

Houtteman, Ivan. 2011. "Living in the Navel of Waag: Ritual Traditions among the Daasanech of South West Ethiopia." Ph.D. Dissertation. Universiteit Gent.

Jaspers, Karl. 1949. *Vom Ursprung und Ziel der Geschichte.* Zurich: Artemis-Verlag.

Kaplan, Steven. 1984. *The Monastic Holy Man and the Christianization of Early Solomonic Ethiopia.* Wiesbaden: Franz Steiner Verlag.

______. 1985. "The Ethiopian Holy Man as Outsider and Angel." *Religion* 15, 235–49.

______. 2007. "Monasteries." In: *Encyclopaedia Aethiopica 3*: 987–93.

Legesse Asmarom. 1973. *Gada: Three Approaches to the Study of African Society*. New York: Free Press.

______. 2006. *Oromo Democracy*. Trenton, NJ: Red Sea Press.

Levine, Donald N. 1985. *Wax and Gold: Tradition and Innovation in Ethiopian Culture.* Chicago: University of Chicago Press.

______. 1998. "Social Theory as a Vocation." <http://www.donlevine.com/uploads/1/1/3/8/11384462/stasvocationcopy.pdf>

______. (1974) 2000. *Greater Ethiopia: The Evolution of a Multiethnic Society*. Chicago: University of Chicago Press.

______. 1995. *Visions of the Sociological Tradition*. Chicago: University of Chicago Press.

______. 1996. "The Battle of Adwa as a 'Historic' Event." In Pamela S. Brown & Fassil Yirgu (eds.), *One House: the Battle of Adwa 1896–100 Years.* Chicago: Nyala

Publishing. 1–8.
______. 2003. "Amhara," in *Encyclopaedia Aethiopica*, Institute of African and Ethiopian Studies, Hamburg University.
______. 2004a. "Reconfiguring the Ethiopian Nation in a Global Era." *International Journal of Ethiopian Studies* Vol. 1, No. 2: 1–15.
______. 2004b. "Kwillo amekkiru we-ze-senay atsni'u." Talk at Addis Ababa University on Occasion of Receiving an Honorary Doctorate. www.eineps.org/forum
______. 2005a. "The Continuing Challenge of Weber's Theory of Rational Action." In *Economy and Society* at 2000, ed. Charles Camic and P. Gorski. Stanford. 101–126.
______. 2005b. "Modernity and Its Endless Discontents." In *After Parsons: A Theory of Social Action for the Twenty-First Century*, ed. R. C. Fox, V. M. Lidz, and H. J. Bershady. New York: Russell Sage. 148–68.
______. 2006. *Powers of the Mind: The Reinvention of Liberal Learning in America*. Univ. of Chicago Press.
______. 2007. "Ethiopia's Missed Chances—1960, 1974, 1991, 1998, 2005—And Now: II." <http://www.donlevine.com/ethiopia/uploads/1/1/3/8/11384462/ethiopias-missed-chance.pdf>
______. 2011. "Ethiopia's nationhood reconsidered." *Análise Social* 41, 2. August: 311–27.
Lewis, Herbert S. 1965. *Jimma Abba Jifar: An Oromo Monarchy Ethiopia 1830–1932*. Trenton, NJ: Red Sea Press.
Lidz, Victor and Talcott Parsons. 1972. *Readings on Premodern Societies.* Englewood Cliffs, NJ: Prentice-Hall.
Marcus, Harold. 1987. Haile Selassie I: The Formative Years, 1892–1936. London: The University of California Press, Ltd.
Maimire, Mennasemay. 2010. "A Critical Dialogue Between Fifteenth and Twenty First Century Ethiopia." *The International Journal of Ethiopian Studies* 5, 1: 1–37.
Mittwoch, Eugen. 1934 "Die angeblichen abessinschen Philosophen des 17 Jahrhunderts." Abessinische Studien, ed. E. Mittwoch. Berlin and Leipzig: 1–18.
Munro-Hay, Stuart. 1991. *Aksum, an African Civilisation of Late Antiquity*. Edinburgh: Edinburgh University Press.
Pankhurst, Alula and Getachew Assefa. 2008. *Grassroots Justice in Ethiopia: The Challenge of Customary Dispute Resolution.* Addis Ababa: French Centre of Ethiopian Studies.
Parsons, Talcott. 1961. Introduction to: Herbert Spencer, *The Study of Sociology*. Ann Arbor, MI: University of Michigan Press: v–x.
______. 1966. *Societies: Evolutionary and Comparative Perspectives*. Englewood Cliffs, NJ: Prentice-Hall.
______. 1971a. *The System of Modern Societies.* Englewood Cliffs, NJ: Prentice-Hall.
______. 1971b. "Comparative Studies and Evolutionary Change." In Ivan Valier (ed.), *Comparative Methods in Sociology: Essays on Trends and Applications*: 97–139.
______. 1977. *The Evolution of Societies*. Jackson Toby, ed. Englewood Cliffs, NJ: Prentice-Hall.
Perham, Margery. 1969. Government of Ethiopia, Revised Edition. London: Faber and Faber.
Tzadua, Paulos. 2005. "Fethanagast." In *Encyclopaedia Aethiopica 2*: 534–5.
Redfield, Robert. 1953. *The Primitive World and Its Transformations*. Ithaca, NY: Cornell University Press.
Shack, William A. 1966. *The Gurage: A People of the Ensete Culture*. London: Oxford University Press.
Shack, William A. and Habte Mariam Marcos. 1974. *Gods and Heroes: Oral traditions of the*

Gurage of Ethiopia. Oxford: Oxford University Press.

Shils, Edward A. 1981. *Tradition*. Chicago: University of Chicago Press.

Stauder, Jack. 1971. *The Majangir: Ecology and Society of a Southwest Ethiopian People*. London: Cambridge University Press.

______. 1972. "Anarchy and Ecology: Political Society among the Majangir." Southwestern Journal of Anthropology 28 no. 2, 153–168.

Strecker, Ivo. 1988. *The Social Practice of Symbolization: An Anthropological Analysis*. London-Atlantic Highlands, NJ: Berg Publishers.

Tamrat, Taddesse. 1972. *Church and State in Ethiopia 1270–1527*. Oxford.

Weber, Max. 1921. *Gesammelte Aufsätze zur Religionssoziologie*. Tübingen.

Wilkinson, David. 2007. "Global Civilization: Yesterday, Today and Tomorrow." In *World Civilizations*, ed. Robert Holton, in Encyclopedia of Life Support Systems (EOLSS), Oxford, UK [http://www.eolss.net].

Index

J

K

L

M

T

U

V

W

Y

Z